Gender, Nutrition, and the Human Right to Adequate Food

This book introduces the human right to adequate food and nutrition as an evolving concept and identifies two structural "disconnects" fueling food insecurity for a billion people, and disproportionally affecting women, children, and rural food producers: the separation of women's rights from their right to adequate food and nutrition, and the fragmented attention to food as commodity and the medicalization of nutritional health. Three conditions arising from these disconnects are discussed: structural violence and discrimination frustrating the realization of women's human rights, as well as their private and public contributions to food and nutrition security for all; many women's experience of their and their children's simultaneously independent and intertwined subjectivities during pregnancy and breastfeeding being poorly understood in human rights law and abused by poorly regulated food and nutrition industry marketing practices; and the neoliberal economic system's interference both with the autonomy and self-determination of women and their communities and with the strengthening of sustainable diets based on democratically governed local food systems. The book calls for a social movement-led reconceptualization of the right to adequate food toward incorporating gender, women's rights, and nutrition, based on the food sovereignty framework.

Anne C. Bellows is professor and graduate program director of the Food Studies Program in the Department of Public Health, Food Studies and Nutrition at Syracuse University.

Flavio L. S. Valente is the secretary general of FIAN International, an international human rights organization that advocates for the realization of the right to adequate food and nutrition, based in Heidelberg.

Stefanie Lemke joined the Centre for Agroecology, Water and Resilience, Coventry University, UK in 2015. From 2013 to 2015, she was acting chair, Department of Gender and Nutrition, University of Hohenheim.

María Daniela Núñez Burbano de Lara is a research associate at the Institute of Social Sciences in Agriculture at the University of Hohenheim.

Routledge Research in Gender and Society

17 Gender, Race and National
   Identity
   Nations of Flesh and Blood
   Jackie Hogan

18 Intimate Citizenships
   Gender, Sexualities, Politics
   Elżbieta H. Oleksy

19 A Philosophical Investigation
   of Rape
   The Making and Unmaking of the
   Feminine Self
   Louise du Toit

20 Migrant Men
   Critical Studies of
   Masculinities and the Migration
   Experience
   *Edited by Mike Donaldson,
   Raymond Hibbins, Richard
   Howson and Bob Pease*

21 Theorizing Sexual Violence
   *Edited by Renée J. Heberle and
   Victoria Grace*

22 Inclusive Masculinity
   The Changing Nature of
   Masculinities
   Eric Anderson

23 Understanding Non-
   Monogamies
   *Edited by Meg Barker and Darren
   Langdridge*

24 Transgender Identities
   Towards a Social Analysis of
   Gender Diversity
   *Edited by Sally Hines and Tam
   Sanger*

25 The Cultural Politics of Female
   Sexuality in South Africa
   Henriette Gunkel

26 Migration, Domestic Work
   and Affect
   A Decolonial Approach on
   Value and the Feminization
   of Labor
   Encarnación Gutiérrez-Rodríguez

27 Overcoming Objectification
   A Carnal Ethics
   Ann J. Cahill

28 Intimate Partner Violence in
   LGBTQ Lives
   Edited by Janice L. Ristock

29 Contesting the Politics of
   Genocidal Rape
   Affirming the Dignity of the
   Vulnerable Body
   Debra B. Bergoffen

30 Transnational Migration,
   Media and Identity of
   Asian Women
   Diasporic Daughters
   Youna Kim

31 **Feminist Solidarity at the Crossroads**
Intersectional Women's Studies for Transracial Alliance
Edited by Kim Marie Vaz and Gary L. Lemons

32 **Victims, Gender and *Jouissance***
Victoria Grace

33 **Gender, Development and Environmental Governance**
Theorizing Connections
Seema Arora-Jonsson

34 **Street Sex Workers' Discourse**
Realizing Material Change Through Agential Choice
Jill McCracken

35 **Gender, Ethnicity, and Political Agency**
South Asian Women Organizing
Shaminder Takhar

36 **Ecofeminism and Systems Thinking**
Anne Stephens

37 **Queer Women in Urban China**
An Ethnography
Elisabeth L. Engebretsen

38 **Gender and Rural Migration**
Realities, Conflict and Change
Edited by Glenda Tibe Bonifacio

39 **Gender and Neoliberalism**
The All India Democratic Women's Association and Globalization Politics
Elisabeth Armstrong

40 **Asexualities**
Feminist and Queer Perspectives
Edited by Karli June Cerankowski and Megan Milks

41 **Cross-Cultural Women Scholars in Academe**
Intergenerational Voices
Edited by Lorri J. Santamaría, Gaëtane Jean-Marie, and Cosette M. Grant

42 **Muslim Women, Transnational Feminism and the Ethics of Pedagogy**
Contested Imaginaries in Post-9/11 Cultural Practice
Edited by Lisa K. Taylor and Jasmin Zine

43 **The Embodied Performance of Gender**
Jack Migdalek

44 **Gendering Globalization on the Ground**
The Limits of Feminized Work for Mexican Women's Empowerment
Gay Young

45 **New Dynamics in Female Migration and Integration**
Edited by Christiane Timmerman, Marco Martiniello, Andrea Rea and Johan Wets

46 **Masculinities and Femininities in Latin America's Uneven Development**
Susan Paulson

47 **Gender, Nutrition, and the Human Right to Adequate Food**
Toward an Inclusive Framework
Edited by Anne C. Bellows, Flavio L. S. Valente, Stefanie Lemke, and María Daniela Núñez Burbano de Lara

Gender, Nutrition, and the Human Right to Adequate Food

Toward an Inclusive Framework

**Edited by
Anne C. Bellows, Flavio L. S. Valente,
Stefanie Lemke, and María Daniela
Núñez Burbano de Lara**

Routledge
Taylor & Francis Group

LONDON AND NEW YORK

First published 2016
by Routledge

2 Park Square, Milton Park, Abingdon, Oxon OX14 4RN
711 Third Avenue, New York, NY 10017, USA

Routledge is an imprint of the Taylor & Francis Group, an informa business

First issued in paperback 2017

Library of Congress Cataloging-in-Publication Data
Gender, nutrition, and the human right to adequate food : toward an inclusive
   framework / edited by Anne C. Bellows, Flavio L. S. Valente, Stefanie
   Lemke, and María Daniela Núñez Burbano de Lara.
      pages cm. — (Routledge research in gender and society ; 47)
   Includes bibliographical references and index.
   1. Food security—Developing countries.   2. Nutrition policy—
Developing countries.   3. Women—Developing countries—Social
conditions.   4. Women's rights—Developing countries.   I. Bellows,
Anne C., editor.
   HD9018.D44G45 2016
   363.809172'4—dc23   2015027608

ISBN: 978-0-415-71445-7 (hbk)
ISBN: 978-1-138-29824-8 (pbk)

Typeset in Sabon
by Apex CoVantage, LLC

This book celebrates

The memory of all those women and men who gave or lost their lives in the struggle for the human rights we enjoy today, which we have the obligation to continue defending for our children and grandchildren.

The lives of those women and men who today, with their struggle, make visible the need for all of us to mobilize to ensure that human rights are guaranteed for all.

Let's celebrate their memory and lives, not with a minute of silence—they would not like us to be silent—but with a thundering minute of applause.

This book is dedicated

To our gentle, determined, and tireless friend, Roseane do Socorro Gonçalves Viana, who left us a powerful message of hope and belief in the essential goodness of each and every person, of the need to take on our individual and collective responsibilities to ensure the welfare and dignity of all and each and every one, that all struggles are important and must be respected, and, most of all, that the voices of the affected must be heard.

Contents

List of Figures   xi
List of Tables   xiii
List of Case Studies   xv
Foreword   xix
Preface   xxv
Acknowledgments   xli

1   The Evolving Nature of the Human Rights System and
    the Development of the Right to Adequate Food and
    Nutrition Concept   1
    ANNE C. BELLOWS, MARÍA DANIELA NÚÑEZ BURBANO DE LARA,
    AND ROSEANE DO SOCORRO GONÇALVES VIANA

2   Gender, Nutrition, and the Right to Adequate Food: Introducing
    Two Structural Disconnects and the Human Rights Processes
    Necessary to Address Them   58
    ANNE C. BELLOWS AND MARÍA DANIELA NÚÑEZ BURBANO DE LARA

3   Violence and Women's Participation in the Right to Adequate
    Food and Nutrition   108
    ANNE C. BELLOWS AND ANNA JENDEREDJIAN

4   Maternal, Infant, and Young Child Feeding: Intertwined
    Subjectivities and Corporate Accountability   162
    LIDA LHOTSKA, VERONIKA SCHERBAUM, AND ANNE C. BELLOWS

5   Sustainable Food Systems, Gender, and Participation:
    Foregrounding Women in the Context of the Right to Adequate
    Food and Nutrition   254
    STEFANIE LEMKE AND ANNE C. BELLOWS

6   Closing Protection Gaps through a More Comprehensive
    Conceptual Framework for the Human Right to Adequate
    Food and Nutrition   341
    FLAVIO L. S. VALENTE, ANA MARÍA SUÁREZ FRANCO, AND R. DENISSE
    CÓRDOVA MONTES

    Glossary of Abbreviations and Acronyms   409
    Chronological Glossary of Human Rights Instruments and
        Other International Frameworks and Documents
        Mentioned in This Volume   415
    Contributors   423
    Index   427

Figures

3.1 How discrimination against women is policed and maintained through violence (adapted from HRC 2012b, 4)   110

4.1 Label from Bear Brand coffee creamer (© 2011 Bryan Watt)   195

4.2 Canadian advertisement in the City of Gatineau allowing and supporting breastfeeding in public spaces (© Maryse Arendt)   198

6.1 The Food Security Matrix (Source: A. Eide 1989, 29)   353

Tables

1.1 Human rights characteristics 5

1.2 Timeline of the struggle for the legally binding *Convention on the Elimination of All Forms of Discrimination against Women* (CEDAW) 7

1.3 ICESCR article 2: General human rights obligations of international cooperation, progressive realization, and non-discrimination 14

1.4 Human rights principles (PANTHER) 28

2.1 List of general comments issued by the Committee on Economic, Social and Cultural Rights (CESCR) 67

2.2 References to individuals and groups of individuals facing human rights violations in general comments issued by the Committee on Economic, Social and Cultural Rights (CESCR) 68

4.1 Form of child malnutrition in relationship to treatment approaches, caring, and counseling aspects 211

6.1 People's and food sovereignty conceptual framework of the human right to adequate food and nutrition: the People's and Food Sovereignty Matrix 370

6.2 The People's and Food Sovereignty Matrix: sustainable supply of adequate food 372

6.3 The People's and Food Sovereignty Matrix: stable access to adequate food 373

6.4 The People's and Food Sovereignty Matrix: adequate food 375

6.5 The People's and Food Sovereignty Matrix: eating, self-determination, and well-being 377

Case Studies

1.1 Pre-CEDAW regional organizing across the Americas that facilitated early ratification of CEDAW by select states 9

1.2 Post-CEDAW regional organizing across the Americas that promoted related regional, as well as Brazilian national law 11

3.1 Public participation, structural violence, and conformity with social expectations in Armenia 117

3.2 Public participation and fear of violence in public and private spaces in South Africa 121

3.3 Women's limited mobility as an obstacle for entrepreneurial expansion in Mexico 121

3.4 The invisibility of marginalized women and challenges for related research—United States/Mexico 123

3.5 National action plans (NAPs) on violence against women and their intersections with the right to adequate food and nutrition 131

3.6 Measures by the Indian Government to prevent child marriage, a prerequisite to the right to adequate food and nutrition for women 134

3.7 Microlending programs: the impact of women's success on household stability 140

3.8 Brot für die Welt: working with men in mainstreaming women 142

4.1 CRC Committee: *General Comment 16 on State Obligations Regarding the Impact of the Business Sector on Children's Rights* 169

4.2 UNICEF, UN Global Compact, and Save the Children: *Children's Rights and Business Principles Initiative* 172

4.3 Conflicts of Interest Coalition 176

4.4 Nestlé's nutrition education program to teen mothers in India 177

4.5 Impact of breastfeeding 184

4.6 Guidance on complementary feeding 186

4.7 Powdered infant formula (PIF), intrinsic contamination, and state and corporate response-related 2007 WHO guidelines 189

4.8   Bear Brand marketing in Lao People's Democratic Republic   194
4.9   Ethiopia: breastfeeding culture   197
4.10 Canada: breastfeeding in public   198
4.11 China: lack of breastfeeding support in emergencies   203
4.12 Botswana: diarrhea risk associated with not breastfeeding   206
4.13 Excerpt from the *WHO Guidelines on HIV and Infant
      Feeding 2010: An Updated Framework for Priority Action*   208
4.14 Categories of emergency response to hunger and malnutrition
      with respect to maternal, infant, and young child nutrition   209
4.15 Indonesia: locally made, locally sourced RUFs—Nias biscuits
      for moderately/mildly wasted children   215
4.16 Indonesia: intensive nutrition education   218
5.1   Brazil: toxic contamination of agricultural products
      compromises food and nutrition security of mothers and infants   264
5.2   Uganda: women cannot access markets due to social norms   266
5.3   South Africa: insecurity of tenure of female farmworkers   267
5.4   Kenya: enforcing women's rights with regard to land ownership   267
5.5   Ready-to-use supplementary food (RUSF)   270
5.6   South Africa: violence against women and women-led
      households for greater security   273
5.7   Application of SLA in studies of agricultural programs and
      women's livelihoods in South Africa   279
5.8   South Africa: land reform policies lead to benefits   281
5.9   Sustainable livelihoods, nutrition security, HIV/AIDS,
      and gender   282
5.10 South Africa: the historical legacy and negative perceptions
      regarding land and farming   294
5.11 Application of the human rights framework by grassroots
      and social movements in the agrarian sector   297
5.12 FAO *Right to Food Guidelines* and application by civil
      society   298
5.13 Brazil: the National School Feeding Program   301
5.14 South Africa: social protection gaps in the agricultural sector?   302
5.15 Using law for rural women's empowerment in West Africa:
      Women in Law and Development in Africa (WiLDAF)   304
5.16 Mobilizing poor working women for economic equality:
      Women in Informal Employment Globalization and
      Organizing (WIEGO)   304
5.17 Building feminist democracy in Mesoamerica: Just
      Associates (JASS)   305
5.18 Men speak out against violence against women   307

5.19 PROMESA: a promise for poor farmers and indigenous
       communities in Panama   308
5.20 Equipo Mujeres en Acción (EMAS): a Mexican women's
       organization integrating men   309
6.1 Women's human right to adequate food and nutrition in India 361

Foreword

I am deeply grateful to Anne C. Bellows, Stefanie Lemke, María Daniela Núñez Burbano de Lara, and Flavio Valente for providing me with the opportunity to express my appreciation for their work. With this book, they help us understand how challenging gender-based violence is essential to the eradication of hunger and malnutrition. Women and girls, they recall, are overrepresented among the victims of violations of the right to food: worldwide, about 60 percent of the undernourished are women or girls (ECOSOC 2007, para. 14; WFP 2009, 5). This in itself is unacceptable and calls for combating gender discrimination in access to food to become a global priority. For this reason alone, this book deserves to be widely read and discussed: it provides a gender lens through which to examine the failures of the mainstream food system we have inherited from the previous century.

But there is more, of course. Gender empowerment is the single most important determinant of improved nutritional outcomes: a cross-country study of developing countries covering the period 1970–1995 found that 43 percent of the reduction of hunger was attributable to the progress of women's education, almost as much as increased food availability (26 percent) and improvements to the health environment (19 percent) during that period combined; 12 additional percent of the reduction of hunger were attributable to increased life expectancy of women, so that we owe in total 55 percent of the gains against hunger during those twenty-five years to an improvement of women's situation within societies (Smith and Haddad 2000).

Thus, by combating the abuses women and girls face and by investing more in them, using an approach that is empowering and enlarges their real freedoms, the gains accrue to the entire society. In order to achieve this, this volume shows, the question of *power*—and of its abuse by those holding it in any society—needs to be addressed directly. This explains the focus of the book on the political economy of food systems, as well as the insistence of the authors on using the human right to adequate food and nutrition as a tool to challenge existing hierarchies and the routines that perpetuate male domination. Indeed, there is a mutually reinforcing relationship between the expansion of the social and economic opportunities for women, in particular by improving their access to education and resources, and the improvement of their role in decison-making within the household and within society: greater economic independence will improve the bargaining position of women within the household and increase their voice in public decision-making, while empowerment in turn can accelerate the removal of the obstacles to the expansion of their opportunities as economic agents.

By putting the emphasis on power and the political economy of food systems, this book forces us to pay attention to a number of questions that are generally dismissed as irrelevant, or conveniently ignored: who makes the decisions in food systems reform? Under the influence of which interests? On the basis of which information? Taking as departure point which framing of the problem of hunger and malnutrition? And are women and girls involved in providing the framing and in designing solutions, or are they excluded? The first contribution of this book is in providing us with this new lens through which food systems reform can be analyzed, encouraging us to rethink our routine ways of searching for answers.

The second contribution of the book is to link questions related to gender empowerment to the right to adequate food and nutrition. The right to adequate food and nutrition as a human right goes beyond the requirement of food security alone, for three reasons: first, because it acknowledges that adequate education and health are essential in ensuring that food intakes translate into improved health and nutritional outcomes; second, because it insists on dietary diversity and access to healthy foods as components of adequate nutrition that cannot be reduced to a requirement of access to minimum calorie requirements; and third, because of the dimension of state accountability that an approach focused on the right to adequate food and nutrition entails.

Gender sensitive policies empowering women within households in a human rights framework can make a significant contribution at all three levels. First, the provision of childcare services and the redistribution of power within the household not only should allow women to make the choices that matter for infants but should also ensure that men contribute to giving such care and that this activity is valued as it should. Second, the gender dimension is crucial to ensure that investments in agriculture will translate into improved health or nutritional outcomes. Such investments should ensure access to sufficiently diverse and balanced diets, allowing all individuals to have access to the full range of macro- and micro-nutrients that are necessary to all, at all ages, to lead active and healthy lives, and they should allow for a reduction in rural poverty, taking into account the income effects of various paths of agricultural development. Support to agriculture shall be especially effective in improving nutritional outcomes if such support increases the incomes of the poorest households, and within these households, benefits women in particular. And a greater role of women in making decisions regarding the priorities of agricultural research and development will generally result in a greater attention being paid to the nutritional needs of the family, rather than to profit maximization only.

Third, finally, the right to adequate food and nutrition implies that whatever support is provided to women and girls—including in particular their protection from discrimination—is a matter of human rights. Women and girls are not simply beneficiaries of programs based on charity and the support provided to them is not simply instrumental, a means to improve food and nutrition security: instead, women and girls are rights holders, who have claims against duty bearers, quite apart from the contribution gender empowerment can make to the reduction of overall rates of hunger and malnutrition.

Women's empowerment and the adoption of gender sensitive policies are key also because of the contribution both can make to gender role shifting. Indeed, it is broadly acknowledged that public services should be strengthened in order to alleviate the burdens and time poverty that many women face—in particular by the provision of child care in rural areas, but also by the provision of piped water and access to clean energy sources—in order to reduce the time women and girls spend fetching water or fuelwood. It is also largely accepted that the unpaid work women and girls disproportionately contribute within the household should be recognized. *Reduction* and *recognition* are incomplete, however, unless accompanied by the *redistribution* of roles (Elson 2010; Eyben and Fontana 2011). Consistent with its preamble, which recognizes that "a change in the traditional role of men as well as the role of women in society and in the family is needed to achieve full equality between men and women," article 5(a) of the *Convention on the Elimination of All Forms of Discrimination against Women* (CEDAW; UN General Assembly 1979) provides in this regard that states parties shall seek to "modify the social and cultural patterns of conduct of men and women, with a view to achieving the elimination of prejudices and customary and all other practices which are based on the idea of the inferiority or the superiority of either of the sexes or on stereotyped roles for men and women." Indeed, until the responsibilities in the non-monetary economy are more fairly shared between women and men, such responsibilities will continue to be undervalued and neglected—and those who perform them will not be supported as they should. "Redistribution initiatives are about supporting men's and women's own efforts to change gender norms that prevent men assuming equal roles in care responsibilities, making it easier for men to become more involved in and respected for sharing the family's caring responsibilities as well as for doing paid care work" (Eyben and Fontana 2011, 10).

None of this can be achieved without improving the participation of women at all levels of decision-making that affect the transformation of food systems. When they adopted the outcome document *Keeping the Promise: United to Achieve the Millennium Development Goals* at the sixty-fifth session of the United Nations General Assembly in September 2010, the heads of state and government committed to "improve the numbers and active participation of women in all political and economic decision-making processes, including by investing in women's leadership in local decision-making structures and processes, encouraging appropriate legislative action and creating an even playing field for men and women in political and Government institutions" (UN General Assembly 2010, para. 72(f)).

Improved representation of women at the local level is just as important as their improved representation in national parliaments and executives. In fact, it could be even more significant: the decisions made at the local level are of great practical importance to what matters most to women's ability to contribute to the realization of the right to food, as such decisions concern the allocation of land, the choice of which crops to grow, or how the available labor shall be shared between the plots of land. In addition, it is by participation in local decision-making that women can most easily challenge the dominant representations concerning power and voice. This is one reason why enhancing leadership and participation of women in rural institutions is one of the four pillars of the initiative launched in September 2012 jointly by UN Women, the Food and Agriculture Organization of the United Nations (FAO), the International Fund for Agricultural Development (IFAD), and the World Food Programme (WFP). The program, Accelerating Progress toward the Economic Empowerment of Rural Women, will be implemented during its initial five-year phase in Ethiopia, Guatemala, Kyrgyzstan, Liberia, Nepal, Niger, and Rwanda. It is premised on the idea that economic and political empowerment are mutually supportive and should go hand in hand: the expansion of economic opportunities for women and their enhanced role as economic agents improve their status within the community and can create the necessary social consensus for a greater role of women in rural institutions and local governance and, at the same time, women's political empowerment can facilitate the adoption of reforms in public policies that will improve their status in the economy. The important implication is that neither economic nor political empowerment should be seen as a prerequisite of each other: instead, both processes should go hand in hand, leading in time to a virtuous cycle in which women's economic emancipation facilitates their ability to have "voice" in decision-making, which in turn shall help remove the current obstacles they face in expanding their economic opportunities.

For all the reasons outlined above, this book makes a major contribution to our understanding of the root causes of hunger and malnutrition and of the importance of challenging the violence against women and girls as a key determinant of both. But it also is remarkable by the methodological démarche that it adopts. This collection of essays is the result of a process of co-construction between two non-governmental organizations, FIAN International and the Geneva Infant Feeding Association (GIFA)—the latter part of the International Baby Food Action Network (IBFAN)—and academic researchers working within the Gender Nutrition Rights (GNR) research group based in Syracuse University, the

University of Hohenheim, and Coventry University. As such, it offers a clear demonstration of the need for social actors and scientists to collaborate both in the framing problems and the identification of solutions, in a mode of research that is truly transdisciplinary.

Such a collaboration between different types of knowledge is an essential condition for policy relevant science to have an impact. The implementation of policy proposals will only succeed if they are perceived as legitimate both by those to whom they are addressed and by the intended beneficiaries. Such legitimacy in turn depends on involvement of those being addressed in shaping these proposals and ensuring that they are informed by their views and concerns. It also depends on such proposals addressing not only the symptoms—for instance, high rates of stunting among children or growing incidence of obesity—but also the causes of the problems identified, including in particular the political economy of food systems. Finally, it depends on the policy proposals including mechanisms for self-correction: feedback loops allowing for policy revision that can be activated by social actors when unintended and undesirable consequences of existing policies are perceived. In short, legitimate policy proposals are proposals that involve social actors, both ex ante and ex post, that include a requirement of participation at all stages, and that go beyond "fixes" in order to lead food systems to a sustainable trajectory by addressing the causes of failure.

I welcome this book as a major contribution not simply to the rights of women and girls as a central question of food systems reform, but also as a new and promising way to advance science.

Olivier De Schutter
Former United Nations special rapporteur on the
right to food (2008–2014); member of the United Nations
Committee on Economic, Social and Cultural Rights

REFERENCES

Elson, D. 2010. "Gender and the Global Economic Crisis in Developing Countries: A Framework for Analysis." *Gender & Development* 18(2): 201–12.

Eyben, R. and M. Fontana. 2011. *The Bellagio Initiative: The Future of Philanthropy and Development in the Pursuit of Human Wellbeing. Caring for Wellbeing.* Brighton, London, New York: Institute for Development Studies (IDS), the Resource Alliance, and the Rockefeller Foundation.

Smith, L. C. and L. Haddad. 2000. *Explaining Child Malnutrition in Developing Countries: A Cross-country Analysis.* Research Report 111. Washington, D.C.: International Food Policy Research Institute (IFPRI).

United Nations Economic and Social Council (ECOSOC). 2007. *Strengthening Efforts to Eradicate Poverty and Hunger, Including through the Global Partnership for Development. Report of the Secretary-General. E/2007/71, 1 June 2007.* New York: United Nations Economic and Social Council (ECOSOC).

United Nations General Assembly. 1979. *Convention on the Elimination of All Forms of Discrimination against Women. 18 December 1979.* New York: United Nations (UN) General Assembly.

———. 2010. *Resolution Adopted by the General Assembly on 22 September 2010. 65/1. Keeping the Promise: United to Achieve the Millennium Development Goals. A/RES/65/1, 19 October 2010.* New York: United Nations (UN) General Assembly.

World Food Programme (WFP). 2009. *WFP Gender Policy: Promoting Gender Equality and the Empowerment of Women in Addressing Food and Nutrition Challenges.* Rome: World Food Programme (WFP).

Preface

The food crisis of 2008 was not an isolated incident or unique event from which the world economy and food security has re-stabilized. Rather, as Valente and Suárez Franco (2010, 455) state, "[the 2008 food crisis] is not new for more than 840 million people who have constantly been subjected to hunger over the last thirty years, millions of whom died of malnutrition and associated diseases, or had their quality of life severely affected by the consequences of malnutrition."

The United Nations' (UN) Food and Agriculture Organization (FAO)'s estimates of persons experiencing food insecurity has been reevaluated with an improved methodological instrument called the prevalence of undernourishment (PoU) indicator (FAO, WFP, and IFAD 2012).[1] New estimates of global hunger suggest that the increase in hunger during 2007–2010, the period characterized by food price and economic crises, was lower than previously estimated.[2] The 2012 edition of the FAO's yearly report *The State of Food Insecurity in the World* advises that 868 million people suffered from food insecurity in the 2010–12 time period at the global level (FAO, WFP, and IFAD 2012), less than previous projections in excess of one billion (e.g., FAO and WFP 2010). These more recent calculations have led some to think that "the worries [about world hunger] may be overdone and so are the demands that accompany them" (J.P. 2012). We could not disagree more with this statement. Eight hundred and seventy million hungry people are just as much of a disgrace as one billion. Popular demands to address the human right to adequate food and nutrition are more necessary than ever and are increasing. The new assessment method adjusts benchmarks; it does not dispute trends.

Although estimates of food insecurity differ, the geography and sociodemographic profile of the food insecure remains unaltered (FAO, WFP, and IFAD 2012; HRC 2011, 6). Among the most food insecure population groups are food producing peasants, including small-scale and family farm holders, landless farmers surviving as tenants or agricultural workers, hunters and gatherers, pastoralists and fisherfolk, more particularly those living in higher risk environments and remote areas, as well as non-farm rural households, and the urban poor (HRC 2012a, 4; Scherr 2003, 15).

Within these, women and girls face violations of their right to adequate food and nutrition at a 60:40 ratio relative to men and boys (ECOSOC 2007) and comprise 70 percent of the poor (HRC 2012b; World Bank, FAO, and IFAD 2009). Obviously, not all women everywhere are hungry and gender does not connote the "last" or "worst" basis for discrimination but is further complicated by differences of age, social status, sexuality, and dis/ability, among others. Nevertheless, available data reveal that the structural power inequalities reflected in food and nutrition insecurity according to different status of livelihood, rural-urban location, nation, ethnicity, race, and class are consistently compounded by and manifested within gender discrimination.

As the chapters in this volume stress, knowledge of women's contribution to family and community, despite socially ingrained gender-based discrimination, is firmly established and extends back at least as far as Ester Boserup's (1970) classic *Woman's Role in Economic Development*. Indeed, since Boserup, programs have attempted to address women in development generally, and the ongoing disparities in women's and girls' access to economic, social, and cultural rights, including the human right to adequate food and nutrition, in particular. That said, the obvious question to ask and the question that drives this volume is, *why, when so many call for the inclusion of women and a gender perspective in food and nutrition security, is the food and nutrition security status of women and girls still not improving?* The collaborative effort of this volume's authors attempts to address this question by embracing a more inclusive framework for the human right to adequate food and nutrition. Answering the question has consequences beyond the improvement of the nutritional status of women. At the heart of our inquiry is an analysis of social power imbalances that we recognize in gender relations, but that are further reflective of and rooted in macroeconomic scale inequalities. These disparities are leveraged and reinforced through the escalating reach and domination of the corporate private sector in the realm of public policy making arena.

A full realization of women's right to adequate food and nutrition indeed is closely linked to the realization of the right to adequate food and nutrition for *all* members of society and, further, can only be achieved in the context of holistic progress toward the realization of *all* human rights across the life span: economic, social, and cultural, as well as civil and political human rights. The moral logic of simple justice and equality and the social expediency of investment in women's well-being to leverage their own, their families', and their communities' livelihoods and stability would seem self-evident drivers of food and nutrition policy. Yet the barriers to underrepresented voices in policy have increased. Since the UN Global Compact was launched in 2000 (its "blueprint for change" was recently praised once more by the UN secretary general as we finalize this volume's manuscript in early 2015),[3] the involvement of the corporate private sector has been advanced in public decision-making under the guise of including all "stakeholders" in policy development. As we write, *corporate private* global economic actors in policy development are compromising the independence, integrity, and trustworthiness of *public* policy making by essentially allowing the entity that needs to be regulated to establish the rules on regulation, or, in other words, permitting the fox to build the henhouse. One of today's greatest challenges is an incomprehensible blindness to the fundamentally different nature of market-based actors whose primary institutional interest is the fiduciary duty to their shareholders to maximize profits.[4] A full realization of human rights requires attention to non-discrimination and public participation by social actors who seek the prevention of and recourse for human rights violations. This differs from so-called policy "inclusiveness" that essentially opens new channels for corporate private interests and broadens the sector's capacity to stymie policies and regulations deemed " 'unfriendly' to profit maximization" (Richter 2014).

It has long since been established that women are the key to food and nutrition security as well as well-being at the household level (i.e., IFPRI 2005; Kent 2002; Lemke et al. 2003; Maxwell and Smith 1992; Quisumbing and Smith 2007; Smith and Haddad 2000). Further, composite indicators for gender equality positively correlate with food security and social stability at the national level (UN 2002; von Grebmer et al. 2009).[5] Already in 1984 it was asserted that the realization of the right to adequate food which "depends on an immense, economically uncompensated work input by women" is simultaneously frustrated by gender-based social and cultural prejudice (Gussow, Muchena, and W. B. Eide 1984, 69). In the decade that opened doors to civil society participation in UN engagements, gender mainstreaming was introduced at the 1995 UN Fourth World Conference for Women in Beijing as the most effective means to address development as well as discrimination (Moser and Moser 2005). The 1995 Conference for Women did not, however, link women's rights and gender mainstreaming with gender-based violations of the right to adequate food and nutrition. Neither did it address the complexities of mother-child interrelated rights, biology, and specifically, nutritional health, before and during pregnancy and breastfeeding. Finally, while gender mainstreaming promoted women's participation in public policy, the top-down approach overlooked or ignored the real barriers, including structural violence, to women's public participation. Nevertheless, a major step forward occurred a year later at the 1996 FAO World Food Summit in Rome where the new food sovereignty movement began to press for women's inclusion in rights-based and security approaches to food and nutrition, this time from the grassroots. Over the years, evolving UN frameworks and institutions have attempted to address the effective exclusion of women from access to universal human rights.

And yet, the former UN special rapporteur on the right to food, Olivier De Schutter, points to the paradox of a wide range of available human rights instruments designed to protect women's and girls' rights that are nevertheless juxtaposed against a consistently higher incidence of food and nutrition rights violations among women and girls than among boys and men (HRC 2012b, para. 1). Likewise, the Human Rights Council (HRC) Advisory Committee, in its 2011 study on discrimination in the context of the right to food, found that "[t]he intersection between women's rights and the right to food provides a rich overview of a number of interrelated dimensions of discrimination against women related to [reduced] access to land, property and markets, which are inextricably linked to access to education, employment, health care and political participation" and further that "[g]overnments are not living up to their international commitments to protect women from discrimination, as the gap between de jure equality and de facto discrimination continues to persist and resist change" (HRC 2011, para. 29).

Discrimination against women, as an inherent violation of the human rights principle of equality and non-discrimination, forms the lens through which the lack of significant progress on the realization of women's right to adequate food and nutrition is framed and addressed in this volume. The UN Committee on Economic Social and Cultural Rights (CESCR) defines discrimination as

> any distinction, exclusion, restriction or preference or other differential treatment that is directly or indirectly based on the prohibited grounds of discrimination and which has the intention or effect of nullifying or impairing the recognition, enjoyment or exercise, on an equal footing, of Covenant rights. Discrimination also includes incitement to discriminate and harassment. (CESCR 2009, para. 7)

We, the authors of this cooperative writing project, and with particular attention dedicated in chapters 3 and 6, argue that discrimination, as an arbiter of social inequality, is very specifically policed and maintained by diverse forms of violence. Avoidance of or discomfort with the descriptor *violence* allows social and economic systems to label the most marginalized and most discriminated against groups as "vulnerable," transferring the quality of weakness and victimhood to those de facto denied their human rights. Simultaneously, the mantle of "patron" and "benefactor" is bestowed to entities that "share" their largesse with the *under*privileged. In other words, discrimination becomes a vaguely defined cultural concept that results in compromised human livelihoods that require help. We claim that the benefactors' control over "sharing" effectively regulates discriminated against groups' right to self-determination, the foundation for human dignity. We argue that consistent patterns of "food insecurity" are *violations* of the human right to adequate food and nutrition brought about for three overlapping reasons: because a political economy chooses not to prioritize attention to hunger, because the hungry are not those shaping the political economy, and because diverse forms of structural violence maintain the separation, that is, they *manifest discrimination* between the hungry and the policy makers.

ACADEMIA-CIVIL SOCIETY COLLABORATION

This book is the result of a collaboration between a group of university-based researchers and two international public interest non-governmental organizations (NGOs), all of whom were focused on aspects of under-recognized food and nutritional justice within the human right to adequate food and nutrition framework. Since 2008–9, FIAN International, the Geneva Infant Feeding Association (GIFA), and the Gender Nutrition Rights (GNR) research group which is based at Syracuse University, the University of Hohenheim, and Coventry University have been working synergistically to leverage the capacity of all concerned to foreground women and a gender analysis into the promotion of a human rights-based approach to food and nutrition security. Our book and our ongoing work seek to contribute to the capacity and momentum for action and human rights enforceability through the full engagement and self-determination of all women and men in the pursuit of nutritional well-being, with human dignity.

Through an expanded conceptual framework, namely the food sovereignty framework, for the human right to adequate food and nutrition that integrates the dimensions of gender, women's rights, and nutrition, our academic-civil society partnership seeks to address three conditions that impede women's right to adequate food and nutrition. First, we identify violence against women and girls as an under-examined barrier to the fulfilment of self-determination and their participation as autonomous and participatory members in development and food security strategies in general and their right to adequate food and nutrition in particular. Second, we argue that the neglect of women's and girls', and also men's and boys' overall nutritional needs throughout their life cycle is a result of the current focus on malnutrition during pregnancy, lactation, and infancy. Third, we strongly reject as erroneous the presumption that the state and international market systems provide better support for food security and nutritional well-being than do local and regional systems, of which women are key actors. Overall, we press for corporate adherence to the international health standards and human rights framework, especially the *International Covenant on Economic, Social and Cultural Rights* (ICESCR; UN General Assembly 1966), the *Convention on the Elimination of All Forms of Discrimination against Women* (CEDAW; UN General Assembly 1979), the *Convention on the Rights of the Child* (CRC; UN General Assembly 1989), and the *International Code of Marketing of Breast-milk Substitutes* (WHO 1981), among others. We denounce the negative impact of conflicts of interest and corruption on the integrity and coherence with human rights of policy-making and implementation.

Cooperation between academic and public interest civil society organizations takes advantage of the strengths and weaknesses of both groups. Civil society actors, organized into peoples' organizations or working in civil society organizations (CSOs), must react in real time to current events. Peoples' organizations, supported by CSOs, provide leadership for social progress and they usually house the most current knowledge on policy issues because they are engaged in them. What civil society actors often lack is the time to leverage their knowledge and experience into the kind of publications that drive public policy debates. The academy has a greater luxury of time and the workplace incentive to teach, research, and write on those same subjects, but just as often without the flexible capacity of direct participation in policy development. Cooperation between civil society and academic sectors offers huge benefits, but it is also based on trust and understanding as our very different demands pull us in different directions.

We do affirm, however, that the process of elaborating this book catalyzed multiple layers of collaboration among the different members of the group, beyond the original project scope. Teaching and related research activities were enriched by expanded and immediate introduction to the rapidly changing landscape of the human right to adequate food and nutrition, for example, through ongoing advocacy, case documentation, and the elaboration of new human rights instruments. At the same time, position papers, statements, and reports, elaborated by the civil society members of the group, were made more precise due to contributions from the academic partners. The political and social processes we were, and are, involved in shaped the book, the discussions, the research, the analyses, and the conclusions we reached; they influenced the way we acted and reacted in face of social and political challenges. We matured together.

Looking back, it is now clear to us that our collaboration grew far beyond the writing of the book, and that the way forward will demand even broader cooperation with other social actors, in particular with peoples' movements and organizations, which with their daily struggles make visible the abuses of power and violence that continue to permeate our societies. It is only with them, as partners, that human dignity for all can be achieved.

The collaborators of this book share the understanding that academic efforts must listen to the voice and cries of the individuals, groups, and communities we work with. We must hear not only the questions that their lives pose to us but their answers to them as well. The validation of the knowledge produced in these joint academic, grassroots, and activist initiatives is not to be left to the traditional academic peer review evaluations alone, but to the reality check of whether the analyses, concepts, and tools resulting from them are effective and useful in supporting ongoing struggles for more justice, equity, and less hunger and malnutrition.

Readers will realize that the chapters and the book as a whole represent a snap shot that depicts the state of the art at a specific point in time. From the moment we decided to stop tweaking the individual chapters, many things have continued to change in the fields covered by them. In some cases, there have been changes due to the impact of knowledge produced and advocacy advanced by our joint efforts. An unwelcome example has been the increasing rhetorical co-optation of "rights-based approaches" by actors whose objective has been more to circumvent criticism and nominally adapt to the direction of global food governance than it is to embrace and to work toward the implementation of, let alone to comply with, a *human rights legal framework*. As this publication goes to press, we find ourselves thinking about future fora to further improve and advance this language and issue. We do anticipate that some of our analyses may inevitably be modified as "facts on the ground" change. We welcome shared communication and dialogue on the changing landscape of the human right to adequate food and nutrition and, among other things, invite inquiry on what might have happened since the final editing of the book.

WHO WE ARE AND HOW WE BEGAN

FIAN International is an international human rights organization, grounding its work in twenty-nine years of case documentation and campaigning for the redress and/or prevention of violations of the human right to adequate food and nutrition, and related rights, in countries worldwide, working in close cooperation with, and technically and politically supporting the affected communities' struggle for redress and prevention of recurrence of violations. This engagement provides means to identify systematic trends in violations, to contribute to the international standard setting on the right to adequate food and nutrition, and to link civil society counterparts with the aim of mutual support and education. FIAN International brings this largely national-scale experience to international fora like the HRC, the CESCR, and the Committee on the Elimination of Discrimination against Women (CEDAW Committee), as well as the UN Committee on World Food Security (CFS). Although FIAN International has staff and members throughout the world that are dedicated to women's and gender issues, this project leveraged capacity at the headquarters office, which in turn expanded a gender focus to international governance initiatives.

The Geneva Infant Feeding Association (GIFA) works within the network of over 270 members of the International Baby Food Action Network (IBFAN) based in 168 countries. The network has thirty-four years of experience in working on corporate accountability issues in the infant and young child feeding arena, helping to bridge nutrition and food issues. GIFA is IBFAN's liaison office with the UN, international institutions, and NGOs. The IBFAN network specializes in assisting governments in setting up legally binding mechanisms that regulate marketing practices of infant food manufacturers and in monitoring these practices against the *International Code of Marketing of Breast-milk Substitutes* (hereinafter, *Code*) and subsequent World Health Assembly resolutions relevant to the *Code*.[6] GIFA brings related information to international policy makers, in particular the World Health Organization (WHO), the United Nations Children's Fund (UNICEF), and the Committee on the Rights of the Child (CRC Committee).

While GIFA's focus on maternal, infant, and young child well-being has tremendous resonance for women's lives, until joining with the project partners, GIFA had not focused its traditional advocacy, policy, or evaluation work through the lens of women's human rights.

The GNR research group began at the University of Hohenheim and expanded to Syracuse University (2013) and Coventry University (2015). The GNR group embraces a human rights-based framework in its work and engages theoretical and practical approaches to nutrition security and sustainable food systems in the local, regional, and international arenas. Teaching and research emphasize social justice, gender analysis, human rights, engaged civil society, and food and identity. We employ quantitative, qualitative, and diverse mixed methods as well as participatory approaches, and we collaborate across disciplines, sectors, and levels.

The collaboration leading to this book began in 2008, through an effort at the University of Hohenheim to bring experts from diverse fields and sectors who were working on the human right to adequate food on campus to update faculty and students on cutting edge issues unfolding at FAO and WHO. These initial lectures and workshops developed into consultations that plotted common areas of interest and potential areas of cooperation, in particular between the Department of Gender and Nutrition at Hohenheim and FIAN International. In May 2011, the Department of Gender and Nutrition at Hohenheim and FIAN International co-organized a public workshop meeting entitled Gender, Nutrition and the Right to Adequate Food to present our ideas and to initiate public discussion with representatives from international human rights bodies. To these ends, we collaborated with Olivier de Schutter, former UN special rapporteur on the right to food, Ismat Jahan, member of the CEDAW Committee, and Asako Hattori, senior legal adviser from the UN Office of the High Commissioner for Human Rights (OHCHR). The public workshop was followed by a closed afternoon meeting with the morning panel participants and other right to adequate food experts who reviewed the collaborative work achieved so far and helped develop strategies for follow-up. The perspectives of these experts are further captured in a public workshop report that was compiled from the public dialogue.[7] One outcome of this meeting was a closer collaboration with GIFA on the eventual development of the book project and related advocacy, which for the partnership included engagement with the CFS, CRC Committee, CEDAW Committee, and WHO (WHO secretariat and its governing bodies, executive board, and the World Health Assembly).

THE ORGANIZATION OF THE BOOK

Each chapter of the volume reflects work by key authors, but they have each been reviewed by all or most of the authors at various stages of their evolution to maintain a consistency of ideas and process. Furthermore, the book benefitted from external reviewers, but the final product of each chapter remains the responsibility of the key authors.

The first chapter of this volume, "The Evolving Nature of the Human Rights System and the Development of the Right to Adequate Food and Nutrition Concept," provides an overview of the international human rights concepts, framework, and system as an evolving social construct that constantly changes, even as we have worked on this volume. For some, this present background will be repetitive. For many, perhaps especially those in the United States, one of the miniscule handful of countries that has ratified neither the 1966 ICESCR which enshrines the right to adequate food, nor the 1979 CEDAW, nor the 1989 CRC, many aspects of the volume's approach will be new. We present background on the evolutive nature of human rights generally, and more specific information on the ICESCR, CEDAW, and more recent developments including the 1999 CESCR interpretive *General Comment 12 on the Right to Adequate Food* (CESCR 1999), the *Voluntary Guidelines to Support the Progressive Realization of the Right to Adequate Food in the Context of National Food Security*, published by the FAO in 2005, and a procession of global governance reforms that have been unfolding since the 2008 international food crisis. Critical to this discussion is the role of public interest civil society in shouldering forward progressive transformations of human rights-based approaches to food and nutrition.

Chapter 2 of this volume, "Gender, Nutrition, and the Right to Adequate Food: Introducing Two Structural Disconnects and the Human Rights Processes Necessary to Address Them," identifies two structural "disconnects" that frustrate women's right to adequate food and nutrition and that magnify three existing conditions that further impede women's food security on the ground. The first disconnect refers to the structural isolation of women's rights from the human right to adequate food and nutrition within the legally binding language of key international human rights treaties. This disconnect is primarily reflected in the invisibility of women in the ICESCR, the omission of women's right to adequate food and nutrition in CEDAW, and the singular attention paid to pregnant and breastfeeding women's nutritional status in the aforementioned conventions as well as in the CRC. The chapter's analysis of the first structural disconnect is supplemented through a brief review of the general comments and general recommendations issued by the CESCR and CEDAW Committee, respectively, regarding their use of a language that refers to the discriminated against, and especially the women among them, as *vulnerable*. Vulnerability implies weakness as opposed to the abuse of power that leads to violations of human rights. The second disconnect is intertwined in the first and reveals a focus on nutrition as primarily a function of reproduction and not the sovereign human right of all people at all times, and further, that nutrition is isolated from the right to adequate food by an emphasis on mass production and globalized trade of food stuffs and the over-medicalization of nutritional health.

The first condition that is leveraged by the disconnects, violence against women and girls, is addressed in chapter 3 of this volume entitled "Violence and Women's Participation in the Right to Adequate Food and Nutrition." We present violence as an under-examined barrier to women's human right to adequate food and nutrition and their participation as autonomous and participatory members of efforts to address hunger and malnutrition. Gender-based violence, of which discrimination is a primary form, impedes women from engaging in their own right to adequate food and nutrition and from acting on behalf of their families and communities to the full extent of their capabilities. Structural violence engenders violations of women's human rights and at the same time impedes their protection. Furthermore, structural violence is a cause of systematic violations of the human right to adequate food and nutrition, including malnutrition, of infants, children, and women. In order to approach the goal of including women and a gender perspective in food security ("gender mainstreaming"), research and policy must pay attention to the challenges women face, most particularly in relation to structural violence as a basis of discrimination and social injustice that impedes the realization of women's basic human rights and their participation in civil society.

Chapter 4 of this volume, "Maternal, Infant, and Young Child Feeding: Intertwined Subjectivities and Corporate Accountability," investigates a second condition that interferes with women's right to adequate food and nutrition, namely the structural and legal separation of women's rights and both (*a*) their control over reproductive choice and nutritional needs before, during, and after pregnancy and (*b*) their material and psychological connection to fetuses, infants, and young children during the most crucial time of human nutrition and health, a period generating short and long term developmental consequences. The chapter presents on women's malnutrition in the context of current policy intervention on maternal, infant, and young child health and nutrition. The chapter focuses on the CRC and reports on recent general comments issued by the CRC Committee—namely *General Comment 15 on the Right of the Child to the Enjoyment of the Highest Attainable Standard of Health* (hereinafter, *CRC General Comment 15*; CRC Committee 2013a) and *General Comment 16 on State Obligations regarding the Impact of the Business Sector on Children's Rights* (hereinafter *CRC General Comment 16*; CRC Committee 2013b)—that critique inadequate short-term, transnational, and market-based solutions to hunger and malnutrition. The corporate private sector must not interfere with others' strategies to build self-determination and autonomy through the promotion and protection of local and national food systems that begin with breastfeeding support and the appropriate introduction of culturally specific and locally grown complementary foods. *CRC General Comment 15* and *CRC General Comment 16* strongly urge state parties to build legally binding human rights frameworks that require corporate accountability to standards that protect children's nutritional health. Women's human right to adequate food and nutrition can only be achieved within the context of commitment to the realization of all of their economic and political human rights. Further, the critical nutrition needs of pregnant and lactating women and of the youngest children must not supersede the human right to adequate food and nutrition of all children and adults, female and male.

As related in chapter 5 of this volume, "Sustainable Food Systems, Gender, and Participation: Foregrounding Women in the Context of the Right to Adequate Food and Nutrition," the structural disconnects support a third condition which leads to the presumption that international market systems provide better support for food security and nutritional well-being than do local and regional systems. The impact of this presumption leads to food and nutrition insecurity and inequality at the community level and among marginalized women in particular. There is a need to address the constructed and artificial separation in policy, program, trade, and ideology of "food" as something to produce and "nutrition" in the context of macro- and micro-nutrient sufficiency and health. The patronizing impetus to deliver external charitable nutrition "cures," especially in non-emergency situations as a "malnutrition prevention strategy," reifies discrimination against women and communities. This chapter provides alternative theoretical and practical frames that integrate food and nutrition security in a food systems approach, among them food sovereignty, sustainable diets, and agroecology. Central to the discussion is a gender perspective that takes into consideration discrimination and violence which women face, posing barriers to their participation in providing food and nutrition security for them, their families, and their communities. The chapter presents strategies that have yielded positive results for women in overcoming these barriers, participating in governance, and gaining a political voice and greater economic participation. It is further argued that men have to be more actively integrated in food and nutrition security strategies that seek to incorporate a gender perspective, providing case studies and initiatives from various regions that aim to address specifically men. These diverse approaches are cost effective and sustainable, in part because they build capacity and self-determination in local food systems through local governance. Local food governance in turn becomes actively linked to inter-scalar food governance systems that facilitate inclusive participation across geographies and socioeconomic differences.

To broaden rights holders' capacity and to hold states accountable, in particular for violations against women and girls, chapter 6 of this volume, "Closing Protection Gaps through a More Comprehensive Conceptual Framework for the Human Right to Adequate Food and Nutrition," introduces an expanded conceptual framework for the right to adequate food and nutrition that uses food sovereignty as the overarching framework and integrates the dimensions of gender, women's rights, and nutrition. It is our view that the human rights framework, in spite of limitations inherent to all social constructs, is the most potent tool available to human beings to promote a more precise diagnosis of the root causes of inequities and vio-lence observed in society. In this context, a participatory social movement-led reconceptualization of the human right to adequate food and nutrition is to be supported as the best way to overcome the artificial fragmentation and dislocation of the conceptual, legal, and institutional frameworks and the associated ineffective policies against hunger and malnutrition. At the same time, the new framework is seen as a potent tool to facilitate the unifica-tion of a social struggles agenda which could contribute to a needed shift in power correlation. For this new framework to be implemented, we recom-mend the creation of precedent through casework aligned with advocacy at the national, regional, and international levels. Further, we urge human rights treaty bodies to better coordinate their work on the human right to adequate food and nutrition and related rights, and to take steps forward in the task of evolutive interpretation through their joint or independent gen-eral comments and recommendations on the basis of this casework.

The making of this book benefitted from the input of many persons: people in struggle for their rights, in particular women and girls, human rights defenders, researchers, friends, colleagues, family; experts and those with new and open perspectives; people who agreed and disagreed. In the end, while the gift of insights is shared, and without them this book would have been impossible, the responsibility for error is ours.

Anne C. Bellows, Flavio L. S. Valente, Stefanie Lemke,
and María Daniela Núñez Burbano de Lara

NOTES

1. The methodology used to derive the prevalence of undernourishment (PoU) indicator incorporates, among others, (*a*) new data from demographic, health, and household surveys that revise minimum dietary energy requirements, by country; (*b*) new estimates of dietary energy supply, by country; (*c*) country specific estimates of food losses at the retail distribution level; and (*d*) techni-cal improvements to the methodology. By revising estimates back to 1990, the model draws conclusions of changes in food security from different previous year(s') baseline(s) (FAO, WFP, and IFAD 2012, 12–14, technical annex).

2. According to FAO, WFP, and IFAD (2012, 10–11), reasons to reduce the food insecurity estimates between 2007–2010 are based on two points: first, the transmission of economic shocks (in terms of slower gross domestic product (GDP) growth and higher prices for domestic staple foods) to many devel-oping countries was less pronounced than initially anticipated and, second, the PoU methodology does not capture short-term shocks but rather chronic undernourishment based on habitual consumption of dietary energy.

3. To see the summary of UN Secretary General Ban Ki-moon's address to the UN Global Compact board of January 9, 2015, please visit the webpage "Ban Calls on Global Compact to Help End Poverty, Transform Lives, Pro-tect Planet" at the UN News Centre website at http://www.un.org/apps/news/story.asp?NewsID=49770#.VNklgHco42h (last accessed February 10, 2015).

4. As Dr. Margaret Chan, director general of the World Health Organization (WHO), states in this context: "I am deeply concerned by . . . efforts by

industry to shape the public health policies and strategies that affect their products. When industry is involved in policy-making, rest assured that the most effective control measures will be downplayed or left out entirely. This, too, is well documented, and dangerous. In the view of WHO, the formulation of health policies must be protected from distortion by commercial or vested interests." For the Dr. Chan's full address at the Eighth Global Conference on Health Promotion in 2013 in Helsinki, please visit the website of WHO at http://www.who.int/dg/speeches/2013/health_promotion_20130610/en/ (last accessed on February 11, 2015).

5. For example, the 2002 UN *Women, Peace, and Security* study found that increasing violations of women's rights constituted a reliable indicator of escalating intra-national conflict (UN 2002). The UN secretary general's 2009 report *Women and Peace and Security* identifies special needs of women associated with conflict escalation, prevention, resolution and peace-building to include violations associated with sexual violence, security and access to social services, access to political participation, and access to education (UN Security Council 2009). Empirical data drives findings linking gender discrimination and hunger in the IFPRI and Welthungerhilfe *Global Hunger Index* (GHI) (von Grebmer et al. 2009).

6. As of May 2014, WHA resolutions relevant to the *International Code of Marketing of Breast-milk Substitutes* comprise resolutions WHA35.26 (WHA 1982), WHA37.30 (1984), WHA39.28 (1986), WHA41.11 (1988), WHA43.3 (1990), WHA47.5 (1994), WHA49.15 (1996), WHA54.2 (2001), WHA55.25 (2002), WHA58.32 (2005), WHA59.11 (2006a), WHA59.21 (2006b), WHA61.20 (2008), WHA63.23 (2010), and WHA65.6 (2012b).

7. Department of Gender and Nutrition, University of Hohenheim, and FIAN International. 2011. *Gender, Nutrition and the Right to Adequate Food. 20th May 2011. Public Workshop Report.* University of Hohenheim, Stuttgart, Germany. Available online at http://www.fian.org/en/library/publication/detail/gender_nutrition_and_right_to_adequate_food; accessed December 15, 2014.

REFERENCES

Boserup, E. 1970. *Woman's Role in Economic Development.* London: Earthscan.

Food and Agriculture Organization of the United Nations (FAO). 2005. *Voluntary Guidelines to Support the Progressive Realization of the Right to Adequate Food in the Context of National Food Security.* Rome: Food and Agriculture Organization of the United Nations (FAO).

Food and Agriculture Organization of the United Nations (FAO) and United Nations World Food Programme (WFP). 2010. *The State of Food Insecurity in the World: Addressing Food Insecurity in Protracted Crises.* Rome: Food and Agriculture Organization of the United Nations (FAO).

Food and Agriculture Organization of the United Nations (FAO), United Nations World Food Programme (WFP), and International Fund for Agricultural Development (IFAD). 2012. *The State of Food Insecurity in the World: Economic Growth is Necessary but Not Sufficient to Accelerate Reduction of Hunger and Malnutrition.* Rome: Food and Agriculture Organization of the United Nations (FAO).

Gussow, J., O. Muchena, and W.B. Eide. 1984. "Women and Food—Equity and Development?" In *Food as a Human Right*, edited by A. Eide, W.B. Eide, S. Goonatilake, J. Gussow and Omawale, 69–88. Tokyo: United Nations University.

International Food Policy Research Institute (IFPRI). 2005. *Women: Still the Key to Food and Nutrition Security*. Washington, D.C.: International Food Policy Research Institute (IFPRI).

J.P. 2012. "Not a Billion after All." *The Economist*, October 1, 2012.

Kent, G. 2002. "A Gendered Perspective on Nutrition Rights." *Agenda* 17 (51): 43–50.

Lemke, S., H.H. Vorster, N.S. Jansen van Rensburg, and J. Ziche. 2003. "Empowered Women, Social Networks and the Contribution of Qualitative Research: Broadening our Understanding of Underlying Causes for Food and Nutrition Insecurity." *Public Health Nutrition* 6 (8): 759–64.

Maxwell, S. and M. Smith. 1992. "Household Food Security: A Conceptual Review." In *Household Food Security: Concepts, Indicators, Measurements—A Technical Review*, edited by S. Maxwell and T.R. Frankenberger, 1–72. New York: United Nations Children's Fund (UNICEF); International Fund for Agricultural Development (IFAD).

Moser, C. and A. Moser. 2005. "Gender Mainstreaming since Beijing: A Review of Success and Limitations in International Institutions." *Gender and Development* 13 (2): 11–22.

Quisumbing, A.R. and L.C. Smith. 2007. "Case Study No. 4–5. Intrahousehold Allocation, Gender Relations, and Food Security in Developing Countries." In *Food Policy for Developing Countries: Case Studies*, edited by P. Pinstrup-Andersen and F. Cheng, 13 pp. Ithaca, New York: Cornell University.

Richter, J. 2014. "Letters World Health Organization: Time to Turn the Tide: WHO's Engagement with Non-State Actors and the Politics of Stakeholder Governance and Conflicts of Interest." *British Medical Journal* 348: g335.

Scherr, S. 2003. *Halving Global Hunger. Background Paper of the Millennium Project Task Force on Hunger*. New York: United Nations Development Programme (UNDP).

Smith, L.C. and L. Haddad. 2000. *Overcoming Child Malnutrition in Developing Countries: Past Achievements and Future Choices*. Food, Agriculture, and the Environment Discussion: Paper 30, edited by International Food Policy Research Institute (IFPRI). Washington, D.C.: International Food Policy Research Institute (IFPRI).

United Nations (UN). 2002. *Women, Peace and Security: Study Submitted by the Secretary-General Pursuant to Security Council Resolution 1325 (2000)*. New York: United Nations (UN).

United Nations Committee on Economic, Social and Cultural Rights (CESCR). 1999. *General Comment No. 12: The Right to Adequate Food (Art. 11 of the Covenant). E/C.12/1999/5, 12 May 1999*. New York: United Nations Economic and Social Council (ECOSOC).

———. 2009. *General Comment No. 20: Non-Discrimination in Economic, Social and Cultural Rights (Art. 2, Para. 2, of the International Covenant on Economic, Social and Cultural Rights). E/C.12/GC/20, 2 July 2009*. New York: United Nations Economic and Social Council (ECOSOC).

United Nations Committee on the Rights of the Child (CRC Committee). 2013a. *General Comment No. 15 (2013) on the Right of the Child to the Enjoyment of the Highest Attainable Standard of Health (Art. 24). CRC/C/GC/15, 17 April 2013*. New York: United Nations (UN).

———. 2013b. *General Comment No. 16 (2013) on State Obligations regarding the Impact of the Business Sector on Children's Rights. CRC/C/GC/16, 17 April 2013*. New York: United Nations (UN).

United Nations Economic and Social Council (ECOSOC). 2007. *Strengthening Efforts to Eradicate Poverty and Hunger, Including through the Global Partnership for Development (E/2007/71)*. New York: United Nations (UN).

United Nations General Assembly. 1966. *International Covenant on Economic, Social and Cultural Rights. 16 December 1966, United Nations, Treaty Series, Vol. 993, p. 3.* New York: United Nations (UN) General Assembly.

———. 1979. *Convention on the Elimination of All Forms of Discrimination against Women. 18 December 1979.* New York: United Nations (UN) General Assembly.

———. 1989. *Convention on the Rights of the Child, 20 November 1989, United Nations, Treaty Series, Vol. 1577, p. 3.* New York: United Nations (UN) General Assembly.

United Nations Human Rights Council (HRC). 2011. *Study of the Human Rights Council Advisory Committee on Discrimination in the Context of the Right to Food. A/HRC/16/40, 16 February 2011.* New York: United Nations (UN).

———. 2012a. *Final Study of the Human Rights Council Advisory Committee on the Advancement of the Rights of Peasants and Other People Working in Rural Areas. A/HRC/19/75, 24 February 2012.* New York: United Nations (UN) General Assembly.

———. 2012b. *Report Submitted by the Special Rapporteur on the Right to Food, Olivier De Schutter: Women's Rights and the Right to Food. A/HRC/22/50, 24 December 2012.* New York: United Nations (UN) General Assembly.

United Nations Security Council. 2009. *Women and Peace and Security. Report of the Secretary-General. S/2009/465, 16 September 2009.* New York: United Nations Security Council.

Valente, F. L. S. and A. M. Suárez Franco. 2010. "Human Rights and the Struggle against Hunger: Laws, Institutions, and Instruments in the Fight to Realize the Right to Adequate Food." *Yale Human Rights & Development Law Journal* 13 (2): 435–61.

von Grebmer, K., B. Nestorova, A. R. Quisumbing, R. Fertziger, H. Fritschel, R. Pandya-Lorch, and Y. Yohannes. 2009. *2009 Global Hunger Index: The Challenge of Hunger: Focus on Financial Crisis and Gender Inequality.* Bonn, Washington, D.C., Dublin: Welthungerhilfe; International Food Policy Research Institute (IFPRI); Concern Worldwide.

World Bank, Food and Agriculture Organization of the United Nations (FAO), and International Fund for Agricultural Development (IFAD). 2009. *Gender in Agriculture Sourcebook.* Washington, D.C. World Bank Publications.

World Health Assembly (WHA). 1982. *WHA Resolution 35.26. Thirty-fifth World Health Assembly.* Geneva: World Health Assembly (WHA).

———. 1984. *WHA Resolution 37.30. Thirty-seventh World Health Assembly.* Geneva: World Health Assembly (WHA).

———. 1986. *WHA Resolution 39.28. Thirty-ninth World Health Assembly.* Geneva: World Health Assembly (WHA).

———. 1988. *WHA Resolution 41.11. Forty-first World Health Assembly.* Geneva: World Health Assembly (WHA).

———. 1990. *WHA Resolution 43.3. Forty-third World Health Assembly.* Geneva: World Health Assembly (WHA).

———. 1994. *WHA Resolution 47.5. Forty-seventh World Health Assembly. Infant and Young Child Nutrition.* Geneva: World Health Assembly (WHA).

———. 1996. *WHA Resolution 49.15. Forty-ninth World Health Assembly.* Geneva: World Health Assembly (WHA).

———. 2001. *WHA Resolution 54.2. Fifty-fourth World Health Assembly. Infant and Young Child Nutrition.* Geneva: World Health Assembly (WHA).

———. 2002. *WHA Resolution 55.25. Fifty-fifth World Health Assembly. Infant and Young Child Nutrition.* Geneva: World Health Assembly (WHA).

———. 2005. *WHA Resolution 58.32. Fifty-eighth World Health Assembly. Infant and Young Child Nutrition.* Geneva: World Health Assembly (WHA).

———. 2006a. *WHA Resolution 59.11 Fifty-ninth World Health Assembly. Nutrition and HIV/AIDS.* Geneva: World Health Assembly (WHA).

———. 2006b. *WHA Resolution 59.21. Fifty-ninth World Health Assembly. Infant and Young Child Nutrition.* Geneva: World Health Assembly (WHA).

———. 2008. *WHA Resolution 61.20. Sixty-first World Health Assembly.* Geneva: World Health Assembly (WHA).

———. 2010. *WHA Resolution 63.23. Sixty-third World Health Assembly. Infant and Young Child Nutrition.* Geneva: World Health Assembly (WHA).

———. 2012b. *WHA Resolution 65.6. Sixty-fifth World Health Assembly. Comprehensive Implementation Plan on Maternal, Infant and Young Child Nutrition.* Geneva: World Health Assembly (WHA).

World Health Organization (WHO). 1981. *International Code of Marketing of Breast-milk Substitutes.* Geneva: World Health Organization (WHO).

Acknowledgments

We, the combined group of authors associated with this book, extend our most sincere thanks to the many people who helped our group project from earliest stages through the production of the final manuscript.

Many thanks go to those who were involved in the preparatory and initial stages, even before it became clear that the project would turn into a book. Their critical and enthusiastic insight played a substantial role in the manuscript's final creation. This includes those who took part in the Gender, Nutrition, and the Right to Adequate Food conference held at the University of Hohenheim and cooperatively organized by the formerly existing university's Department of Gender and Nutrition and FIAN International in 2011. Particular thanks is imparted to the public workshop panelists, namely Olivier De Schutter (member of the United Nations Committee on Economic, Social and Cultural Rights, at that time United Nations special rapporteur on the right to food), Asako Hattori (representative of the United Nations Office of the High Commissioner for Human Rights), and Ismat Jahan (member of the United Nations Committee on the Elimination of Discrimination against Women), as well as to Hans-Peter Liebig, at that time rector of the University of Hohenheim, for his opening words, and especially to the participants who, during the closed expert meeting of that conference, shared with us their views of how our initial position paper could be further improved. Together we discussed possible strategies to engage our thesis through public policy advocacy, publication, teaching, and research. Specifically, we extend our gratitude to Christine Bruckner, Christine Chemnitz, Olivier De Schutter, Asako Hattori, Irmgard Jordan, Gertrude Klaffenböck, Kristin Kraejet, Isabella Rae, Martin Remppis, Fatima Shabodien, Ina Verzivolli, and Bernhard Walter. For their funding support of this conference, our gratitude goes to the European Commission's EcoFair Trade Dialogue Project, Glopolis, Heinrich-Böll Foundation, Misereor, Foundation fiat panis, FIAN International, and the no longer active Research Center for Gender and Nutrition at the University of Hohenheim.

We say thank you also to those involved in the workshop which took place the following year at the congress World Nutrition *Rio2012* held in Rio de Janeiro, Brazil, which was organized by the Department of Gender and Nutrition of the University of Hohenheim together with FIAN International and the Geneva Infant Feeding Association, Swiss member of the International Baby Food Action Network (IBFAN-GIFA). Workshop panelists included Emma Siliprandi (Food and Agriculture Organization of the United Nations, Regional Office for Latin America and the Caribbean, formerly of the Center of Food Studies and Research at the State University of Campinas), and Ina Verzivolli (Albanian State Agency on Protection of Children's Rights, Ministry of Social Welfare and Youth, formerly IBFAN-GIFA).

A special mention must go to those who provided their invaluable knowledge and acumen in regard to specific chapters of this book, in particular Martin Wopold-Bosien, Jennifer L. Wilkins, Leila Srour, Maryse Arendt, and Alison Linnecar. Thanks also to Maryse Arendt and Bryan Watt for granting us the copyright permissions to make use of their art work.

We feel greatly indebted to all those involved with the numerous smaller and larger tasks and undertakings that assisted in the many stages leading to completion of this book, namely Marion Büttner, Ana Cristina Eisermann, Shahin Ghaziani, Dyah Inayati, Shauna Keeler, Elisabeth Kilian, Fabiola López, Stefanie Loveless, María Isabel Matute Girón, Margo Elena Mejía, Josephine Montford, Ratna Purwestri, Samira Sahamishirazi, Julia Skibowski, Caroline Stiller, and Fereshteh Yousefi. This extends to the administrative support and assistance provided by Kathleen Heckert and the indomitable Julia Rietze. A huge word of thanks goes to Katharine Cresswell Riol, without whose thoroughness and steady support this book would have taken far longer to complete. Her assistance was particularly valuable in regard to the proofreading process, literature research, bibliographic management, and the development and completion of the index.

Deep gratitude is expressed to the anonymous reviewers who supplied their beneficial and well-received feedback on the book proposal, and to our editor at Routledge, Max Novick, for his patience and support.

All of us authors individually know and are grateful for where our inspiration and endurance originate: from those who do and have nurtured us every day, from forthright colleagues, from those we met for a day or a moment who took the time to share an insight that changed our lives, from giants whom we never met but whose ideas and lives live on to guide us and give us hope.

1 The Evolving Nature of the Human Rights System and the Development of the Right to Adequate Food and Nutrition Concept

Anne C. Bellows, María Daniela Núñez Burbano de Lara, and Roseane do Socorro Gonçalves Viana

INTRODUCTION

The food crisis of 2008 was not an isolated incident or unique event from which the world economy and food security has now restabilized. Calculations of individuals living in hunger and with food and nutrition insecurity range from 870 million to over one billion.[1] But although estimates of food insecurity differ, the geography and sociodemographic profile of the food insecure remains unaltered (FAO, WFP, and IFAD 2012). The most food and nutrition insecure groups comprise peasant farmers, small landholders, landless workers, fisherfolk, and hunters and gatherers (HRC 2010; see also Scherr 2003, table 3.1).[2] As a crosscutting category of these groups, women and girls face violations of their right to adequate food and nutrition more often than do boys and men; they comprise about 60 percent of the hungry (ECOSOC 2007) and 70 percent of the poor (World Bank, FAO, and IFAD 2009; HRC 2012a). Paradoxically, not only are women's and girls' rights protected through a wide range of human rights instruments (HRC 2012a, para. 1), it has furthermore long since been established that women are key to food security and well-being at the household level (Smith and Haddad 2000; Kent 2002; IFPRI 2005; Quisumbing and Smith 2007; see also Maxwell and Smith 1992; Lemke, Bellows, and Heumann 2009), and that composite indicators for gender discrimination are positively correlated with hunger and social instability at the national level (UN 2002; von Grebmer et al. 2009).[3]

The moral logic of simple justice and equality, as well as the social expediency of investment in women's well-being to leverage family and community livelihoods would seem self-evident. And yet, women's rights have had to be specifically and independently articulated; further, interference with these rights affects not only women but the communities to which they belong. Already in 1984 it was asserted that the realization of the right to adequate food and nutrition "depends on an immense, economically uncompensated work input by women" that social and cultural prejudice frustrates (Gussow, Muchena, and W.B. Eide 1984, 69). Indeed, these arguments buoyed the promotion and mainstreaming of a gender perspective in all spheres of society as the means to address discrimination at the 1995 United Nations (UN) Fourth World Conference for Women in Beijing (Moser and Moser 2005; see also chapter 3 of this volume). Yet not even at this conference did advocacy, policy, and analysis identify or address the existing link between women's rights, nutrition, and the human right to adequate food, losing a good opportunity to effectively include a gender perspective in efforts to promote food and nutrition security.[4] The obvious question to ask, therefore, is: *when so many call for the inclusion of women and a gender perspective in food and nutrition security, why is the food and nutrition security status of women and girls not improving?* This volume attempts to address this question by embracing a more inclusive framework for the human right to adequate food, one that includes the long neglected gender and nutrition dimensions. Answering this question has consequences beyond the improvement of the nutritional status of women alone. The full realization of women's rights, including women's right to adequate food and nutrition, is closely linked to the realization of the right to adequate food and nutrition of all members of society.

At the core of our project is our intention to demonstrate how growing public interest civil society participation immeasurably strengthens the human rights system's evolutive process and, we argue, legitimizes related global governance objectives by broadening participation through the messy and absolutely necessary conditions of democracy.[5] At the same time, our presentation introduces the contemporary struggle over the future of the global governance of food and nutrition policy. These developments currently pit a human rights-based approach and, importantly, its legal framework, that champion the participation of the most socially and economically marginalized against the so-called "neoliberal agenda" that promotes free trade, private sector deregulation, and public-private partnerships (PPP) as central to social stability and economic security. What is portrayed as "free trade" or "free trade agreements" is actually exceedingly regulated, but in favor of protecting and enhancing already powerful private interests and investments, aims that are at odds with human rights.

This chapter introduces the evolving nature of the human rights system, a characteristic that makes it possible to advance continually the human rights conceptual and legal frameworks and related support mechanisms to close existing and emerging gaps in human rights protection and achieve social justice objectives, including gender equity. Although this evolutive process began a long time before the foundational *Charter of the United Nations* was signed in San Francisco in 1945 (UN 1945), the establishment of an international organization with the mandate to oversee and promote the respect and protection of universal human rights reflects an evolution in rights thinking and marks the starting point of our analysis. This chapter illustrates how, since then, the human rights development endeavor has worked and continues to work step by step to overcome its own limitations and to strive toward the ideals it sets forth for itself. This chapter's presentation is by no means comprehensive in terms of all that has and is happening with regards to human rights in general and the right to adequate food and nutrition in particular. Likewise, this discussion introduces a narrative about human rights that is very young and vibrant, whose history has only begun. In the chapters that follow, some of these additional achievements and developments related to the human right to adequate food and nutrition framework will be taken up.

Human rights principles and states parties' obligations under international law lay the foundation for a realization of human rights.[6] This framework represents the crucial difference between food security and nutrition on one hand, and the human right to adequate food, on the other hand, or as we will argue, the human right to adequate food *and nutrition* (see chapters 5 and 6 of this volume). In this chapter, we explain how the human rights framework creates the legal condition of rights holders' enhanced status as rights claimers to an accountable state that must adhere to measurable obligations. In this approach based on human dignity, rights holders are recognized as subjects and not mere recipients of charity. As described by Kelsen (1967, 134), "the right—the reflex of the legal obligation—is equipped with the legal power of the entitled individual to bring about by a law suit the execution of a sanction as a reaction against the nonfulfillment of the obligation whose reflex is his right." Beyond utopian dream or legalistic parlay and despite massive resistance, we have faith that the human rights system must and will continue to evolve into an increasingly accessible and effective resource and institution.

HUMAN RIGHTS CONCEPTS, FRAMEWORKS, AND SYSTEM AS EVOLVING SOCIAL CONSTRUCTS

The premise of this volume is aligned with the argument that international law is evolutionary in character, meaning that the assumptions and language use that support the development of legal instruments reflect an evolving society and must, therefore, be considered as flexible constructions that may need improving or expansion over time (see, e.g., Brownlie 2008; De Schutter 2010; Henkin 1978; Hunt 2008; Ishay 2008; Lauren 2003). Supporting this position, we note that the 1969 *Vienna Convention on the Law of Treaties* points to the need to use outside sources in interpreting international law treaties (UN 1969, art. 32). Quoting Micheline Ishay (2008, 3), "[i]n our day, the manifold meanings of human rights reflect the process of historical continuity and change that helped shape their present substance." Although this process of historical continuity and change might be traced back to ancient civilizations and world religions, the history of universal human rights as part of international law dates back only to the mid-twentieth century. The *Universal Declaration of Human Rights* (UDHR) adopted by the UN General Assembly in 1948 embeds the idea that all governments in their role as representatives of society have the obligation to respect universally the inherent and inalienable equality, dignity, and autonomy of all individuals through the progressive realization of their interdependent, interrelated, and indivisible rights.

Human rights are not defined by state or non-state charity and benevolence, but rather through empowered dignity, inclusive leadership, and self-determination. The evolution of human rights from an abstract legal and idealistic tract to a living, debated, and justiciable force, wherein dignity has tangible qualities, and for which indicators can be developed and benchmarks set, has only begun. The framework of defining, claiming, and being accountable for the realization of human rights is shaped by what often appears to be rigid constructions of the international legal system. However, this framework has the capacity to change with newly introduced knowledge and adequate pressure. From a sociopolitical perspective, the path to realize human rights is in large part advanced by those persons who suffer oppression and discrimination. When they recognize and are able to articulate endured privations as violations of their human rights, they begin to develop the capacity to organize and stand up against these violations (Valente and Suárez Franco 2010, 439). As Valente and Suárez Franco (2010, 458) observe, "[i]n the process [rights holders/claimants] defend and 'build' their rights and eventually get them codified into national and international law."

The UDHR provides the visionary framework for human dignity and self-determination whence subsequent declarations and treaty laws have advanced. But already at its beginnings, the Cold War between the free market driven, democratic West and the socialist East dominated the era and its oppositional ideologies generated a structural demarcation of the human rights system. While the declared intention of human rights is that they are indivisible, inalienable, and available for all persons, everywhere (see Table 1.1), the UDHR also wrought the blueprint of their institutionalized partition.[7] Economic, social, and cultural rights, like the right to adequate food and nutrition, education, health care, and work, were consolidated in the socialist block, while civil and political rights that protect individuals' and groups' freedoms to guarantee their capacity to participate in civil and political life, like the freedoms of speech and association, were promoted in Western democracies. After long debate, this artificial separation resulted in the issuance of two separate covenants in 1966, the *International Covenant on Economic, Social and Cultural Rights* (ICESCR; UN General Assembly 1966b) and *the International Covenant on Civil and Political Rights* (ICCPR; UN General Assembly 1966a).[8] The practical administration of these two covenants developed separate institutional structures that did not prioritize mechanisms to realize the interrelatedness and indivisibility of human rights.

Table 1.1 Human rights characteristics

Characteristic	Explanation
Universal	Human rights are applicable worldwide to every human being, regardless of political, economic, cultural, or creed-based system.
Inalienable	Human rights are inherent in all human beings, simply on the basis of being human. They cannot be taken away, sold, parted with, or renounced. Exceptionally and in very specific situations, human rights can be limited through due legal process to guarantee public well-being.
Interrelated	Improvement in the realization of any one human right is a function of the realization of the other human rights.
Interdependent	The level of enjoyment of any one human right is dependent on the level of realization of a human being's other human rights.
Indivisible	All civil, cultural, economic, political, and social human rights are equally important. Improving the enjoyment of any human right cannot be done at the expense of the realization of any other human right. Moreover, the content of a human right should not be fragmented, for example, by separating the human right to use of and control over natural and productive resources from the human right to adequate food and nutrition.

Source: adapted from OHCHR (2012, 11).

The 1950s and 1960s witnessed an acceleration of opposition to colonialism and institutionalized racial discrimination, the resurfacing of a women's movement after World War II, resistance to the exponential growth of transnational corporations (TNCs), and the beginning of environmental activism. Not all of these struggles were shaped in the frame of international and universal human rights. They were, however, reflected in the gap between states parties' commitment to recognize and realize progressively "the equal and inalienable rights of all members of the human family" (UN General Assembly 1948, preamble) and the concrete reality of non-compliance with this commitment (Valente and Suárez Franco 2010, 441). Over the years, social movement energy has forced forward group rights agendas on many fronts (Stammers 1999, 2005). Part of the evolutionary trajectory was supported through the 1993 World Conference on Human Rights in Vienna that reinvigorated the call for the integration of civil and political with economic, social, and cultural rights, reaffirming their indivisible nature and rejecting a rank order approach to their realization (UN General Assembly 1993b, para. 5; A. Eide 2005, esp. 19–22; Valente and Suárez Franco 2010, 458). Successes over time include the adoption by the UN General Assembly of the legally binding *International Covenant on the Elimination of All*

Forms of Racial Discrimination (ICERD) in 1965 (UN General Assembly 1965a), the *Convention on the Elimination of All Forms of Discrimination against Women* (CEDAW) in 1979 (UN General Assembly 1979), the *Convention against Torture and Other Cruel, Inhuman or Degrading Treatment or Punishment* (CAT) in 1984 (UN General Assembly 1984), the *Convention on the Rights of the Child* (CRC) in 1989 (UN General Assembly 1989), the *International Convention on the Protection of the Rights of All Migrant Workers and Members of Their Families* (ICMW) in 1990 (UN General Assembly 1990), the *International Convention for the Protection of All Persons from Enforced Disappearance* (CPED; UN General Assembly 2006), as well as the *Convention on the Rights of Persons with Disabilities* (CRPD; UN General Assembly 2007a) and the legally non-binding *Declaration on the Rights of Indigenous Peoples* (UN General Assembly 2007b), both in 2007. These post-1966 UN instruments speak to the ongoing need for continuous improvement in human rights assumptions, laws, monitoring, and accountability mechanisms. Currently, the process continues. There are, for instance, diverse intergovernmental working groups established by the United Nations Human Rights Council (HRC) concerned with the development of further human rights instruments, including the Open-ended Intergovernmental Working Group on a United Nations Declaration on the Rights of Peasants and Other People Working in Rural Areas (established 2012; see HRC 2012b) and the Open-ended Intergovernmental Working Group on a Legally Binding Instrument on Transnational Corporations and Other Business Enterprises with Respect to Human Rights (established 2014; see HRC 2014).

The Slowly Evolving Institutional Framework for Realizing Women's Human Rights: An Example of Evolutionary Perseverance

As much as we find hope in the evolutionary capacity of human rights concepts, framework, and system, we stress that the process is slow and painstaking. As an example of a long struggle to confront the limitations of the existing human rights system and to force the development of a new institutional legal mechanism to address human rights violations, we present the winding course traversed by women's rights activists in achieving the status of a legally binding convention in CEDAW (see table 1.2). While diffuse and sporadic efforts to bring attention to women's rights certainly started in many parts of the world long before the mid-twentieth century, *universal* women's rights initiatives began in 1946 with the establishment of the Sub-commission on Women's Rights as one of the earliest UN projects. Although it took over thirty years before the UN General Assembly finally adopted CEDAW as international treaty law in 1979, the convention paradoxically entered into force less than two years after its adoption, faster than any previous human rights treaty (CEDAW Committee 1995).

Table 1.2   Timeline of the struggle for the legally binding *Convention on the Elimi-nation of All Forms of Discrimination against Women* (CEDAW)

Year	Stage of progress
1946	Commission on the Status of Women (CSW) is established as sub-commission of the Commission on Human Rights (CHR)
1952	UN General Assembly *Resolution 640 (VII). Convention on the Political Rights of Women;* adopted 20 December 1952, enters into force 7 July 1954 (see UN General Assembly 1952)
1957	UN General Assembly *Resolution 1040 (XI). Convention on the Nationality of Married Women;* adopted 29 January 1957, enters into force 11 August 1958 (see UN General Assembly 1957)
1962	UN General Assembly *Resolution 1763 (XVII) A. Convention on Consent to Marriage, Minimum Age for Marriage and Registration of Marriages;* adopted 7 November 1962, enters into force 9 December 1964 (scc UN General Assembly 1962)
1963	UN General Assembly *Resolution 1921 (XVIII). Draft Declaration on the Elimination of Discrimination against Women;* adopted 5 December 1963: Economic and Social Council (ECOSOC) should invite CSW to draft a declaration to combine, in one single instrument, international standards articulating the equal rights of men and women (see UN General Assembly 1963)
1965	UN General Assembly *Resolution 2018 (XX). Recommendation on Consent to Marriage, Minimum Age for Marriage and Registration of Marriage;* adopted 1 November 1965 (see UN General Assembly 1965b)
1967	UN General Assembly *Resolution 2263 (XXII). Declaration on the Elimination of Discrimination against Women;* adopted 7 November 1967 (see UN General Assembly 1967)
1968	UN Economic and Social Council (ECOSOC) *Resolution 1325 (XLIV). Implementation of the Declaration on the Elimination of Discrimination against Women:* adoption of voluntary reporting system on rights status and violation (see ECOSOC 1968, 13)
1972	CSW considers preparation of binding covenant
1973	Working group formed to study covenant possibilities
1974	Working group delivers report. At its twenty-fifth session, CSW decides to create one single, comprehensive, and internationally binding instrument
1975	Call for a convention at the World Conference on the International Women's Year, Mexico City, 19 June-2 July 1975
1976	CSW working groups prepare the text of the *Convention on the Elimination of All Form of Discrimination against Women* (CEDAW)
1977–1979	UN General Assembly (working group of the Third Committee)[1] debates CEDAW text

(*Continued*)

Table 1.2 (Continued)

Year	Stage of progress
1979	UN General Assembly *Resolution 34/180. Convention on the Elimination of All Forms of Discrimination against Women;* adopted 18 December 1979 with 130 to zero votes and ten abstentions (see UN General Assembly 1979)
1980	Sixty-four states sign the convention and two states submit instruments of ratification at the World Conference of the United Nations Decade for Women: Equality, Development and Peace, Copenhagen, 17 July 1980
1981	CEDAW enters into force 3 September 1981, thirty days after ratification by the twentieth state, in accordance with article 27 of CEDAW
1999	UN General Assembly *Resolution 54/4. Optional Protocol to the Convention on the Elimination of All Forms of Discrimination against Women;* adopted 6 October 1999: the UN General Assembly, acting without a vote, adopts the optional protocol containing two procedures by which (*a*) individual women or groups of women may submit claims to the CEDAW Committee and (*b*) the committee may initiate inquiries into situations of grave or systematic violations of women's rights (UN General Assembly 1999)[2]
2000	*Optional Protocol to the Convention on the Elimination of All Forms of Discrimination against Women* enters into force 22 December 2000, following the ratification of the tenth state party to the convention

Source: adapted from CEDAW Committee (1995, paras. 6–14).

[1] The Third Committee, the Committee for Social, Humanitarian and Cultural Affairs (SOCHUM), is one of the Six Main Committees that the UN General Assembly has called into being to manage its diverse tasks. Among others, it examines the reports of the special procedures of the Human Rights Council (HRC), interacting with special rapporteurs, independent experts, and chairs of working groups of the HRC. The Third Committee discusses issues relating to a range of social, humanitarian affairs and human rights, such as the advancement of women, the protection of children, indigenous issues, the treatment of refugees, the promotion of fundamental freedoms through the elimination of racism and racial discrimination, and the right to self- determination (UN General Assembly 2014).

[2] For an overview of the history of the *Optional Protocol to the Convention on the Elimination of All Forms of Discrimination against Women*, please visit the website of the Division for the Advancement of Women, Department of Economic and Social Affairs (DAW/DESA 2009).

While states, upon signature of a treaty, provide a preliminary endorsement of the proposed instrument and commit themselves to refrain from acts that would undermine its objectives, their signature does not automatically create a legally binding obligation toward the treaty. The treaty does not become functional—that is, it does not *enter into force*—until it is either ratified at the national level, or directly acceded to by a non-signatory state following a process of domestic approval procedures. The number of state instruments of ratification or accession that are necessary before a treaty enters into force is set out in the treaty text and usually varies among treaties. In the case of women's rights, CEDAW entered into force as international treaty thirty days after the twentieth instrument of ratification or accession was deposited with the UN secretary general (UN General Assembly 1979, art. 27).

At this writing during the beginning phases of the twenty-first century, we see that universal human rights are still in early stages of development. Table 1.2 shows how thirty-three years passed between the 1946 establishment of the Commission on the Status of Women (CSW) and the 1979 resolution of CEDAW, thirty-five years before a women's rights treaty entered into force. Many early CEDAW attempts were frustrated, but the work continued and today, the struggle is not only to implement and realize the promised rights, but to reinterpret and expand upon them.

The development of international treaty law is a result of, and an influence on, national and regional campaigns. CEDAW is no exception. Intense local, regional, and national struggles form a history that leveraged the potential of an international women's human rights movement. This social movement continues to provide political fodder to push CEDAW and other women's rights initiatives to stages of human rights implementation, monitoring, recourse, and remedy. Likewise, the achievement of CEDAW on the international level supports political traction for women's human rights movements at the local, regional, and state levels. The following two case studies (1.1 and 1.2) present early and late twentieth century examples of regional and national lobbying work on women's rights in the Americas.

Case study 1.1 Pre-CEDAW regional organizing across the Americas that facilitated early ratification of CEDAW by select states

The *Equal Rights Amendment* (ERA) was penned by United States (US) American suffragist leader, Alice Paul, and introduced for the first of many unsuccessful attempts to the US Congress in 1923. It reads simply,

> Section 1. Equality of rights under the law shall not be denied or abridged by the United States or by any State on account of sex.
> Section 2. The Congress shall have the power to enforce, by appropriate legislation, the provisions of this article.
> Section 3. This amendment shall take effect two years after the date of ratification. (Francis 2013)

After the ERA was drafted for and presented (unsuccessfully) in the United States, the demand for equal rights for women and men was taken up by women's groups for regional adoption at the Sixth International Conference of the American States in Havanna in 1928 with the objective of introducing it into national and international political debates across the hemisphere (Brewer Boeckel 1929). The exclusively male contingent, comprising country delegates in attendance and discussing women's rights in their absence, refused to allow anyone else to speak on their floor, or to open review of an equal rights treaty. Nevertheless, after much protest and campaigning, women succeeded in having their voices heard at a conference's plenary and public session. Although an equal rights treaty was not adopted, the decision was made to establish an Inter-American Commission of Women (CIM, after the Spanish name Comisión Interamericana de Mujeres) of the Organization of American States (OAS) which became in the same year the first intergovernmental agency dealing with women's rights in the world.[9] CIM immediately embraced equal rights for women as its official struggle and, together with women's groups, made a second equally failed attempt to introduce the treaty at the Seventh Conference of American States in Montevideo in 1933 (OAS 2013). With women in formal attendance, CIM did play a key role in successfully leveraging adoption of the 1933 *[Inter-American] Convention on the Nationality of Women* (OAS 1933), the first international, albeit regional, instrument, securing women the right to retain their citizenship in the event of marrying a man of different nationality (Benedek 2012, 175; OAS 2013).[10] This convention helped to leverage further constitutional reforms on behalf of women in the region and generated precedence for the development of the 1957 UN *Convention on the Nationality of Married Women* (UN General Assembly 1957; see table 1.2).

Almost half a century later, CIM participated in pushing the majority of regional states toward early ratification of the 1979 CEDAW: in 1980 Barbados, Cuba, Dominica, and Guyana; in 1981 Canada, Ecuador, El Salvador, Haiti, Mexico, Nicaragua, Panama, Saint Vincent and the Grenadines, and Uruguay; and in 1982 Colombia, Dominican Republic, Guatemala, Peru, and Saint Lucia (UN 2013b). The United States, which spawned the ERA, never ratified it.[11] Without the ERA in place and having expended political energy in its pursuit, the political will was never built in the United States to ratify CEDAW as an international treaty, even though the country signed CEDAW in 1980.

Case study 1.2 describes the development in the 1990s of an early regional convention on violence against women in the Americas that, in turn, helped with related constitutional law reforms in Brazil. At the international level, attention to violence against women had not been specifically incorporated into CEDAW. In 1992, the CSW took up the issue and in 1993 introduced and passed the *Declaration on the Elimination of Violence against Women* (DEVAW; UN General Assembly 1993a) at the World Conference on Human Rights in Vienna. The following year, CIM engaged the issue at the regional level.

Case study 1.2 Post-CEDAW regional organizing across the Americas that promoted related regional, as well as Brazilian national law

In 1994 at the twenty-fourth regular session of the General Assembly of the OAS, CIM facilitated the adoption of the *Inter-American Convention on the Prevention, Punishment, and Eradication of Violence against Women* (OAS 1994), known as the *Convention of Belém do Pará* on account of the Brazilian city where the assembly took place.[12] The convention states that women have the right to live free from violence, and that violence against women—physical, sexual, and psychological, both in the public and private spheres—constitutes a violation of human rights and fundamental freedoms (OAS 1994, arts. 1–3).[13]

Brazilian women, who were mobilized in social movements of the 1970s and 1980s, had forced through public policies for women in the 1988 national constitution, such as the extension of the maternity rights, as well as labor rights for urban and rural women (Pedrosa 2010). Brazil ratified the *Convention of Belem do Pará* in 1995 and upon its entry into force, the activist Brazilian women's movement pushed for national legislation to address violence against women, originating the law 11.340/2006, known as the *Maria da Penha Law* (Special Secretariat for Women's Policies [Brazil] 2006). In line with the *Convention of Belém do Pará*, article 6 of the *Maria da Penha Law* defines domestic violence as a human rights violation (Special Secretariat for Women's Policies [Brazil] 2006, 11) and dictates the creation of special courts for complaints of domestic and family violence against women with the specific and appropriate civil and penal competence to handle these violation complaints. We note, with respect to the discussion in chapter 3 of this volume, that the *Maria da Penha Law* links women's freedom from violence to the assurance of the right to adequate food.[14]

Claiming human rights is a slow and uneven process. It rarely moves forward on a steady, straightforward path. Neither does it start or stop at one specific political scale: the local, national, regional, or international. Rather, the evolution of the human rights system responds to the synergies of leadership, precedence, cooperation, opportunity, and perhaps most of all, perseverance across political scales.

THE EVOLUTION OF THE HUMAN RIGHT TO ADEQUATE FOOD AND NUTRITION CONCEPT AND FRAMEWORK

This section provides a rudimentary introduction to the concepts, frameworks, and system of human rights in general, and of the human right to adequate food and nutrition in particular. It is by no means comprehensive (see, among others, De Schutter 2013; De Schutter and Cordes 2011; W. B. Eide and Kracht 2005a, 2007; Kent 2005, 2008; Ziegler et al. 2011). The intention is to underscore the ongoing evolution that marks the development of the right to adequate food and nutrition frameworks, as well as the role of civil society in fostering that process. For many experts in this field, the presentation may appear quite basic. We hope that for those newer to the field of human rights, this background introduction will offer a foundation for reading the subsequent chapters.

The Legal Foundation of the Right to Adequate Food and Nutrition in the Human Rights System

As evidenced above, changing existing legal constructions or introducing new ones is a slow process. Leverage of the CEDAW achievement necessitated grassroots, national, and international organizing. Struggles persisted over time at all scales of geography and political life, balancing out failures with successes. On any day, in any year, we witness human rights as a snapshot in an unfolding process of striving toward greater equity and justice. In a similar spirit, we present the right to adequate food and nutrition as part of the machinery of international law, and at the same time, as the common inspiration of a diversity of social movements whose aspirations and concrete expectations *vis-à-vis* the state differ by location, with time, and in concert with greater knowledge of human rights principles. The "snapshot" of today attempts to freeze a moment of time, while concurrent efforts are unfolding to strategically organize and carry forward struggles with ever changing challenges (see Randolph and Hertel 2013). Accordingly, definitions, understanding and interpretation, implementation, monitoring and reporting, justiciability, and the enforcement of the right to adequate food and nutrition evolve even as we grasp and portray the picture of today.

A first reference to the right to adequate food and nutrition can be found in article 25.1 of the UDHR in the context of the right to an adequate standard of living:

> Everyone has the right to a standard of living adequate for the health and well-being of himself and of his family, including food, clothing, housing and medical care and necessary social services, and the right to security in the event of unemployment, sickness, disability, widowhood, old age or other lack of livelihood in circumstances beyond his control. (UN General Assembly 1948, art. 25.1)

This first articulation of the right to adequate food and nutrition was further elaborated in article 11 of the ICESCR, again as an element of the right to an adequate standard of living (UN General Assembly 1966b, art. 11.1), and included a reference to the fundamental right to be free from hunger (UN General Assembly 1966b, art. 11.2):[15]

1. The States Parties to the present Covenant recognize the right of everyone to an adequate standard of living for himself and his family, including adequate food, clothing and housing, and to the continuous improvement of living conditions. The States Parties will take appropriate steps to ensure the realization of this right, recognizing to this effect the essential importance of international co-operation based on free consent.
2. The States Parties to the present Covenant, recognizing the fundamental right of everyone to be free from hunger, shall take, individually and through international co-operation, the measures, including specific programmes, which are needed:

   (a) To improve methods of production, conservation and distribution of food by making full use of technical and scientific knowledge, by disseminating knowledge of the principles of nutrition and by developing or reforming agrarian systems in such a way as to achieve the most efficient development and utilization of natural resources;
   (b) Taking into account the problems of both food-importing and food-exporting countries, to ensure an equitable distribution of world food supplies in relation to need. (UN General Assembly 1966b, art. 11)

Article 11 of the ICESCR comprised the sum total of treaty-based language on the right to adequate food and nutrition until after the end of the Cold War in the late 1980s and early 1990s.[16] In 1974, the *Universal Declaration on the Eradication of Hunger and Malnutrition*, adopted by the World Food Conference in Rome (World Food Conference 1974) and endorsed by the UN General Assembly in the same year (UN General Assembly 1974), addressed the global scale problem of production and consumption, but framed it in terms that proclaimed that "every man, woman and child has the inalienable right to be free from hunger and malnutrition in order to develop their physical and mental faculties" (World Food Conference 1974, para. 1). This did not, however, move states toward a human rights-based approach that has the objective of dignity and self-determination, as much as it strove to organize charitable relief through trade mechanisms. A comprehensive interpretation of the right to adequate food and nutrition, however, does not start and stop with article 11, but can and should grow from its nested existence within the overall human rights framework. At the heart of later constructions of the right to adequate food and nutrition is ICESCR article 2 which iterates provisional mechanisms for realizing the covenant's protected human rights: international cooperation, progressive realization to the maximum of available resources, and non-discrimination (see table 1.3).

Table 1.3   ICESCR article 2: General human rights obligations of international cooperation, progressive realization, and non-discrimination (UN General Assembly 1966b)

ICESCR article 2.1	
"Each State Party to the present Covenant undertakes to take steps, individually and through *international assistance and co-operation*, especially economic and technical, to the *maximum of its available resources*, with a view to *achieving progressively the full realization* of the rights recognized in the present Covenant by all appropriate means, including particularly the adoption of legislative measures." (emphasis added)	
General obligation of international cooperation	As reiterated in ICESCR article 11.2, more developed states must support other less developed states with resources to fulfill progressively human rights obligations. At the same time, less developed countries must, where necessary and available, accept this support: external assistance is thus considered part of the *available resources* (OHCHR 2005, 14). Additionally, cooperation is needed to facilitate the adoption and implementation of regulations and other mechanisms to ensure the protection of human rights internationally, particularly as regards human rights' extraterritorial dimension (cf. Maastricht University and ICJ 2011).

General obligation of progressive realization to the maximum of available resources	States parties have a duty to use the maximum available resources to realize ratified human rights. This obligation disallows regression from a higher to a lower level of enjoyment of a right (OHCHR 2005, 12),[1] or justification of "sustained levels of chronic or extreme poverty" and "endows States with an immediate minimum core obligation to ensure the satisfaction of, at the very least, minimum essential levels of all economic, social and cultural rights" (Sepúlveda Carmona and Nyst 2012, 18).

ICESCR article 2.2

"The States Parties to the present Covenant undertake to guarantee that the rights enunciated in the present Covenant will be exercised *without discrimination* of any kind as to race, colour, sex, language, religion, political or other opinion, national or social origin, property, birth or other status." (emphasis added)

General obligation of non-discrimination	States parties are obliged to "desist from discriminatory behavior," "to alter laws and practices which allow discrimination," and to "prohibit [third parties] from discriminating in any field of public life" (OHCHR 2005, 13). Social power inequities can necessitate additional legal protection, including judicial and other recourse mechanisms in case of violations for groups such as women, children, and minority populations (cf. CESCR 2009).

[1] The only time that regression on the progressive realization of an economic, social, or cultural right is justified is "by reference to the totality of the rights provided for in the Covenant and in the context of the full utilization of a State's maximum available resources" (OHCHR 2005, 12). In other words, an exception for the parallel obligation of non-retrogression is only acceptable when a state has fully utilized all of its available resources to their maximum extent for the realization of the totality of rights provided for in the covenant as a whole, and yet fails to realize progression in all of the constituent rights individually.

In part IV of the ICESCR, articles 16–22 outline states parties reporting functions through which compliance with covenant obligations shall be monitored. Regardless of these mechanisms and reporting procedures, Philip Alston (1984, 173–74) believed that the framework with which to operationalize the right to adequate food and nutrition was inadequate and he called forcefully for a "spelling out [of] the normative implications of the right to food" because, without such articulation, "the concept of the right to food as a human right [would] continue to be abused for rhetorical purposes while being ignored for all practical purposes."

Both Alston (1984, 164–65) and Asbjørn Eide (1989, para. 79) believed that the "spelling out" of a human right to adequate food and nutrition should incorporate and benefit from a myriad of other human rights documents besides the 1948 UDHR article 25.1 and the 1966 ICESCR articles 2 and 11. These include, among others,

- UDHR article 2 stating that "everyone is entitled to all the rights and freedoms set forth in this Declaration, without distinction of any kind"
- UDHR article 3 providing for everyone's right to life
- UDHR article 22 on the realization of economic, social, and cultural rights through national efforts and international cooperation
- UDHR article 28 providing that "everyone is entitled to a social and international order in which the rights and freedoms set forth in [the] Declaration can be fully realized"
- article 1 of both the ICESCR and ICCPR on the right to self-determination
- ICCPR article 6 on every human being's inherent right to life,
- the four 1949 Geneva Conventions (ICRC 1949) and their two Additional Protocols of 1977 (ICRC 1977a, b) regulating the rights of civilians and former combatants in war time.

The 1990s brought many changes to the development of the right to adequate food and nutrition. In his 1999 report *The Right to Adequate Food and to Be Free From Hunger: Updated Study on the Right to Food* (hereinafter, *Updated Study on the Right to Food*), submitted to the UN Sub-Commission on the Promotion and Protection of Human Rights, A. Eide pointed to the 1989 adoption of the CRC and its rapid entry into force in 1990 as a turning point that "strengthened the place of the right to food and nutrition in international human rights law" (A. Eide 1999, para. 5).

The Role of Civil Society in Shaping Interpretation of The Right to Adequate Food and Nutrition

The first half of the 1990s ushered in a series of UN world conferences beginning with the World Summit for Children in New York in 1990, and including the United Nations Conference on Environment and Development (Rio de Janeiro 1992), the World Conference on Human Rights (Vienna 1993), the International Conference on Population and Development (Cairo 1994), the Fourth World Conference on Women (Beijing 1995), the World Summit for Social Development (Copenhagen 1995), the Second United Nations Conference on Human Settlements (Istanbul 1996) and, of particular relevance here, the World Food Summit (Rome 1996). The problem of extensive hunger and malnutrition in the world was addressed in almost all of these conferences (A. Eide 1999, para. 5). In no small part, the rising space and voice of public interest civil society spurred UN work in general, and the attention to food and agriculture in particular. Indeed Nora McKeon, in her 2009 book *The United Nations and Civil Society: Legitimating Global Governance—Whose Voice?*, presents the case that civil society's democratic engagement at the global level since the 1990s has not only helped shape policy, but has at the same time reinforced the legitimacy to the UN as a global governance mechanism.

The UN Committee on Economic, Social and Cultural Rights (CESCR) was established in 1987 as a body of independent experts to carry out the monitoring functions of the ICESCR and to prepare non-legally binding general comments to provide guidance and interpretation on the content of specific provisions, as well as on crosscutting themes of the ICESCR (CESCR 1989; see Riedel 2005).[17] In 1993, the CESCR *Rules of Procedure of the Committee* were revised, endorsing and institutionalizing the participation of civil society in ICESCR monitoring and reporting (CESCR 1993, rule 69). Rule 69.1 allows non-governmental organizations (NGOs), in consultative status with the HRC, to issue independent and supplemental shadow reports to the periodic states parties' reports to the CESCR. Additionally, rules 69.2 and 69.3 offer these NGOs the opportunity both to meet for a "short period of time" with working groups before CESCR sessions, as well as to present "relevant oral information" during sessions. These new procedures invite civil society to engage procedurally to bring up issues that might be overlooked or ignored in official reports, or that were inadequately addressed from a civil society perspective.

Another boost for civil society participation came in 1993 with the recommendation of the World Conference on Human Rights Preparatory Committee to issue an optional protocol to the ICESCR to provide formal mechanisms for individual complaints of rights violations under the covenant (see World Conference on Human Rights Preparatory Committee 1993, para. 18; UN General Assembly 1993b, para. 75).[18] Optional protocols provide "a more extensive and in-depth framework of inquiry to a specific case" (World Conference on Human Rights Preparatory Committee 1993, para. 34) and more effective mechanisms and procedures for individual and group recourse to a UN body (World Conference on Human Rights Preparatory Committee 1993, para. 35). Additionally, they play an important role in elaborating the procedure of response open to and for individual and group complaints of state violations of human rights obligations (World Conference on Human Rights Preparatory Committee 1993, para. 38; see also A. Eide 2005, 30; ESCR-Net 2013; NGO Coalition for an Optional Protocol to the ICESCR and ESCR-Net 2008). Similar optional protocols to the ICCPR and CEDAW had already been adopted by the UN General Assembly in 1966 and 1999, respectively (UN General Assembly 1966c, 1999). However, due to remaining dissention on the nature and justiciability of economic, social, and cultural rights in comparison to civil and political rights, among other issues (see Arambulo 1999), the first draft of the ICESCR optional protocol was only presented by the CESCR to the UN Commission on Human Rights (CHR) in 1997. The adoption of the *Optional Protocol to the International Covenant on Economic, Social and Cultural Rights* was delayed even longer and only occurred in 2008 (UN General Assembly 2009). On February 6, 2013 Uruguay provided the tenth ratification of the ICESCR optional protocol, allowing for its entering into force three months later, in accordance with article 18.1 (FIAN International 2013).[19]

Since the early 1990s, civil society had been organizing resistance against the global political economy of food and trade that was becoming increasingly dominated by wealthy countries, global financial institutions, and particularly by corporate giants of the early globalized agrofood industry. A. Eide refers to this staggering shift of economic and political power as the transition from the wealth of nations to the wealth of corporations (A. Eide 2005, 18–19). Coalitions of civil society organizations (CSOs) demanded an interrogation of the "practically binding" structural adjustment conditionalities imposed on national social policies by the International Monetary Fund (IMF) and the World Bank according to the principles of the Consensus of Washington (CIDSE 2008; CIDSE and IATP 2009). As A. Eide writes, in return for credit, the international financial institutions had "in effect taken over what should be the area of democratic decision-making by elected politicians in the affected countries" (A. Eide 2005, 17). La Via Campesina, roughly translated as The Peasants' Way, initiated a worldwide farmers' organization challenge in 1993 that protested the 1994 Uruguay Round of the General Agreement on Tariffs and Trade (GATT) and the 1995 creation of the World Trade Organization (WTO). La Via Campesina critiqued the presumptions inside the GATT and WTO that international trade and free markets would optimize food supply, and by extension, food security (Ballenger and Mabbs-Zeno 1992; Healy, Pearce, and Stockbridge 1998; Watkins 1991). Compounding the IMF imposed stranglehold over state autonomy, the 1994 GATT further restrained governments' use of public sector tools, including subsidies, tariffs, and regulations to realize the right to adequate food and nutrition of those under their jurisdiction and to protect the sustainability of their own food systems and economies (see, e.g., Forum for Food Sovereignty 2007; Isaah 2007; Paasch 2008; Paasch, Garbers, and Hirsch 2007). La Via Campesina countered with the thesis of *food sovereignty*, not only objecting to the global interference in national policy, but relocating the idea of food governance, as well as food security in the human and democratic rights of peoples as determined at the most local of levels and by those most engaged in the production of food, particularly at smaller scales (see, e.g., Desmarais 2007; Windfuhr and Jonsén 2005; see also chapters 5 and 6 of this volume).

CSOs, social movements, and human rights organizations raised objections to the hegemonic impulses of the globalizing agrofood corporations, international financial institutions, and wealthy countries in the 1990s (Valente and Suárez Franco 2010, 452). This critique coalesced at the Civil Society Forum on Food Security that brought together almost one thousand organizations in a program running parallel to the 1996 World Food Summit in Rome. Among other objectives, civil society organized to exert pressure to revisit, reinterpret, and expand the understanding of the right to adequate food and nutrition, and to address some of the inadequacies of the ICESCR language (NGO Forum to the World Food Summit 1996). Concurrently, FAO member states present at the World Food Summit called upon UN human rights institutions "[t]o clarify the content of the right to adequate food and the fundamental right of everyone to be free from hunger, as stated in the International Covenant on Economic, Social and Cultural Rights and other relevant international and regional instruments, and to give particular attention to implementation and full and progressive realization of this right as a means of achieving food security for all" (FAO 1996, objective 7.1).

By mandate from the Civil Society Forum on Food Security, FIAN International, the World Alliance for Nutrition and Human Rights (WANAHR), and the Jacques Maritain International Institute cooperated to elaborate the desired reinterpretation of the ICESCR through the drafting of the 1997 *International Code of Conduct on the Right to Adequate Food* (hereinafter, *Code of Conduct*; FIAN International, WANAHR, and Institute Jacques Maritain International 1997). In an indirect reference to the evolutive process of human rights frameworks, Michael Windfuhr (1998), cofacilitator of the *Code of Conduct*, describes the dialectical process that went on inside the civil society movement during the drafting of the document. Producing this analysis of the right to adequate food and nutrition, he writes, required both "'unlearning' the reductionist human rights concept, which focused entirely on civil and political rights, as well as the reductionist concepts of food security that focus only or mostly on agricultural productivity and harvest yields" to the detriment of nutrition and food access (Windfuhr 1998, 7).

By 2000, over one thousand NGOs around the world endorsed the intention to enact the *Code of Conduct* into the global human rights framework (Kracht 2000, cited in W. B. Eide and Kracht 2005b, 104). The first steps were to place it on the agendas of both the CHR and the Committee on World Food Security (CFS; Windfuhr 1998; SCN 1999).[20] Although ultimately and almost immediately rejected, the code was widely praised for its contribution to the 1999 issuance and adoption by the CESCR of *General Comment 12 on The Right to Adequate Food* (hereinafter, *General Comment 12*; CESCR 1999, para. 2; see also Oshaug 2005, 259–60; Albrecht, Germann, and Ratjen 2007, 8; Valente and Suárez Franco 2010, 453; SCN 1999, para. 4). The *Code of Conduct* also helped to propel forward the 2002 creation of a CFS Intergovernmental Working Group (IGWG) and the execution of its mandate established at the World Food Summit: five years later (Rome, 2002) to negotiate a set of voluntary guidelines on the implementation of the right to adequate food (see Albrecht, Germann, and Ratjen 2007, 8; W. B. Eide and Kracht 2005b, 104).

General Comment 12 on the Right to Adequate Food

The UN high commissioner for human rights had ultimate responsibility to follow up on the 1996 World Food Summit call for clarification of the right to adequate food concept. As a result, chronologically parallel and in collaboration with the NGO organizing effort described above, a series of UN sponsored expert consultations was established between 1997 and 2001 reflecting the ideas that a collective of practitioners and academics working on the right to adequate food and nutrition had been theorizing. One outcome was the previously mentioned *Updated Study on the Right to Food* by Asbjørn Eide in 1999. Another closely related outcome was the issuance by the CESCR of *General Comment 12* (CESCR 1999) in the same year.[21]

The *Updated Study on the Right to Food* reintroduces two ideas central to the eventual shape of contemporary understandings on the right to adequate food and nutrition: (*a*) a rights-based approach to food *and nutrition* and (*b*) the specific obligations of states parties to the ICESCR to respect, protect, and fulfill the human right to adequate food and nutrition. While the latter concept of specific obligations was adopted into the content of *General Comment 12*, the link of nutrition to the right to adequate food was not successfully or completely included (see also chapters 2, 5, and 6 of this volume).

Although non-legally binding in nature itself, *General Comment 12* represents "the authoritative [UN] interpretation of the right to food in the International Bill of Rights" (Suárez Franco and Ratjen 2007, 4). It provides an interpretation of the right to adequate food and nutrition from A. Eide's *Updated Study on the Right to Food* that incorporates the food security dimensions of availability, accessibility, adequacy, and sustainability. In that report, "the links between the notion of 'sustainability' in terms of long-term availability and 'accessibility' of adequate food, and how both are intrinsically linked to the notion of food security, implying food being accessible for both present and future generations" were emphasized (W. B. Eide 2005, 86). The authoritative definition for the right to adequate food and nutrition, as cobbled together from three paragraphs of *General Comment 12*, reads:

> The right to adequate food is realized when every man, woman and child, alone or in community with others, have physical and economic access at all times to adequate food or means for its procurement. The core content of the right to adequate food implies . . . the availability of food in a quantity and quality sufficient to satisfy the dietary needs of individuals, free from adverse substances, and acceptable within a given culture [and] the accessibility of such food in ways that are sustainable

and that do not interfere with the enjoyment of other human rights. . . . Accessibility encompasses both economic and physical accessibility. (CESCR 1999, paras. 6, 8, and 13)

General Comment 12 identifies the respective obligations of states parties and provides them with guidance on the implementation of the legally binding ICESCR provisions relevant for the progressive realization of the right to adequate food and nutrition (see Valente and Suárez Franco 2010, 442). These states parties' specific obligations to *respect, protect,* and *fulfill* were first introduced in a report submitted to the Sub-commission on Prevention of Discrimination and Protection of Minorities in 1987 and published in the Human Rights Study Series in 1989 (A. Eide 1989). The concept of those specific obligations has evolved since. The right to adequate food and nutrition, like all other economic, social, cultural, civil, and political rights, imposes on states parties these three levels of specific obligations.

The first level obligation, to *respect,* requires that states do not interfere, both within and beyond their territories, with existing access to food or to resources for producing food or with existing and working processes of growing, accessing, and consuming food for local populations in ways that make it impossible to maintain traditions and self-determination (although these traditions are subject to review for their adherence to other human rights principles like non-discrimination).

The second level of specific obligations provides that states should, within their jurisdiction, adopt measures to *protect* individuals from efforts by other non-state actors (individuals or enterprises) to deprive or interfere with food access, for example, through land eviction or water contamination. As Oshaug, W. B. Eide, and A. Eide (1994, 494) point out, "[t]his is probably the most important aspect of the right to food and other survival rights: the state not as provider, but as protector." The specific obligation of protect prescribes to states, for example, to regulate large corporate private sector involvement in activities that might diminish local and national autonomy over food and nutrition security, such as privatizing public commons resources like water, seed genetics, or land,[22] or by interfering with breastfeeding practices, the universally acknowledged best and safest nutrition for infants and young children, through aggressive marketing of breastmilk substitutes. It is expected that national scale law shall be designed to augment state capacity to extend legal accountability for human rights abuses to the corporate private sector. Furthermore, states must protect against violations engaged by individuals and groups, both inside and outside family households. Protecting women from discrimination and violence inside, as well as outside the household and family space, including by extension the violence of food-related abuses such as withholding food, falls within the domain of state obligations (see also chapter 3 of this volume).

According to *General Comment 12,* the third level specific obligation, to *fulfill,* includes two obligations. It asserts that states should proactively engage in enhancing people's autonomous capacity at the local and national level to produce, access, and use food and nutrition resources (*fulfill/facilitate*), and that states have the obligation to provide to those, who for emergency or non-emergency reasons outside their control, need resources (e.g., food donations and cash transfers) to fulfill the right (*fulfill/provide*).

General Comment 12 should not be interpreted as definitive with respect to state specific obligations; they have the potential to evolve. Possible future inclusions might consider the 1997 *Maastricht Guidelines on Violations of Economic, Social and Cultural Rights*, that assign the elements of obligation of *conduct* ("action reasonably calculated to realize the enjoyment of a particular right") and obligation of *result* (the achievement of "specific targets to satisfy a detailed substantive standard") for all three levels of specific obligations (ICJ 1997, para. 7). Additionally, CESCR *General Comment 14 on the Right to the Highest Attainable Standard of Health* (CESCR 2000) adds the aspect of *promote* to the third level obligation of *fulfill*. This *promote* aspect requires states parties to disseminate information and educate their administrations and populace about the respective right. To underscore the practical side of this obligation, *General Comment 14* further specifies that "the obligation to fulfil requires States to adopt appropriate legislative, administrative, budgetary, judicial, promotional and other measures towards the full realization of the right to health" (CESCR 2000, para. 33).

Moreover, the specific states party obligations of respect, protect, and fulfill are not limited to national boundaries. The extraterritorial character of these obligations is rather defined, among others, through the ICESCR general obligation of international cooperation (UN General Assembly 1966b, article 2).[23] In this context, *General Comment 12*, paragraph 36 reads,

> In the spirit of article 56 of the Charter of the United Nations, the specific provisions contained in articles 11, 2.1, and 23 of the Covenant and the Rome Declaration of the World Food Summit, States parties should recognize the essential role of international cooperation and comply with their commitment to take joint and separate action to achieve the full realization of the right to adequate food. In implementing this commitment, States parties should take steps to respect the enjoyment of the right to food in other countries, to protect that right, to facilitate access to food and to provide the necessary aid when required. States parties should, in international agreements whenever relevant, ensure that the right to adequate food is given due attention and consider the development of further international legal instruments to that end. (CESCR 1999, para. 36)

A. Eide's (1999) and *General Comment 12*'s incorporation of the dimensions of food security and specific states parties' obligations was developed into the Food Security Matrix, a tabular form to identify, classify, and analyze progressive realization of the right to adequate food and nutrition (see W. B. Eide 2005, 93). Used, for example, by Damman, W. B. Eide, and Kuhnlein (2008), the matrix attempts to provide an analytical format to capture the human rights dimensions of food security. Whether and how a state meets its obligations to respect, protect, and fulfill household food security is the logic of the table. While absolutely groundbreaking in terms of clarifying what a state must do, the matrix does not provide a dimension to the voice of rights holders. Democratic participation in policy making is an intrinsic part of what both A. Eide (1999, paras. 35, 63, 70, 87, 93, 100, 103) and *General Comment 12* (CESCR 1999, para. 23) promoted. Chapter 6 of this volume revisits the matrix with a vision of analyzing states parties' obligations as duty bearers in cross section with the democratic food sovereignty of rights holders.

Paragraph 20 of *General Comment 12* notes that only states are parties to the ICESCR and, therefore, they alone carry ultimate accountability to comply with the rights articulated in the covenant. Nevertheless, "all members of society—individuals, families, local communities, non-governmental organizations, civil society organizations, as well as the private business sector—have responsibilities in the realization of the right to adequate food" (CESCR 1999, para. 20; see also para. 27). To this end, "[t]he State should provide an environment that facilitates implementation of these responsibilities" (CESCR 1999, para. 20), by which *General Comment 12* moves toward expanding rights holders participation and regulating corporate activity. Attempting to counter the uneven influence exercised by large corporations and financial institutions that overwhelm both the rights holders represented by public interest civil society and the duty bearers of governments, paragraph 20 continues, "[t]he private business sector—national and transnational—should pursue its activities within the framework of a code of conduct conducive to respect of the right to adequate food, agreed upon jointly with the Government and civil society."

The corporate private sector and civil society are handled separately because of their vastly different power and because of their dissimilar status: members of civil society are human rights *holders*; corporations and businesses are not. Through the issuance of the CESCR general comments, civil society participation has become increasingly institutionalized in the design and implementation of the human right to adequate food and nutrition at the national level.[24] In this respect, paragraph 23 of *General Comment 12* reads,

> The formulation and implementation of national strategies for the right to food requires *full compliance with the principles of* accountability, transparency, *people's participation*, decentralization, legislative capacity and the independence of the judiciary. (CESCR 1999, para. 23, emphasis added)

Civil society engagement on behalf of public interest, particularly when it challenges existing power structures, can place participants in danger of facing reprisals for their work exposing human rights violations. As discussed by Lauren (2003, 2), human rights defenders "all directly threatened those with power who refused to share it voluntarily, those with vested interests or prevailing prejudice who wanted special privilege, and those government leaders who hid behind the claims of national sovereignty and insisted that they were immune from ever being held accountable for any abuses they might commit."

It is, therefore, critical to have the mandated respect *and protection* of civil society participation in right to adequate food and nutrition work at the national and international levels, especially of "human rights advocates and other members of civil society who assist vulnerable groups" (CESCR 1999, para. 35). We know that law alone rarely protects those who struggle against more powerful groups. That is why, to leverage states parties protection of human rights defenders, civil society must be able to participate in the public actions that uphold the right to adequate food and nutrition including monitoring, reporting, and using recourse and remedy mechanisms to hold competent authorities accountable.

The articulation of the core content of right to adequate food in *General Comment 12* further provided a blueprint for the CHR in its resolution 2000/10 to appoint a special rapporteur on the right to food "to respond fully to the necessity for an integrated and coordinated approach in the promotion and protection of the right to food" (CHR 2000, para. 10). UN special rapporteurs—also called special procedures of the HRC—are independent experts working to examine, monitor, advise, and publicly report on different specific human rights issues, one of which is food and nutrition (OHCHR 2013). Sociologist Jean Ziegler held the first two consecutive appointments (September 2000-April 2008) as UN special rapporteur on the right to food, contributing, among other things, directly to the development of the *Right to Food Guidelines* and then producing reports to help governments implement them (Valente and Suárez Franco 2010, 454; CHR 2005). Law professor Olivier De Schutter was appointed the second UN special rapporteur on the right to food (May 2008-April 2014). De Schutter is credited with immediately organizing a special session of the HRC on the global food crisis in 2008, from which a resolution was adopted that called for a rights-based approach to the fight against hunger and for a review of "any policy or measure which could have a negative impact on the realization of the right to food" (HRC 2008, 4; see also Golay and Büschi 2012; Valente and Suárez Franco 2010).[25] The third mandate holder, research professor and lawyer Hilal Elver, was appointed by the HRC to take the vacancy of this special procedure in May 2014 and assumed her functions in June of the same year. While her tenure is just beginning as this book is being finalized, it is clear that the first two rapporteurs on the right to food have had tremendous positive impact on the development of content and implementation of the human right to adequate food and nutrition.[26]

The Promotion of a Human Rights Framework for Food and Nutrition Security

Efforts to mainstream the so-called "human rights–based approach" into the programs, policies, and activities of all UN specialized agencies began with the 1997 UN secretary general's report *Renewing the United Nations: A Programme for Reform* (UN Secretary General 1997). The main feature of the human rights-based approach is that it is founded on the understanding that states are human rights duty bearers and that individuals and groups of individuals are human rights holders. The construction of how these two actor groups relate to and with each other is further framed within human rights instruments. The human rights-based approach is centered on the universality and indivisibility of human rights. For example, the human right to adequate food and nutrition cannot be viewed independently from, for example, the human right to the highest attainable standard of health, or the human rights of women or of children.

Subsequent publications to the 1997 UN secretary general's report adopting the human rights-based approach include the *Human Development Report 2000: Human Rights and Human Development* by the United Nations Development Programme (UNDP; UNDP 2000), the 2000 UN General Assembly adoption of the *United Nations Millennium Declaration* (UN General Assembly 2000), and the 2003 United Nations Development Group (UNDG) adoption of the *UN Statement of Common Understanding on Human Rights-Based Approaches to Development Cooperation and Programming* (hereinafter, *Common Understanding*; UNDG 2003, att. 1; see also Golay and Büschi 2012, 13–14).

In the context of the right to adequate food and nutrition, A. Eide, in his previously mentioned *Updated Study on the Right to Food*, reflects upon the importance of state efforts to "elaborate a human rights-based strategy to ensure freedom from hunger and the enjoyment of the right to food" (A. Eide 1999, para. 66), referencing examples from Brazil and South Africa (A. Eide 1999, paras. 67–70). When reporting on the adoption of the human rights-based approach to food and nutrition by UN and other intergovernmental agencies, A. Eide writes that UNICEF "has taken an explicit political decision to make the realization of the rights contained in the Convention on the Rights of the Child and the Convention on the Elimination of All Forms of Discrimination against Women the heart of its mandate" and "uses these two human rights instruments in its struggle against hunger and malnutrition by emphasizing the responsibility of Governments and other actors arising from these conventions, and by a reorientation of the understanding of the nutrition problem" (A. Eide 1999, para. 102). With UNICEF as a model, A. Eide recommended training and the development of learning materials on human rights related to food and nutrition for UN specialized agencies and other bodies adopting the human rights-based approach (A. Eide 1999, para. 135.a.iii).

Using the language of "human right–based approaches," attempts to employ human rights frameworks and principles expanded rapidly but without coordination, and some have argued, with more compulsion than conviction. Notably, the imperative of promoting civil society participation and social policy development appears lacking. Uvin (2007, 599) asserts that the great number of policy statements, guidelines, and documents published during the 1990s by bilateral and multilateral aid agencies on the incorporation of human rights in their mandate were "little more than thinly disguised presentations of old wine in new bottles," basically "colonis[ing] the human rights discourse" and claiming "that human rights is what these developing agencies were doing all along." Moreover, the same author, quoting Donelly (1999, 611) and Windfuhr (2000, 25), maintains that the rhetorical exercise of inserting a "rights-based approach" into development literature ignores fundamental power-based relationships between states parties, rights holders, and corporations. This failure obscures the essential difference between charity or benevolence bestowed and human rights claimed, and perpetuates existing hegemonic power structures (Uvin 2007, 599–600).

We warn, however, that the human rights-based approach discourse leaves margin for states and other actors to only selectively apply aspects of the approach that serve their interests.[27] As witnessed during the course of writing this volume, rights-based rhetoric has been increasingly coopted as just another buzzword. Actors, whose objective has been more to circumvent criticism and only nominally adapt to the present direction of democratic and global food governance rather than to embrace and to work toward the implementation of, let alone to comply with, a *human rights framework*, including its legal components, threaten the foundational imperative of holding states accountable for the realization and protection of the human right to adequate food and nutrition.

The human rights framework is made manifest by realizing the roles of rights holders and duty bearers in a relationship based on obligation and accountability. From a global public sector perspective, this engages the state as democratic manager of the public good, serving as effective representative of the people's will, in line with universal human rights principles. The human rights framework is systemic and organic, and given its evolutive character, resists a singular interpretation that is anchored in time.

As with the advancement of the human rights-based approach, the actual promotion and implementation of the human rights framework is largely attributable to the work of NGOs and CSOs (Uvin 2007, 602). In the specific context of food and nutrition security, Valente and Suárez Franco (2010, 453) maintain that "[t]he advances observed in the incorporation of the rights-based approach and in the strengthened civil society participation are, to a great extent, a result of the strong alliance built among the civil society organizations, social movements, and human rights organizations around the defense of the banner of food sovereignty and the promotion of the right to adequate food." This effort from civil society has been necessary to overcome varying degrees of reluctance from states and active resistance from the international corporate private sector (see, e.g., De Schutter 2006; Deva and Bilchitz 2013; Holt-Giménez 2011; McKeon 2009).

Regardless of who invests more in a human rights framework, its objective is a dialogue between rights holders and duty bearers. In this dialogue, rights holders are able to shape their participation with dignity and with the representation of the most marginalized. They are empowered to demand policy transparency and to hold governments, and through them non-state actors, accountable through recourse and remedy mechanisms, for the progressive realization of the right to adequate food and nutrition. The 2003 UN *Common Understanding* provides a framework for the growth and range of rights-based initiatives. The *Common Understanding* clarifies in three points that all development work shall (*a*) further realize human rights as explicated in the UDHR and other international human rights instruments, (*b*) follow associated standards and principles, and (*c*) contribute to the development of the capacities of duty bearers to meet their obligations and of rights holders to claim their rights. Effectively adhering to the *Common Understanding* requires that the duties of monitoring and evaluation of both outcomes and processes be guided by human rights standards and principles; it also commands thorough observance of the recommendations of international human rights bodies and mechanisms in programming. Basic principles include incorporating focus on the participation of marginalized and excluded groups, as well as local ownership of development (Anderson 2013, 113–14).

One of the most contemporary articulations of human rights principles is presented by FAO under the mnemonic acronym PANTHER, comprised by the initial letters of the concepts of *p*articipation, *a*ccountability, *n*on-discrimination and focus on vulnerable groups, *t*ransparency, *h*uman dignity, *e*mpowerment, and *r*ule of law (FAO 2013b, 10; Diokno 2013). These principles are further described in table 1.4, in terms of expectations of public sector conduct in the context of the human rights-based approach.

The application of the human rights framework to food and nutrition security programs involves the identification of rights holders and the recognition of their rights, including their right to claim recourse and remedy for rights violations. At the same time, the process through which food and nutrition security programs and policies are designed and implemented must itself share and relocate decision-making authority with those previously identified rights holders. The commitment to move toward a human right to adequate food and nutrition requires a paradigm shift in public policy and social organization (Golay and Büschi 2012; W. B. Eide 2005). Rights holders' public participation reallocates power over policy processes and puts powerful recourse and remedy tools at their disposal. While human rights initiatives might be embraced intuitively or emphatically, actual changes in decision-making authority are almost always traumatic because of struggles

Table 1.4 Human rights principles (PANTHER)

Participation

The public sector must conduct:
- Active encouragement of people to organize and to genuinely, freely, actively participate in decision-making
- Outreach to, and inclusion of, those most affected by public decisions into the decision-making
- Mandated incorporation of people's views (voluntary, legally recognized, free) in all public decisions and actions
- Formal mechanisms for claim holders and other actors to question policies, bring complaints, demand compensation/restitution, hold governments, and through them non-state actors, accountable
- Involvement of people in the monitoring of public policy implementation.

Accountability

The public sector is accountable for:
- Human rights obligations of conduct and of result
- Responsiveness with public decisions, actions, and performance to those most affected by social exclusion and discrimination
- Fairness in conduct, treatment, and actions
- Responsibility for policies, decisions, actions, services, goods, for associated performance, and for related consequences
- Inclusiveness, collaborative with defined processes of genuine, voluntary, active, free, and full participation and involvement
- Competency, effectiveness, efficiency, and professionalism in actions and performance
- Timely delivery of resources, institutions, goods, and services implicit in human rights
- Making available monitoring and remedy mechanisms that allow rights holders to monitor their authorities and to seek remedy in cases of threat or enactment of violation of their human rights.

Non-discrimination (focus on marginalized and excluded groups)

The public sector must guarantee:
- The enjoyment of all human rights without distinction of any kind, exclusion, restriction, or preference based on race, color, ethnic origin, sex, gender stereotypes, prejudices and expected roles, language, religion, political or other opinion, national or social origin, descent, inherited social status, property, birth, disability, age, nationality, marital and family status, sexual orientation and gender identity, health status, place of residency, economic and social situation, and membership in group.[1]

Transparency

The public sector must commit to the principle that:
- All public actions and decisions are visible, free from obscurity, unhidden, clear, and distinct

- Public documents, decisions, rules, regulations, and processes are readily, timely, understandably, and freely accessible, and complete
- Claim holders and other actors are able to see openly into all activities of duty bearers
- Persons and communities affected by development projects, especially indigenous peoples, have the right to free, prior, and informed consent.

Human dignity

The public sector must make manifest that human dignity:
- Implies that human beings are an end in themselves and cannot be used as mere means to reach the aims of others
- Implies that people shall not be humiliated or put in a situation of impotence based on an authority's arbitrary decision or conduct and that, shall this ever happen, recourse mechanisms shall be available for affected people to claim the respect, protection, and fulfillment of their human dignity
- Implies that human beings are rights holders and not charity recipients; therefore, when claiming their human rights, they are holding authorities accountable and not asking for charity
- Founds the basis and aim of all human rights, resting on the intrinsic value or worth of the human person
- Is non-negotiable, irreversible, and the same at all places and at all times
- Demands that those most vulnerable to human rights deprivations require special human rights measures and protection
- Encourages resort to safeguards (anticipatory and proactive measures), rather than safety nets (reactionary measures).

Empowerment

The public sector must:
- Recognize that human beings are subjects of human rights and as such have the right to influence public policy making, implementation, and monitoring, without discrimination.
- Acknowledge, respect, and build people's capacity to seek appropriate solutions to injustices they may face
- Make available mechanisms that allow people to take part in public life.

Rule of law

The public sector should guarantee:
- That the primacy of human rights is applied, especially in situations in which human rights are put in conflict with rights of a different nature (i.a., commercial law)
- That conflicts be resolved impartially, on the basis of fact, in accordance with law, and without improper influence or pressure
- The availability and accessibility of independent and impartial judicial or administrative forums to act on conflicts

(Continued)

Table 1.4   (Continued)

Rule of law   (Continued)

- Provision of appropriate remedies and effective redress mechanisms, including appeals mechanisms
- Inclusion of efficient monitoring mechanisms to support the impartial and just implementation of regulations
- The respect, protection, and security of human rights defenders and their activities, in particular as regards threats, intimidation, and violence on the part of powerful social actors.

Source: adapted from Diokno (2013).

[1] Temporary special measures constitute legitimate differentiation under human rights instruments, when these are intended to correct discrimination, when the criteria for such differentiation are reasonable and objective, and when the aim is to achieve legitimate purposes.

over sharing political and economic power (Stammers 1999, 2005). Such resistance is compounded by the fact that the practical administrative and legal machinery to support such changes is complex and very much still evolving.

The Voluntary Guidelines to Support the Progressive Realization of the Right to Adequate Food in the Context of National Food Security

The 1996 *Rome Declaration on World Food Security and World Food Summit Plan of Action* not only called for guidance on the interpretation of the right to adequate food as referenced in the ICESCR, but also "invite[d] the UN High Commissioner for Human Rights, in consultation with relevant treaty bodies, and in collaboration with relevant specialized agencies and programmes of the UN system and appropriate intergovernmental mechanisms, . . . *to propose ways to implement and realize these rights* as a means of achieving the commitments and objectives of the World Food Summit, taking into account the possibility of formulating voluntary guidelines for food security for all" (FAO 1996, objective 7.4(e); emphasis added).

As previously noted, civil society almost immediately created the 1997 *Code of Conduct*. And although ultimately unsuccessful in developing legally binding procedures for the fulfillment of states parties' obligations, it nevertheless helped to shape *General Comment 12* and lay the groundwork for the non-binding and voluntary-based system that would follow. In 2002, the International Planning Committee on Food Sovereignty (IPC) was established on an ad hoc basis as an international network for CSOs, and in particular peoples' organizations, to continue advancing their work after the 1996 World Food Summit.[28] Facilitating the participation of small and medium-scale farmers, fisherfolks, agricultural workers, and indigenous peoples, the IPC held a Civil Society Forum for Food Sovereignty parallel to the 2002 World Food Summit: five years later, which was organized by the FAO (IPC 2014).

At the FAO summit, 179 participating states reaffirmed the human right to adequate food and "invite[d] the FAO Council to establish at its [123rd] Session an Intergovernmental Working Group [IGWG], with the participation of stakeholders . . . to elaborate, in a period of two years, a set of voluntary guidelines to support Member States' efforts to achieve the progressive realisation of the right to adequate food in the context of national food security" (FAO 2002, para.10). This action built upon the momentum of the 1996 World Food Summit, the 1997 *Code of Conduct*, and the 1999 *General Comment 12*. However, refusing to incorporate the proposed *Code of Conduct*, and developing instead the *voluntary guidelines*, weakened the human rights principle of states parties' accountability. In the 2002 NGO/CSO political statement and action agenda delivered and facilitated by the IPC (NGO/CSO Forum on Food Sovereignty 2002a, b), CSOs rejected the declaration of the World Food Summit: five years later for maintaining the "same strategies . . . with weakened commitments, as reflected in the downgrading of the Code of Conduct on the Right to Food to a set of voluntary guidelines" and called for "a totally new human sustainable development paradigm having as one of its central goals the promotion of food and nutritional security for all within the overarching framework of a human rights based approach to food sovereignty with gender equity" (NGO/CSO Forum on Food Sovereignty 2002b).

The previously mentioned IGWG of the CFS was established in 2002 and the *Voluntary Guidelines to Support the Progressive Realization of the Right to Adequate Food in the Context of National Food Security* (hereinafter, *Right to Food Guidelines*) were adopted unanimously by the FAO Council in November 2004, after two years of negotiations (FAO 2005, iii). Arne Oshaug, member of the official Norwegian delegation to the World Food Summit in 1996 and 2002, as well as to the IGWG meetings, describes the political and practical frustrations experienced in the development of the *Right to Food Guidelines*. In concert with the determination not to create a legally binding instrument, the subject of acceptable language was paramount at the IGWG meetings. Debates over usage of states "may wish to" versus "should" or "will" proceeded at length (Oshaug 2005, 264). Likewise, attempts to include a separate guideline addressing the rule of law principle (see table 1.4) with its emphasis on recourse and remedy mechanisms were similarly rejected (Oshaug 2005, 274). In the end, drafters of the *Right to Food Guidelines* reflected the intentions of those states most critical of a human rights framework for adequate food and nutrition (Oshaug 2005, 277) and outlined only recommendations for state action, not binding responsibilities and obligations.

Despite this resort to the weakest possible language, the *Right to Food Guidelines* must be recognized for being both the first intergovernmental negotiation on the development of guidelines for countries to act upon their duties as states parties to an individual right within the ICESCR (Oshaug 2005, 276) and "the only complete set of rights-based guidelines to promote food and nutritional security for all" (Valente 2010, 14). This step forward is, therefore, also welcomed as "open[ing] up the possibility of putting human rights principles, tools, and instruments at the service of the elaboration of rights-based strategies to promote food and nutritional security, including the respective international and national governance, monitoring and accountability mechanisms" (Valente and Suárez Franco 2010, 459). While the *Right to Food Guidelines* could have been much stronger in outlining human rights principles and obligations, they play an important role in the identification of violations and risks of violations of the right to adequate food and nutrition for policy makers and victims of violations, as well as for civil society in general. Further, as Oshaug (2005, 276–77) highlights, the *Right to Food Guidelines* serves as "a unique document that provides the basis for further development of practical tools for human rights based policies and programs," including strategies for monitoring the realization of the right to adequate food and nutrition.

The *Right to Food Guidelines* attempts to "empower individuals and civil society to make demands on their governments" (FAO 2005, guideline 1.2) and to participate in public consultations and decision-making processes on right to adequate food and nutrition policies (see, e. g., guidelines 3.8 and 18.2), as well as to monitor state obligations regarding the human right to adequate food (guideline 18.1) as relevant right to adequate food and nutrition "stakeholders" (guideline 6).[29] However, the gap between UN policy that attempts to embrace civil society participation and the realistic engagement of local actors at immense social, geographic, and economic distance from the UN presents enormous obstacles. The challenge of making the *Right to Food Guidelines* accessible for civil society use was taken up in the 2007 civil society-based manual *Screen State Action against Hunger! How to Use the Voluntary Guidelines on the Right to Food to Monitor Public Policies* published by Welthungerhilfe (Aid for World Hunger) and FIAN International (Suárez Franco and Ratjen 2007). This manual can be understood as a contribution by civil society to the *fulfill/promote* obligation of states to educate civil society and other actors about human rights in general, and about the human rights framework for adequate food and nutrition in particular.

Global Governance and Food and Nutrition Policy

It has been argued that the 2008 food crisis was not a new event in a smoothly running global food system. Rather, it reflects chronic food and nutrition insecurity at the worldwide scale that was aggravated by a relatively sudden and steep rise in food prices. This price instability was and remains connected with market speculation, competition for agricultural production dedicated to agrofuels instead of food, and a trend toward so-called "large-scale land acquisition projects," (commonly called "landgrabbing") which in turn are fueled by food trade and speculation, agrofuels, and foreign country food security projects (Valente and Suárez Franco 2010, 445 ff.; see also Exner et al. 2013; Liberti 2013; Wolford et al. 2013). The food crisis prompted more than sixty riots in countries of the global South between 2007 and 2009 (Boincean et al. 2013; Department of State [United States] 2009), pointing to the incapacity of the deregulated international food market to guarantee national food and nutrition security and intensifying destabilization of local and national food and nutrition systems (Valente 2010, 13). The former special rapporteur on the right to food, Olivier De Schutter, insisted in several reports that addressing the global food crisis demanded attention to root structural causes of hunger, essentially linking the right to adequate food and nutrition to all human rights necessary to achieve this human right (OHCHR 2008b; Valente and Suárez Franco 2010, 455–56).

The international community responded to the global food crisis with three separate institutional proposals to improve food governance. The UN secretary general's office introduced the UN High Level Task Force (HLTF) on the Global Food Security Crisis. The Group of Eight (G8) chartered a Global Partnership on Agriculture, Food Security and Nutrition (GPAFS) that was subsequently adopted by the Group of Twenty Finance Ministers and Central Bank Governors (G20). The Group of Seventy-Seven (G77), in coordination with the FAO, supported a revitalization of the mandate and the work of the CFS (Boincean et al. 2013, 6).[30] As described elsewhere (CSM 2011; Paasch 2008; Valente and Suárez Franco 2010, 447–49), the struggle between these three proposals reflected lines of global political and economic power as manifested in consolidated blocks of states, corporate finance and influence, and the efforts of transnational coalitions of public interest civil society and social movement actors. While the infrastructure of a global governance system for food, nutrition, and agriculture certainly continues to be a matter of negotiation and struggle, the evolution of the CFS has played a dominant role therein.

Revitalizing the CFS entailed a complete review and overhaul of the organization. The proposal for reform was not first introduced in the context of the food crisis, although it gained traction there. Established originally in 1974 as an intergovernmental body wherein member countries each cast one equal ballot, the CFS had the mandate "to serve as a forum in the United Nations System for review and follow-up of policies concerning world food security including production and physical and economic access to food" (FAO 2013a). In the late 1990s after the 1996 World Food Summit and in response to changes in the UN system, the CFS had already attempted to take steps to modernize its terms of reference and general rules. High on this agenda was broadening non-state, multistakeholder participation in CFS activities with particular emphasis on civil society due to its cooperative work and active lobbying during and after the World Food Summit (Duncan and Barling 2012, 147–49). In 2006 and 2007, in the wake of work on *the Right to Food Guidelines* and before the abysmal failure of states and the international community to reach Millennium Development Goal 1 (halve extreme poverty and hunger by 2015) was forced to world attention due to major riots, the CFS was preparing options to formalize continued multistakeholder participation in its operations in the coming years (CFS 2007, para. 31; 2008, paras. 3, 18; FAO 2006, para. 15). By 2008, the thirty-fourth session of the CFS proposed ambitious reform modifications that "opened the way to an unprecedented increase in participation of social movements, particularly small-scale food producer organizations, within the global governance related to food security and nutrition" (Boincean et al. 2013, 6), in other words, those populations most affected by hunger and malnutrition before, during, and after the 2007–2008 food (price) crisis.

The CFS finalized its reform process in 2009 (CFS 2009). With its one-country-one-vote principle, the CFS retains equality between, and decision-making authority exclusively for, member states in an arrangement that has been called the "most democratic option at present for multilateral decision-making" (Duncan and Barling 2012, 151; see also Valente 2010, 14). The thirteen member CFS bureau of state representatives is balanced by a fourteen member advisory group of social actors that participates by providing guidance, policy recommendations, and state monitoring. The advisory group includes representatives of UN agencies and bodies with food and nutrition interests, four civil society representatives, one representative from international agricultural research bodies, one corporate private sector representative, and one representative from philanthropic bodies.[31]

From a human rights perspective, the advisory group itself is a heterogeneous complement of state aligned actors (UN agencies and bodies), rights holders (civil society), and other private actors that the state has the responsibility to regulate according to its legal and democratic obligations to rights holders and the populace of voters. Struggles persist over the makeup of this delicate balance of social actors within the advisory group. It may be argued, for example, that the corporate private sector is buttressed in the CFS by the participation of the World Bank and the Consultative Group on International Agricultural Research (CGIAR) Consortium, both of which tend to lend broad support for mainstream agroindustrial model development that essentially ignores the human rights framework. At the same time, however, "[p]resently, the private sector is lobbying to get an equal number of seats on the Advisory Group as civil society. Their attempts thus far have been unsuccessful" (Duncan and Barling 2012, 149–50). Despite such unresolved disputes, at this writing we can say that the CFS has achieved a high level of legitimacy and broad recognition as being the most inclusive international and intergovernmental platform on food security and nutrition worldwide.

Two important characteristics are signature of today's CFS. Notably, the CFS reform evolved not isolated from, but interdependently with that of the HLTF and GPFAS. While the HLTF was accorded CFS key partnership and membership status in the advisory group (CFS 2009, paras. 2 (box), 6(i), 11(i), 25), the CFS was tasked to "explor[e] synergies" with the GPFAS (CFS 2009, paras. 2, 4). At the same time, the CFS reform document explicitly articulates a human rights perspective on food security and identifies related key documents, including the *Right to Food Guidelines*, as shaping its mission (see Boincean et al. 2013, 6). Thus, the reformed CFS may become "a key platform for coordination and exchange of best practices, as well as a forum to promote accountability" (Golay and Büschi 2012, 8; see also CSM 2012; Valente and Suárez Franco 2010, 449; Brem-Wilson 2010).

The CFS reform document called on "[c]ivil society organizations/NGOs and their networks . . . to autonomously establish a global mechanism for food security and nutrition which will function as a facilitating body for CSO/NGOs consultation and participation in the CFS" (CFS 2009, para. 16). At the 2009 People's Food Sovereignty Forum, a civil society CFS Contact Group was thus formed to facilitate the participation of CSO and NGO representatives in the process of reform of the CFS (Duncan and Barling 2012, 155).[32] The Contact Group's mandate was to continue as the civil society interface with the CFS bureau and to oversee the preparation of what in 2010 became the *Proposal for an International Food Security and Nutrition Civil Society Mechanism for Relations with CFS* (hereinafter, *CSM Proposal*; CFS 2010).

The Civil Society Mechanism (CSM) outlines the role, functions, organizing principles, and governing structure of the civil society participation in the CFS (see CSM 2013). Its goal was to create flexible representation in a so-called Coordination Committee of the most food and nutrition insecure groups in the world, including smallholders, agricultural and food workers, artisanal fisherfolk, pastoralists, indigenous people, the landless, and women and youth, and additionally taking gender and geographic balance into consideration. Participation by social movements, in addition to NGOs, is highlighted in recognition of the fact that social movements still have neither the necessary credentials nor often the organizational capacity to gain UN observer and participation status in other fora (see Duncan and Barling 2012, 156–57).

Importantly, the Coordination Committee does not serve to represent civil society at the CFS. Instead it facilitates a communicative and networking function between the CFS and the larger civil society membership of CSM, particularly through the establishment of CSM working groups that participate in the CFS work streams and so-called Open-Ended Working Groups (CFS 2011). This participatory approach builds on the extensive experience and networks of CSOs that have been establishing themselves across a range of policy areas since the early 1990s. This historical strength is also connected to one of the CSM's challenges: the organizational and financial demands of managing a diverse membership, multiple languages, technical and political issues, and ensuring meaningful engagement of all those most affected by food and nutrition insecurity (Duncan and Barling 2012, 152–58).

Correspondingly, the CFS provided the opportunity for private sector associations, private philanthropic organizations, and other private constituencies active in areas related to food security, nutrition, and the right to adequate food to establish a coordination mechanism for participation in the CFS (CFS 2009, para. 17). In 2011, one year after the *CSM Proposal* was introduced into the CFS, the International Agri-Food Network (IAFN) as mediating interface for corporate private sector representation on the CFS advisory group issued a draft *CFS Private Sector Modalities* statement (IAFN 2011) that was presented to the CFS at its Priorities Information Session of 21 March 2012 (CFS Working Space 2014). The IAFN welcomes, whether multinational or national corporation, or small or medium enterprise (IAFN 2011, para. 12), all "private sector food actors who want to participate [in the network], with a particular emphasis on those active in the area of food and nutrition at any level, particularly those that represent food producers, input suppliers, agro-retailers, grain traders, food manufacturers and retailers, and other actors directly involved in producing and selling" (IAFN 2011, para. 5). The IAFN outlines the role of the private sector focal point as facilitating private sector perspectives through, among others, negotiation and input into decision-making of the CFS (IAFN 2011, para. 11).

Reifying and reflecting the struggle over a commitment to a human rights-based approach to food and nutrition within the CFS in particular, and among the diverse convictions about global food governance more generally, the IAFN draft engages very specific human rights language out of context. Section I "Accountability and Evaluation" expresses the expectation that the private sector focal point and members are "accountable" to each other and to the CFS (IAFN 2011, para. 35(a)). The critical position of accountability as the obligation of duty bearers to rights holders is elided throughout this document. With the exception of the reference in paragraph 2 to the CFS terms of participation being limited to non-state actors "active in areas related to food security, nutrition, and the right to food"(CFS 2009, para. 17), the *CFS Private Sector Modalities* makes no further reference to human rights or a rights-based approach.

The Global Strategic Framework for Food Security and Nutrition

The major objective of the CFS reform is to become "the foremost inclusive international and intergovernmental platform" (CFS 2009, para. 4) with the mandate to create and carry forward a *Global Strategic Framework for Food Security and Nutrition* (GSF; CFS 2009, para. 6(iii)). After a challenging two year negotiation process, CFS member states finally adopted the first version of the GSF during its thirty-ninth session in October 2012. However, as Boincean et al. (2013) highlight in their manual for the use of the GSF by social movements and CSOs,

> [I]n terms of content, nothing in the GSF is new. What is new, however, is the process: the GSF represents a document of global intergovernmental

consensus on matters related to food security and nutrition, including extremely important demands and perspectives of social movements and civil society groups. (Boincean et al. 2013, 5)

By building upon already existing international instruments (CFS 2009, para. 6(iii)), the GSF is to "provide an overarching framework and a single reference document with practical guidance on core recommendations for food security and nutrition strategies, policies and actions validated by the wide ownership, participation and consultation afforded by the CFS" (CFS 2012b, para.7). As explicitly stated in the 2013 FAO publication *The Human Right to Adequate Food in the Global Strategic Framework for Food Security and Nutrition: A Global Consensus,*

> *The Global Strategic Framework for Food Security and Nutrition (GSF) is the first global framework adopted by consensus, by governments, that systematically mainstreams the right to adequate food and human rights into policies relevant to food security and nutrition at the global, regional and national levels. The GSF requires all stakeholders to implement and ensure the coherence of these policies with regard to the right to adequate food. (FAO 2013c, 4)*

The first version of the GSF (CFS 2012b) draws upon the ICESCR, the *Rome Declaration on World Food Security and World Food Summit Plan of Action*, CESCR *General Comment 12*, and the FAO *Right to Food Guidelines*, documents that have all been discussed in previous sections of this chapter. Moreover, the GSF builds on the 2009 *Declaration of the World Summit on Food Security* (FAO 2009) and the *Voluntary Guidelines on the Responsible Governance of Tenure of Land, Fisheries and Forests in the Context of National Food Security* (FAO 2012), among others (see CFS 2012b, paras. 12–13, 18). However, in his submissions to the first and second drafts of the first GSF version, the former UN special rapporteur on the right to food noted his regret that the progressive realization of the right to adequate food and nutrition was not as fully articulated as the ultimate goal of the GSF as he had previously proposed (De Schutter 2012a, 2012b).[33]

The GSF is meant to be a "dynamic and living document that reflects the current international consensus among governments, which will be regularly updated to include outcomes and decisions of the CFS" (CFS 2012c, para. 5; see also Valente 2010, 14; Boincean 2013, 12; Wopold-Bosien 2013, 31).[34] Regular updates will integrate the annual activity and latest decisions of the CFS; broader revisions are anticipated every three to four years. All members of the CFS Advisory Group, including those from civil society and the private sector, will have the opportunity and the mandate to participate in the updating and revision process (Boincean et al. 2013, 12).

The GSF provides new strength to the human rights approach to food and nutrition policy. With respect to its embrace of existing international instruments, the GSF places great emphasis on the employment of policy coherence by decision and policymakers across the fields of trade, agriculture, health, natural resource management, and economic or investment policy (CFS 2012b, para. 9). Further, the GSF recognizes the rights-based approach of identifying and acting upon the root causes of hunger and malnutrition (CFS 2012b; see, e.g., parts II and IV) by prioritizing the participation of and policy focus on the most marginalized and excluded, including smallholder farmers, agricultural and food workers, artisanal fisherfolk, indigenous peoples, and the landless, with particular attention to women and youth (CFS 2012b, footnote 1; see also FAO 2013c). Following the identification of those most affected by food insecurity, the GSF "builds on a holistic understanding of rights holders and the articulation of their claims" (FAO 2013c, 7; see CFS 2012b, paras. 20, 75). Furthermore, the GSF explicitly includes and supports the application of the PANTHER principles (see table 1.4 in this chapter) to guide the decision-making, implementation, monitoring, and evaluation processes of all food and nutrition security policies, strategies, and program recommendations (CFS 2012b, para. 20; see also FAO 2013c, 7, 9, 14–15).

The GSF provides extensive language on the needs for and processes of implementing and monitoring food and nutrition policy. Unlike the premise in the draft *CFS Private Sector Modalities*, the use of the term "accountability" in the GSF clearly falls under the institutional domain of an open and international system of human rights, not the closed familiarity of private corporations (CFS 2012b, esp. paras. 92–93; see also FAO 2013c, 8).[35] Paragraph 93 identifies five principles that should apply to monitoring and accountability systems:

a) They should be human rights-based, with particular reference to the progressive realization of the right to adequate food.
b) They should make it possible for decision-makers to be accountable.
c) They should be participatory and include assessments that involve all stakeholders and beneficiaries, including the most vulnerable.
d) They should be simple, yet comprehensive, accurate, timely and understandable to all, with indicators disaggregated by sex, age, region, etc., that capture impact, process, and expected outcomes.
e) They should not duplicate existing systems, but rather build upon and strengthen national statistical and analytical capacities. (CFS 2012b, para. 93).

The GSF reflects a global struggle of civil society, corporate power, and states. Civil society, and indeed the CFS as a whole, seeks to expand participation by the most marginalized and excluded. However, greater engagement by non-traditionally represented persons and groups presents challenges of organization structure, financial mechanism, and political culture that the CFS has yet to fully adapt to in order to facilitate this broader and truly active involvement. Internal frictions within civil society resulting from, for example, "insider status" and "knowing the ropes" present an ongoing need for self-examination and adherence to the CSM rules that attempt to balance structure, continuity, and space for new voices of change (Duncan and Barling 2012, 156–57). According to several observers, ongoing challenges concern different strategic approaches, resources, and experience available to NGOs on the one hand and social movements on the other. To secure the legitimacy of the CSM, the leadership role of social movements, as organizations of rights holders most affected by food insecurity, must be ensured (M. Wopold-Bosien, pers. comm.).[36]

Communication presents additional challenges. Internal consultation is complicated by the multiplicity of languages, unequal educational preparation in literacy, and a lack of ready or affordable access to internet, telephone, or other communication infrastructure. External communication, that is, interaction and knowledge exchange between diverse civil society members and others, can be complicated by the embrace of participants with forms of information sharing that do not conform to common international protocol, for example, testimony, storytelling, and cultural and gender specific styles of communication. To truly embrace diversity and the voices of the marginalized, the CSM must remain flexible and responsive to its constituencies (Duncan and Barling 2012, 152–58).

As civil society copes with processes of expansion, the "private sector" may face challenges with an increasingly teleological vision of itself that eclipses diversity from its participation in decision-making in the CFS. The private sector fuels the economy. And yet, when fronted by the largest multinational corporations, it appears that the voices of small and medium business persons, including and especially the women among them, are closed out of what has become called "private sector representation." Indeed, smallholder farmers, artisanal fisherfolk, pastoralists—they are entrepreneurs. They are the traditional heart of economic development behind local and regional food systems. Nevertheless, these small-scale members of the private sector are more often aligned in international food and nutrition policy and decision-making with public interest civil society and social movements because of their priority attention on addressing violations of the realization of their basic human rights in the context of food and nutrition. In the CFS and other UN settings, what passes for the "private sector" today are actually the interests of large multinational corporations. We can say that the majority of global entrepreneurs are completely obscured by the monopoly holders of capital and other resources, a group that should be specified as the *corporate* private sector.

Global food and nutrition governance is tasked with the democratic evolution of strategies to improve the economic and social security of all persons with attention to the most marginalized. We argue that the best vision to date for this objective is people's and food sovereignty, a framework concept for the human right to adequate food and nutrition that includes women's rights and a gender perspective as well as the right's nutritional dimension. This argument is further developed in the volume's final chapter.

CHALLENGES LOOKING FORWARD

This chapter introduced the message that the concepts, frameworks, and system of human rights in general, and of the human right to adequate food and nutrition in particular, are of an evolutive nature. We have focused in particular on the growing role and participation of public interest civil society in addressing the constant need to update the legal and conceptual frameworks of human rights to meet the gaps of protection that are generated by rights holders' realities. This process has surely not finished and indeed our presentation is at best rudimentary. Many recent and contemporary initiatives, beyond the scope of this chapter, are changing the landscape of human rights; most reflect or respond to the escalating struggle between liberal trade policy and the human rights framework for adequate food and nutrition. These include but are certainly not limited to (*a*) the powerful field of extra-territorial obligations that extend state duties to the activities of its constituents beyond a state's geographic border, (*b*) the *Optional Protocol to the International Covenant on Economic, Social and Cultural Rights* (UN General Assembly 2009) that came into force in 2013 and that provides recourse to the international human rights system for rights violation complaints by individuals and groups, and (*c*) vociferous disagreement over the legitimacy of the public-private partnership (PPP) approach. This latter PPP argument is waged, for example, by maternal, infant, and young child advocates who see a conflict of interest when corporate violators of international regulatory codes on marketing infant and young child nutrition and food substitutes are invited to participate in decision-making on the same public nutrition and food policy themes (Gupta 2012; IBFAN 2011, 2012; see also chapter 4 of this volume).

In the next chapter, we turn to the question of women's food and nutrition security status that drives this volume and introduce two disconnects that, we argue, frustrate the realization of a universal human right to adequate food and nutrition in general, and women's enjoyment of those rights, more particularly.

NOTES

1. In the 2012 edition of its yearly report *The State of Food Insecurity in the World*, the Food and Agriculture Organization (FAO) of the United Nations (UN) reevaluated its estimates of food insecure persons back to 1990 (FAO, WFP, and IFAD 2012). The revised food insecurity figures rate the increase in hunger during 2007–2010, the period characterized by food price and economic crises, as less severe than originally estimated, and the amount of people who suffered from food insecurity in the 2010–12 time period at the global level as amounting to 868 million, less than the projections in excess of one billion (FAO and WFP 2010). These new calculations have led some to think that "the worries [about world hunger] may be overdone and so are the demands that accompany them" (J.P. 2012). Thomas Pogge (2008, 10–13)

gives a short but insightful analysis of how language, baselines, and targets used in the definition and measurement of poverty have been manipulated to portray more social progress than actual in reality. This leads to a level of uncertainty regarding the is accuracy of the present official statistics indicating improvements in global poverty and hunger.

2. The reform document of the Committee on World Food Security (CFS), when referring to small-scale food producers or smallholder farmers, includes also agriculture and food workers, artisanal fisherfolk, pastoralists, indigenous peoples, and the landless, with particular attention to women and youth (CFS 2009, para. 11, ii; see also CFS 2012b, note 1).

3. For example, the 2002 *Women, Peace, and Security* study by the UN secretary general found that increasing violations of women rights constituted a reliable indicator of escalating intranational conflict (UN 2002). The secretary general's 2009 report *Women and Peace and Security* identifies special needs of women associated with conflict escalation, prevention, resolution, and peace-building to include violations associated with sexual violence, security, and access to social services, access to political participation, and access to education (UN Security Council 2009). Empirical data drives findings linking gender discrimination and hunger in the IFPRI and Welthungerhilfe (Aid for World Hunger) Global Hunger Index (GHI; see von Grebmer et al. 2009).

4. As proposed by the CFS in its 2012 report, *Coming to Terms with Terminology*, we adopt the term "food and nutrition security" to best express "a single integrated development goal to help guide policy and programmatic action effectively" (CFS 2012a, 2).

5. Public interest civil society can engage powerful political agency to realize human rights. However, not all civil society organizations (CSOs), and particularly not all non-governmental organizations (NGOs), represent a free and engaged public interest aligned with a human rights-based framework. Some NGOs prevail with corporate backing serving as a functional arm of large industrial holdings and their investors (see also chapter 4 of this volume), as opposed to a public interest civil society organization. Other NGOs may be dedicated to civil society, but do not use a human right–based approach, even in cases when they may claim to (Windfuhr 1998, 7; Jenderedjian and Bellows forthcoming). These latter may, for example, approach support from a charity rather than a human rights-based perspective that emphasizes empowerment, participation, transparency, and other principles introduced in this chapter.

6. The government of a country that has voluntarily consented, by means of ratification or accession, to be legally bound by an international treaty, and for which this treaty is in force, is called a state party to the respective treaty (see UN 1969).

7. The UDHR contains thirty articles. The first five and last three had few political overtones at the time of inception, and focused on the universal dignity of the person, on her/his rights to life, on liberty and freedom from slavery and torture, on the responsibilities of rights holders to their communities, and the obligation to uphold respect for the human rights accorded to others. The remainder of the UDHR articles are divided into the political and civil rights championed by the geopolitical West (articles 6–21), and the economic, social, and cultural rights promoted by the East (articles 22–27; see UN General Assembly 1948).

8. On the issuance of two separate treaties, A. Eide and Rosas (2001, 3) write, "[w]hen the United Nations Commission on Human Rights had completed its work on the Declaration and started to draft conventions on human rights which would be legally binding on the states ratifying them, the Commission split on the question of whether there should be one or two covenants.

The question was turned over to the General Assembly, which, in a resolution adopted in 1950, emphasized the interdependence of all categories of human rights and called upon the Commission to adopt a single convention. The next year, however, the Western states were able to reverse the decision, asking the Commission to divide the rights contained in the UDHR into two separate international covenants, one on civil and political rights (CCPR) and the other on economic, social and cultural rights (CESCR)." See also A. Eide (2001).

9. Florence Brewer Boeckel (1929, 237) writes, "An International Committee of Women led by Miss Doris Stevens, Chairman of the Committee on International Action of the [US] National Woman's Party, and Mrs. Jane Norman Smith, Chairman of the Council of the same organization, accompanied by representative women of Latin American countries, attended the [1928] Conference to present their demand, that the countries in the Pan American Union, by treaty, accord the women of this hemisphere equal rights with men. This was the first time in history that women had sought to obtain equality by means of an international treaty. As a result, also for the first time, women were given an opportunity to address the Conference on this subject. Later their request for a special committee of women to deal with laws affecting women, was granted by the adoption of [a] resolution."

10. At the 1933 OAS conference, the failed ERA was only signed by Cuba, Ecuador, Paraguay, and Uruguay. For more information, please see Benedek (2012, 175) or visit the website of the OAS (OAS 2013).

11. In 1972, the ERA was again presented to, and accepted by, the US House of Representatives and the Senate, and then sent to the state legislatures for ratification. The deadline for ratification expired on 30 June 1982. After ten years of a polarizing debate, the United States again failed to adopt the ERA into its constitution.

12. At the time of this writing, the *Convention of Belém do Pará* has been signed by all member states to the OAS, with exception of Canada and the United States, a total of thirty-two states. It entered into force in 1995 (CIDH 2010).

13. The 2011 *Council of Europe Convention on Preventing and Combating Violence against Women* (also known as *Istanbul Convention*; see Council of Europe 2011) is another prominent, but more recent regional advance in the protection of women against violence (OAS and Council of Europe 2014).

14. Article 3 of the *Maria da Penha Law* reads,

    Women are ensured the conditions for the effective exercise of the rights to life, security, health, food, education, culture, housing, access justice, sport, leisure, work, citizenship, freedom, dignity, respect and family and community living. (Special Secretariat for Women's Policies [Brazil] 2006, 10)

15. For a detailed legal analysis of ICESCR article 11, please see, for example, Alston (1984, 166 ff.).

16. ICESCR article 11 went through the drafting committee relatively quickly due to FAO's direct involvement in the article drafting process (Alston 1984, 165–66).

17. As of April 2014, the Committee has issued a total of twenty-one general comments (OHCHR 2014).

18. The CESCR first contemplated the idea of adopting an optional protocol to the ICESCR in 1990 during its fifth session (see Arambulo 1999).

19. To verify the most current state of ratification of the optional protocol to the ICESCR, visit the UN Treaty Collection website (UN 2013a).

20. Established originally in 1974 as an intergovernmental body, the CFS had the mandate "to serve as a forum in the United Nations System for review and

follow-up of policies concerning world food security including production and physical and economic access to food" (FAO 2013a).

21. Several CESCR general comments that followed *General Comment 12 on the Right to Adequate Food* also addressed the right to adequate food and nutrition, including *General Comment 14 on the Highest Attainable Standard of Health* (CESCR 2000), *General Comment 15 on the Right to Water* (CESCR 2003), *General Comment 18 on the Right to Work* (CESCR 2006), *General Comment 19 on the Right to Social Security* (CESCR 2008), and *General Comment 20 on Non-Discrimination in Economic, Social, and Cultural Rights* (CESCR 2009; see also Valente and Suárez Franco 2010, 453).

22. In the context of the privatization of water, see, for example, Bakker (2007); Mehta, Veldwisch, and Franco (2012); as well as Shiva (2002). In the context of seeds, see Goodmann (2009), ICFFA (2006), and Shiva (2001, esp. chap. 6 "Can Seed be Owned?"). For a discussion of the diverse impacts of (trans) national commercial land transactions and land speculation ("large-scale land acquisition" or "landgrabbing") on poverty and food and nutrition insecurity, see, for example, Borras (2013), Borras and Franco (2010a, 2010b, 2012), De Schutter (2011), Li (2011), and the 2013 special issue of the journal *Globalizations* on *Land Grabbing and Global Governance*, among many other contributions available on the issue.

23. For more information on the extraterritorial dimension of human rights, see the *Maastricht Principles on Extraterritorial Obligations of States in the Area of Economic, Social and Cultural Rights* (Maastricht University and ICJ 2011). See also Coomans and Künnemann (2012), De Schutter et al. (2012), and Künnemann (2013, 2014).

24. Institutionalization of civil society participation in the design and implementation of the right to adequate food and nutrition includes the centralization of a civil society role in the extended development of national framework laws on the right to adequate food and nutrition, as well as in the establishment of goals, monitoring, and recourse procedures (see CESCR 1999, para. 29).

25. For more information on the HRC special session on the 2008 world food crisis, visit the *News and Events* website of the UN Office of the High Commissioner for Human Rights (OHCHR; OHCHR 2008a).

26. The special rapporteur on the right to food is required to submit a report at the annual sessions of the CHR (until March 2006) and of the HRC (from June 2006 on) and a report to the General Assembly on his or her activities, themes identified, and studies undertaken (CHR 2000). These reports can be retrieved from the OHCHR website at http://www.ohchr.org/EN/Issues/Food/Pages/Annual.aspx (last accessed 28 January 2015). Additionally, these official reports, as well as other briefing notes and documents, can be retrieved from the private websites of the two former special rapporteurs. Please go to http://www.righttofood.org/publications/un-reports/ (last accessed 28 January 2015) for Jean Ziegler's reports and http://www.srfood.org/en/documents (last accessed 28 January 2015) for Olivier De Schutter's documents. At this time of writing, a website for the current special rapporteur, Hilal Elver, has not yet been created.

27. Although in past publications we have also referred to the "human rights–based approach," we now employ this terminology with extreme care, having found its use light and leaving margin for abuse as states and non-state actors selectively pick and choose what they want from the "approach."

28. Officially set up in 2003, the International Planning Committee for Food Sovereignty (IPC) is the only international network that aggregates globally large CSOs and NGOs, representing together hundreds of millions of food producers, whose goal is to play an active role in global governance and accountability in

order to support the ability of governments to protect the interests of small food producers and consumers. The IPC broadens the scope of political negotiation for civil society within FAO, through the participation of new social actors in decision-making, as well as through the inclusion of their contents, methodologies, and militancy, thereby establishing an effective democracy (TNI 2014).

29. Instead of "stakeholders", we prefer the term "actors" or "constituencies" due to a tendency of the corporate private sector to adopt "stakeholder" status allowing it to appear to participate on equal footing with public interest civil society when instead it sometimes overpowers the political realm.

30. The Group of Eight (G8), the governments of eight of the world's wealthiest countries, includes Canada, France, Germany, Italy, Japan, Russia, the United Kingdom, and the United States, with the European Union also represented as observer. The Group of Twenty Finance Ministers and Central Bank Governors (G20) is a group of the key national finance actors (ministers and governors) from the twenty major national economies, that is, from nineteen countries and the European Union. The countries include Australia, Japan, South Africa, France, Turkey, the United States, Saudi Arabia, Russia, Mexico, South Korea, China, Canada, Italy, Indonesia, India, Germany, the United Kingdom, Brazil, and Argentina. Finally, the Group of Seventy-Seven (G77) was established in Geneva on 15 June 1964 by seventy-seven countries signatories of the *Joint Declaration of the Seventy-Seven Developing Countries Made at the Conclusions of the United Nations Conference on Trade and Development* (Group of Seventy-Seven 1964). In the meantime, the number of countries members of the G77 has increased to 133; however, the original name has been retained "due to its historic significance" (Group of Seventy-Seven 2014).

31. For the period of 2013–15, the thirteen state members of the CFS bureau are Netherlands (chair), Afghanistan, Argentina, Australia, Brazil, Congo, France, Pakistan, Philippines, Sudan, Switzerland, Uganda, and United States. The fourteen CFS advisory group members for the same period are as follows: (*a*) six UN bodies: FAO, World Food Programme (WFP), International Fund for Agricultural Development (IFAD), the special rapporteur on the right to food, HLTF on the Global Food Security Crisis, and UN Standing Committee on Nutrition (SCN); (*b*) four CSOs/NGOs: World Forum of Fish Harvesters & Fish Workers (WFHFF), Mouvement International de la Jeunesse Agricole (MIJARC), Indigenous Caucus (ICAZA), and World Alliance of Mobile Indigenous Peoples (WAMIP); (*c*) one international agricultural research body: Consultative Group on International Agricultural Research (CGIAR) Consortium; (*d*) one international financial and trade institution: World Bank; and (*e*) two private sector/philanthropic foundations: Bill and Melinda Gates Foundation, and International Agri-Food Network (IAFN). For this and more information on the previous bureau, please visit the website of the CFS at http://www.fao.org/cfs/cfs-home/cfs-about/cfs-members/en/ (last accessed February 2, 2015).

32. The CFS Contact Group consisted of three male and one female representatives from Le Réseau des Organizations Paysannes et de Producteurs de l'Afrique de l'Ouest (ROPPA), the International Planning Committee for Food Sovereignty (IPC), Oxfam International, and the Mouvement International de la Jeunesse Agricole et Rurale Catholique (MIJARC; Duncan and Barling 2012, 155).

33. The CFS reform document (CFS 2009, para. 11(i)) provides for the engagement of the UN special rapporteur on the right to food and of the OHCHR in the work of the CFS. The former special rapporteur on the right to food, Olivier De Schutter, participated very actively in the process of revitalizing the CFS and submitted various comments on the GSF. The documents are available on De Schutter's website (De Schutter 2014).

34. At the time of writing, the CFS adopted, at its fortieth session in October 2013, a second version of the GSF. The main addition of this amended document relates to recommendations to "[s]tates, international and regional organizations and all other appropriate stakeholders" on the issue of social protection for food security and nutrition (CFS 2013, 32).

35. The first version of the GSF states,

> Accountability for commitments and for results is crucial, especially for advancing the progressive realization of the right to adequate food, and it is noted that those countries making the greatest progress on food security and nutrition are those that have demonstrated the greatest political will, with a strong political and financial commitment that is open and transparent to all stakeholders. Objectives to be monitored should include nutritional outcomes, right to food indicators, agricultural sector performance, progress towards achievement of the MDGs, particularly MDG1, and regionally agreed targets. (CFS 2012b, para. 92)

36. Formerly the Right to Food Accountability program coordinator at FIAN International, Heidelberg, as of February 2015 Martin Wopold-Bosien serves as chair of the Civil Society Mechanism (CSM) to the Committee on World Food Security (CSM).

REFERENCES

Albrecht, K., J. Germann, and S. Ratjen. 2007. *D:49 How to use the Voluntary Guidelines on the Right to Food: A Manual for Social Movements, Community-Based Organisations and Non-Governmental Organisations.* Heidelberg: FIAN International.

Alston, P. 1984. "International Law and the Right to Food." In *Food as a Human Right*, edited by A. Eide, W. B. Eide, S. Goonatilake, J. Gussow, and Omawale, 162–74. Tokyo: United Nations University.

Anderson, M. 2013. "Beyond Food Security to Realizing Food Rights in the US." *Journal of Rural Studies* 29: 113–22.

Arambulo, K. 1999. *Strengthening the Supervision of the International Covenant on Economic Social and Cultural Rights: Theoretical and Procedural Aspects.* School of Human Rights Research (Book 3). Antwerpen, Groningen, Oxford: Intersentia.

Bakker, K. 2007. "The 'Commons' versus the 'Commodity': Alter-Globalization, Anti-Privatization and the Human Right to Water in the Global South." *Antipode* 39 (3): 430–55.

Ballenger, N. and C. Mabbs-Zeno. 1992. "Treating Food Security and Food Aid Issues at the GATT." *Food Policy* 17 (4): 264–76.

Benedek, W. 2012. *Understanding Human Rights—Manual on Human Rights Education.* Graz: European Training and Research Centre for Human Rights and Democracy (ECT).

Boincean, S., A. Ferrante, G. Henriques, N. Landívar, S. Longley, and M. Wolpold-Bosien. 2013. *Using the Global Strategic Framework for Food Security and Nutrition to Promote and Defend the People's Right to Adequate Food: A Manual for Social Movements and Civil Society Organization.* Heidelberg: International Alliance of Catholic Development Agencies (CIDSE), International Union of Food, Agricultural, Hotel, Restaurant, Catering, Tobacco and Allied Workers' Associations (IUF), La Via Campesina, and FIAN International.

Borras, S. J. 2013. "The Challenge of Global Governance of Land Grabbing: Changing International Agricultural Context and Competing Political Views and Strategies." *Globalizations* 10: 161–79.

Borras, S. J. and J. C. Franco. 2010a. "Contemporary Discourses and Political Contestations around Pro-Poor Land Policies and Land Governance." *Journal of Agrarian Change* 10 (1): 1–32.

———. 2010b. "From Threat to Opportunity? Problems with the Idea of a 'Code of Conduct' for Land-Grabbing." *Yale Human Rights and Development Law Journal* 13 (2): 507–23.

———. 2012. "Global Land Grabbing and Trajectories of Agrarian Change: A Preliminary Analysis." *Journal of Agrarian Change* 12 (1): 34–59.

Brem-Wilson, J. 2010. *The Reformed Committee on World Food Security: A Briefing Paper for Civil Society*, edited by International Planning Committee for Food Sovereignty (IPC), Center Internazionale Crocevia (CIC), and Mundubat. Bilbao: International Planning Committee for Food Sovereignty (IPC).

Brewer Boeckel, F. 1929. "Women in International Affairs." *ANNALS of the American Academy of Political and Social Science* 143: 230–48.

Brownlie, I. 2008. *Principles of Public International Law*. Seventh ed. New York: Oxford University Press.

Committee on World Food Security (CFS). 2007. *Report of the 33rd Session of the Committee on World Food Security. CL 132/10, 7–10 May 2007*. Rome: Food and Agriculture Organization of the United Nations (FAO).

———. 2008. *Proposals to Strengthen the Committee on World Food Security (CFS) to Meet New Challenges. CFS:2008/6, 14–17 October 2008*. Rome: Food and Agriculture Organization of the United Nations (FAO).

———. 2009. *Reform of the Committee on World Food Security. Final Version. CFS 2009/2 Rev.2., 14, 15 and 17 October 2009*. Rome: Food and Agriculture Organization of the United Nations (FAO).

———. 2010. *Proposal for an International Food Security and Nutrition Civil Society Mechanism for Relations with CFS. Document Prepared by Action-Aid International, the Governance Working Group of the International Planning Committee for Food Sovereignty and Oxfam. CFS:2010/9, 11–14 and 16 October 2010*. Rome: Food and Agriculture Organization of the United Nations (FAO).

———. 2011. *Guidelines for Participation in CFS Open Ended Working Groups*. Rome: Committee on World Food Security (CFS).

———. 2012a. *Coming to Terms with Terminology: Food Security, Nutrition Security, Food Security and Nutrition, Food and Nutrition Security (Revised Draft 25 July 2012)*. Rome: Committee on World Food Security (CFS).

———. 2012b. *Global Strategic Framework for Food Security and Nutrition: First Version. Consolidated Version Agreed in the Plenary of the CFS Open-Ended Working Group for GSF— 27–29 June and 19 July 2012. Committee on World Food Security Thirty-Ninth Session. CFS 2012/39/5 Add.1, 15–20 October 2012*. Rome: Food and Agriculture Organization of the United Nations (FAO).

———. 2012c. *First Version of the Global Strategic Framework for Food Security and Nutrition (GSF). Preamble and Decision Box. CFS 2012/39/5, 15–20 October 2012*. Rome: Committee on World Food Security (CFS).

———. 2013. *Global Strategic Framework for Food Security and Nutrition: Second Version (2013). Committee on World Food Security Fortieth Session. CFS 2013/40/5 Add.1, 7–11 October 2013*. Rome: Food and Agriculture Organization of the United Nations (FAO).

Committee on World Food Security (CFS) Working Space. 2014. "CFS Priorities Information Session." Rome: Committee on World Food Security (CFS), accessed April 4, 2014, http://www.fao.org/cfs/workingspace/cfs-news/details/en/c/143593/.

Coomans, F. and R. Künnemann. 2012. *Cases and Concepts on Extraterritorial Obligations in the Area of Economic, Social and Cultural Rights*. Cambridge: Intersentia.

Coopération Internationale pour le Développement et la Solidarité (CIDSE). 2008. *CIDSE Statement: Food Price Crisis Highlights the Need for Real Reform in Trade and Agricultural Policies, September 2008*. Brussels: Coopération Internationale pour le Développement et la Solidarité (CIDSE).

Coopération Internationale pour le Développement et la Solidarité (CIDSE) and Institute for Agriculture and Trade Policy (IATP). 2009. *Global Food Responsibility: The European Union and the United States Must Chart a New Path*. Brussels: Coopération Internationale pour le Développement et la Solidarité (CIDSE).

Council of Europe. 2011. *Council of Europe Convention on Preventing and Combating Violence Against Women and Domestic Violence, 11 May 2011*. Strasbourg: Council of Europe.

Damman, S., W.B. Eide, and H.V. Kuhnlein. 2008. "Indigenous Peoples' Nutrition Transition in a Right to Food Perspective." *Food Policy* 33 (2): 135–55.

De Schutter, O. 2006. *Transnational Corporations and Human Rights*. Studies in International Law. Portland: Hart Publishing.

———. 2010. *International Human Rights Law: Cases, Materials, Commentary*. Cambridge: Cambridge University Press.

———. 2011. "How Not to Think of Land Grabbing: Three Critiques of Large-Scale Investments in Farmland." *Journal of Peasant Studies* 38 (2): 249–79.

———. 2012a. *Comments on the Second Draft of the Global Strategic Framework for Food Security and Nutrition of the Committee on World Food Security*. New York: United Nations (UN).

———. 2012b. *Submission to the Consultation on the First Draft of the Global Strategic Framework for Food Security and Nutrition of the Committee on World Food Security*. New York: United Nations (UN).

———. 2013. *Economic, Social and Cultural Rights as Human Rights*. Edward Elgar.

———. "Global Governance." Olivier De Schutter: United Nations Special Rapporteur on the Right to Food, last modified 2014, accessed April 7, 2014, http://www.srfood.org/en/global-governance.

De Schutter, O. and K.Y. Cordes. 2011. *Accounting for Hunger: The Right to Food in the Era of Globalisation*. Studies in International Law. Oxford and Portland: Hart Publishing.

De Schutter, O., A. Eide, A. Khalfan, M. Orellana, M. Salomon, and I. Seiderman. 2012. "Commentary to the Maastricht Principles on Extraterritorial Obligations of States in the Area of Economic, Social and Cultural Rights." *Human Rights Quarterly* 34: 1084–169.

Department of State [United States]. "Remarks with Secretary of Agriculture Tom Vilsack on a Conference Call to Discuss Food Security on World Food Day." Department of State [United States]: Diplomacy in Action, last modified October 16, 2009, accessed November 3, 2013, http://m.state.gov/md130663.htm.

Desmarais, A.A. 2007. *La Via Campesina: Globalization and the Power of Peasants*. London: Pluto Press.

Deva, S. and D. Bilchitz, eds. 2013. *Human Rights Obligations of Business: Beyond the Corporate Responsibility to Respect?* New York: Cambridge University Press.

Diokno, M.S.I. 2013. "Chapter 4. Human Rights (PANTHER) Principles in Development Planning." Human Rights Based Approach Development Toolkit, accessed February 28, 2013, http://www.hrbatoolkit.org/?page_id=116.

Donelly, J. 1999. "Human Rights, Democracy, and Development." *Human Rights Quarterly* 21 (3): 608–32, quoted in Uvin, P. 2007. "From the Right to Development to the Rights-Based Approach: How 'Human Rights' Entered Development." *Development in Practice* 17 (4–5): 597–606.

Duncan, J. and D. Barling. 2012. "Renewal through Participation in Global Food Security Governance: Implementing the International Food Security and Nutrition Civil Society Mechanism to the Committee on World Food Security." *International Journal of Sociology of Agriculture and Food* 19 (2): 143–61.

Eide, A. 1989. *Right to Adequate Food as a Human Right.* Human Rights Study Series 1. New York: United Nations (UN) Centre for Human Rights.

———. 1999. *The Right to Adequate Food and to be Free from Hunger: Updated Study on the Right to Food. Submitted by Mr. Asbjørn Eide in Accordance with Sub-Commission Decision 1997/108 (E/CN.4/Sub.2/1999/12).* New York: United Nations (UN).

———. 2001. "Economic, Social and Cultural Rights as Human Rights." In *Economic, Social and Cultural Rights: A Textbook*, edited by A. Eide, C. Krause, and A. Rosas. Second ed., 9–28. New York: Springer.

———. 2005. "The Importance of Economic and Social Rights in the Age of Economic Globalisation." In *Food and Human Rights in Development—Volume I: Legal and Institutional Dimensions and Selected Topics*, edited by W. B. Eide and U. Kracht, 3–40. Antwerpen: Intersentia.

Eide, A. and A. Rosas. 2001. "Economic, Social and Cultural Rights: A Universal Challenge." In *Economic, Social and Cultural Rights: A Textbook*, edited by A. Eide, C. Krause, and A. Rosas. Second ed., 3–7. New York: Springer.

Eide, W. B. 2005. "From Food Security to the Right to Food." In *Food and Human Rights in Development—Volume I: Legal and Institutional Dimensions and Selected Topics*, edited by W. B. Eide and U. Kracht, 67–97 Antwerpen: Intersentia.

Eide, W. B. and U. Kracht, eds. 2005a. *Food and Human Rights in Development—Volume I: Legal and Institutional Dimensions and Selected Topics.* Antwerpen: Intersentia.

———. 2005b. "The Right to Adequate Food in Human Rights Instruments: Legal Norms and Interpretations." In *Food and Human Rights in Development—Volume I: Legal and Institutional Dimensions and Selected Topics*, edited by W. B. Eide and U. Kracht, 99–118. Antwerpen: Intersentia.

———. 2007. *Food and Human Rights in Development—Volume II: Evolving Issues and Emerging Applications.* Antwerpen: Intersentia.

Exner, A., P. Fleissner, L. Kranzl, and W. Zittel, eds. 2011. *Kämpfe um Land. Gutes Leben im Post-Fossilen Zeitalter [Struggles for Land. Good Life in the Post-fossil Age].* kritik & utopie. Wien: Mandelbaum.

FIAN International. "Press Release 7 February 2013. Optional Protocol to be Brought into Force with Uruguay Ratification." Heidelberg: FIAN International, accessed February 7, 2013, http://www.fian.org/news/article/detail/optional_protocol_to_be_brought_into_force_with_uruguay_ratification/.

FIAN International, World Alliance for Nutrition and Human Rights (WANAHR), and Institute Jacques Maritain International. 1997. *International Code of Conduct on the Human Right to Adequate Food.*

Food and Agriculture Organization of the United Nations (FAO). 1996. *Rome Declaration on World Food Security and World Food Summit Plan of Action.* Rome: Food and Agriculture Organization of the United Nations (FAO).

———. 2002. "Appendix: Declaration of the World Food Summit: Five Years Later." In *Report of the World Food Summit: Five Years Later—Rome, 10–13 June 2002*, 80–88. Rome: Food and Agriculture Organization of the United Nations (FAO).

———. 2005. *Voluntary Guidelines to Support the Progressive Realization of the Right to Adequate Food in the Context of National Food Security.* Rome: Food and Agriculture Organization of the United Nations (FAO).

———. 2006. *Report of the Council of FAO. CL 131/REP, 20–25 November 2006.* Rome: Food and Agriculture Organization of the United Nations (FAO).

———. 2009. *Declaration of the World Summit on Food Security. WSFS 2009/2, 16–18 November 2009.* Rome: Food and Agriculture Organization of the United Nations (FAO).

———. 2012. *Voluntary Guidelines on the Responsible Governance of Tenure of Land, Fisheries and Forests in the Context of National Food Security.* Rome: Food and Agriculture Organization of the United Nations (FAO).

———. 2013a. "About CFS." Committee on World Food Security, last modified March 11, 2013, accessed November 3, 2013, http://www.fao.org/cfs/cfs-home/cfs-about/en/.

———. 2013b. *Guidance Note: Integrating the Right to Adequate Food into Food and Nutrition Security Programmes.* Rome: Food and Agriculture Organization of the United Nations (FAO).

———. 2013c. *The Human Right to Adequate Food in the Global Strategic Framework for Food Security and Nutrition: A Global Consensus.* Rome: Food and Agriculture Organization of the United Nations (FAO).

Food and Agriculture Organization of the United Nations (FAO) and United Nations World Food Programme (WFP). 2010. *The State of Food Insecurity in the World: Addressing Food Insecurity in Protracted Crises.* Rome: Food and Agriculture Organization of the United Nations (FAO).

Food and Agriculture Organization of the United Nations (FAO), United Nations World Food Programme (WFP), and International Fund for Agricultural Development (IFAD). 2012. *The State of Food Insecurity in the World: Economic Growth is Necessary but Not Sufficient to Accelerate Reduction of Hunger and Malnutrition.* Rome: Food and Agriculture Organization of the United Nations (FAO).

Forum for Food Sovereignty. 2007. *Declaration of Nyéléni.* Sélingué, Mali.

Francis, R. W. 2013. "The ERA: A Brief Introduction." Alice Paul Institute (API), ERA Task Force of the National Council of Women's Organizations (NCWO) [United States], accessed December 12, 2013, http://www.equalrightsamendment.org/history.htm.

Golay, C. and M. Büschi. 2012. *The Right to Food and Global Strategic Frameworks: The Global Strategic Framework for Food Security and Nutrition (GSF) and the UN Comprehensive Framework for Action (CFA).* Rome: Food and Agriculture Organization of the United Nations (FAO).

Goodman, Z. 2009. *Seeds of Hunger: Intellectual Property Rights on Seeds and the Human Rights Response.* Backgrounder No. 2: THREAD Series, edited by C. Dommen, Geneva: 3D—Trade-Human Rights-Equitable Economy.

Group of Seventy-Seven. 2014. "About the Group of 77." The Group of 77 at the United Nations. Group of Seventy-Seven, last modified 2014, accessed April 7, 2014, http://www.g77.org/doc/.

———. 1964. *Joint Declaration of the Seventy-Seven Developing Countries Made at the Conclusion of the United Nations Conference on Trade and Development. 15 June 1964.* Geneva: Group of Seventy-Seven.

Gupta, A. 2012. "International Baby Food Action Network (IBFAN) Statement on the Promotion and Use of Commercial Fortified Foods as Solutions for Child Malnutrition." *Indian Pediatrics* 49 (4): 295–96.

Gussow, J., O. Muchena, and W. B. Eide. 1984. "Women and Food—Equity and Development?" In *Food as a Human Right,* edited by A. Eide, W. B. Eide, S. Goonatilake, J. Gussow, and Omawale, 69–88. Tokyo: United Nations University.

Healy, S., R. W. Pearce, and M. Stockbridge. 1998. *The Implications of the Uruguay Round Agreement on Agriculture for Developing Countries: A Training Manual.* Training Materials for Agricultural Planning. Vol. 41. Rome: Food and Agriculture Organization of the United Nations (FAO).

Henkin, L. 1978. *The Rights of Man Today.* Boulder: Westview Press.

Holt-Giménez, E., ed. 2011. *Food Movements Unite! Strategies to Transform Our Food Systems*. Oakland: Food First Books.

Hunt, L. 2008. *Inventing Human Rights: A History*. New York: WW Norton.

Inter-American Commission on Human Rights (CIDH). 2010. "Inter-American Convention on the Prevention, Punishment and Eradication of Violence against Women. 'Convention of Belém do Pará.'" Washington, D.C.: Inter-American Commission on Human Rights (CIDH), accessed April 7, 2014, http://www.cidh.org/Basicos/English/Basic14.Conv%20of%20Belem%20Do%20Para%20Ratif.htm.

International Agri-Food Network (IAFN). 2011. *CFS Private Sector Modalities*. International Agri-Food Network (IAFN).

International Baby Food Action Network (IBFAN). 2011. *Statement on the Promotion and Use of Commercial Fortified Foods as Solutions for Child Malnutrition*. Geneva: International Baby Food Action Network (IBFAN).

———. 2012. *IBFAN Discussion Paper. The Scaling-Up Nutrition (SUN) Initiative: IBFAN's Concern about the Role of Businesses*. Geneva: International Baby Food Action Network (IBFAN).

International Commission on the Future of Food and Agriculture (ICFFA). 2006. *Manifesto on the Future of Seeds*. Toscana: Arsia.

International Commission of Jurists (ICJ). 1997. *Maastricht Guidelines on Violations of Economic, Social and Cultural Rights. 26 January 1997*. Geneva: International Commission of Jurists (ICJ).

International Committee of the Red Cross (ICRC). 1949. *The Geneva Conventions of 12 August 1949*. Geneva: International Committee of the Red Cross (ICRC).

———. 1977a. *Protocol Additional to the Geneva Conventions of 12 August 1949, and Relating to the Protection of Victims of International Armed Conflicts (Protocol I), 8 June 1977, 1125 UNTS 3*. Geneva: International Committee of the Red Cross (ICRC).

———. 1977b. *Protocol Additional to the Geneva Conventions of 12 August 1949, and Relating to the Protection of Victims of Non-International Armed Conflicts (Protocol II), 8 June 1977, 1125 UNTS 609*. Geneva: International Committee of the Red Cross (ICRC).

International Food Policy Research Institute (IFPRI). 2005. *Women: Still the Key to Food and Nutrition Security*. Washington, D.C.: International Food Policy Research Institute (IFPRI).

International Food Security & Nutrition Civil Society Mechanism (CSM). 2011. *Civil Society Working Document on the Global Strategic Framework for Food Security and Nutrition: Draft—December 2011*. Rome: International Food Security & Nutrition Civil Society Mechanism (CSM).

———. 2012. *The Committee on World Food Security (CFS): A Guide for Civil Society*. Rome: International Food Security & Nutrition Civil Society Mechanism (CSM).

———. 2013. "What Is the CSM?" Rome: International Food Security & Nutrition Civil Society Mechanism (CSM), accessed March 11, 2013, http://www.csm4cfs.org/about_us-2/what_is_the_csm-1.

International Network for Economic, Social and Cultural Rights (ESCR-Net). 2013. "Section 2: Improving Supervision of the ICESCR: An Optional Protocol." Issues & Resources, accessed February 19, 2013, http://www.escr-net.org/docs/i/425247.

International Planning Committee for Food Sovereignty (IPC). 2014. "About Us. History." International Planning Committee for Food Sovereignty (IPC), last modified 2014, accessed April 3, 2014, http://www.foodsovereignty.org/about-us/.

Isaah, M. 2007. *Right to Food of Tomato and Poultry Farmers: Report of an Investigative Mission to Ghana*. Heidelberg: FIAN International, Send Foundation, Both Ends, Germanwatch, and UK Food Group.

Ishay, M. 2008. *The History of Human Rights: From Ancient Times to the Globalization Era*. California: University of California Press.

J.P. 2012. "Not a Billion after All." *The Economist*, October 1, 2012.

Jenderedjian, A. and A.C. Bellows. Forthcoming. "Diffusion of Human Rights and Development Concepts: NGOs' Application of Human Rights-based Approaches to Development and Gender Mainstreaming in Armenia and Georgia in Addressing Food Security." Manuscript in preparation.

Kelsen, H. 1967. *Pure Theory of Law*. Second ed. California: University of California Press.

Kent, G. 2002. "A Gendered Perspective on Nutrition Rights." *Agenda* 17 (51): 43–50.

———. 2005. *Freedom from Want: The Human Right to Adequate Food*. Washington, D.C.: Georgetown University Press.

———, ed. 2008. "Global Obligations for the Right to Food." In *Human Rights, Environmental Justice, and Popular Democracy*, edited by J. Blau, K. Gould, and A. Moncada. Plymouth: Rowman and Littlefield.

Kracht, U. 2000. "World Food Summit Commitment 7.4: The Right to Adequate Food, Note on Follow-Up. Background Document 7, International Encounter on the Fight to Food and Nutrition, Phase I: Review and Outlook. Oslo, June 18–21, 2000", cited in Eide, W.B. and U. Kracht, eds. 2005b. "The Right to Adequate Food in Human Rights Instruments: Legal Norms and Interpretations." In *Food and Human Rights in Development—Volume I: Legal and Institutional Dimensions and Selected Topics*, edited by W.B. Eide and U. Kracht, 99–118. Antwerpen: Intersentia.

Künnemann, R. 2013. *Twelve Reasons to Strengthen Extraterritorial Human Rights Obligations*. Heidelberg: ETO Consortium.

———. 2014. *Fourteen Misconceptions about Extraterritorial Human Rights Obligations* Heidelberg: ETO Consortium.

Lauren, P.G. 2003. *The Evolution of International Human Rights: Visions seen*. Philadelphia: University of Pennsylvania Press.

Lemke, S., A.C. Bellows, and N. Heumann. 2009. "Gender and Sustainable Livelihoods: Case Study of South African Farm Workers." *International Journal of Innovation and Sustainable Development* 4 (2–3): 195–205.

Li, T.M. 2011. "Forum on Global Land Grabbing: Centering Labor in the Land Grab Debate." *Journal of Peasant Studies* 38 (2): 281–98.

Liberti, S. 2013. *Land Grabbing. Journeys in the New Colonialism* [Land Grabbing. Come il Mercato delle Terre Crea il Nuovo Colonialismo], translated by E. Flanelly. London and New York: Verso.

Maastricht University and International Commission of Jurists (ICJ). 2011. *Maastricht Principles on Extraterritorial Obligations of States in the Area of Economic, Social and Cultural Rights*. Maastricht, Geneva: Maastricht University; International Commission of Jurists (ICJ).

Maxwell, S. and M. Smith. 1992. "Household Food Security: A Conceptual Review." In *Household Food Security: Concepts, Indicators, Measurements—A Technical Review*, edited by S. Maxwell and T.R. Frankenberger, 1–72. New York: United Nations Children's Fund (UNICEF) and International Fund for Agricultural Development (IFAD).

McKeon, N. 2009. *The United Nations and Civil Society: Legitimating Global Governance—Whose Voice?* edited by United Nations Research Institute for Social Development (UNRISD). London: Zed Books.

Mehta, L., G.J. Veldwisch, and J. Franco. 2012. "Water Grabbing? Focus on the (Re) Appropriation of Finite Water Resources." *Water Alternatives* 5 (2): 193–207.

Moser, C. and A. Moser. 2005. "Gender Mainstreaming since Beijing: A Review of Success and Limitations in International Institutions." *Gender and Development* 13 (2): 11–22.

NGO Coalition for an Optional Protocol to the ICESCR and International Network for Economic, Social and Cultural Rights (ESCR-Net). 2008. *Statement of the NGO Coalition for an Optional Protocol to the ICESCR and the International Network for Economic, Social and Cultural Rights.* Paris: Worldwide Human Rights Movement (FIDH).

NGO Forum to the World Food Summit. 1996. *NGO Forum Statement to the World Food Summit. Profit for Few or Food for All? Food Sovereignty and Security to Eliminate the Globalisation of Hunger, 17 November 1996,* http://www.converge.org.nz/pirm/food-sum.htm#ngo.

NGO/CSO Forum on Food Sovereignty. 2002a. *Food Sovereignty: A Right for All. Political Statement of the NGO/CSO Forum for Food Sovereignty.* Rome: NGO/CSO Forum for Food Sovereignty.

———. 2002b. *Food Sovereignty: An Action Plan of the NGO/CSO Forum for Food Sovereignty.* Rome: NGO/CSO Forum for Food Sovereignty.

Organization of American States (OAS). 1933. *[Inter-American] Convention on the Nationality of Women, 26 December 1933.* Montevideo: Organization of American States (OAS).

———. 1994. *Inter-American Convention on the Prevention, Punishment and Eradication of Violence against Women (Convention of Belém do Pará), 9 June 1994.* Washington, D.C.: Organization of American States (OAS).

———. 2013. "About CIM: Brief History of the Commission." Washington, D.C.: Organization of American States (OAS), accessed December 12, 2013, http://www.oas.org/en/cim/history.asp.

Organization of American States (OAS) and Council of Europe. 2014. *Regional Tools to Fight Violence Against Women: The Belém do Pará and Instanbul Conventions.* Washington, D.C., Strasbourg Cedex: Inter-American Commission of Women (CIM) and Council of Europe.

Oshaug, A. 2005. "Developing Voluntary Guidelines for Implementing the Right to Adequate Food: Anatomy of an Intergovernmental Process." In *Food and Human Rights in Development—Volume I: Legal and Institutional Dimensions and Selected Topics,* edited by W. B. Eide and U. Kracht, 259–82. Antwerpen and Oxford: Intersentia.

Oshaug, A., W. B. Eide, and A. Eide. 1994. "Human Rights: A Normative Basis for Food and Nutrition-Relevant Policies." *Food Policy* 19 (6): 491–516.

Paasch, A. 2008. "Time for a Human Right to Food Framework of Action." *Contact: A Publication of the World Council of Churches* 186: 20–21.

Paasch, A., F. Garbers, and T. Hirsch. 2007. *Die Auswirkungen der Liberalisierung des Reismarkts auf das Recht auf Nahrung: Fallstudien aus Ghana, Honduras und Indonesien. [The Effects of the Liberalization of the Rice Market on the Right to Food: Case Studies from Ghana, Honduras and Indonesia]* Stuttgart: Brot für die Welt, FIAN International, and Globales Ökumenisches Aktionsbündnis.

Pedrosa, C. M. 2010. "O Cuidado as Pessoas que Sofreram Violência Sexual—Desafios à Inovação de Práticas e á Incorporação da Categoria Gênero no Programa Iluminar Campinas." *[The Care of Persons Who Suffered Sexual Violence—Challenges for the Innovation of Practices and for the Incorporation of the Gender Category into the Program 'Enlighten Campinas']* Doctoral Thesis, Universidade de São Paulo.

Pogge, T. 2008. *World Poverty and Human Rights.* 2nd ed. Cambridge and Malden: Polity Press.

Quisumbing, A. R. and L. C. Smith. 2007. "Case Study #4–5. Intrahousehold Allocation, Gender Relations, and Food Security in Developing Countries." In *Food Policy for Developing Countries: Case Studies,* edited by P. Pinstrup-Andersen and F. Cheng, 13 pp. Ithaca, New York: Cornell University.

Randolph, S. and S. Hertel. 2013. "The Right to Food: A Global Perspective." In *The State of Economic and Social Human Rights: A Global Overview,* edited by L. Minkler, 21–60. New York: Cambridge University Press.

Riedel, E. 2005. "Allgemeine Bemerkungen zu Bestimmungen des Internationales Paktes über Wirtschaftliche, Soziale und Kulturelle Rechte der Vereinten Nationen." *[General Comments on the Provisions of the United Nations International Covenant on Economic, Social and Cultural Rights]* In *Die 'General Comments' zu den VN-Menschenrechtsverträgen: Deutsche Übersetzung und Kurzeinführungen [The General Comments to the UN Human Rights Treaties: German Translation and Short Introductions]*, edited by Deutsches Institut für Menschenrechte, 160–73. Baden-Baden: Nomos Verlagsgesellschaft.

Scherr, S. 2003. *Halving Global Hunger. Background Paper of the Millennium Project Task Force on Hunger*: United Nations Development Programme (UNDP).

Sepúlveda Carmona, M. and C. Nyst. 2012. *The Human Rights Approach to Social Protection*. Finland: Ministry for Foreign Affairs of Finland.

Shiva, V. 2001. *Protect Or Plunder? Understanding Intellectual Property Rights*. London: Zed Books.

———. 2002. *Water Wars: Privatization, Pollution and Profit*. Cambridge: South End Press.

Smith, L. C. and L. Haddad. 2000. *Overcoming Child Malnutrition in Developing Countries: Past Achievements and Future Choices*. Food, Agriculture, and the Environment Discussion: Paper 30. Washington, D.C.: International Food Policy Research Institute (IFPRI).

Special Secretariat for Women's Policies [Brazil]. 2006. *Maria Da Penha Law. Law n. 11.340 of August 7, 2006. Retrains Domestic and Family Violence against Women*. Brasilia: Precidency of the Republic [Brazil].

Stammers, N. 1999. "Social Movements and the Social Construction of Human Rights." *Human Rights Quarterly* 21 (4): 980–1008.

———. 2005. "The Emergence of Human Rights in the North: Towards Historical Re-Evaluation." In *Inclusive Citizenship: Meanings and Expressions*, edited by N. Kabeer, 50–68. London and New York: Zed Books.

Suárez Franco, A. M. and S. Ratjen. 2007. *Screen State Action against Hunger! How to Use the Voluntary Guidelines on the Right to Food to Monitor Public Policy*. Bonn and Heidelberg: Welthungerhilfe and FIAN International.

Transnational Institute (TNI). 2014. "International Planning Committee for Food Sovereignty." Creative Commons License, accessed April 7, 2014, http://www.tni.org/network/international-planning-committee-food-sovereignty.

United Nations (UN). 1945. *Charter of the United Nations, 26 June 1945, 1 UNTS XVI*. San Francisco: United Nations (UN).

———. 1969. *Vienna Convention on the Law of Treaties. 23 May 1969, United Nations Treaty Series, Vol. 1155, p. 331*. New York: United Nations (UN).

———. 2002. *Women, Peace and Security: Study Submitted by the Secretary-General Pursuant to Security Council Resolution 1325 (2000)*. New York: United Nations (UN).

———. 2013a. "Multilateral Treaties Deposited with the Secretary-General: Chapter IV. Human Rights. 3.a Optional Protocol to the International Covenant on Economic, Social and Cultural Rights." United Nations Treaty Collection. New York: United Nations (UN), accessed March 11, 2013a, http://treaties.un.org/Pages/ViewDetails.aspx?src=TREATY&mtdsg_no=IV-3-a&chapter=4&lang=en.

———. 2013b. "Multilateral Treaties Deposited with the Secretary-General: Chapter IV. Human Rights. 8. Convention on the Elimination of All Forms of Discrimination against Women." United Nations Treaty Collection. New York: United Nations (UN), accessed December 12, 2013b, http://treaties.un.org/Pages/ViewDetails.aspx?src=TREATY&mtdsg_no=IV-8&chapter=4&lang=en.

United Nations Commission on Human Rights (CHR). 2000. *Commission on Human Rights Resolution 2000/10 the Right to Food. E/CN.4/RES/2000/10, 17 April 2000*. Geneva: Nations High Commissioner for Human Rights (HCHR).

———. 2005. *The Right to Food: Report of the Special Rapporteur on the Right to Food, Jean Ziegler. E/CN.4/2005/47, 24 January 2005.* New York: United Nations Economic and Social Council (ECOSOC).

United Nations Committee on Economic, Social and Cultural Rights (CESCR). 1989. *Report on the Third Session (6–24 February 1989). Economic and Social Council Officila Records. Supplement No. 4.* New York: United Nations (UN).

———. 1993. *Rules of Procedure of the Committee. Provisional Rules of Procedure Adopted by the Committee at its Third Session (1989). E/C.12/1990/4/Rev.11 September 1993.* New York: United Nations Economic and Social Council (ECOSOC).

———. 1997. *Seventeenth Session. Summary Record of the 46th Meeting. E/C.12/1997/SR.46, 3 December 1997.* New York: United Nations Economic and Social Council (ECOSOC).

———. 1999. *General Comment No. 12: The Right to Adequate Food (Art. 11 of the Covenant). E/C.12/1999/5, 12 May 1999.* New York: United Nations Economic and Social Council (ECOSOC).

———. 2000. *General Comment No. 14: The Right to the Highest Attainable Standard of Health (Art. 12 of the Covenant). E/C.12/2000/4, 11 August 2000.* New York: United Nations Economic and Social Council (ECOSOC).

———. 2003. *General Comment No. 15: The Right to Water (Arts. 11 and 12 of the Covenant). E/C.12/2002/11, 20 January 2003.* New York: United Nations Economic and Social Council (ECOSOC).

———. 2006. *General Comment No. 18: The Right to Work (Art. 6 of the Covenant). E/C.12/GC/18, 6 February 2006.* New York: United Nations Economic and Social Council (ECOSOC).

———. 2008. *General Comment No. 19: The Right to Social Security (Art. 9 of the Covenant). E/C.12/GC/19, 4 February 2008.* New York: United Nations Economic and Social Council (ECOSOC).

———. 2009. *General Comment No. 20: Non-Discrimination in Economic, Social and Cultural Rights (Art. 2, Para. 2 of the International Covenant on Economic, Social and Cultural Rights). E/C.12/GC/20, 2 July 2009.* New York: United Nations Economic and Social Council (ECOSOC).

United Nations Committee on the Elimination of Discrimination against Women (CEDAW Committee). 1995. *Progress Achieved in the Implementation of the Convention on the Elimination of All Forms of Discrimination against Women: Report by the Committee on the Elimination of Discrimination against Women at the United Nations Fourth World Conference on Women in Beijing. A/CONF.177/7, 21 June 1995.* Geneva: United Nations Committee on the Elimination of Discrimination against Women (CEDAW Committee).

United Nations Development Group (UNDG). 2003. "Attachment 1: The Human Rights Based Approach to Development Cooperation. Towards a Common Understanding among UN Agencies." In *Second Interagency Workshop on Implementing a Human Rights-Based Approach in the Context of UN Reform,* edited by United Nations Development Group (UNDG), 17–19. Stamford: United Nations Development Group (UNDG).

United Nations Development Programme (UNDP). 2000. *Human Development Report 2000: Human Rights and Human Development.* New York: United Nations Publications.

United Nations Division for the Advancement of Women of the Department of Economic and Social Affairs (UN DAW/DESA). 2009. "History of the Optional Protocol." New York: United Nations (UN), last modified 2009, accessed March 28, 2014, http://www.un.org/womenwatch/daw/cedaw/protocol/history.htm.

United Nations Economic and Social Council (ECOSOC). 1968. *Resolutions Supplement No.1: Economic and Social Council Official Records, Forty-Fourth Session (6–31 May 1968).* New York: United Nations (UN).

————. 2007. *Strengthening Efforts to Eradicate Poverty and Hunger, Including through the Global Partnership for Development (E/2007/71).* New York: United Nations (UN).

United Nations General Assembly. 1948. *Universal Declaration of Human Rights, Adopted by General Assembly Resolution 217 A(III) of 10 December 1948.* Geneva: United Nations Office of the High Commissioner for Human Rights (OHCHR).

————. 1952. *Convention on the Political Rights of Women. A/RES/640(VII), 20 December 1952.* New York: United Nations (UN) General Assembly.

————. 1957. *Convention on the Nationality of Married Women. A/RES/1040(XI), 29 January 1957.* New York: United Nations (UN) General Assembly.

————. 1962. *Convention on Consent to Marriage, Minimum Age for Marriage and Registration of Marriages. 7 November 1962.* New York: United Nations (UN) General Assembly.

————. 1963. *Draft Declaration on the Elimination of Discrimination Against Women. A/RES/1921(XVIII), 5 December 1963.* New York: United Nations (UN) General Assembly.

————. 1965a. *International Convention on the Elimination of all Forms of Racial Discrimination, 21 December 1965, United Nations, Treaty Series, Vol. 660, p. 195.* New York: United Nations (UN) General Assembly.

————. 1965b. *Recommendation on Consent to Marriage, Minimum Age for Marriage and Registration of Marriages. A/RES/2018(XX), 1 November 1965.* New York: United Nations (UN) General Assembly.

————. 1966a. *International Covenant on Civil and Political Rights. 16 December 1966, United Nations, Treaty Series, Vol. 999, p. 171.* New York: United Nations (UN) General Assembly.

————. 1966b. *International Covenant on Economic, Social and Cultural Rights. 16 December 1966, United Nations, Treaty Series, Vol. 993, p. 3.* New York: United Nations (UN) General Assembly.

————. 1966c. *Optional Protocol to the International Covenant on Civil and Political Rights, 19 December 1966, United Nations, Treaty Series, Vol. 999, p. 171.* New York: United Nations (UN) General Assembly.

————. 1967. *Declaration on the Elimination of Discrimination Against Women. A/RES/2263(XXII), 7 November 1967.* New York: United Nations (UN) General Assembly.

————. 1974. *World Food Conference. A/RES/3348, 17 December 1974.* New York: United Nations (UN) General Assembly.

————. 1979. *Convention on the Elimination of All Forms of Discrimination against Women. 18 December 1979.* New York: United Nations (UN) General Assembly.

————. 1984. *Convention against Torture and Other Cruel, Inhuman or Degrading Treatment or Punishment, 10 December 1984, United Nations, Treaty Series, Vol. 1465, p. 85.* New York: United Nations (UN) General Assembly.

————. 1989. *Convention on the Rights of the Child, 20 November 1989, United Nations, Treaty Series, Vol. 1577, p. 3.* New York: United Nations (UN) General Assembly.

————. 1990. *International Convention on the Protection of the Rights of all Migrant Workers and Members of their Families. A/RES/45/158, 18 December 1990.* New York: United Nations (UN) General Assembly.

————. 1993a. *Declaration on the Elimination of Violence against Women. A/RES/48/104, 20 December 1993.* New York: United Nations (UN) General Assembly.

————. 1993b. *Vienna Declaration and Programme of Action. A/CONF.157/23, 12 July 1993.* New York: United Nations (UN) General Assembly.

————. 1999. *Optional Protocol to the Convention on the Elimination of All Forms of Discrimination against Women: Resolution / Adopted by the General Assembly. A/RES/54/4, 15 October 1999.* New York: United Nations (UN) General Assembly.

————. 2000. *United Nations Millennium Declaration, Resolution / Adopted by the General Assembly. A/RES/55/2, 18 September 2000.* New York: United Nations (UN) General Assembly.

————. 2006. *International Convention for the Protection of all Persons from Enforced Disappearance. A/RES/61/177, 20 December 2006.* New York: United Nations (UN) General Assembly.

————. 2007a. *Convention on the Rights of Persons with Disabilities. A/RES/61/106, 24 January 2007.* New York: United Nations (UN) General Assembly.

————. 2007b. *United Nations Declaration on the Rights of Indigenous Peoples: Resolution / Adopted by the General Assembly. A/RES/61/295, 2 October 2007.* New York: United Nations (UN) General Assembly.

————. 2009. *Optional Protocol to the International Covenant on Economic, Social and Cultural Rights: Resolution / Adopted by the General Assembly [on the Report of the Third Committee (A/63/435)]. A/RES/63/117, 5 March 2009.* New York: United Nations (UN) General Assembly.

————. 2014. "Social, Humanitarian & Cultural—Third Committee." New York: United Nations (UN), accessed March 28, 2014, http://www.un.org/en/ga/third/index.shtml.

United Nations Human Rights Council (HRC). 2008. *Report of the Human Rights Council in its Seventh Special Session. A/HRC/S-7/2, 17 July 2008.* Geneva: United Nations Human Rights Council (HRC).

————. 2010. *Preliminary Study of the Human Rights Council Advisory Committee on Discrimination in the Context of the Right to Food. A/HRC/13/32, 22 February 2010.* New York: United Nations (UN) General Assembly.

————. 2012a. *Report Submitted by the Special Rapporteur on the Right to Food, Olivier De Schutter: Women's Rights and the Right to Food. A/HRC/22/50, 24 December 2012.* New York: United Nations (UN) General Assembly.

————. 2012b. *Resolution Adopted by the Human Rights Council 21/19. Promotion and Protection of the Human Rights of Peasants and Other People Working in Rural Areas. A/HRC/RES/21/19, 11 October 2012.* New York: United Nations (UN) General Assembly.

————. 2014. *Bolivia (Plurinational State of), Cuba, Ecuador, South Africa, Venezuela (Bolivarian Republic of): Draft Version. 26/ . . . Elaboration of an International Legally Binding Instrument on Transnational Corporations and Other Business Enterprises with Respect to Human Rights. A/HRC/26/L.22/Rev.1, 25 June 2014.* New York: United Nations (UN) General Assembly.

United Nations Office of the High Commissioner for Human Rights (OHCHR). 2005. *Economic, Social and Cultural Rights: Handbook for National Human Rights Institutions.* Professional Training Series. Vol. 12. New York: United Nations (UN).

————. 2008a. "Human Rights Council Opens Special Session on World Food Hunger." Geneva: United Nations Office of the High Commissioner for Human Rights (OHCHR), last modified May 22, 2008a, accessed April 4, 2014, http://www.ohchr.org/EN/NewsEvents/Pages/DisplayNews.aspx?NewsID=8525&LangID=E#.

————. 2008b. "Statement of the Special Rapporteur on the Right to Food, Mr. Olivier De Schutter." Geneva: United Nations Office of the High Commissioner for Human Rights (OHCHR), last modified May 22, 2008b, accessed April 4, 2014, http://www.ohchr.org/EN/NewsEvents/Pages/DisplayNews.aspx?NewsID=8477&LangID=E.

————. 2012. *Human Rights Indicators: A Guide to Measurement and Implementation.* New York: United Nations (UN).

————. 2013. *Directory of Special Procedures Mandate Holders.* New York: United Nations (UN).

————. 2014. "Committee on Economic, Social and Cultural Rights—General Comments." Geneva: Office of the United Nation High Commissioner for Human Rights (OHCHR). United Nations (UN), last modified 2014, accessed April 7, 2014, http://tbinternet.ohchr.org/_layouts/treatybodyexternal/TBSearch.aspx?Lang=en&TreatyID=9&DocTypeID=11.

United Nations Secretary General. 1997. *Renewing the United Nations: A Programme for Reform. A/51/950, 14 July 1997.* New York: United Nations (UN) General Assembly.

United Nations Security Council. 2009. *Women and Peace and Security. Report of the Secretary-General. S/2009/465, 16 September 2009.* New York: United Nations (UN) Security Council.

United Nations Standing Committee on Nutrition (SCN). 1999. *Report from the Fifth Meeting of the SCN Working Group on Nutrition, Ethics and Human Rights.* Geneva: United Nations High Commissioner for Human Rights (HCHR).

Uvin, P. 2007. "From the Right to Development to the Rights-Based Approach: How 'Human Rights' Entered Development." *Development in Practice* 17 (4–5): 597–606.

Valente, F.L.S. 2010. "It is Time for a Rights-Based Global Strategic Framework on Food Security and Nutrition." *Right to Food and Nutrition WATCH* 2010: 13–15.

Valente, F.L.S. and A.M. Suárez Franco. 2010. "Human Rights and the Struggle Against Hunger: Laws, Institutions, and Instruments in the Fight to Realize the Right to Adequate Food." *Yale Human Rights and Development Law Journal* 13 (2): 435–61.

von Grebmer, K., B. Nestorova, A.R. Quisumbing, R. Fertziger, H. Fritschel, R. Pandya-Lorch, and Y. Yohannes. 2009. *2009 Global Hunger Index: The Challenge of Hunger: Focus on Financial Crisis and Gender Inequality.* Bonn; Washington, D.C.; Dublin: Welthungerhilfe, International Food Policy Research Institute (IFPRI), and Concern Worldwide.

Watkins, K. 1991. "Agriculture and Food Security in the GATT Uruguay Round." *Review of African Political Economy* 18 (50): 38–50.

Windfuhr, M. 1998. "NGOs and the Right to Adequate Food." In *The Right to Food in Theory and Practice*, edited by Food and Agriculture Organization of the United Nations (FAO), 6–13. Rome: Food and Agriculture Organization of the United Nations (FAO).

———. 2000. "Economic, Social and Cultural Rights and Development Cooperation." In *Working Together. The Human Rights Approach to Development Cooperation. Stockholm Workshop, 16–19 October 2000. Part 1*, edited by A. Frankovits and P. Earle. Stockholm: Swedish International Development Cooperation Agency (SIDA), quoted in Uvin, P. 2007. "From the Right to Development to the Rights-Based Approach: How 'Human Rights' Entered Development." *Development in Practice* 17 (4–5): 597–606.

Windfuhr, M and J. Jonsén. 2005. *Food Sovereignty: Towards Democracy in Localized Food Systems.* Warwickshire: ITDG Publishing.

Wolford, W., S.M. Borras Jr., R. Hall, I. Scoones, and B. White. 2013. "Governing Global Land Deals: The Role of the State in the Rush for Land." *Development and Change* 44 (2): 189–210.

Wopold-Bosien, M. 2013. "A Human Rights-Based Global Framework for Food Security and Nutrition." *Right to Food and Nutrition WATCH* 2013: 31–32.

World Bank, Food and Agriculture Organization of the United Nations (FAO), and International Fund for Agricultural Development (IFAD). 2009. *Gender in Agriculture Sourcebook.* Washington, D.C.: World Bank.

World Conference on Human Rights Preparatory Committee. 1993. *Status of Preparation of Publications, Studies and Documents for the World Conference. Note by the Secretariat. Addendum. Contribution Submitted by the Committee on Economic, Social and Cultural Rights. A/CONF.157/PC/62/Add.5, 26 March 1993.* New York: United Nations (UN) General Assembly.

World Food Conference. 1974. *Universal Declaration on the Eradication of Hunger and Malnutrition, U.N. Doc. E/CONF.65/20.* Rome.

Ziegler, J., C. Golay, C. Mahon, and S.A. Way. 2011. *The Fight for the Right to Food: Lessons Learned.* International Relations and Developments. Basingstoke; New York: Palgrave Macmillan.

2 Gender, Nutrition, and the Right to Adequate Food

Introducing Two Structural Disconnects and the Human Rights Processes Necessary to Address Them

Anne C. Bellows and María Daniela Núñez Burbano de Lara

INTRODUCTION

Why, when so many call for the inclusion of women and a gender per-spective in food and nutrition security, is the food and nutrition security status of women and girls still not improving? The thesis of this volume is grounded upon the combined authors' broad discussion and practical actions that addressed women's continued exclusion from food and nutri-tion equity. This experience isolated two structural "disconnects" that frus-trate advocacy for, as well as theoretical explanation of, the development of necessary policy and analysis to improve gender-based inequalities in achieving the human right to adequate food and nutrition. Chapter 2 of this volume introduces these two disconnects that, we argue, frustrate the potential of positive change in women's access to the right to adequate food and nutrition. The disconnects are foundational to the analyses developed in depth in chapter 3 "Violence and Women's Participation in the Right to Adequate Food and Nutrition," chapter 4 "Maternal, Infant, and Young Child Feeding: Intertwined Subjectivities and Corporate Accountability," and chapter 5 "Sustainable Food Systems, Gender, and Participation: Fore-grounding Women in the Context of the Right to Adequate Food and Nutri-tion" of this volume. Chapter 6, "Closing Protection Gaps through a More Comprehensive Conceptual Framework for the Human Right to Adequate Food and Nutrition," returns to the disconnects, providing a vision for pro-gressive action and research moving forward.

The first disconnect describes the structural isolation of women's rights from the human right to adequate food and nutrition. The second disconnect reflects upon the separation of nutrition from the human right to adequate food and its attachment to medicalized health interventions. As elaborated later, this disconnect eclipses women's autonomy and self-determination through contemporary emphases on industrial scale food production and the rapid commercialization and globalization of medical nutrition prod-ucts. These two disconnects encumber not only women but also all members of society whose sovereignty over their own and their communities' welfare in general, and enjoyment of the right to adequate food and nutrition in particular, are closely intertwined with women's rights, autonomy, and self-determination. In the spirit of the introduction to the evolutive character of human rights in chapter 1 of this volume, this chapter outlines the ongoing project of improving universal and interdependent objectives of the human right to adequate food and nutrition.

DISCONNECT ONE: THE STRUCTURAL ISOLATION OF WOMEN'S RIGHTS FROM THE HUMAN RIGHT TO ADEQUATE FOOD AND NUTRITION

The structural isolation of women's rights from the human right to adequate food and nutrition frustrates women's capacity as rights holders to claim this right for themselves, their families, and their communities, and to hold governments accountable for related violations. The disconnect at the policy level derives, on the one hand, from the invisibility of women as self-determining beings with regard to the right to adequate food and nutrition within the 1948 *Universal Declaration of Human Rights* (UDHR; UN General Assembly 1948) and its legally binding counterpart, the 1966 *International Covenant on Economic, Social and Cultural Rights* (ICESCR; UN General Assembly 1966), and, on the other hand, from the omission of women's right to adequate food and nutrition in the 1979 *Convention on the Elimination of All Forms of Discrimination against Women* (CEDAW; UN General Assembly 1979). The absence of women's agency with respect to food and nutrition is reified in the effective instrumentalization of women as passive feeders of infants in the 1989 *Convention on the Rights of the Child* (CRC; UN General Assembly 1989). Important steps to remedy these flaws have been initiated at the United Nations (UN) level, including the 2008 study written by Isabella Rae and published by the Food and Agriculture Organization (FAO), *Women and the Right to Food: International Law and State Practice*. As shall be discussed, however, there is more to do, including looking closely at some institutional reforms that may in fact contribute to sociocultural patterns of patronization and gender discrimination. The static trend of women's greater experience with hunger and food and nutrition insecurity surely makes clear that policies, as well as culture, have not caught up to the ideals inherent in human rights legal reforms to date.

Invisibility of Women's Right to Adequate Food and Nutrition in the *Universal Declaration of Human Rights* (UDHR) and the *International Covenant on Economic, Social and Cultural Rights* (ICESCR)

In its opening preamble, the 1948 UDHR recognizes that "the inherent dignity and . . . equal and inalienable rights of all members of the human family is the foundation of freedom, justice and peace in the world" (UN General Assembly 1948, preamble). The core principle of non-discrimination and equality is established at the beginning of the UDHR text, "[a]ll human beings are born free and equal in dignity and rights" (UN General Assembly 1948, art. 1) and "[e]veryone is entitled to all the rights and freedoms set forth in this Declaration, without distinction of any kind, such as race, colour, sex, language, religion, political or other opinion, national or social origin, property, birth or other status" (UN General Assembly 1948, art. 2). Nevertheless, article 25 on the right of everyone to an adequate standard of living, including food, clothing, housing, medical care, and social services, conflates the rights of men, women, and children and then erases the individuality and dignity of women and children by ordinating the flow of rights through a (presumed) male head of the family household. The rights holder is identified in the expression "of himself and of his family," never giving name to females of any age, nor to male children, nor possibly to adult males who have not achieved "male head of household" status.

> Everyone has the right to a standard of living adequate for the health and well-being *of himself and of his family*, including food, clothing, housing and medical care and necessary social services, and the right to security in the event of unemployment, sickness, disability, widowhood, old age or other lack of livelihood in circumstances beyond his control. (UN General Assembly 1948, art. 25.1; emphasis added)

Sixteen years later, the foundational treaty document for the right to adequate food and nutrition, the 1966 ICESCR, followed suit. The ICESCR provides for the exercise and enjoyment of economic, social, and cultural rights without discrimination of any kind (UN General Assembly 1966, art. 2.2), and with the obligation "to ensure the equal rights of men and women" to all rights set forth in the covenant (UN General Assembly 1966, art. 3). Yet once again, with the right to adequate food and nutrition marginally expanded in the ICESCR under article 11, one sees reproduced the patronizing formulation of the UDHR that insists upon a patriarchal head of household, eliding women's and children's personhood thereunder.

> The States Parties to the present Covenant recognize the right of everyone to an adequate standard of living *for himself and his family*, including adequate food, clothing and housing, and to the continuous improvement of living conditions. (UN General Assembly 1966, art. 11.1; emphasis added)

As it stands, the ICESCR renders women, children, and possibly non-dominant males as economically, socially, and culturally invisible with respect to a right to adequate food and nutrition (cf. Bellows 2003), compromising their standing as rights holders with the capability of presenting claims to and demanding accountability from the state.[1]

In 1999, more than thirty years after the adoption of the ICESCR, the United Nations Committee on Economic, Social and Cultural Rights (CESCR) issued *General Comment 12 on the Right to Adequate Food* (hereinafter, *General Comment 12*; CESCR 1999b). *General Comment 12* provides an extensive interpretation of the two short paragraphs comprising article 11 of the ICESCR.[2] Among other critical issues addressed in *General Comment 12*, the opening paragraph acknowledges the inherent gender discrimination in the 1966 language, noting that the right to adequate food and nutrition "applies to everyone; thus the reference in article 11.1 to 'himself and his family' does not imply any limitation upon the applicability of this right to individuals or to female-headed households" (CESCR 1999b, para. 1). Paragraph 6 reemphasizes the human rights characteristic of universality, stating that the human right to adequate food and nutrition applies to "every man, woman and child, alone or in community with others." *General Comment 12* makes clear that the social gender and family norms of 1948 and 1966 and the resulting legal construction of men organizing the lives of women and children are archaic and will not be carried forward in UN language. *General Comment 12*, paragraph 26, presses further, by stating:

> The strategy should give particular attention to the need to prevent discrimination in access to food or resources for food. This should include: guarantees of full and equal access to economic resources, *particularly for women*, including the right to inheritance and the ownership of land and other property, credit, natural resources and appropriate technology; measures to respect and protect self-employment and work which provides a remuneration ensuring a decent living for wage earners and their families (as stipulated in article 7 (a) (ii) of the Covenant); maintaining registries on rights in land (including forests). (CESCR 1999b, para. 26; emphasis added)

Further, in 2005, CESCR *General Comment 16 on The Equal Right of Men and Women to the Enjoyment of All Economic, Social and Cultural Rights* (hereinafter, *General Comment 16*; CESCR 2005) reiterated women's right to "access to or control over means of food production" and additionally, that "customary practices under which women are not allowed to eat until the men are fully fed, or are only allowed less nutritious food" must be addressed (CESCR 2005, para. 28).[3]

The arc of this volume and the focus of this and forthcoming chapters are, however, dedicated to the observation that ongoing gender discrimination and patriarchal presumption narrate the social conditions that perpetuate the greater collective challenge that women continue to face in achieving food and nutrition security. The disavowal in *General Comment 12* of the language of ICESCR article 11.1 in no way suffices as summary declaration that discrimination against women is overcome. Rather, it brings attention to the shape and reality of discrimination that women today still confront.

Omission of Women's Right to Adequate Food and Nutrition in the *Convention on the Elimination of All Forms of Discrimination against Women* (CEDAW)

The intention of the 1979 CEDAW was to protect women with respect to interference with any and all of women's human rights. Yet the drafters overlooked the inclusion of women's right to adequate food and nutrition. In part II (UN General Assembly 1979, arts. 7–9), CEDAW devotes great attention to civil and political rights associated with voting and political and public participation. Part IV (UN General Assembly 1979, arts. 15, 16) addresses judicial rights and protections, including the right to citizenship, property ownership, and rights in marriage and parenthood. Among the economic, social, and cultural rights outlined in articles 10 to 14, CEDAW stresses education, social security and employment, health care, economic and social activities, and the particular rights of rural women (UN General Assembly 1979, arts. 10–14). The convention does not, however, incorporate language addressing women's right to adequate food and nutrition (see also chapter 3 of this volume).

CEDAW references the terms "food" and "nutrition" in three places. First, the preamble notes that "in situations of poverty women have the least access to *food*, health, education, training and opportunities for employment and other needs" (UN General Assembly 1979, preamble; emphasis added). The CEDAW preamble describes conditions of discrimination against women, making clear that "women" is not a homogenous group; they experience discrimination differently, for example, the poor often more acutely than their counterparts. The preamble is, however, descriptive; it does not contain the substance of the rights articulated in the parties' actual agreement. The embedded concern about poor women's access to food is not transposed into a formal right to adequate food and nutrition in the treaty document.

Second, CEDAW article 12.2 describes states parties' obligations for women "in connection with pregnancy, confinement and the post-natal period, granting free services where necessary, *as well as adequate nutrition during pregnancy and lactation*" (UN General Assembly 1979, art. 12.2; emphasis added). Article 12.2 enshrines the concept of a human right to adequate nutrition, but limits it to pregnant and breastfeeding women; it is not presented as a universal human right. As written in 1979, article 12.2 is selectively attuned to women's biological or essentialist capacity to have children. At the expense of all women (and girls), article 12.2 addresses only a time limited stage of physical maternal connection to a fetus, infant, or young child.

Finally, under article 14 dedicated to rural women, CEDAW protects women's rights to farm-related resources, including "credit and loans, marketing facilities, appropriate technology and equal treatment in land and agrarian reform as well as in land resettlement schemes" (UN General

Assembly 1979, art. 14.2(g)), and to living conditions, for example, with respect to housing, sanitation, and water (UN General Assembly 1979, art. 14.2(h)). Article 14 addresses rural women and rural women's work and has been linked to women's right to adequate food and nutrition by the former UN special rapporteur on the right to food, Olivier De Schutter (HRC 2012a), the Human Rights Council Advisory Committee (HRC 2012b), and others (e.g., ESCR-Net and IWRAW Asia Pacific 2013, 14). Article 14 makes, however, no reference to food or nutrition, provoking FIAN International et al. (2013a, b) to call for explicit recognition of the relationship between women's rights and the human right to adequate food and nutrition. Article 14 focuses on the means to expand gender equality in rural work. While this certainly can be argued to constitute part of a right to adequate food and nutrition, it just as certainly does not embrace its entirety. Critically, CEDAW article 14 cannot serve as a replacement provision for the right to adequate food and nutrition because it specifically excludes urban and peri-urban women and because it concentrates on equality in rural work and does not encompass access to food through non-rural work or non-food production means.

In an example of the need for greater harmonization between human rights instruments, CESCR *General Comment 12* is clear that food production is only one way to achieve food and nutrition security. Physical and economic access to adequate food and nutrition can be achieved in three ways: (*a*) through one's own food production (including farming, gathering, fishing, shepherding, etc.), (*b*) through access to paid work and the adequate resources with which to buy food, and (*c*) through access to social protection services ("special programmes") whereby the state steps in under specific conditions of emergency or chronic need (CESCR 1999b, paras. 12, 13).

CEDAW article 14 made great strides by addressing some of the specific needs of rural farm women; however, its limitations highlight the need for an unencumbered articulation of the right to adequate food and nutrition in CEDAW.

As in the case of the ICESCR, the human rights treaty body monitoring the implementation of CEDAW, the United Nations Committee on the Elimination of Discrimination against Women (CEDAW Committee), has developed interpretations to expand and sometimes to improve the language of the treaty. The CEDAW Committee's 1999 interpretive *General Recommendation 24 on Women and Health* (hereinafter, *General Recommendation 24*; CEDAW Committee 1999) revisits CEDAW article 12 and strengthens it significantly by extending "the right to nutritional well-being" across women's entire lives without regard to whether or not they have children:

> The Committee notes that the full realization of women's right to health can be achieved only when States parties fulfil their obligation to respect, protect and promote women's *fundamental human right to*

nutritional well-being throughout their life span by means of a food supply that is safe, nutritious and adapted to local conditions. Towards this end, States parties should take steps to facilitate physical and economic access to productive resources especially for rural women, and to otherwise ensure that the special nutritional needs *of all women* within their jurisdiction are met. (CEDAW Committee 1999, para. 7; emphasis added)

General Recommendation 24 was enormously progressive in 1999, already linking local food production, supply, and physical and economic access with safe and nutritious consumption over the life span. Although urban women are not specifically named, *General Recommendation 24* speaks of "all women within [states parties'] jurisdiction." In some ways, it anticipates the divide between rights associated with food and production and rights to nutritional well-being and health (see discussion on this disconnect later in this chapter). However, *General Recommendation 24* does not make the link between women's right to adequate food and nutrition and the capacity of women to augment the well-being and realization of that right for women's family members and their communities that depend upon women's rights to self-determination and autonomy (cf. IFPRI 2005; Kent 2002; Lemke, Bellows, and Heumann 2009; Lemke et al. 2003; Maxwell and Smith 1992; Smith and Hadad 2000; Quisumbing and Smith 2007). In other words, the objectives of human dignity and self-determination empower individual capability on behalf of others. An often overlooked characteristic of women's right to adequate food and nutrition is that it includes their capacity to feed others (Van Esterik 1999). Further, as in the discussion of article 14 above, *General Recommendation 24* beautifully, but exclusively, links women's right to nutritional well-being to food production alone, not to other processes of obtaining food and nutrition security, including through reimbursement from all forms of paid work and social protection.

The Instrumentalization and Patronization of Women's Right to Adequate Food and Nutrition

The structural violence of discrimination, *not vulnerability*, disconnects and isolates women as well as other discriminated against groups from successfully achieving the human right to adequate food and nutrition (see chapter 3 of this volume). Discrimination against women oppresses personal autonomy and self-determination and results, among others, in food and nutrition insecurity. Aid without attention to structural discrimination and other forms of human rights violations reinforces this oppression. In the words of chapter 1 of this volume in the context of states' specific obligations to progressively realize the human right to adequate food and nutrition, states are obliged to *respect* functioning forms of self-determination, to *protect* individuals and groups from third parties' interference with that functioning self-determination, to *facilitate* support (including the availability of adequate information on individuals' and collective human rights and their claim mechanisms) to *fulfill* self-determination efforts, and lastly, to *provide* resources as necessary to fulfill needs beyond individuals' and communities' capacities to care for themselves. The notion of women's "vulnerability" dwells upon the exclusive and thus inappropriate application of the dimension of fulfill/provide at the expense of attention to the dimensions of respect, protect, and fulfill/facilitate of self-determination and autonomy.

Nutrition policy that focuses only on women when they are pregnant or lactating and girls as future mothers violates the totality of girls' and women's human rights over their life spans. These rights include women's rights in reproductive health-related decisions such as partner choice and pregnancy, other economic rights such as education, housing, medical care, and fair access to work, and their right to be free from gender stereotypes such as the expectations that women provide household food production and preparation work. When nutrition policy becomes focused only on the physical demands of pregnancy and lactation, it aligns its purpose to "help" or a patronizing form of the fulfill/provide dimension of states' human rights obligations. Such policy equates pregnancy and lactation and its narrow vision of the lives of women and girls with "vulnerability" and need, not coincidentally facilitating an entry for medicalized nutrition products and related marketing to address "the problem." While doctors and public health professionals may individually specialize in maternal health and nutrition, nutrition public policy must be linked to broader strategies that respect and empower non-discriminatory and economically secure livelihoods for all women and girls, and all men and boys. Nutrition policy must protect rights holders from overenthusiastic and sometimes predatory medical marketing, not open the door for it. And finally, nutrition policy must support and facilitate women's own plans—whether aligned to or separate from market-based nutrition products—for their own, their families', and their communities' nutritional health.

The term "vulnerability" sits on a knife's edge, defining the difference between many food security approaches and the human rights framework for adequate food and nutrition: the difference between charity *bestowed* and human rights *claimed*. Talk of vulnerability as "weakness," "defenselessness," "victimhood," and "need," instead of vulnerability as the consequence of *marginalization, injustice,* and *human rights violations* leverages band-aid intervention programs to "help the weak" instead of wrestling the impenetrability of privileged groups whose power rests upon conditions of inequality. The Brazilian educator Paolo Freire writes, "the oppressed must be their own example in the struggle for their redemption" (Freire 1970, 54) because they will wait in vain for acts of concession from the powerful. Nineteenth century social reformer and former escaped slave, Frederick Douglass, is often quoted for saying, "[p]ower concedes nothing without a demand. . . . Find out what any people will quietly submit to and you have found out the exact measure of injustice and wrong which will be imposed upon them" (Douglass 1857, quoted in Foner 1999, 367). And as political philosopher Martha Nussbaum writes, "[g]ender justice cannot be successfully pursued without limiting male freedom[s]," like, for example, arbitrarily earning more than women or sexually harassing them (Nussbaum 2011, 72). The discriminated against must lead in the development of their own strategies to address injustice. Such work arises from a position of capability and through an analysis of social power, not from help for "the vulnerable" and "the victims" (see also chapters 3 and 6 of this volume).

In terms of the language used in UN treaties most directly relevant to the human right to adequate food and nutrition, women are never described as vulnerable within the 1979 CEDAW, neither is any group defined in those terms within the 1966 ICESCR nor the 1989 CRC. However, in the longer articulations of the rights contained in these treaties found in general comments and general recommendations issued by the respective human rights treaty bodies, populations facing greater violations are alternately called "vulnerable," "marginalized," and "disadvantaged," or some combination of these terms.[4] These designations by no means exclusively include women, or women and children, although sometimes women as a group are referred to as vulnerable or marginalized.[5] While the practice of referring to discriminated against individuals and groups as vulnerable has gradually diminished in the general comments issued by the CESCR since 1999 (see tables 2.1 and 2.2), other UN documents like the 2000 *United Nations Millennium Declaration* (UN General Assembly 2000), the 2004 FAO *Voluntary Guidelines to Support the Progressive Realization of the Right to Adequate Food in the Context of National Food Security* (FAO 2005; hereinafter, *Right to Food Guidelines*), the 2012 FAO *Voluntary Guidelines on the Responsible Governance of Tenure of Land, Fisheries and Forests in the Context of National Food Security* (FAO 2012; hereinafter, *Voluntary Guidelines on Land, Fisheries and Forests Tenure*), and the 2012 *Global Strategic Framework for Food Security and Nutrition* (GSF) of the Committee on World Food Security (CFS; CFS 2012) continue its usage.[6]

We observe "vulnerability" often associated with pregnant and breastfeeding women. Women's nutritional status during maternity in general, and most specifically during pregnancy and breastfeeding, indeed warrants particular attention because of the heightened physical demands on the mother to gestate new life and produce food for it. In this particular moment, women physically manifest the most local of food systems: the most caring, the best quality, and the most cost efficient and sustainable food and nutrition, where the food miles between producer and consumer are, so to speak, less than negligible. Calling pregnant and breastfeeding women "vulnerable" is a misnomer that can serve, if misused, to rob women of their capability and autonomy and becomes an avenue to patronize, commercialize, and build dependency.[7]

Table 2.1 List of general comments issued by the Committee on Economic, Social and Cultural Rights (CESCR)

	General comment		ICESCR article addressed
Number	Year of issuance	Title	
1	1989	*Reporting by States Parties*	—
2	1990	*International Technical Assistance Measures*	22
3	1990	*The Nature of States Parties Obligations*	2, para. 1
4	1991	*The Right to Adequate Housing*	11, para. 1
5	1994	*Persons with Disabilities*	—
6	1995	*Economic, Social and Cultural Rights of Older Persons*	—
7	1997	*The Right to Adequate Housing (Forced Evictions)*	11, para. 1
8	1997	*Relationship between Economic Sanctions and Respect for ESC Rights*	—
9	1998	*The Domestic Application of the Covenant*	—
10	1998	*The Role of National Human Rights Institutions in the Protection of Economic, Social and Cultural Rights*	—
11	1999	*Plans of Action for Primary Education*	14
12	1999	*The Right to Adequate Food*	11
13	1999	*The Right to Education*	13
14	2000	*The Right to the Highest Attainable Standard of Health*	12
15	2003	*The Right to Water*	11, 12
16	2005	*The Equal Right of Men and Women to the Enjoyment of All Economic, Social and Cultural Rights*	3
17	2006	*The Right of Everyone to Benefit from the Protection of the Moral and Material Interests Resulting from Any Scientific, Literary or Artistic Production of Which He or She Is the Author*	15, para. 1(c)
18	2006	*The Right to Work*	6
19	2008	*The Right to Social Security*	9
20	2009	*Non-Discrimination in Economic, Social and Cultural Rights*	2, para. 2
21	2009	*Right of Everyone to Take Part in Cultural Life*	15

Source: website of the United Nations Office of the High Commissioner for Human Rights (OHCHR) at http://tbinternet.ohchr.org/_layouts/treatybodyexternal/TBSearch.aspx?Lang=en& TreatyID=9&DocTypeID=11 (last accessed February 16, 2015).

Table 2.2 References to individuals and groups of individuals facing human rights violations

CESCR General Comment[1]	vulnerable (stand-alone)	vulnerable *or* disadvantaged	vulnerable *and* disadvantaged	vulnerable *or* marginalized	vulnerable *and* marginalized
		used to refer to discriminated against individuals and groups			
No. 1 (1989)		3			
No. 2 (1990a)	9[2]				
No. 3 (1990b)	12				
No. 4 (1991)			13		
No. 5 (1994)			9		
No. 6 (1995)	17				17[3]
No. 7 (1997a)	10,* 16				
No. 8 (1997b)	4, 5, 6, 8, 10, 14, 15				
No. 9 (1998a)			10		
No. 10 (1998b)					
No. 11 (1999a)	4				
No. 12 (1999b)	13,[4] 28, 35, 38				
No. 13 (1999c)	6(b)(i), 38				
No. 14 (2000)	18			12(b),* 35,* 37, 40, 43(a, f), 52, 62, 65	
No. 15 (2003)	13			12(c)(iii), 44(c), 59, 60	37(h)
No. 16 (2005)					
No. 17 (2006a)					
No. 18 (2006b)					
No. 19 (2008)					
No. 20 (2009a)					27[5]
No. 21 (2009b)					

[1] Please see Table 2.1 for the full titles of the general comments.
[2] "poor and vulnerable"
[3] "vulnerable, marginal and unprotected"
[4] "socially vulnerable" and "physically vulnerable"
[5] "social groups that are vulnerable and have suffered and continue to suffer marginalization"

general comments issued by the Committee on Economic, Social and Cultural Rights (CESCR)

organized according to relevant paragraphs in the General Comment

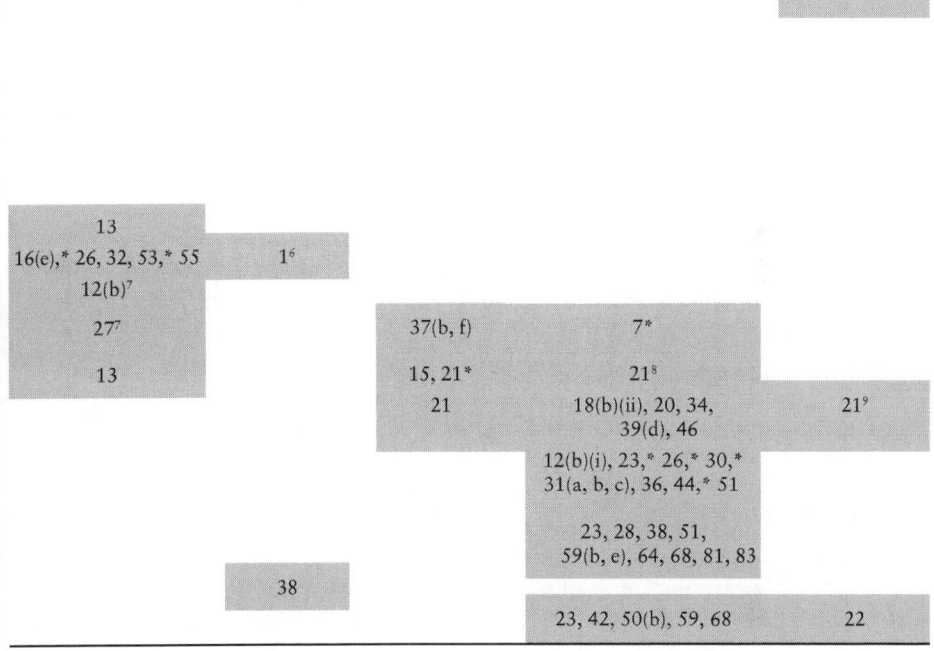

disadvantaged (stand-alone)	marginalized (stand-alone)	disadvantaged or marginalized	disadvantaged and marginalized	discriminated against
8(e), 19				
				25
13 16(e),* 26, 32, 53,* 55 12(b)[7]	1[6]			
27[7]		37(b, f)	7*	
13		15, 21*	21[8]	
		21	18(b)(ii), 20, 34, 39(d), 46	21[9]
			12(b)(i), 23,* 26,* 30,* 31(a, b, c), 36, 44,* 51	
			23, 28, 38, 51, 59(b, e), 64, 68, 81, 83	
	38			
			23, 42, 50(b), 59, 68	22

[6] "economically and socially marginalized"
[7] "socially disadvantaged"
[8] "poorest and most disadvantaged and marginalized"
[9] "those subjected to discrimination"

If women's basic human rights are already violated through discrimination and other forms of structural violence, a woman brings in corpus to pregnancy the burden of human rights violations which compromise her own and her child's well-being and nutritional health. Naming these women "vulnerable" suggests that it is the female condition of pregnancy and lactation that leads to "weakness," instead of identifying the human rights violations and their social determinants, such as discrimination, that create maternal, infant, and young child malnutrition. Subsequent chapters of this volume carry relevant examples.

The vulnerability label must not define pregnant and breastfeeding women. While they truly do have greater physical, psychological, economic, and social demands that include food and nutrition and that are essential to address, they also remain individuals with capabilities and dignity. Pregnant and lactating women require self-determination and autonomy with regard to the well-being of themselves and their offspring, especially in connection with the locus of mother-baby intertwined food and nutrition systems (see chapter 4 of this volume).

Yet, women's nutritional status during maternity, and most specifically pregnancy and breastfeeding, demarcates institutional and programmatic attention to women's right to adequate food and nutrition, whereby "special protection," "appropriate care," and "special measures and appropriate services" frame states parties' obligations under ICESCR, CRC, and CEDAW, respectively. Under the rubrics of "special protection . . . to mothers during a reasonable period before and after childbirth" (UN General Assembly 1966, art. 10.2) and "appropriate pre-natal and post-natal health care for mothers" (UN General Assembly 1989, art. 24.2(d)), women's health is promoted with the primary objective of family, infant, and child well-being. Moreover, states parties are called upon to adopt "special measures . . . aimed at protecting maternity" which "shall not be considered discriminatory" (UN General Assembly 1979, art. 4.2) and "ensure appropriate services in connection with pregnancy, confinement and the post-natal period," including adequate nutrition (UN General Assembly 1979, art. 12.1).

CEDAW articles 4.2 and 12.1 attracted sufficient attention that the CEDAW Committee found it necessary to elaborate upon the correct meaning of these "special measures" as different from "help to the vulnerable," and in 2004 issued *General Recommendation 25 on Temporary Special Measures* (hereinafter, *General Recommendation 25*; CEDAW Committee 2004):

> The term "special", though being in conformity with human rights discourse, also needs to be carefully explained. Its use sometimes casts women and other groups who are subject to discrimination as weak, vulnerable, and in need of extra or "special" measures in order to participate or compete in society. However, the real meaning of "special" in the formulation of [CEDAW] article 4, paragraph 1, is that the measures are designed to serve a specific goal. (CEDAW Committee 2004, para. 21)

Despite this clarification in *General Recommendation 25*, the singular attention to women's right to adequate food and nutrition in the context of reproduction still collapses and instrumentalizes this right, and in the process the very breadth and possibility of women's experience. Within the more accurately labelled "discriminated against" category, it is imperative that associated responses (e.g., special protection and measures) promote women's autonomy and capability and do not engage in the inverse, that is, patronizing women by instrumentalizing "vulnerability" to deny self-determination and foster dependency. The goal is to enable women's autonomy and participation in the development of self-determined, food and nutrition secure communities, wherein all persons can realize human rights over the life course. The avenue is to identify and overcome human rights violations that stand in the way.

* * *

In summary, we argue that there is a need to overcome the disconnect between the human right to adequate food and nutrition and the full spectrum of women's human rights over the life span. To this end, each of the chapters in this volume presses for the evolution of international human rights instruments (e.g., ICESCR, CEDAW, CRC), frameworks (e.g., the current framework for the right to adequate food and nutrition), and related policy, as well as their integration at regional, national, and local levels. Harmonization of law, policies, and programs on the right to adequate food and nutrition of women as food producers and critical arbiters of household and community food and nutrition security requires addressing the role of the violences that perpetuate discrimination and facilitate patronizing approaches to "vulnerable" females (see chapter 3 of this volume). In the specific context of the mother and child intertwined subjectivities during pregnancy and lactation (see chapter 4 of this volume), human rights instruments need to reflect the balanced, independent, and yet still interconnected rights. As we have contended in this section, discrimination cannot be equated with vulnerability; discrimination generates human rights violations. This distinction and correct understanding is critical to protect women's, as well as men's and children's capacity to achieve and engender food and nutrition security, food sovereignty, and the realization of all human rights, from their own standpoints of autonomy and self-determination.

DISCONNECT TWO: THE STRUCTURAL ISOLATION OF NUTRITION FROM THE HUMAN RIGHT TO ADEQUATE FOOD

The second disconnect presents the structural isolation of nutrition from the human right to adequate food and how this disconnect interferes with the realization of women's right to adequate food and nutrition. Our discussion centers on a review of the separation of food production and nutrition in UN human rights instruments and proceeds to related public policy and private sector engagement that places inordinate attention on food production and medicalizes the meaning and practice of nutrition (see also chapter 5 of this volume).[8]

Policy and research attention to food and separately to nutrition diverged early along lines demarcated in the 1966 ICESCR, the 1979 CEDAW, and the 1989 CRC (W. B. Eide 2005). "Food" attracted the attention of agriculturalists and agricultural economists seeking to boost production efficiencies and to commoditize food for the sake of maximizing global scale trade potential. "Nutrition" was traditionally linked to health and focused on discrete population groups like children (especially infants and young children), pregnant and lactating women, seniors, and others. While some developments promoted wholesome nutrition and sustainable diets based on local food systems, nutrition products grew most prominently inside medical health markets. Industrial scale production and global circulation of food stuffs has been promoted with sufficient attention targeted neither to equitable distribution, access, and control over the means, methods, and production mode choices at the local level, nor to the nutritional and cultural adequacy of the produced and circulated food stuffs for the people consuming them. In other words, policy that identifies the answer to food insecurity in terms of "produce more" clearly overlooks the fact that steadily increasing production has not changed the demographics or geographies of hunger and malnutrition. Further, such policy is more intimately linked to market-led and food price volatility prone solutions based on comparative advantage and agribusiness profit than on support for local food production initiatives, sovereignty, and autonomy. At the same time, a pharmaceutical-based approach to micronutrient supplementation of highly processed foods and food substitutes has obstructed needed emphasis on promoting equitable and affordable access to culturally adequate and high quality food in local food systems, including breastfeeding and appropriate complementary foods for infants and young children, as well as culturally adapted nutrition education for all genders and ages. We argue that policy attention for food *and* nutrition must apply the human rights framework and focus primarily on local and national food systems that are managed under an inclusive governance scheme, embracing and respecting women's contribution to food and nutrition security, as well as people's and food sovereignty.

As expounded on in chapter 6 of this volume, the immeasurable variations of food customs and traditions, their practices of discrimination notwithstanding,[9] provide defining contours of the culture of a community and even family. Millennia of trial and error have produced a wealth of cropping, animal husbandry, and foraging knowledge that has established sustainable livelihoods and durable customs. At the heart of local food systems is the rich life of commensality, how we feed and care for each other, which is eclipsed through the separated concentrations on large-scale food production and medicalized nutrition. Food nurtures; food begins with healthy soils and seas and feeds into the physical and mental well-being of individuals and groups. Food defined identity and purpose support the will and capacity to claim the human right to adequate food *and* nutrition as an entitlement, never charity. This is the claim of people's sovereignty in a food system, the resolve to interact as necessary with the global economic system from a position of autonomy instead of dependency in order to safeguard food and nutrition security.

Attention to Nutrition in the *International Covenant on Economic, Social and Cultural Rights* (ICESCR), the *Convention on the Elimination of All Forms of Discrimination against Women* (CEDAW), and the *Convention on the Rights of the Child* (CRC)

In the 1948 UDHR, food is referenced only one time as one of many aspects constituting the human right to an adequate standard of living (UN General Assembly 1948, art. 25(1); see also chapter 1 of this volume). Nutrition does not appear at all. In the 1966 ICESCR, nutrition is cited one time in article 11 which addresses the human right to an adequate standard of living, including adequate food, clothing, and housing. Article 11.2(a) asserts that states parties shall,

> improve methods of production, conservation and distribution of food by making full use of technical and scientific knowledge, *by disseminating knowledge of the principles of nutrition* and by developing or reforming agrarian systems in such a way as to achieve the most efficient development and utilization of natural resources. (UN General Assembly 1966, art. 11.2(a); emphasis added)

"[D]isseminating knowledge of the principles of nutrition," commonly known as nutrition education, is enumerated as one of the means to realize a right to adequate food and nutrition. Nutrition education is, however, rarely delegated the task of linking food production and community nutritional health within the geography and culture of a local food system. Nutrition knowledge, like methods of food production, was conceived in this era of early outer space travel as a function of scientific discovery and technical competence. Industrial scale productivity, commoditization, and the dawn of globalized trade vastly overshadowed the waning field of home economics as well as the dawning grassroots environmental movement and evolution of alternative local food production models. "Principles of nutrition" easily subsumed the late nineteenth and twentieth century discipline of home economics that arguably both colluded in defining women's role as dependent consumers outside the paid workplace and, at the same time, disseminated cooking and other knowledge that augmented women's capability and autonomy to protect their families' nutritional health by preparing what was available. In other words, home economics reinforced the structural discrimination of gender stereotyping at the same time that it empowered women within the constraints of their gender role.

The science of nutrition became increasingly linked to the patronizing wisdom of the centralized state in the geopolitical East and to the market driven economy in the West. Local knowledge, especially that controlled by women, was demeaned. Neither the East nor West strove for local political and economic autonomy and capacity, what Amartya Sen (1985) called "capability" (see also Agarwal, Humphries, and Robeyns 2006; Nussbaum 2011; Nussbaum and Sen 1993).[10] For the centrist state governance model supported by the ideological leader of economic, social, and cultural rights, the former Soviet Union, self-determination through a food and nutrition systems model that linked local food production and nutritional health would probably have seemed dangerously independent and suspiciously close to political and civic self-rule. From the opposite ideological vantage point and with the United States as flagship, the goal of equitable living standards (in the context of the human rights to food, nutrition, and health, among others) would most likely have appeared inconsistent with the market mechanism of supply and demand, consumer loyalty and dependence, and promotion of international trade.

The right of everyone to be free from hunger (UN General Assembly 1966, art. 11.2) is a fundamental but also a minimal right; it constitutes a "subnorm" and "should be seen only as the first step toward realization of the primary norm" (Alston 1984, 167). Freedom from hunger implies a government's obligation to address rudimentary quantity needs. It is with the adoption of CEDAW in 1979 and CRC in 1989 that nutrition as a human right is introduced into the UN treaty language. However, this first conception of a right to nutrition does not devise it as a universal human right, but rather a selective and discontinuous right available through articles 12 of CEDAW and 24 of CRC, which are designed to promote the right to the highest attainable standard of health of infants and young children, women who are their mothers during the period of pregnancy and breastfeeding, and also older children through age seventeen (UN General Assembly 1979, art. 12.2; 1989, arts. 24.2(c), (e)). UN treaty language has not been expanded to embrace the nutritional needs and rights of adult men in general or of women who are not pregnant or breastfeeding, reducing the human right to adequate food and nutrition to only some of its dimensions (see chapter 4 of this volume for further discussion).

The right to nutrition is linked in these articles to the promotion of the right to the highest attainable standard of health. The frames of anti-hunger and improved and sustainable food availability and access are obscure or completely absent. CEDAW article 12.2 reads:

> States Parties shall ensure to women appropriate services in connection with pregnancy, confinement and the post-natal period, granting free services where necessary, as well as *adequate nutrition during pregnancy and lactation.* (UN General Assembly 1979, art. 12.2; emphasis added)

Likewise, the CRC lays out the right of children of all ages (0–17) to the provision of adequate nutritious food in the context of primary health care (UN General Assembly 1989, art. 24.2(c)). This construction erases adult men and women. It further fails to link the right to nutrition to food systems, opening nutrition to pharmaceutical cooptation.

> States Parties . . . shall take appropriate measures . . . [t]o combat disease and malnutrition, including within the framework of primary health care, through, inter alia, the application of readily available technology and *through the provision of adequate nutritious foods* and clean drinking-water, taking into consideration the dangers and risks of environmental pollution. (UN General Assembly 1989, art. 24.2(c); emphasis added)

Article 24.2(e) of the CRC seeks to secure universal access to nutrition education, although the focus of this education is infants and young children, not the learners themselves.

> States Parties . . . shall take appropriate measures . . . [t]o ensure that all segments of society, in particular parents and children, are informed, have access to education and are supported in the use of *basic knowledge of child health and nutrition, the advantages of breastfeeding,* hygiene and environmental sanitation and the prevention of accidents. (UN General Assembly 1989, art. 24.2(e); emphasis added)

For the development of the 1989 CRC, the United Nations Children's Fund (UNICEF) defined and promoted the right to nutrition as the combination of access to food, health, and care as necessary components to ensure adequate nutrition to children (Jonsson 1981; see also UNICEF 1998, 20, 24; Windfuhr 1998, 8). According to Jonsson (1993; 1996), UNICEF consciously selected the formulation of "a right of the child to nutrition" over "a child's right to adequate food" because the former recognized a more complex construction to alimentation needs than guaranteed by food production alone. However, the outcome of this choice was the separation of child nutrition from a local food systems approach, leaving it more greatly exposed to the introduction of "formulated" foods and growing reliance on the industry that produces them.

The CRC consciously anchors nutrition in the right of children of all ages to an adequate standard of living in article 27, and, therefore, to their "physical, mental, spiritual, moral and social development" (UN General Assembly 1989, art. 27.1), noting further that this right to nutrition is subject to social protection measures of direct material assistance and support programs (UN General Assembly 1989, art. 27.3).

> States Parties, in accordance with national conditions and within their means, shall take appropriate measures to assist parents and others responsible for the child to implement this right and shall in case of need *provide material assistance and support programmes, particularly with regard to nutrition*, clothing and housing. (UN General Assembly 1989, art. 24.3; emphasis added)

The CRC places the right of children to nutrition under the same umbrella as the ICESCR does with the right of everyone to food and to be free from hunger, namely under the umbrella of the right to an adequate standard of living, and explicitly provides for social protection measures that are part of states parties obligations under ICESCR to fulfill/provide (see chapters 1 and 6 of this volume and previous mention in this chapter). The CRC misses the opportunity to link nutrition to the breadth of what the adequate standard of living encompasses, including food production and the four pillars of food security: adequacy, access, utilization, and sustainability.

The 1989 CRC's inclusion of nutrition in article 27 and its unequivocal identification of breastfeeding as best food practice for infants and young children in article 24 is a groundbreaking expansion of the ICESCR's right to adequate food and nutrition scope. Nevertheless, and linking this analysis back to the first disconnect presented earlier in this chapter, the right of children to nutrition is introduced through an instrumentalization of women as the physical conduit of healthy children through pregnancy and breastfeeding (see also chapter 4 of this volume). A more thorough evolution of the human right to adequate food and nutrition demands attention to the development of the capabilities to demand respect, self-determination, and the protection of food and nutrition security for all. While the CRC links nutrition to a child's physical, mental, spiritual, moral, and social development, a still more holistic approach would require the care, competence, and well-being of adults around them who manage children's access to food and nutrition security. A local food systems approach needs local governance that foregrounds the leadership and participation of those who feed, especially under conditions of market unpredictability and various emergency conditions (see chapters 4 and 5 of this volume). In the case of infants and young children, this is particularly, although certainly not exclusively, women. In the case of older children, both girls and boys, young people need to learn about and be empowered to participate in the inclusive and non-discriminatory governance of their local food systems.

Representing a major change since the 1966 ICESCR, nutrition was incorporated into a late twentieth century *regional* human rights instrument as a component of the right to food (*sic*; not adequate food): article 12 of the 1988 *Additional Protocol to the [1969] American Convention on Human Rights in the Area of Economic, Social and Cultural Rights* (hereinafter, *Protocol of San Salvador*; OAS 1988). The *Protocol of San Salvador* reaffirmed "within the framework of [American hemisphere] democratic institutions, a system of personal liberty and social justice based on respect for the essential rights of man [*sic*]" (OAS 1988, preamble).[11] Article 12 on the right to food reads:

1. Everyone has the *right to adequate nutrition* which guarantees the possibility of enjoying the highest level of physical, emotional and intellectual development.
2. In order to promote the exercise of this right and eradicate malnutrition, the States Parties undertake to *improve methods of production, supply and distribution of food*, and to this end, agree to promote greater international cooperation in support of the relevant national policies. (OAS 1988, art. 12; emphasis added)

Article 12 of the *Protocol of San Salvador* encompasses here both the *universal* right to adequate nutrition (art. 12.1) and the ICESCR-based state obligation to address production, supply, and distribution of food (art. 12.2). In other words, this regional treaty enhances the project of bringing food and nutrition under one human rights, food systems-based umbrella.

The previously discussed 1999 CESCR *General Comment 12* also links food and nutrition; however, the scope of this expansion is narrow. *General Comment 12* reflects upon the existence of hunger and malnutrition noting that "[e]very State is obliged to ensure for everyone under its jurisdiction access to the minimum essential food which is sufficient, *nutritionally adequate* and safe, to ensure their freedom from hunger" (CESCR 1999b, para. 14; emphasis added) and that the obligations to strive for "*food and nutrition security* for all" should be contextualized in national legislation (CESCR 1999b, para. 21; emphasis added). Although nutrition and food are explicitly mentioned together in both paragraphs 14 and 21, *General Comment 12*, like the *Protocol of San Salvador*, does not yet develop nutrition within food systems, nor self-determination with inclusive food governance in the right to adequate food and nutrition framework (see also chapter 6 of this volume).

In 2000, the CESCR issued *General Comment 14 on the Right to the Highest Attainable Standard of Health* (hereinafter, *General Comment*

14; CESCR 2000). *General Comment 14* identifies food and nutrition as part of the underlying social determinants of health (CESCR 2000, para. 4). In paragraph 27, with particular reference to indigenous peoples, *General Comment 14* integrates food and nutrition in a profoundly new paradigm grounded beyond individual rights in groups' cultures, the vitality of their collectives, and the way human relationships with the environment and each other shape food, nutrition, and health. We quote at length:

> States should provide resources for indigenous peoples to design, deliver and control such services so that they may enjoy the highest attainable standard of physical and mental health. The *vital medicinal plants, animals and minerals necessary to the full enjoyment of health* of indigenous peoples should also be protected. The Committee notes that, in indigenous communities, *the health of the individual is often linked to the health of the society as a whole and has a collective dimension.* In this respect, the Committee considers that development-related activities that lead to the displacement of indigenous peoples against their will from their traditional territories and environment, *denying them their sources of nutrition and breaking their symbiotic relationship with their lands*, has a deleterious effect on their health. (CESCR 2000, para. 27; emphasis added)

Paragraph 27 lays critical groundwork from which to build a more holistic understanding of the human right to adequate food and nutrition. *General Comment 14* reflects upon the specific cultural situation of indigenous peoples in terms of their interrelationship with the physical landscape, the diverse fruits of the land, human health, and cultural well-being. It is this interrelationship that is crucial to the idea of self-determination, dignity, and people's sovereignty in active local food systems and food economies. *General Comment 14* presents a new frame of the right to adequate food and nutrition, but paradigmatically, it is only ascribed to indigenous peoples. Perhaps it was easier in *General Comment 14* to absorb this new holistic outlook by "naturalizing" it to a social "other," that is, indigenous peoples. The idea, however, is relevant not only to those identified as indigenous individuals and communities but to all human beings. Indeed, we propose that against the negotiated and ordered rights to use land, relationships with land and culture are relevant to the realization of the right to adequate food and nutrition for all. Just as nutrition must be the right of all people, not just children and pregnant and breastfeeding women, so too must the vision of paragraph 27 in *General Comment 14* be universalized to expand the human right to adequate food and nutrition to self-determination in food systems, where leadership and participation include and represent communities' most marginalized constituents.

In 2004, FAO member states adopted the aforementioned *Right to Food Guidelines* to recommend actions for governments to progressively realize the right to adequate food and nutrition, including implementations and monitoring. Guideline 10 integrates and expands upon progress in incorporating nutrition in the right to adequate food by addressing dietary diversity, availability, and sustainability (FAO 2005, guideline 10.1); nutrition education (FAO 2005, guideline 10.2); inclusive participation and non-discrimination, in particular with respect to women and girls (FAO 2005, guidelines 10.3, 10.8, 10.10); promotion of best feeding practices for infants and young children centered on breastfeeding (FAO 2005, guidelines 10.5, 10.6); the intersection of the right to adequate food and nutrition with the right to health, education, and sanitary infrastructure to promote intersectoral collaboration (FAO 2005, guideline 10.7); and the vital part of culture in dietary and eating patterns (FAO 2005, guidelines 10.9, 10.10).[12]

The *Right to Food Guidelines* suggests how governments can promote the right to adequate food, including nutrition. Whereas there is notable reference to the connection between food and culture, nowhere is there an expression of the sensitive relationship between land, people, and sustainable food systems that *General Comment 14* offers (at least for indigenous peoples). The *Right to Food Guidelines* additionally does not articulate an express connection between food systems, inclusive participatory food governance, and food and nutrition policy. Without a food systems and local governance analysis, efforts for governments to comply with and rights holders to claim a right to adequate food and nutrition more easily remain compartmentalized in separate production and nutrition policy silos.

Since the endorsement of the *Right to Food Guidelines*, attention to the integration of food and nutrition has grown considerably, particularly with the reform of the CFS housed at the FAO. The 2009 CFS reform document states:

> Food security exists when all people, at all times, have physical, social and economic access to sufficient, safe and nutritious food that meets their dietary needs and food preferences for an active and healthy life. The four pillars of food security are availability, access, utilization and stability. The nutritional dimension is integral to the concept of food security and to the work of CFS. (CFS 2009, 1)

The aforementioned *Global Strategic Framework for Food Security and Nutrition* (GSF; CFS 2012, 2013, 2014) is a document created by governments within the CFS in cooperation with a wide range of constituencies, including public interest civil society and the (corporate) private sector, and approved by the CFS plenary of governments. Although legally non-binding, the GSF is built upon "existing frameworks, guidelines and coordination processes at all levels" (CFS 2013, 6), including legally binding international human rights instruments (cf. CFS 2013, 14), in order to merge them into one living document and process designed to be flexible enough to embrace and incorporate the evolutive character of human rights (FAO 2013, 6–7). The purpose is to "provide an overarching framework and a single reference document with practical guidance on core recommendations for food security and nutrition strategies, policies and actions validated by the wide ownership, participation and consultation afforded by the CFS" (CFS 2013, 5).[13] States, in exchange with interested constituencies, should "ensure that agricultural policies and public investment give priority to food production and improving levels of nutrition, especially of the most vulnerable populations, and increase the resilience of local and traditional food systems and biodiversity [including for] . . . sustainable smallholder food production" (CFS 2013, 17).

As discussed at greater length elsewhere in the volume (see chapters 1, 5, and 6), global food governance efforts struggle between the human rights framework that foregrounds people's food sovereignty and market-based approaches that seek to maximize food production and financial returns of global trade. The CFS houses and the GSF as a living document reflects those struggles. At a moment, therefore, when nutrition and food appear to be more linked, conflicts over how nutrition and food are connected increase.

Despite the holistic and indivisible nature of human rights, the two separate constructions are (*a*) the right to adequate food as the need to improve quantity of supply, without due attention to the related adequacy of the food or the ability of communities and nations to become food sovereign, and (*b*) the right to nutrition as the selective right of children and pregnant and lactating women to nutritional health. These constructions have impeded the incorporation of nutrition into local food sovereignty and systems approaches, especially as concerns maternal, infant, and young child feeding, and further facilitated its domination by the medical nutrition industry. Of course, we recognize and applaud the great strides that the inclusion of nutrition under the right to adequate food umbrella has made since the 1948 UDHR and the 1966 ICESCR through the behest of diverse social movements. However, much more needs to be done. Respect and consideration, protection, and promotion of the cultural knowledges and quotidian practices of nutrition need to be leveraged into institutional and policy strategies for food security. Individuals and groups must be able to define and claim the human right to adequate food and nutrition instead of receiving it as charity.

Noting that the majority, although by no means the entirety, of household and community oriented nutrition work is done by women, compounded by structural gender-based discrimination and violences against women, we argue and elaborate further in the next section that nutrition is devalued and patronized by production oriented and medicalized approaches to food security and health.

Overemphasis on Food Production and the Medicalization of Nutrition

The overemphasis on food production and the medicalization of nutrition have unfolded in waves of policy changes, technical developments and market opportunities, and popular struggles to participate in the identification and implementation of solutions for hunger and malnutrition. Since the 1960s, agricultural research and policy has focused on the concern that population growth could surpass the ability to supply sufficient food to meet people's needs. This approach, labeled the "production paradigm" by Welch and Graham (1999, 2), was emphasized at the 1974 World Food Conference as the strategy to reduce global undernutrition rates through significantly increased investments in agricultural research that culminated in the development of green revolution technologies (Dangour, Kennedy, and Taylor 2013, 194; Welch and Graham 1999, 2; cf. HRC 2011, para. 4). A decade later, a shift toward the "sustainability paradigm" (Welch and Graham 1999, 3) began to address the growing concerns about the detrimental environmental effects of agriculture, but still focused on improving productivity, albeit while preserving the natural resource base. During the 1980s and 1990s, the commoditization of food was sealed through the negotiation of the Agreement on Agriculture during the Uruguay Round (1986–1994) at the General Agreement on Tariffs and Trade (GATT). Concurrently, micronutrient deficiency increasingly became recognized as a public health concern as well, particularly in those countries in which green revolution technologies had been introduced (Welch and Graham 1999, 1–2; Underwood 2000, referenced in Pinstrup-Andersen 2000, 353). This opened a door to the marketable pharmaceutical "fix" to chronic malnutrition, heralding what we call the "micronutrient deficiency paradigm." In response, the "food systems paradigm" evolved as "an agriculture which aims not only at productivity and sustainability, but also at better nutrition" (Welch and Graham 1999, 9). Beyond the food systems paradigm, research today on food production and nutrition increasingly addresses what we call the "governance paradigm," that is, the shape of public decision-making as influenced by public, private, and civil society actors that participate in and prompt public policy on food and nutrition (see chapter 5 of this volume for further discussion on the disconnect of food production and nutrition).

Integrating nutritional goals into agricultural research and programming has progressed slowly since the early 1980s (Levin et al. 2003). The United Nations Administrative Committee on Co-ordination/Sub-Committee on Nutrition (ACC/SCN), together with the Consultative Group on International Agricultural Research (CGIAR), convened a first CGIAR-wide workshop on this issue in 1984 (Pinstrup-Andersen, Berg, and Forman 1984, 1–2). The meeting was not successful, however, in foregrounding nutritional considerations into agricultural research which remained focused on production technologies to solve hunger.[14] Fifteen years passed before a second

CGIAR-wide workshop was convened in 1999 to follow-up nutrition-related findings and recommendations made at the first conference (Bouis 2000; Pinstrup-Andersen 2000, 355). Similarly, whereas in 1992 the FAO and the World Health Organization (WHO) jointly organized the first International Conference on Nutrition (ICN) to foster an integrated nutrition and agriculture approach to research (FAO and WHO 1992, para. 9), actual work on malnutrition remained divided in separate medical and food production tracks. At present, the appearance and rampant increase of population scale overweight, obesity, and related noncommunicable diseases (NCDs) concurrently with hunger and undernutrition in low, middle, and high income countries alike (WHO 2008) has brought back policy direction into question. The 2014 Second International Conference on Nutrition (ICN2) addressed this phenomenon known as "nutrition transition" with the aim to incorporate nutrition into agricultural programming and policy to enhance human well-being (Dangour et al. 2012, 224; Nugent 2011, 3; Fan, Pandya-Lorch, and Fritschel 2012, 1; World Bank 2007).

Proposed strategies to bridge the agriculture-nutritional health divide generally neglect the role and context of human dignity and self-determination in the endeavor of linking food production and nutrition on behalf of human well-being. They have failed to tackle the power imbalances that have directed or kept attention away from real, long-term solutions that strengthen community and national capacity to provide food and nutrition for its members and citizens through local and national sustainable food systems. In the case of ICN2, the conference failed to take into account the negative impact of the agroindustrial model, including its pursuit of large-scale land acquisitions, commonly known as landgrabs, on human health, environments, and livelihoods. More specifically, ICN2 refused to recognize these and other human rights violations that are faced by marginalized groups, especially low income women and all persons living in poverty, to be social determinants of malnutrition (Public Interest Civil Society Organizations' and Social Movements' Forum 2014).

Inordinate Attention to Food Production

Inordinate attention to food production ignores population capability to access food that is adequate in quantity *and* quality, as well as nutrition as a function of food adequacy and access (cf. HRC 2011). Despite Sen's empirical studies revealing that food and nutrition security is tied far less to the capacity to produce enough food for all than it is to the capability of individuals and groups to establish democratically based entitlements (Sen 1981), the existence of world hunger and malnutrition continues to be addressed primarily through the Malthusian lens of uncontrolled and dangerous population growth and the determined scientific and technological challenge of producing enough to feed it. The FAO projects that, by 2050, the world population will have increased by one third to 9.1 billion and will require an increase of food production of 70 percent, including a 74 percent increase in meat production (FAO 2009). These figures carry assumptions that the global population growth will be mostly in the developing world and that this new population will be richer, more urban, and will eat more meat. In addition to the 70 percent boost in food production, farmland will be pressed and expanded for ever increasing agrofuel yields. Overpopulation, it is alleged, demands technological salvation.

We dispute neither the realities of population growth nor the adverse effects of climate change on some world regions. We question, however, the 2009 FAO study assumptions that of the 70 percent increase needed in food output, 80 percent should come from enhanced yields and 20 percent from expanded arable lands, and further, that deregulated markets are necessary to promote trade and support for farmers who can operate at larger and higher technological scales (FAO 2009). Data show that from 1960–2000, increases in food production have consistently outstripped population growth (HRC 2014, para. 10; see also Holt-Giménez 2012; Patel 2007; Sen 1999) and production surpluses have coexisted with food insecurity and malnutrition (Altieri and Rosset 1999; Poppendieck 2014). On the one hand, it is widely acknowledged that the technological developments that are termed the green revolution resulted in a boost in crop yields, enhanced incomes for some of the rural poor particularly in Asia, and an improvement, although slow, of the poverty and undernutrition status in both rural and urban areas through a decline in food prices (Berger 2003, referenced in Wahlqvist et al. 2012, 663; Kennedy and Bouis 1993; World Bank 2007). On the other hand, the green revolution led to significant environmental problems through the overuse of pesticides and fertilizers, the substantial reduction of water tables due to the irrigation requirements of the introduced high yield varieties, and a process of land consolidation primarily benefitting large holder farmers able to afford the necessary chemical inputs and agricultural machines. Many small-scale farmers were forced off of their lands to either become wage laborers or migrate to the cities (Lipton 1989; Rosegrant and Hazell 2001; Timmer 2000, all referenced in Wahlqvist et al. 2012, 663). As Wahlqvist et al. (2012, 663) put it, "[t]he success of the Green Revolution in Asia raised expectations that such dramatic increases in crop yields could be repeated . . . but, notwithstanding the lives it must have saved, its legacy is a mixed one," challenging "the principles of both sustainability and equity." In fact, the lower food prices attributed to the green revolution reflect the non-inclusion of these and other ecological, health, and social costs of the expansion of this input intensive agroindustrial model.

As De Schutter writes in his final report to the HRC as special rapporteur on the right to food:

Any prescription to increase [crop] yields that ignores the need to transition to sustainable production and consumption, and to reduce rural poverty, will not only be incomplete; it may also have damaging impacts, worsening the ecological crisis and widening the gap between different categories of food producers. (HRC 2014, para. 15)[15]

With specific reference to food and nutrition policy, the 2009 FAO report caps a long era starting with Reagan and Thatcher's dismantling of less industrialized countries' initiatives to retain or gain control over and put limits on the rapidly growing power of transnational corporations (TNCs; A. Eide 2005; Palmer 2009; Walton and Seddon 1994) and the encroachment on democratic governance by both national and transnational businesses seeking to "partner" with governments (Lhotska, Bellows, and Scherbaum 2012; Palmer 2009; Richter 2004; Schuftan and Holla 2012).

Since Sen (1981), many have observed the terrible irony that attention to increased food production is often focused on commodity exports rather than domestic consumption (e.g., Coomans and Künneman 2012; FAO 2006; HRC 2014). As Wahlqvist et al. (2012, 663–4) claim, international trade can benefit local systems when they are "vulnerable to disruptions from natural disasters and other crises." Under normal conditions, however, market imperfections, power asymmetries, and externalities are likely to disadvantage and suppress local production, leading to a vicious cycle of greater dependency on food imports and food aid, thus reinforcing concession to global markets.

The large-scale food production and related large-scale land acquisition focus on high macronutrient (especially grains) and luxury crops, as well as agrofuels for export. These production priorities challenge rural consumer ability to grow, access, or purchase a diversified and nutritious diet within local rural economies. Local communities, regions, and nations must retain capability to sustain themselves through local and regional resources when global markets, whose geographical commitments are guided by profit potential, fail to do so (Friedmann 1993; Lappé, Collins, and Rosset 1998; Madeley 2000; Magdoff, Bellamy Foster, and Buttel 2000; Palmer 2009; Shiva 1998, 2000).[16] Complete loss of self-sufficiency capability threatens the food and nutrition security of the poorest food producers and consumers, both urban and rural, and especially of the women among them. It can only be "rebuilt through long, difficult and costly efforts" (Mehmet 1999, referenced in Wahlqvist et al. 2012, 664).

Large-scale production efficiencies in fact lead to nutrition and other *inefficiencies*. Related farm operations are often dedicated to maximizing yield and are less efficient in terms of total calorie and nutrient output (in food) compared to total inputs (in the form of fossil energy and agrochemicals). Dominant forms of intense grain-based animal production foster meat centered consumption, additionally contributing to diet-related chronic diseases associated with diets both rich in lower priced, calorie dense, and nutrient poor foods and lacking in nutrient dense counterparts such as fruits, vegetables, and whole grains (Dangour et al. 2012, 224). The logic of production efficiencies, overproduction, and the production of nutritionally poor and calorie dense food is linked to the rise of multinational food retailers who have been both responding to and creating new demands for profitable, low quality convenience foods, particularly among young consumers (Wahlqvist et al. 2012).

The Medicalization of Nutrition

This section introduces a theme that is expanded on in chapters 4, 5, and 6 of this volume, namely the disconnect of food and nutrition from the vantage point of the pharmaceutical industry's dedication to addressing micronutrient deficiency, particularly from the 1990s forward. The first part of our discussion of the food-nutrition disconnect argued that global agrifood interests pursue maximized commodity output without emphasis on or respect for food quality, adequacy, access, or community and national food culture and self-determination. This second part now presents the case that growth of the nutritional products market (i.e., nutrient supplemented, fortified, or enriched products) at the commodity scale has not been aligned with food systems approaches in general and food sovereignty in particular. In common, corporate food and nutrition interests patronize the authority of both non-industrial scale and non-market-based actors, including those who produce for their own consumption, women who breastfeed (excluding paid wet nurses), and those who barter or trade for and with food in locally based, direct markets. The heady promotion of industrialized nutrition products targets consumers, especially women consumers, without regard for them as human rights holders and autonomous governors of their own food and nutritional well-being.

Both the agribusiness and pharmaceutical sectors rely on the almost unassailable mantle of scientific expertise, technology, and marketplace efficiency to promote their respective commodities. At the same time that basic research and technology advances on nutritional products emerged to service the "micronutrient deficiency paradigm" (mentioned earlier), maximizing commodity production was augmented with developments in agricultural biotechnology (Williams 2009; Lang 2006, unnumbered table). In the early paradigm stages, research and development efficiencies were sought in the commonalities of the two industrial streams. The new "agribiotech" field began with small start-up ventures that were consolidated in the 1990s by large life science companies seeking to integrate agricultural and medical applications of genetic engineering (Falkner 2009, 228, 245; Williams 2009).

The global trade in food and in pharmaceuticals, including processed food nutrients, began, however, to establish independent market streams later in the 1990s. From the mid-1990s onward, genetically modified crops began to attract significant popular disapproval, posing a growing threat to commercialization that similar research approaches in pharmaceuticals did not experience. Falkner (2009, 228) reports that, anxious to avoid public resistance to the pharmaceuticals, the life sciences industry split apart previously entwined agricultural and medical research and production streams. A key example is the United Kingdom's Astra and Sweden's Zeneca, two large pharmaceutical firms with stakes in agribiotechnology that merged in December 1998 to form AstraZeneca. A year later, AstraZeneca and Novartis, the Swiss pharmaceuticals producer, both spun off respective agrichemical and agribiotechnological businesses and merged them to form Syngenta. In 2000, Monsanto and Pharmacia & Upjohn merged their pharmaceutical operations to create a separate company that focused more exclusively on agribiotechnology under the name of Monsanto (Falkner 2009, 228).

Pharmaceutical interests aligned themselves with the food retail instead of the agricultural sector. Pharmaceutical and so-called "consumer packaged goods" (CPG) companies consolidated to sell dietary supplements throughout the 1990s, with pharmaceutical companies like Warner-Lambert, Centrum, and Bayer, and CPG companies such as Procter & Gamble, Nestlé, and Kraft launching and buying supplement product lines (Stephens 2013). Two kinds of micronutrient supplement products emerged. "Nutraceuticals," a term first coined in 1991 by the US Foundation for Innovation in Medicine (DeFelice 1991, cited in Kottke 1998, 1178) are composed of synthetic compounds rather than food or food derived ingredients.[17] "Functional foods," a category of pharmaceutical production that originated in 1988 with a Japanese soft drink containing dietary fiber, are manufactured food products, including snacks, meal accompaniments, and drinks that are "positioned in the market place for particular and identified physiological and health reasons" (Wahlqvist and Wattanapenpaiboon 2002, 1). Boundaries between nutraceuticals and functional foods have increasingly blurred and, in 1997, the *Journal of Nutraceuticals, Functional and Medical Foods* provided a research and industry platform to express future market directions to address the prevention and cure of micronutrient deficiency (Kottke 1998, 1778).[18] Globally marketed nutraceuticals and functional foods are generally highly processed foods made anywhere from commodities that can be sourced also from anywhere. Exceptions could conceivably include locally sourced and manufactured products, such as the ready-to-use-foods (RUFs) described below and expanded upon in chapter 4 of this volume. Nutraceuticals are, however, seldom linked to local food systems and even more rarely, if ever, under the purview of local or regional food governance systems.

The expansion of commercialized nutritional products and services is connected to medical nutrition, an academic field linked with clinical nutrition counseling and therapy. Academically, the term medical nutrition has roots in the concept of medical nutrition therapy (MNT) which was initiated in 1994 by the American Dietetic Association.[19] MNT clarifies a two stage process to identify and engage specific nutritional services to treat illness, injury, or disease conditions including through the determination of (*a*) patient nutritional status and (*b*) "treatment, which includes nutrition therapy, counseling, and the use of specialized nutrition supplementations" (Green Pastors et al. 2002). In the commercial sector, medical nutrition is more directly connected to the development of nutrition supplements. The Medical Nutrition International Industry (MNI), an organization established in 2006, states in its website that

> MNI was founded by leading international companies in specialized medical nutrition [with t]he mission . . . to bring together companies that provide products and services to optimize patient outcome through specialized nutritional solutions

and that its goals are to

> [b]uild an environment which promotes the transition of clinical nutrition research into standard practice, and work with regulatory authorities and scientific bodies to shape a regulatory and reimbursement framework which supports the health needs of patients throughout the world.[20]

In this statement, MNI clarifies its intent to legitimize members' medical nutrition products for the global market with the imprimatur of academic research and government policy. To encourage research that benefits its industry members, MNI supports nutritional product development through an annual MNI Grant for the Best Initiative to Fight Malnutrition—so far granted exclusively to member organizations of the European Society for Clinical Nutrition and Metabolism (ESPEN).[21] To gain public sector patronage, MNI strives to participate in public decision-making bodies in order to, among other things, participate in shaping a public policy framework that identifies industry nutritional products as part of a functional standard in clinical nutrition practice.

A clinical condition of injury or disease might very well make it necessary to apply medical nutrition therapy to support the convalescence and, in some cases, even the survival of patients. However, the application of medical nutrition therapy has expanded from treating clinical needs of an individual to a population-based response to treat chronic undernourishment, especially in less industrialized countries, as in the case of the extensive and inappropriate use of ready-to-use-foods (RUFs).

RUFs were first developed in the mid-1990s as ready-to-use therapeutic foods (RUTFs) for the treatment of severe acute malnutrition in the context of emergency and under close medical supervision. They could be classified either or both as a nutraceutical and a functional food. Acclaimed by some as "one of the most successful examples of Functional Foods" (Asian Development Bank 2000, referred to in Wahlqvist and Wattana-penpaiboon 2002, 6), RUTF applications have increasingly shifted toward commercial ready-to-use supplementary foods (RUSFs) for the prevention of malnutrition, marketed as nutrition boosters. As explained in detail in chapter 4 of this volume, this shift away from local food systems has been heavily criticized for providing very young children with energy dense and thus less healthy, highly processed, waste producing, and cash demanding snacks ("The Global Game Plan of Big Snack [Editorial]" 2011; Monteiro 2010). Illustrative of the ongoing corporate promotion of RUTFs as the only legitimate malnutrition treatment, the summary report of session 4, panel 2 of the Preparatory Technical Meeting for the International Conference on Nutrition (ICN2) exclusively addressing opportunities for the further expansion of the corporate approach of "[a]pplying value chain interventions to markets for more nutritious foods" (Henson and Humphrey 2013, 2), reads:

> Ready-to-Use Therapeutic Foods (RUTFs) are now widely used to treat severe acute malnutrition. The model developed by international organizations and national governments is based on tight control of production and public distribution. This model avoids many of the value chain challenges facing companies looking to market nutrition-ally-enhanced products, including establishing the nutritional value of the product in the mind of the consumers, establishing new distribution channels, securing a sustainable finance model, certifying the quality of the product, eliminating or controlling opportunistic claims by low-cost imitators and ensuring affordability. (Henson and Humphrey 2013, para. 10)

As described in the chapters throughout this volume, chronic malnutrition is a function of poverty, discrimination, and the denial of self-determination at the individual and community levels, conditions of human rights violations heavily tilted toward women, as well as children, rural food producers, and the poor in general. Micronutrient supplementation will not satisfy these human rights violations that form the root cause of malnutrition and hunger. Nutraceuticals and functional foods will not provide any more than the stop gap measure of a pill. Medicalized nutrition might ameliorate the metabolic disorder of an individual but it does not feed people sustainably, adequately, affordably, or accessibly over time. Because it does not address these criteria of well-functioning food and nutrition systems, the role of medical nutrition in the health needs of persons throughout the world is highly questionable in the context of promoting food and nutrition security. Even more importantly, medical nutrition does nothing to attend to the human rights violations, including gender discrimination, at the root of conditions of malnutrition and the intergenerational recycling of poverty. Governments' human rights obligations call for their accountability to empower individuals and communities, not the corporate business sector.

Despite the lack of hard scientific support for the claimed health benefits of nutrient components alone or in combination "beyond the correction of deficiencies" (Wahlqvist and Wattanapenpaiboon 2002, 4), functional foods are being strongly promoted in rich and poor countries alike as a promising approach for addressing the increasing rates of overweight, obesity, and related NCDs (Garnett 2014, 12). Obesity and food-related diseases serve thus as an entry point for the food industry to exacerbate fear and manufacture demand for health enhancing products to which it is "ideally placed to respond to" (Scrinis 2013, 4). With its "goal of optimizing your consumption of beneficial nutrients" rather than "just avoiding the bad nutrients," this increasingly dominant discourse requires that we "keep up with the latest nutrition research and expert advice if we are to identify the whole foods or processed 'functional foods' that deliver the desired health benefits" (Scrinis 2013, 4).

Sometimes called "nutritionism," medical—and medicalized—nutrition is a reductive process of transforming the wealth of food, that is, its links to land, water, and human traditions and relations, into foodstuffs as an avenue to deliver narrowly defined nutrient units to defined diseases without attention to dynamic relationships between food, the body, and the physical and social environment around us (Kimura 2013; Scrinis 2008, 2013; Pollan 2008; Dixon and Banwell 2004). The good that medical nutrition seeks to do is further complicated by its alliance with industry that simultaneously blames, victimizes, and profits from those whose capability to demand their right to adequate food and nutrition and to feed others has been violated. Nutritionism, as well as the inordinate focus on agricultural productivities, obstructs attention to human rights, to food systems, and to culture and spirituality.

***

We have seen that medicalized nutrition and efforts to maximize agricultural production developed different pathways in the late twentieth century. The field of biofortification—the process of genetically altering agricultural products to increase crop nutrient load for humans—represents one location where the research and marketing efforts for biotechnological innovation in agricultural production and medicalized nutrition are again coalescing. Similar to the aim of RUTFs' distribution, biofortification aims at reaching "malnourished rural populations who may have limited access to diverse diets, supplements, and commercially fortified foods. Marketed surpluses of these crops may make their way into retail outlets, reaching consumers in rural and eventually urban areas" (SCN 2014, 20; see also Wahlqvist et al. 2012, 662; Bouis and Islam 2012). Mirroring the medicalized market frame of nutraceuticals and functional foods, the current promotion of biofortification is viewed as "the most direct approach to increasing the relevance of agricultural research to nutrition" and with promises of high cost effectiveness (Haddad 2000, 369; see also Meenakshi et al. 2010; Saltzman et al. 2013).[22]

The corporate private sector may of course develop markets, including those based on agribiotechnology and medicalized nutrition products. The effects of these products may prove beneficial for human health and well-being. The preeminence of commodified food and nutrition products however, cannot be presumed to be natural or best. As will be discussed in the following chapters of this volume, best food and nutrition choices and practices need to be established in accordance with local preferences and with respect to people's and food sovereignty. What advances the human right to adequate food and nutrition of women and other marginalized groups in the context of their human rights in general over the life span constitutes best choice and practice; it will differ by location and according to different groups.

CONSTRUCTIVE PATHS FORWARD

As articulated with specific goals and recommendations here and at the end of each of the subsequent chapters of this volume, developing policy to meet progressive realization requires the definitive articulation of women's human right to adequate food and nutrition in documents issued by UN human rights treaty bodies such as the CESCR, the CEDAW Committee, and the CRC Committee, as well as the CFS and others. Women's human rights, the totality of them across the life cycle including their right to self-determination, must be embraced in order that progressive realization of the right to adequate food and nutrition be availed by any and all humans—women, men, infants, girls, and boys—as individuals and in communities. Most food security policies and programs identify women as the main provider of food and nutritional care for entire families. These policies and programs place additional responsibilities on women without calling for a just redistribution of family and community-based care work, or calling the state, as primary duty bearer, to comply with its obligations to respect, protect, facilitate, and provide resources as necessary that are required to guarantee the realization of the right to adequate food and nutrition. Concurrently, food and nutrition policies and programs characterize women and girls as "vulnerable," essentially patronizing them as weak without addressing discrimination and structural violence that deny agency to demand human rights, including the capacity to control partner choices and reproductive lives. Food and nutrition efforts must be reunited under a human rights umbrella where priority is placed on overcoming root causes of hunger and malnutrition. Self-determined, culturally imbued, and community-based autonomous food systems are the foundation of what is known as people's and food sovereignty (see especially chapter 6 of this volume), the suppression of which fuels the market-based separation of food and nutrition. Peoples' and food sovereignty that foregrounds a full and lifecycle approach to women's human rights is necessary both to counter the mesmerizing influence of industrial food and nutrition products and to bolster states' political will to harness the coercive power of TNCs.

We close this chapter by underscoring attention to one general and three specific findings and recommendations.

- A reconnection of women's rights and of nutrition with the human right to adequate food, as well as an embrace and the incorporation of a people's and food sovereignty framework in food and nutrition policy, are critical for the achievement of the progressive realization of the human right to adequate food and nutrition. This general point is detailed at length in chapters 3 through 6 of this volume.
- The Organization of American States (OAS) 1988 *Protocol of San Salvador* brings food and nutrition under one food systems-based, human right to adequate food and nutrition umbrella. We recommend consideration of the *Protocol of San Salvador* as a model for replication at international and other regional levels with the proviso that specific language supporting women's human rights to adequate food and nutrition be included. Among other venues for an enhanced replication of the *Protocol of San Salvador*, we urge the CEDAW Committee to consider the issuance of a *General Recommendation on the Human Right to Adequate Food and Nutrition and Women*. Additionally, at this writing, the CEDAW Committee is finalizing its *General Recommendation on Rural Women*. We encourage the committee to consider inclusion of our holistic concept of the human right to adequate food and nutrition.
- Respected and durable cultural traditions of commensality, gastronomy, and food-based identity (adjusted for gender and other forms of discrimination) represent a holistic social determinate of communities' food and nutrition security; ideally, they help to unite food and nutrition in community practice and policy. The CESCR 2000 *General Comment 14 on the Right to the Highest Attainable Standard of Health* underlines attention to the social determinants of health, an approach that needs to be considered in the policy addressing the right to adequate food and nutrition. Further, *General Comment 14* develops exceptional food systems and cultural relevance language with respect to indigenous communities' relationship to land, food,

health, and well-being. This excellent language needs to be digested, reconsidered, and reflected in the CESCR's, the CEDAW Committee's, and the CRC Committee's concluding observations to states' periodic reports, with respect to, among others, the right to self-determination, food and nutrition security, and health, in all communities and particularly for the most marginalized among them, especially women.

• The CFS 2012 *Global Strategic Framework for Food Security and Nutrition* (GSF) outlines global governance approaches for food and nutrition security prioritizing the human rights legal framework in a living document design. The CFS and its 2012 GSF stress women's human rights and propose practical steps to realize gender equity in food and nutrition policy and practice. The CFS is currently the most democratic space for sharing diverse global experience and developing food and nutrition policy with a long-term development outlook (De Schutter 2014). States need to truly recognize, protect, and strengthen this popularly legitimated arena as the key political space where food and nutrition policy (such as that of the ICN2) is discussed and decided upon, instead of bypassing it—or tolerating and supporting it being bypassed—in order to safeguard only the interests of the corporate private sector.

NOTES

1. For a discussion of the concept of human capability or the capabilities approach, see Sen (1985); Nussbaum and Sen (1993); Agarwal, Humphries, and Robeyns (2006); and Nussbaum (2011).
2. Article 11 of the ICESCR reads:

   1. The States Parties to the present Covenant recognize the right of everyone to an adequate standard of living for himself and his family, including adequate food, clothing and housing, and to the continuous improvement of living conditions. The States Parties will take appropriate steps to ensure the realization of this right, recognizing to this effect the essential importance of international co-operation based on free consent.
   2. The States Parties to the present Covenant, recognizing the fundamental right of everyone to be free from hunger, shall take, individually and through international co-operation, the measures, including specific programmes, which are needed:

      (a) To improve methods of production, conservation and distribution of food by making full use of technical and scientific knowledge, by disseminating knowledge of the principles of nutrition and by developing or reforming agrarian systems in such a way as to achieve the most efficient development and utilization of natural resources;
      (b) Taking into account the problems of both food-importing and food-exporting countries, to ensure an equitable distribution of world food supplies in relation to need. (UN General Assembly 1966, art. 11)

3. Paragraph 28 of CESCR *General Comment 16* also makes explicit reference to women's access to land: "[i]mplementing [ICESCR] article 3 in relation to article 11(1) requires that women have a right to own, use or otherwise control housing, *land* and property on an equal basis with men, and to access necessary resources to do so" (CESCR 2005, para. 28; emphasis added).

4. A screening of the twenty-one CESCR general comments (as of February 2015) for the terms "vulnerable," "disadvantaged," "marginalized," and "discriminated against" as label for discriminated against individuals and groups of individuals revealed the following (see also Table 2.2):

- The term "discriminated against" is only used in *General Comment 5 on Persons with Disabilities* (CESCR 1994; hereinafter *General Comment 5*), *General Comment 21 on the Right of Everyone to Take Part in Cultural Life* (CESCR 2009b), and *General Comment 17 on the Right of Everyone to Benefit from the Protection of the Moral and Material Interests Resulting from any Scientific, Literary or Artistic Production of which He or She Is the Author* (CESCR 2006a; hereinafter, *General Comment 17*). The first two prohibit discrimination of disabled workers (CESCR 1994, para. 25) and discrimination of all persons on the grounds of culture (CESCR 2009b, para. 22), respectively, rather than referring to specific individuals or groups; 2006 *General Comment 17*, however, does refer to "those subjected to discrimination" (CESCR 2006a, para. 21).

- "Vulnerable" and "disadvantaged" are the preferred labels to refer to discriminated against groups from the 1989 *General Comment 1 on Reporting by States Parties* (hereinafter, *General Comment 1*) to the issuance of *General Comment 16* in 2005, except for the 1998 *General Comment 10 on The Role of National Human Rights Institutions in the Protection of Economic, Social and Cultural Rights*, which does not mention any of the terms "vulnerable," "disadvantaged," "marginalized," or "discriminated;" see CESCR 1998b).

  In most cases, these terms are used as the stand-alone labels "vulnerable" (CESCR 1990b, para. 12; 1995, para. 17; 1997a, paras. 10, 16; 1997b, paras. 4, 5, 6, 8, 10, 14, 15; 1999a, para. 4; 1999b, paras. 13, 28, 35, 38; 1999c, para. 6(b)(i), 38; 2000, para. 18; 2003, para. 13) or "disadvantaged" (CESCR 1991, paras. 8(e), 19; 1999c, paras. 16(e), 26, 32, 53, 55; 2000, para. 12(b); 2003, para. 27; 2005, para. 13), but in some cases also as the two combinations "vulnerable *or* disadvantaged" (CESCR 1989, para. 3, emphasis added) and "vulnerable *and* disadvantaged" (CESCR 1991, para. 13; 1994, para. 9; 1998a, para. 10, emphasis added).

- Although the description "marginal" is used in the 1995 *General Comment 6 on The Economic, Social and Cultural Rights of Older Persons*, placing older persons "among the most vulnerable, marginal [*sic*] and unprotected groups" (CESCR 1995, para. 17), it is only with the issuance of *General Comment 13 on the Right to Education* (hereinafter, *General Comment 13*) in the year 1999 that a shift in language toward the concepts of marginalization and discrimination starts to become visible. *General Comment 13* introduces the term "marginalized," which becomes used in an increasingly systematic way in the following general comments, either as a stand-alone term (CESCR 1999c, para. 1; 2009a, paras. 27, 38) or in combination with "vulnerable" (CESCR 2000, paras. 12(b), 35, 37, 40, 43(a), (f), 52, 62, 65; 2003, paras. 12(c)(iii), 37(h), 44(c)(ii), 59, 60).

- Most noteworthy is the almost complete discontinuation of the label "vulnerable" from the 2005 issuance of *General Comment 16* (with the exception of paragraph 38 in the 2009 *General Comment 20 on*

Non-Discrimination in Economic, Social and Cultural Rights, where "vulnerable" appears one last time in combination with "marginalized;" see CESCR 2009a, para 27). The language of CESCR general comments moves toward a combination of the terms "disadvantaged" and "marginalized," initially with both conjunctions "and" (i.e., "disadvantaged *and* marginalized") and "or" (i.e., "disadvantaged *or* marginalized;" see CESCR 2003, paras. 7, 37(b), (f); 2005, paras. 15, 21; 2006a, paras. 21, 18(b)(ii), 20, 34, 39(d), 46) and later with consistent reference to "disadvantaged *and* marginalized" (CESCR 2006b, paras. 12(b)(i), 23, 26, 30, 31, 36, 44, 51; 2008, paras. 23, 28, 38, 51, 59(b), (e), 64, 68, 81, 83; 2009b, paras. 23, 42, 50(b), 59, 68).

5. Women are in some cases explicitly included under one of these labels: in *General Comment 7 on the Right to Adequate Housing: Forced Evictions* in "vulnerable individuals and groups" (CESCR 1997a, para. 10), in *General Comment 13* in "disadvantaged groups" (CESCR 1999c, paras. 16(e), 53), in *General Comment 14 on the Right to Highest Attainable Standard of Health* in "vulnerable or marginalized groups" (CESCR 2000, paras. 12(b), 35), in *General Comment 15 on the Right to Water* in "disadvantaged and marginalized farmers" (CESCR 2003, para. 7), and in *General Comment 16* in "poorest and most disadvantaged or marginalized men and women" (CESCR 2005, para. 21). From *General Comment 17* on, women are no longer explicitly included within the disadvantaged and/or marginalized groups, except in *General Comment 18 on the Right to Work,* which mentions women as a separate cluster *along* with the "disadvantaged and marginalized" (CESCR 2006b, paras. 23, 26, 30, 44).

Inside the general recommendations issued by the CEDAW Committee, women are generally not treated as being vulnerable per se; these general recommendations regulate instead the conditions of those women being particularly subjected to discrimination:

- Conditions that make women especially vulnerable to HIV infection in *General Recommendation 15 on Women and AIDS* (CEDAW Committee 1990, (b))
- Women who are physically or mentally disabled in *General Recommendation 18 on Disabled Women* (CEDAW Committee 1991), *General Recommendation 24 on Women and Health* (CEDAW Committee 1999, paras. 6, 25; hereinafter, *General Recommendation 24*), and *General Recommendation 28 on The Core Obligations of States Parties under Article 2 of the Convention on the Elimination of All Forms of Discrimination against Women* (hereinafter, *General Recommendation 28*; CEDAW Committee 2010b, para. 31)
- Women in prostitution in *General Recommendation 19 on Violence against Women* (CEDAW Committee 1992, para. 15) and *General Recommendation 24* (CEDAW Committee 1999, paras. 6, 18)
- Migrant women in *General Recommendation 24* (CEDAW Committee 1999, para. 6), *General Recommendation 26 on Women Migrant Workers* (CEDAW Committee 2008, esp. paras. 12, 19, 20, 22, 24(i)), and *General Recommendation 28* (CEDAW Committee 2010b, para. 31)
- Women refugees in *General Recommendation 24* (CEDAW Committee 1999, para. 6) and *General Recommendation 28* (CEDAW Committee 2010b, para. 31)
- Internally displaced women in *General Recommendation 24* (CEDAW Committee 1999, para. 6)

- The girl child in *General Recommendation 24* (CEDAW Committee 1999, paras. 6, 12(b)) and *General Recommendation 28* (CEDAW Committee 2010b, para. 21)
- Older women in *General Recommendation 24* (CEDAW Committee 1999, para. 6), *General Recommendation 27 on Older Women and Protection of their Human Rights* (CEDAW Committee 2010a, esp. paras. 27, 49, 50), and *General Recommendation 28* (CEDAW Committee 2010b, para. 31)
- Indigenous women in *General Recommendation 24* (CEDAW Committee 1999, para. 6)
- Female widows in *General Recommendation 29 on Economic Consequences of Marriage, Family Relations and their Dissolution* (CEDAW Committee 2013, para. 49)
- Women deprived of their liberty, asylum seeking, stateless women, lesbian women, and women victims of trafficking in *General Recommendation 28* (CEDAW Committee 2010b, para. 31).

6. The use of the term "vulnerable" to describe discriminated against groups, and women in particular, is continued in other UN documents. For example, all of the Millennium Development Goals (MDGs) iterated in the 2000 *United Nations Millennium Declaration* target attention to vulnerable populations, including MDG 1 on extreme poverty and hunger, MDG 3 on gender equality and women's empowerment, MDG 4 on child mortality, and MDG 5 on maternal mortality (UN General Assembly 2000). Women, however, are not labeled "vulnerable" inside the *United Nations Millennium Declaration*; only children are mentioned explicitly as such (UN General Assembly 2000, paras. 2, 16), along with "all civilian populations that suffer disproportionately the consequences of natural disasters, genocide, armed conflicts and other humanitarian emergencies" (para. 26). In the 2004 *Right to Food Guidelines*, women are mentioned along with but not inside "vulnerable, marginalized and traditionally disadvantaged groups" (FAO 2005, guideline 8.3). However, elsewhere the document refers to "vulnerable groups, especially women, children and the elderly" (FAO 2005, guideline 17.5). The 2012 *Voluntary Guidelines on Land, Fisheries and Forests Tenure* refers to women along with other groups in "women and men, youth and vulnerable and traditionally marginalized people" (FAO 2012, guideline 3B.3), "women and the vulnerable" (FAO 2012, guideline 7.1), "women, the poor and vulnerable groups" (FAO 2012, guideline 17.3), and only includes widows inside the vulnerable groups in "the vulnerable, including widows and orphans" (FAO 2012, guideline 25.6). The 2012 GSF includes women explicitly inside the vulnerable in "vulnerable categories of populations such as women and children" (CFS 2012, para. 44(j)), and "vulnerable groups, especially women, children and the elderly" (para. 75 (step six)).
7. For instance, as pursued in chapter 4 of this volume, the period of pregnancy and lactation attracts private sector interests that can profit by altering breastfeeding-based mother/baby food systems through the introduction of non-traditional feeding cultures and products.
8. For an in-depth discussion on the disconnect between food production and nutrition at the level of scientific discourse, please see chapter 5 of this volume. Chapter 5 further elaborates on the different paradigms and theoretical frameworks that developed as a result of this separation.
9. As noted in chapter 3 of this volume, we know that food practices sometimes reflect discrimination and prompt violence, as in the case of gender and age-based food deprivation, to which purpose the CESCR has expressly stated in *General Comment 14* that tradition and culture (including food traditions) may not trump or jeopardize human rights (CESCR 2000, para. 35).

10. For a brief explanation of the concept of capability and how it is understood and used in the context of this volume's chapters, please go to chapter 6, footnote 25.

11. As of July 2014, the *Protocol of San Salvador* has been signed, ratified, or acceded to by Argentina, Bolivia, Brazil, Colombia, Costa Rica, Ecuador, El Salvador, Guatemala, Honduras, Mexico, Nicaragua, Panama, Paraguay, Peru, Suriname, and Uruguay (see the website of the Department of International Law of the Organization of American States (OAS) at http://www.oas.org/juridico/english/sigs/a-52.html; accessed July 16, 2014).

12. Beyond guideline 10 on nutrition, the theme of realizing women's and girls' right to adequate food and nutrition permeates the *Right to Food Guidelines* with regard to economic development policies (FAO 2005, guideline 2.5); national development strategies (FAO 2005, guidelines 3.5, 3.8, 3.9); legal frameworks (FAO 2005, guideline 7.4); access to resources, assets, and land in particular (FAO 2005, guidelines 8.3, 8.4, 8.6, 8.9, 8.10); education and awareness raising (FAO 2005, guidelines 11.2); support for vulnerable groups (FAO 2005, guideline 13.4); and monitoring, indicators, and benchmarks (FAO 2005, guideline 17.5). Although guideline 16.7 does not specify for gender or other variables, it calls for disaggregated data collection on behalf of early warning systems "to prevent or mitigate the effects of natural or human-made disasters."

13. For more information on the incorporation of the human right to adequate food and nutrition in the GSF, please go to chapter 1 of this volume.

14. As Pinstrup-Andersen (2000, 354–5) reflects back, "[t]he 1984 meeting was heavily influenced by the troubles experienced by the Centro Internacional de Mejoramiento de Maiz y Trigo (CIMMYT) in the development of quality protein maize (QPM), the first major effort by a CGIAR centre to breed for nutritional quality."

15. See also, as noted in HRC 2014, footnotes 18 and 19, French National Institute for Agricultural Research (INRA) and French Agricultural Research Centre for International Development (CIRAD; 2009), Wezel and Soldat (2009), Wise and Sundell (2013).

16. As a case in point, Sundaram (2010, cited in Wahlqvist et al. 2012, 663–4) reports that cheap imports of grain and rice have driven local farmers out of business in Mexico and the Philippines, respectively. What happens when both global and disrupted local markets fail to supply Mexican and Philippine communities with the basic crops they need to survive?

17. In 1991, nutraceuticals were very broadly defined as "any object that may be considered a food or a part of food and provides medical or health benefits, including the prevention and treatment of disease" (DeFelice 1991, cited in Kottke 1998, 1178), ranging from isolated nutrients and dietary supplements to genetically engineered foods, herbal products, and processed foods (Andlauer and Fürst 2002, 172).

18. Some of the private organizations working on nutraceutical products include the American Nutraceutical Association, the Foundation for Innovative Medicine, the American Herbal Products Association, and the Council for Responsible Nutrition (Kottke 1998, 1178). The *Journal of Nutraceuticals, Functional and Medical Foods* is now called the *Journal of Dietary Supplements.*

19. The [United States] Academy of Nutrition and Dietetics (until 2012 the American Dietetic Association) states on its website that "Medical Nutrition Therapy (MNT) is the legal definition of nutrition counseling provided by a registered dietitian," and further that "[t]he application of medical nutrition therapy (MNT) and lifestyle counseling as a part of the Nutrition Care Process is an integral component of the medical treatment for managing specific disease states

and conditions. As such, it should be the initial step in the management of these situations." For more information, please visit: http://www.eatright.org/Health-Professionals/content.aspx?id=6442451339; accessed August 9, 2014.

20. These quotes were taken from the MNI webpage "About MNI and MNI Objectives" (http://www.medicalnutritionindustry.com/about/; accessed August 9, 2014). MNI members include Abbott Nutrition, Baxter, Braun, Fresenius Kabi, Nestlé Health Science, and Nutricia.

21. Past grantees include the Irish Society for Clinical Nutrition and Metabolism (IrSPEN) in 2013, the Greek Society for Clinical Nutrition and Metabolism (GRESPEN) in 2012, the Spanish Society for Parenteral and Enteral Nutrition (SENPE) in 2011, the Dutch Society on Parenteral and Enteral Nutrition (NESPEN) in 2010, the Danish Association of Parenteral and Enteral Nutrition (DAPEN) and The Danish National Board of Health in 2009, and the British Association for Parenteral and Enteral Nutrition (BAPEN) in 2008. For more information on the MNI annual grant, please visit the MNI website at http://www.medicalnutritionindustry.com/mni-grant/2014-grant; accessed August 9, 2014.

22. Prominent and debated examples of the implementation of biofortified crops are the introduction of vitamin A fortified rice (also known as golden rice) in the Philippines (Kimura 2013; Medina 2012; Solon 2000, 516) and orange-fleshed sweet potato in Mozambique (Hagenimana and Low 2000; World Bank 2007, 33–36). For further information on ongoing research and the introduction of biofortified crops and target countries by CGIAR centers, see, for example, Bouis and Islam (2012) and the section entitled "Current Research by the Consultative Group on International Agricultural Research (CGIAR) Related to Human Nutrition" in the *Food and Nutrition Bulletin* "Special Issue on Improving Human Nutrition through Agriculture" (Bouis 2000).

REFERENCES

Agarwal, B., J. Humphries, and I. Robeyns, eds. 2006. *Capabilities, Freedom and Equality: Amartya Sen's Work from a Gender Perspective*. India: Oxford University Press.

Alston, P. 1984. "International Law and the Right to Food." In *Food as a Human Right*, edited by A. Eide, W. B. Eide, S. Goonatilake, J. Gussow, and Omawale, 162–74. New York: United Nations University.

Altieri, M. A. and P. Rosset. 1999. "Ten Reasons Why Biotechnology Will Not Ensure Food Security, Protect the Environment and Reduce Poverty in the Developing World." *AgBioForum* 2 (3 and 4): 155–62.

Andlauer, W. and P. Fürst. 2002. "Nutraceuticals: A Piece of History, Present Status and Outlook." *Food Research International* 35: 171–76.

Asian Development Bank. 2000. *Manila Forum 2000: Strategies to Fortify Essential Foods in Asia and the Pacific. Proceedings of a Forum on Food Fortification Policy for Protecting Populations in Asia and the Pacific from Mineral and Vitamin Deficiencies. 21–24 February 2000*. Manila: Asian Development Bank, referenced in Wahlqvist, M. L. and N. Wattanapenpaiboon. 2002. "Can Functional Foods Make a Difference to Disease Prevention and Control?" In *Globalization, Diets and Noncommunicable Diseases*. Geneva: World Health Organization (WHO).

Bellows, A. C. 2003. "Exposing Violences: Using Women's Human Rights Theory to Reconceptualize Food Rights." *Journal of Agricultural and Environmental Ethics* 16 (3): 249–79.

Berger, M. T. 2003. *The Battle for Asia: From Decolonization to Globalization.* London: Routledge, referenced in Wahlqvist, M. L., J. McKay, Y.-C. Chang, and Y.-W. Chiu. 2012. "Rethinking the Food Security Debate in Asia: Some Missing Ecological and Health Dimensions and Solutions." *Food Security* 4: 657–70.

Bouis, H. E., ed. 2000. "Special Issue on Improving Human Nutrition through Agriculture." *Food and Nutrition Bulletin* 21 (4): 347–583.

Bouis, H. E. and Y. Islam. 2012. "Biofortification: Leveraging Agriculture to Reduce Hidden Hunger." In *Reshaping Agriculture for Nutrition and Health*, edited by S. Fan and R. Pandya-Lorch, 83–92. Washington, D.C.: International Food Policy Research Institute (IFPRI).

Committee on World Food Security (CFS). 2009. *Reform of the Committee on World Food Security. Final Version. CFS 2009/2 Rev.2., 14, 15 and 17 October 2009.* Rome: Food and Agriculture Organization of the United Nations (FAO).

———. 2012. *Global Strategic Framework for Food Security and Nutrition: First Version. Consolidated Version Agreed in the Plenary of the CFS Open-Ended Working Group for GSF—27–29 June and 19 July 2012. Committee on World Food Security Thirty-Ninth Session. CFS 2012/39/5 Add.1, 15–20 October 2012.* Rome: Food and Agriculture Organization of the United Nations (FAO).

———. 2013. *Global Strategic Framework for Food Security and Nutrition: Second Version (2013). Committee on World Food Security Fortieth Session. CFS 2013/40/5 Add.1, 7–11 October 2013.* Rome: Food and Agriculture Organization of the United Nations (FAO).

———. 2014. *Committee on World Food Security. Forty-First Session "Making a Difference in Food Security and Nutrition." Global Strategic Framework for Food Security and Nutrition (GSF): Third Version (2014). August 2014, CFS 2014/41/14.* Rome: Food and Agriculture Organization of the United Nations (FAO).

Coomans, F. and R. Künnemann. 2012. *Cases and Concepts on Extraterritorial Obligations in the Area of Economic, Social and Cultural Rights.* Cambridge: Intersentia.

Dangour, A. D., R. Green, B. Häsler, J. Rushton, B. Shankar, and J. Waage. 2012. "70th Anniversary Conference on 'From Plough through Practice to Policy.' Symposium 1: Food Chain and Health. Linking Agriculture and Health in Low- and Middle-Income Countries: An Interdisciplinary Research Agenda." *Proceedings of the Nutrition Society* 71: 222–28.

Dangour, A. D., and A. Taylor. 2013. "Commentary: The Changing Focus for Improving Nutrition." *Food and Nutrition Bulletin* 34 (2): 194–98.

De Schutter, O. 2014. "The Reform of the CFS: The Quest for Coherence in Global Governance." In *Rethinking Food Systems: Structural Challenges, New Strategies and the Law*, edited by N. C. S. Lambeck, P. Claeys, A. Wong, and L. Brilmayer, 219–37. Dordrecht: Springer Science and Business Media.

DeFelice, S. L. 1991. *The Nutraceutical Initiative: A Proposal for Economic and Regulatory Reform.* The Foundation for Innovative Medicine, cited in Kottke, M. K. 1998. "Scientific and Regulatory Aspects of Nutraceutical Products in the United States." *Drug Development and Industrial Pharmacy* 24 (12): 1177–95.

Dixon, J. and C. Banwell. 2004. "Re-Embedding Trust: Unravelling the Construction of Modern Diets." *Critical Public Health* 14 (2): 117–31.

Douglass, F. 1857. "West India Emancipation, Speech Delivered at Canandaigua, New York, August 3, 1857," quoted in Foner, P. S., ed.1999. *Frederick Douglas: Selected Speeches and Writings*, abridged and adapted by Y. Taylor. Chicago: Chicago Review Press.

Eide, A. 2005. "The Importance of Economic and Social Rights in the Age of Economic Globalisation." In *Food and Human Rights in Development—Volume I:*

Legal and Institutional Dimensions and Selected Topics, edited by W. B. Eide and U. Kracht, 3–40. Antwerpen: Intersentia.

Eide, W. B. 2005. "From Food Security to the Right to Food." In *Food and Human Rights in Development—Volume I: Legal and Institutional Dimensions and Selected Topics*, edited by W. B. Eide and U. Kracht, 67–97. Antwerpen: Intersentia.

Falkner, R. 2009. "The Troubled Birth of the 'Biotech Century': Global Corporate Power and Its Limits." In *Corporate Power in Global Agrifood Governance*, edited by J. Clapp and D. Fuchs, 225–51. Massachusetts: Massachusetts Institute of Technology.

Fan, S., R. Pandya-Lorch, and H. Fritschel. 2012. "Overview." In *Reshaping Agriculture for Nutrition and Health*, edited by S. Fan and R. Pandya-Lorch, 1–11. Washington, D.C.: International Food Policy Research Institute (IFPRI).

FIAN International, Center for Women's Global Leadership (CWGL), Geneva Infant Feeding Association (GIFA), International Collective in Support of Fishworkers (ICSF), International Union of Food Workers (IUF), International Women's Rights Action Watch (IWRAW) Asia Pacific, National Fisheries Solidarity Movement (NAFSO), Coordination Nationale des Organisations Paysannes du Mali (CNOP), Programme on Women's Economic, Social and Cultural Rights (PWESCR), and World Forum of Fish Harvesters and Fish Workers (WFF). 2013a. *Oral Statement on Rural Women's Right to Adequate Food and Nutrition Submitted by FIAN International, Center for Women's Global Leadership (CWGL), Geneva Infant Feeding Association (GIFA), International Collective in Support of Fishworkers (ICSF), International Union of Food Workers (IUF), International Women's Rights Action Watch Asia Pacific (IWRAW), National Fisheries Solidarity Movement (NAFSO), Coordination Nationale Des Organisations Paysannes Du Mali (CNOP), Programme on Women's Economic Social and Cultural Rights (PWESCR), and World Forum of Fish Harvesters and Fish Workers (WFF) to the Committee on the Elimination of Discrimination against Women on Its General Discussion on Rural Women, 56th Session, 7 October 2013*.

———. 2013b. *Written Contribution on Rural Women's Right to Adequate Food and Nutrition Submitted by FIAN International, Center for Women's Global Leadership (CWGL), Geneva Infant Feeding Association (GIFA), International Collective in Support of Fishworkers (ICSF), International Union of Food Workers (IUF), International Women's Rights Action Watch Asia Pacific (IWRAW), National Fisheries Solidarity Movement (NAFSO), Coordination Nationale Des Organisations Paysannes Du Mali (CNOP), Programme on Women's Economic Social and Cultural Rights (PWESCR), and World Forum of Fish Harvesters and Fish Workers (WFF) to the Committee on the Elimination of Discrimination against Women on its General Discussion on Rural Women, 56th Session, 7 October 2013*.

Food and Agriculture Organization of the United Nations (FAO). 2005. *Voluntary Guidelines to Support the Progressive Realization of the Right to Adequate Food in the Context of National Food Security*. Rome: Food and Agriculture Organization of the United Nations (FAO).

———. 2006. *Livestock's Long Shadow: Environmental Issues and Options*. Rome: Food and Agriculture Organization of the United Nations (FAO).

———. 2009. *How to Feed the World in 2050. Executive Summary*. Rome: Food and Agriculture Organization of the United Nations (FAO).

———. 2012. *Voluntary Guidelines on the Responsible Governance of Tenure of Land, Fisheries and Forests in the Context of National Food Security*. Rome: Food and Agriculture Organization of the United Nations (FAO).

———. 2013. *The Human Right to Adequate Food in the Global Strategic Framework for Food Security and Nutrition: A Global Consensus*. Rome: Food and Agriculture Organization of the United Nations (FAO).

Food and Agriculture Organization of the United Nations (FAO) and World Health Organization (WHO). 1992. "Plan of Action for Nutrition" in *Food, Nutrition and Agriculture—5/6—International Conference on Nutrition*. http://www.fao.org/docrep/u9920t/u9920t00.htm, accessed November 5, 2014.

Foner, P. S., ed. 1999. *Frederick Douglas: Selected Speeches and Writings*, abridged and adapted by Y. Taylor. Chicago: Chicago Review Press.

Freire, P. 1970. *Pedagogy of the Oppressed*. New York: Herder and Herder.

French National Institute for Agricultural Research (INRA) and French Agricultural Research Centre for International Development (CIRAD). 2009. *Agrimonde: Scenarios and Challenges for Feeding the World in 2050. Summary Report*. Paris, Montpellier: French National Institute for Agricultural Research (INRA); French Agricultural Research Centre for International Development (CIRAD).

Friedmann, H. 1993. "The Political Economy of Food: A Global Crisis." *New Left Review*, 29–57.

Garnett, T. 2014. "Three Perspectives on Sustainable Food Security: Efficiency, Demand Restraint, Food System Transformation. What Role for Life Cycle Assessment?" *Journal of Cleaner Production* 73: 10–18.

"The Global Game Plan of Big Snack [Editorial]." 2011. *World Nutrition* 2 (2): 55–61.

Green Pastors, J., H. Warshaw, A. Daly, M. Franz, and K. Kulkarni. 2002. "The Evidence for the Effectiveness of Medical Nutrition Therapy in Diabetes Management." *Diabetes Care* 25 (3): 608–13.

Haddad, L. 2000. "A Conceptual Framework for Assessing Agriculture-Nutrition Linkages." *Food and Nutrition Bulletin* 21 (4): 367–73.

Hagenimana, V. and J. Low. 2000. "Potential of Orange-Fleshed Sweet Potatoes for Raising Vitamin A Intake in Africa." *Food and Nutrition Bulletin* 21 (4): 414–18.

Henson, S. and J. Humphrey. 2013. *Preparatory Technical Meeting for the International Conference on Nutrition (ICN2). Rome, 13–15 November 2013. Session 4. What Are the Policy Lessons Learned and What Are the Success Factors. Panel 2: The Influence of Agrofood Policies and Programmes on the Availability, Affordability, Safety and Acceptability of Food. Summary*. PTM-ICN2 2013/06. Rome; Geneva: Food and Agriculture Organization of the United Nations (FAO); World Health Organization (WHO).

Holt-Giménez, E. 2012. "We Already Grow Enough Food for 10 Billion People—and Still Can't End Hunger." *The Huffington Post FOOD—The Blog*, 2 May 2012.

International Food Policy Research Institute (IFPRI). 2005. *Women: Still the Key to Food and Nutrition Security*. Washington, D.C.: International Food Policy Research Institute (IFPRI).

International Network for Economic, Social and Cultural Rights (ESCR-Net) and International Women's Rights Action Watch (IWRAW) Asia Pacific. 2013. "Part Two: An Overview of Women's ESC Rights under ICESCR and CEDAW." In *Claiming Women's Economic, Social and Cultural Rights. A Resource Guide to Advancing Women's Economic, Social and Cultural Rights Using the Optional Protocol and Convention on the Elimination of All Forms of Discrimination against Women and the Optional Protocol and International Covenant on Economic, Social and Cultural Rights*, edited by International Network for Economic, Social and Cultural Rights (ESCR-Net) and International Women's Rights Action Watch (IWRAW) Asia Pacific. New York, Kuala Lumpur: International Network for Economic, Social and Cultural Rights (ESCR-Net); International Women's Rights Action Watch (IWRAW) Asia Pacific.

Jonsson, U. 1981. "The Causes of Hunger." *Food and Nutrition Bulletin* 3 (2): 9.
———. 1993. *Nutrition and the United Nations Convention on the Rights of the Child*. Innocenti Occasional Papers, Child Rights Series, Vol. 5, edited by United Nations Children's Fund International Child Development Centre (UNICEF ICDC). Florence: United Nations Children's Fund International Child Development Centre (UNICEF ICDC).
———. 1996. "Nutrition and the Convention on the Rights of the Child." *Food Policy* 21 (1): 41–55.
Kennedy, E. and H. E. Bouis. 1993. *Linkages between Agriculture and Nutrition: Implications for Policy and Research*. Washington, D.C.: International Food Policy Research Institute (IFPRI).
Kent, G. 2002. "A Gendered Perspective on Nutrition Rights." *Agenda* 17 (51): 43–50.
Kimura, A. H. 2013. *Hidden Hunger: Gender and the Politics of Smarter Foods*. New York: Cornell University Press.
Kottke, M. K. 1998. "Scientific and Regulatory Aspects of Nutraceutical Products in the United States." *Drug Development and Industrial Pharmacy* 24 (12): 1177–95.
Lang, T. 2006. "Agriculture, Food, and Health: Perspectives on a Long Relationship." In *Understanding the Links between Agriculture and Health*, edited by C. Hawkes and M. T. Ruel, 5–6. Washington, D.C.: International Food Policy Research Institute (IFPRI).
Lappé, F. M., J. Collins, and P. Rosset, with L. Esparza. 1998. *World Hunger: Twelve Myths*. New York: Institute for Food and Development Policy.
Lemke, S., A. C. Bellows, and N. Heumann. 2009. "Gender and Sustainable Livelihoods: Case Study of South African Farm Workers." *International Journal of Innovation and Sustainable Development* 4 (2–3): 195–205.
Lemke, S., H. H. Vorster, N. S. Jansen van Rensburg, and J. Ziche. 2003. "Empowered Women, Social Networks and the Contribution of Qualitative Research: Broadening our Understanding of Underlying Causes for Food and Nutrition Insecurity." *Public Health Nutrition* 6 (8): 759–64.
Levin, C. E., J. Long, K. R. Simlet, and C. Johnson-Welch. 2003. *Cultivating Nutrition: A Survey of Viewpoints on Integrating Agriculture and Nutrition*. Discussion Paper BRIEFS. Washington, D.C.: International Food Policy Research Institute (IFPRI).
Lhotska, L., A. C. Bellows, and V. Scherbaum. 2012. "Conflicts of Interest and Human Rights-Based Policy-Making: The Case of Maternal, Infant, and Young Children's Health and Malnutrition." In *Right to Food and Nutrition WATCH* 2012: 31–36.
Lipton, M. 1989. *New Seeds and Poor People*. Baltimore: Johns Hopkins University Press, referenced in Wahlqvist, M. L., J. McKay, Y.-C. Chang, and Y.-W. Chiu. 2012. "Rethinking the Food Security Debate in Asia: Some Missing Ecological and Health Dimensions and Solutions." *Food Security* 4: 657–70.
Madeley, J. 2000. *Hungry for Trade: How the Poor Pay for Free Trade*. London: Zed Books.
Magdoff, F., J. Bellamy Foster, and F. H. Buttel, eds. 2000. *Hungry for Profit: The Agribusiness Threat to Farmers, Food, and the Environment*. Penang: New York: Monthly Review Press.
Maxwell, S. and M. Smith. 1992. "Household Food Security: A Conceptual Review." In *Household Food Security: Concepts, Indicators, Measurements—A Technical Review*, edited by S. Maxwell and T. R. Frankenberger, 1–72. New York; Rome (IFAD headquarters): United Nations Children's Fund (UNICEF); International Fund for Agricultural Development (IFAD).

Medina, C. P. 2012. *Who Needs Golden Rice? PANAP Rice Sheets.* Penang: Pesticide Action Network Asia and the Pacific (PANAP).

Meenakshi, J. V., N. L. Johnson, V. M. Manyong, H. Degroote, J. Javelosa, D. R. Yanggen, F. Naher, C. Gonzalez, J. Garcia, and E. Meng. 2010. "How Cost-Effective is Biofortification in Combating Micronutrient Malnutrition? An *Ex Ante* Assessment." *World Development* 38 (1): 64–75.

Mehmet, Ö. 1999. *Westernizing the Third World: The Eurocentricity of Economic Development Theories.* London: Routledge, referenced in Wahlqvist, M. L., J. McKay, Y.-C. Chang, and Y.-W. Chiu. 2012. "Rethinking the Food Security Debate in Asia: Some Missing Ecological and Health Dimensions and Solutions." *Food Security* 4: 657–70.

Monteiro, C. 2010. "The Big Issue Is Ultra Processing: There Is No Such Thing as a Healthy Ultra-Processed Product." *World Nutrition* 2 (7): 333–49.

Nugent, R. 2011. *Bringing Agriculture to the Table: How Agriculture and Food Can Play a Role in Preventing Chronic Disease.* Chicago: Chicago Council on Global Affairs.

Nussbaum, M. 2011. *Creating Capabilities: The Human Development Approach.* Cambridge: Belknap of Harvard University Press.

Nussbaum, M. and A. Sen, eds. 1993. *The Quality of Life.* New York: Oxford Clarendon Press.

Organization of American States (OAS). 1988. *Additional Protocol to the [1969] American Convention on Human Rights in the Area of Economic, Social and Cultural Rights.* Washington, D.C.: Organization of American States (OAS).

Palmer, G. 2009. *What is Complementary Feeding? A Philosophical Reflection to Help a Policy Process. A Discussion Paper Developed for the International Baby Food Action Network (IBFAN).* Geneva: International Baby Food Action Network—Geneva Infant Feeding Association (IBFAN-GIFA).

Patel, R. 2007. *Stuffed and Starved: The Hidden Battle for the World Food System.* London: Melville House.

Pinstrup-Andersen, P. 2000. "Improving Human Nutrition through Agricultural Research: Overview and Objectives." *Food and Nutrition Bulletin* 21 (4): 352–55.

Pinstrup-Andersen, P., A. Berg, and M. Forman, eds. 1984. *International Agricultural Research and Human Nutrition.* Washington, D.C.: International Food Policy Research Institute (IFPRI); United Nations Administrative Committee on Co-ordination/Sub-Committee on Nutrition (ACC/SCN).

Pollan, M. 2008. *In Defense of Food: An Eater's Manifesto.* New York: Penguin Press.

Poppendieck, J. 2014. *Breadlines Knee-Deep in Wheat: Food Assistance in the Great Depression, Updated and Expanded.* California: University of California Press.

Public Interest Civil Society Organizations' and Social Movements' Forum. 2014. *Public Interest Civil Society Organizations' and Social Movements' Forum Declaration to the Second International Conference on Nutrition (ICN2), Rome, 21 November 2014.*

Quisumbing, A. R. and L. C. Smith. 2007. "Case Study No. 4–5. Intrahousehold Allocation, Gender Relations, and Food Security in Developing Countries." In *Food Policy for Developing Countries: Case Studies,* edited by P. Pinstrup-Andersen and F. Cheng. Ithaca, New York: Cornell University.

Rae, I. 2008. *Women and the Right to Food: International Law and State Practice.* Rome: Food and Agriculture Organization of the United Nations (FAO).

Richter, J. 2004. *Public-Private Partnerships and International Health Policy Making: How Can Public Interest Be Safeguarded?* Helsinki: Development Policy Information Unit of the Ministry for Foreign Affairs of Finland.

Rosegrant, M. W. and P. Hazell. 2001. *Transforming the Rural Asian Economy: The Unfinished Revolution*. Oxford: Asian Development Bank; Oxford University Press, referenced in Wahlqvist, M. L., J. McKay, Y.-C. Chang, and Y.-W. Chiu. 2012. "Rethinking the Food Security Debate in Asia: Some Missing Ecological and Health Dimensions and Solutions." *Food Security* 4: 657–70.

Saltzman, A., E. Birol, H. E. Bouis, E. Boy, F. F. De Moura, Y. Islam, and W. H. Pfeiffer. 2013. "Biofortification: Progress toward a More Nourishing Future." *Global Food Security* 2: 9–17.

Schuftan, C. and R. Holla. 2012. "Two Contemporary Challenges: Corporate Control over Food and Nutrition and the Absence of a Focus on the Social Determinants of Nutrition." *Right to Food and Nutrition WATCH* 2012: 24–30.

Scrinis, G. 2008. "On the Ideology of Nutritionism." *Gastronomica* 8: 139–48.

———. 2013. *Nutritionism. The Science and Politics of Dietary Advice*. New York: Columbia University Press.

Sen, A. 1981. *Poverty and Famines: An Essay on Entitlements and Deprivation*. Oxford: Clarendon Press.

———. 1985. *Commodities and Capabilities*. Oxford: Elsevier.

———. 1999. *Development as Freedom*. Oxford: Oxford University Press.

Shiva, V. 1998. *Biopiracy: The Plunder of Nature and Knowledge*. Cambridge: Green Books.

———. 2000. *Stolen Harvests: The Hijacking of the Global Food Supply*. London: Zed Books.

Smith, L. C. and L. Haddad. 2000. *Overcoming Child Malnutrition in Developing Countries: Past Achievements and Future Choices. Food, Agriculture, and the Environment Discussion Paper 30*. Washington, D.C.: International Food Policy Research Institute (IFPRI).

Solon, F. S. 2000. "Food Fortification in the Philippines: Policies, Programmes, Issues and Prospects." *Food and Nutrition Bulletin* 21 (4): 515–20.

Stephens, G. 2013. "Column: Pharmaceuticals & Dietary Supplements Converge: It Appears the Relationship between these Two Markets May Not Be as Adversarial as It Was in Years Past." *Neutraceuticals World*, 9 September 2013.

Sundaram, J. K. 2010. "Lessons from the 2008 World Food Crisis." *Economic and Political Weekly* XLV (12): 35–40, referenced in Wahlqvist, M. L., J. McKay, Y.-C. Chang, and Y.-W. Chiu. 2012. "Rethinking the Food Security Debate in Asia: Some Missing Ecological and Health Dimensions and Solutions." *Food Security* 4: 657–70.

Timmer, C. P. 2000. "The Macrodimensions of Food Security: Economic Growth, Equitable Distribution, and Food Price Stability." *Food Policy* 25 (3): 283, referenced in Wahlqvist, M. L., J. McKay, Y.-C. Chang, and Y.-W. Chiu. 2012. "Rethinking the Food Security Debate in Asia: Some Missing Ecological and Health Dimensions and Solutions." *Food Security* 4: 657–70.

Underwood, B. A. 2000. "Overcoming Micronutrient Deficiencies in Developing Countries: Is There a Role for Agriculture?" *Food and Nutrition Bulletin* 21 (4): 356–60, referenced in Pinstrup-Andersen, P. 2000. "Improving Human Nutrition Through Agricultural Research: Overview and Objectives." *Food and Nutrition Bulletin* 21 (4): 352–55.

United Nations Children's Fund (UNICEF). 1998. *The State of the World's Children 1998: Focus on Nutrition*. New York: United Nations Children's Fund (UNICEF).

United Nations Committee on Economic, Social and Cultural Rights (CESCR). 1989. *General Comment No. 1: Reporting by States Parties (Third Session, 1989), E/1989/22, Annex III*. New York: United Nations Economic and Social Council (ECOSOC).

————. 1990a. *General Comment No. 2: International Technical Assistance Measures (Art. 22 of the Covenant), E/1990/23, 2 February 1990.* New York: United Nations Economic and Social Council (ECOSOC).

————. 1990b. *General Comment No. 3: The Nature of States Parties' Obligations (Art. 2, para. 1, of the Covenant). E/1991/23, 14 December 1990.* New York: United Nations Economic and Social Council (ECOSOC).

————. 1991. *General Comment No. 4: The Right to Adequate Housing (Art. 11 (1) of the Covenant). E/1992/23, 13 December 1991.* New York: United Nations Economic and Social Council (ECOSOC).

————. 1994. *General Comment No. 5: Persons with Disabilities. E/1995/22, 9 December 1994.* New York: United Nations Economic and Social Council (ECOSOC).

————. 1995. *General Comment No. 6: The Economic, Social and Cultural Rights of Older Persons, E/1996/22, 8 December 1995.* New York: United Nations Economic and Social Council (ECOSOC).

————. 1997a. *General Comment No. 7: The Right to Adequate Housing (Art.11.1): Forced Evictions, E/1998/22, 20 May 1997.* New York: United Nations Economic and Social Council (ECOSOC).

————. 1997b. *General Comment No. 8: The Relationship between Economic Sanctions and Respect for Economic, Social and Cultural Rights, E/C.12/1997/8, 12 December 1997.* New York: United Nations Economic and Social Council (ECOSOC).

————. 1998a. *General Comment No. 9: The Domestic Application of the Covenant, E/C.12/1998/24, 3 December 1998.* New York: United Nations Economic and Social Council (ECOSOC).

————. 1998b. *General Comment No. 10: The Role of National Human Rights Institutions in the Protection of Economic, Social and Cultural Rights, E/C.12/1998/25, 10 December 1998.* New York: United Nations Economic and Social Council (ECOSOC).

————. 1999a. *General Comment No. 11: Plans of Action for Primary Education (Art. 14 of the Covenant). E/1992/23, 10 May 1999.* New York: United Nations Economic and Social Council (ECOSOC).

————. 1999b. *General Comment No. 12: The Right to Adequate Food (Art. 11 of the Covenant). E/C.12/1999/5, 12 May 1999.* New York: United Nations Economic and Social Council (ECOSOC).

————. 1999c. *General Comment No. 13: The Right to Education (Art. 13 of the Covenant). E/C.12/1999/10, 8 December 1999.* New York: United Nations Economic and Social Council (ECOSOC).

————. 2000. *General Comment No. 14: The Right to the Highest Attainable Standard of Health (Art. 12 of the Covenant). E/C.12/2000/4, 11 August 2000.* New York: United Nations Economic and Social Council (ECOSOC).

————. 2003. *General Comment No. 15: The Right to Water (Arts. 11 and 12 of the Covenant). E/C.12/2002/11, 20 January 2003.* New York: United Nations Economic and Social Council (ECOSOC).

————. 2005. *General Comment No. 16: The Equal Right of Men and Women to the Enjoyment of all Economic, Social and Cultural Rights (Art. 3 of the Covenant). E/C.12/2005/4, 11 August 2005.* New York: United Nations Economic and Social Council (ECOSOC).

————. 2006a. *General Comment No. 17: The Right of Everyone to Benefit from the Protection of the Moral and Material Interests Resulting from any Scientific, Literary or Artistic Production of Which He Or She Is the Author (Art. 15, para. 1 (c) of the Covenant). E/C.12/GC/17, 12 January 2006.* New York: United Nations Economic and Social Council (ECOSOC).

———. 2006b. *General Comment No. 18: The Right to Work (Art. 6 of the Covenant). E/C.12/GC/18, 6 February 2006.* New York: United Nations Economic and Social Council (ECOSOC).

———. 2008. *General Comment No. 19: The Right to Social Security (Art. 9 of the Covenant). E/C.12/GC/19, 4 February 2008.* New York: United Nations Economic and Social Council (ECOSOC).

———. 2009a. *General Comment No. 20: Non-Discrimination in Economic, Social and Cultural Rights (Art. 2, para. 2, of the International Covenant on Economic, Social and Cultural Rights). E/C.12/GC/20, 2 July 2009.* New York: United Nations Economic and Social Council (ECOSOC).

———. 2009b. *General Comment No. 21, The Right of Everyone to Take Part in Cultural Life (Art. 15, para. 1a of the Covenant on Economic, Social and Cultural Rights), E/C.12/GC/21, 21 December 2009.* New York: United Nations Economic and Social Council (ECOSOC).

United Nations Committee on the Elimination of Discrimination against Women (CEDAW Committee). 1990. *General Recommendation No. 15—Ninth Session, 1990, Women and AIDS.* Geneva: United Nations Committee on the Elimination of Discrimination against Women (CEDAW Committee).

———. 1991. *General Recommendation No. 18—Tenth Session, 1991, Disabled Women.* Geneva: United Nations Committee on the Elimination of Discrimination against Women (CEDAW Committee).

———. 1992. *General Recommendation No. 19—Eleventh Session, 1992, Violence against Women.* Geneva: United Nations Committee on the Elimination of Discrimination against Women (CEDAW Committee).

———. 1999. *General Recommendation No. 24: Article 12 of the Convention (Women and Health). A/54/38/Rev.1, Chap. I.* Geneva: United Nations Committee on the Elimination of Discrimination against Women (CEDAW Committee).

———. 2004. *General Recommendation No. 25, on Article 4, Paragraph 1, of the Convention on the Elimination of all Forms of Discrimination against Women, on Temporary Special Measures.* Committee on the Elimination of Discrimination against Women (CEDAW Committee).

———. 2008. *General Recommendation No. 26—Forty-Second Session, 2008, Women Migrant Workers.* Geneva: United Nations Committee on the Elimination of Discrimination against Women (CEDAW Committee).

———. 2010a. *General Recommendation No. 27—Forty-Seventh Session, 2010, Older Women and Protection of their Human Rights.* Geneva: United Nations Committee on the Elimination of Discrimination against Women (CEDAW Committee).

———. 2010b. *General Recommendation No. 28—Forty-Seventh Session, 2010, The Core Obligations of States Parties under Article 2 of the Convention on the Elimination of All Forms of Discrimination against Women.* Geneva: United Nations Committee on the Elimination of Discrimination against Women (CEDAW Committee).

———. 2013. *General Recommendation No. 29—Fifty-Fourth Session, 2013, Article 16, Economic Consequences of Marriage, Family Relations and their Dissolution.* Geneva: United Nations Committee on the Elimination of Discrimination against Women (CEDAW Committee).

United Nations General Assembly. 1948. *Universal Declaration of Human Rights, Adopted by General Assembly Resolution 217 A(III) of 10 December 1948.* Geneva: United Nations Office of the High Commissioner for Human Rights (OHCHR).

————. 1966. *International Covenant on Economic, Social and Cultural Rights. 16 December 1966, United Nations, Treaty Series, Vol. 993, p. 3.* New York: United Nations General Assembly.

————. 1979. *Convention on the Elimination of all Forms of Discrimination against Women. 18 December 1979.* New York: United Nations General Assembly.

————. 1989. *Convention on the Rights of the Child, 20 November 1989, United Nations, Treaty Series, Vol. 1577, p. 3.* New York: United Nations General Assembly..

————. 2000. *United Nations Millennium Declaration, Resolution Adopted by the General Assembly. A/RES/55/2, 18 September 2000.* New York: United Nations General Assembly.

United Nations Human Rights Council (HRC). 2011. *Report Submitted by the Special Rapporteur on the Right to Food, Olivier De Schutter, at the Nineteenth Session of the United Nations Human Rights Council. A/HRC/19/59, 26 December 2011.* New York: United Nations General Assembly.

————. 2012a. *Report Submitted by the Special Rapporteur on the Right to Food, Olivier De Schutter: Women's Rights and the Right to Food. A/HRC/22/50, 24 December 2012.* New York: United Nations General Assembly.

————. 2012b. *Final Study of the Human Rights Council Advisory Committee on Rural Women and the Right to Food. Report Presented at the Twenty-Second Session of the United Nations Human Rights Council. A/HRC/22/72, 27 December 2012.* New York: United Nations General Assembly.

————. 2014. *Report of the Special Rapporteur on the Right to Food. Olivier De Schutter. Final Report: The Transformative Potential of the Right to Food. A/HRC/25/57, 24 January 2014.* New York: United Nations General Assembly.

United Nations Standing Committee on Nutrition (SCN). 2014. *Findings from a Review of Country Level Programming in Nutrition-Sensitive Agriculture.* Geneva: United Nations Standing Committee on Nutrition (SCN).

Van Esterik, P. 1999. "Right to Food; Right to Feed; Right to be Fed. The Intersection of Women's Rights and the Right to Food." *Agriculture and Human Values* 16 (2): 225–32.

Wahlqvist, M. L. and N. Wattanapenpaiboon. 2002. "Can Functional Foods Make a Difference to Disease Prevention and Control?" In *Globalization, Diets and Noncommunicable Diseases.* Geneva: World Health Organization (WHO).

Wahlqvist, M.L., J. McKay, Y.-C. Chang, and Y.-W. Chiu. 2012. "Rethinking the Food Security Debate in Asia: Some Missing Ecological and Health Dimensions and Solutions." *Food Security* 4: 657–70.

Walton, J.K. and D. Seddon. 1994. *Free Markets and Food Riots: The Politics of Global Adjustment.* Cambridge MA; Oxford: Blackwell.

Welch, R.M. and R.D. Graham. 1999. "A New Paradigm for World Agriculture: Meeting Human Needs—Productive, Sustainable, Nutritious." *Field Crops Research* 60: 1–10.

Wezel, A. and V. Soldat. 2009. "A Quantitative and Qualitative Historical Analysis of the Scientific Discipline of Agroecology." *International Journal of Agricultural Sustainability* 7 (1): 3–18.

Williams, M. 2009. "Feeding the World? Transnational Corporations and the Promotion of Genetically Modified Food." In *Corporate Power in Global Agrifood Governance*, edited by J. Clapp and D. Fuchs, 155–85. Cambridge, Massachusetts: Massachusetts Institute of Technology.

Windfuhr, M. 1998. "NGOs and the Right to Adequate Food." In *The Right to Food in Theory and Practice*, 6–13. Rome: Food and Agriculture Organization of the United Nations (FAO).

Wise, T. A. and K. Sundell. 2013. *Rising to the Challenge: Changing Course to Feed the World in 2050*. Washington, D.C.: ActionAid USA.

World Bank. 2007. *From Agriculture to Nutrition: Pathways, Synergies and Outcomes*. Washington, D.C.: The International Bank for Reconstruction and Development; World Bank.

World Health Organization (WHO). 2008. *The Global Burden of Disease: 2004 Update*. Geneva: World Health Organization (WHO).

3 Violence and Women's Participation in the Right to Adequate Food and Nutrition

Anne C. Bellows and Anna Jenderedjian

INTRODUCTION

Violence against women is an under-examined barrier to women's right to adequate food and nutrition and their participation in development and food security strategies. This volume was introduced with the question: "When so many call for the inclusion of women and a gender perspective in food and nutrition security, why is the food and nutrition security status of women and girls not improving?" Part of the answer is that violence impedes women from engaging in their own right to adequate food and nutrition and from acting on behalf of their families and communities to the full extent of their capabilities.[1] Furthermore, this violence is rarely acknowledged or anticipated when attempting to address women's particular over-representation among the food and nutrition insecure and to mainstream them into right to adequate food and nutrition work.

Hunger and food insecurity is, in effect, a form of violence against adults and children. The human right to adequate food and nutrition is considered so basic that the United Nations (UN) special rapporteur on torture and other cruel, inhuman, or degrading treatment or punishment, Juan E. Méndez, points out that forcibly withholding food in detention centers, prisons, or schools must be recognized—along with deprivation of water, clothing, health care, and minimum space—as torture or cruel, inhuman, and degrading treatment (HRC 2011a, para. 66; HRC 2011b).

Gender discrimination in public and private spheres is a primary form of violence to individual dignity and rights. Discrimination leverages tolerance for passive and active forms of violence. It persuades against, and reduces capacity to acknowledge and act upon the reality of physical and psychological violences. Silence on the topic of discrimination and related violence constitutes their de facto sanction. Ignoring the violence promoted by gender discrimination propagates a cultural institution of women's "vulnerability" and their lack of self-determination in the domestic and public spheres that support and normalize violence. Violence limits women's capacity to withstand unstable social and economic conditions, excludes them from avenues of judicial redress, and restricts their participation in civil society processes of change. The political will to address violence against women has been uneven and often shallow. With the advent in 2011 of the reorganized UN Entity for Gender Equality and the Empowerment of Women (UN Women) office and the (former) leadership of the Chilean President Michelle Bachelet (2006–2010; since 2014), a new level of confrontation with the passive acceptance of violence against women began.[2] Nevertheless, this attention has not, we argue, adequately addressed or incorporated food-related violence against women, thus limiting the scope of attention both to women's rights and to the right to adequate food and nutrition.

This chapter begins with a discussion of violence as a constituent of the cycle of gender discrimination that frustrates women's realization of the right to adequate food and nutrition. The second section of the chapter, "Violence and women's right to adequate food and nutrition," introduces the theory of structural and other forms of violence and reviews how structural violence reveals itself in food and nutrition practice. The third section, "Violence and women's public participation," opens the subject of violence as a barrier to women's participation in public life. The fourth section, "Institutional and formal recognition of violence against women," presents on the evolution of policy on violence against women at the international and national scales. The fifth section, "Women's right to adequate food and nutrition: linking gender mainstreaming with approaches to address violence against women," examines (*a*) gender mainstreaming as a strategy to move women into public life, but that may underestimate how structural violence hinders as much or more than it fosters women's public participation and self-determination; and (*b*) other ways in which development organizations are trying to address violence against women. Finally, the section "Summary and recommendations" offers practical steps to address structural violence against women in various institutional and organizational settings.

Violence against Women and the Cycle of Gender Discrimination

Gender discrimination directly interferes with women's and girls' access to the right to adequate food and nutrition. This point was addressed by Olivier De Schutter, former UN special rapporteur on the right to food, in his 2012 report to the UN Human Rights Council (HRC), wherein he introduces a cycle of discrimination that results in women's compromised self-determination within both family and society, hampering women's access to decent work, productive resources, and social protection (HRC 2012b, 4). As seen in figure 3.1, the cycle of discrimination goes beyond the largely private space of the household to influence women's experience in the more public spaces of employment and civic life. We argue that this cycle of disempowerment entrenches itself across generations because it is policed with the threat and use of violence designed to repel challenges for change.

A recent article in *The Lancet*, for instance, documents that approximately one-quarter (24 percent) of 9,961 men surveyed by male interviewers

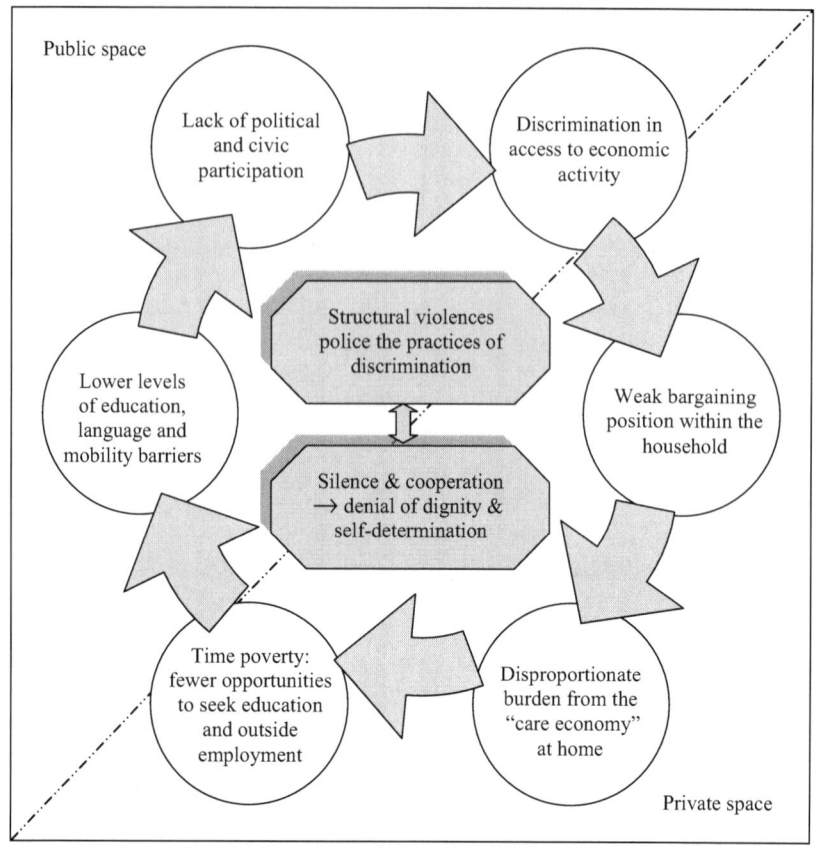

Figure 3.1 How discrimination against women is policed and maintained through violence (adapted from HRC 2012b, 4)

in six Asian countries reported that they had perpetrated forced sex, or sex against the will (i.e., rape) of an intimate partner or non-partner (Jewkes et al. 2013, Table 2). When force is used to bend an individual's will under social conditions that do not interfere, object, or protect that person, that someone is likely to adjust her or behavior to "keep the peace" and safeguard her or his own well-being as well as those for whom she or he cares. Lack of protection from the most basic physical violations reflects a continuum of silence to discrimination that can obstruct women's participation in private and public life. Efforts to promote women's and girls' human right to adequate food and nutrition must overcome not only broad structural aspects of gender-based discrimination, but the overt and covert tools—including violence—that sustain them. The unwillingness to acknowledge and address this violence undermines the strategies, objectives, and goals to mainstream women and a gender perspective into policies and programs related to the right to adequate food and nutrition.

Any type of discrimination associated with groups' minority status, such as ethnicity, religion, race, sexual orientation, class, or disability, reinforces structural violence, creating an "intersection" of interrelated discriminations and oppressions (Carastathis 2014; Crenshaw 1989; Hancock 2007; Mohanty 2003). Violence and its social consequences are often harsher for women than for men in the context of intersectionality, negatively affecting women's positions at work, in the family, and in the community. Violence can result in isolation, reinforce both gendered undernourishment and risks of violence, and place women's health and well-being, as well as that of their children, at risk.

Food-Related Violences

Bellows (2003) proposes the term "food violences" to characterize periodic or chronic physical, psychological, and political harm associated with food availability and food-related work. Notably, the trauma of hunger, malnutrition, and food poisoning that is due, for example, to environmental mismanagement and toxins in the food, affects not only those who eat that food but also those with the social role and responsibility to feed others. Those who feed through food preparation and breastfeeding have the best experience and knowledge of what their households need. "Feeders" require the economic and political capacity to keep themselves and those for whom they care free from food violences. A right to adequate food and nutrition must protect the interests of both "eaters"—as a universal group—and "feeders"—as a subset of them (Bellows 2003, 251).

Recognizing that women are key to family and community food security has brought critically needed attention to their economic contribution and associated rights, ranging from inheritance and education to participation in public policy (see also chapter 5 of this volume). However, this critical assessment can shift work and social responsibility to women without addressing their individual human rights and the barriers they face, especially violence, in accessing their rights. Not addressing violence partially explains why so little progress is being made in addressing the implacability of women's food insecurity. Violence interferes with women's basic human rights to dignity and self-determination, the foundation of the capability necessary to advance claims on rights and entitlements.

In this chapter, we approach the links between violence against women and the violation of women's right to adequate food and nutrition in terms of the correlation between food-based work and discrimination, of how violence relates to poor nutrition and food access, and of the extended impact of these relationships on children.

Women's food-based work can instigate gender-based violence. An existing body of literature reports ethnographic observations of retaliatory abuse for cooking transgressions, like burning food or preparing it at the wrong time. Whitehead (1994) reports cases where violence is perpetrated if, for example, meals are prepared too late, food is insufficient in quantity or quality, or the food is too cold, too hot, etc.. Inadequate food work is perceived as a violation of the husband's exclusive rights to the wife's services or as a breach in the marriage contract. Basically, "the demands for meals and food may symbolize the wider right to command and control which husbands are asserting" (Whitehead 1994, 126–27; see also Beardsworth and Keil 1997; Burgoyne and Clark 1984; DeVault 1991; Dobash 1979). However, besides food-related violence by husbands, other powerful women and men in the family may find violence appropriate and justifiable. From both a woman's original and in-law families, violence can be perpetrated by senior women, for example, mothers (-in-law), grandmothers (-in-law), non-husband adult males, and even sons if food expectations are not met. The cycle of violence can draw in older women who may reinforce gender discrimination by reproducing learned violence in order to protect the small measure of freedom from food labor that may have been earned through age or the availability of a younger protégé.

Research has established many cases wherein gendered power relationships and associated violence have resulted in women and girls eating last, least, and most poorly in the private household space (Kikafunda and Lukwago 2005; Musaiger 1993; Rosalina et al. 2007; Sasson 2012). Intimate partner violence (IPV) affects not only the nutritional status of women but also that of their children: an analysis of Bangladesh's cross-sectional demographic and health surveys by Ziaei, Naved, and Ekström (2012) reveals that women's exposure to violence in the private sphere is associated with increased risk of having a stunted preschool-aged child. Similar results on the negative consequences of intimate partner violence on children's nutritional status were found in different geographic contexts.[3] Based on the growing need for finding links between IPV and its impact on children's nutritional status, Yount, Di Girolamo, and Ramakrishnan (2011) review the gaps in research and propose a conceptual interdisciplinary framework that models how IPV against mothers influences a child's growth and nutrition prenatally and through the toddler years.

We note further that, as the primary "feeders" for their families, women are targeted by corporations in both the Global South and North to increase household food purchases from the global market chain. An increasing consumption of ultra-processed food leads to reduced reliance on local food systems, loss of cultural dietary preferences, and a correlated growth in non-communicable disease (Moodie et al. 2013). As described further in chapter 4 of this volume, a most acute form of industry-based food violence is an attack on the "intertwined subjectivity" of mothers and their infants and young children through the aggressive marketing of breastmilk substitutes and the inappropriate content and timed introduction of complementary foods. This promotional force constitutes a violation of, among others, the *International Code of Marketing of Breast-milk Substitutes* (WHO 1981) and subsequent World Health Assembly (WHA) resolutions. Such violations result in often dangerous and costly feeding practices for infants and young children, especially in the areas with unclean or limited water sources and minimal access to fuel and refrigeration. Critically, the loss of women's control over their infants' nutrition affects their own and their communities' food sovereignty and self-determination at the local level, with regard to the reproduction of sustainable food traditions, including breastfeeding.

We argue that research is needed that can demonstrate the effect of violence against women on their ability to participate (i.e., "mainstream") in strategies to secure their own, their families', and their communities' right to adequate food and nutrition. In order to approach the goal of including women and a gender perspective in food and nutrition security strategies, research and policy must pay attention to the challenges women face, most particularly structural violence that impedes access to women's basic human rights, generally, and when participating in civil society, specifically. This is no easy task. For some, gender research is considered passé. For those who do engage in this field of research, unexpected difficulties often surface: women and girls can be hard to reach because of their restricted mobility in public space and their interaction with non-family members being frequently supervised or controlled. Consequently, related data gathering can be time consuming, unfamiliar, and resource intensive. Nevertheless, a growing number of researchers and policy analysts are developing and applying methodologies that provide improved avenues of human rights research and reporting as well as the attendant responses of policy and accountability.

VIOLENCE AND WOMEN'S RIGHT TO ADEQUATE FOOD AND NUTRITION

Violence takes multiple forms and impacts individual and group survival, well-being, freedom, and identity. It is manifested through "avoidable insults inflicted on basic human needs and more generally life, and lower[s] the real satisfaction level of needs below what is potentially feasible" (Galtung 1990, 292). Violence targeted at an individual or group survival is referred to as direct or personal violence and is identified through events entailing either a passive threat or active force delivered by persons individually or on behalf of groups as actors (Galtung 1969). Galtung introduces two other forms of violence: structural (1969) and, later, cultural (1990). Structural violence is a process aligned with social injustice that "is built into [social] structure and shows up as unequal power and consequently as unequal life chances" (Galtung 1969, 171). Cultural violence is defined by those aspects of structural or direct violence that are legitimized under the terms of cultural practice, tradition, and institution (Galtung 1990, 291). Structural violence is exercised in, and reflective of, societies that are polarized by wealth distribution, life expectancy, and health status, or where there is systematic physical assault or economic or social injustice (Galtung 1969). Structural violence begets poverty, the deprivation of material necessities, and repression; the lack of human rights creates prejudice and humiliation and denies dignity (Ulvin 1998). Structural violence serves to maintain uneven and discriminatory social relations that build upon prejudice directed against diverse groups, for example, ethnic, racial, political, or sexual minorities, rural peoples, the elderly or infirm, the differently abled, or women and children, etc.

Those in discriminated against groups experience structural violence differently. As introduced in diverse theories, such as intersectionality, multiracial feminism, and matrices of domination, uneven power relations overlap, either protecting or further weakening prospects of survival, dignity, self-determination, and identity (see Collins 1990; Crenshaw 1991; Crosby 1995; Fox-Genovese 1994; Hooks 1984; Lorde 1984; May 2015; Nadasen 2005; Zinn and Dill 1996). Wealth can diminish the effects of discrimination, as can location. An impoverished, undereducated, rural-based, and older female farmer from a minority group, for example, will more likely have limited access to health services relative to a younger, urban, and employed woman professional from the dominant ethnic group. Members of discriminated against groups, including women, might claim that they have faced no encounters with structural violence or discrimination. Indeed, it is not uncommon to hear the assertion from women, as well as from men, that there is no longer any discrimination against women. These elites within discriminated groups who do not recognize their social advantages contribute to the perpetuation and invisibility of structural violence. We maintain that each member of discriminated against groups (the elites therein included, although perhaps to a lesser or different extent) remains subject to group-based structural violence. Social support is required to protect all members of discriminated groups against violations of their human rights. Those who experience multiple forms of disempowerment must define and demand rights guarantees from their unique vantage points. Social structures of protection must be flexible enough to evolve and improve over time (see chapters 1 and 6 of this volume).

Systematic violations of human rights are symptoms of deeply embedded structural violence (Farmer 1999). As stated by Ho (2007, 15), "when economic and social structures conspire to limit one's agency to the extent that fundamental human needs cannot be met, then structural violence becomes a structural violation of human rights." A deeply embedded structure refers to a set of beliefs or actions that we take for granted and that we believe are natural. Both Farmer (1999) and Ho (2007) show us how human rights violations—loss of dignity, self-determination, and even life—become accepted as normal and "natural." Consider, for example, the following violations: (*a*) many (poor) women die in childbirth, (*b*) (minority) women are underrepresented in politics because they struggle against cultural norms to command respect, and (*c*) food and pharmaceutical industries promote the popular belief that modern science can produce better nutrition for infants than can mothers (especially illiterate ones). Deplorably, we have come to view human rights violations of discrimination, patronization, and structural violence as inevitable and non-surprising. Perhaps the greatest tragedy of violence, however, is when the individual or groups experiencing the violence themselves believe that it is normal and natural. Bourdieu and Wacquant (1992, 140) have called this "symbolic" or "soft violence," referring to the function of normalizing the terms of structural rights violations, that is, when dominated groups, along with their more powerful counterparts, accept violence and injustice as normal or self-evident.

When systematic human rights violations, like hunger, malnutrition, and poverty, are perceived as normal or natural, they become associated with "characteristics" or "failures" of individuals or groups and not with the failings of the state. For example, we might hear that women are too vulnerable, disempowered, and weak to secure adequate food and nutrition for themselves. Shifting the analysis to the "failures" of an individual who is experiencing human rights violations is a form of symbolic, soft, or structural violence and leverages the capacity of the state to apply superficial programs to "help" these "vulnerable" groups and not address structural issues of inequality, discrimination, and violence that deny women social justice and human rights.

Addressing Structural Violence as a Human Rights Violation in Policy and Research

Structural violence must be addressed as a human rights violation that presses states to meet their obligations to respect, protect, and fulfill individuals' right to be free from discrimination. In the context of human rights, states' obligations impose accountability mechanisms on states' actions, through which rights holders can seek recourse and redress for rights violations. We differ here, for example, from Shepherd (2012), who discusses the "structural violence of hunger" but writes about it as a problem of existing power structures and privileged actors as opposed to a human rights violation. Shepherd borrows from Booth (2007, 112) to describe a process of emancipating vulnerable populations from the oppressions that "stop them carrying out what they would freely choose to do," claiming it will provide a foundation for accountability by all actors and for improving institutional arrangements that perpetuate structural violence.[4] Shepherd further highlights states' responsibility for creating an enabling environment for the emancipation of marginalized groups with constrained self-help capacity and frames a strategy that sounds rights-based but is never articulated outside of food security and vulnerability. As such, Shepherd's plan cannot invoke state obligations and legal accountability. Further, his proposed strategy calls upon the state to "secure" an enabling environment that is vague and possibly easy to manipulate (Shepherd 2012, 206–7). This further reflects a paternalistic approach of emancipating "the vulnerable," versus the clear outline of the respect, protect, and fulfill obligations associated with a human rights-based approach and, importantly, its legal framework. A human rights-based approach to addressing the structural violence of hunger must include an analysis and construction of rights holders—those who face discrimination, and duty bearers, those who have the obligation to respect, protect, and fulfill rights holders' human rights. Duty bearers include those who can help leverage the voice of rights holders experiencing violations, for example, the operators of recourse mechanisms (Burity, Cruz, and Franceschini 2011; Suárez Franco 2011; Valente and Beghin 2006; Viana and Bellows 2014; see also chapters 1 and 6 of this volume).

Despite the clear violation of human rights within existing structural power relations, articulating the terms of *violence* is complicated. Researchers, activists, and policy makers live in social systems of female-male interdependency that are built not only upon long-term strategies for household and community survival, but also upon tradition, family, respect, and love. Interrogating the inconsistencies of power, control, and violence easily threatens the psychological and tangible stability of "the norm." This risk moderates personal testimony, dilutes critical analysis, and weakens political resolve, reinforcing and normalizing oppression. Work in the public sphere is typically in male majority settings that often remain resistant to addressing violence in the context of food and nutrition systems. Sometimes, efforts to identify and confront violence—whether by a rights holding individual, a researcher, or a policy maker—face ridicule or opposition. *Fear of diverse forms of violence in consequence of the expression of a voice is a most essential form of structural violence*: fear of alienating those we care about intimately, fear of accusations of turning a human rights crisis into a political platform for "women's vulnerability" at the expense of food insecure men and children, as well as women. The fear of bearing witness to one's own or others' violation, or articulating a relatively straightforward thesis based on extensive literature and field experience, reflects restraint on personal dignity, intellectual freedom, and self-determination.

Whether as a vague threat or shattering brutality, the punishing function of violence maintains lines of sociocultural rights, norms, and distributions. In this way, violence creates and upholds social structure, including systematic gender discrimination that becomes tolerated as normal even by those who suffer from it.[5] Addressing structural violence, therefore, may trigger surprise and resistance from those experiencing violation because normalized conditions of discrimination and abuse have become foundational to cultural or familial stability. Change disturbs the established equilibrium and those suffering injustice will carry the brunt of adjustment to change, however indispensable and obligatory that change is.

Domestic violence constitutes a grave aspect of structural violence. The 2010 publication by the UN Department of Economic and Social Affairs (UN DESA), *The World's Women 2010: Trends and Statistics*, shows data on women's attitudes toward wife beating acquired in 2009 from the Macro

International website "MEASURE DHS STATcompiler" (Macro International 2009). Aggregated scores for thirty-three countries demonstrate that women tolerate and expect male abuse in general and that poor performance in food work may specifically trigger violence considered reasonable by respondents (UN DESA 2010, 137–38). Presented with five possible scenarios, women were asked whether husbands were justified in beating wives in cases wherein she (*a*) burnt the food (21 percent, yes), (*b*) argued with him (29 percent), (*c*) refused to have sex with him (25 percent), (*d*) went out without telling him (36 percent), and (*e*) neglected the children (41 percent). We note that data vary considerably across different countries. For example, in Jordan and Ethiopia approximately 60 percent of respondent women consider "burning the food" as an acceptable reason for physical violence. If these women are conditioned to accept violence as normal, they will not report beating to the police. Indeed, such an act would probably be viewed as justification for further aggression. Police, most of who tend to be male and married, have little incentive to enforce laws prohibiting violence against women unless they are specifically trained and directed to do so.

Perhaps most daunting to efforts to identify and confront violence limiting women's public participation are women and men's complicit behaviors in familial compacts regarding gendered movement and roles. Women obey and respect; men protect and provide. Obeying and respecting encompass certain food work (e.g., cooking for husband and family) and rules (e.g., being available and able to meet eating expectations of husband and family). Protecting and providing presume the right to make rules. In this compact, women achieve recognition and status for their special or "unique" capability to meet their duties (e.g., cooking better than anyone else *and, not coincidentally, being recognized as the key to food security*), men do not (need to) enact violence against women because the women obey and respect (e.g., women stay home to cook and they do not leave without permission), and women accept work and rules, achieve status, and are not violated.

Case study 3.1 Public participation, structural violence, and conformity with social expectations in Armenia

In an Armenian civil society development project managed by Anna Jenderedjian, coauthor of this chapter, and dedicated to building an environmental education curriculum with public school teachers, including school gardens, some women declined participation in trainings with the justification: "I cannot; my husband will not allow me." Whether true or an excuse, the reason was accepted or at least acknowledged because of the soft, but implicit, threat of violence associated with the terms of potential disobedience and a disruption of roles and terms of women's mobility. It is important to note that the justification was not: "I am afraid of my husband's reaction." Instead, it demonstrated accepted and expectable gendered reactions. "Will not allow" refers back to the compact and acceptance of the terms of "obey and respect" for women and "protect and provide" for men. There is pride and status in "my husband will not allow me," a pronouncement signifying that the women who perform their roles are regarded as "good wives," earn protection, and, consequently, do not face discipline. These acts of obedience and respect are made to the rule-making protector who notably holds the power both of fending off and perpetrating violence.

Slippage between benign and malignant aspects of the power relations inside family compacts can be overlooked until there is an emergency, at which time the crisis is labeled an exception. In an all too common example, on October 1, 2010, a twenty-year-old woman was beaten to death by her husband and mother-in-law (Barsoumian 2010). The neighbors and the press were appalled, pronouncing this a brutal outrage that had no place in society. Men were held up by women and men alike as nurturing and loving; the isolated aspect of this aberration of behavior was stressed. Looking more closely, the press discovered that the murdered woman had twice in vain sought police protection against the violent behavior of her husband since she married in 2008, being turned away due to the "private family matter" and "unimportant" nature of the claim.

Perpetuation of any kind of physical violence is outlawed in Armenia. Nevertheless, when attempting to report against their husbands, women face resistance from police officials and courts (Shirinian 2010), who attempt to "reconcile" husband and wife and avoid their separation, often without registering offences as official crimes (Amnesty International 2008, 28). In the case here under review, the woman's efforts for relief and to run away were not unknown to her neighbors and extended family. Thus, the threat of violence against women is not overtly acknowledged but rather woven into compliance, duty, tradition, and love. In this way, discussing structural violence generally, or violence by men against women more specifically, becomes taboo. It is off limits from acceptable discourse.

Women's groups believe that the situation could be improved by the adoption of a law on domestic violence. In May 2013, this draft law was rejected by the Parliament of Armenia on the grounds that it would be unenforceable, and it was recommended that some of the proposed changes should rather be integrated into the current legislation (Aleksanyan 2013).

Withholding food reinforces structural violence and can attain, with respect to Méndez (HRC 2011a, b), the status of torture.[6] Controlling food access and consumption patterns can further manipulate women and girls to conform to gender norms of behavior according to diverse cultural situations. Research has compiled evidence of family and household patterns of withholding food in order to discipline or control women. Offenders include employers of female migrant home care workers in Israel (Ayalon 2009) and the UK (Eziefula and Brown 2010), in-laws (especially mothers-in-law who may be reenacting experienced abuse), and husbands in Bangladesh (Dalal, Rahman, and Jansson 2009) and India (Raj et al. 2011).[7]

Restricted access to food is certainly not limited to consciously withholding food to discipline or punish. Often women's, and sometimes children's, social status is so low that their hunger is socially invisible or (un) consciously ignored as a function of tradition. A 2004 study in Nepal, for example, revealed uneven intra-household food distribution in 70 percent of homes, with husbands, children, and elders tending to eat first and women last (United Mission to Nepal 2004, 5).

Over- and under-nutrition due to Food-Related Cultural Violence

Controlled food consumption patterns involve direct and indirect forms of forced over- or under-nutrition. Undereating to attain sociocultural norms of thinness is evidenced particularly for women in the Global North; however, this behavior is also increasingly present among men and, with globalized culture norms, throughout the world. In a clinical study in Denmark by Støving et al. (2011, 363), of 1,015 patients with eating disorders, 96 percent were female. In a study of 4,598 adolescent girls and boys in the ninth and tenth grades in the United States, the prevalence of unhealthy weight habits, such as restricting a diet to only one meal per day, vomiting, using diet pills and laxatives, etc., was found to be associated with gender (54.2 percent of girls, 32.1 percent of boys interviewed; see Vander Wal 2012, Table 2). Among those affected, the association varied by race and ethnicity, with eating disorders being most common among non-Hispanic white girls and boys (Vander Wal 2012, 399). A study about the impact of exposure to Western popular culture on dietary behaviors and preferred body image among female adolescents in Fiji, a society where large body image had been considered a beauty ideal for both men and women as recently as the 1980s, revealed both increasing eating pathologies and the desire to be thinner (Becker et al. 2011).

Cases also exist where women are compelled to transform their bodies into a cultural ideal of fatness. In Mauritania, for example, a practice exists that forces girls to consume enormous quantities of food in a practice known as *leblouh*, with the aim of achieving cultural beauty standards and enhancing their chances of a good marriage. Men are typically the ones to decide whether or not to "fatten" a girl because males are generally required to supply the necessary extra food (Popenoe 2004). Women (other than mothers who are considered too soft to impose the work of overeating), however, verbally or physically impose the feeding process (Popenoe 2004; see also Ouldzeidoune et al. 2013).

VIOLENCE AND WOMEN'S PUBLIC PARTICIPATION

> The agrarian reform processes of the past discriminated against women since in most cases we were not direct beneficiaries of the reforms. As peasant and indigenous women we were excluded from the reforms through various legal, institutional, cultural and structural mechanisms. (GCAR 2003, para. 2)

This statement, made by delegates attending the 2003 International Seminar Agrarian Reform and Gender convoked by La Via Campesina's Global Campaign for Agrarian Reform (GCAR),[8] illustrates that structural violence against women limits their capacity to participate publicly in food-related policy that has a direct impact on their lives. It denies women their dignity and self-determination.

The opportunity and growing capacity to claim one's right to participate in public life can change an individual's life and the direction of social development. This is the promise, for example, of gender mainstreaming (UN OSAGI 2002). At the same time, without understanding, acknowledging, and addressing structural violence, urging women into public political life can put them at risk of violence. The failure to recognize this threat jeopardizes gender mainstreaming success. Certainly, there is an imperative to include and center women—whose voices have heretofore been excluded—in public policy. Yet some of these women have fears that violence will be exerted against themselves, their children, and their possessions when they leave the household space. These apprehensions restrain women's physical and political mobility and can prevent their public participation. Those who try to include historically marginalized women must understand the potential and real violence faced from women's families and communities when they transcend traditional cultural compacts related to physical space and social interactions. Complexities of time and expense that are associated with public engagement can trigger violence: the time it takes to participate publically and what that means to women whose workload is, on average, much higher than that of men. Female household members need resources to move into public space, but they often do not have control over the management of these resources. It is irresponsible, if not dangerous, to talk of including women in public life in general, and in efforts to advance the right to adequate food and nutrition in particular, without broad recognition of the costs of this public participation, particularly those associated with the fear of violence.

Case study 3.2 Public participation and fear of violence in public and private spaces in South Africa

Particularly in more rural and higher risk areas, women often keep close to their homes to protect their children and their material possessions. The intention of drawing women out to participate powerfully in the construction of their own lives can, in fact, put them in danger. In a South African study on food security and the right to adequate food and nutrition under land and agrarian reform by Stefanie Lemke, coauthor of chapter 5 of this volume, the difficulties associated with women leaving their homes to participate in a group meeting became explicit. Even when workshop meetings were organized by a women's group for women farmers and farm workers with every available support to facilitate their participation, participant women expressed their apprehensions. Living in isolated rural settings, many women worried that when they left no one would care for or feed their children while they are gone. Worse, these women dreaded the children's potential exposure to abuse in their absence. Finally, these women remained anxious that the material goods of their household would remain unprotected in their absence.

Research demonstrates that women consistently reinvest a higher percentage of their income into family and household well-being than do men (Quisumbing et al. 1995; Schmeer 2005; Thomas 1993). This has led to public policy that supports paid working opportunities, including entrepreneurialism, for women. A resulting problem is, however, that structural conditions of discrimination and the real or implied threat of social and personal violence can inhibit the development of successful enterprises at the point of their expansion and success.

Case study 3.3 Women's limited mobility as an obstacle for entrepreneurial expansion in Mexico

In an indigenous community of the Mezquital Valley, Mexico, a women's cooperative has succeeded during the past two decades in maintaining traditional patterns of cultivation and use of agave (also known as century plant or maguey) through the production of syrup from its sap. The otherwise increasing neglect of traditional practices in this semiarid and marginalized region has been both cause and consequence of mass migration to the United States and the associated flow of remittances back to Mexico. As stated by several members during interviews conducted in October 2011 by M. Daniela Núñez B. de L., coauthor of chapters 1 and 2 of this volume, the cooperative has furthermore enabled members to access credits and grants, reforestation projects, and cultivation and manufacturing training programs. The cooperative's main contribution for some respondents lies in its provision of additional income, for other respondents, in the creation of a space for them to interact and reaffirm their self-confidence as women in the light of their sons' or partners' absence.

Notwithstanding women's greater participation in local public life when male family members are gone, the freedom of the majority of the cooperative members to move beyond the community borders for an extended period was stated to have remained restricted by the fear of their partners' disapproval, even when the partner was reported to be abroad. According to some informants, former cooperative members decided to leave the organization when appointed to administrative tasks requiring them to leave the community on a regular basis in order to avoid confrontations with partners. Unrestrained mobility was described as the privilege of those women who had chosen not to have a partner, or who, having also endured such confrontations in the past, had been able to convince their family members of the significance of their entrepreneurship. Respondents further explained that these few women were the ones taking on the representation of the cooperative and the marketing of their products at regional, national, and international fairs.

Violence and the Invisibility of Women's Experience

Including women's profile in research and policy often meets unexpected challenges requiring time, patience, adjusted outreach strategies, amended investigation methods, and additional resources. Female research subjects and study participants may face family, cultural, or social resistance to meeting with strangers, attending public events, or filling out a questionnaire. Women shouldering irregular migration status or housebound conditions due to health, age, pregnancy, childcare, or other reasons often avoid contact with "outsiders" who are not part of their social group. As a result, they are particularly prone to being left out of research analysis and policy formulation. The recruitment and training of peer interviewers for outreach and to build confidence with community participants in research projects may need to be pulled from a small population pool wherein local networks are extensive, compromising research imperatives of confidentiality and subjects' autonomy to participate in or withdraw from research at will. Many research projects do not plan for these hurdles, do not expect them, do not know how to cope with them, and are not able or choose not to exert the effort necessary to include women into their studies. As a result, especially those women facing the greatest social marginalization figure least representatively into analyses of public and private life, including those related to productive food systems and nutritional health.

Case study 3.4 The invisibility of marginalized women and challenges for related research—United States/Mexico

Community-based public health and nutrition research organized by Anne C. Bellows, coauthor of this and other chapters of this volume, in the US state of New Jersey with Mexican immigrant women was complicated, even when trained female community researchers with similar migration histories collaborated on research design and conducted the interviews.[9] Immigrants in the United States, both documented and otherwise, often face blatant discrimination and social distrust. As the largest immigrant group, Latina and Latino immigrants certainly face this exclusion. The anxiety of irregular status imposes a severe psychological burden and fear for both women and men, reproduces itself into a more stressed and violence prone domestic life, and increases suspicion of outsiders (especially those who come asking questions, like researchers). In a research project on health and dietary practice, peer interviewers were selected who shared experiences with police, judicial, educational, and medical authorities *vis-à-vis* their precarious migration status with the survey respondents. These community-based peer interviewers were able to help address many of the research barriers of language, cultural familiarity, and trust.

Nonetheless, interviews always needed to end early in the afternoons so that the women respondents could pick up and complete their jobs of cooking and other household tasks before their male partners and other family members returned home. The sense of the women respondents' discomfort and even fear was palpable to interviewers as the end of an afternoon approached and the respondents began to worry about how to end the interview and finish their expected household work. When research focus group meetings were organized in a public space like a school or library, attendance often entailed layers of deception by the interviewees so that their departure would not be criticized or missed at home. Interviewed women typically brought their children along, in part because the men were not expected to look after them, but also because women provoked less suspicion of "illicit" behavior when in the company of children.

Overall, the interviewed women generally appreciated the attention that came with interviews because it countered the invisibility with which the women struggle. Nevertheless, they felt exposed and vulnerable because of the unwritten rules that they had broken or stretched by engaging in a non-household oriented event that called on their individuality— rules that carried the structural violence of surveillance and enforcement.

Policy, Women, and the Consequence of Not Acknowledging Violence as the Arbiter of Discrimination

Structural violence that poses barriers to women's participation in public policy and employment must be confronted to improve food and nutrition security for women, their families, and their communities and, at the same time, to expose and deconstruct the violence and discrimination that obstruct change. As is the case of a growing number of national social protection policies, Brazil targets its cash transfer Bolsa Família program to women.[10] As reported in a study conducted by the Brazilian Institute for Social and Economic Analysis (Ibase) in 2008 and referenced by da Fosenca Menezes, Brait-Poplawski, and Menezes Santarelli Roversi (2012, 26–27), "women are more aware of the family's needs and tend to spend the grant on food and other expenditures to meet their children's needs and domestic tasks that are generally undertaken by women" (see also OECD 2007). In attempting to measure the social impacts of Bolsa Família on women's social status, the referenced Ibase survey reports that interviewed female program participants claimed that their involvement led to "greater financial independence (49 percent); greater role in decision-making about expenditure (39 percent); and more respect from partners (27.4 percent)" (see da Fonseca Menezes Brait-Poplawski, and Menezes Santarelli Roversi 2012, 34).

Barriers to women's access to public life are generally not understood in terms of structural violence. As Holmes and Jones (2010) notice, there is often a divide between social protection objectives on the one hand and gender equality and self-determination on the other. In their analysis of social programs in Ethiopia, Bangladesh, Ghana, India, Mexico, and Peru, only two (those of Bangladesh and Mexico) consider the impact of gender role transformations in addition to targeting women as their primary beneficiary groups. Indeed, programs that do not focus on empowerment and equality might further reinforce traditional social roles and responsibilities of women, stressing the obligations of "good mothers" in a private space and further "marginalizing" already excluded (largely self-exempted) men from unrecognized household and child care work, as Molyneux (2006) states.[11] Bolsa Família does not improve women's professional opportunities or empower men in the co-responsibility of caring for the family. We suggest, therefore, that social protection programs like Bolsa Família may divert some needed material resources to women, but the fundamental conditions of discrimination and violence against women remain entrenched. Such programs should strive to reshape conditions that reinforce social inequality and leverage the potential to take further steps toward justice and human rights, including the right to adequate food and nutrition. At the same time, social protection programs targeted at women must be carefully designed not to reinforce gender stereotypes that reify conditions of gender discrimination and (re)launch violence.

Examples in the report *Promoting Pro-Poor Growth: Social Protection* (OECD 2009) demonstrate that social protection targeted at women can both increase and decrease the incidence of domestic violence. Another report by Samson (2008) on the impact of cash transfers on the protection and care of vulnerable children and on the empowerment of families in the context of HIV epidemic in Papua New Guinea finds cash transfer programs, designed to increase women's autonomy, to be successful in reducing their exposure to violence. Concurrent evidence from Bangladesh, however, suggests that domestic violence can increase with cash transfers to women (Luttrell and Moser 2004). Holmes and Jones (2010) report similarly diverse outcomes: whereas in Vietnam social protection has reduced tensions in the household, it has had either no impact or produced increased tensions in India. Social protection policy design instruments must, therefore, take multiple risks and outcomes into account and devise locally tailored programs with participatory evaluation mechanisms that promote women's right to adequate food and nutrition while protecting their physical, psychological, and socioeconomic well-being overall (OECD 2009, 171–73).

INSTITUTIONAL AND FORMAL RECOGNITION OF VIOLENCE AGAINST WOMEN

Institutional and formal recognition of violence against women evolved through long-term local and regional grassroots organizing that successfully orchestrated global scale attention and action in the 1990s. The development of international frameworks defining violence against women as a human rights violation provided an institutional structure that propelled further action at the state level.

International Recognition of Violence against Women

The legal and enforceable understanding that women hold the human right to bodily integrity and absolute freedom from violence against their persons is astonishingly new. Indeed, it remains controversial and contested across the globe. This section introduces the evolution of institutional and formalized recognition of violence against women as a violation of women's fundamental human rights, first at the international, and then at the national levels.

The *Convention on the Elimination of All Forms of Discrimination against Women* (CEDAW; UN General Assembly 1979) outlines the linkages between discrimination and violations of women's freedom, dignity, and well-being. The strength of CEDAW lies in the demands placed on states parties to redress discrimination and prevent further violations, develop processes and terms of accountability, and support the mechanism of the *Optional Protocol to the Convention on the Elimination of All Forms of Discrimination against Women* (UN General Assembly 1999) that articulates procedural steps for claims of violations.[12] During the Fourth World Conference on Women in Beijing in 1995, national governments and the UN agreed to promote gender mainstreaming in programs and policies. The goal was to maximize women's profile in the work and politics of public life and, in particular, to foreground their participation in public policy-making with respect to its impact on women's own lives.

This 1979 convention neither addresses women's right to adequate food and nutrition nor the subject of violence against women. The practice of discrimination as a form of structural violence is not articulated, nor is violence as the constructive medium to maintain discrimination expressed. Twenty years after the adoption of CEDAW, the UN Committee on the Elimination of Discrimination against Women (CEDAW Committee) addressed violence against women in its 1999 *General Recommendation 24 on Women and Health* (hereinafter *General Recommendation 24*; see CEDAW Committee 1999). Violence against women as a barrier to their participation in public life generally, and with specific respect to their right to adequate food and nutrition, is not mentioned in *General Recommendation 24*. In the same year, the UN Committee on Economic, Social and Cultural Rights (CESCR) issued *General Comment 12 on the Right to Adequate Food* (CESCR 1999) that introduces substantive issues arising from the human right to adequate food and nutrition. Whereas this general comment clearly articulates the intention not to discriminate against women (CESCR 1999, para. 1), there is no mention of a link to gendered food violations and violence against women.

Only in the early 1990s was violence against women enumerated in UN resolutions and law. In 1992, the UN Commission on the Status of Women (CSW) established a special working group with a mandate to draw up a draft declaration on violence against women.[13] In 1993, the resolution of the UN Commission on Human Rights (CHR) *Integrating the Rights of Women into the Human Rights Mechanisms of the United Nations* (see CHR 1993) was introduced and further developed at the June World Conference on Human Rights in Vienna.[14] Thereafter, the UN General Assembly adopted, with its 1993 resolution 48/104, the *Declaration on the Elimination of Violence against Women* (DEVAW; see UN General Assembly 1993). In its opening preamble, DEVAW specifically states that "violence against women is an obstacle to the achievement of equality, development and peace" that "impairs or nullifies [women's] enjoyment of those rights and freedoms." Article 1 of the same declaration reads, "violence against women means any act of gender-based violence that results in, or is likely to result in, physical, sexual or psychological harm or suffering to women, including threats of such acts, coercion or arbitrary deprivation of liberty, whether occurring in public or in private life." Article 2 underscores that there is no space wherein violence against women is tolerated, neither at the levels of the household, community, and institution nor at the state level. Article 3 reiterates that women should have full access to all human rights under UN law and provides examples, among others, from the *International Covenant of Economic, Social and Cultural Rights* (ICESCR; UN General Assembly 1966), although none specifically from article 11 on the right to adequate food. Article 4 of DEVAW compels states parties to protect women from violence and prohibits state recourse to excuses of custom, tradition, or religious consideration. Article 4(e) further proposes that states "[c]onsider the possibility of developing national plans of action to promote the protection of women against any form of violence." Article 5 states that the diverse "organs and specialized agencies of the United Nations system should, within their respective fields of competence, contribute to the recognition and realization of the rights and the principles set forth in the present Declaration."

With specific reference to DEVAW's article 4, the 1995 *Beijing Declaration and Platform for Action* articulated at the Fourth World Conference on Women urges all states to "[p]romote research, collect data and compile statistics, especially concerning domestic violence relating to the prevalence of different forms of violence against women" (UN 1995, strategic objective D.2., para. 130(a)). The World Health Organization (WHO), in cooperation with key public health research institutions, women's organizations, and participating countries, developed a common methodology and trained interviewers to survey twenty-four thousand women in fifteen sites and ten countries to evaluate domestic violence in the private sphere of the household (García-Moreno et al. 2005). Notably however, neither DEVAW nor the *Beijing Declaration and Platform for Action* link violence against women with violations of their right to adequate food and nutrition. Further, they link violence with trespass on women's liberty in the public and private spaces, but not expressly with active policy and participation in public decision-making.

The 1999 CEDAW Committee's *General Recommendation 24* mentioned earlier highlights the link between women's health and violence against women (paras. 5, 12(b), 12(d), 15, 15(a), 15(b), 25, 29, 30(f)). Paragraph 9 calls upon states parties to "report on their health legislation, plans and policies for women with reliable data disaggregated by sex on the incidence and severity of diseases and conditions hazardous to women's health and nutrition and on the availability and cost-effectiveness of preventive and curative measures." In the following year, the CESCR issued *General Comment 14 on the Right to the Highest Attainable Standard of Health* (hereinafter *General Comment 14*; see CESCR 2000). *General Comment 14* acknowledges in article 10 that since the drafting of the ICESCR in 1966, "the world health situation has changed dramatically and the notion of health has undergone substantial changes and has also widened in scope." As a result, new determinants of health, such as gender differences and resource distribution, must be taken into account, as must conditions of violence and war.[15] Under this rubric, *General Comment 14* carries forward the work of DEVAW and the Beijing Platform, determining that violence against women is a justiciable violation of the ICESCR in general, and of women's human right to health in particular. Risks to women's health include gender-based violence, with particular emphasis on domestic violence, against which the state is specifically obliged to protect women and prosecute perpetrators under the treaty law (CESCR 2000, paras. 21, 35, 36, 51).

General Comment 14 states that "the reference in article 12.1 of the Covenant [ICESCR] to 'the highest attainable standard of physical and mental health' is not confined to the right to health care. On the contrary, the drafting history and the express wording of article 12.2 acknowledge that the right to health embraces a wide range of socio-economic factors that promote conditions in which people can lead a healthy life, and extends to the underlying determinants of health" (CESCR 2000, para. 4). In addition to gender and violence considerations, adequate and safe food and proper nutrition constitute another set of underlying health determinants (CESCR 2000, paras. 4, 11, 36). Paragraph 11 goes further to identify the importance of self-determination as a critical health determinant in the realization of the highest attainable standard of health, namely, the participation of the population in all health-related decision-making at the community, national, and international levels.

With specific attention to the case of indigenous groups, *General Comment 14* states that "the health of the individual is often linked to the health of the society as a whole and has a collective dimension" that is reflective of the "symbiotic relationship" with indigenous lands (CESCR 2000, para. 27). Herein is found valuable precedence that can be linked to women's greater participation in the human right to adequate food and nutrition, the denial of which constitutes structural violence and the foundation of a human rights violation. First, women's nutritional health is indeed connected to the health of the social collectivities around them, both through the biology of reproduction and lactation and through their sociocultural-based labors on behalf of the food and nutritional well-being of families and communities. Second, as critical agriculturalists, fishing folk, pastoralists, and other types of food producers, women's work is integrated throughout the food system; this work requires participation and representation in public sector decision-making in the context of food and nutrition. Third, women need respect for, and protection of, their dignity and self-determination in the pursuit of their right to adequate food and nutrition *vis-à-vis* possible obstacles posed from state and non-state actors. For indigenous groups, such interference has come from state and corporate actors' intent upon access to traditional indigenous lands, the source of many indigenous people's food and nutrition security, as well as their cultural and spiritual heritage.

As recognized for indigenous groups, denial of, or interference with, women's human right to adequate food and nutrition constitutes a form of structural violence against women; it impedes their dignity, self-determination, and capacity to contribute to an adequate standard of living for themselves, their families, their communities, and wider publics. For example, women's undisputed authority over the best nutritional practices for infants and young children through breastfeeding is regularly threatened through industry efforts to circumnavigate international rules on marketing breastmilk substitutes (see chapter 4 of this volume for a more in-depth discussion on this issue). Additionally, discrimination against women in terms of access to agricultural training and credit, equal work and pay opportunities, and land inheritance rights forces rural women into dependency and undermines their potential for autonomy and equal social and economic participation (please see also chapter 5 of this volume).

CESCR *General Comment 14* provides important tools to extend the specific legal obligations of the state to protect women against gender-based violence. However, while it recognizes food, nutrition, and participatory decision-making as underlying determinants of health, it does not expressly connect gender-based violence with restricted or constrained public participation. In this way, women's right to participate in policy concerning their right to adequate food and nutrition as a function of health is not clearly articulated; the omission constitutes a missed opportunity and reinforces barriers that impede these rights.

General Comment 14 comes very close to a holistic approach to women's right to adequate food and nutrition; it regards (*a*) violence against women as a violation of their human rights and as detriment to peace and social stability, (*b*) food and nutrition as instrumental to health and linked to individuals, communities, and nature, and (*c*) the need for all persons, women in particular, to participate in public policy as related to their own and their communities' well-being. These pieces all stand alone, however, without a unified vision and a link to a food systems approach that should connect production, distribution, access, nutrition, and health and their various cultural manifestations. Integrated, they could illuminate and address key challenges to achieving women's right to adequate food and nutrition, as well as families' and communities' potential for food and nutrition security. To date, no international instrument has shaped such a holistic premise.

In 2010, two important UN reports provided further guidance on addressing violence against women: the *Handbook for Legislation on Violence against Women* (UN DAW/DESA 2010a), and its *Supplement to the Handbook for Legislation on Violence against Women: Harmful Practices against Women* (UN DAW/DESA 2010b). The handbook is targeted at policy makers, civil society organizations, and other interested parties and contains recommendations for adoption and implementation of national legislation to prevent violence against women. The supplement expands the range of harmful practices against women and girls to include, among other things, issues related to nutrition and violence, such as forced feeding, nutritional taboos, and discrimination in food allocation (UN DAW/DESA 2010b, 7).[16] The handbook and the supplement are important tools for national reports on violence against women.[17] These UN guidelines take positive initial steps to connect violence against women with women's participation in public life and with food and nutrition-related violences. However, as follows our critique of *General Comment 14*, these UN efforts miss the opportunity to link and thereby strengthen women's public voice on food-related violences.

National Recognition of Violence against Women

Whereas the understanding of gender-based violence as an issue of human rights, dignity, self-determination, and security for women is improving, the available data to support this understanding remains limited. Inconsistencies persist in terms of adequate theoretical tools, research methodologies, and standardized indicators of violence to measure and interpret the impact of structural violence on women's participation in public life over their life course. As a case in point, the UN Statistics Division's dataset on gender-based violence that demonstrates the magnitude of this human rights violation, shows huge variation among nations. Discrepancies in data collection methodologies may well account for some of the significant differences between countries.[18] At the same time and despite the progress made, some countries still have no laws prohibiting violence against women, and among many of those that have adopted such laws, the enforcement remains weak (OECD Development Centre 2010).

As a response to the World Conference on Human Rights (Vienna 1993) and post-Beijing calls to design a policy response against violence, the UN General Assembly reemphasized in 2006 the need for countries to develop so-called National action plans (NAPs) to address violence against women. It called for (*a*) a multisectoral approach that targets spheres of education, health, judicial systems, social protection, etc., (*b*) policy measures for violence prevention, and (*c*) support programs dedicated to victims of sexual and physical violence (UN General Assembly 2007, para. 8). In 2008, the UN secretary general launched the campaign "UNiTE to End Violence against Women" to facilitate the adoption and implementation of NAPs in all countries by 2015 (UN 2013). In the same year, the UN General Assembly again called on states to address the structural causes of violence in NAPs and other policy mechanisms, such as poverty eradication strategies (UN General Assembly 2009, paras. 16(a), (f), (g), and 17). Also relevant to this context are the resolutions of the UN Security Council on sexual violence in conflict and post-conflict situations, such as *Security Council Resolution 2106 (2013) [on Sexual Violence in Armed Conflict]* on rape as a crime against humanity and weapon of war (UN Security Council 2013).

NAPs are recommended to be multisectoral, as well as adaptive and responsive to each state's specific political, economic, social, and historical context (UN Women 2012a). However, relatively few countries' NAPs use broader definitions of violence against women focusing both on private and public aspects of women's lives.[19] In practice, the majority of NAPs are framed by the research and programming areas of WHO that specifically identify sexual and intimate partner violence, trafficking, and the psychological and sexual trespass against women's bodily integrity. In comparison, minor attention is paid to the impact of violence on women's engagement in public life.

The result is that policy designed to address discrimination against women in public life and spaces—for example with regard to paid work or civic participation—does not have adequate capacity to recognize how structural violence undermines dignity and self-determination and frustrates gender mainstreaming goals. *Without an adequate understanding and capacity, efforts to mainstream women into the arena of human rights and public policy, including the right to adequate food and nutrition and policy related to food and nutrition security, are incomplete.*

Case study 3.5 National action plans (NAPs) on violence against women and their intersections with the right to adequate food and nutrition

A review of the NAPs listed on the UN Women online database *The UN Secretary-General's Database on Violence against Women* (UN Women 2012b) demonstrates that they are primarily focused on domestic violence, sexual harassment, and trafficking. The analysis of the NAPs included in this database through 2012 revealed that NAPs rarely connect violence against women with food and nutrition or with rural livelihoods. Those found are grouped below by category.

Food deprivation. The most commonly addressed intersection of violence against women and the right to adequate food and nutrition is the crime of withholding food. The Australian *National Council's Plan for Australia to Reduce Violence against Women and their Children* uniquely defines food deprivation as a form of physical abuse

(National Council to Reduce Violence against Women and their Children [Australia] 2009, 187), while the Ukranian National Campaign "Stop Violence!" counts it as a form of economic violence within the family (Ministry for Family, Youth and Sports [Ukraine] 2008, 6). Tanzania's government, in its *National Strategy for Gender Development*, repudiates taboos based on traditions that deny women and girls certain foods (Ministry of Community Development, Gender and Children (MCDCG) [Tanzania] 2005, 13, 21). In its *National Action Plan for the Prevention of Domestic Violence in Chile*, food access needs of the elderly are emphasized (National Service for Women [Chile] 2011, 8, 34). Connected with their reports on preventing and combating human trafficking, Ireland includes the denial of food and drink as a means for controlling victims of this crime (Department of Justice, Equality and Law Reform [Ireland] 2009, 228), Canada promotes its Prenatal Nutrition Program to produce positive health outcomes in vulnerable children and their families (Government of Canada 2012, 24), and Moldova links ensuring food for young children from socially vulnerable families with the prevention of human trafficking (National Committee to Combat Trafficking in Human Beings [Moldova] 2010,12).[20]

Correlation of abuse and malnutrition. In its *National Strategy on Domestic, Sexual and Gender-based Violence*, Ireland includes impaired nutritional status as one of the health outcomes correlated with violence (Cosc—National Office for the Prevention of Domestic, Sexual and Gender-based Violence [Ireland] 2010, 46). The United States points to research-based evidence linking improved socioeconomic factors, including better nutrition, with a reduction in gender-based violence (USAID 2012, 19).

Forced sex for food and punishment related to food work expectations. Liberia's NAP alone explicitly articulates these two issues. "Many Liberian women and girls, regardless of age, marital status and ethnic affiliation suffer various forms of violence and exploitation including, gang rape, sexual slavery, forced sex in exchange for food and survival, forced and early marriage" (Ministry of Gender and Development [Liberia] 2006, 9). This NAP's definition of physical violence includes situations when the "wife is beaten or abused for not performing her duties according to husband's expectations (refuses sex, food is late to be prepared, etc.)" (Ministry of Gender and Development [Liberia] 2006, 37).

Gender violence and economic insecurity. In its *National Strategy to Combat Violence against Women*, Algeria reports extending the powers of judges to decide by order, among other things, for food pensions for women (Ministry for the Family and the Status of Women

[Algeria] 2007, 48). Haiti's NAP introduces the need for socioeconomic rehabilitation of violated women through vocational training, microcredit, and productive jobs, in particular for the support of food security (Ministry for the Status of Women and Women's Rights [Haiti] 2005, 18).

HIV/AIDS, gender-based violence, and food insecurity. Per the Zambian NAP on gender-based violence, HIV/AIDS as a form of violence disproportionally affects women. Among other things, "AIDS increases girls and women's vulnerability to poverty and vice versa. It also decreases inter-generational transfer of life skills and knowledge about agriculture and other livelihoods, and reduces adult labour resulting in lower agriculture production and increased food insecurity. The link between [p]overty, gender inequality and HIV/AIDS is inseparable" (Gender in Development Division [Zambia] 2008, 5).

Women in prisons. Algeria reports addressing nutritional needs of pregnant female prisoners through article 50 of its 2005 Code of the Organization of Prisons and the Social Reintegration of Detainees (Ministry for the Family and the Status of Women [Algeria] 2007, 49).

Extra-national development policy. In addressing links between violence against women and food-related abuse, Sweden's International Development Cooperation Agency (Sida) targets its own development aid policy toward this end, referring to protection needs of encamped refugee women foraging for food, fuel, and water (Gender Secretariat [Sweden] 2007, 10), and additionally, women's and girls' property, land, and inheritance rights (Gender Secretariat [Sweden] 2007, 19). Similarly, the United States links the relationship of food-based development aid, for example, the Global Food Security Initiative (Feed the Future), with a goal of "full integration of activities to empower women and prevent and respond to gender-based violence" (USAID 2012, 8–9).

Isolated rural livelihoods. Belize's NAP introduces a special set of measures for rural women who are victims of gender-based violence in order to ensure their access to justice and support in the environment where food-related labors put them at increased risk of violence because of the isolation and lack of service infrastructure in many or most areas (Lewis 2010, goal 2, objective 2–4).

Right to adequate food and nutrition. In South Africa's *365 Day National Action Plan to End Gender Violence*, the country recommits itself to its constitutional guarantees of providing "socio-economic rights such as right to adequate housing, health care services, food, water, and social security" (Government of South Africa 2007, 58).

> *Nutrition education.* Albania introduces the plan to develop "curricula on nutrition, hygiene and family planning for young men and women" (Ministry of Labour, Social Affairs and Equal Opportunities [Albania] 2006, 78). Mongolia's NAP seeks to "[i]ncrease advocacy and facilitate access to information regarding proper nutrition, safe food consumption of clean water and first aid medical services" to achieve gender equality in rural development (National Committee on Gender Equality [Mongolia] 2002, 12).

Women's right to adequate food and nutrition cannot be addressed without attention to the status of all of their human rights over their lifetimes. It is imperative to analyze and attend to discrimination, violence, and structural inequity before, for example, narrowly conceived food and nutrition security intervention programs can make sustainable changes in the incidence and prevalence of malnutrition. Whereas nutrition interventions provide short-term relief for select populations, no sustainable change in hunger, food security, or malnutrition is possible without elimination of human rights violations of poverty, discrimination, and violence against women (see more related discussions in chapters 4, 5, and 6 of this volume). The following case study from India addresses the impact on female children and adolescents who are forced into the adult roles of sexual partnerships and procreation that constitutes child marriage. Our objective is to demonstrate that malnutrition cannot be attended to without coming to terms with violations of women's and girl's basic human rights across their life spans, including the travesty of child marriage.

Case study 3.6 Measures by the Indian Government to prevent child marriage, a prerequisite to the right to adequate food and nutrition for women

India's *National Plan of Action for Children 2005* includes, among its priorities for action, (*a*) nutrition discrimination against girls as a harmful practice, (*b*) the necessity of reducing infant and child mortality, (*c*) the elimination of child marriage particularly, but not only, as it concerns girls, and (*d*) the need to protect adolescents from all forms of physical, emotional, and psychological violence and discrimination, including early pregnancy (Government of India 2005). These issues form critical underpinnings of girls' and women's basic human rights to dignity and self-determination generally, as well as to the progressive realization of their right to adequate food and nutrition.[21]

One aspect of violence protection for girls concerns the reduction of child marriage. According to the most recent available statistics from the Third National Family Health Survey (NFHS-3) carried out in 2005–2006, UNICEF (2013) reports that 47 percent of marriages in India are child marriages.[22] Of these, 56 percent occur in rural areas and 29 percent in urban areas, with 75 percent of child marriages overall taking place within the poorest wealth quintile and only 16 percent within the richest. The close link between poverty and child marriage in rural areas, where most of the early marriages take place, has also been reported by Ghosh (2011). In a survey of twenty- to twenty-four-year-old women in Bihar, 18 percent of married women were married at the age of fifteen and 60 percent were married at the age of eighteen; the median age at marriage was eighteen (Sajeda 2011, Table 1).[23]

Partner violence in marriage also threatens women, perhaps especially child brides who are isolated from their families and whose youth further complicates their ability to stand up for their rights. According to the NFHS-3, 34 percent of women between fifteen and forty-nine years of age experienced physical violence at some point since age fifteen; in 85.3 percent of the cases, the husband was responsible (IIPS and Macro International 2007, 497, 500). Abuse of wives and young children for "disciplinary" purposes usually has a customary rather than a formal and legally condoned character. Devastatingly for women's health, dignity, and self-determination, more women even than men (54 percent of women versus 51 percent of men) tolerate the idea and the practice of hitting or beating a wife as deserved punishment for various transgressions (IIPS and Macro International 2007, 475–77). The correlation between IPV and maternal-child health is indisputable. Among mothers who have experienced IPV, infant and child mortality amounted to 79.2 and 103.6 out of 1,000 births among infants and children, respectively, compared to 59.1 and 74.8 out of 1,000 births, respectively, for those infants and children whose mothers did not experience IPV (Silverman et al. 2011, 22–27).[24] The acceptance and expectation of IPV demands special training for police in order to deliver necessary and appropriate protection for both women and for children.

Child marriage can serve as a form of "sexual service" and bondage in circumstances where there are no traditional securities of adult unions. One result of this situation includes girls carrying out pubescent age pregnancies, as well as relegation to sexual and household bondage. If and when these children are abandoned as extremely young mothers, they are left with very limited options, particularly given their lack of education, unstable social and familial networks, inexperience with paid work, and the stigma of already being "married." Other outcomes of child marriage include child brides' own undernourished status, as well as the likely cyclical and intergenerational reproduction of malnutrition in children (see also chapter 4 of this volume).

In an important attempt to abolish the violence of child marriage, India adopted *The Prohibition of Child Marriage Act* in 2006 (Ministry of Law and Justice (Legislative Department) [India] 2007). The act breaks legal and historical precedence in India by declaring child marriage voidable and prescribes the minimum age for marriage of boys and girls to continue to be 21 and 18, respectively.[25] The act requires the former husband or his parents to pay maintenance money to the girl until her remarriage. Additionally, the act prosecutes the solemnization of a child marriage or cohabitation with a child bride.

Changing cultural practice is slow and the optimistic law has also had to concede serious limitations. The act appears to have driven child marriage underground to a possibly greater extent than it has prevented it. As reported by Ghosh (2011, 204), only six police cases of child marriage were registered in 2008 following the act's adoption in West Bengal, a state with an otherwise relatively high rate of child marriage in India. The law also does not regard child marriage invalid unless one of the contracting parties objects to it within a stipulated period, nor does it prohibit the cohabitation of a child bride with her husband. Furthermore, in the case of divorce or separation, the act does not protect the child bride from non-payment or irregular transfers of maintenance money by the former husband before the woman's (eventual) remarriage (see Ghosh 2011).

In this context, the right to adequate food and nutrition for girls and women rests not in their ability to navigate a difficult world with autonomy. Legal advances notwithstanding, traditional harmful practices consign the fate of many girls and women, sometimes a majority of them, to a system of human bondage that denies basic human rights, including sexual and reproductive rights. Thus, efforts related to nutrition discrimination and infant-child mortality must, necessarily, establish and protect girls' and women's basic right to dignity in the context of partner selection, sexual choice, and reproductive lives. Any other approach will prove unsustainable and unsuccessful.

Providing nutrition interventions, like micronutrient supplementation, food fortification, nutrition education, or cheap or free food, may provide short-term relief for select populations. However, it does not realize the right to adequate food and nutrition for child-age mothers, nor will any of these options empower women unless they include an assessment of, and engagement with, the structural violence routinely faced by these young women. If we hope to mainstream women into food and nutrition security policy, girls must not grow up with the expectation, much less the acceptance, of being sold off into forced marriage or of violent retaliation if they do not fulfill their husbands', other male household members', or elder female in-laws' household expectations. Attention to, and respect for, all which frames human capabilities for self-determination is the critical lens through which food and nutrition intervention for women and girls must be addressed.

Human rights place governments under the obligation to protect the interdependence and indivisibility of women's human rights, including their bodily integrity, reproductive rights, access to education, etc., in addition to their right to adequate food and nutrition. Human rights characteristics of interdependence and indivisibility recognize that the right to adequate food and nutrition will not and cannot be successfully addressed in isolation. The systematic conditions of discrimination and marginalization that conspire against individuals' and groups' food secure status must be addressed. Otherwise, intervention is only a so-called "band-aid," a short-term fix whose affect will quickly wear away because the conditions leading to poverty and want remain constant. For example, girls will have a greater range of life options and human securities if richer men and well-off parents searching for a bride for their sons are not allowed to enact the violence of essentially buying young girls, and, likewise, if poorer families do not sell off their daughters in order to achieve greater economic and social security. The greater range of life options in turn will result in girls' and women's improved self-determination in establishing positive nutritional status for themselves, their children, their families, and their communities. To realize the right to adequate food and nutrition, as also other economic and political rights, states must acknowledge and carry out their obligation to respect, protect, and fulfill girls' and women's human rights to dignity, self-determination, and non-discrimination through legal mechanisms, institutional reform, and a refusal to allow traditional harmful practices to take precedence over basic human rights.

WOMEN'S RIGHT TO ADEQUATE FOOD AND NUTRITION: LINKING GENDER MAINSTREAMING WITH APPROACHES TO ADDRESS VIOLENCE AGAINST WOMEN

Mainstreaming a gender perspective is the process of assessing the implications for women and men of any planned action, including legislation, policies or programmes, in all areas and at all levels. It is a strategy for making women's as well as men's concerns and experiences an integral dimension of the design, implementation, monitoring and evaluation of policies and programmes in all political, economic and societal spheres, so that women and men benefit equally and inequality is not perpetuated. The ultimate goal is to achieve gender equality. (UN General Assembly 1997, 27)

Challenges to Mainstreaming Women in Food and Nutrition Human Rights and Security

The concept of gender mainstreaming was proposed at the 1985 Third World Conference on Women in Kenya, developed in the subsequent decade, and formally introduced during the 1995 Fourth World Conference on Women in Beijing. Although critiqued for cultural insensitivity, Western bias, coopting feminist analysis, technocratic and apolitical practice, and superficial buy-in devoid of needed investment for change (Eerdewijk and Davids 2014; Ferree 2011; Ferree and Pudrovska 2011; Parpart 2014; Smyth 2007; Spivak 1999; Tiessen 2007; True 2011), gender mainstreaming operates as a strategy for many national states and development agencies to design planned actions with a view toward how those actions would have different and specific implications for women and men. The critique notwithstanding, gender mainstreaming provides a now widely accepted framework for centering women in public policy decision-making with regard to women realizing the right to adequate food and nutrition for themselves, their families, and their communities. We argue, however, that gender mainstreaming programs in practice underestimate the power and potential of structural violence as a barrier to women's public participation. Therein lies part of the answer to the book's question of why women continue to experience worse conditions of hunger and malnutrition at the same time as so many claim to recognize and address injustice toward women.

The goal of gender mainstreaming is gender equality, which, in turn, is often understood to be achievable through women's empowerment. Empowerment is considered by many development organizations and increasingly by nation states as a key component of gender mainstreaming and the human rights-based approach, where the ability of rights holders to "protect and advance their rights and interests" (CLEP 2008, 3) is fundamental for participation in establishing rights claims. No universal agreement exists, however, on the concept or measurement of empowerment. In fact, it is a highly contested term that is criticized for the patronizing assumption that powerful groups can bestow, that is, *empower*, weaker groups.[26] The counter belief asserts that marginalized groups must claim power for themselves through a process of internal "conscientization" and external confrontation, not collaboration or partnership with groups that are more powerful.[27] Powerful individuals and groups do not, as a rule, cede power voluntarily. Therein lies the fundamental challenge to the gender mainstreaming effort.

Alston (2009, 141) writes that the key point of gender mainstreaming is to change "the system" to incorporate women, rather than "changing women to fit the system." But whereas proponents have concentrated on reconstructing public sector reception to women's participation, less attention has been given to resistance that women face when departing their households and changing their roles. When gender mainstreaming inadvertently provokes retaliatory violence at women for venturing into culturally unauthorized public spaces, the effect reasserts gendered social norms of power and hierarchy. Few development initiatives and even less research identify and dedicate attention to gender-based violence as an inhibitor of gender mainstreaming, especially perhaps, within the field of food and nutrition security.

On the operational implementation level, gender mainstreaming has been criticized as inadequately planned, lacking political commitment, underfunded, and limited by top-down design by international development organizations (Moser and Moser 2005) and national state agencies (Jones and Holmes 2011; Kusakabe 2005; Schech and Mustafa 2010). Perhaps this is normal as the excitement and theory of program planning at international meetings trickle down through to the grudging realities and dissimilar politics of state budgeting departments and then attempts to implement and adapt progressive new social strategies face the particular realities and resistances at the local level. However, is there still enough commitment behind the relatively popular gender mainstreaming policy to begin to address structural violence as a barrier to women's public participation? We argue: yes—with reservation. Since 1995, many states, as well as public and private development and aid organizations, have adopted gender mainstreaming policies in the areas of food and nutrition security and rural development.[28] The majority of UN institutions (e.g., the Food and Agriculture Organization (FAO) and the International Fund for Agricultural Development (IFAD) and international non-governmental development organizations (e.g., CARE International, Mercy Corps, and Oxfam) working in the field of agriculture recognize the profound importance of empowering women to promote food and nutrition security. Yet, despite the rhetoric of sponsoring gender mainstreaming, in the words of Moser and Moser, its "implementation remains inconsistent" (Moser and Moser 2005, 11) and the formal and symbolic support "evaporate[s]" (Moser and Moser 2005, 15) in practice. The 2009 *Gender in Agriculture Sourcebook* reiterates Moser and Moser's comment and states that "[e]ven when gender is emphasized at the project design stage, it is sometimes lost in the daily grind of project implementation" (World Bank, FAO, and IFAD 2009, 667). Popular policy statements devoid of practical program design, timelines, implementation expectations, monetary support, and monitoring and evaluation to determine accountability, frustrate the intention of gender mainstreaming. For example, the study by Alston (2009) demonstrates that a gender mainstreaming initiative adopted in Australia into national agricultural and drought policy specifically discriminated against women. In Northern Ireland, Shortall and Byrne

(2009, 296) note that the Department of Agriculture and Rural Development "regularly states a commitment to engaging women in their Rural Development Programmes, but how this will be done is never explicitly stated." Research in Tanzania conducted by Mkenda-Mugittu (2003) concludes that gender mainstreaming commitments are often limited to formal and numerical requirements, such as ensuring a certain percentage of women attendance during meetings or a specific ratio of microcredit loans being given to women. The emphasis on "hard data" can effectively detract attention from understanding existing gender gaps, recognizing the social paradigm shifts necessary to effecting real change, and setting realistic output goals and indicators (Mannell 2012; Mukhopadhyay 2013).

Persons claiming to engage gender mainstreaming in the development organizations they represent sometimes give the distinct impression that related efforts to include women in their agenda serve political and agencies funders' goals more than they represent the agencies' own priorities. Such pro forma approaches to gender mainstreaming may, in particular, turn a blind eye to structural violence risks that women face when recruited for gender mainstreaming ends. Tabbush (2010), for example, finds "unrecognized violence" (abstract, 332) that includes high rates of domestic abuse, homicide, and power struggles in the streets to be a major obstacle for women's participation in community-based food aid delivery programs in Buenos Aires that had been designed to include women. In another food distribution example, Grabska (2011) explains how in Sudanese refugee camps well-intentioned aid workers, who saw women as disempowered victims and men as bullies in the food lines, sought to protect women's and children's interests by prioritizing women's access to relief food. This oversimplification of gender roles and women's greater food access was experienced as demeaning to men in public and kindled their retaliation toward the women, putting the women at even more risk.

This short review of literature illustrates how, despite stated goals and political good will, gender mainstreaming is occasionally—or often—only superficially implemented without attention to quality or evaluation. The review also suggests that gender mainstreaming requires more commitment, money, time, and research. The following case study reviews studies on the impact of gendered microcredit intervention and empowerment programs on household stability and violence against women.

Case study 3.7 **Microlending programs: the impact of women's success on household stability**

Microlending to support women's entrepreneurial growth, family welfare, and economic autonomy has been a gender equity and development strategy for lower income groups in poorer and richer countries alike since the 1980s. Early reports of success led to a massive adoption of the program, in many instances without consistent attention to diverse cultural needs and sensitivities that have, in some cases, resulted in increased violence and reinforced existing power relations (Fernando 1997; Hashemi, Schuler, and Riley 1996; Schuler et al. 1996). Indeed, initial attention to the social empowerment aspects of participants' lending support groups and other cooperative tools has ebbed as microcredit itself has become significant in banking enterprises in some locations.

A diverse and still inconclusive body of recent research shows that women's inclusion in microcredit programs can be perceived as intimidating for family leaders (husband, father, or mother-in-law). Data suggest that where microcredit intervention is not carefully planned and articulated within the community, women's success in programs coexists with increased incidence of diverse forms of domestic violence. In Bangladesh, for example, Naved and Persson (2005, 13) report that augmented economic income increases the risk of domestic violence for both urban and rural women. In a meta-analysis of thirty studies on the relationship between an increase of women's income and domestic violence in low and middle income countries, Vyas and Watts (2009) find no clear correlation and identify varying outcomes of microcredit programs even within one country. Among other points, the authors suggest that initial rises in violence associated with women's economic empowerment may diminish over time. A further review of research on microcredit and intra-household relationships in South Asia concludes that most women apply for microcredit in response to their husbands' request. In this tenuous situation, women do not control loan use; however, they carry the legal and financial responsibility in the case of mismanagement and default (Balasubramanian 2012).

Research on the impacts of microenterprise programs should analyze and compare measures of success, including prevention of violence in the context of changing household roles and power relations, social mobility, and economic empowerment. In one such study, Kim et al. (2007, 1798) write that two years after graduating from a twelve month microfinance training program in South Africa *that also included training on domestic violence*, participating women reported that in the "past year physical or sexual violence by intimate partner was reduced by more than half among the intervention group." Women also claimed greater participation in community civic life, as well as a stronger voice in household decision-making.

Development Organizations and Violence against Women in Food and Nutrition Security Initiatives

Development organizations promoting women's participation in food and nutrition security projects find that gender-based discrimination and violence disrupt their objectives. Normally, this interference is located outside the organization, but sometimes, it is subtly exacerbated from within NGOs that have a strong patriarchal culture, with men running the organization and being paid and women carrying out the bulk of the work in part-time, volunteer, or a combination of part-time and unpaid capacities.[29] A number of development organizations are beginning to develop and test means to address discrimination and structural violence directly. For example, in some situations, it is argued that the terms of violence must first be discussed with women among women. In other cases, no change of violence can be imagined without men's involvement.[30] Different factors that may influence training approaches to addressing violence include program size, limited resources, cultural differences, gender makeup of the organizational staff, and the range of projects that the organization embraces.[31] The following case study introduces how the relief organization Brot für die Welt is addressing violence against women.[32]

Case study 3.8 Brot für die Welt: working with men in mainstreaming women

The German ecumenical organization Brot für die Welt (Bread for the World) works with its local partner organizations in Asia, Latin America, Eastern Europe, and Africa to improve food security, promote education, health, and democracy, and overcome violence. The core of the agency's and its partner organizations' work is based on the awareness that many of the current gender roles are disadvantageous not only for women, but also for men. Brot für die Welt strives to integrate gender mainstreaming strategies into projects. In its experience, the promotion of gender equality through gender mainstreaming appears to be most successful when development organizations recognize the need for concomitant engagement by women and men, sometimes working together, sometimes separately. In accordance with the different contexts in which the partner organizations develop their work, Brot für die Welt reports some successful measures for addressing and reducing gender discrimination. These include addressing a wife and a husband as a couple instead of identifying a single head of household, developing women's leadership skills, conducting masculinity workshops, and providing access to credit for women (Brot für die Welt 2009).

Political and natural emergencies disrupt codes of conduct and diminish systems of community protection and policing. Lower status and discriminated against groups can face heighted exposure to social approbation, including gender-based violence in the context of post-disaster crisis and food relief (Al Gasseer et al. 2004; Benelli, Mazurana, and Walker 2012; Pingali, Alinovi, and Sutton 2005; Rodríguez, Quarantalli, and Dynes 2007; True 2012). Response programs to such emergencies can be ill equipped to guarantee a safe and protected environment for those in crisis to travel to, procure, and return safely from points where food, water, and cooking fuel are distributed. Sensitivity to risks faced by women, including potential exposure to gender-based violence, can be uneven, as well as constrained by knowledge, understanding, and limited options in a commonly masculinized emergency management response (Clifton and Gell 2001; Ojaba, A.I. Leonardo, and M.I. Leonardo 2002). Emergency programs have tried various strategies to facilitate women's access to food on behalf of themselves and their families (Gribble et al. 2011; Rossi 2009). For example, many emergency programs now stipulate that women should receive food directly to decrease the diversion of donated food for cash sales.[33] However, allowing women to stand before men in waiting lines for relief supplies can incite anger or jealousy among men that has repercussions for women's safety. The necessity for women to travel to distribution sites, sometimes through spaces in which they customarily are not allowed, with or without escort, and possibly leaving their few possessions and children unprotected, can generate dangerous predicaments (Gell 1999). The program strategy to supply food to women alone, therefore, carries with it many problems and may not be able to ensure women's and families' right to, and need for, adequate food and nutrition in emergencies. One clear conclusion is that the potential exposure to gender-based violence must figure into emergency relief planning. To the maximum extent possible, evaluating potential risk and planning related safety measures must include women from affected communities (Clifton and Gell 2001).

Reflective gender mainstreaming remains central to any policy, program, and project aimed at improving food and nutrition security. Any intervention design must consider potential changes in social and gender structures and assess the opportunities and risks associated with gender-based violence. This includes any social protection program that is based on states' obligation to fulfill the right to adequate food and nutrition, especially for marginalized groups with constrained self-help capacity.

Violence and the Ongoing Need for Gender Mainstreaming

We have argued that gender-based structural violence lies at the heart of why women's and gender perspectives are not adequately attended to in food and nutrition policy, and women's and girls' food and nutrition status are not improving. The roots of structural violence lie in efforts to maintain and police uneven social power relations. The acceptance of violence—physically and psychologically enacted or threatened—as normal parades under various guises. This includes certain traditional practices of discrimination that "other cultures" enact, as well as the rebuff by elite groups that believe that they themselves are unaffected and who state that "the 'gender problem' is long since solved," and even, "remaining voices are hysterical."

Indeed, an emerging paradigm shift is slowly beginning to address structural violence as a factor delimiting women's public sector engagement in social and economic lives and their participation in policy interventions. Such changes need, however, to grow much further. Developing, monitoring, and evaluating policy around violence against women must take into consideration violations concerning women's and girls' right to adequate food and nutrition. Likewise, those engaged in food and nutrition security work must recognize, anticipate, plan for, and monitor the structural violence that women must overcome to participate in efforts to realize the capability to demand their basic economic, social, and cultural human rights.

The claim that gender as a category of discrimination is passé and not relevant for further inquiry and action requires scrutiny. On the one hand, gender mainstreaming has been integrated into the legal systems of many countries since the *Beijing Declaration and Platform for Action* (UN 1995), for example, through the introduction of quota systems for women in elite political structures, such as parliaments and other governmental bodies. On the other hand, less effort has been made in addressing women's participation when low income status, extreme poverty, rurality, or other factors magnify, complicate, and differentiate discrimination (see HRC 2012a).[34] In other words, gender mainstreaming is too often not fully achieved and even stalls in the service of relatively powerful women who then join the ranks of those saying the "gender problem" has been solved. The result of closing the door on the very open issue of gender discrimination both reinforces discrimination against low income, less educated, rural, and other marginalized groups, and frustrates opportunities to evolve a universal and determined embrace for women's right to dignity and self-determination. Recognizing the lines of advantage and discrimination among women would benefit, we argue, from an examination of the social theory of intersecting power relations and a closer examination of the human rights principle of non-discrimination. To this end, gender mainstreaming programs should invite civil society oversight, including participating NGOs and, importantly, their beneficiaries, for monitoring and advocating on behalf of gender mainstreaming education broad recruitment for participation. This, we hope, will encourage a focus on more discriminated against groups of women who face the most aggressive forms of structural violence, directly inhibiting their capability to participate socially and publically in food and nutrition policy, security, and human rights.

SUMMARY AND RECOMMENDATIONS

In summary, women's and girls' right to adequate food and nutrition is predicated upon the fulfillment of their basic rights with dignity, as outlined in CEDAW, and must be in accordance with ICESCR article 11 and *General Comment 12*. Mainstreaming women and girls into food and nutrition security programs must address the structural conditions of gender-based violence in private and public spheres, as well as gender discrimination more generally. To this end, we make the following recommendations:

General Recommendations Related to Economic, Social, and Cultural Rights and the Right to Adequate Food and Nutrition

To progress toward the goal of including women and a gender perspective in food and nutrition security, civil society organizations, researchers, and policy makers must recognize that (*a*) women's right to adequate food and nutrition is not realizable in isolation from all of their human rights and (*b*) the multiple barriers of structural violence that women face when being "mainstreamed" into existing food, nutrition, and agriculture programs should be addressed. Adequate resources to address, and for redress and resolve, must be available for research and policy development with respect to challenges in women's lives.

Recommendations Related to the United Nations Committee on Economic, Social and Cultural Rights (CESCR)

The CESCR reviews states parties' periodic reports on the right to adequate food and nutrition, as well as the parallel civil society reports. According to the 2005 FAO *Voluntary Guidelines to Support the Progressive Realization of the Right to Adequate Food in the Context of National Food Security* (FAO 2005),[35] the states parties' review should include attention to the critical engagement of civil society in the development of democratic processes of participation in prioritizing goals, monitoring the progressive realization, data collection and interpretation, and reporting (FAO 2005, esp. guidelines 1, 6, 13, 37). The CESCR should consider how well states parties' and civil society reports incorporate women's specific access to, and violations of, the right to adequate food and nutrition, and also, the degree to which their own voices and presence are reflected in the reporting.

Recommendations Related to the United Nations Committee on the Elimination of Discrimination against Women (CEDAW Committee)

The CEDAW convention does not specifically articulate women's unrealized right and unequal access to food and nutrition as a form of discrimination against women. Unlike topics such as employment, political representation, and education, national and international gender mainstreaming programs are rarely constructed to attend to the right to adequate food and nutrition. One outcome is that related food and nutrition human rights violations against women are rarely included in states parties' periodic reports on discrimination against women for submission to the CEDAW Committee. National and international gender mainstreaming objectives and programs that promote women's right to adequate food and nutrition would benefit if the CEDAW Committee made public more comments on related violations. Further, those comments should be framed in terms of structural violence against women. Consideration of issuing a *General Recommendation on the Human Right to Adequate Food and Nutrition and Women* is encouraged (see also chapter 6 of this volume). Additionally, the incorporation of the right to adequate food and nutrition into other new and existing general recommendations would be welcomed.

Violations of women's right to adequate food and nutrition should be framed in the context of violence against women. The *Declaration on the Elimination of Violence against Women* (DEVAW) does not have its own committee; violations are handled by the CEDAW Committee. The range of violence against women identified in articles 1–4 of DEVAW has been narrowly interpreted in the practice of monitoring violence through WHO and NAPs. The result is a monitoring and accountability approach that is not designed in theory or practice to analyze structural violence as measured in loss of public voice and participation. The CEDAW Committee should in general apply DEVAW to its review of gender mainstreaming in states parties' periodic reports, and in specific with regard to violations of women's access to adequate food and nutrition.

Recommendations for States and Civil Society Organizations

First of all, governments must create and maintain space for civil society to participate in the formulation of NAPs and further, governments should commit to take steps to implement the NAPs recommendations. Further, governments' NAPs against gender-based violence must recognize connections between violence against women and food, for example, food deprivation, forced sex for food, punishment related to food work expectations, cultural food taboos, and types of economic violence. At the same time, any gender mainstreaming effort should reflect on the human rights framework, prioritize the involvement and participation of those whose rights are discriminated against, and be shaped and implemented with an attention to any actual and potential risks of violences. By this, we mean that gender mainstreaming efforts should include an analysis and construction of rights holders (those who face discrimination) and duty bearers (those who have the obligation to respect, protect, and fulfill the human rights of the rights holders, including the operators of the recourse mechanisms who can help leverage the voice of rights holders experiencing violations; see also chapters 1 and 6 of this volume).

Recommendations for Researchers

Academic research should further investigate the linkages between structural violence, women's right to adequate food and nutrition, and gender mainstreaming. Participatory and action-based research methods must be integrated into study designs that prioritize strategies to include marginalized and isolated women's experience into published knowledge and policy development. Further studies should include difficult to reach and understudied groups that experience violence, such as the elderly, persons with irregular immigration status, and traumatized women, men, and children. Researchers must pay close attention to, and mitigate, violence that women may face for participation in research projects that takes them outside of culturally bound roles.

NOTES

1. For a discussion of human capability or the capabilities approach, see Agarwal et al. (2005), Nussbaum (2011), Nussbaum and Sen (1993), and Sen (1985).
2. In July 2010, the UN General Assembly created UN Women, bringing together under one roof the Division for the Advancement of Women (DAW), the International Research and Training Institute for the Advancement of Women (INSTRAW), the Office of the Special Adviser on Gender Issues and Advancement of Women (OSAGI), and the United Nations Development Fund for Women (UNIFEM).
3. The negative consequences of IPV on children's nutritional status have been documented for India (Ackerson and Subramanian 2008), Brazil (Hasselmann and Reichenheim 2006), Egypt, Honduras, Kenya, Malawi, and Rwanda (Rico et al. 2011), Liberia (Sobkoviak, Yount, and Halim 2012), and Nicaragua (Salazar et al. 2012).
4. For a more detailed discussion on the use of the concept of vulnerability, please see chapter 2 of this volume.
5. For analogies between the theory and practice of women's rights, human rights, and the right to adequate food and nutrition movements *vis-à-vis* diverse violences, please see Bellows (2003).
6. As mentioned in the opening section of this chapter, the UN special rapporteur on torture and other cruel, inhuman or degrading treatment or punishment, Juan E. Méndez, points out that forcibly withholding food in detention centers, prisons, or schools must be recognized as torture or cruel, inhuman, and degrading treatment (HRC 2011a, para. 66; HRC 2011b).
7. Regarding family and household-based food withholding, Ayalon (2009) states that, in Israel, out of 245 interviewed female migrant home care workers, 43.7 percent reported receiving inadequate food, 24.9 percent experienced physical harassment, and 24.9 percent reported sexual harassment. Eziefula and Brown (2010) refer to a study conducted among migrant domestic workers from resource poor countries in London in 2005–2006, where 86 percent of the respondents reported working over sixteen hours a day, 70 percent

reported psychological abuse, 23 percent physical abuse, and 71 percent food deprivation. Raj et al. (2011) report on in-law aggression toward pregnant women (especially by mothers-in-law who may be reenacting experienced abuse) that includes food denial, forced heavy domestic labor, and efforts to prevent medical care. Dalal, Rahman, and Jansson (2009) interviewed 4,411 married women in Bangladesh between fourteen and forty-nine years of age, of which 5 percent claimed to have suffered food-related abuse, including full or partial restriction of food intake by an intimate partner.

8. The GCAR was initiated by La Via Campesina and its member organizations, such as Coordinadora Latinoamericana de Organizaciones del Campo (CLOC) and FIAN International. The International Seminar Agrarian Reform and Gender took place in Cochambamba, Bolivia, in June 2003. For more information about the GCAR, please see Borras (2008). For information on the topics discussed during the seminar, please see Monsalve Suárez (2006).

9. For background information on this community-based public health and nutrition research involving Mexican immigrant women in the US state of New Jersey, see Bellows, Alcaraz Velasco, and Vivar (2010) and Schefske et al. (2010).

10. Further examples of national social protection policies that target women are Malawi's Zomba Cash Transfer Program, Nicaragua's Social Safety Net (*Red de Protección Social*), Chile's Chile in Solidarity (*Chile Solidario*), Colombia's Families in Action program (*Familias en Acción*), and the US Special Supplemental Nutrition Program for Women, Infants and Children (WIC).

11. Please see chapter 5 of this volume for a critical discussion of the concept of empowerment.

12. See also chapter 1 of this volume for a brief discussion of the history of CEDAW.

13. The CSW was originally established in February 1946 as a sub-commission of the Commission on Human Rights (CHR), but reached a short time later (on 21 June 1946) the status of a full commission reporting to the UN Economic and Social Council (ECOSOC). For more information on the CSW, please visit the webpage "A Brief History of the CSW" at the website of UN Women (UN Women 2014).

14. HRC *Resolution 6/30. Integrating the Human Rights of Women throughout the United Nations System* (HRC 2007) expands the related CHR 1993 resolution by decreeing its relevance through the UN system and across UN agencies, calling for the inclusion of women's rights in all phases of the universal periodic review and all special procedures and other human rights mechanisms of the HRC and its Advisory Committee (14 December 2007).

15. Consider also concurrent further developments of the understanding of health and its determinants in UN Security Council (2000, 2002), Rehn and Sirleaf (2002), Lindsey (2001), UNDP (2003), and Legros and Brown (2001).

16. The *Supplement to the Handbook for Legislation on Violence against Women: Harmful Practices against Women* describes the nature of harmful practices against women and girls as follows: "Women throughout the world may be exposed to a wide range of 'harmful practices' across their life cycle, including prenatal sex selection and female infanticide, child marriage, dowry-related violence, female genital mutilation, so-called 'honour' crimes, maltreatment of widows, inciting women to commit suicide, dedication of young girls to temples, restrictions on a second daughter's right to marry, dietary restrictions for pregnant women, forced feeding and nutritional taboos, marriage to a deceased husband's brother and witch hunts" (UN DAW/DESA 2010b, 3).

17. Although there has not yet been much progress made by states in regard to addressing violence associated with food practices and behaviors in their national reports, we note that India's *National Plan of Action for Children* does

include nutrition discrimination against girls as a harmful practice (Government of India 2005, 18).

18. For example, figures on the proportion of women who have experienced physical violence at least once in their lives range from roughly 10 percent of all adult women in China, Hong Kong, and Azerbaijan to 50–60 percent in the Czech Republic and Zambia (UN DESA 2010, 131).

19. Sri Lanka's NAP, for example, uses the definition of violence against women found in article 1 of DEVAW (UN General Assembly 1993), meaning "any act of gender-based violence that results in, or is likely to result in, physical, sexual or psychological harm or suffering to women, including threats of such acts, coercion or arbitrary deprivation of liberty, whether occurring in public or in private life." Haiti's *National Plan on Violence against Women (2006–2011)* uses the definition from article 1 of the *Inter-American Convention on the Prevention, Punishment and Eradication of Violence against Women (Convention of Belém Do Pará)* (OAS 1994), "understood as any act or conduct, based on gender, which causes death or physical, sexual or psychological harm or suffering to women, whether in the public or the private sphere."

20. For further examples of how food deprivation is addressed in NAPs to reduce violence against women, see National Women's Institute [Honduras] (2010) and Ministry of Gender and Development [Liberia] (2006).

21. For more information about the general obligation of states parties to the ICESCR to progressively realize the human right to adequate food and nutrition, please see chapters 1 and 6 of this volume, as well as the *Voluntary Guidelines to Support the Progressive Realization of the Right to Adequate Food in the Context of National Food Security* (FAO 2005).

22. UNICEF calculates these figures of child marriage as the percentage of women aged between twenty and twenty-four who were married or in union before the age of eighteen.

23. This cited report on child marriage shows even worse cases than the Indian context. For example, in Rajshahi, Bangladesh, 45 percent of girls are married by age fifteen, 82 percent are married by age eighteen, and the median age at marriage is fifteen (Sajeda 2011, Table 1).

24. Compare population analyses in Honduras, Kenya, and Malawi that demonstrate that mothers' exposure to physical or sexual violence by intimate partners is highly correlated with children's malnourishment rates (Rico et al. 2011).

25. Under the 2006 Indian *Prohibition of Child Marriage Act*, the marriage is "voidable" because the contracting party who was a "child" at the time of the marriage has the option to nullify the marriage within two years of attaining majority. There is provision for the return of all valuables, money, ornaments, and gifts in marriage when declaring the nullity order (Ghosh 2011, 201).

26. According to the *Encyclopedia of Women and Gender*, "disempowerment" refers to a heightened sense of vulnerability and lack of control over one's own life and choices that may be produced under certain circumstances (Worell 2001, 851). Toomey (2011) makes a classification of various community development approaches that have a disempowerment rather than empowerment potential and cause dependency, passivity, and disbelief in the community members' own strength. See also chapter 5 of this volume.

27. "Conscientization" (*conscientização*, per Freire 1970) is defined by the Freire Institution as the "process of developing a critical awareness of one's social reality through reflection and action, [in which] action is fundamental because it is the process of changing the reality" (Freire Institute 2013).

28. Gender mainstreaming policies in the areas of food and nutrition security and rural development adopted by states and development and aid organizations have generally not applied a human rights-based approach, let alone the human

rights framework (please see chapter 1 of this volume for more information on the emergence of this approach).

29. Gender experts of Brot für die Welt and the Association of World Council of Churches related Development Organisations in Europe (APRODEV), in discussion with Anne C. Bellows, February 2012.

30. Vlachová and Biason (2003) point to the complex and multidimensional aspects of gender-based violence, recognizing violence experienced by men and boys exerted by other males under conditions of war and peace. Both women and men can be consciously or unconsciously indoctrinated to violence—whether as victim or offender—as a means to power and control. The authors call to "move beyond the common narrative of 'men as perpetrators and women as victims', and begin to envision them as partners in the solution by equally placing men and women into strategies of prevention and intervention" (Vlachová and Biason 2003, 28, note 2). One example of the involvement of men in gender mainstreaming efforts is given by the Farmer Field and Life Schools program, launched in Uganda by the FAO, together with UNIFEM and the United Nations Fund for Population Activities (UNFPA). In this approach, women and men cooperate in participatory trainings covering issues related to agricultural practices and life skills, including gender-based violence (FAO 2010). For more information on gender sensitive peacebuilding, please see New Tactics in Human Rights (2013).

31. The special issue "Beyond Gender Mainstreaming" of the journal *Gender and Development*, published in November 2012, includes a selection of articles that address the problems that organizations face when addressing violence. See, in particular, the papers by Mannell (2012) on the experiences of NGOs in South Africa, Horton (2012) on the development efforts in post-disaster Haiti, and van Eerdewijk and Dubel (2012) on the experiences of Dutch development agencies.

32. For more examples of effective practice in gender mainstreaming, see also chapter 5 of this volume.

33. Examples of emergency programs that have developed strategies that prioritize women's food access are (*a*) the operations of the German International Cooperation Agency (GIZ) in post-earthquake Leogane, Haiti, in 2010, where women's and children's food distribution centers were protected by military forces to avoid clashes (Metz 2010), (*b*) the work of the Cooperative for Assistance and Relief Everywhere (CARE) in Horn of Africa in 2011 that prioritized women's safety in access to food with design of specific projects to address the needs in different localized contacts (CARE 2012), and (*c*) the work of Action Against Hunger in Ivory Coast that combined unconditional cash transfers with food distribution (Truelove and Watson 2012).

34 Public programs, as well as civil society and community-based organizations, need internal systems of strong accountability and transparency mechanisms to avoid cases of "corporate clientelism," political favoring, and other forms of discrimination in their own circles. Even advanced social support programs can improve their efficiency and transparency by providing space for individual and public oversight by the service clients and civil society organizations. For example, the Mexican program PROGRESA/Oportunidades that provides social protection benefits to women and their families has been criticized for reoccurring power abuses, such as solicitation of benefit shares, political proselytism, and intimidation by the state actors and institutional intermediaries (Hevia 2008).

35. For more information on the history of and background on the *Voluntary Guidelines to Support the Progressive Realization of the Right to Adequate Food in the Context of National Food Security*, please see chapter 1 of this volume.

REFERENCES

Ackerson, L. K. and S. V. Subramanian. 2008. "Domestic Violence and Chronic Malnutrition among Women and Children in India." *American Journal of Epidemiology* 167 (10): 1188–96.

Agarwal, B., J. Humphries, and I. Robeyns, eds. 2005. *Amartya Sen's Work and Ideas: A Gender Perspective*. London: Routledge.

Al Gasseer, N. A., E. Dresden, G. B. Keeney, and N. Warren. 2004. "Status of Women and Infants in Complex Humanitarian Emergencies." *Journal of Midwifery and Women's Health* 49 (4 Suppl. 1): 7–13.

Aleksanyan, M. 2013. "Domestic Abuse Law Dumped in Armenia." *Caucasus Reporting Service (CRS)* 689. http://iwpr.net/report-news/domestic-abuse-law-dumped-armenia

Alston, M. 2009. "Drought Policy in Australia: Gender Mainstreaming or Gender Blindness?" *Gender, Place and Culture—A Journal of Feminist Geography* 16 (2): 139–54.

Amnesty International. 2008. *No Pride in Silence: Domestic and Sexual Violence against Women in Armenia*. London: Amnesty International.

Ayalon, L. 2009. "Evaluating the Working Conditions and Exposure to Abuse of Filipino Home Care Workers in Israel: Characteristics and Clinical Correlates." *International Psychogeriatrics* 21 (1): 40.

Balasubramanian, S. 2012. "Why Micro-Credit May Leave Women Worse Off: Non-Cooperative Bargaining and the Marriage Game in South Asia." *The Journal of Development Studies* 49 (5): 609–23.

Barsoumian, N. 2010. "Domestic Abuse? What Abuse? . . . She Fell and Died!" *The Armenian Weekly*, 10 October 2010.

Beardsworth, A. and T. Keil. 1997. *Sociology on the Menu: An Invitation to the Study of Food and Society*. London: Routledge.

Becker, A. E., K. E. Fay, J. Agnew-Blais, A. N. Khan, R. H. Striegel-Moore, and S. E. Gilman. 2011. "Social Network Media Exposure and Adolescent Eating Pathology in Fiji." *The British Journal of Psychiatry* 198 (1): 43–50.

Bellows, A. C. 2003. "Exposing Violences: Using Women's Human Rights Theory to Reconceptualize Food Rights." *Journal of Agricultural and Environmental Ethics* 16 (3): 249–79.

Bellows, A. C., G. Alcaraz Velasco, and T. Vivar. 2010. "Gardening as Tool to Foster Health and Cultural Identity in the Context of International Migration: Attitudes and Constraints in a Female Population." *Acta Horticulturae* 881: 785–92.

Benelli, P., D. Mazurana, and P. Walker. 2012. "Using Sex and Age Disaggregated Data to Improve Humanitarian Response in Emergencies." *Gender and Development* 20 (2): 219–32.

Booth, K. 2007. *Theory of World Security*. Vol. 105. Cambridge: Cambridge University Press.

Borras, S. M., Jr. 2008. "La Vía Campesina and its Global Campaign for Agrarian Reform." *Journal of Agrarian Change* 8 (2 and 3): 258–89.

Bourdieu, P. and L. Wacquant. 1992. *An Invitation to Reflexive Sociology*. Chicago: University of Chicago Press.

Brot für die Welt. 2009. *Gender Mainstreaming in Practice: Nine Examples of Good Practice from Four Continents*. Stuttgart: Diakonisches Werk der EKD e.V.

Burgoyne, J. and D. Clark. 1984. *Making a Go of It: A Study of Stepfamilies in Sheffield*. London: Routledge.

Burity, V., L. Cruz, and T. Franceschini. 2011. *Exigibilidade: Mechanisms to Claim the Human Right to Adequate Food in Brazil*. Rome: Food and Agricultural Organization of the United Nations (FAO).

Carastathis, A. 2014. "The Concept of Intersectionality in Feminist Theory." *Philosophy Compass* 9 (5): 304–14.

Clifton, D. and F. Gell. 2001. "Saving and Protecting Lives by Empowering Women." *Gender and Development* 9 (3): 8–18.

Collins, P.H., ed. 1990. *Black Feminist Thought: Knowledge, Consciousness, and Politics of Empowerment*. New York: Routledge.

Commission on the Legal Empowerment of the Poor (CLEP). 2008. *Making the Law Work for Everyone: Volume I—Report of the Commission on Legal Empowerment of the Poor*. New York: United Nations Development Program (UNDP).

Cooperative for Assistance and Relief Everywhere (CARE). 2012. *Update: Horn of Africa Food Security Emergency*. Atlanta: Cooperative for Assistance and Relief Everywhere (CARE).

Cosc—National Office for the Prevention of Domestic, Sexual and Gender-based Violence [Ireland]. 2010. *National Strategy on Domestic, Sexual and Gender-Based Violence 2010–2014*. Dublin: Department of Justice, Equality and Law Reform.

Crenshaw, K. 1989. "Demarginalizing the Intersection of Race and Sex: A Black Feminist Critique of Antidiscrimination Doctrine, Feminist Theory and Antiracist Politics." *University of Chicago Legal Forum* 140: 139–67.

———. 1991. "Mapping the Margins: Intersectionality, Identity Politics, and Violence Against Women of Color." *Stanford Law Review* 43 (6): 1241–99.

Crosby, C. 1995. "Dealing with Difference." In *Women's Rights Human Rights: International Feminist Perspectives*, edited by J. Peters and A. Wolper, 130–43. New York: Routledge.

da Fonseca Menezes, F.A., L. Brait-Poplawski, and M. Menezes Santarelli Roversi. 2012. *Aspects of Social Security in Brazil: From Fome Zero to Brasil Sem Miséria*. Stuttgart; Rio de Janiero: Diakonisches Werk der EKD e.V.; Instituto Brasileiro de Análises Sociais e Econômicas (Ibase).

Dalal, K., F. Rahman, and B. Jansson. 2009. "Wife Abuse in Rural Bangladesh." *Journal of Biosocial Science* 41 (5): 561–73.

De Vault, M.L. 1991. *Feeding the Family: The Social Organization of Caring as Gendered Work*. Chicago: University of Chicago Press.

Department of Justice, Equality and Law Reform [Ireland]. 2009. *National Action Plan to Prevent and Combat Trafficking of Human Beings in Ireland: 2009–2012*. Dublin: Department of Justice and Equality.

Dobash, R. 1979. *Violence Against Wives: A Case against the Patriarchy*. New York: Free Press.

Eziefula, C. and M. Brown. 2010. "The Health of Recent Migrants from Resource-Poor Countries." *Medicine* 38 (1): 60–65.

Farmer, P. 1999. "Pathologies of Power: Rethinking Health and Human Rights." *American Journal of Public Health* 89 (10): 1486–96.

Fernando, J.L. 1997. "Nongovernmental Organizations, Micro-Credit, and Empowerment of Women." *The Annals of the American Academy of Political and Social Science* 554 (1): 150–77.

Ferree, M.M. 2011. "Globalization and Feminism: Opportunities and Obstacles for Activism in the Global Arena." In *Global Feminism: Transnational Women's Activism, Organizing, and Human Rights*, edited by M.M. Ferree and A. M. Tripp, 1–23. New York: New York University Press.

Ferree, M.M. and T. Pudrovska. 2011. "Transnational Feminist NGOs on the Web: Networks and Identities in the Global North and South." In *Global Feminism: Transnational Women's Activism, Organizing, and Human Rights*, edited by M.M. Ferree and A. M. Tripp, 247–72. New York: New York University Press.

Food and Agriculture Organization of the United Nations (FAO). 2010. "Farm Schools in Uganda Engage Women and Men in Gender-Based Violence Prevention." Food and Agriculture Organization of the United Nations (FAO), published

November 25, 2010, accessed November, 2013, http://www.fao.org/gender/gender-home/gender-projects/gender-projectsdet/en/?dyna_fef[uid]=48118.

———. 2005. *Voluntary Guidelines to Support the Progressive Realization of the Right to Adequate Food in the Context of National Food Security*. Rome: Food and Agriculture Organization of the United Nations (FAO).

Fox-Genovese, E. 1994. "Difference, Diversity and Divisions in an Agenda for the Women's Movement." In *Color, Class and Country: Experiences of Gender*, edited by G. Young and B. Dickerson, 232–48. London: Zed Books.

Freire Institute. "Concepts used by Paulo Freire." Freire Institute, accessed September 13, 2013, http://www.freire.org/paulo-freire/concepts-used-by-paulo-freire.

Freire, P. 1970. *Pedagogy of the Oppressed*. New York: Herder and Herder.

Galtung, J. 1969. "Violence, Peace, and Peace Research." *Journal of Peace Research* 6 (3): 167–91.

———. 1990. "Cultural Violence." *Journal of Peace Research* 27 (3): 291–305.

García-Moreno, C., J. Hafm, M. Ellsberg, L. Heise, and C. Watts. 2005. *WHO Multi-Country Study on Women's Health and Domestic Violence Against Women: Initial Results on Prevalence, Health Outcomes and Women's Responses*. Geneva: United Nations World Health Organization (WHO).

Gell, F. 1999. "Gender Concerns in Emergencies." In *Gender Works: Oxfam Experiences in Policy and Practice*, edited by F. Porter, I. Smyth and C. S. Sweetman, 37–46. Oxford: Oxfam GB.

Gender in Development Division [Zambia]. 2008. *National Action Plan on Gender-Based Violence (NAP-GBV) 2008–2013*. Lusaka: Gender in Development Division [Zambia].

Gender Secretariat [Sweden]. 2007. *Action Plan for Sida's Work against Gender-Based Violence 2008–2010*. Stockholm: Department for Democracy and Social Development of the Swedish International Development Cooperation Agency (Sida).

Ghosh, B. 2011. "Child Marriage, Society and the Law: A Study in a Rural Context in West Bengal, India." *International Journal of Law, Policy and the Family* 25 (2): 199–219.

Global Campaign for Agrarian Reform (GCAR). 2003. *International Seminar "Agrarian Reform and Gender:" Declaration of Cochabamba (4–8 June 2003, Cochabamba, Bolivia)*. Global Campaign for Agrarian Reform (GCAR).

Government of Canada. 2012. *National Action Plan to Combat Human Trafficking*. Ottawa: Her Majesty the Queen in Right of Canada.

Government of India. 2005. *National Plan of Action for Children 2005*. New Delhi: Government of India.

Government of South Africa. 2007. *365 Day National Action Plan to End Gender Violence*. Pretoria: Planning Task Team.

Grabska, K. 2011. "Constructing 'Modern Gendered Civilised' Women and Men: Gender-Mainstreaming in Refugee Camps." *Gender and Development* 19 (1): 81–93.

Gribble, K. D., M. McGrath, A. MacLaine, and L. Lhotska. 2011. "Supporting Breastfeeding in Emergencies: Protecting Women's Reproductive Rights and Maternal and Infant Health." *Disasters* 35 (4): 720–38.

Hancock, A. M. 2007. "When Multiplication Doesn't Equal Quick Addition: Examining Intersectionality as a Research Paradigm." *Perspectives on Politics* 5 (1): 63–79.

Hashemi, S. M., S. R. Schuler, and A. P. Riley. 1996. "Rural Credit Programs and Women's Empowerment in Bangladesh." *World Development* 24 (4): 635–53.

Hasselmann, M. H. and M. E. Reichenheim. 2006. "Parental Violence and the Occurrence of Severe and Acute Malnutrition in Childhood." *Paediatric and Perinatal Epidemiology* 20 (4): 299–311.

Hevia, F. 2008. "Between Individual and Collective Action: Citizen Participation and Public Oversight in Mexico's Oportunidades Programme." *IDS Bulletin* 38 (6): 64–72.

Ho, K. 2007. "Structural Violence as a Human Rights Violation." *Essex Human Rights Review* 4 (2): 1–17.

Holmes, R. and N. Jones. 2010. *Rethinking Social Protection using a Gender Lens*. London: Overseas Development Institute (ODI).

Hooks, B. 1984. *Feminist Theory: From Margin to Center*. London: Pluto Press.

Horton, L. 2012. "After the Earthquake: Gender Inequality and Transformation in Post-Disaster Haiti." *Gender and Development* 20 (2): 295–308.

Instituto Brasileiro de Análises Sociais e Econômicas (Ibase). 2008. *Repercussões do Programa Bolsa Família Na Segurança Alimentar e Nutricional Dos Seus Beneficiários. [Repercussions of the Bolsa Família Program on the Food and Nutrition Security of Its Beneficiaries]* Rio de Janeiro: Instituto Brasileiro de Análises Sociais e Econômicas (Ibase), quoted in da Fonseca Menezes, F. A., L. Brait-Poplawski, and M. Menezes Santarelli Roversi. 2012. *Aspects of Social Security in Brazil: From Fome Zero to Brasil Sem Miséria*. Stuttgart; Rio de Janeiro: Diakonisches Werk der EKD e.V.; Instituto Brasileiro de Análises Sociais e Econômicas (Ibase), 26.

International Institute for Population Sciences (IIPS) and Macro International. 2007. "Domestic Violence." In *National Family Health Survey (NFHS-3)*. Vol. 1. Mumbai: International Institute for Population Studies (IIPS).

Jewkes, R., E. Fulu, T. Roselli, and C. Garcia-Moreno. 2013. "Prevalence of and Factors Associated with Non-Partner Rape Perpetration: Findings from the UN Multi-Country Cross-Sectional Study on Men and Violence in Asia and the Pacific." *The Lancet Global Health* 1 (4): e208–e218.

Jones, N. and R. Holmes. 2011. "Why is Social Protection Gender-Blind? The Politics of Gender and Social Protection." *IDS Bulletin* 42 (6): 45–52.

Kikafunda, J. K. and F. B. Lukwago. 2005. "Nutritional Status and Functional Ability of the Elderly Aged 60 to 90 Years in the Mpigi District of Central Uganda." *Nutrition* 21 (1): 59–66.

Kim, J. C., C. H. Watts, J. R. Hargreaves, L. X. Ndhlovu, G. Phetla, L. A. Morison, J. Busza, J. D. H. Porter, and P. Pronyk. 2007. "Understanding the Impact of a Microfinance-Based Intervention on Women's Empowerment and the Reduction of Intimate Partner Violence in South Africa." *American Journal of Public Health* 97 (10): 1794–1802.

Kusakabe, K. 2005. "Gender Mainstreaming in Government Offices in Thailand, Cambodia, and Laos: Perspectives from Below." *Gender and Development* 13 (2): 46–56.

Legros, D. and V. Brown. 2001. "Documenting Violence against Refugees." *The Lancet* 357 (9266): 1429.

Lewis, D. 2010. *The National Gender-Based Violence Plan of Action 2010–2013*. Belize: Women's Department of the Ministry of Human Development and Social Transformation [Belize].

Lindsey, C., ed. 2001. *Women Facing War*. Geneva: International Committee of the Red Cross (ICRC).

Lorde, A. 1984. *Sister Outsider: Essays and Speeches*. Crossing Press Feminist Series. Berkeley: Ten Speed Press.

Luttrell, C. and C. Moser. 2004. *Gender and Social Protection*. London: Overseas Development Institute.

Macro International. "MEASURE DHS: Demographic and Health Surveys." United States Agency for International Development (USAID), accessed August, 2009, http://www.measuredhs.com/, quoted in United Nations Department of Economic and Social Affairs (UN DESA). 2010. *The World's Women 2010: Trends and Statistics*. New York: United Nations (UN), 137–38.

Mannell, J. 2012. "'It's Just Been such a Horrible Experience.' Perceptions of Gender Mainstreaming by Practitioners in South African Organisations." *Gender and Development* 20 (3): 423–34.

May, V. M. 2015. *Pursuing Intersectionality: Unsettling Dominant Imaginaries*. New York: Taylor & Francis.

Metz, M. 2010. "Emergency Food Assistance in Haiti: Lessons Learnt from a Post-Earthquake GTZ Operation in Leogane." *Humanitarian Exchange Magazine* (48): 25–28.

Ministry for Family, Youth and Sports [Ukraine]. 2008. *National Campaign Stop Violence!* Kiev: Ministry for Family, Youth and Sports [Ukraine].

Ministry for the Family and the Status of Women [Algeria]. 2007. *Stratégie Nationale De Lutte Contre La Violence l'Égard Des Femmes. [National Strategy for the Struggle against Violence against Women]* Algier: Ministry for the Family and the Status of Women [Algeria].

Ministry for the Status of Women and Women's Rights [Haiti]. 2005. *Plan National De Lutte Contre Les Violences Faites Aux Femmes: Prévention, Prise En Charge Et Accompagnement Des Victimes De Violences Specifiques Faites Aux Femmes 2006–2011. [National Plan for the Struggle against Violence against Women: Prevention, Support and Attendance of Victims of Violence Specifically Committed against Women 2006–2011]* Haiti: Ministry for the Status of Women and Women's Rights [Haiti].

Ministry of Community Development, Gender and Children (MCDGC) [Tanzania]. 2005. *National Strategy for Gender Development.* Dar es Salaam: Ministry of Community Development, Gender and Children (MCDGC) [Tanzania].

Ministry of Gender and Development [Liberia]. 2006. *National Plan of Action for the Prevention and Management of Gender-Based Violence in Liberia (GBV-POA).* Monrovia: Ministry of Gender and Development [Liberia].

Ministry of Labour, Social Affairs and Equal Opportunities [Albania]. 2006. *National Strategy on Gender Equality and Domestic Violence 2007–2010.* Albania: Ministry of Labour, Social Affairs and Equal Opportunities [Albania].

Ministry of Law and Justice (Legislative Department) [India]. 2007. *The Prohibition of Child Marriage Act, 2006*, Public Law Part II—Section 1, *The Gazette of India.*

Mkenda-Mugittu, V. F. 2003. "Measuring the Invisibles: Gender Mainstreaming and Monitoring Experience from a Dairy Development Project in Tanzania." *Development in Practice* 13 (5): 459–73.

Mohanty, C. T. 2003. *Feminism Without Borders: Decolonizing Theory, Practicing Solidarity.* Durham: Duke University Press.

Molyneux, M. 2006. "Mothers at the Service of the New Poverty Agenda: Progresa/Oportunidades, Mexico's Conditional Transfer Programme." *Social Policy and Administration* 40 (4): 425–49.

Monsalve Suárez, S. 2006. "Gender and Land." In *Promised Land: Competing Visions of Agrarian Reform*, edited by P. Rosset, R. Patel and M. Courville, 192–207. New York: Food First Books.

Moodie, R., D. Stuckler, C. Monteiro, N. Sheron, B. Neal, T. Thamarangsi, P. Lincoln, and S. Casswell. 2013. "Profits and Pandemics: Prevention of Harmful Effects of Tobacco, Alcohol, and Ultra-Processed Food and Drink Industries." *The Lancet* 381 (9867): 670–79.

Moser, C. and A. Moser. 2005. "Gender Mainstreaming since Beijing: A Review of Success and Limitations in International Institutions." *Gender and Development* 13 (2): 11–22.

Mukhopadhyay, M. 2013. "Mainstreaming Gender or Reconstituting the Mainstream? Gender Knowledge in Development." *Journal of International Development* 26 (3): 356–67.

Musaiger, A. O. 1993. "Socio-Cultural and Economic Factors Affecting Food Consumption Patterns in the Arab Countries." *The Journal of the Royal Society for the Promotion of Health* 113 (2): 68–74.

Nadasen, P. 2005. *Welfare Warriors: The Welfare Rights Movement in the United States.* New York: Routledge.

National Committee on Gender Equality [Mongolia]. 2002. *National Program on Gender Equality*. Ulaanbaatar: Government of Mongolia.

National Committee to Combat Trafficking in Human Beings [Moldova]. 2010. *National Plan for Prevention and Combating of Trafficking in Human Beings for the Years 2010–2011*. Moldova: National Committee to Combat Trafficking in Human Beings [Moldova].

National Council to Reduce Violence against Women and their Children [Australia]. 2009. *Time for Action: The National Council's Plan for Australia to Reduce Violence Against Women and their Children, 2009–2021*. Canberra: Commonwealth of Australia.

National Service for Women [Chile]. 2011. *Plan Nacional de Acción para la Prevención de la Violencia Intrafamiliar en Chile: Septiembre 2011-Agosto 2012. [National Action Plan for the Prevention of Intrafamily Violence in Chile: September 2011–August 2012]* Santiago de Government of Chile.

National Women's Institute [Honduras]. 2010. *La Política Nacional de la Mujer: Segundo Plan de Igualdad y Equidad de Género de Honduras 2010–2022. [National Women's Policy: Honduras' Second Plan of Gender Equality and Equity 2010–2022]* Tegucipalpa: National Women's Institute [Honduras].

Naved, R.T. and L.Å. Persson. 2005. "Factors Associated with Spousal Physical Violence against Women in Bangladesh." *Studies in Family Planning* 36 (4): 289–300.

New Tactics in Human Rights. "Joining Forces: Engaging Men as Allies in Gender-Sensitive Peacebuilding." Accessed November, 2013, https://www.newtactics.org/conversation/joining-forces-engaging-men-allies-gender-sensitive-peacebuilding.

Nussbaum, M. 2011. *Creating Capabilities: The Human Development Approach*. Cambridge: Belknap of Harvard University Press.

Nussbaum, M. and A. Sen, eds. 1993. *The Quality of Life*. New York: Oxford Clarendon Press.

Ojaba, E., A.I. Leonardo, and M.I. Leonardo. 2002. "Food Aid in Complex Emergencies: Lessons from Sudan." *Social Policy and Administration* 36 (6): 664–84.

Organisation for Economic Cooperation and Development (OECD). 2007. *Promoting Pro-Poor Growth: Policy Guidance for Donors*. DAC Guidelines and Reference Series. Paris: Organisation for Economic Cooperation and Development (OECD).

———. 2009. *Promoting Pro-Poor Growth: Social Protection*. DAC Guidelines and Reference Series. Paris: Organisation for Economic Cooperation and Development (OECD).

Organisation for Economic Cooperation and Development (OECD) Development Centre. 2010. *Atlas of Gender and Development: How Social Norms Affect Gender Equality in Non-OECD Countries*. Paris: Organisation for Economic Cooperation and Development (OECD).

Organization of American States (OAS). 1994. *Inter-American Convention on the Prevention, Punishment and Eradication of Violence against Women (Convention of Belém do Pará), 9 June 1994*. Washington, D.C.: Organization of American States (OAS).

Ouldzeidoune, N., J. Keating, J. Bertrand, and J. Rice. 2013. "A Description of Female Genital Mutilation and Force-Feeding Practices in Mauritania: Implications for the Protection of Child Rights and Health." *Plos One* 8 (4): e60594.

Parpart, J.L. 2014. "Exploring the Transformative Potential of Gender Mainstreaming in International Development Institutions." *Journal of International Development* 26 (3): 382–95.

Pingali, P., L. Alinovi, and J. Sutton. 2005. "Food Security in Complex Emergencies: Enhancing Food System Resilience." *Disasters* 29 (Suppl. 1): S5–S24.

Popenoe, R. 2004. *Feeding Desire: Fatness, Beauty, and Sexuality among Saharan People*. New York: Routledge.

Quisumbing, A. R., Lynn R. Brown, H. S. Feldstein, L. Haddad, and C. Peña. 1995. *Women: The Key to Food Security*. Washington, D.C.: International Food Policy Research Institute (IFPRI).

Raj, A., S. Sabarwal, M. R. Decker, S. Nair, M. Jethva, S. Krishnan, B. Donta, N. Saggurti, and J. G. Silverman. 2011. "Abuse from In-Laws during Pregnancy and Post-Partum: Qualitative and Quantitative Findings from Low-Income Mothers of Infants in Mumbai, India." *Maternal and Child Health Journal* 15 (6): 700–12.

Rehn, E. and E. Sirleaf, eds. 2002. *Women, War and Peace: The Independent Experts' Assessment on the Impact of Armed Conflict on Women and Women's Role in Peacebuilding*. New York: United Nations Development Fund for Women (UNIFEM).

Rico, E., B. Fenn, T. Abramsky, and C. Watts. 2011. "Associations between Maternal Experiences of Intimate Partner Violence and Child Nutrition and Mortality: Findings from Demographic and Health Surveys in Egypt, Honduras, Kenya, Malawi and Rwanda." *Journal of Epidemiology and Community Health* 65 (4): 360–67.

Rodríguez, H., E. L. Quarantalli, and R. R. Dynes. 2007. *Handbook of Disaster Research*. New York: Springer.

Rosalina, T., L. Wibowo, A. A. Kielmann, and A. A. Usfar. 2007. "Food-Poverty Status and Food Insecurity in Rural West Lombok Based on Mothers' Food Expenditure Equivalency." *Food and Nutrition Bulletin* 28 (2): 135–48.

Rossi, L. 2009. "Targeting the Most Vulnerable in the Food Crisis." *CAB Reviews: Perspectives in Agriculture, Veterinary Science, Nutrition and Natural Resources* 4: 1–8.

Sajeda, A. 2011. *Programs to Address Child Marriage: Framing the Problem*. New York: Population Council.

Salazar, M., U. Högberg, E. Valladares, and L. Å. Persson. 2012. "Intimate Partner Violence and Early Child Growth: A Community-Based Cohort Study in Nicaragua." *BMC Pediatrics* 12: 82.

Samson, M. 2008. *Cash Transfers to Improve the Protection and Care of Vulnerable Children and to Empower Families in the Context of the HIV Epidemic in Papua New Guinea: Conceptual Framework*. Bangkok; New York: Papua New Guinea's Department for Community Development; Papua New Guinea's Institute of National Affairs; United Nations Children's Fund (UNICEF).

Sasson, A. 2012. "Food Security for Africa: An Urgent Global Challenge." *Agriculture and Food Security* 1 (2): 1–16.

Schech, S. and M. Mustafa. 2010. "The Politics of Gender Mainstreaming Poverty Reduction: An Indonesian Case Study." *Social Politics: International Studies in Gender, State & Society* 17 (1): 111–35.

Schefske, S. D., A. C. Bellows, C. Byrd-Bredbenner, C. L. Cuite, H. Rapport, T. Vivar, and W. K. Hallman. 2010. "Nutrient Analysis of Varying Socioeconomic Status Home Food Environments in New Jersey." *Appetite* 54 (2): 384–89.

Schmeer, K. K. 2005. "Married Women's Resource Position and Household Food Expenditures in Cebu, Philippines." *Journal of Marriage and Family* 67 (2): 399–409.

Schuler, S. R., S. M. Hashemi, A. P. Riley, and S. Akhter. 1996. "Credit Programs, Patriarchy and Men's Violence against Women in Rural Bangladesh." *Social Science and Medicine* 43 (12): 1729–42.

Sen, A. 1985. *Commodities and Capabilities*. Oxford: Elsevier.

Shepherd, B. 2012. "Thinking Critically about Food Security." *Security Dialogue* 43 (3): 195–212.

Shirinian, S. "Domestic Violence against Women in Armenia." Glendale: United Human Rights Council, last modified May 26, 2010, accessed July 1, 2013, http://www.unitedhumanrights.org/2010/05/domestic-violence-against-women-in-armenia.

Shortall, S. and A. Byrne. 2009. "Gender and Sustainability in Rural Ireland." In *A Living Countryside? The Politics of Sustainable Development in Rural Ireland*, edited by J. McDonagh, T. Varley, and A. Shortall, 287–303. Surrey: Ashgate.

Silverman, J. G., M. R. Decker, D. M. Cheng, K. Wirth, N. Saggurti, H. L. McCauley, K. L. Falb, B. Donta, and A. Raj. 2011. "Gender-Based Disparities in Infant and Child Mortality Based on Maternal Exposure to Spousal Violence: The Heavy Burden Borne by Indian Girls." *Archives of Pediatrics and Adolescent Medicine* 165 (1): 22–27.

Smyth, I. 2007. "Talking of Gender: Words and Meanings in Development Organisations." *Development in Practice* 17 (4–5): 582–88.

Sobkoviak, Y. M., K. M. Yount, and N. Halim. 2012. "Domestic Violence and Child Nutrition in Liberia." *Social Science and Medicine* 74 (2): 103–11.

Spivak, G. C. 1999. *A Critique of Postcolonial Reason: Toward a History of the Vanishing Present*. Cambridge: Harvard University Press.

Støving, R. K., A. Andries, K. Brixen, N. Bilenberg, and K. Hørder. 2011. "Gender Differences in Outcome of Eating Disorders: A Retrospective Cohort Study." *Psychiatry Research* 186 (2–3): 362–66.

Suárez Franco, A. M. 2011. "The Challenges in Accessing Justice when Claiming the Right to Adequate Food." *Right to Food and Nutrition WATCH* 2011: 39–46.

Tabbush, C. 2010. "'The Elephant in the Room': Silencing Everyday Violence in Rights-Based Approaches to Women's Community Participation in Argentina." *Community Development Journal* 45 (3): 325–34.

Thomas, D. 1993. "The Distribution of Income and Expenditure within the Household." *Annales d'Economie Et De Statistique* (29): 109–35.

Tiessen, R. 2007. *Everywhere/Nowhere: Gender Mainstreaming in Development Agencies*. Bloomfield: Kumarian Press.

Toomey, A. H. 2011. "Empowerment and Disempowerment in Community Development Practice: Eight Roles Practitioners Play. *Community Development Journal* 46 (2): 181–95.

True, J. 2011. "Feminist Problems with International Norms: Gender Mainstreaming in Global Governance." In *Feminism and International Relations: Conversations about the Past, Present and Future*, edited by J. A. Tickner and L. Sjoberg, 73–88. New York: Routledge.

———. 2012. *The Political Economy of Violence against Women*. Oxford: Oxford University Press.

Truelove, S. and M. Watson. 2012. *WFP/ACF Unconditional Mobile Cash Transfer in Abidjan, Ivory Coast—External Evaluation: Executive Summary*. London: Action Against Hunger UK.

Ulvin, P. 1998. *Aiding Violence: The Development Enterprise in Rwanda*. Hartford: Kumarian Press.

United Mission to Nepal. 2004. *Food Security and Hunger Survey in Nepal: A Report Submitted to Bread for the World and Church Development Service—Germany (EED)*. Katmandu: United Mission to Nepal.

United Nations (UN). 1995. *Beijing Declaration and Platform for Action, Adopted at the Fourth World Conference on Women. 27 October 1995*: New York: United Nations (UN).

———. "United Nations Secretary General's Campaign UNite to End Violence against Women." United Nations Web Services Section, Department of Public Information, United Nations, accessed March 24, 2014, http://endviolence.un.org/index.shtml.

United Nations Children's Fund (UNICEF). "Statistics by Area/Child Protection: Percentage of Women Aged 20–24 Who Were First Married/in Union before the Age of 18." Childinfo: Monitoring the Situation of Women and Children. New York: United Nations Children's Fund (UNICEF), accessed May 25, 2013, http://www.childinfo.org/marriage_countrydata.php.

United Nations Commission on Human Rights (CHR). 1993. *Integrating the Rights of Women into the Human Rights Mechanisms of the United Nations. E/CN.4/RES/1993/46, 8 March 1993.* Geneva: United Nations Commission on Human Rights (CHR).

United Nations Committee on Economic, Social and Cultural Rights (CESCR). 1999. *General Comment No. 12: The Right to Adequate Food (Art. 11 of the Covenant). E/C.12/1999/5, 12 May 1999.* New York: United Nations Economic and Social Council (ECOSOC).

———. 2000. *General Comment No. 14: The Right to the Highest Attainable Standard of Health (Art. 12 of the Covenant). E/C.12/2000/4, 11 August 2000.* New York: United Nations Economic and Social Council (ECOSOC).

United Nations Committee on the Elimination of Discrimination against Women (CEDAW Committee). 1999. *CEDAW General Recommendation No. 24: Article 12 of the Convention (Women and Health). A/54/38/Rev.1, Chap. I.* Geneva: United Nations Committee on the Elimination of Discrimination against Women (CEDAW Committee).

United Nations Department of Economic and Social Affairs (UN DESA). 2010. *The World's Women 2010: Trends and Statistics.* New York: United Nations (UN).

United Nations Development Programme (UNDP). 2003. *Gender Approaches in Conflict and Post-Conflict Situations.* New York: United Nations Development Programme (UNDP).

United Nations Division for the Advancement of Women of the Department of Economic and Social Affairs (UN DAW/DESA). 2010a. *Handbook for Legislation on Violence against Women.* New York: United Nations (UN).

———. 2010b. *Supplement to the Handbook for Legislation on Violence against Women: Harmful Practices against Women.* New York: United Nations (UN).

United Nations Entity for Gender Equality and the Empowerment of Women (UN Women). 2012a. *Handbook for National Action Plans on Violence Against Women.* New York: United Nations Entity for Gender Equality and the Empowerment of Women (UN Women).

———. "The UN Secretary General's Database on Violence Against Women." New York: United Nations Entity for Gender Equality and the Empowerment of Women (UN Women), accessed November, 2012b, http://sgdatabase.unwomen.org/home.action.

———. "A Brief History of the CSW." New York: United Nations Entity for Gender Equality and the Empowerment of Women (UN Women), accessed March 25, 2014, http://www.unwomen.org/en/csw/brief-history.

United Nations General Assembly. 1966. *International Covenant on Economic, Social and Cultural Rights. 16 December 1966.* United Nations, Treaty Series, Vol. 993, p. 3. New York: United Nations General Assembly.

———. 1979. *Convention on the Elimination of all Forms of Discrimination against Women. 18 December 1979.* New York: United Nations General Assembly.

———. 1993. *Declaration on the Elimination of Violence against Women. A/RES/48/104, 20 December 1993.* New York: United Nations General Assembly.

———. 1997. *Report of the Economic and Social Council for 1997—Chapter IV: Coordination of the Policies and Activities of the Specialized Agencies and Other Bodies of the United Nations System. Part A. Mainstreaming the Gender Perspective into all Policies and Programmes in the United Nations System; Definition of the Concept of Gender Mainstreaming.* New York: United Nations (UN).

————. 1999. *Optional Protocol to the Convention on the Elimination of all Forms of Discrimination against Women: Resolution / Adopted by the General Assembly. A/RES/54/4, 15 October 1999.* New York: United Nations General Assembly.

————. 2007. *Intensification of Efforts to Eliminate all Forms of Violence against Women: Resolution / Adopted by the General Assembly. A/RES/61/143, 30 January 2007.* New York: United Nations General Assembly.

————. 2009. *Intensification of Efforts to Eliminate all Forms of Violence against Women: Resolution / Adopted by the General Assembly. A/RES/63/155, 30 January 2009.* New York: United Nations General Assembly.

United Nations Human Rights Council (HRC). 2007. *Resolution 6/30. Integrating the Human Rights of Women throughout the United Nations System.* Geneva: United Nations Office of the High Commissioner for Human Rights (OHCHR).

————. 2011a. *Report of the Special Rapporteur on Torture and Other Cruel, Inhuman or Degrading Treatment or Punishment, Juan E. Méndez. A/HRC/16/52, 1 March 2011.* New York: United Nations General Assembly.

————. 2011b. *Report of the Special Rapporteur on Torture and Other Cruel, Inhuman or Degrading Treatment or Punishment, Juan E. Méndez. Addendum: Summary of Information, Including Individual Cases, Transmitted to Governments and Replies Received. A/HRC/16/52/Add.1, 1 March 2011.* New York: United Nations General Assembly.

————. 2012a. *Report of the Special Rapporteur on Extreme Poverty and Human Rights, María Magdalena Sepúlveda Carmona. A/67/278, 9 August 2012.* New York: United Nations General Assembly.

————. 2012b. *Report Submitted by the Special Rapporteur on the Right to Food, Olivier De Schutter: Women's Rights and the Right to Food. A/HRC/22/50, 24 December 2012.* New York: United Nations General Assembly.

United Nations Office of the Special Adviser on Gender Issues and Advancement of Women (UN OSAGI). 2002. *Gender Mainstreaming: An Overview.* New York: United Nations (UN).

United Nations Security Council. 2000. *Security Council Resolution 1325 (2000) [on Women and Peace and Security]. S/RES/1325 (2000), 31 October 2000.* New York: United Nations Security Council.

————. 2002. *Report of the Secretary-General on Women, Peace and Security. S/2002/1154, 16 October 2002.* New York: United Nations Security Council.

————. 2013. *Security Council Resolution 2106 (2013) [on Sexual Violence in Armed Conflict]. S/RES/2106 (2013), 24 June 2013.* New York: United Nations Security Council.

United States Agency for International Development (USAID). 2012. *Strategy to Prevent and Respond to Gender-Based Violence Globally.* Washington, D.C.: Department of State.

Valente, F. L. S. and N. Beghin. 2006. *Realization of the Human Right to Adequate Food and the Brazilian Experience: Inputs for Replicability*, translated by H. M. Lemos and P. Coelho. Rome: Food and Agricultural Organization of the United Nations (FAO).

van Eerdewijk, A. and I. Dubel. 2012. "Substantive Gender Mainstreaming and the Missing Middle: A View from Dutch Development Agencies." *Gender and Development* 20 (3): 491–504.

van Eerdewijk, A. and T. Davids. 2014. "Escaping the Mythical Beast: Gender Mainstreaming Reconceptualised." *Journal of International Development* 26 (3): 303–16.

Vander Wal, J. S. 2012. "The Relationship between Body Mass Index and Unhealthy Weight Control Behaviors among Adolescents: The Role of Family and Peer Social Support." *Economics and Human Biology* 10 (4): 395–404.

Viana, R. S. G. and A. C. Bellows. 2014. " 'Teacher, We Are Hungry.' The Violation of *Quilombola* Students' Right to Adequate Food: A Case Study." *International Journal of Human Rights* 18 (7–8): 774–94.

Vlachová, M. and L. Biason. 2003. "Violence Against Women as a Challenge for Security Sector Governance." In *Challenges of Security Sector Governance*, edited by H. Hänggi and T. Winkler. Geneva: Geneva Centre for the Democratic Control of Armed Forces (DCAF).

Vyas, S. and C. Watts. 2009. "How does Economic Empowerment Affect Women's Risk of Intimate Partner Violence in Low and Middle Income Countries? A Systematic Review of Published Evidence." *Journal of International Development* 21 (5): 577–602.

Whitehead, A. 1994. "Food Symbolism, Gender Power and the Family." In *Food: Multidisciplinary Perspectives*, edited by B. Harris-White and R. Hoffenberg, 116–29. Cambridge: Blackwell.

Worell, J., ed. 2001. *Encyclopedia of Women and Gender: Sex Similarities and Differences and the Impact of Society on Gender*. Orlando: Academic Press.

World Bank, Food and Agriculture Organization of the United Nations (FAO), and International Fund for Agricultural Development (IFAD). 2009. *Gender in Agriculture Sourcebook*. Washington, D.C.: World Bank Publications.

World Health Organization (WHO). 1981. *International Code of Marketing of Breast-milk Substitutes*. Geneva: World Health Organization (WHO).

Yount, K. M., A. M. Di Girolamo, and U. Ramakrishnan. 2011. "Impacts of Domestic Violence on Child Growth and Nutrition: A Conceptual Review of the Pathways of Influence." *Social Science and Medicine* 72 (9): 1534–54.

Ziaei, S., R. T. Naved, and E. C. Ekström. 2012. "Women's Exposure to Intimate Partner Violence and Child Malnutrition: Findings from Demographic and Health Surveys in Bangladesh." *Maternal and Child Nutrition* 10(3): 347–59.

Zinn, M. and B. Dill. 1996. "Theorizing Difference from Multiracial Feminism." *Feminist Studies* 22 (2): 321–31.

4 Maternal, Infant, and Young Child Feeding

Intertwined Subjectivities and Corporate Accountability

Lida Lhotska, Veronika Scherbaum, and Anne C. Bellows

INTRODUCTION

In this chapter, we propose that nutritional issues of mothers and children must be engaged simultaneously and that childbearing and the potential of healthy, well-nourished offspring and mothers must be framed through the lens of women's fundamental human rights over their life spans. In considering the balance of power that shapes decisions and practices influencing the realization of maternal, infant, and young child nutrition and health, we discuss the role of non-state actors, in particular the private for-profit sector, in relation to policies and programs, and their potential impact on the realization of the right to adequate food and nutrition of women, infants, and young children.

We present the subject of infant and young child feeding, with emphasis on protection, promotion, and support of early, exclusive, and continued breastfeeding as well as safe and adequate complementary feeding. We introduce our topic in the context of the right to adequate food and nutrition and how this right is intrinsically connected with the fulfillment of all children's and women's rights. Two specific issues contextualize our topic: HIV/AIDS and emergency situations. These additional challenges to infant and young child feeding tend to be approached on a needs basis as a "service delivery" type of intervention, rather than through a holistic human rights approach defined in part by dialogue between rights holders and duty bearers. Finally, we introduce the Scaling Up Nutrition (SUN) initiative and query the extent to which it offers opportunities or challenges to addressing malnutrition, hunger, and human rights in the context of maternal, infant, and young child nutrition and health.

SELF-DETERMINATION AND DIGNITY IN THE CONTEXT OF HUMAN RIGHTS AND MATERNAL AND CHILD HEALTH AND NUTRITION

The right to adequate food and nutrition is not narrowly understood as only the right to adequate food stuffs, which might compose a safe, culturally, and nutritionally adequate diet, but also as a right to feed (cf. Van Esterik 1999). The human right to feed incorporates the right to dignity and self-determination with respect to the social processes of producing and providing food, preparing food for oneself and others, eating and promoting nutritional well-being to support physical and mental health, and an active and healthy social life.

The right to adequate food and nutrition should ensure a progressive realization of the highest possible standard of physical and mental health for every woman, man, girl child, boy child, and female and male infant. The universality of human rights identifies all rights holders equally, as individuals with dignity and entitled to respect. Women's right to adequate food and nutrition is inalienable; it depends neither on motherhood nor marital status, nor on the reproductive or productive stage of a woman's life. Children have a right to adequate food and nutrition regardless of their age, gender, or developmental stage. Men also have this human right regardless of fatherhood status or productivity.

As articulated in the 2005 update of the 1990 *Innocenti Declaration on the Protection, Promotion and Support of Breastfeeding* by the World Health Organization (WHO) and the United Nations Children's Fund (UNICEF), breastfeeding is the norm and the only natural form of feeding infants and young children (WHO and UNICEF 2005). Breastfeeding extends the dyadic biological and developmental connection between mother and child *ex utero* through babies' physical and emotional dependency on the mother. Whereas babies can survive on substitutes for mothers' milk (referred to as "breastmilk substitutes" or "formula feeding"), at least in settings where they are prepared and used as safely as possible, breastfeeding has vast positive short- and long-term nutritional and overall health impacts on both mother and child that are "precious and valuable" (Rothman 2008, 1) and cannot be equaled by any substitute.[1] Breastfeeding is recommended to start within the first hour after birth and thereafter to be an infant's exclusive form of nutrition for the first six months of life, followed by continued breastfeeding for two years or beyond along with the gradual introduction of adequate, safe, and properly fed complementary foods (Lamberti et al. 2011; WHO 2009; WHO and UNICEF 2003). As breastfeeding is the biological norm, Cattaneo (2008) posits that the time and resources invested toward researching breastfeeding benefits would be better spent by promoting interventions to support optimal breastfeeding habits and by exposing the health risks of formula feeding.

Women uniquely have the capacity to gestate and breastfeed; hence, we can impute a right to women to nourish their unborn child in utero and breastfeed her/him in infancy and early childhood. We emphasize most urgently, however, that women's and children's right to adequate food, nutrition, and health must not be interpreted as, or equated with, a duty of a woman to breastfeed. At the same time, any effort to deter women from receiving access to information about, and support for, best infant and young child feeding practices at home, at work, or in other public or private spaces also constitutes an infringement on women's right to feed. Both of these approaches reflect discrimination and violence against women's self-determination and dignity.

Human rights instruments and the systems in place to ensure the progressive realization of the right to adequate food and nutrition and of health, as presently constructed, do not adequately embrace what we are introducing under the term the "intertwined subjectivities" of mother and child during pregnancy, childbirth, and breastfeeding.[2] A child's health and nutritional status is largely and directly dependent on that of the mother's at the time of conception, throughout pregnancy, in infancy, and, more broadly, in the context of family socioeconomic condition. It is further influenced by the environment in which mother and child live, by conditions, options, and pressures at various levels, all influencing decisions related to infant and young child feeding in general, and breastfeeding in particular. In turn, a woman's decision to breastfeed or not breastfeed and her capacity to carry out this decision, have health, infant development, social, cultural, and economic implications. Currently, however, there is no comprehensive framework or convention tackling the rights, needs, and capabilities of both mother and child during this critical period of biological, emotional, social, and legal interconnectedness.

A focus on nutrition during pregnancy and lactation must not, however, diminish attention to women's nutritional needs over their life spans. Whether or not childbearing is relevant in a woman's life, her right to adequate food and nutrition must be recognized, respected, protected, and fulfilled throughout her entire life span (as must also be men's). Nevertheless, a key component of a woman's health in maternity is the cumulative outcome of her own nutritional well-being as fetus, infant, girl child, and adolescent, who throughout motherhood projects her health status forward in her own offspring. In maternal and child nutrition, older women often have the role of caregiver for children and traditionally pass nutritional health-related knowledge and practice to younger women, thereby contributing to the nutritional well-being of families and communities and future generations. The former United Nations (UN) special rapporteur on the right to health, Anand Grover, and other experts in the field suggest that encouraging older persons to remain physically, politically, socially, and economically active for as long as possible will benefit not only the individual, but society as a whole (HRC 2011b).

Chapters one and two in this volume introduce aspects of the *Convention on the Elimination of All Forms of Discrimination against Women* (CEDAW; UN General Assembly 1979) and the *Convention on the Rights of the Child* (CRC; UN General Assembly 1989). Both international treaties have long histories of active lobbying, beginning well before the 1945 *Charter of the United Nations* (UN 1945). Both achieved success after the "development decades" of the 1960s and 1970s when it became recognized that universality in law did not produce equal access to rights for discriminated against groups like women, children, refugees, and indigenous peoples. Notably, human rights for women and children were developed largely separately. The complex interconnectedness of mother and child in pregnancy, infancy, and breastfeeding has yet to be adequately addressed. Adopted by the UN General Assembly in 1959, the *Declaration of the Rights of the Child* states that "the child, by reason of his [*sic*] physical and mental immaturity, needs special safeguards and care, including appropriate legal protection, before as well as after birth" (UN General Assembly 1959, opening section). In 1994, the International Conference on Population and Development in Cairo affirmed women's reproductive rights and included reproductive health as a basic human right for women. These landmark developments proclaim the individual and inalienable rights of infants and young children on the one hand, and women on the other. The separation of these rights declarations dodges, however, the unique physical and empathic aspects of pregnancy and breastfeeding and, in doing so, disadvantages the potential of related policy and programs.

Ongoing de facto discrimination against women and children is evident. Girls face more discrimination than boys, although the level of childhood gender discrimination overall is under scrutiny and more research is advised (UNICEF 2011).[3] According to *Resolution 7/14 on the Right to Food* of the UN Human Rights Council (HRC; see HRC 2008), in many countries girls are twice as likely as boys to die from malnutrition and preventable childhood disease, and it is estimated that almost twice as many women as men suffer from malnutrition. Despite the stated protections of CEDAW for women and the CRC for children, each year half a million women die from mostly preventable complications of pregnancy and childbirth. For every death, approximately twenty women suffer from injury, infection, disease, or disability as a result of complications arising from pregnancy and childbirth (UNICEF 2010, 26).

Approximately two-thirds of infant deaths occur within the first twenty-eight days; one in seven children in Sub-Saharan Africa die before their fifth birthday; and one in four children under the age of five are underweight (UNICEF 2010, 14, 22). Due both to unequal access to nutrition and bargaining capacity in negotiating sexual relations, girls and women aged fifteen to twenty-four in Sub-Saharan Africa are at least twice as likely to become infected with HIV than their male counterparts (UNICEF 2010, 30). HIV infection has an immense impact on both maternal nutritional health status and on the manner in which infants of HIV infected mothers are fed. Existing reproductive health vulnerabilities and risks are quickly magnified both by man-made and natural disaster emergencies; they are exacerbated by inadequate reproductive health services. Women and young children are particularly affected by emergency situations; gender-based violence, mental health, and psychosocial issues have an impact on a mother's ability to provide optimal feeding and care for an infant or a young child (ENN 2011b; Ziaei, Naved, and Ekström 2012).[4]

As argued also in chapters three and six of this volume, interventions in support of mother-child health and nutrition must not treat pregnancy and lactation as periods isolated from the rest of life and the longer-term well-being of women and children. The heightened challenges and demands of pregnancy, lactation, and infancy are magnified when correlated with discrimination against women and children. A malnourished and pregnant child bride who is sold into marriage by her impoverished family is a case in point. Short-term nutritional interventions in the context of such massive gender-based violations may be improving the birth weight of the newborn but will not improve the girl's future or her capacity to claim her human right to adequate food and nutrition, let alone any other rights. Truly addressing maternal and child nutritional health must begin by addressing women's and children's human rights overall. Eglantyne Jebb, founder of Save the Children in 1919, identified the overlapping violations connecting child and maternal well-being in the context of larger human rights as follows:

> Mankind as a whole is responsible for the world as a whole, and the people of every race should unite to get rid of such evils as child slavery, premature marriage, child labor and neglect and starvation of children.[5]

More attention is needed to investigate how gender roles and relations impact maternal and child health (cf. Tolhurst, Raven, and Theobald 2009). Women and children are not just members of society who require aid during maternity and infancy. Neither do women deserve blame for the malnutrition and ill-health they and their children face under diverse conditions, including poverty, crisis, and corporate abuse. Women and children are rights holders with demands for justice, dignity, respect, and equality. In the context of pregnancy, infancy, and breastfeeding, their human rights concurrently intertwine and exist individually.

ACCOUNTABILITY, THE BALANCE OF POWER BETWEEN STATE AND NON-STATE ACTORS, AND INTERTWINED SUBJECTIVITIES

States parties to the 1966 *International Covenant on Economic, Social and Cultural Rights* (ICESCR; UN General Assembly 1966), which entered into force in 1976, are obligated to protect, respect, and fulfill the human right to adequate food and nutrition for all persons. This requires that organizers of related projects, programs, and food distribution mechanisms (whether public relief, market-based, or traditional/alternative social exchange) respect the dignity and self-determination of state party populations.[6]

The legal and binding obligations of the ICESCR extend to non-state actors, such as transnational corporations (TNCs), through states parties' obligations to protect every human being against human rights abuses caused by non-state actors. In this sense, states parties are obliged to regulate, monitor, investigate, and sanction non-state actors abusing human rights; victims of such abuses must have recourse and remedy mechanisms available (CESCR 2011). Therefore, non-state actors abusing the right to adequate food and nutrition and related rights shall be held accountable.

The practical question then is: how can states parties and the private for-profit and private non-profit sectors operating in, or from (with respect to extraterritorial obligations), a state's domain be held accountable to their legal obligations to realize progressively the human right to adequate food and nutrition? In other words, what kind of oversight processes will help to determine whether the action and spirit of related policies, projects, and programs serve the population well and proactively?

States parties must fulfill their treaty-linked obligations with utmost transparency and in democratic dialogue with their population. However, transparency and dialogue alone do not ensure treaty compliance. Monitoring, evaluation, regulation, and recourse mechanisms are necessary in order to hold states parties and non-state actors accountable. Therefore, beyond the ratification process, the ICESCR treaty obligations should be transposed into national legislation. Ratification and associated national and international legislation provide states parties with leverage to regulate and monitor treaty obligations, making even more explicit the requirement that all sectors—whether public, private for-profit, private non-profit, or some hybrid thereof—must operate within the context of these national obligations to international law. Women and children, as well as men, should not have to depend on legally non-binding ("voluntary") initiatives by corporations to have their rights protected.

Along with other TNCs, the agrofood industry has become increasingly consolidated and powerful. At the international level, there is presently no global regulatory system that effectively regulates and monitors TNC activities to ensure that they comply with human rights international law standards and do not have a negative impact on the right to adequate food and nutrition in countries where they source, process, market, and trade their goods. At the national level, therefore, it is all the more critical that states assume fully the obligation to protect their citizens from corporate abuses and violations of human rights, and that they hold these businesses accountable to their responsibility to respect human rights in their countries and extraterritorially. The 2011 *Maastricht Principles on Extraterritorial Obligations of States in the Area of Economic, Social and Cultural Rights*, which do not establish new elements of human rights law but clarify extraterritorial obligations of states on the basis of standing international law, provide an important new guidance (Maastricht University and ICJ 2012).

At both the international and national levels, it has been difficult for states parties to hold non-state actors accountable, particularly those in the business sector, due to mutual dependencies: income to govern and free license to operate. Recent forms of the international development model, like public-private partnerships (PPPs) and multistakeholder initiatives (MSIs), often conflate public and private for-profit interests, confusing what should be distinct roles and responsibilities of publicly elected servants. These governing hybrid arrangements tend not to be transparent (Ollila 2003); they squeeze out democratic participation, stifle government incentive to monitor and regulate, and sidestep accountability demands of binding obligations, settling instead for soft promises of working on behalf of public interests (Richter 2001).

With specific attention to maternal and infant/child care, the following illustrates aspects of sectoral power imbalance *vis-à-vis* policy and programming on the right to adequate food and nutrition.

United Nations Human Rights Committees

At the regional and global levels, UN treaty bodies monitor the progressive realization of human rights. In Geneva, specific treaty bodies, known as human rights committees, specifically or additionally examine states parties' accountability *vis-à-vis* the right to adequate food and nutrition. These include the Committee on Economic, Social and Cultural Rights (CESCR), the Committee on the Elimination of Discrimination against Women (CEDAW Committee), and the Committee on the Rights of the Child (CRC Committee). As duty bearers to the international laws, states parties are required regularly to submit status reports to treaties' respective human rights committees.[7] Through this evolving model, human rights committees review national state party reports, publicly respond with an evaluation of progress to date, and issue concluding observations and recommendations designed to propel the state party forward. The objective is to hold states parties accountable through transparent reporting and committee's feedback thereby: (*a*) permitting country residents to push their elected representatives to follow committee recommendations, and (*b*) advancing the progressive realization of specific human rights and holding non-state actors accountable for any abuses of these human rights.

Non-state actors play significant roles at the national and international levels in how states parties proceed with the fulfillment of their human rights obligations. The unequal balance of power between, on the one hand, the private for-profit sector (most specifically at the corporate level), and, on the other hand, public interest non-governmental organizations (NGOs) and other public interest members of the civil society, namely civil society organizations (CSOs), results in—as a reliable generalization—greater influence on the public sector, including governments, by the private for-profit sector than by the public interest actors from civil society.

National and international NGOs and other members of civil society may submit alternative national reports to the human rights committees. This process helps counter the weight of private sector interests and democratize human rights treaty bodies' processes by bolstering the profile and interests of civil society. CSOs are particularly encouraged to coordinate such alternate reports (OHCHR 2008).[8]

Furthermore, the UN General Assembly and HRC have requested all international organizations "to promote policies and projects that have a positive impact on the right to food . . . and to avoid any actions that could have a negative impact on the realization of the right to food" (OHCHR 2010, 23–24).[9] As described in chapter one of this volume, this reflects the obligation of progressive realization and non-retrogression of human rights.

Human rights treaty bodies have the mandate to issue so-called general comments (see, CESCR and CRC Committee) or general recommendations (see, CEDAW Committee) on thematic issues. The CESCR has, for example, issued:

- *General Comment 12 on the Right to Adequate Food* (CESCR 1999)
- *General Comment 14 on the Right to the Highest Attainable Standard of Health* (CESCR 2000)
- *General Comment 16 on the Equal Right of Men and Women to the Enjoyment of All Economic, Social and Cultural Rights* (CESCR 2005)
- *General Comment 20 on Non-Discrimination in Economic, Social and Cultural Rights* (CESCR 2009).

Through general comments or recommendations, human rights committees provide authoritative interpretations of the content of particular human rights treaty provisions. Motivation to prepare such interpretations arises from a united request, such as the call from state and non-state actors coming out of the 1996 World Food Summit that stimulated the generation of *General Comment 12 on the Right to Adequate Food* (for further discussion, see chapter one of this volume). Authors of this volume, for example, advocate that the CEDAW Committee issue a *General Recommendation on the Human Right to Adequate Food and Nutrition and Women* (see esp. chapter six of this volume). Increasingly, the argument is being made, and authors in this volume support it, that international treaties and their general comments and recommendations have relevance for the accountable obligations not only of state party duty bearers but, also, of non-state actors (Right to Food and Nutrition WATCH Consortium 2011).

Case study 4.1 CRC Committee: *General Comment 16 on State Obligations Regarding the Impact of the Business Sector on Children's Rights*

In 2011, the CRC Committee launched a process to develop a general comment on child rights and the business sector. This general comment had the potential of becoming a unifying framework that could guide states parties in establishing regulatory instruments to protect children's rights and emphasize business' legal obligations to respect those rights. With reference to the focus of this chapter, it was important to ensure that such a regulatory framework include provisions that require businesses to:

- Refrain from unethical marketing of products that undermine optimal infant and young child feeding
- Refrain from undermining known best nutrition and health practices
- Operate in ways that do not monopolize local markets thereby threatening and/or destroying local food and nutrition economies and leading to dependency on global markets at the cost of local initiatives for self-reliance and dignity.

Effective NGO advocacy ensured that *General Comment 16 on State Obligations Regarding the Impact of the Business Sector on Children's Rights* (hereinafter referred to as *General Comment 16*), issued by the CRC Committee in February 2013, urges states parties to implement and enforce internationally agreed standards.

The Committee acknowledges that voluntary actions of corporate responsibility by business enterprises such as social investments, advocacy and public policy engagement, voluntary codes of conduct, philanthropy and other collective actions can advance children's rights. States should encourage such voluntary actions and initiatives as a means to create a business culture which respects and supports children's rights. However, *it should be emphasised that such voluntary actions and initiatives are not a substitute for State action and regulation of businesses in line with obligations under the Convention and its protocols or for businesses to comply with their responsibilities to respect children's rights.* (CRC Committee 2013b, para. 9; emphasis added)

While *General Comment 16* includes reference to "voluntary actions of corporate responsibility," states are nonetheless required to implement and enforce internationally agreed upon standards concerning children's rights, health, and business. This includes the 1981 *International Code of Marketing of Breast-milk Substitutes* (hereinafter referred to as *Code*; WHO 1981) and relevant subsequent World Health Assembly (WHA) resolutions. In conclusion, what *General Comment 16* provides is critically important as it represents a stronger framework to uphold international nutrition standards for children, despite the fact that it does not have the required regulatory power to hold businesses accountable to those standards.

Corporate Accountability, Corporate Social Responsibility, and Global Multistakeholder Cooperation

Corporate social responsibility (CSR) suggests ethical business behavior, but upon closer examination is a slippery concept that holds different meanings for different persons and institutions.

> The term [social responsibility] is a brilliant one; it means something, but not always the same thing, to everybody. To some it conveys the idea of legal responsibility or liability; to others, it means socially responsible behavior in an ethical sense; to still others, the meaning transmitted is that of "responsible for," in a causal mode; many simply equate it with a charitable contribution; some take it to mean socially conscious; many of those who embrace it most fervently see it as a mere synonym for "legitimacy," in the context of "belonging" or being proper or valid; a few see it as a sort of fiduciary duty imposing higher standards of behavior on businessmen than on citizens at large. (Votaw 1973, 11; quoted in Carroll 1999, 280)

In theory, CSR leads to a harmonization between corporate interests and social development, including human rights. However, since in practice businesses cannot and will not relinquish their organizational orientation of profit making, their ethical focus is always in competition with business success (Friedman 1970), especially when businesses are so large that "stakeholders" have no grounded understanding of business impacts. Richter writes: "Relying on corporate self-interest while refraining from any meaningful checks on corporate practices is akin to building on quicksand" (Richter 2003, 44).

CSR is designed as a *voluntary* concession on the part of business, not adherence to legally binding obligations that engender oversight, regulation, sanctions, and democratic or civil society commentary on business practice. Therefore, when businesses enter into MSIs or PPPs with public organizations in the name of CSR and social development, the opportunity to develop clear binding frameworks and expectations for accountability in corporate practice becomes remote. Indeed, such multistakeholder schemes and PPPs can sidetrack initiatives to develop legally binding regulatory tools and structures for human rights frameworks applied to business practice.

Attempting *mandatory*, instead of legally non-binding, guidelines for businesses quickly reveals the implausibility of relying on CSR to steer businesses toward adherence to international codes and law. In 2003, the UN Sub-Commission on the Promotion and Protection of Human Rights *unanimously* adopted the UN *Draft Norms on Responsibilities of Transnational Corporations and Other Business Enterprises with Regard to Human Rights* (hereinafter referred to as *Norms;* UN 2003). The *Norms* articulated a range of legal obligations on corporations, drawn from existing human rights, labor rights, and environmental standards. Formal obligations were placed on TNCs and other business enterprises, their officers, and their workers to respect generally recognized responsibilities and norms in UN treaties and other international instruments. The 1981 *Code*, that sets rules for the marketing of infant formula, other forms of breastmilk substitutes, and feeding bottles and teats, was on the list of instruments identified in the 2003 *Norms*.

The TNCs mounted an immediate and ferocious opposition to the *Norms*. Among others, the International Chamber of Commerce and the International Organization of Employers described the proposed draft norms as "counterproductive to the UN's ongoing efforts to encourage companies to support and observe human rights norms by participating in the Global Compact" (ICC and IOE 2003, 2). The UN Global Compact was launched in 2000 by UN Secretary General Kofi Annan and is described on its website as "a strategic policy initiative for businesses that are committed to aligning their operations and strategies with ten universally accepted principles in the areas of human rights, labor, environment and anti-corruption."[10] TNC resistance to the *Norms* resulted in their eradication from the UN agenda in 2004. In 2006, the UN Commission on Human Rights was disbanded and replaced by the HRC.[11] And so, UN-TNC multistakeholder approaches now fully reflect a shift toward what Utting already in 2002 described as "lukewarm voluntary initiatives [that] have crowded out important mechanisms and institutional arrangements involving new forms of international law, oversight or monitoring of TNC activities, mediation or arbitration disputes, and critical research into regulatory alternatives and the social, environmental and developmental impact of TNCs" (Utting 2002, 646). CSR distracts us from creating any meaningful change or enforcement of international regulations.

Case study 4.2 UNICEF, UN Global Compact, and Save the Children: *Children's Rights and Business Principles Initiative*

The United Nations Children's Fund (UNICEF) with Save the Children and in partnership with the UN Global Compact developed the *Children's Rights and Business Principles* (CRBP) with the intention to launch them in spring 2012.[12] The CRBP effort is based on the CSR model championed by the UN Global Compact wherein the focus is on legally non-binding measures rather than on states parties' obligations to monitor and regulate state and non-state actors *vis-à-vis* the impact of business on children's rights, including the right to adequate food and nutrition. As the UN Joint Inspection Unit (JIU) concluded in their evaluation of the UN Global Compact:

> [The UN Global Compact annual reviews] are basically a self-assessment exercise of business participants' progress in implementing the ten principles . . . [and] do not depict an independent,

unbiased and comprehensive picture of the Global Compact successes and failures, opportunities and risks. The Inspectors are of the opinion that other performance review mechanisms should be put in place to increase effectiveness and accountability. (Fall and Zahran 2010, para. 135)[13]

The International Baby Food Action Network (IBFAN) was concerned about the UN Global Compact approach and warned already in its July 2011 comments on the initiative that "[a]s currently presented, the CRBPI will be another opportunity for business to improve its image by its association with the UN system, without any real strategy proposed by the UN to ensure that children's rights are protected" (IBFAN 2011a).

This concern was heard, despite strong opposition by the infant food industry. When the CRBP initiative was launched in the course of 2012, both globally as well as nationally in a number of countries with plans to pilot its implementation in 2013, its principle 6.b. directed businesses to "[c]omply with the standards of business conduct in World Health Assembly instruments related to marketing and health in all countries. Where national law prescribes a higher standard, business must follow that standard" (UNICEF, UN Global Compact, and Save the Children 2012, 26).

Now, the legally non-binding CRBP engage the same language as the UN CRC Committee's *General Comment 16*, issued in 2013 (further discussion to follow). It remains to be seen, however, whether the CRBP will reinforce or compromise the expected positive impact of *General Comment 16* on the fulfillment of children's rights. The latter is feared by public interest NGOs.

Blocking Corporate Accountability: Conflict of Interest

The WHO and UNICEF 2003 *Global Strategy for Infant and Young Child Feeding* (hereinafter referred to as *IYCF Global Strategy*) defines the appropriate roles of companies in relation to infant and young child feeding. The definition of the roles is essential to addressing and minimizing risks posed by conflicts of interest caused by too close interaction between baby food companies and public sector decision makers. The two roles identified by the *IYCF Global Strategy* as appropriate for the baby food companies to engage in are: (a) comply with the 1981 *International Code of Marketing of Breast-milk Substitutes* and subsequent relevant WHA resolutions, and (b) meet specific quality, safety, and labeling standards set by the *Codex Alimentarius*. Limiting business activity to these roles reduces the risk of corporate interference with public policy making related to the *Code* and subsequent relevant WHA resolutions. If companies employed their considerable resources to fulfill these two roles, they would best contribute to the overall aim of the *IYCF Global Strategy* "to improve—through optimal feeding—the nutritional status, growth and development, health, and thus the survival of infants and young children" (WHO and UNICEF 2003, para 6). Nevertheless, infant food manufacturers have continued to pursue involvement beyond these stipulated roles. Many of them have entered the domain of public health policy making and implementation by joining UN-backed initiatives such as the recent nutrition-oriented initiative that started in 2008, Scaling Up Nutrition (SUN), to which we return later in this chapter.

Despite clear conflicts of interest, the public sector consciously and perversely invites private corporate entities to participate in public sector decision-making. Shortly after the introduction of the UN Global Compact, the public-private partnership Global Alliance for Improved Nutrition (GAIN) was launched at the 2002 UN General Assembly Special Session on Children.[14] On GAIN's Board of Directors sit the corporate partners that manufacture much of the processed foods that have tipped the global diet toward less locally sustainable diets and higher rates of noncommunicable diseases (NCDs; see, e.g., Moodie et al. 2013).[15] Among the original members of GAIN's Board of Directors was DANONE, the second largest infant food manufacturer and a known *Code* violator (Lhotska 2008). Due to the pressure from public interest NGOs, DANONE was forced to step down from the board but continued until recently to be a GAIN partner. Brittania Industries Ltd., for which DANONE formerly was a major shareholder and whose stated purpose is to "[h]elp people enjoy life—through healthy snacking,"[16] is still represented on the board of GAIN, encouraging consumption of junk foods.

The fact that at the UN level there is no comprehensive ethical and policy framework to adequately deal with conflicts of interest and help to delineate appropriate from inappropriate roles for business, together with the failure to pass the *Norms*, enables commercial actors to filter inappropriately into the responsibilities of public interest actors, thus increasing risks to the integrity, independence, and trustworthiness of public sector actors in public policy making.

There are various guidelines on cooperation between UN agencies and the business community. They include, for instance, the UN *Guidelines on Cooperation between the United Nations and the Business Community* (2000, 2009), the WHO *Guidelines on Working with the Private Sector to Achieve Health Outcomes* (2000), and the WHO *Policy on WHO Engagement with Global Health Partnerships and Hosting Arrangements* (2010a). These documents contain a number of useful tenets. For example, the UN 2009 guidelines list among its general principles for cooperation that any UN business arrangements should "[a]dvance UN goals" (UN 2009, para.

12.a) and "should not diminish the UN's integrity, independence, and impartiality" (para. 12.d). Furthermore, they should be based on a "[c]lear delineation of responsibilities and roles" (para 12.c) and be "transparent" (para. 12.f), meaning that "information on the nature and scope of major cooperative arrangements should be available . . . to the public at large" (para. 12.f). The problem is that there is a clear gap between such guidelines and UN agencies' practices.

The words "conflicts of interest" appear in various global UN policy documents. However, the argument of transparency is often used by UN leaders to curtail any debate about the need for effective conflict of interest safeguards. Transparency about *who and what*, that is, who has what role and represents what social sector—and thus what their primary interests are—is an essential requirement and first step toward addressing conflicts of interest. Nevertheless, this so-called "revelation" is not a sufficient safeguard against harmful effects on policy making and program implementation caused by profit motivated conflicts of interest that have not been dealt with appropriately.

Therefore, despite reference to conflicts of interest in several UN documents, the "United Nations family" has no comprehensive ethical and policy framework to help adequately deal with both institutional and individual conflicts of interest and to help differentiate appropriate from inappropriate roles for business (Conflicts of Interest Coalition 2011; Richter 2004).[17]

We present two definitions that may help to better understand and address this issue:

- "A[n individual] conflict of interest is a set of conditions in which professional judgment concerning a *primary interest* . . . tends to be unduly influenced by a *secondary interest*" (Thompson 2005, 290; emphasis added)
- "Institutional conflicts of interest arise when an institution's own financial interest or those of its senior officials pose risk of undue influence on decisions involving the institution's primary interest" (Lo and Field 2009, 218).

Conflicts of interest do occur, for example, when the wish of UN agencies to attract private sector resources (secondary interest) conflicts with their duty to work toward the fulfillment of their "core missions" as expressed in their constitutional mandates and functions (primary interests). Conflict of interest policies and laws are of a very particular nature: "Whether they are at the individual or the institutional level, conflict of interest policies seek to *prevent* compromised decisions" (Lo and Field 2009, 218; emphasis added).

Increasingly, public interest civil society actors are concerned about the lack of comprehensive safeguards against conflicts of interest and the role that industry front groups present when they attempt to pass as genuine NGOs and thereby organize to exercise inappropriate pressure on UN policy and action.

Case study 4.3 Conflicts of Interest Coalition

The trend of businesses positioning themselves within civil society was challenged at the September 2011 UN High-Level Meeting on Prevention and Control of Non-Communicable Diseases by the Conflicts of Interest Coalition.[18] A *Statement of Concern* (Conflicts of Interest Coalition 2011), endorsed in the same month by 145 national, regional, and global networks and organizations working in public health, including medicine, nutrition, cancer, diabetes, heart disease, lung disease, mental health, infant feeding, food safety, and development, called on the UN to:

- Recognize and distinguish between industries, including business interest non-governmental organizations (BINGOs) and public interest non-governmental organizations (PINGOs) that are both currently under the "civil society" umbrella without distinction
- Develop a code of conduct that sets out a clear framework for interacting with the private sector and managing conflicts of interest and that differentiates between policy development and appropriate involvement in implementation.

The UN member states ignored the *Statement of Concern*, recognizing conflicts of interest only in the context of the tobacco industry and public health, and calling generally for expanded collaborative partnerships at all levels among all actors.

The October 2011 comment in *The Lancet* by Beaglehole et al. (2011) describes the summit as an impressive success. The comment emphasizes the idea of a NCD partnership that would "include all key stakeholders—civil society, UN agencies, including WHO, the World Bank, and the private sector"—and stresses the need for "transparent rules of engagement for all partners" (Beaglehole et al. 2011, 1283–84). However, *The Lancet* essay fails to acknowledge the risks for conflicts of interest and the need for clear policy to safeguard against these. Therefore, those concerned with the improvement and protection of public health continue to share one worry: the influence of industry sectors whose policies and practices conflict with those of public health (WPHNA 2011).

In January 2012, the executive board of WHO attempted to rectify this failure at its hundred-and-thirtieth session and in resolution

EB130.R7, forwarded to the sixty-fifth session of the WHA for adoption, requested WHO's director general "to develop, in a consultative manner, WHO's input, called for in paragraph 64 of the Political Declaration of the [Summit] concerning options for strengthening and facilitating multisectoral action for the prevention and control of noncommunicable diseases through effective and transparent partnership, while safeguarding public health from any potential conflict of interest, and submit it to the Secretary-General by the end of 2012" (WHO 2012a, EB130/R.7, para. 2.2). This wording did not survive intensive lobbying by industry and industry friendly governments at the sixty-fifth WHA session (WHA 2012a).

The decision was taken to develop a global coordination mechanism "to improve coordination of activities which address functional gaps that are barriers to the prevention and control of noncommunicable diseases" (WHA 2013, para. 15) and "with a view to perform collectively, in a coordinated and coherent manner, a set of actions for Member States, international partners and the private sector, and WHO comprised in the WHO Global NCD Action Plan 2013–2020" (WHO 2013b, para. 3). The global coordinating mechanism is understood as yet another MSI, with the corporate sector seen as an equal partner.

The policy shift toward closer cooperation between the UN and the corporate sector has created an environment in which many have come to believe there seems to be no alternative to having private sector actors as "partners" and "stakeholders" in any public initiative. We face a crisis of insufficient scrutiny of the actual conduct of corporate "partners," for example, baby food manufacturers; all seem accepted. In 2011, for instance, the UN secretary general called on all actors to contribute to the 2010 Every Woman Every Child initiative in terms of policy, service, and product delivery, and through financial support.[19] Thus, the private sector actors can relatively easily use UN initiatives to gain influence in public policy making arenas that intersect with their market goals and, at the same time, "bluewash" their tarnished images through association with the UN.[20]

Case study 4.4 Nestlé's nutrition education program to teen mothers in India

As already described, in 2011 the UN called on all actors in the secretary general's 2010 Every Woman Every Child initiative to submit their commitments in policy, service, or product delivery area, and financial commitments. Nestlé's initial, and no longer available, internet commitment statement to the implementation of the UN Secretary general's Every Woman Every Child initiative follows (emphasis added):

> Nestlé commits to *expanding nutrition education to teenage girls in all its milk villages in India before they reach the age of marriage, so that they will have the nutritional knowledge to best feed their children when they reach childbearing age.* Nestlé also aims to double the number of countries covered by its Healthy Kids Global Program launched in 2010, and already has programs in over 50 countries reaching 5 million children.[21]

This initial Nestlé statement almost explodes with the revelation that the corporation views teenage girls not as young women with human rights, including reproductive rights, but rather in a narrow biological straitjacket that identifies them as potential future consumers and feeders of inferior Nestlé products for infants and young children. Some concerns within the UN must have been raised, as the original commitment was reworded. Nestlé rethought the transparency of this statement and, today, the 2011 corporation's pledge found on the UN Foundation's website of the initiative reads:

> Nestlé's commitment to *Every Woman Every Child* is anchored in continuing and scaling up a host of programs, including the expansion of Nestlé Healthy Kids Global Programme (HKP). . . . HKP has been designed to address today's complex health challenges, such as poor nutrition and obesity, by teaching school-age children the value of good nutrition and physical activity.[22]

This Nestlé case study raises a set of fundamental questions: why does the UN accept a commitment that goes beyond the roles defined for infant food manufacturers by the *Code* and the WHO and UNICEF *IYCF Global Strategy*? Why does it give its blessing and confer its image on Nestlé, a known *Code* violator? Why does it allow a corporation with clear ulterior motives to take on a role of a nutrition educator for children? Why does it not challenge the company to refrain from marketing infant foods in violation of the *Code* and from producing and marketing unhealthy foods high in salt, fat, and sugar for children?

A strategy that allows Nestlé, the world's largest manufacturer of breastmilk substitutes, to educate teenage girls on infant and young child feeding contradicts the foundational purpose of the *Code*: namely, to ensure that parents receive unbiased and complete information about breastfeeding and the risks of artificial feeding. With the intention to prevent manufacturers from influencing women's infant feeding decisions, the *Code* explicitly prohibits any contact between baby food manufacturers and pregnant women and mothers of infants and young children. We are distressed to see Nestlé unethically programming nutrition education for girls as objects of child and teen marriage and reproduction and accepting the possible denial of their human rights in personal relationships and reproduction. We further observe with great reservation Nestlé's expectation to expand the number of countries in its HKP, wondering why the UN accepts such a commitment. In its pretense of social beneficence, CSR promotes ongoing ignorance and dependence. While businesses expand their profits and create a superficial identity by which their deeds are regarded as heroic, in reality their efforts are shamelessly exploiting women, children, and infants as opportunities to generate "good PR" and new customers.

THE INDEPENDENT AND INTERTWINED SUBJECTIVITIES OF WOMEN AND CHILDREN

Respect, protection, and fulfillment of the right to adequate food and nutrition of women and children depend upon understanding their unique intertwined relationship in pregnancy, childbirth, and breast-feeding stages. Unfortunately, legal and programmatic structures on behalf of maternal, infant, and young child nutritional health have an under-conceptualized framework for addressing the rights and needs of this population cohort.

Independent and Intertwined Subjectivities of Women and Children

As supported in the 1995 *Declaration for Women's Reproductive and Sexual Rights and Health* (WABA 1995), women as independent subjects hold human rights to reproductive and sexual autonomy rights which embrace the full range of decisions related to partnerships and marriage, sexuality, conception, and motherhood (cf. Labbok, Smith, and Taylor 2008). Women require full access to the right to the highest attainable standard of physical and mental health, as well as the right to adequate food and nutrition, regardless of whether or not they themselves have children. CEDAW affirms that women's dignity and freedom require that childbearing be an outcome of informed decision (UN General Assembly 1979, arts. 10(h), 11.2, 12, and 14.2(b)).

The realization of reproductive and sexual rights is crucial for women's and children's right to health and for the reduction of their mortality and morbidity ("Women's Choice is Key to Reduce Maternal Deaths" 2012). Enormous violations of women's rights are evidenced in the inexcusable maternal mortality rates which constitute the biggest inequality in health worldwide and are tied to gender discrimination and the immense gaps between rich and poor globally, and within nations. Maternal mortality is caused directly by obstetric complications aggravated by poor availability and access to quality services for delivery. Indirect mortality risk factors include early marriage, female genital mutilation (FGM), structural violence against women (Paruzzolo et al. 2010), inadequate contraception (Ahmed et al. 2012; Richter 1996; UNFPA 2012), absence of skilled individuals during maternal labor (Gabrysch et al. 2009), and poorly performed abortions (DSW et al. 2009; Grimes et al. 2006; Sedgh et al. 2012; Singh, Sedgh, and Hussain 2010).[23] Also exacerbating maternal mortality rates during pregnancy and childbirth are nutritional deficiencies like anemia often caused by food discrimination, violence against girls and women (see also chapter three of this volume), cultural food taboos (Gao et al. 2013; UN DESA 2010, xi), and nutrition depletion complicated by multiple pregnancies and inadequate child spacing (Central Statistical Agency [Ethiopia] and ORC Macro 2006). These foods, nutrition, and other violations of a woman's human rights mark the subjectivity of a fetus, infant, or young child *not* as uniquely independent, but concurrently as a physical, psychological, and intergenerational extension of the mother. Violations the mother faced and faces during pregnancy set the stage for infant and child rights to adequate food and nutrition through the recycling of the mother's nutrition status in utero to her child.

"Intertwined subjectivities" is the term we introduce to grasp the independent and yet critically interconnected rights, needs, and capacities of women and children in the stages of pregnancy, childbirth, and breastfeeding/lactation. The nutrition practices of pregnant and breastfeeding women and their children, from the antenatal and newborn period through the first years of life, are influenced in many ways: by the balance between women's own choices and the available options to nurture themselves and their babies; by the quality and accessibility of knowledge about and support for best nutrition practices; and by dominant cultural patterns, as well as medical recommendations and marketing tactics for consumption. Health practice might be expected to address nutrition concerns for this intertwined cohort as an organic whole, reflecting the biological and psychological mother-child interdependence in eating, nutrition, and generational reproduction. Yet modern medical practice—and the corporate sector that supports it—often adopts a compartmentalized or fragmented approach that isolates the stages of pregnancy, birthing, and child health and nutrition, functionally separating breastfeeding as the third link after pregnancy and child birth from its essential role in the reproductive cycle. The intimacy of pregnancy continues for mother and newborn after birth. While an infant does not appear to have any direct influence over whether her/his mother decides to breastfeed, the birth itself and the newborn behavior of the baby influence mothers' hormones and provide a positive stimulus for breastfeeding. In support, WHO strategies recommend a "continuum of care" to overcome the structural separation of birth during the extended reproductive period (see, e.g., WHO 2005, esp. chaps. 5 and 6).

Partners in the World Alliance for Breastfeeding Action (WABA) argue that breastfeeding is best framed as a reproductive and sexual right (WABA 1995). If women are denied the opportunity to freely choose breastfeeding, for example, through violations of codes for marketing breastmilk substitutes, they are stripped of bodily integrity and denied the opportunity to enjoy the full potential of their body for "health, procreation and sexuality" (Correa and Petchesky 2007, 113). Consistent with the ethical principles that underpin reproductive and sexual rights, this means that women are denied full personhood in equal measure with men because men have no equivalent bodily function over which they are denied autonomy (Correa and Petchesky 2007; Olbricht 1985). To "freely choose" breastfeeding means, at minimum, having access to best practice information, support to engage in the best practices of breastfeeding, and freedom from marketing interference of other forms of child feeding, as defined in the *Code* and the subsequent WHA resolutions.[24] The choice and the practice of breastfeeding expands and extends the interim period of intimate connection in the mother-infant/young child dyad, defying the absolute separateness of individual subjectivities and rights, and demanding attention to the shifting and intertwined rights and needs of both individual subjects.

The confluence of human rights and breastfeeding is a complicated subject that demonstrates how women's and children's right to adequate food and nutrition must be considered in the context of both the pre- and postnatal intertwined (mother-child) dyad, as well as through the broadest interpretation of their individual and full human rights. In recognizing the right of a child to the highest attainable standard of health, states parties are required:

> To ensure that all segments of society, in particular parents and children, are informed, have access to education and are supported in the use of basic knowledge of child health and nutrition, the advantages of breastfeeding, hygiene and environmental sanitation and the prevention of accidents. (UN General Assembly 1989, art. 24(e))

The intersection of rights of women to breastfeed, of women to decide whether or not to breastfeed, and of infants to receive the best possible nutrition, evokes strong and sometimes divisive professional, emotional, legal, and ethical commitments and perspectives. If women are given complete and unbiased information and support and have all the obstacles to breastfeeding eliminated, including marketing interference, they are likely to choose breastfeeding over formula feeding. It is thus essential that related debates do not lose sight of the larger frame of corporate actors' participation—and state actors' complicity through lack of regulation—in the social and commercial manipulation and misinformation regarding the normative value of breastfeeding.

Infants' capacity to exercise their right to adequate food and nutrition and to health depends upon other people. Due to the immediate and direct dependence of infants on their mothers, the nutritional status of infants is determined not only by the quality of the food, health services, and care they receive directly, but also by the food, health services, and care received by the mother herself (Ashworth and Ferguson 2009; Bhutta and Labbok 2011; Trickey and Newburn 2012). Mothers, and fathers as well (Sherriff and Hall 2011), should be entitled to parental nutrition-related services and information in-line with internationally recognized best practices, codes, and regulations, as well as the right to be protected from undue influences from commercial interests not only because of their own rights and needs, but also because of their legal responsibility to provide for their children. Pregnant women and mothers must have the right to work, as well as protection in public and work places that safeguards their health and allows them to breastfeed their children as needed. These requirements are necessary components to ensure the progressive realization of infants' right to adequate food and nutrition (cf. Kent 2002; 2005, 171).

Intertwined Subjectivities in Utero: Re/Production of Nutrition Status over the Intergenerational Life Cycle

Nutritional well-being in an adult typically reflects one stage in an intergenerational health cycle that includes positive and/or negative nutritional status during childhood, in utero, and reaching back even to a child's mother's nutritional status prior to and during pregnancy.

Malnutrition continues to afflict the woman of childbearing age and later years. Poor nutrition, literally and figuratively, reproduces itself in the form of intergenerational cycles of growth failure, (leaving malnourished girls at nutritional disadvantage in subsequent generations), with serious consequences for maternity, childbirth, and infant physical and mental health (i.e., the risk of intellectual deficits). Childhood stunting increases the incidence of low birth weight (LBW) babies in adolescents and adult women. For LBW newborns, especially those born into poor living conditions, LBW is a special risk factor for health problems during infancy as well as later in life, for example, in regards to pneumonia, diabetes, hypertension, coronary heart disease, and growth failure. LBW girls are more likely to become short statured (stunted) adult women who face increased risk of complications during childbirth, including heightened risk of dying and having LBW babies themselves (ACC/SCN and IFPRI 2000; Save the Children 2006; SCN 2010).

Incidence of poverty and gendered malnutrition over the life span are the dependent links between child health and survival, and maternal nutritional, cultural, and economic status; they begin their influence even before conception. Fetal programming theory (Godfrey and Barker 2000) asserts that disease susceptibility (e.g., affecting blood pressure and insulin levels) starts in the mother's womb and influences children's and adults' health as they mature. Maternal malnutrition can impair the growth of fetal organs leading to permanent changes in structure and functioning of the fetus' body (Godfrey and Barker 2000; Thurnham 2012; A. F. Williams 2009).[25]

In 2000, the concept of "nutrition throughout the life cycle" began inspiring intervention strategies to improve the nutritional status of women before and during pregnancy with the *Fourth Report on the World Nutrition Situation: Nutrition throughout the Life Cycle* of the UN Administrative Committee on Coordination/Subcommittee on Nutrition (ACC/SCN) in collaboration with the International Food Policy Research Institute (IFPRI; see ACC/SCN and IFPRI 2000).[26] This report failed, however, to describe either the role or potential of breastfeeding to address the critical window of child development from conception until two years of age or the intergenerational nature of a life cycle approach. Further, therefore, breastfeeding's potential, as a best nutrition practice because of its capacity to even out much of the negative impact of discrimination and poverty on nutrition status, was not emphasized.

Ten years later, the *Sixth Report on the World Nutrition Situation* reiterates the importance of the life cycle approach, arguing that birth weight can be rapidly improved even in populations of short statured adult women by improving their diet through quantity and quality (SCN 2010). Although the 2010 report fails to emphasize the importance of breastfeeding (Thurnham 2012), the progressive text does link maternal malnutrition to social discrimination (i.e., early marriage and teen pregnancy), and promotes nutritional and family planning activities, not only to augment newborn birth weight but to redress and reverse social inequalities and to make concrete contributions to the "progressive realization of the rights of the girl child and of the adolescent mother" (SCN 2010, 63).

Intertwined Subjectivities *Ex Utero:* Infant and Young Child Nutrition

As earlier stated, breastfeeding is the norm and the only best practice for infant feeding up to approximately six months of a child's life (WHO and UNICEF 2005). The benefits accrue to all mothers regardless of age of conception, wealth or poverty, or other factor, as well as to their infants and young children. These benefits last across the life cycles. Best practice breastfeeding benefits families, communities, and nation states through the engagement of a local, renewable, lowest cost, and best quality nutrition and public health resource.

Case study 4.5 Impact of breastfeeding

The impact of breastfeeding on mothers. Immediate postpartum breastfeeding results in less postpartum bleeding, synchronization of mother-child sleep patterns, enhanced self-esteem, lower rates of postpartum depression, decreased incidence of osteoporosis through improved calcium metabolism, better return to pre-pregnancy weight, delay of the return of fertility,[27] and risk reduction for type 2 diabetes, coronary heart disease, and ovarian, breast, and other reproductive cancers later in life. These outcomes in turn lower the risk of maternal death from postpartum bleeding and reduce postpartum trauma while fostering mother-baby bonding through sleep synchronization and intensive skin to skin contact that releases anti-stress hormones (Groer and Davis 2006; LINKAGES 2001; Scherbaum, Rouw, and Hormann 2011; Stuebe 2009).

The impact of breastfeeding on children. Relative to artificially fed infants, immediate and continued postpartum breastfeeding provides immeasurable immunological protection from the colostrum (first milk), especially immediately after birth: enhanced immune functions; self-regulation of nourishment intake; protection against diarrhea, respiratory diseases, otitis media, and urinary tract infections; promotion of correct development of jaw and teeth; improved cognitive development; greater visual and hearing functions; and decreased risk of chronic diseases like obesity, cancer, adult cardiovascular diseases, allergic conditions, and diabetes mellitus (Gartner et al. 2005; Gillman et al. 2001; Lamberti et al. 2011; Scherbaum and Bellows 2009; Scherbaum, Rouw, and Hormann 2011; Stuebe 2009; WHO 2007, 2009).

According to a meta-study review by Edmond et al. (2006), early initiation of breastfeeding could prevent 16 percent of neonatal deaths if all infants were breastfed from day one and 22 percent if breastfeeding started within the first hour of birth. Jones et al. (2003) calculated that up to 13 percent of under five-year-old deaths could be prevented through breastfeeding promotion and 6 percent through appropriate complementary feeding (introduced below). The nutritional impact of continued breastfeeding, which starts from a completed six months of exclusive breastfeeding up to two years old or beyond, is often poorly understood. As continued lactation provides about one-half of an infant's energy needs up to the age of one year and up to one-third during the second year of life (Brown, Dewey, and Allen 1998; WHO 2009), it also reduces the pressure on complementary feeding to fill the tremendous nutrient gaps within a few months in case of rapid secession of breastfeeding.

Positive impacts of breastfeeding on both child and mother. A meta-analysis by Gale et al. (2012) suggests that breastfeeding may have a small protective effect against the development of obesity among children and mothers. Compared with breastfeeding, formula feeding is associated with altered body composition for infants, including a higher fat mass.[28]

Positive impacts of breastfeeding beyond the child-mother dyad. Breastfeeding can strengthen family ties, promote family nutritional security, has short and long-term economic advantages (e.g., less spending on formula, feeding utensils, medical care, etc.; Ball and Wright 1999; Rouw, Hormann, and Scherbaum 2015), and assists birth spacing as a natural birth control. Breastfeeding saves time (e.g., from fetching water and fuel, preparing bottles, taking a sick child to the health center, shopping for formula, etc.). Breastmilk is a renewable resource at the heart of local food systems and the transfer of mother's milk to her baby saves resources (e.g., water, fuel, energy committed to the production of cartons, bottles, and teats, as well as the cost of transport and disposal of waste produced by bottle feeding). Countries can economize large amounts of cash, often in foreign exchange, that is presently dedicated to the purchase and distribution of commercial breastmilk substitutes; they can save health care expenses for preventable, acute, and chronic illnesses. The direct "cost" of breastfeeding in the form of increased nutrient requirements for breastfeeding mothers is relatively small compared to the costs of artificial feeding, amounting to approximately 300 to 500 additional kilocalories of a well-balanced diet (LINKAGES 2009).[29] During the late 1990s in India, for example, women produced approximately 3,900 million liters of milk over a two year period at the national level. If this milk were purchased in the form of tinned cow's milk, the cost would have been about USD three billion (Gupta and Khanna 1999).

Beyond the recommended six months of exclusive breastfeeding both in developing and developed-country setting (Kramer and Kakuma 2012), most infants need to receive other foods to meet their nutritional needs and to become accustomed to the eating habits of the family and community (Palmer 2011). These additional foods complement the child's breastmilk diet and thus frame the terminology of "complementary feeding." It is recommended that breastfeeding itself continue for two years or longer as the complementary foods are gradually introduced. Research from more industrialized countries indicates that complementary food should be introduced under the protection of breastfeeding and definitely not before the age of four months in order to prevent or minimize the development of allergies in young children (Grimshaw et al. 2013, Krawinkel 2011a, b; Scherbaum, Rouw, and Hormann 2011).[30]

WHO's global public health recommendation for the introduction of complementary foods at six months has been repeatedly challenged. However, as Cattaneo et al. (2008) write, such "papers on the timing of complementary feeding are based on weak evidence and do not justify a change of the current policies for 6 months of exclusive breastfeeding as a public health recommendation."

During the complementary feeding period (six to twenty-four months), a baby should gradually become accustomed to eating family foods (Burgess, Bijlsma, and Ismael 2009). However, these timings are only approximations. Children do not sit without help or start walking and talking at the same given age and, similarly, children do not need additional foods exactly at the same time (Rapley 2006). Nevertheless, although it does not correspond to the physiological realities of all children, the six month cut off point is a necessary public health policy decision and a public health tool as it also helps to prevent baby food companies from marketing their complementary foods at too early an age. The six to twenty-four month window is of utmost importance because it is the time when rates of malnutrition usually peak (Dewey and Adu-Afarwuah 2008). Especially for infants at six to eight months, the timely and appropriate introduction of complementary foods, which also includes dietary diversity and iron rich foods, is associated with significantly reduced risk of underweight and stunting (Marriott et al. 2012; WHO and UNICEF 2003). Yet, complementary feeding frequently begins too early or too late and complementary foods are often nutritionally inadequate and unsafe.[31] During the transitional period when complementary feeding begins, infants are particularly vulnerable (WHO 2003). If a complement is introduced too early, there is an increased risk of diarrheal disease and the development of allergic diseases; if too late, the risk of malnutrition increases (Kaufmann and Scherbaum 2003; Lamberti et al. 2011).

While article 24 of the 1989 CRC (UN General Assembly 1989) refers to children's rights related to the "provision of adequate nutritious foods and clean drinking-water" as well as to the right of parents to learn the "use of basic knowledge of child health and nutrition," the convention does not specify how to go about it, especially in the case of adequate complementary feeding. In 2003, the aforementioned *IYCF Global Strategy* (WHO and UNICEF 2003) provided broad guidance on complementary foods.

Case study 4.6 Guidance on complementary feeding

To ensure children's nutritional needs are met, the following criteria should be followed, the first four of which were introduced by WHO and UNICEF (2003) and the fifth by Black and Aboud (2011):

- *Timely introduction.* Complementary foods are introduced when the need for energy and nutrients exceeds that provided through exclusive and frequent breastfeeding.

- *Adequate.* Complementary foods provide sufficient energy, protein, and micronutrients to meet a growing child's nutritional needs.
- *Safe.* Complementary foods are hygienically stored and prepared, and fed to children with clean hands using clean utensils and not bottles and teats.
- *Properly fed.* Complementary foods are given consistent with the child's signals of appetite and satiety, and meal frequency and feeding method—actively encouraging the child, even during illness, to consume sufficient food using fingers, spoon, or self-feeding—as suitable for the age.
- *Responsive feeding, loving care, and stimulation.* Complementary foods need to be introduced in an environment of love and care that extends and complements the stimulation and responsive feeding approach of breastfeeding.

During the onset of complementary feeding, clean water, how foods are offered, and food quality are all more important than quantity (Flax et al. 2010; Phuka et al. 2012). Exclusive breastfeeding protects infants from compromised water supplies, whereas the safe introduction of complementary feeding depends upon reliable and clean water access. In September 2010, the HRC provided a welcome reaffirmation regarding human rights to water and sanitation (HRC 2010), although this is only a first step in acknowledging the problem. Continued non-exclusive breastfeeding provides ongoing immunological support as water is introduced in many forms and older infants' diets expand. Complementary food quality must emphasize nutrients like zinc and iron that breastmilk increasingly does not supply in sufficient quantity, starting at approximately six months. Basic nutrition knowledge and adaptive local food systems support infant and young child health, and family and community economic security (Palmer 2011).

CHALLENGES TO BEST PRACTICE INFANT AND YOUNG CHILD FEEDING

The intertwined subjectivities of mother and child as related to infant and young child feeding evolve not only in the context of the biology and health status of both, but also in everyday life realities. Whether or not mothers breastfeed their babies and how and whether they are able to provide safe and adequate complementary foods from sustainable local food economies is strongly influenced by socioeconomic factors, commercial and cultural pressures, and the conditions and contexts in which they live, including states of emergencies and chronic health crises.

Commercial and Social Challenges

Women and families have a human right to full and accurate information about best nutrition and feeding practices for infants and young children (i.a., foundational sources include article 11.2(a) of the ICESCR (UN General Assembly 1966), article 24.2(e) of the CRC (UN General Assembly 1989), and the *Code*, especially article 4 (WHO 1981)). Priorities imposed by profit and misguided cultural tradition can interfere with this right, the latter providing leverage to industry to propel their markets in violation of internationally agreed rules of marketing.

Commercial Challenges and Commerciogenic Malnutrition

Popularization of the idea that animal milk and milk products are equal or superior to (human) mother's milk for infant health presents ethical, moral, and legal challenges. These include for the principal of "do no harm," a disavowal of the dignity of human families, and a disparagement of human rights to adequate food and nutrition and to the highest attainable standard of health, not to mention a lack of respect for the right to full and unbiased information (cf. Palmer 2009).

The practice of breastfeeding has been under attack in many industrialized countries since before the development of the infant formula market. However, this market, introduced in the late nineteenth century and expanding ever since, represents a particular challenge. Already in the 1930s, propaganda for, and the malnutrition and death risks from, breastmilk substitutes was faulted. In a talk to the Singapore Rotary Club in 1939, Cicely Williams stated, "misguided propaganda on infant feeding should be punished as the most criminal form of sedition, and that these deaths should be regarded as murder" (Allain 1986; quoted in Richter 2001, 45–46). Nineteenth century misinformation of breastmilk substitutes as medically superior nutrition for infants established a trend that gradually took on an increased commercial dimension and which continues to today. From the late 1950s to 1970s, a massive promotion and distribution of breastmilk substitutes at a worldwide scale virtually eliminated the breastfeeding culture in many countries. The term "commerciogenic malnutrition" was coined to describe the negative impact of inappropriate marketing of breastmilk substitutes on infant health and nutritional status (Jellife 1971; see also Brady 2012; Palmer 2009; Sobel et al. 2011).

Boycotts of certain companies, US senate hearings, and, finally, the 1979 Joint WHO/UNICEF Meeting on Infant and Young Child Feeding, established the need to develop an international code that would set rules for the marketing of breastmilk substitutes (WHO and UNICEF 1979). In 1981, the WHA, the highest international decision-making body in public health, adopted the aforementioned *Code*. This policy instrument laid out marketing guidelines to "contribute to the provision of safe and adequate nutrition for infants, by protection and promotion of breast-feeding, and by ensuring the proper use of breast-milk substitutes, when these are necessary, on the basis of adequate information and through appropriate marketing and distribution" (WHO 1981, art. 1). As expanded further in this chapter, states parties to the CRC have the obligation to adopt the *Code* into their national legislation and support it.

The *Code* does not say that women are obligated to breastfeed their infants, nor does it invite the state to intervene in relationships between mothers, fathers, and their infants. The *Code* is not designed to prohibit the availability or use of infant formula and other breastmilk substitutes, but it aims at ensuring their proper use when these are necessary. The *Code* aims to end types of marketing that interfere with the right of mothers and caregivers to make informed decisions that dissuade mothers from breastfeeding or that encourage early supplementation of breastmilk. Adequate *Code* implementation removes profit driven obstacles to breastfeeding; it assures that parents can make informed decisions about best infant feeding practices that are free from commercial pressures.

In response to new marketing strategies, the 1981 *Code* has since been clarified and amplified by fifteen subsequent relevant WHA resolutions with the same status as the *Code*.[32] Normally, the WHA addresses only its member states. As a result of companies continually hiding behind a rhetoric of being in agreement with the aims and principles of the *Code* and yet violating its provisions around the world (IBFAN 2014), the 2010 WHA focused its *Resolution 63.23 on Infant and Young Child Nutrition* with a call directly to companies "to comply fully with their responsibilities" under the *Code* and its resolutions (WHA 2010, para. 2).

Frustrated health workers, mothers, families, communities, and policy makers have led campaigns to counter the destructive effects of breastmilk substitute marketing and formula feeding, and to escalate efforts to promote and support breastfeeding (Brady 2012; Coutsoudis, Coovadia, and King 2009). Yet, the multibillion dollar industry lobby has often succeeded in weakening any legal or other national measures that governments are urged to put in place to implement the *Code* in order to protect infants from the harmful effects of artificial feeding.

An example of marketing with incomplete information or disinformation concerns powdered infant formula (PIF). A case study of PIF and industry resistance to related public policy guidelines follows.

Case study 4.7 Powdered infant formula (PIF), intrinsic contamination, and state and corporate response-related 2007 WHO guidelines

For artificial feeding with PIF to be as safe as possible, its preparation requires hygienic conditions and access to resources such as adequate amounts of clean water, fuel, etc. In the past, and despite imperfect conditions and a lack of resources, mothers have been both implicitly and explicitly blamed for the poor health results obtained with artificial feeding because of their failure to carefully read and follow the instructions on labels.

Labels on PIF products have been shown to be inadequate, inaccurate, and misleading, creating a public health risk. PIF is not a sterile product and has been associated with severe invasive infections caused by intrinsic contamination, that is, contamination associated with the manufactured product PIF itself and not contamination introduced from an external (extrinsic) source. These infections can lead to death or lifelong disability (Bowen and Braden 2006; Friedemann 2008; Iversen and Forsythe 2004). *Enterobacter sakazakii,* now renamed as a new genus with many subspecies, *Cronobacter,* was detected in 14 percent of unopened tins of powdered formula in a 1988 study (and linked to serious illness and death in infants; Muytjens, Roelofs-Willemse, and Jaspar 1988), and in nearly 2.5 percent (two out of eighty-two tested samples) of tested powdered infant formula in a 2003 study (Iversen and Forsythe 2004). Not even hygienic production of PIF for infant consumption appears to guarantee control of *Cronobacter*; less than hygienic conditions further amplify risk (Iversen and Forsythe 2004). In other words, for over twenty-five years it has been established that PIF is not a sterile product. *Cronobacker sakazakii,* a species of *Cronobacter,* is resistant to heat. To inactivate the bacteria, formula preparation requires using water that is first boiled and then allowed to cool slightly, but not below 70°C (158°F). Notably, this high temperature process also kills healthy heat sensitive probiotic bacteria (FAO and WHO 2001) and along with them, one set of the PIF industry's valuable and highly visible marketing health claims.[33]

In 2007, WHO, together with the Food and Agriculture Organization of the United Nations (FAO), adopted the *Safe Preparation, Storage and Handling of Powdered Infant Formula Guidelines* (hereinafter referred to as *PIF Guidelines*; WHO and FAO 2007). In the 2008 *WHA Resolution 61.20,* states are called upon to take measures to reduce the risk of intrinsic contamination, including improved product labeling and food safety measures (IBFAN Africa 2008; WHA 2008). To date, few states have implemented the *PIF Guidelines.* One example of appropriate national action is *Guidance for Parents* issued by the Department of Health (DH) and the Food Standards Agency (FSA) of the UK (DH and FSA [United Kingdom] n.d.). In an additional example, after cases of fatal invasive *Cronobacter* infections in the United States in 2011, the Centers for Disease Control and Prevention (CDC) published on their website revised consumer recommendations on January 13, 2012. These recommendations emphasize breastfeeding to prevent infections and include the warning that "[p]owdered infant formula is not sterile" and the need to "[u]se hot water (158 degrees F/70 degrees C and above) to make formula."[34]

Manufacturing companies have resisted the *PIF Guidelines*. Some companies do state that their PIF product is not sterile. However, the great majority do not notify consumers about the need to use boiled water cooled to no less than 70°C. Not incidentally, this keeps the blame for PIF-related child illness focused on parents, and, most particularly, on mothers, while at the same time allowing PIF manufacturers to maintain unjustified marketing claims for probiotic products.

As stated by Elisabeth Sterken, director of INFACT Canada, an advocacy organization that promotes breastfeeding, "[t]o subvert health needs to marketing needs is unconscionable" (quoted in Collier 2009, E46). An important testimony about how profits are put before health comes from Dr. Yasmine Motarjemi, who served as corporate food safety manager and assistant vice president of Nestlé from 2000 until 2010, when she was dismissed by Nestlé. Dr. Motarjemi was becoming "uncomfortable" with the company and repeatedly alerted its leadership about food safety problems, for example, about industry known excessive and dangerous levels of vitamins A and D in baby products. Dr. Motarjemi highlighted in her testimony a number of examples where Nestlé's leadership did not heed her alerts and was not prepared to consider an internal audit. She stated, "il faut que des bébés meurent pour que les choses soient prises au sérieux [babies have to die for matters to be taken seriously]" (Bonvin 2013, 56).[35] This story further underscores that companies cannot self-regulate, and that, therefore, governments must fulfill their obligation to protect consumers through laws that are monitored and enforced and that hold manufacturers of baby foods and feeding products accountable.

The 1989 CRC places breastfeeding protection, promotion, and support on the child rights agenda. Since 1989, the CRC Committee has on numerous occasions recommended to countries under review that they implement or strengthen national implementation of the *Code* and adopt additional policies, programs, and initiatives in support of breastfeeding, by, among others, curbing commercial pressure to market infant formula.[36] The CRC Committee's *General Comment 15 on the Right of the Child to the Enjoyment of the Highest Attainable Standard of Health* (hereinafter referred to as *General Comment 15*; CRC Committee 2013a) clearly stipulates that states parties to the CRC have the *obligation* to implement the *Code* as a national law.

> Exclusive breastfeeding for infants up to 6 months should be protected and promoted and breastfeeding should continue together with appropriate complementary foods preferably until two years of age as feasible. States' obligations in this area are defined in the "*protect, promote and support framework*," adopted unanimously by the World Health Assembly [WHO and UNICEF 2003 *IYCF Global Strategy*]. States are required to introduce into national law, implement and enforce internationally agreed standards concerning children' right to health, including the International Code on Marketing of Breast-milk Substitutes, as well as the WHO Framework Convention on Tobacco Control. Special measures should be taken to promote community and workplace support to mothers in relation to pregnancy and lactation, and feasible and affordable child-care services, and compliance to the [International Labor Organization] ILO Maternity Protection Convention 2000 (No. 183). (CRC Committee 2013a, para. 44; italics in the original)

Once states introduce the *Code* into national legislation, they have clear power to regulate private sector companies' actions with regard to the protection of children's right to health and adequate food and nutrition against unethical business behavior. Nevertheless, and in advance of all countries' adopting in full such legislation, the CRC Committee's *General Comment 15* goes on to clarify companies' responsibility to not threaten the welfare of children, a responsibility which extends to complying with the *Code* and to refraining from promoting foods of poor nutritional value.

> Among other responsibilities and in all contexts, private companies should: refrain from engaging children in hazardous labor while ensuring they comply with the minimum age for child labor; comply with the International Code of Marketing of Breast-milk Substitutes; limit advertisement of energy-dense, micronutrient-poor foods, and drinks containing high levels of caffeine or other substances potentially harmful to children. (CRC Committee 2013a, para. 81)

We note that "responsibility" is frequently misunderstood as the *voluntary* commitment of corporations. However, responsibilities to respect human rights are always ethical *obligations*, that is, not voluntary, even if they are not enforced by law.

In March 2013, the CRC Committee also adopted the aforementioned *General Comment 16* (CRC Committee 2013b). Paragraphs 18 and 57 establish common ground in the dangers of private sector market promotion of poor quality food products, tobacco, alcohol, and other toxic substances. Paragraph 57 further upholds states' obligations to regulate companies' practices in accordance with international standards protecting and enhancing children's welfare.

> States are also required to implement and enforce internationally agreed standards concerning children's rights, health and business including the World Health Organization . . . International Code of Marketing of Breast-milk Substitutes and relevant subsequent World Health Assembly resolutions. (CRC Committee 2013b, para. 57)

As of 2011, thirty-five countries implemented most provisions of the *Code* as law. Thirty-five implemented many provisions as legally enforceable measures; forty-eight countries have mostly chosen to maintain a narrow scope, not taking into account the fifteen subsequent relevant WHA resolutions (most EU countries are in this category). Seven countries incorporated parts of the *Code* into other laws. Thirty-five countries have some legally, non-binding (voluntary) measures in place which generally offer less protection either due to dominant industry influence and/or lack of independent monitoring mechanisms. Finally, there are sixteen countries known to be in the process of drafting national measures based on the *Code*: nine countries are studying the *Code* and its implementation and, for the remaining thirteen countries, there is either no further available information or no action has been taken (ICDC and IBFAN 2014).

One important initiative in support of breastfeeding is the Baby-Friendly Hospital Initiative (BFHI) launched by WHO and UNICEF in 1991, following the adoption of the 1990 *Innocenti Declaration on the Protection, Promotion, and Support of Breastfeeding* (WHO and UNICEF 1990).[37] Through a ten-step program, the BFHI aims to create an environment supportive of breastfeeding in health care settings at the community level. It calls on baby food companies to end free supplies of breastmilk substitutes to hospitals worldwide. As this call was not heeded by companies (Rosenberg et al. 2008),[38] the 1994 *WHA Resolution 47.5* ultimately prohibits any "donations of free or subsidized supplies of breastmilk substitutes and other products covered by [the *Code*] in any part of the health care system" (WHA 1994, para. 2.2).

The *Innocenti Declaration on Infant and Young Child Feeding* (UNICEF 2005) builds upon and expands the 1990 declaration (WHO and UNICEF 1990) to more directly address violations of the *Code* by private sector corporations. The 2005 declaration reiterates that "inappropriate feeding practices—sub-optimal or no breastfeeding and inadequate complementary feeding—remain the greatest threat to child health and survival globally." The document issues a call for action to all parties, including "[a]ll manufacturers and distributors of products within the scope of the International Code" to "[e]nsure full compliance with all provisions of the International Code and subsequent relevant World Health Assembly resolutions in all countries, independently of any other measures taken to implement the Code" (UNICEF 2005).

Case study 4.8 Bear Brand marketing in Lao People's Democratic Republic[39]

Marginal rates of exclusive breastfeeding in low income countries such as Laos are exacerbated by misleading marketing campaigns that can have a powerful influence on child feeding practices and increase risks for undernutrition and infant mortality (Slesak et al. 2009; Barennes et al. 2012). Among Lao children, 31 percent are moderately or severely underweight, 7 percent experience wasting, and 48 percent are stunted, placing Laos among the worst affected countries for stunting. Among Lao adults, the female literacy rate is 77 percent that of males' (UNICEF 2012b). Countries such as Laos with poor nutritional and educational status can be particularly vulnerable to the negative effects of aggressive marketing of breastmilk substitutes.

The case of Nestlé's marketing of the Bear Brand coffee creamer in Laos was reported by Barennes et al. in 2008 and has received considerable attention, as this product has been falsely understood and commonly used as a breastmilk substitute for decades. The Bear Brand logo used for a highly sweetened coffee creamer (sugar being its main ingredient) was identical to the logo used on a canned sterilized cows' milk product as well as on the so-called "follow-up" infant formula. The logo presented a cartoon image of a baby bear being held by its mother in the breastfeeding position (see figure 4.1). Although the Bear Brand logo displayed a warning that "[t]his product is not to be used as a breast milk substitute" in English, Thai, and Lao as well as an illustration of a feeding bottle with a cross through it, the 2008 investigation of Lao consumers by Barennes et al. showed that 80 percent of respondents did not read the text warning and only 2 percent identified the contents correctly as coffee creamer. Thus, the Bear Brand logo not only effectively portrayed the message that the product was acceptable as a breastmilk substitute,[40] it also promoted what WHO has labeled a completely unnecessary product (i.e., follow-up formula products that are needlessly promoted for use after six months) by displaying and selling it together with infant formulas.[41]

Coffee creamer is nutritionally unacceptable as a breastmilk substitute and infants who are fed the product exclusively are at high risk of protein-calorie malnutrition (Barennes et al. 2008). The questionable marketing practice of using the same logo of a breastfeeding bear and her infant on coffee creamer, infant formula, and follow-up infant formula has thus resulted in inappropriate infant and young child feeding practices nationwide, resulting in severe malnutrition and even death in both rural and urban populations (Barennes et al. 2008, 2012).

Figure 4.1   Label from Bear Brand coffee creamer (© 2011 Bryan Watt)

Another study by Barennes et al. (2012) conducted in 2009 also revealed that Lao mothers with high socioeconomic status are showing a greater tendency to use breastmilk substitutes before six months, in part due to higher exposure to advertising. The authors recommend that "action should be taken to decrease the impact of misleading advertising, which influences mothers to switch from traditional breastfeeding to BMS [breastmilk substitutes]" and that sustained educational interventions are needed in order to reverse this vicious cycle (Barennes et al. 2012, e30634).

In an open letter to Nestlé dated 24 May, 2011, a group of nineteen Laos-based international NGOs, including Save the Children, Oxfam, CARE International, and World Vision, announced, "We won't be applying for your prize money, Nestlé." They explained that they would not take funding from the food giant while Nestlé "continues to make millions of dollars of profit, at the expense of infants and children in Asia, through violations of the International Code of Marketing of Breast-milk Substitutes." The open letter specifically mentions Bear Brand as an example of the unethical marketing that violates the *Code*.[42]

In response to the publicity of malnutrition and deaths from inappropriate marketing that accompanied the 2008 study, the Bear Brand logo in Thailand and Laos was modified. The baby bear now sits on the mother's lap, not in the breastfeeding position (Srour 2014, pers. comm.).[43] Furthermore, in the same year Nestlé announced that they had stopped distribution of Bear Brand coffee creamer in Laos and also prevented an independent company that had licensed the brand from using the Bear Brand trademark on coffee creamer (Stieger 2009). Nevertheless, the study conducted by Barennes et al. in 2009 indicated that the licensed trademark had remained widely available throughout Laos and Thailand, still being a cause for concern; note that 14.5 percent of respondents in Laos continued to report using coffee creamer as a breastmilk substitute for their infants before the age of six months (Barennes et al. 2012; Srour 2014, pers. comm.).

Commercial challenges to highest quality infant and young child feeding extend beyond interfering with breastfeeding to product development and marketing practices that promote overweight, as well as underweight malnutrition. Known as the "double burden of malnutrition," overweight and obesity affect as many individuals worldwide as do hunger and underweight malnutrition, and contribute greatly to increasing rates of NCDs (HRC 2011a; SCN NGO/CSO 2010; Swinburn et al. 2011). The structural link between overweight and the agrofood industry is found in the government subsidies and prices that support agricultural production linked to high fat, sugar, and salt content foods, as identified in the 2011 report to the HRC by the former special rapporteur on the right to food, Olivier De Schutter (HRC 2011a). De Schutter recommends in his report that states should "[a]dopt statutory regulation on the marketing of food products, as the most effective way to reduce marketing of foods high in saturated fats, trans-fatty acids, sodium and sugar (HFSS foods) to children, as recommended by WHO, and restrict marketing of these foods to other groups" (HRC 2011a, para. 50(c)).

Similar to the phenomenon of a vicious intergenerational cycle of undernutrition, the condition of overweight and obesity has a propensity to pass from mother to child (Ludwig and Currie 2010; Phelan 2010; Poston 2012; Ruchat and Mottola 2012; Sen et al. 2012). Overweight and obesity—most commonly thought to be associated with wealthy countries—are being increasingly pronounced among lower and middle income, urban, and female populations and can occur even in the same household and individual (Doak et al. 2000, 2005; Gardner et al. 2012; Gustafsson, Persson, and Hammarström 2012; Mason 2012; Uauy, Garmendia, and Corvalán 2014; Varela-Silva et al. 2012). Additionally, the phenomenon of coexisting overweight and underweight has been observed among persons living in protracted emergency settings and dependent on food assistance, for example, among Western Saharan refugees (Grijalva-Eternod et al. 2012). The frequent coexistence of underweight/wasting and stunting in young children and overweight and stunting in adults in the same household or person requires specific interventions to tackle this burden of malnutrition in all its forms (Uauy, Garmendia, and Corvalán 2014; Varela-Silva et al. 2012).

Cultural and Social Challenges

Industrial marketing of breastmilk substitutes prey upon and augment diverse cultural pressures that also exert influence on mothers' decisions about, and capacities to, breastfeed. These cultural traditions differently define breastfeeding. For example, in stages, wherein breastmilk is healthy or taboo, adequate or insufficient; spatially, in terms of public or private places where feeding or denying a hungry infant is judged acceptable or not; functionally, with regard to whether a woman should work for free (e.g., at home) or for pay (e.g., in an office) during the breastfeeding period. It is important to understand the widespread acceptance of adverse as well as positive cultural traditions in order to implement policy and regulation which can withstand both commercial pressure and disruptive cultural norms that distort women's and families' right of access to full and complete information about best practices for infant and young child feeding.

Case study 4.9 Ethiopia: breastfeeding culture

Work conducted by chapter coauthor Veronika Scherbaum found that newborns in many parts of Ethiopia are often not immediately breast-fed because the critically valuable colostrum is considered contaminated due to its color and consistency, and is further believed to cause colic, stomach cramps, and worm infestations.

Women from poor families begin their productive work activities as soon as twelve days after birth. Beliefs that a mother's sweat can contaminate her breastmilk often force women to leave children at home instead of bringing them to fields or markets. At home they may be bottle fed by alternate caregivers or, if left unattended, fed a home brewed alcohol to pacify them and assure their sleep until the mother returns.

Long-term breastfeeding is normal in Ethiopia, especially in rural areas, and generally lasts as long as the child wishes to do so, or until the mother gets pregnant again.[44] Nevertheless, early child weaning is induced with the beginning of a new pregnancy mainly because of the belief that the lactating child might take up the nutritional means of the unborn baby. It is, moreover, widely believed that mother's milk quality diminishes in pregnancy causing worm infestation and yellow teeth in the lactating child, and that it can provoke jealousy from the unborn sibling. Additionally, people believe that a woman who is sick with any illness should not breastfeed her infant for fear that a mother's spoiled milk could potentially transfer her disease to the infant (Scherbaum 1996, 1997).

Breastfeeding and breastmilk constitute the core of sustainable local food systems and should be buttressed by the appropriate introduction of culturally relevant, geographically sustainable, and nutritionally adequate complementary foods. Nevertheless, problematic cultural beliefs can easily be exploited and shaped by mass media (Brown and Peuchaud 2008) and corporate marketing (Brady 2012). Marketing campaigns can lead to the displacement of breastfeeding and local foods that are often less expensive in comparison with globally traded food products. The result is that families bleed their budgets to purchase lower quality feeding options for their infants and young children (Palmer 2011).

Notably in the United States but also in other industrialized countries, breastfeeding practice is discouraged by the media's aggravated sexualization of breasts, and enshrined in restricted rights to breastfeed in public and workplace settings (Olbricht 1985). This interference with maternal, infant, and young child feeding results simultaneously in the loss of breastfeeding's positive health impact and its cultural invisibility (Kolinsky 2010; Mulford 2008; Sowden et al. 2009; Wolf 2008).

Case study 4.10 Canada: breastfeeding in public

In 2009, a mother who worked as a pharmacist filed a complaint because she was asked to move away from the border of the municipal swimming pool where she was breastfeeding. She had refused to move because, while breastfeeding, she was keeping an eye on her two other children playing at the pool.

**L'allaitement est permis
en tout temps!**

La Ville de Gatineau permet
l'allaitement des enfants en
tout temps dans tous ses
édifices.

Figure 4.2 Canadian advertisement in the City of Gatineau allowing and supporting breastfeeding in public spaces (© Maryse Arendt)

Her complaint to the ombudsman of the City of Gatineau was successful. She received financial compensation and both a public and written apology. Moreover, on 1 October 2009, the administration of the city issued a decree that no one is allowed to disturb a breastfeeding woman, or to prohibit her from breastfeeding in any public place.[45] The city also initiated the organization of specially designated breastfeeding spaces, noting that these places were not to be understood as the only public locations where women were allowed to exercise their right to breastfeed in public (see Arendt 2012). Figure 4.2 shows the signs displayed in public places of the City of Gatineau.

The 1979 CEDAW defines maternity as a "social function" (UN General Assembly 1979, art. 5(b)) and requires states parties to take steps to prevent workplace discrimination against women on the grounds of maternity (or marriage; UN General Assembly 1979, art. 11.2(a-d)). Additionally, the 1989 CRC provides vague umbrella wording that could leverage attention to women's right to breastfeed in public and at work:

> States Parties shall render appropriate assistance to parents and legal guardians in the performance of their child-rearing responsibilities and shall ensure the development of institutions, facilities and services for the care of children. (UN General Assembly 1989, art. 18.2)
> States Parties shall take all appropriate measures to ensure that children of working parents have the rights to benefit from child-care services and facilities for which they are eligible. (UN General Assembly 1989, art. 18.3)

The older and more conservative 1966 ICESCR is more concerned with achieving maternity leave from work for a "reasonable period before and after childbirth" (UN General Assembly 1966, art. 10.2) than with promoting women's right to paid employment, and, with it, workplace adaptation for mothers returning to work with breastfeeding demands.

The 1990 and 2005 *Innocenti Declarations* clearly articulate the unequivocal "breastfeeding rights of working women" and the need to eliminate "obstacles to breastfeeding within the health system, the workplace and the community" (UNICEF 1990). Governments are further called upon "to adopt maternity protection legislation and other measures that facilitate six months of exclusive breastfeeding for women employed in all sectors, with urgent attention to the non-formal sector" (UNICEF 2005).

In May 2012, the ILO released its *Maternity Protection Resource Package—From Aspiration to Reality* (ILO 2012). This tool is designed to help organizations and individuals everywhere to strengthen and extend the fundamental right of maternity protection to all women in all types of economic activity. The *Maternity Protection Resource Package* delivers the message that universal and comprehensive maternity protection at work is both possible and desirable because it contributes to equitable economic growth, social cohesion, and decent work for all women and men. The package elaborates on the 2000 ILO *Maternity Protection Convention* (No. 183; ILO 2000a) and its accompanying *Maternity Protection Recommendation* (No. 191; ILO 2000b), the former of which states:

1. A woman shall be provided with the right to one or more daily breaks or a daily reduction of hours of work to breastfeed her child.
2. The period during which nursing breaks or the reduction of daily hours of work are allowed, their number, the duration of nursing breaks and the procedures for the reduction of daily hours of work shall be determined by national law and practice. These breaks or the reduction of daily hours of work shall be counted as working time and remunerated accordingly. (ILO 2000a, art. 10)

The 2000 ILO *Maternity Protection Convention* further sets maternity leave at six weeks compulsory leave after birth (ILO 2000a, art.4.4) and not less than fourteen weeks total (ILO 2000a, art. 4.1). The *Maternity Protection Recommendation* further advises member states to extend maternity leave to at least eighteen weeks (ILO 2000b, para. 1(1)).

Emergencies and Chronic Health Crises

Under bilateral or multilateral conditions, states are obligated under the ICESCR to cooperate internationally to respect, protect, and fulfill the "fundamental right of everyone to be free from hunger" (UN General Assembly 1966, art. 11(2)). Whether in the context of natural or man-made disaster, states are required to help each other and affected states must facilitate safe and unimpeded access for international assistance to reach populations in need (Harper 2009; Kent 2014). The goal of intervention is to assist in resolving the crisis and establishing local and state self-determination.

Crises take many forms and all create short or longer term aid dependencies. An emergency may be "acute," "sudden," "urgent," or "chronic." Each has varied causes and a range of associated complexities. Acute emergencies generally put the health and survival of a population at immediate risk, often leaving people unable to feed themselves and requiring a response designed to ensure survival and prevent further damage (Toole and Waldman 1997). Chronic health difficulties, like food insecurity and HIV/AIDS, tend to produce self-replicating individual and social ordeals because underlying structural conditions, like poverty, discrimination, and dependency, are not addressed. Acute and urgent emergencies often evolve into chronic crises. If an emergency situation continues over years or even decades, for

example, due to persisting political instability, relief food and nutrition programming changes and begins to resemble those in non-emergency settings.

Self-determination vs. Dependency: Best Practice and Local Knowledge in Emergencies

A chronic emergency reflects dependency and can be reproduced through
misguided policy, as well as through the replacement of available
resources, labor, and capability with new, external market-based goods. An
under-examined aspect of dependency is its character of mutuality. Dependency can as often reflect public agencies' and industry's respective reliance
on employment and market development as it does willingness by a "needy"
group to forego traditional or typical livelihoods in order to survive on
handouts (Maren 1997; Moyo and Ferguson 2009; Poppendieck 1999).

Across the diversity of emergency and chronic crisis conditions, infants
and young children under five as well as women who are most engaged
in their nutrition and in the feeding of their families and communities in
crisis, face specific and severe challenges related to food and nutrition security (ENN 2011c; Gasser et al. 2004; IASC 2006; IFE Core Group and
UNICEF 2006). Planning for, implementing, and evaluating food- and
nutrition-related emergencies and chronic health crises must remain flexible
to on-site needs and include as quickly as possible participation from these
most affected and most engaged group members.

The centralization of women's feeding experience together with their,
men's, and older children's knowledge about the local food and nutrition
system, not only benefits all stages of intervention in crisis processes, it also
transforms "emergency victims" into *actors engaged in self-determination
in a crisis*. This approach channels aid workers and crisis-affected actors
toward the construction of a crisis response that can be resolved into local
self-determination instead of chronic dependency. However, whereas it may
be possible to ensure that women have a presence in village distribution
committees or that they themselves receive food aid directly as required, for
example, by the World Food Program (WFP), gender equity goals face resistance on diverse fronts. Traditional leadership might try to deny women de
facto participation and to force them to accept food aid distributed according to local power relationships. Whereas every effort should be made to
include women in decision-making and implementation, this must not subject them to potential violence in retaliation for transgressing traditional
roles (ENN 2011a; see also chapter three of this volume). Additionally, in
order to expand market reach, purveyors of processed nutrition goods have
tried to patronize women in particular and local knowledge in general in the
attempt to overrule common sense and known best practice with the sug-
gestion that breastfeeding and local foods are not modern, scientific, or progressive. The roots of this insidious misinformation lie perhaps in an effort
to curtail women's independence and equality. Women's social experience,

biological capacity, and local knowledge concerning infant and young child feeding leverages a point of gender equity; their employment of the non- or only slightly monetized economy of breastfeeding promotes social wealth equity.

UNICEF and WHO guidelines for exclusive, followed by extended and continued, breastfeeding (e.g., UNICEF 2005; WHO and UNICEF 1990, 2003, 2005) become even more critical in emergencies. Under all categories of emergency and chronic health crises, respiratory tract infections and diarrheal diseases remain the most common cause of death in infants and young children (Black et al. 2008; Lozano et al. 2012). Both are associated with undernutrition, the risk of which is exacerbated by poor breastfeeding practices. As previously described, breastmilk substitutes carry risks of increased illness and mortality in the best of circumstances. In emergencies, this risk increases because conditions to ensure stable access to adequate amounts of infant formula, sufficient clean water, and an energy infrastructure for refrigeration, boiling water, etc., are not in place, either in the short-term or for the minimum of the first twelve months of a baby's life (provided other sources of protein and micronutrients become available thereafter; Gribble and Berry 2011; Gribble et al. 2011). Studies in northern Iraq (Scherbaum 2003), Lebanon, and Indonesia (Assefa et al. 2008; MacLaine and Corbett 2006), the Democratic People's Republic of Korea (Rawas 2008), and China (Bengin et al. 2010) have shown that the indiscriminate use of breastmilk substitutes during emergency situations interferes with women's options to feed their children and often does more harm than good.

Donations of breastmilk substitutes by companies and other actors, including governments, NGOs, and the public, and their untargeted distribution, expose both breastfed and non-breastfed infants to increased risk of malnutrition, morbidity, and mortality. These donations, many of which are made in good faith and honest charity, are delivered in quantities that far exceed need. They are then indiscriminately distributed to all infants, although they may not be of the right type and may be labeled in a non-local language. Donations can undermine breastfeeding practices, especially where related nutrition education may not exist or may be suspended during emergency. Donations of breastmilk substitutes are not recommended by the 2007 *Infant and Young Child Feeding in Emergencies: Operational Guidance for Emergency Relief Staff and Programme Managers* (IFE Core Group 2007), guidance supported in 2010 by *WHA Resolution 63.23 on Infant and Young Child Nutrition* (WHA 2010, 1(8)). Nevertheless, they remain common and are often delivered in violation of the *Code*, as a sales inducement by companies or by aid groups that bypass donation coordination structures (IBFAN and ICDC 2009; IFE Core Group 2007; IRIN Asia 2013). By not preventing these *Code* violations, the state fails to protect, and non-state actors deny respect to, women's and children's right to adequate food and nutrition in the particular context of emergencies.

Case study 4.11 China: lack of breastfeeding support in emergencies

In 2008, a major earthquake shook China's Sichuan Province. During this emergency, a certified Baby-friendly Hospital in Deyang distributed a one-week supply of infant formula. As the hospital streamlined its operations to cope with the flood of disaster victims, one of the first services dropped was support for new mothers to breastfeed their children adequately. The hospital staffs' explanations for reintroducing infant formula and curtailing breastfeeding education and support demonstrated a serious misunderstanding both of how lactation works and the nature of its crucial importance in emergencies. Not only was this a direct violation of the Baby-friendly Hospital Initiative, but also of the *Infant and Young Child Feeding in Emergencies: Operational Guidance for Emergency Relief Staff and Programme Managers* (IFE Core Group 2007; Bengin et al. 2010).

As witnessed by coauthor of this chapter, Veronika Scherbaum, in a 2012 conference of pediatricians in Deyang, China, medical training largely overlooks the function and importance of breastfeeding. As such, medical doctors, nurses, and other support staff are unprepared to protect and support the viability of breastfeeding in the context of emergencies. Further, they are particularly vulnerable to unscrupulous donations of breastmilk substitute from manufacturers taking advantage of crisis situations to promote their products.

Self-determination and HIV: Challenges of a Public Health Approach vs. the Human Rights Framework

A woman's right to make an informed decision about feeding her child has gone through troubling changes in the HIV/AIDS context because the HIV virus can be passed from the mother to the infant through pregnancy, labor, and breastfeeding. Over the past twenty-five years, HIV transmission through breastfeeding has created one of the most painful dilemmas in public health. Breastfeeding, a life line and an example of the most perfect situation in which the child is not only provided with adequate food but also with optimal care and health by a mother, who herself also benefits from this practice, has become a potential transmitter of a deadly disease (Dunn et al. 1992).

There are multiple and shifting lenses to this troubling debate. First of all, there is the slowly accumulating research-based literature that helps shape public policy, often shifting it in surprising directions. At the time of this writing, the most up-to-date research indicates that "in the absence of antiretroviral prophylaxis, greater than 90% of infants exposed to HIV-1 via breastfeeding remain uninfected, despite daily mucosal exposure to the virus for up to two years" (Fouda et al. 2013, 1). The authors of the quoted paper identified an innate HIV neutralizing protein called Tenascin-C in breastmilk.

Second, this latest information comes at a time where a wide range of approaches are engaged to counsel HIV infected mothers about breastfeeding. More specifically, there is a *public health approach* in which the state determines health counseling directives with specific advice, and a *human rights framework* wherein HIV infected mothers have the right to make their own decision about breastfeeding based on non-directive counseling and access to full information, including all feeding options to consider.

Third, there is the context of richer and poorer countries with vastly different access to information, medical services, community support, and judicial review, which all together frustrate the simplicity of saying "women can make informed choices." In poorer contexts and countries, *there is no choice* if the means to affordable, feasible, acceptable, sustainable, and safe (AFASS) feeding of infants with replacement foods (no breastmilk involved) is not there for the greater part of the population.[46] In richer contexts and countries, full HIV prophylaxis/treatment and other medical interventions to prevent, to the highest degree possible, HIV transmission to children are generally available through all three stages: pregnancy, delivery, and breastfeeding. In these wealthy locations the public health approach directive is often taken, recommending all avoidance of breastfeeding. However, this then means that HIV infected, fully informed women, who might want to elect to breastfeed, are also not provided a choice and can face serious child protection-related charges if they do so.

Under these shifting lenses, the international policy on HIV and infant feeding has changed several times since the last decade of the twentieth century. With reports such as the October 2013 publication by Fouda et al., these adaptations are likely to continue as new evidence from research and the field comes in.

Initially, the right to make an informed decision about how to feed the child was, at least in theory, with the mother. The most recent policy guidelines were issued in 2010 (WHO 2010b) and reiterated in 2013 (WHO 2013a),[47] based on evidence showing that antiretroviral (ARV) interventions to either the HIV infected mother or to the HIV exposed infant significantly reduce the risk of postnatal transmission of HIV through breastfeeding during the first six (high quality evidence) to twelve (low quality evidence) months of life. The 2013 WHO *Consolidated Guidelines on the Use of Antiretroviral Drugs for Treating and Preventing HIV Infection* (WHO 2013) now call on national and subnational authorities (instead of individual health workers) to "decide whether [maternal and child] health services will mainly counsel and support mothers to be known to be infected with HIV to either breastfeed and receive ARV interventions or avoid all breastfeeding given their particular context" (WHO 2013a, 104). The guidelines continue to strongly recommend that, whenever promotion of and support for breastfeeding and ARV interventions are the preferred strategy to improve the HIV-free survival of infants exposed to HIV, "[m]others known to be infected with HIV (and whose infants are HIV uninfected or of unknown HIV status) should exclusively breastfeed their infants for the first 6 months of life, introducing appropriate complementary foods thereafter, and continue breastfeeding for the first 12 months of life. Breastfeeding should then only stop once a nutritionally adequate and safe diet without breast-milk can be provided" (WHO 2013a, 104). These guidelines explain that these new recommendations do not remove a mother's right to make decisions regarding infant feeding and are fully consistent with respecting individual human rights. When highly effective interventions are available, the explanation goes, it is justifiable for health authorities to promote and support a single approach. The UN hopes that this new policy will help considerably to reduce HIV transmission to infants while being strongly supportive of six months of exclusive breastfeeding and continued breastfeeding by HIV infected mothers, for at least twelve months, with adequate and safe complementary foods.

A 2012 UNICEF report, still unpublished at the time of writing, provides the first in-depth overview of the adoption and implementation of the 2010 WHO guidelines in the African setting (UNICEF 2012a).[48] Twenty-five countries responded to a standardized questionnaire revealing that almost all of the countries had adopted the 2010 WHO *Guidelines on HIV and Infant Feeding*. In terms of the adoption of the guidelines recommendations, the majority of countries followed, with some variation, the key recommendation that mothers should breastfeed while on ARV treatment. This 2012 UNICEF draft report notes challenges related to the implementation of these national guidelines: only half of the countries have an implementation plan in place, and only one-fifth have estimated the actual cost of plan implementation. This obviously slows implementation, beginning with building adequate capacity among health workers. The 2012 UNICEF draft report further anticipates major challenges in assessing the impact of implementing the 2010 WHO guidelines because a majority of countries still do not routinely collect data on infant feeding practice in the general population. Several of these challenges, such as vertical adaptation process of national guidelines leading to lack of awareness and the beginning of mixed and confused messages by health workers to mothers and the general public, have been already described (Sagoe-Moses et al. 2012). Inadequate ARV drug coverage and poor adherence to treatment throughout breastfeeding place infants exposed to HIV at risk of infection and represent additional challenges, as stated in the 2013 consolidated guidelines (WHO 2013a, 105–6).

The 2010 and 2013 WHO guidelines reveal the reality that one cannot have public health directives and also claim there is still a mother's right to decide how to feed her infant. If public policy does not promote breastfeeding as an option, mothers do not have the means of making an informed decision protected from reprimand. At the same time, public health officials struggle to make sound decisions given evolving evidence and limited resources.

When the context of HIV and emergencies intersect, the risks posed by artificial feeding may become more apparent than under normal circumstances. The case study of Botswana below describes what happened following a public health decision to discourage breastfeeding despite uncertain AFASS conditions, all exacerbated by a weather-caused emergency. It brings into question the potential for danger when public health approaches are favored over an approach engaging the human rights framework, especially when they elect options like breastmilk substitutes through which women lose capacity to control the conditions of feeding, becoming dependent upon external sources.

Case study 4.12 Botswana: diarrhea risk associated with not breastfeeding

In early 2006, heavy rains in Botswana resulted in alarming increases in infant diarrhea and mortality. In this case study, adapted from the Emergency Nutrition Network (ENN) website story, "Diarrhoea Risk Associated with Not Breastfeeding in Botswana: Summary of Report and Presentation," the infant health crisis overwhelmed the medical system; children were increasingly dying.[49] In twelve health districts, there were 22,500 cases of diarrhea, with 470 deaths in children under five years old (2.1 percent mortality) compared to 9,166 cases and twenty-one deaths for the entire country (0.2 percent mortality) in the first quarter of 2005.

Most of the cases appeared to be associated with bottle feeding. An investigation by the Ministry of Health of Botswana with support from the US CDC revealed widespread water contamination from various pathogens in affected districts. Among them was enteropathogenic *Escherichia coli*, previously linked to diarrhea from unsafe bottle feeding caused by lack of sufficient sterilization capacity. Additionally, the CDC identified a variety of risk factors (adjusted for socioeconomic status, age, and mother's HIV status) that were associated with children's hospitalization for diarrhea. The agency found that poor hand washing, standing water near home, overflowing latrines, and the storage of drinking water were major risk factors for diarrhea. Notably, the most statistically significant risk factor was the variable not breastfeeding. In one village visited, 30 percent of the formula-fed babies died during the diarrhea outbreak; no breastfed babies died.

In 2005, the HIV prevalence among pregnant women in Botswana was 33.4 percent. HIV infected mothers were advised not to breastfeed. Infant formula for twelve months was made available to all HIV infected mothers; 63 percent of them used it in 2005. Among HIV non-infected mothers or mothers of unknown HIV status, a CDC site survey found that 20 percent of infants had been weaned from the breast before the age of six months.

Among the HIV infected mothers, problems were reported with adequate and consistent formula supply. Although most of their babies were given the appropriate amount of formula at birth, only 51 percent received ongoing and adequate amounts of formula. Mothers reported returning to clinics on multiple occasions each month but were still not given adequate formula.

It appears that a combination of not breastfeeding, water contamination, the inability to sterilize bottles, nipples, and water, and the irregular and insufficient supply of formula impairing the babies' overall nutritional health increased risk for contracting and perishing from this diarrhea outbreak. The CDC recommended a review of the national formula feeding policy, including a reevaluation of the conviction that formula saves lives in the context of HIV infection. The 2010 World Breastfeeding Trends Initiative (WBT*i*) Botswana Assessment Report indicates that the country had yet to put in place a comprehensive infant and young child feeding policy that includes guidance for HIV and infant feeding in emergencies (WBT*i* 2010; see also Creek et al. 2006).

In 2012, WHO issued guidelines entitled *HIV and Infant Feeding 2010: An Updated Framework for Priority Action* (WHO 2012b) and published online "Questions and Answers on Infant Feeding in the Context of HIV."[50] The updated framework places strong emphasis on *Code* implementation and on ensuring that "financial support and other incentives for programmes and health professionals working in infant and young child feeding do not create conflicts of interest" (WHO 2012b, 7). The framework, if implemented, has the potential to ensure progress in insuring the right to adequate food and nutrition for infants and young children affected by HIV/AIDS.

Case study 4.13 Excerpt from the WHO *Guidelines on HIV and Infant Feeding 2010: An Updated Framework for Priority Action*

Implement and enforce the [1981] International Code of Marketing of Breast-milk Substitutes and subsequent relevant World Health Assembly resolutions (the Code)

Actions required [by policy makers, program managers, regional advisory bodies, public health authorities, country coordinating mechanisms, UN staff, professional bodies, NGOs and other interested actors, including the community]:

- Implement existing measures to give effect to the Code, and, where appropriate, strengthen and adopt new measures.
- Monitor Code compliance.
- Define the relevance of the Code in the context of HIV, and ensure the prevalence of HIV is not used as a pretext to misinform and undermine the Code and breastfeeding.
- Ensure that the response to the HIV pandemic does not include the introduction of non Code-compliant donations of breast-milk substitutes or the promotion of breast-milk substitutes.
- In countries that have decided to provide breast-milk substitutes for the infants of HIV positive mothers (either from birth or when they stop breastfeeding), establish appropriate criteria for whom should receive it, for how long, and for adequate procurement and distribution systems, in accordance with the provisions of the Code in order to protect breastfeeding and avoid spill over of breast-milk substitutes to the general population.
- Ensure that the conduct of manufacturers and distributors at every level conforms to the Code.
- Ensure that financial support and other incentives for programs and health professionals working in infant and young child health do not create conflicts of interest. (WHO 2012b, 7; emphasis in the original)

Complementary Feeding in Emergency Situations

Local and traditional foods usually can provide adequate nutrition for older infants and young children during the six to twenty-four months complementary feeding stage when balanced with ongoing breastfeeding and further bolstered by culturally adapted nutrition education (Inayati, Scherbaum, Purwestri, Wirawan et al. 2012a). In the context of emergencies and chronic health crises, however, regular food conduits can be interrupted, placing particular burden on very young children. Responses to emergencies and chronic health crises that result in mild, moderate, and severe forms of child malnutrition require individual evaluation of needs and the assignment of different forms of nutritional support as necessary (cf. case study 4.13). Interventions aiming at improved micronutrient status during the complementary feeding stage range from inclusion of micronutrient rich foods to provision of micronutrient fortified foods (e.g., blended foods) or products for home fortification.

Virtually the same global recommendations for safe and appropriate infant and young child feeding practices that are in alignment with human rights frameworks apply in emergency situations as is the case under normal circumstances (Sphere Project 2011).[51] Emergency aid must not undermine good infant and young child feeding practice, but rather must support it. The wide variety of response options that exist for different phases of food and nutrition crises can generally be divided into two objectives: preventing undernutrition and treating acute malnutrition with therapeutic care. These response categories are described in the following case study.

Case study 4.14 Categories of emergency response to hunger and malnutrition with respect to maternal, infant, and young child nutrition

1. Preventing undernutrition

   General food distribution (e.g., cereals, legumes, oil, salt, etc.). Intends to meet immediate and medium-term needs of households that lost access to food, restore and protect livelihoods, and support nutrition and health of children, pregnant and lactating women, people living with HIV/AIDS, and other vulnerable groups.

   Supplementary feeding, blanket approach. As an addition to the general rations this is often performed at the onset of a crisis when nutritional assessments are not yet available. It aims to prevent deterioration of the nutritional status of at risk groups and reduce the prevalence of moderate acute malnutrition (MAM) in children under five years old.

   Supplementary feeding, targeted approach. Provides nutritional support to children with MAM, pregnant/lactating women, and other vulnerable individuals of the affected population. Skilled support for breastfeeding and infant feeding should be an integral part of these programs.

2. Treating acute malnutrition

Therapeutic care. This is aimed at children with severe acute malnutrition (SAM). Children without medical complications can be treated in the community with use of RUTFs. Those with medical complications require hospitalization and treatment with specially formulated milks (F75, F100) and/or RUTFs. In both settings, skilled support for breastfeeding and infant feeding is essential (Ashworth and Burgess 2003; Collins et al. 2006; Golden 2010; WHO 1999).

Assessment of the category of emergency response is critical for determining an appropriate and adequate nutritional intervention response (ENN 2011b; Khan and Munshi 1983; Roberts et al. 2001; Toole and Waldman 1988). Cooperation by all involved in an emergency response, including multisectoral efforts, industry, and individual engagement, is critical. We note, however, that despite technical guidance, obtuse confusion characterizes much engagement in maternal, infant, and young child nutrition in crises, especially regarding the use of ready-to-use foods (RUFs/RUTFs) in different settings. Table 4.1 and the following discussion present an overview of different forms of malnutrition and the associated appropriate response of professional supervision, counseling, treatment, and care.

Treating acute malnutrition with therapeutic care. RUTFs are not a stand-alone miracle food product. They must be integrated into a larger emergency relief plan (Paul et al. 2012). The development and testing phase of RUTFs for SAM in older infants and young children during crises began in the mid-1990s. The peanut, milk powder, sugar, and vitamin and mineral supplement was designed for use in the context of weekly supervision in community-based programs.[52] Distributing RUTF paste/spread without close medical supervision can be dangerous for severely wasted children because of the potential of relapse cases.[53] To avoid frustrating overall public health objectives, it must be organized within a framework that includes available, timely, and effective treatment for diarrhea, pneumonia, and malaria (Bhutta 2009).

RUTFs and other RUFs increase a child's need for access to clean drinking water. RUFs' own low water content decreases the risk of bacterial contamination. Their use, however, increases a child's need for safe drinking water due to their high renal solute loads which exceed that of children's diets that are composed of less concentrated local traditional foods, combined with continued breastfeeding (Purwestri, Scherbaum, Inayati, Wirawan, Suryantan, Bloem, Pangaribuan, Stuetz et al. 2012; Purwestri et al. 2013).

Table 4.1 Form of child malnutrition in relationship to treatment approaches, caring, and counseling aspects

Form of child malnutrition	Indicator	Main contributing factors	Professional supervision	Caregiver counseling and support[2]	Form of treatment accompanying care
Severe acute malnutrition (SAM) with complications (often no appetite)	<-3 WHZ and/or oedema	Emergency/chronic food insecurity and/or infectious diseases and/or inadequate care	Inpatient care daily supervision	Exclusive breastfeeding (zero to six months) Support for relactation Gradual and appropriate introduction of semisolid and solid complementary foods with continued breastfeeding (six to twenty-four months) Loving care and psychosocial support	Medical and nutritional rehabilitation with therapeutic milk (F-75, F-100)[3] and/or RUTF[4]
Severe acute malnutrition (SAM) without complications (child can eat well, at least during admission period)	<-3 WHZ no oedema	Emergency/chronic food insecurity and/or inadequate care Refeeding syndrome (e.g., cardiac failure, gastrointestinal disturbance)	Outpatient care Weekly supervision Immediate referral system to hospital in case the child gets ill		Community-based rehabilitation RUTF[5] etc.[6]
Moderate acute malnutrition (MAM)	<-3 to ≥ -2 WHZ	Emergency/chronic food insecurity and/or inadequate care Refeeding syndrome (e.g., cardiac failure, gastrointestinal disturbance)	Outpatient care Weekly supervision Referral system to hospital in case the child gets ill	Transition to best combinations of locally available, safe, and adequate family foods through interactive and culturally sensitive nutrition/health communication activities	Community-based rehabilitation and prevention with MAM RUTF[7] RUSF,[8] RUF biscuits,[9] LNS,[10] CSB,[11] etc.[f]

(Continued)

Table 4.1 (Continued)

Form of child malnutrition	Indicator	Main contributing factors	Professional supervision	Caregiver counseling and support[2]	Form of treatment accompanying care
Mild acute malnutrition	<-2 to ≥ -1 WHZ	Emergency/chronic food insecurity and/or inadequate care	Outpatient care Weekly or monthly supervision Referral system to hospital in case the child gets ill		Community-based rehabilitation and prevention with MAM RUF biscuits,[h] RUTF;[12] CSB,[k] micronutrient powder,[13] etc.[f]

Acronyms: CSB: Corn Soya Blend; LNS: Lipid-based Nutrient Supplements; RUF: Ready-to-Use Food; RUSF: Ready-to-Use Supplementary Food; RUTF: Ready-to-Use Therapeutic Food; WHZ: Weight for Height Z score.

[1] We recognize that the dynamics of health and nutrition rehabilitation (e.g., individual children are crossing assessment categories in different directions during the recovery, default, or relapse process) cannot be adequately reflected in this box.

[2] For published evidence for culturally appropriate nutrition education, please see Guldan et al. (2000) and Inayati, Scherbaum, Purwestri, Wirawan et al. (2012a).

[3] F-75, F-100 (WHO 1999).

[4] For more information on RUTF for SAM in hospital-based interventions, please see Diop et al. (2003).

[5] For more information on RUTF for SAM in community-based rehabilitation, please see Collins and Sadler (2002) and Ciliberto et al. (2006).

[6] Ongoing research into new forms of RUFs.

[7] For more information on RUTF for MAM, please see Isanaka et al. (2009).

[8] For more information on RUSF for MAM, please see Lagrone et al. (2010) and Matilsky et al. (2009).

[9] For more information on RUF biscuits for MAM, please see Scherbaum et al. (2009), Scherbaum et al. (2015), Purwestri, Scherbaum, Inayati, Wirawan, Suryantan, Bloem, Pangaribuan, Koeniger et al. (2012), Purwestri, Scherbaum, Inayati, Wirawan, Suryantan, Bloem, Pangaribuan, Stuetz et al. (2012), and Purwestri et al. (2013).

[10] For more information on LNS for MAM, please see Chaparro and Dewey (2010).

[11] For more information on CSB form of MAM, please see Matilsky et al. (2009).

[12] For more information on RUTF and CSB for mildly wasted children, please see Patel et al. (2005).

[13] For more information on micronutrient powder with and without nutrition education, please see Inayati, Scherbaum, Purwestri, Wirawan, et al. (2012b).

Patent rights and compulsory licensing for RUTFs keep prices high and limit global distribution. While patents benefit product innovators, many argue that lifesaving products should be treated differently. Plumpy'nut, a fortified peanut butter spread, was the first RUTF to appear on the market and is a registered trademark of the private French company Nutriset. Nutriset aggressively protects its patent in Europe and North America, but is reportedly more liberal about licensing in developing countries (Rice 2010).

Preventing undernutrition and the deterioration of mild and moderate forms of malnutrition. The development of RUFs has shifted from emergencies with SAM associated with famine and conflict toward commercial innovations of ready-to-use supplementary foods (RUSFs) and related products to address less severe forms of chronic malnutrition and its prevention (e.g., MAM). These RUSFs generally differ from RUTFs in having a lower energy and protein content, a micronutrient composition designed for MAM cases, or simply the recommended daily allowance (RDA) of vitamins and minerals, and the capability to be implemented without medical supervision. Additionally, a marketing niche is developing for RUFs designed for malnutrition prevention in both mildly malnourished and well nourished, in other words, *all* children. These latter products have been widely criticized as creating a high sugar, high fat snack food for very young children that is marketed as a nutrition booster and which predisposes dietary development away from local foods and toward less healthy, more processed, waste producing, and cash demanding food options ("The Global Game Plan of Big Snack [Editorial]" 2011; Monteiro 2010).

Despite new RUF developments, the majority of nutrition intervention programs to date and for all levels of child malnutrition use RUTFs because research is still more available on RUTFs than on RUSFs (Lagrone et al. 2010; Matilsky et al. 2009). Whereas research supports the use of RUTFs for treating severe malnutrition, controversy remains over its role for prevention of moderate and mild forms of undernutrition (Hendricks 2010), wherein, for example, RUTFs are being distributed without clinical oversight and conceivably without monitoring actual and appropriate consumption by the malnourished child. We note that unsupervised distribution can lead to risks of over- or under-consumption because, for instance, of the sharing of RUTFs with other children in the family.

Extended use of RUTFs for moderate and mild cases of malnutrition is part of a disturbing trend wherein solutions for child malnutrition, both its prevention and treatment, become increasingly medicalized with the use of fortified commercial foods as "quick fixes," thereby evading underlying and basic causative factors of malnutrition (IBFAN 2011b). This "medicalization" disregards local knowledge about local food and nutrition systems (IAASTD 2009), effectively jeopardizing the perpetuation and potential of a family's skills to feed itself and induct its youngest members into traditions of food knowledge and sharing (HRC 2011a; Lhotska, Bellows, and Scherbaum 2012; Palmer 2011). Heavily promoted and initially subsidized commercial RUSFs for moderately malnourished children threaten families' food and nutrition security, especially in low income households. At the onset, RUSFs are usually distributed free of charge, creating demand and undermining traditional and sustainable nutrition practices. Once product dependency is secure, the full cost is reinstated, burdening households (IBFAN 2011b; Sachs, Fanzo, and Sachs 2010).[54]

Of significant danger is that RUFs are marketed as the best solution for young child nutrition and malnutrition prevention *without mentioning the best practice of continued breastfeeding* through age two years and from six months, only with a *gradual introduction of semisolid and solid foods that ideally come from the traditional foods that the family eats*. Through the omission of this information, RUFs continue a market pattern of impeding breastfeeding practice and additionally interfering with traditional family and community foods and eating patterns (Arie 2010). We note additionally that policy attention to women's own food and nutritional status, while recognized in the context of reproduction, has not always given adequate attention to the importance of breastfeeding.[55] In an example of industry assertion that medical product intervention is essential to address *moderate* malnutrition, an article in *Le Temps*, for example, reports that "[t]he industry lobby tries to impose a therapeutic solution involving a ready-to-use industrial product by claiming that over 70% of children suffering from moderate malnutrition cannot be successfully treated without commercial products." The *Le Temps* piece goes on to state that the children's rights NGO, Foundation Terre des Hommes, contradicts the industry claim based on its experience in Guinea (Papart 2010).

Promoting nutrition in sustainable local/regional food economies. Good nutrition is a component of the human right to adequate food and nutrition and should be secured as a function of individual, local, and national self-determination, not through chronic extensions of international emergency aid or global market dependency. Marketing claims allege that RUFs address chronic hunger and micronutrient deficiencies due to long-term poor diets. However, neither should donations disrupt the integrity and continuity of local production, according to the 2005 *Voluntary Guidelines to Support the Progressive Realization of the Right to Adequate Food in the Context of National Food Security* (FAO 2005, guideline 15.1), nor, according to Sachs, Fanzo, and Sachs (2010), should "the main solution lie [not in purchasing commercialized RUFs, but] in more productive local agriculture, . . . a more diverse mix of nutritious crops, and much greater public awareness regarding feasible and low-cost approaches to a healthy diet." RUFs must not become part of a daily diet because political leaders and public authorities do not or cannot fulfill their basic obligation to provide clean and adequate water, support locally sustainable food economies and systems, and communicate practical nutritional information. Available aid must be directed to supporting processes of rebuilding self-determination in local and national capacity for environmentally sustainable food production. We note that market claims have also sidetracked attention away from the environmental drawbacks of prepackaged foods that include the increased carbon footprint of long distance, internationally traded goods, and the lack of local accommodation to process waste from prewrapped and pre-prepared RUFs (Manary 2006).

Concerned about the absence of guidelines to govern the marketing of RUSFs, members of the United Nations Standing Committee on Nutrition (SCN) NGO/CSO constituency drafted such a document in 2010 to fill the gap. The *Draft Guidelines for the Marketing of Ready to Use Supplemental Foods for Children* urge governments and the international community to take necessary steps to address unethical marketing of RUSFs to prevent repetition of the dramatic scenario in the marketing of breastmilk substitutes where market dependency destroys autonomous and traditional feeding culture (SCN NGO/CSO 2010). Mirroring the 1981 *Code*, the guidelines specifically state that unethical marketing of RUSFs must be prevented and that these products should not be marketed to the general public. Neither should free samples of RUSFs be directly or indirectly provided to pregnant women, mothers, or family members by manufacturers and distributors.[56] The *Draft Guidelines for the Marketing of Ready to Use Supplemental Foods for Children* are a step in the right direction regarding principles underpinning the right to adequate food and nutrition, although they fall short in their scope to heed *WHA Resolution 63.23* (WHA 2010) which calls unequivocally for an end to the inappropriate promotion of foods for infants and young children.

To maximize self-determination and minimize dependency on international food aid, local production of different forms of RUFs, as needed, requires more support and attention, especially in lower income countries with a high prevalence of different forms of acute malnutrition (Enserink 2008; Manary 2006; Manary et al. 2004). Using locally available cereals and/or legumes, milk powder, oil, sugar, and a vitamin-mineral premix, local RUF production engages local labor, benefitting and stabilizing local/regional food and agricultural economies and reducing RUF costs (Dibari et al. 2012; J. Guimón and P. Guimón 2012).

Case study 4.15 Indonesia: locally made, locally sourced RUFs—Nias biscuits for moderately/mildly wasted children

Following the tsunami of December 2004 and the earthquake of March 2005, a food crisis developed affecting Nias Island in Western Sumatra, Indonesia. In response, a project was initiated to create an affordable, sustainable, and local alternative to globally marketed RUFs. Researchers, in cooperation with local aid and community groups, developed, tested, and locally produced RUFs in the form of fortified cereal, nut, and legume-based (RUF-Nias) biscuits according to nutritional requirements, taste, shelf life, cost, and local source ability standards (Scherbaum, Shapiro et al. 2009), and then further field-tested them on moderately and mildly wasted children within daily (semi-urban areas) and weekly (rural areas) distribution and supervision program settings. Small-scale local production of RUF-Nias biscuits was undertaken every week at the village level, creating job opportunities for women and vastly reducing the cost of the RUF-Nias biscuits. Over six weeks, 79 percent of children in the project significantly improved their nutritional status (Purwestri, Scherbaum, Inayati, Wirawan, Suryantan, Bloem, Pangaribuan, Koeniger et al. 2012; Purwestri, Scherbaum, Inayati, Wirawan, Suryantan, Bloem, Pangaribuan, Stuetz et al. 2012; Purwestri et al. 2013).

A growing body of literature presents evidence of the possibility of local and sustainable development of nutrition alternatives to moderate and mild forms of chronic malnutrition. They include research from Indonesia (Purwestri, Scherbaum, Inayati, Wirawan, Suryantan, Bloem, Pangaribuan, Koeniger et al. 2012; Purwestri, Scherbaum, Inayati, Wirawan, Suryantan, Bloem, Pangaribuan, Stuetz et al. 2012; Purwestri et al. 2013; Scherbaum, Shapiro et al. 2009), India (Beesabathuni and Natchu 2010; Dube et al. 2009; Gera 2010), Uganda (Bukusuba, Muranga, and Nampala 2008; Ickes et al. 2012), Myanmar (Cosgrove et al. 2012), and Kenya and Zambia (Owino et al. 2012).

The use of RUTFs did introduce positive results for children with severe malnutrition treated at community level in clinically moderate conditions in emergency and non-emergency settings. The approach of controlled nutrition intervention has expanded for moderate and mild forms of malnutrition with exceptionally interesting developments in locally controlled and sourced environments. We are very concerned, however, that efforts to address the emergency context of communities struggling with malnutrition has become secondary to the potential of rapid global market expansion of what is essentially a fortified candy bar for very young children. We believe that the terminology, purpose, and prescribed use of the different forms of RUFs are poorly understood by the general public, but possibly also by many manufacturers and policy makers. The confusion benefits commercial expansion at the expense of proper treatment of malnutrition and attacks the integrity, sustainability, and potential of locally procured and culturally significant foods for both mildly malnourished and healthy older infants and young children.

Opportunities to Support and Enhance Best Practices for Both Child and Mother

Previously, pre- and postnatal intervention health programs have tended to concentrate specifically on the mother or the child, not always on both of them. More recently, a few programs have initiated more holistic wellness approaches for mothers, infants, and young children, and their communities around them, during the intertwined maternal-child stage of life, including the 1991 BFHI (UNICEF and WHO 1991), the 1992 Integrated Management of Childhood Illness (IMCI) strategy, the 2003 WHO and UNICEF *IYCF Global Strategy*, the 2010 development by UNICEF of an integrated infant and young child feeding (IYCF) approach across non-emergency and emergency settings, that includes participatory and culturally adapted nutrition education in food systems.[57]

The 1991 BFHI initially focused on newborns and the protection and promotion of breastfeeding. Over the years, as BFHI implementation advanced at the national level, it became clear that the focus of the initiative must evolve and cover mother friendly care as well. This message was clearly spelled out at the international level as the 2003 *IYCF Global Strategy* states that the health and nutrition status of women, and in turn their babies, requires accurate information and support from their families, communities, and responsible health and non-health institutions during both non-emergency and emergency situations. The recognition that optimal breastfeeding depends upon a healthy mother-child dyad and a supportive environment, led to the development of a revised 2009 BFHI training package (UNICEF and WHO 2009). The updated package introduces mother friendly care and community support modules to ensure antenatal, labor, delivery, and postnatal care for women's health and well-being. It also includes information on the importance of mother-infant-community support to continue best practice breastfeeding in emergencies and in the context of the HIV pandemic.

WHO published online in 2010 and updated in 2011 a "Continuum of Care Fact Sheet: Reproductive, Maternal, Newborn and Child Health" that integrates the health and wellness needs of women, infants, and young children during the period of their intertwined subjectivities.[58] Embedded in these strategies is the UNICEF/WHO IMCI strategy, to date adopted as health policy by more than eighty countries.[59] The IMCI approach entails a component of nutrition interventions such as growth monitoring, assessment of visible signs of severe malnutrition and anemia, and child feeding practices, as well as monitoring and support of the health status of the mother (WHO 2008).[60]

Perhaps the simplest, lowest cost and, theoretically, most accessible opportunity to support and enhance best feeding practices for maternal, infant, and young child well-being is nutrition education. Throughout the world, women and men, in all stages of life, need access to participatory nutrition education so that they can make informed decisions about their own and their children's nutritional well-being, and recognize best practices such as breastfeeding and diversification of diets to maximize micronutrient availability (Aubel 2012).[61] Governments need to support this pro-health knowledge base, both through the advancement of food production that maximizes affordable and available healthy food, and by discouraging the marketing of poor quality food choices (Palmer 2011). Nutrition education should link family and community health with the capacities of local food production and the food economy; it should augment engagement in the operation and self-governance of local and regional food and nutrition systems (Jordan, Reinbott, and Kuchenbecker 2013; Krawinkel 2012).

Feeding others as a right, as a cultural tradition, and as a pleasure must be respected. Nutrition education must likewise adapt to the individuals and customs it addresses. Successful nutrition education should be participatory in design, embracing household and community input. It should strive to provide time and topic intensive sessions. An audience should be attracted that includes men as well as women of diverse generations and ages, and not just caregivers.

Case study 4.16 Indonesia: intensive nutrition education

In the case of addressing malnutrition in mildly wasted children on Nias Island in Western Sumatra, Indonesia, an intensive weekly nutrition educational intervention (INE) program was tested for its impact on the nutrition knowledge and related food practices of children's main caregivers, as well as on the nutritional status of children themselves (Inayati, Scherbaum, Purwestri, Hormann et al. 2012; Inayati, Scherbaum, Purwestri, Wirawan et al. 2012a, b). This INE program introduced culturally appropriate nutrition education that was developed in cooperation with community members and the mothers and caregivers of the mildly wasted children whose condition the program hoped to address. The INE program differed from the existing publicly available, once per month, non-intensive nutrition education (NE) program that also monitored child growth on a monthly basis. The NE program takes a more authoritarian approach with a lecture-based series that does not invite participants' direct engagement with the learning process.[62] While both the INE and NE program were found to increase significantly the nutrition knowledge of mothers, only the INE program appears to have significantly changed the actual measured nutrition practices in the household.

To investigate the best strategy to promote weight gain among mildly wasted children, the INE and NE programs were tested on separated subject groups, with and without the provision of additional micronutrient powders for the mothers/caregivers to administer to the meals of their mildly malnourished children. The best weight gain and most improved hemoglobin results were achieved with the weekly INE program supported by micronutrient powders, followed closely by INE without the micronutrient powders.

Part of the explanation appears to be that without the culturally friendly INE approach, appropriate use, that is, the practice of learned knowledge, of micronutrient powders was low. Whether or not micronutrient powders were distributed for mildly malnourished children at the monthly NE trainings, weight gain and hemoglobin status did not improve significantly with this education approach.

SCALING UP NUTRITION (SUN) AND MARKET DRIVEN APPROACHES TO ADDRESSING MALNUTRITION: OPPORTUNITIES OR CHALLENGES?

As the global community searches for solutions to the food and nutrition crisis and to address uneven progress toward the Millennium Development Goals (MDGs), new efforts are being promoted. One such effort is the Scaling Up Nutrition (SUN) program, announced by the World Bank, UNICEF, WHO, and WFP, along with some developing country partners, CSOs, and bilateral agencies.[63] Launched in 2010, its stated aim is to accelerate action against hunger and address undernutrition with a focus on thirty-six high burden countries where 90 percent of the world's stunted children live. The SUN framework is structured to reflect the findings of the 2008 five-part series published in *The Lancet* entitled "Maternal and Child Nutrition" (Maternal and Child Nutrition Study Group 2008). This open access collection of articles focuses on the so-called "window of opportunity" that encompasses the "1,000 days" from pregnancy and breastfeeding through the first two years of a child's life wherein proper nutrition and care is vital for lifelong physical and mental development. Under conditions of malnutrition, appropriate and cost effective interventions can positively influence growth and cognitive development. Among other advantages, a program that overcomes malnutrition within the one thousand days can benefit both an individual child's earnings potential throughout her/his lifetime, and, also, national economic growth overall.

SUN's strategy has been to develop a broad partnership of "stakeholders," including "government, donor organizations, United Nations agencies, civil society, business, technical and research institutions" to cooperatively address maternal and child malnutrition.[64] The stated aim of this multisectoral PPP is to integrate nutrition issues at the national level into related sectors such as food security (including agriculture), social protection (including emergency relief), and health (including maternal and child health care, immunization, and family planning). SUN's declared emphasis is on the development of strong country strategies that are based on its people's unique needs, constraints, capacities, challenges, and priorities.

However, various social movements, public interest CSOs, and some countries have refused to participate in SUN. Their forbearance lies in the perception of the project as a donor-led process that does not address the central issues of populations most affected by hunger and malnutrition, and that SUN has, as have all PPPs, built-in conflicts of interest. The perspective sharply challenges SUN's image of itself as a social movement. Concern prevails that SUN opens the door wide to profit-driven interests and that it prioritizes market-based, medicalized solutions to malnutrition over developing local capacity to support good nutrition. Such an orientation can threaten best health and nutrition practices and status, as well as promote and commercialize globally marketed supplementary foods (like RUFs) that can depress local food and nutrition economies and systems (Lhotska, Bellows, and Scherbaum 2012; Schuftan 2011; Schuftan and Greiner 2013; Schuftan and Holla 2012).

The SUN program recognizes the private sector's normal and expected imperative of profit over public interest. To that end, SUN warns potential corporate collaborators that they must plan on some population groups simply being outside their reach. The steadily changing "living document" begun in 2011, "Private Sector Engagement Tool Kit," states that "public-private partners that wish to engage in a partnership should at minimum acknowledge and accept that populations below a certain minimum (poverty-line) cannot be served by this [infant and young child feeding] market but need special programs by public sector".[65] But, while SUN identifies populations outside the industry's reach because they are too poor, it fails to close off other population groups that are protected by policy and ethical regulations that prohibit industry-customer interactions, namely the 1981 *Code* and relevant subsequent WHA resolutions. The tool kit does in fact mention the *Code*; however, compliance is falsely identified as the duty of NGOs as opposed to SUN business partners.

> Partners should be aware of each other's mandates, norms & values and act accordingly (e.g., NGO compliancy with International Code of marketing of breastmilk substitutes or private sector goals for business growth).[66]

Until the time of this writing, SUN has not explicitly ruled out any participation by manufacturers of products falling under the scope of the *Code*. Instead, it urges partners to be aware of each other's mandates, norms, and values and to act accordingly.

Nevertheless, under pressure from some public interest NGOs, the SUN Movement Secretariat appears to have begun to take a position *vis-à-vis* its industry partners. The SUN website reports that in 2013 the SUN secretariat began work on conflicts of interest, to be finalized in 2015, and monitoring and evaluation.[67] However, in tune with the introduction earlier in this chapter, SUN proposes to "minimize[e] potential conflicts of interest through shared common codes of conduct" (SUN Road Map Task Team 2010, 15), again supporting self-organized, non-regulated, and voluntary, not binding, adherence to international codes. Unlike the SUN secretariat, the SUN tool kit does not even use the term "conflicts of interest" but only "conflicting priorities."[68]

In its *SUN Movement Progress Report: 2011–2012* (SUN Movement Secretariat 2012a), the SUN secretariat advised "SUN countries" that manufacturers of infant formula whose current marketing practices have been shown to violate the *Code* should be excluded from national programs.

> Different SUN country platforms are establishing clear principles for businesses to engage in the Scaling Up Nutrition SUN Movement. They [the different SUN countries] are supported by the SUN business network and SUN Movement Secretariat—which advises that manufacturers of infant formula whose current marketing practices have been shown to violate the International Code for the Marketing of Breast-milk Substitutes should be excluded. (SUN Movement Secretariat 2012a, 54).

Advice given to "SUN countries" is apparently not considered relevant for the international executive arm of SUN. The SUN secretariat does not seem to be preoccupied by the fact that SUN itself has an inherent conflict of interest when following the PPP model and including industry, such as Unilever and Britannia Industries Ltd., directly, or through members, such as GAIN, on its decision-making Lead Group (IBFAN 2012). Additionally, the SUN partner EPODE International Network has the perennial *Code* violator Nestlé as its core partner.[69]

The SUN secretariat exposes itself and the integrity of public policy to tangible and known risk by partnering with industries that it knows violate international standards and codes, and by recommending countries to eschew. An example of the ability for industry to influence new public policy direction outside of open, transparent, and participatory public and national review can be seen in the SUN secretariat's apparently favorable position with regard to genetically modified seeds. The SUN tool kit presents the Pepsico Frito Lay Company's supported Lays Andinas potato project as a positive example of private-public cooperation to address malnutrition. In other words, technical assistance in nutrition is claimed by one of the biggest makers of snack foods that contribute to the obesity problem and, further, that includes genetic modification of potato seeds in countries with important seed resources and biodiversity in potato plants.

In 2012, SUN updated its 2010 *Road Map for Scaling-Up Nutrition.* The 2012 *SUN Movement: Revised Road Map* (hereinafter referred to as *Revised Road Map*):

> [e]ncourag[es] corporate social responsibility in nutrition: ensure[s] responsible business practices such as those that recognise the vital role of exclusive breast-feeding in protecting the health and wellbeing of children. The Network will ensure that there is no place in the SUN Movement for companies that break the code on the marketing of breast milk substitutes. (SUN Movement Secretariat 2012b, 20)

This may sound like an improvement; however, the *Revised Road Map* disregards the fact that full compliance with the *Code* and all relevant subsequent WHA resolutions includes protection of *non-exclusive, continued* breastfeeding for two years or beyond with adequate complementary feeding. In this slippery rewording, the *Revised Road Map* opens the six to twenty-four plus month period to industry expansion while at the same time calling for respect of the *Code*.

The 2012 *Revised Road Map* attempts to clarify SUN's position on industry conflicts of interest. The text acknowledges potential conflicts of interest, but only as lying "*between* SUN stakeholders" (SUN Movement Secretariat 2012b, 10; emphasis added) or *devolved to* the country level. Further, the *Revised Road Map* states: "[a]ll stakeholders in the Movement use the 2012 World Health Assembly resolution 64–6 on Maternal, Infant and Young Child Nutrition as one of the starting points to resolve conflicts" (SUN Movement Secretariat 2012b, 10). It must be most emphatically stated, however, that no WHO resolution provides guidance on conflict resolution; they only urge that conflicts of interests should be avoided. Moreover, *WHA Resolution 64.6* is related to health workforce strengthening, not to maternal and infant feeding nutrition (see WHA 2011). Perhaps this is a simple typo? Regardless, the statement that "[t]he Movement is guided by the secretariats of specialised UN system agencies and other multi-stakeholder bodies on the handling of such issues" (SUN Movement Secretariat 2012b, 10) is not reassuring. As explained earlier, neither WHO nor UNICEF has a comprehensive conflict of interest policy. SUN, indeed, could set a positive example by developing a sound policy for its own operations. Instead, through its basically flawed design of including industry on its decision-making board (Lead Group), SUN "invites the fox to build the chicken coop." In other words, the corporate actor on the board, whose primary interest and fiduciary duty to shareholders is to maximize profits including by developing new markets for junk food and artificial infant food among high poverty populations, now contributes to health policy development. The central problem is that SUN asks the world to trust industry actors instead of encouraging SUN's partners and member countries to exercise caution and apply an "[at] arm's length" approach and to set up sound policies of engagement with the corporate sector.

In May 2013, the Global Social Observatory (GSO) announced on its website a consultative process on conflict of interest, "Announcement for a Consultation Process on Conflict of Interest in the Scaling Up Nutrition Movement."[70] Paid US$935,449 by the Gates Foundation,[71] this work was delegated by the SUN Movement Lead Group to the GSO, a group whose secretariat is based inside Hagen Resources International (HRI). HRI defines its goal as "help[ing] clients respond to the growing involvement of the United Nations system in issues of importance to conducting global business, including the expanding opportunities for public/private partnerships."[72] The chief executive officer of HRI is Katherine Anne Hagen, who is also the executive director for the GSO and the Council for Multilateral Business Diplomacy. The latter organization claims to be "a responsible voice for business in international affairs." The authors are concerned that GSO is not a neutral or an independent group with regards to considering the subject of business conflicts of interest, and, therefore, not best suited to assist SUN in defining its conflict of interest safeguards.

Authors are apprehensive about the SUN project, anticipating that it is unlikely to achieve nutrition sustainability at the local or national level, can jeopardize best practices, and will serve to build or reinforce poorer countries' dependency on outside sources to feed their young children. We believe that SUN may indeed increase the costs of maternal-child health and that it patronizes women as objects of medical care instead of rights holders with claims, knowledge, and participatory capacity regarding their own and their families' well-being and support. Ready-to-use foods (RUFS, RUSFs, and RUTFs) tend to be produced in industrialized countries by private sector companies, purchased with public funds, and then distributed to countries dealing with a high burden of malnutrition. While ostensibly addressing and changing an undernutrition problem, corporate interests engage because they anticipate the development of new and stable markets, if not dependencies, on their goods into the future. The public policy goal should be to support sustainable strategies that maximize local and national self-determination and avoid dependencies on a global corporate industry.

The greatest capacity to protect and promote family well-being against all odds of poverty and conflict lies with women and their communities, including men and children. Thus, the appropriate strategy must be to support and empower women and their communities and not to patronize them as helpless, victimized, and the newest consumers of rich country exports. Market-based approaches, in particular those involving TNCs in decision-making processes concerning local and community well-being, distort public policies, and degrade and devalue the best practices of breastfeeding and the appropriate introduction of adequate complementary feeding. A short review of internet RUF advertisements quickly reveals that private sector interests collapse the nutritionally relevant distinctions between severe, moderate, and mild forms of undernutrition into medically under-supervised and under-regulated market bonanzas. We recommend research into the unregulated field of marketing these products.

Earlier in this chapter we reported that the blatantly unethical promotion of breastmilk substitutes in the 1950s led to the elimination of breastfeeding culture in many regions, eliciting the new concept of commerciogenic malnutrition, wherein the impact of unethical marketing of inferior and dangerous nutritional products leads to increased morbidity and mortality. This is the outcome we fear from the SUN program because of its central approach on promoting packaged supplementary foods and concurrently ignoring both attention to optimal breastfeeding and local solutions for adequate complementary feeding, as well as their integration into the promotion of equitable and sustainable food systems, economies, and societies.

In his 2011 report to the HRC as the former special rapporteur on the right to food, De Schutter reflects upon the sustainability of nutrition initiatives such as SUN and GAIN. He voices concern that these initiatives are not aligned within a human rights framework and that they "overlook the entitlements that have been established under international law for women, children, minorities, refugees and internally displaced persons, and other groups that may be subjected to marginalization and discrimination" (HRC 2011a). To its credit, the 2012 SUN Movement *Revised Road Map*, issued after the former special rapporteur's 2011 report, mentions rights no less than six times in the following contexts: the 2012 HRC resolution on the right to food, human rights and equity, duty bearers and rights holders, rights-based approaches, and human rights defenders. The document highlights "a rights-based approach" (SUN Movement Secretariat 2012b, 4) as the first of the SUN "Principles of Engagement:"

> For the Movement to function effectively, its members must abide by a "social contract" which establishes a common purpose, agreed behaviours and mutual accountability. The contract is reflected as "Principles of Engagement" and aligns to the framework for development effectiveness as outlined in the Paris/Accra/Busan accords. At all times members should take care to avoid behaving and acting in ways which could disempower—or even harm—those the Movement seeks to serve. This may require members adapting their behaviour to change the duty bearer-rights holder dynamics.
>
> 1) Be rights-based: act in line with a commitment to uphold the equity and rights of all women, men and their children. (SUN Movement Secretariat 2012b, 10)

The problem is that human rights, as legal framework and principle of engagement, are neither elaborated nor is further guidance provided on the "rights-based approach" in the seventy-six page document. There is also the matter of the confusing language suggesting that members may need to adapt "their behavior to change the duty bearer-rights holder dynamics." For private sector businesses that have shown little regard for international codes and regulations, and who have been invited to participate in

SUN despite their violation of those very same, the call for a "rights-based approach" to promoting their goods to address maternal, infant, and young child malnutrition may well appear as much of a pretense to them as it does to us.

How do we move forward to address integrated multisector nutrition engagements? First, there must be clear conflict of interest safeguards to protect public policy goals from the natural and primary profit motive of private sector companies. Second, the private sector can be consulted but must not be in the position of making public policy. Third, states must adopt and enforce international codes and treaties into national legislation in order to strengthen capacity to monitor and regulate mandatory adherence to global human rights norms by corporate interests. The track record on violations of the *Code* unambiguously indicates that such regulation is necessary (IBFAN 2014).

We argue that the path of addressing maternal, infant, and young child nutrition is through attention to all human rights across the life span with particular focus on the reproductive rights of girls and women, as well as on their nutritional needs (and those, also, of all boys and men). Short-term nutrition interventions during the "1,000 days" must be built into a long-term life span approach, not replace it. We recommend that approaches that promote and respect the human rights framework by definition uphold and stimulate people's self-determination, not their dependency. To this end, nutrition interventions must include dedicated emphasis on intensive, locally designed, participatory nutrition and health education, and agricultural policy to disseminate information about nutritional best practices and to integrate them into local food system structures.

Nutrition interventions on behalf of maternal, infant, and young child nutrition during the "window of opportunity" time must include attention to the mother's health before, during, and after birth. This includes both the pregnancy and the protection, promotion, and support of breastfeeding to ensure that mothers, their families, and their communities are protected from commercial pressures for artificial infant feeding, and that they have the education to understand the critical importance of early exclusive and continued breastfeeding with a gradual and appropriate introduction of adequate complementary foods in the six to twenty-four month postnatal period. We note that in this regard, the former special rapporteur on the right to food finds it "troubling that the 1981 International Code of Marketing of Breast-milk Substitutes and subsequent World Health Assembly (WHA) resolutions remain under-enforced, despite the wide recognition that exclusive breastfeeding for the six first months and continued breastfeeding, combined with safe and adequate complementary foods, up to 2 years old or beyond is the optimal way of feeding infants, and reduces the risk of obesity and NCDs later in life" (HRC 2011a, para. 16). He therefore emphasizes that "[c]ountries committed to scaling up nutrition should begin by regulating the marketing of commercial infant formula and other breast-milk substitutes, in accordance with WHA resolution 63.23, and by implementing the full set of WHO recommendations on the marketing of breast-milk substitutes and of foods and non-alcoholic beverages to children, in accordance with WHA resolution 63.14" (HRC 2011a, para. 16).

Families and communities need to understand the absolute necessity of meeting pregnant women's and breastfeeding mothers' extra nutritional demands. A cooperative, participatory approach is important to identify existing local food knowledge and taboos (Scherbaum 1996), as well as service resources to promote best practices in order to maximize the nutritional status of pregnant and breastfeeding women and their children ages zero to twenty-four months. This collective action should evolve into a community-based, local governance mechanism that seeks to strengthen the local food and nutrition system overall and protect it by safeguarding children's and women's human right to adequate food and nutrition. Governments must promote, respect, and protect communities' capacities to provide themselves with adequate food and thus contribute to their rights holders' highest attainable standard of physical and mental health.

Support for these positions comes from the former UN special rapporteur on the right to food, Olivier de Schutter, who writes that he considers the protection of the right to adequate food requires nothing less than direct intervention by states. Regulating private sector marketing practices is essential because "[s]elf- regulation by the agrifood industry has proven ineffective" (HRC 2011a, para. 41). He urges states to "[t]ranspose into domestic legislation the International Code of Marketing of Breast-milk Substitutes and the WHO recommendations on the marketing of breast-milk substitutes and of foods and non-alcoholic beverages to children, and ensure their effective enforcement" (HRC 2011a, para. 50(b)). The CRC Committee in its 2013 *General Comment 15* and *General Comment 16* also strongly urges states to strengthen protection measures through *Code* implementation and by limiting marketing and advertising of energy dense, micronutrient poor foods (CRC Committee 2013a, b).

De Schutter further urges the private sector, consistent with its responsibility to respect the right to adequate food, to "[c]omply fully with the International Code of Marketing of Breast-milk Substitutes, abstaining from promoting breast-milk substitutes, and comply with the WHO recommendations on the marketing of foods and non-alcoholic beverages to children, even where local enforcement is weak or non-existent" (HRC 2011a, para. 51(a)), a call echoed by the CRC Committee *General Comment 15*. Finally, the former special rapporteur insists that the private sector should abstain from "[i]mposing nutrition-based interventions where local ecosystems are able to support sustainable diets, and systematically ensure that such interventions prioritize local solutions and are consistent with the objective of moving towards sustainable diets" (HRC 2011a, para. 51(b)).

We urge states to respond to this call for the respect of local food systems by adopting measures that would regulate marketing of all types of RUFs.

The 2010 SCN NGO/CSO *Draft Guidelines for the Marketing of Ready to Use Supplemental Foods for Children* (SCN NGO/CSO 2010) can serve as a good starting point for governments to challenge marketing and promotional schemes for these products.

RECOMMENDATIONS FOR LEGAL, POLICY, AND PROGRAMMATIC LEVELS

- The first requirement of maternal and child nutritional well-being must be that it is rooted in women's right to self-determination and autonomy with respect to reproductive and partner choices. While the special nutritional demands of pregnant and lactating women as well as infants and young children through the first two years require special attention, women's human rights in general, and women's right to adequate food and nutrition in particular, must not be conflated with motherhood. Likewise, attention to the special needs of maternal and child health must never be interpreted as determining motherhood as intrinsic to female identity and goals, excluding in the process attention to the nutrition status and needs of women of all ages who are not biological mothers.
- Policies and programs must address the special nutritional demands and improve the nutritional status of women, infants, and young children during pregnancy and through the first two years of the child's life.
  - i. Current and future approaches must favor comprehensive policies and programs that respect and pay attention to the intertwined subjectivities of the mother and child, and the time dependent and specific food and nutrition rights and needs of women and children in pregnancy and up to the age of two years old.
  - ii. Women's food and nutrition rights and needs over the life span must not be neglected, noting that interventions in support of mother-child health and nutrition must not treat pregnancy and lactation as periods isolated from the rest of the life and the longer term well-being of women and children.
  - iii. To achieve their right to adequate food and nutrition, women must have non-discriminatory access to their full and indivisible set of women's human rights more generally, including respect for and protection of economic, social, and cultural rights (e.g., clean water, sanitation, housing, health care, and education) and civil and political rights (e.g., participation and self-determination in the context of family, community, and state strategies to fulfill the right to adequate food and nutrition).
- A comprehensive framework or convention is required to address the independent, and yet critically interconnected, rights, needs, and

capacities of women and children in the stages of pregnancy, child-birth, and through age two years old of the child's life in order to tackle the rights, needs, and capabilities of both mother and child during this critical period of biological, emotional, social, and legal interconnectedness. Until so accomplished, relevant treaty bodies should ensure inter-committee coordination to guarantee coherence in recommendations issued for states parties.

- Governments must promote adequate nutrition during pregnancy and lactation, and must protect and promote breastfeeding as a human right (not a duty) to guarantee the highest attainable standard of health and nutritional well-being for both women and children. Women's and children's right to adequate food and nutrition must not be interpreted as, or equated with, a right or a duty of a woman to breastfeed. Such a perspective would reflect rampant discrimination and violence against women and attempt to shift further the burden of obligations to protect, respect, and fulfill the right to adequate food and nutrition from state and non-state actors to women.
- Full, unbiased, and culturally sensitive participatory health and nutrition education is needed throughout the world for women and men in all stages of life so that they can make informed decisions about their own and their children's nutritional well-being, and recognize best practices such as breastfeeding and diversification of diets to maximize macro- and micro-nutrient availability.
- The UN, their relevant agencies, and nation states must take steps to address failure by non-state actors to respect women's and children's right to adequate food and nutrition
- Policies and programs must address the special nutritional demands and improve the nutritional status of women, infants, and young children during pregnancy and through the first two years of the child's life.

    i. A comprehensive ethical and policy framework at the UN level is needed to adequately deal with conflicts of interest and help to delineate the appropriate from the inappropriate roles of private for-profit actors, and thus prevent the harmful impact of profit-motivated conflicts of interest on public policy making and programs.

    ii. Policies and programs, including those focusing on nutritional requirements associated with the intertwined nutritional rights and needs of mothers and children during pregnancy, infancy, and the first two years of a child's life, must not result in trade or technical product dependencies that erode or supplant local capacity.

    iii. Governments must regulate the marketing, promotion, distribution, and ensure the correct use of ready-to-use therapeutic and supplementary food products (RUFs in general, including RUTFs and RUSFs), must give higher priority to and support research into opportunities for local production of alternative forms of these products (if they are needed), and decrease local dependency on external international markets and aid.

iv. Governments must regulate, through legally binding measures, the marketing of breastmilk substitutes in order to fulfill their obligation to protect the right to adequate food and nutrition. As part of this obligation they must prevent violations and/or non-respect of the *International Code of Marketing of Breast-milk Substitutes* and subsequent relevant WHA resolutions by non-state actors.

v. Emergency aid should follow current international policies and guidance in order not to undermine optimal maternal and infant and young child feeding practices but rather to support these through cooperation among diverse agencies, organizations, service providers at all levels, and donors involved in and supporting emergency and disaster relief work.

• The private sector, consistent with its responsibility to respect the right to adequate food and nutrition, should:

i. Comply fully with the provisions of the *International Code of Marketing of Breast-milk Substitutes* and subsequent relevant WHA resolutions, regardless of any other implementation measures taken

ii. Comply with the WHO recommendations on the marketing of foods and non-alcoholic beverages to children, regardless of whether or not local enforcement is weak or non-existent

iii. Abstain from imposing nutrition-based interventions where local ecosystems are able to support sustainable diets, and systematically ensure that such interventions prioritize local solutions and are consistent with the objective of moving toward sustainable adequate diets.

NOTES

1. Not only can the positive short- and long-term nutritional and overall health impacts of breastfeeding on mothers and children not be equaled by substitutes; there is increasing evidence that the protein content (Koletzko 2006) and iron content (Lozoff et al. 2011) in infant formulas has been too high during the last decades, leading to higher risk for childhood overweight/obesity and lower score for spatial memory and visual-motor coordination respectively.

2. For a discussion about disconnects present in the current human rights system, please see chapter two of this volume.

3. According to a 2011 UNICEF report, gender discrimination increases with age. Further, the gender disparities among children may be less than previously thought after disparities in initial survival are taken into account (UNICEF 2011).

4. Recent research from Bangladesh shows that women are more likely to have a stunted child if they have had life time exposure to physical intimate partner violence (IPV; Ziaei, Naved, and Ekström 2012).
5 This statement by Eglantyne Jebb can be found on the Learning to Give website "Save the Children" (http://learningtogive.org/papers/paper395.html; accessed March 28, 2014).
6. Traditional/alternative social exchange includes, but is not limited to, communally owned and distributed goods, local currency-based formal and informal trade, sharing, bartering, gifting, etc.
7. The reporting framework for ICECSR and CRC is the same: the first report by a state party is due two years after ratification and thereafter every five years; for CEDAW, the first report is due one year after ratification and then every four years.
8. For the purposes of this volume, civil society actors are individuals who voluntarily engage in forms of public participation and action around shared interests, purposes, or values that are compatible with the goals of the UN.
9. Please refer to UN General Assembly resolutions 60/165 (2006) and 61/163 (2007), HRC resolutions 7/14 (2008) and 10/12 (2009), and CESCR *General Comment 12 on the Right to Adequate Food* (1999, paras. 40–41).
10. This quote was taken from the UN Global Compact website "Overview of the UN Global Compact" (http://www.unglobalcompact.org/Aboutthegc/index.html; accessed April 14, 2014).
11. The Human Rights Council is an intergovernmental body within the UN system made up of forty-seven states responsible for strengthening the promotion and protection of human rights around the globe. The council was created by the UN General Assembly, March 15, 2006, with the main purpose of addressing situations of human rights violations and making recommendations on them. For more information on the HRC, please visit the website of the OHCHR (http://www.ohchr.org/EN/HRBodies/HRC/Pages/AboutCouncil.aspx; accessed May 23, 2014).
12. For more information on this UNICEF, Save the Children, and UN Global Compact joint initiative, please visit the UNICEF website with reference to *Children's Rights and Business Principles* (http://www.unicef.org/csr/12.htm; accessed April 14, 2014). Note that these *Children's Rights and Business Principles* are sometimes called "Children's Rights and Business Principles Initiative" *(CRBPI)* in documents by the International Baby Food Action Network (IBFAN; see e.g., IBFAN 2011a).
13. For more information on the ten UN Global Compact principles, please refer to the UN Global Compact website (http://www.unglobalcompact.org/AboutTheGC/TheTenPrinciples/index.html; accessed October 15, 2011).
14. For more information about the UN General Assembly Special Session on Children and its supporting events, please visit the UNICEF website on this special session (http://www.unicef.org/specialsession; accessed May 24, 2014).
15. As of May 2014, GAIN's Board of Directors is comprised of the following persons: Jay Naidoo (board chair; co-founder of the investment and management company J&J Group), Joachim von Braun (board vice chair; director of the Center for Development Research (ZEF), Bonn), Shawn K. Baker (board member; director of the Nutrition Global Development Program), Vinita Bali (board member; managing director of the Britannia Industries Ltd., India), Ashok Kumar Bharti (board member; head of the National Confederation of Dalit Organisations), Pierre Henchoz (board member; private banker, Switzerland), Richard Hurrell (board member; professor emeritus of the Institute of Food Science and Nutrition at the Swiss Federal Institute of Technology (ETH)), Kaiser Kabir (board member; CEO and managing director of Renata, Bangladesh),

Anna Lartey (board member; director of the Nutrition division at FAO, Italy), Admassu Tadesse (board member; president and chief executive officer at PTA Bank, Kenya), Stanley Zlotkin (board member; chief of Global Child Health at the Hospital for Sick Children, Canada).

16. This quote on "Britannia purpose" was taken from the presentation *Brittania Industries Limited: Health and Nutrition Initiatives* available online at the website of Britannia Industries Ltd. (www.britannia.co.in/bnf/media/britannia-in-health-nutrition.pdf; accessed May 24, 2014).

17. For general information on the structure and organization of all UN funds, programs, and other entities, please visit the "Structure and Organization" page of the UN website (http://www.un.org/en/aboutun/structure; accessed April 14, 2014).

18. This ad hoc Conflicts of Interest Coalition comprises civil society organizations united by the common objective of safeguarding public health policy making against commercial conflicts of interest through the development of a code of conduct and ethical framework for interactions with the private sector. For more information on the Conflicts of Interest 2011 challenge of the trend of businesses positioning themselves within civil society, please visit the Baby Milk Action website (http://info.babymilkaction.org/node/458; accessed May 24, 2014).

19. The UN 2010 Every Woman Every Child Initiative is designed to accelerate progress toward women's and children's health and the achievement of the Millennium Development Goals (MDGs) 4 and 5—to reduce child mortality and improve maternal health. For more information, please visit the UN Foundation website of the initiative (www.everywomaneverychild.org/about; accessed February 20, 2014).

20. "Bluewash" refers to a process by which corporations figuratively "wrap themselves in the blue flag of the United Nations in order to associate themselves with UN themes of human rights, labor rights, and environmental protection" (taken from the CorpWatch website at www.corpwatch.org/article.php?id=242, accessed May 24, 2014).

21. This initial commitment by Nestlé to Every Woman Every Child was last retrieved from the website of the UN Foundation for the initiative on 6 October 2011 (www.everywomaneverychild.org/commitments/all-commitments/blog).

22. Nestlé's commitment to Every Woman Every Child of 2011 can be found on the website of the UN Foundation for the initiative (www.everywomaneverychild.org/commitments/all-commitments/blog; accessed May 24, 2014).

23. According to Singh, Sedgh, and Hussain (2010), 40 percent of all pregnancies in developing countries are unintended; in developed countries, the percentage increases to 47 percent. Induced abortion is an outcome of unintended pregnancies which is a neglected public health challenge on a global scale. Nearly all cases of induced abortion (97 percent) occur in developing countries, contributing substantially to maternal mortality (Grimes et al. 2006). Research reveals that the rate of unsafe abortions has increased between 1995 and 2008, and that restricted abortion laws do not result in lower abortion rates (Sedgh et al. 2012).

24. Very recently, a study in Germany by Hirsch and Rademacher (2014, 21) revealed that "completely and correctly implemented recommendations [on the nutrition of infants and nursing mothers published by the Healthy Life—Young Families Network in June 2010] can only be found in 30 % of advice leaflets [on infant nutrition] available nationwide."

25. According to A. F. Williams (2009, 167), the mother's "nutrient balance will be largely determined by dietary intake, the size of her nutrient reserve by her body

size and composition, and the availability of nutrients to the fetus by her metabolic competence both to mobilise nutrients from stores and to partition dietary supply between stores and the fetoplacental unit." Optimal nutritional intake must be ensured in women of childbearing age during all stages of pregnancy and while breastfeeding (Thurnham 2012).

26. The Subcommittee on Nutrition was created in April 1977 by the UN Economic and Social Council (ECOSOC) as a subcommittee to the Administrative Committee on Coordination of the UN (ACC). As a result of the 2001 UN reform of the ACC (which was renamed as the Chief Executives Board [CEB]), the Subcommittee on Nutrition continued its functions as the United Nations Standing Committee on Nutrition (SCN).

27. Breastfeeding is central to the Lactational Amenorrhea Method (LAM), a temporary (six month) family planning method, based on natural infertility resulting from "full breastfeeding." This method is 98 percent effective if exclusive breastfeeding is performed and results in neither side effects nor extra cost. Full breastfeeding is the term applied to both exclusive breastfeeding (no other liquid or solid is given to the infant) and almost exclusive breastfeeding (vitamins, water, juice, or ritualistic feeds given infrequently in addition to breastfeeds; see LINKAGES 2001).

28. Excessive postnatal weight gain should be generally avoided, even for infants with low birth weight; research suggests that rapid infant growth, or "catch-up growth," may be associated with an increased risk for obesity, diabetes, hypertension, cardiovascular disease, and osteopenia in later life (Weaver 2006).

29. The extra three to five hundred kilocalories requirement for mothers during lactation assumes that all the energy in breastmilk is derived from the mother's diet and not from energy that might have been stored during pregnancy (LINKAGES 2009, Table 3, note b).

30. In Germany, policy makers changed the international recommendation of exclusive breastfeeding from six months to five months as a cost-cutting strategy to avoid putting into place measures and supporting structures, including services, to support six months of exclusive breastfeeding (Krawinkel 2011b).

31. Especially when a watery, monotonous cereal/roots flour porridge is being offered as complementary food, it is often healthier to support a quick transition to more appropriate family meals containing a higher dietary diversity (see Palmer 2009).

32. As of May 2014, WHA resolutions relevant to the Code comprise resolutions WHA35.26 (WHA 1982), WHA37.30 (1984), WHA39.28 (1986), WHA41.11 (1988), WHA43.3 (1990), WHA47.5 (1994), WHA49.15 (1996), WHA54.2 (2001), WHA55.25 (2002), WHA58.32 (2005), WHA59.11 (2006a), WHA59.21 (2006b), WHA61.20 (2008), WHA63.23 (2010), and WHA65.6 (2012b).

33. The Nestlé infant formula Good Start Probiotic contains *Bifidobacterium lactis*, a strain of bacteria found in breastmilk. The preparation instructions given on the product label and on the website of Nestlé Canada (http://www.nestle-baby. ca/en/products/formula/starter/goodstart_probiotic.htm; accessed May 26, 2014) state that warming the formula to temperatures above 40°C (100°F) will "compromise the *B. lactis*" (see also Collier 2009). Furthermore, and based on its meta-analysis on research related to the supplementation of infant formula with probiotics and prebiotics, the Committee on Nutrition of the European Society for Paediatric Gastroenterology, Hepatology and Nutrition (ESPGHAN) "does not recommend the routine use of probiotic-supplemented formula in infants" (ESPGHAN 2011, 248).

34. For more information on these consumer recommendations by the CDC on *Cronobacter* infection and infant formula, please visit the CDC website (http:// www.cdc.gov/Features/Cronobacter/; accessed April 10, 2014).

35. In the interview by Fabrice Bonvin (2013, 56), Dr. Motarjemi further states: "L'attitude qui prédominait était que 'tan qu'on n'est pas pris, on continue!' Certains me faisaient même comprendre qu'il fallait une crise ou un scandale pour que la direction prenne enfin des mesures. [The prevailing attitude was to say that 'as long as we remain unnoticed, we continue!' Some even made me understand that a crisis or scandal was needed to finally take measures]."

36. For reports on the meetings of the CRC Committee as concerning infant and young child feeding, please visit the IBFAN website (http://ibfan.org/reports-on-the-un-committee-on-the-rights-of-the-child; accessed May 15, 2014).

37. For more information on the history of the BFHI, please visit the WHO website (http://www.who.int/nutrition/topics/bfhi/en/; accessed April 14, 2014).

38. A study in the United States, for example, found that *Code* violating distribution of commercial hospital discharge packs, implying hospital endorsement of formula, resulted in lower rates of exclusive breastfeeding (Rosenberg et al. 2008).

39. The authors would like to thank Dr. med. Leila Srour for her input on the Bear Brand marketing case study in Laos.

40. Barennes et al. (2008, 3) reported that 19 percent of the adults interviewed indicated "giving the coffee creamer with the Bear Brand logo to infants at a mean age of 4.7 months."

41. *WHA Resolution 39.28* called follow-up infant formula "unnecessary" (WHA 1986, para. 3(2)(b)). See also 2013 WHO *Information Concerning the Use and Marketing of Follow-up Formula* wherein it states: "as well as being unnecessary, follow-up formula is unsuitable when used as a breast-milk replacement from six months of age onwards" (WHO 2013c, 1). However, these follow-up products continue to be manufactured, generating huge profits for the baby food industry. They were essentially invented after the adoption of the *Code* in order to get around its rulings (see IBFAN 2014). As described in this chapter in case study 4.8, the Bear Brand logo used on follow-up formulas was also used on creamer products, leading to confusion that proved disastrous for many children (Barennes et al. 2008). These so-called "toddler" or "growing up" milk products have moreover been reported to promote overweight (Gooze, Anderson, and Whitaker 2011).

42. Letter dated May 24, 2011, from eighteen aid agencies working in Lao People's Democratic Republic to the chairman of the board and CEO of Nestlé. It can be located on the Baby Milk Action website (http://info.babymilkaction.org/sites/info.babymilkaction.org/files/Aid%20Agencies%20in%20Laos%20refuse%20to%20apply%20for%20Nestle%20cash_30%20May%202011.pdf; accessed April 14, 2014).

43. Dr. med. Leila Srour is a pediatric continuing medical education coordinator at Health Frontiers (University of Health Sciences, Vientiane) and co-authored the research study by Barennes et al. (2008).

44. As a consequence of long-term breastfeeding, Ethiopian adults can remember themselves suckling at their mother's breast and perceive it as a positive feeling of bonding and security (Asefa Tolessa, pers. comm.; Asefa Tolessa acted as research assistant during the doctoral study of chapter coauthor Veronika Scherbaum).

45. Note de service, service de loisirs, sports et vie communautaire, ville de Gatineau, 1 Octobre 2009 [Memorandum, recreation services, sports, and community life, City of Gatineau, 1 October 2009].

46. For background on replacement feeding for infants that is affordable, feasible, acceptable, sustainable, and safe (AFASS), see the WHO webpage on Breastfeeding, Maternal Health and Everyday Living (http://www.who.int/maternal_child_adolescent/topics/child/nutrition/hivif_qa/general/q13/en;accessed April 14, 2014).

47. Full review of the WHO guidelines on the subject is scheduled for late 2015.

48. *Country Implementation of the 2010 HIV and Infant Feeding Guidelines: Report on Baseline Information.* Unpublished draft by UNICEF from September 2012.

49. The ENN story "Diarrhoea Risk Associated with Not Breastfeeding in Botswana: Summary of Report and Presentation" is available online at http://www.ennonline.net/pool/files/ife/fex-diarrhoearisk-botswana.html (accessed May 28, 2014).

50. The "Questions and Answers on Infant Feeding in the Context of HIV" webpage of the WHO can be found at http://www.who.int/maternal_child_adoles cent/topics/child/nutrition/hivif_qa/en/ (accessed April 10, 2014).

51. In 1997, out of a desire to ensure better quality and stronger accountability in the delivery of humanitarian response, a group of NGOs together with the Red Cross and the Red Crescent Movement initiated the Sphere Project to frame a human rights-based and people-centered humanitarian charter that introduced a set of universal minimum standards in core areas of humanitarian response to emergencies. The Sphere Project's handbook *Humanitarian Charter and Minimum Standards in Humanitarian Response*, periodically updated since 1998, was designed for planning, implementation, monitoring, evaluation, and reporting during humanitarian responses as an advocacy tool, and for disaster preparedness activities and contingency planning. This humanitarian charter "is a statement of established legal rights and obligations and of shared beliefs and commitments of humanitarian agencies, all collected in a set of common principles, rights and duties. Founded on the principle of humanity and the humanitarian imperative, these include the right to life with dignity, the right to receive humanitarian assistance and the right to protection and security" (Sphere Project 2011, 6).

52. The vitamin and mineral supplement was developed in the 1980s and 1990s for treatment of severely malnourished children in hospitals using F-75 or F-100. The same vitamin/mineral premix was later added to RUTF; that means this essential part of RUTF was not invented by researchers of Nutriset. The replacement of part of the milk powder by peanut butter was invented by Dr. A. Briend and M. Lescanne (J. Guimón and P. Guimón 2012).

53. The refeeding syndrome indicates that children who are free of clinical signs of SAM and show some appetite during the initial assessment can rapidly develop fever, symptoms of acute respiratory infection, etc., during the early rehabilitation process (relapse cases). Due to lack of energy and nutrients, the child can be too weak during the initial assessment to develop any medically relevant symptoms. This is one major reason why close supervision is essential, especially during the onset of the recovery process (stabilization/rehabilitation; see Rohrer and Dietrich 2014).

54. Lower cost and intersecting strategies to improve early childhood nutrition include nutrition education and micronutrient powders (MNP or "sprinkles"), the latter of which can fortify locally based food options for improved nutrition (Suchdev et al. 2012, with respect to decreasing rates of anemia and iron and vitamin A deficiency in Western Kenya; Loewenberg 2011, with respect to improved children's health status in poor regions).

55. The importance of adequate dietary intake of pregnant and lactating women and its long-term consequences are slowly being recognized. Due to metabolic/fetal/perinatal programming, the infant is already being imprinted and accustomed to the mother's diet (Aaltonen et al. 2011). In relation to this finding, in an ongoing research project in West Bengal, India, conducted under the supervision of chapter coauthor Veronika Scherbaum, the introduction of dietary diverse complementary foods to infants whose mothers had consumed a monotonous diet on a regular basis was found to be difficult. Infants aged six to twelve months who

were offered a more diversified family diet actually consumed mainly rice if left alone in a non-responsive feeding setting.

56. See also the updated, unfinalized version of the SCN NGO/CSO 2010 *Draft Guidelines for the Marketing of Ready to Use Supplemental Foods for Children*, with more background information, on the ENN Magazine *Field Exchange* on the ENN website (http://fex.ennonline.net/41/draft; accessed May 15, 2014).

57. For more information on the UNICEF integrated, community-based IYCF approach, please visit the UNICEF website (http://www.unicef.org/nutrition/index_58362.html; accessed April 14, 2014).

58. The "Continuum of Care Fact Sheet: Reproductive, Maternal, Newborn and Child Health" webpage can be found on the WHO website (http://www.who.int/pmnch/about/continuum_of_care/en/; accessed March 26, 2014).

59. The IMCI strategy was developed in 1992 by UNICEF and WHO with the aim of prevention, or early detection and treatment, of major culprits of childhood poor health and death. Underlying causes of child health and well-being are scrutinized with the understanding that factors such as nutrition, hygiene, and immunizations are as important as medical treatment in improving health. For further information please visit the WHO website (http://www.who.int/maternal_child_adolescent/topics/child/imci/en/; accessed April 14, 2014).

60. Evaluations of IMCI programs have revealed reductions in morbidity and mortality of children under five years of age, including a decrease in stunting rates (Schellenberg et al. 2003). There is a need, however, for improving equity regarding access to IMCI programs; many regions demand pro-poor criteria when new programs are planned (Victora et al. 2003).

61. Grandparents, particularly paternal grandmothers, are heavily involved in infant and child well-being, and need to be included in nutrition education programming (Aubel 2012).

62. The NE program was designed at national level and was therefore not sensitive toward the local cultural setting and belief system (Inayati, pers. comm.; Dr. sc. agr. Dyah Inayati conducted her doctoral study on the effects of INE on child nutritional status on Nias Island, Indonesia).

63. According to the SUN website, in April 2014 there were fifty developing world countries participating in the SUN project. For more information on the program, please go to http://scalingupnutrition.org/ (accessed April 14, 2014).

64. This quote was taken from the SUN website "Bringing People Together" (http://scalingupnutrition.org/sun-countries/bangladesh/progress-impact/bringing-people-together; accessed April 14, 2014).

65. This quote was taken from slide 20 in section 4.2 ("Overcoming Challenges") of the presentation "Private Sector Engagement Toolkit, 8 September 2011, Work in Progress, *This is a living document*," available online as Portable Document Format file at http://scalingupnutrition.org/wp-content/uploads/2013/02/Business-Network_Private-Sector-Engagement-Toolkit.pdf (accessed April 14, 2014).

66. This quote was taken from slide 26 in section 5.4 ("A Stress Test for PPP") of the presentation "Private Sector Engagement Toolkit, 8 September 2011, Work in Progress, *This is a living document*," available online as Portable Document Format file at http://scalingupnutrition.org/wp-content/uploads/2013/02/Business-Network_Private-Sector-Engagement-Toolkit.pdf (accessed April 14, 2014).

67. For more information on the declared work of the SUN Movement Secretariat on conflicts of interest and monitoring and evaluation, please visit the secretariat's website (http://scalingupnutrition.org/global-support/sun-movement-secretariat; accessed March 30, 2014).

68. This quote was taken from slide 19 in section 4.1 ("Challenges in PPP") of the presentation "Private Sector Engagement Toolkit, 8 September 2011, Work in Progress, *This is a living document,*" available online as Portable Document Format file at http://scalingupnutrition.org/wp-content/uploads/2013/02/Business-Network_Private-Sector-Engagement-Toolkit.pdf (accessed April 14, 2014).

69. For more information about the founding partners of the EPODE International Network, please go to http://www.epode-international-network.com/what-is-ein/ein-founding-partners/nestl%C3%A9 (accessed April 14, 2014).

70. This "Announcement for a Consultation Process on Conflict of Interest in the Scaling Up Nutrition Movement" can be found on the GSO website (http://gsogeneva.ch/; accessed June 2, 2014). For more information on the consultation process, please go to http://gsogeneva.ch/?page_id=1456 (accessed June 2, 2014) and http://scalingupnutrition.org/about/principles-of-engagement-2/preventing-and-managing-conflicts-of-interest (accessed June 2, 2014).

71. Information about the grant amount was retrieved from the Bill & Melinda Gates Foundation website (http://www.gatesfoundation.org/How-We-Work/Quick-Links/Grants-Database/Grants/2013/04/OPP1081893; accessed July 7, 2014).

72. This and more information about HRI can be retrieved from the organization's website (http://hrigeneva.com/?page_id=301; accessed April 8, 2014).

REFERENCES

Aaltonen, J., T. Ojala, K. Laitinen, T. Poussa, S. Ozanne, and E. Isolauri. 2011. "Impact of Maternal Diet during Pregnancy and Breastfeeding on Infant Metabolic Programming: A Prospective Randomized Controlled Study." *European Journal of Clinical Nutrition* 65: 10–19.

Ahmed, S., Q. Li, L. Liu, and A. O. Tsui. 2012. "Maternal Deaths Averted by Contraceptive Use: An Analysis of 172 Countries." *Obstetrical and Gynecological Survey* 67 (11): 685–86.

Allain, A. (ed.). 1986. *Milk and Murder. Address by Dr. Cicely Williams to the Rotary Club of Singapore in 1939.* Penang: International Organization of Consumers Unions (IOCU), quoted in Richter, J. 2001. *Holding Corporations Accountable: Corporate Conduct, International Codes, and Citizen Action.* London: Zed Books.

Arendt, M. 2012. "Allaiter en Public [Breastfeeding in Public]." *baby info* 01–03: 4.

Arie, S. 2010. "Hungry for Profit." *British Medical Journal (Clinical Research Ed.)* 341: c5221.

Ashworth, A. and A. Burgess. 2003. *Caring for Severely Malnourished Children.* Oxford: MacMillan.

Ashworth, A. and E. Ferguson. 2009. "Dietary Counseling in the Management of Moderate Malnourishment in Children." *Food and Nutrition Bulletin* 30 (3 Suppl.): S405–33.

Assefa, F., S. Sukotjo (Ninik), A. Winoto, and D. Hipgrave. 2008. "Increased Diarrhea Following Infant Formula Distribution in 2006 Earthquake Response in Indonesia: Evidence and Actions." *Field Exchange* 34: 30–35.

Aubel, J. 2012. "The Role and Influence of Grandmothers on Child Nutrition: Culturally Designated Advisors and Caregivers." *Maternal and Child Nutrition* 8 (1): 19–35.

Ball, T. M. and A. L. Wright. 1999. "Health Care Costs of Formula-Feeding in the First Year of Life." *Pediatrics* 103 (4 Pt 2): 870–76.

Barennes, H., T. Andriatahina, V. Latthaphasavang, M. Anderson, and L. M. Srour. 2008. "Misperceptions and Misuse of Bear Brand Coffee Creamer as Infant Food: National Cross Sectional Survey of Consumers and Paediatricians in Laos." *British Medical Journal* 337: a1379.

Barennes, H., G. Empis, T. D. Quang, K. Sengkhamyong, P. Phasavath, A. Harimanana, and P. N. Koffi. 2012. "Breast-milk Substitutes: A New Old-Threat for Breastfeeding Policy in Developing Countries. A Case Study in a Traditionally High Breastfeeding Country." *Public Library of Science ONE* 7 (2): February 6, 2014-e30634. doi:10.1371/journal.pone.0030634.

Beaglehole, R., R. Bonita, G. Alleyne, and R. Horton. 2011. "NCDs: Celebrating Success, Moving Forward." *The Lancet* 378 (9799): 1283–84.

Beesabathuni, K. N. and U. C. M. Natchu. 2010. "Production and Distribution of a Therapeutic Nutritional Product for Severe Acute Malnutrition in India: Opportunities and Challenges." *Indian Pediatrics* 47 (8): 702–706.

Bengin, H. G., V. Scherbaum, E. Hormann, and Q. Wang. 2010. "Breastfeeding after Earthquakes." *Birth* 37 (3): 264–65.

Bhutta, Z. A. 2009. "Addressing Severe Acute Malnutrition Where it Matters." *The Lancet* 374 (9684): 94–96.

Bhutta, Z. A. and M. Labbok. 2011. "Scaling Up Breastfeeding in Developing Countries." *The Lancet* 378 (9789): 378–80.

Black, M. M. and F. E. Aboud. 2011. "Responsive Feeding Is Embedded in a Theoretical Framework of Responsive Parenting." *Journal of Nutrition* 141 (3): 490–94.

Black, R. E., L. H. Allen, Z. A. Bhutta, L. E. Caulfield, M. de Onis, M. Ezzati, C. Mathers, J. Rivera, and Maternal and Child Undernutrition Study Group. 2008. "Maternal and Child Undernutrition: Global and Regional Exposures and Health Consequences." *The Lancet* 371: 243–60.

Bonvin, F. 2013. "Interview Yasmine Motarjemi: 'Nestlé Confondait Sécurité Alimentaire et Gestion des Crises' ('Nestlé Confused Food Security and Crises Management')." *Nexus* (84), 54–59.

Bowen, A. B. and C. R. Braden. 2006. "Invasive *Enterobacter Sakazakii* Disease in Infants." *Emerging Infectious Diseases* 12 (8): 1185–89.

Brady, J. P. 2012. "Marketing Breast Milk Substitutes: Problems and Perils throughout the World." *Archives of Disease in Childhood* 97 (6): 529–32.

Brown, J. D. and S. R. Peuchaud. 2008. "Media and Breastfeeding: Friend or Foe?" *International Breastfeeding Journal* 3: 15.

Brown, K., K. Dewey, and L. Allen. 1998. *Complementary Feeding of Young Children in Developing Countries: A Review of Current Scientific Knowledge.* Geneva: World Health Organization (WHO).

Bukusuba, J., F. I. Muranga, and P. Nampala. 2008. "Effect of Processing Technique on Energy Density and Viscosity of Cooking Banana: Implication for Weaning Foods in Uganda." *International Journal of Food Science and Technology* 43 (8): 1424–29.

Burgess, A., M. Bijlsma, and C. Ismael. 2009. *Community Nutrition: A Handbook for Health and Development Workers.* Oxford: Macmillan.

Carroll, A. B. 1999. "Corporate Social Responsibility: Evolution of a Definitional Construct." *Business Society* 38 (3): 268–95.

Cattaneo, A. 2008. "The Benefits of Breastfeeding or the Harm of Formula Feeding?" *Journal of Paediatrics and Child Health* 44 (1–2): 1–2.

Cattaneo, A., C. Williams, C. R. Pallás-Alonso, M. T. Hernández-Aguilar, J. J. Lasarte-Velillas, L. Landa-Rivera, E. Rouw, M. Pina, A. Volta, and A. M. Oudesluys-Murphy. 2011. "ESPGHAN's 2008 Recommendation for Early Introduction of Complementary Foods: How Good Is the Evidence?" *Maternal & Child Nutrition* 7 (4): 335–43.

Central Statistical Agency [Ethiopia] and ORC Macro. 2006. *Ethiopia Demographic and Health Survey (EDHS) 2005*. Addis Ababa: Central Statistical Agency; ORC Macro.

Chaparro, C. M. and K. G. Dewey. 2010. "Use of Lipid-Based Nutrient Supplements (LNS) to Improve the Nutrient Adequacy of General Food Distribution Rations for Vulnerable Sub-Groups in Emergency Settings." *Maternal and Child Nutrition* 6 (Suppl. 1): 1–69.

Ciliberto, M. A., M. J. Manary, M. J. Ndekha, A. Briend, and P. Ashorn. 2006. "Home-based Therapy for Oedematous Malnutrition with Ready-to-use Therapeutic Food." *Acta Paediatrica* 95 (8): 1012–15.

Collier, R. 2009. "Squabble Over Risks of Probiotic Infant Formula." *Canadian Medical Association Journal* 181 (3–4): E46–E47.

Collins, S. and K. Sadler. 2002. "Outpatient Care for Severely Malnourished Children in Emergency Relief Programmes: A Retrospective Cohort Study." *The Lancet* 360 (9348): 1824–30.

Collins, S., K. Sadler, N. Dent, T. Khara, S. Guerrero, M. Myatt, M. Saboya, and A. Walsh. 2006. "Key Issues in the Success of Community-based Management of Severe Malnutrition." *Food and Nutrition Bulletin* 27 (Suppl. 3): S49–S82.

Conflicts of Interest Coalition. 2011. *Conflicts of Interest Coalition: Statement of Concern*. Cambridge: Baby Milk Action/International Baby Food Action Network.

Correa, S. and R. Petchesky. 2007. "Reproductive and Sexual Rights: A Feminist Perspective." In *Culture, Society and Sexuality: A Reader*, edited by R. Parker and P. Aggleton. 2nd ed., 298–315. London: Routledge.

Cosgrove, N., J. Earland, P. James, A. Rozet, M. Grossiord, and C. Salpeteur. 2012. "Qualitative Review of an Alternative Treatment of SAM in Myanmar." *Field Exchange* (42): 7.

Coutsoudis, A., H. M. Coovadia, and J. King. 2009. "The Breastmilk Brand: Promotion of Child Survival in the Face of Formula-Milk Marketing." *The Lancet* 374 (9687): 423–25.

Creek, T. L., A. Kim, L. Lu, A. Bowen, J. Masunge, W. Arvelo, M. Smit, O. Mach, K. Legwaila, C. Motswere, L. Zaks, T. Finkbeiner, L. Povinelli, M. Maruping, G. Ngwaru, G. Tebele, C. Bopp, N. Puhr, S. P. Johnston, A. J. Dasilva, C. Bern, R. S. Beard, and M. K. Davis. 2006. "Hospitalization and Mortality among Primarily Nonbreastfed Children during a Large Outbreak of Diarrhea and Malnutrition in Botswana." *Journal of Acquired Immune Deficiency Syndromes* 53 (1): 14–19.

Department of Health (DH) and Food Standards Agency (FSA) [United Kingdom]. *Guidance for Health Professionals on Safe Preparation, Storage and Handling of Powdered Infant Formula*. London: Department of Health (DH); Food Standards Agency (FSA).

Deutsche Stiftung Weltbevölkerung (DSW), Deutsche Gesellschaft für Technische Zusammenarbeit (GTZ), Internationale Weiterbildung und Entwicklung (InWEnt), International Planned Parenthood Federation (IPPF), Kreditanstalt für Wiederaufbau (KFW), Bayer, and Federal Ministry for Economic Cooperation and Development [Germany]. 2009. *7th International Dialogue on Population and Sustainable Development. Exploring Cultural Diversity and Gender Equality: Towards Universal Access to Sexual and Reproductive Health and Rights*. Berlin: Bayer Schering Pharma AG.

Dewey, K. G. and S. Adu-Afarwuah. 2008. "Systematic Review of the Efficacy and Effectiveness of Complementary Feeding Interventions in Developing Countries." *Maternal and Child Nutrition* 4 (Suppl. 1): 24–85.

Dibari, F., E. H. I. Diop, S. Collins, and A. Seal. 2012. "Low-cost, Ready-to-use Therapeutic Foods Can Be Designed Using Locally Available Commodities with the Aid of Linear Programming." *Journal of Nutrition* 142 (5): 955–61.

Diop, E. H. I., N. I. Dossou, M. M. Ndour, A. Briend, and S. Wade. 2003. "Comparison of the Efficacy of a Solid Ready-to-use Food and a Liquid, Milk-Based Diet for the Rehabilitation of Severely Malnourished Children: A Randomized Trial." *American Journal of Clinical Nutrition* 78 (2): 302–307.

Doak, C. M., L. S. Adair, C. Monteiro, and B. M. Popkin. 2000. "Overweight and Underweight Coexist within Households in Brazil, China and Russia." *Journal of Nutrition* 130 (12): 2965–71.

Doak, C. M., L. S. Adair, M. Bentley, C. Monteiro, and B. M. Popkin. 2005. "The Dual Burden Household and the Nutrition Transition Paradox." *International Journal of Obesity* 29: 129–136.

Dube, B., T. Rongsen, S. Mazunder, S. Taneja, F. Rafiqui, N. Bhandari, and M. K. Bhan. 2009. "Comparison of Ready-to-use Therapeutic Food with Cereal Legume-Based Khichri among Malnourished Children." *Indian Pediatrics* 46 (5): 383–88.

Dunn, D., M. L. Newell, A. Ades, and C. Peckham. 1992. "Risk of Human Immunodeficiency Virus Type 1 Transmission through Breast-Feeding." *The Lancet* 340 (8819): 585–88.

Edmond, K. M., C. Zandoh, M. A. Quigley, S. Amenga-Etego, S. Owusu-Agyei, and B. R. Kirkwood. 2006. "Delayed Breastfeeding Initiation Increases Risk of Neonatal Mortality." *Pediatrics* 117 (3): e380–86.

Emergency Nutrition Network (ENN). 2011a. "Module 11: General Food Distribution." In *Harmonised Training Package (HTP): Resource Material for Training on Nutrition in Emergencies, Version 2.* Oxford, England: Nutrition Works; Emergency Nutrition Network (ENN); Global Nutrition Cluster.

———. 2011b. "Module 15: Priority Health Interventions that Impact Nutrition Status in Emergencies." In *Harmonised Training Package (HTP): Resource Material for Training on Nutrition in Emergencies, Version 2.* Oxford, England: Nutrition Works; Emergency Nutrition Network (ENN); Global Nutrition Cluster.

———. 2011c. "Module 17: Infant and Young Child Feeding." In *Harmonised Training Package (HTP): Resource Material for Training on Nutrition in Emergencies, Version 2.* Oxford, England: Nutrition Works; Emergency Nutrition Network (ENN); Global Nutrition Cluster.

Enserink, M. 2008. "Nutrition Science: The Peanut Butter Debate." *Science* 322 (5898): 36–38.

European Society for Paediatric Gastroenterology, Hepatology and Nutrition (ESP-GHAN) Committee on Nutrition. 2011. "Supplementation of Infant Formula with Probiotics and/or Prebiotics: A Systematic Review and Comment by the ESPGHAN Committee on Nutrition." *Journal of Pediatric Gastroenterology and Nutrition* 52: 238–50.

Fall, P. L. and M. M. Zahran. 2010. *United Nations Corporate Partnerships: The Role and Functioning of the Global Compact. JIU/REP/2010/9.* Geneva: United Nations Joint Inspection Unit (JIU).

Flax, V. L., J. Phuka, Y. B. Cheung, U. Ashorn, K. Maleta, and P. Ashorn. 2010. "Feeding Patterns and Behaviors during Home Supplementation of Underweight Malawian Children with Lipid-Based Nutrient Supplements or Corn-Soy Blend." *Appetite* 54 (3): 504–11.

Food and Agriculture Organization of the United Nations (FAO). 2005. *Voluntary Guidelines to Support the Progressive Realization of the Right to Adequate Food in the Context of National Food Security.* Rome: Food and Agriculture Organization of the United Nations (FAO).

Food and Agriculture Organization of the United Nations (FAO) and World Health Organization (WHO). 2001. *Health and Nutritional Properties of Probiotics in Food Including Powder Milk with Live Lactic Acid Bacteria: Report of a Joint*

FAO/WHO *Expert Consultation on Evaluation of Health and Nutritional Properties of Probiotics in Food Including Powder Milk with Live Lactic Acid Bacteria*. Córdoba: Food and Agriculture Organization of the United Nations (FAO); World Health Organization (WHO).

Fouda, F. H., G. Genevieve, J. D. Jaeger, C. H. Amos, E. L. Kunz, K. Anasti, L. W. Stamper, B. E. Liebl, K. H. Barbasm T. Ohashi, M. A. Moseley, H. Liao, H. P. Erickson, S. M. Alam, and S. R. Permar. 2013. "Tenascin-C Is an Innate Broad-Spectrum, HIV-1–Neutralizing Protein in Breast Milk." *Proceedings of the National Academy of Sciences of the United States of America: Early Edition*. doi:10.1073/pnas.1307336110.

Friedman, M. 1970. "The Social Responsibility of Business is to Increase Its Profits." *New York Times Magazine*. September 13, 1970.

Friedemann, M. 2008. "*Enterobacter Sakazakii* in Powdered Infant Formula." *Bundesgesundheitsblatt Gesundheitsforschung Gesundheitsschutz*. 51 (6): 664–74.

Gabrysch, S., C. Lema, E. Bedriñana, M. A. Bautista, R. Malca, O. M. R. Campbell, and J. J. Miranda. 2009. "Cultural Adaptation of Birthing Services in Rural Ayacucho, Peru." *Bulletin of the World Health Organization* 87 (9): 724–29.

Gale, C., K. M. Logan, S. Santhakumaran, J. R. C. Parkinson, M. J. Hyde, and N. Modi. 2012. "Effect of Breastfeeding Compared with Formula Feeding on Infant Body Composition: A Systematic Review and Meta-Analysis." *American Journal of Clinical Nutrition* 95 (3): 656–69.

Gao, H., C. K. Stiller, V. Scherbaum, H. K. Biesalski, Q. Wang, E. Hormann, and A. C. Bellows. 2013. "Dietary Intake and Food Habits of Pregnant Women Residing in Urban and Rural Areas of Deyang City, Sichuan Province, China." *Nutrients* 5: 2933–54.

Gardner, B., J. Cane, N. Rumsey, and S. Michie. 2012. "Behaviour Change Among Overweight and Socially Disadvantaged Adults: A Longitudinal Study of the NHS Health Trainer Service." *Psychology and Health* 27 (10): 1178–93.

Gartner, L. M., J. Morton, R. A. Lawrence, A. J. Naylor, D. O'Hare, R. J. Shanler, and A. I. Eidelman. 2005. "Breastfeeding and the Use of Human Milk." *Pediatrics* 115 (2): 496–506.

Gasser, M., C. Salzano, R. Di Meglio, and A. Lazarte-Hoyle. 2004. *Local Economic Development in Post-Crisis Situations: Operational Guide*. Geneva: International Labor Office (ILO).

Gera, T. 2010. "Efficacy and Safety of Therapeutic Nutrition Products for Home Based Therapeutic Nutrition for Severe Acute Malnutrition: A Systematic Review." *Indian Pediatrics* 47 (8): 709–18.

Gillman, M. W., S. L. Rifas-Shiman, C. A. J. Camargo, C. S. Berkey, A. L. Frazier, H. R. H. Rockett, A. E. Field, and G. A. Colditz. 2001. "Risk of Overweight Among Adolescents Who Were Breastfed as Infants." *Journal of the American Medical Association* 285 (19): 2461–67.

"The Global Game Plan of Big Snack [Editorial]." 2011. *World Nutrition* 2 (2): 55–61.

Godfrey, K. M. and D. J. P. Barker. 2000. "Fetal Nutrition and Adult Disease." *American Journal of Clinical Nutrition* 71 (5 Suppl.): 1344s–52s.

Golden, M. H. 2010. "Evolution of Nutritional Management of Acute Malnutrition." *Indian Pediatrics* 47 (8): 667–78.

Gooze, R. A., S. E. Anderson, and R. C. Whitaker. 2011. "Prolonged Bottle Use and Obesity at 5.5 Years of Age in US Children." *Journal of Pediatrics* 159 (3): 431–36.

Gribble, K. D. and N. J. Berry. 2011. "Emergency Preparedness for Those Who Care for Infants in Developed Country Contexts." *International Breastfeeding Journal* 6 (1): 16.

Gribble, K. D., M. McGrath, A. MacLaine, and L. Lhotska. 2011. "Supporting Breastfeeding in Emergencies: Protecting Women's Reproductive Rights and Maternal and Infant Health." *Disasters* 35 (4): 720–38.

Grijalva-Eternod, C. S., J. C. K. Wells, M. Cortina-Borja, N. Salse-Ubach, M. C. Tondeur, C. Dolan, C. Meziani, C. Wilkinson, P. Spiegel, and A. J. Seal. 2012. "The Double Burden of Obesity and Malnutrition in a Protracted Emergency Setting: A Cross-Sectional Study of Western Sahara Refugees." *Public Library of Science Medicine* 9 (10): February 12, 2014. doi:10.1371/journal.pmed.1001320.

Grimes, D. A., J. Benson, S. Singh, M. Romero, B. Ganatra, F. E. Okonofua, and I. H. Shah. 2006. "Unsafe Abortion: The Preventable Pandemic." *The Lancet* 368 (9550): 1908–19.

Grimshaw, E. C., J. Maskell, E. M. Oliver, R. C. G. Morris, K. D. Foote, E. N. C. Mills, G. Roberts, and B. M. Margetts. 2013. "Introduction of Complementary Foods and the Relationship to Food Allergy." *Pediatrics* 132 (6): e1529–38.

Groer, M. W. and M. W. Davis. 2006. "Cytokines, Infections, Stress, and Dysphoric Moods in Breastfeeders and Formula Feeders." *Journal of Obstetric, Gynecologic, and Neonatal Nursing (JOGNN)* 35 (5): 599–607.

Guimón, J. and P. Guimón. 2012. "How Ready-to-use Therapeutic Food Shapes a New Technological Regime to Treat Child Malnutrition." *Technological Forecasting and Social Change* 79 (7): 1319–27.

Guldan, G. S., H. C. Fan, X. Ma, Z. Z. Ni, X. Xiang, and M. Z. Tang. 2000. "Culturally Appropriate Nutrition Education Improves Infant Feeding and Growth in Rural Sichuan, China." *Journal of Nutrition* 130 (5): 1204–11.

Gupta, A. and K. Khanna. 1999. "Economic Value of Breastfeeding in India." *National Medical Journal of India* 12 (3): 123–27.

Gustafsson, P. E., M. Persson, and A. Hammarström. 2012. "Socio-Economic Disadvantage and Body Mass over the Life Course in Women and Men: Results from the Northern Swedish Cohort." *European Journal of Public Health* 22 (3): 322–27.

Harper, E. 2009. *International Law and Standards Applicable in Natural Disaster Situations.* Rome: International Development Law Organization (IDLO).

Hendricks, K. M. 2010. "Ready-to-use Therapeutic Food for Prevention of Childhood Undernutrition." *Nutrition Reviews* 68 (7): 429–35.

Hirsch, J. and C. Rademacher. 2014. "Implementation of the Recommendations Made by the '*Gesund ins Leben*' Network as Found in Advice Leaflets on the Nutrition of Infants: How and How Well Have the Recommendations Been Implemented Two Years Later?" *Ernährungs Umschau* 61 (2): 27–31.

Ickes, S. B., S. B. Jilcott, J. A. Myhre, L. S. Adair, H. Thirumurthy, S. Handa, M. E. Bentley, and A. S. Ammerman. 2012. "Examination of Facilitators and Barriers to Home-based Supplemental Feeding with Ready-to-use Food for Underweight Children in Western Uganda." *Maternal and Child Nutrition* 8 (1): 115–29.

Inayati, D. A., V. Scherbaum, R. C. Purwestri, E. Hormann, N. N. Wirawan, J. Suryantan, S. Hartono, M. A. Bloem, R. V. Pangaribuan, H. K. Biesalski, V. Hoffmann, and A. C. Bellows. 2012. "Infant Feeding Practices Among Mildly Wasted Children: A Retrospective Study on Nias Island, Indonesia." *International Breastfeeding Journal* 7 (3): doi:10.1186/1746-4358-7-3.

Inayati, D. A., V. Scherbaum, R. C. Purwestri, N. N. Wirawan, J. Suryantan, S. Hartono, M. A. Bloem, R. V. Pangaribuan, H. K. Biesalski, V. Hoffmann, and A. C. Bellows. 2012a. "Combined Intensive Nutrition Education (INE) and Micronutrient Powder (MNP) Supplementation Improved Nutritional Status of Mildly Wasted Children in Nias Island, Indonesia." *Asia Pacific Journal Clinical Nutrition* 21 (3): 361–73.

Inayati, D. A., V. Scherbaum, R. C. Purwestri, N. N. Wirawan, J. Suryantan, S. Hartono, M. A. Bloem, R. V. Pangaribuan, H. K. Biesalski, V. Hoffmann, and A. C. Bellows. 2012b. "Improved Nutrition Knowledge and Practice Through

Intensive Nutrition Education: A Study Among Caregivers of Mildly Wasted Children on Nias Island, Indonesia." *Food and Nutrition Bulletin* 33 (2): 117–27.

Infant and Young Child Feeding in Emergencies (IFE) Core Group. 2007. *Infant and Young Child Feeding in Emergencies: Operational Guidance for Emergency Relief Staff and Programme Managers*. Oxford: Infant and Young Child Feeding in Emergencies (IFE) Core Group.

Infant and Young Child Feeding in Emergencies (IFE) Core Group and UNICEF. 2006. *Making it Matter: Proceedings of a Strategy Meeting Held by the Infant and Young Child Feeding in Emergencies (IFE) Core Group*. Oxford: Emergency Nutrition Network (ENN).

Integrated Regional Information Networks (IRIN) Asia. 2013. *Pressure in Philippines to End Ban on Formula Milk Aid*. Integrated Regional Information Networks (IRIN) Asia.

Inter-Agency Standing Committee (IASC). 2006. *Gender Handbook in Humanitarian Action*. Geneva: Inter-Agency Standing Committee (IASC).

International Assessment of Agricultural Knowledge, Science and Technology for Development (IAASTD). 2009. *Agriculture at a Crossroads: International Assessment of Agricultural Knowledge, Science and Technology for Development: Synthesis Report*, edited by B. D. McIntyre, H. R. Herren, J. Wakhungu and R. T. Watson. Washington, D.C.: Island Press.

International Baby Food Action Network (IBFAN). 2011a. *Comments on the 'Children's Rights and Business Principles Initiative'*. Geneva: International Baby Food Action Network (IBFAN).

———. 2011b. *Statement on the Promotion and Use of Commercial Fortified Foods as Solutions for Child Malnutrition*. Geneva: International Baby Food Action Network (IBFAN).

———. 2012. *IBFAN Discussion Paper. The Scaling Up Nutrition (SUN) Initiative: IBFAN's Concern about the Role of Businesses*. Geneva: International Baby Food Action Network (IBFAN).

———. 2014. *Breaking the Rules—Stretching the Rules: Evidence of Violations of the International Code of Marketing of Breastmilk Substitutes and Subsequent Resolutions, Compiled from January 2011 to December 2013*. Geneva: International Baby Food Action Network—International Code Documentation Centre (IBFAN-ICDC).

International Baby Food Action Network (IBFAN) Africa. 2008. *WHA Resolution 61.20–2008: Eighth Plenary Meeting (A61/VR/8)*.

International Baby Food Action Network (IBFAN) and International Code Documentation Centre (ICDC). 2009. *The Code and Infant Feeding in Emergencies*. Malaysia: International Code Documentation Centre (ICDC).

International Chamber of Commerce (ICC) and International Organization of Employers (IOE). 2003. *Joint Written Statement Submitted by the International Chamber of Commerce and the International Organization of Employers, Non-Governmental Organizations in General Consultative Status. Commission on Human Rights, Sub-Commission on Promotion and Protection of Human Rights, Item 4, Economic, Social and Cultural Rights, E/CN.4/Sub.2/2003/NGO/44, 29 July 2003*. New York: United Nations Economic and Social Council (ECOSOC).

International Code Documentation Centre (ICDC) and International Baby Food Action Network (IBFAN). 2014. *State of the Code by Country 2014*. International Baby Food Action Network (IBFAN).

International Labour Organization (ILO). 2000a. *C183—Maternity Protection Convention, 2000 (No.183)*.

———. 2000b. *R191—Maternity Protection Recommendation (No. 191)*.

———. 2012. *Maternity Protection Resource Package: From Aspiration to Reality for All*.

Isanaka, S., N. Nombela, A. Djibo, M. Poupard, D. Van Beckhoven, V. Gaboulaud, P. J. Guerin, and R. F. Grais. 2009. "Effect of Preventive Supplementation with Ready-to-use Therapeutic Food on the Nutritional Status, Mortality, and Morbidity of Children Aged 6 to 60 Months in Niger: A Cluster Randomized Trial." *Journal of the American Medical Association (JAMA)* 301 (3): 277–85.

Iversen, C. and S. Forsythe. 2004. "Isolation of *Enterobacter Sakazakii* and Other Enterobacteriaceae from Powdered Infant Formula Milk and Related Products." *Food Microbiology* 21 (6): 771–77.

Jellife, D. B. 1971. "Commerciogenic Malnutrition? Time for a Dialogue." *Food Technology* 25: 55–61.

Jones, G., R. W. Steketee, R. E. Black, Z. A. Bhutta, and S. S. Morris. 2003. "How Many Child Deaths Can We Prevent This Year?" *The Lancet* 362 (9377): 65–71.

Jordan, I., A. Reinbott, and J. Kuchenbecker. 2013. *Preliminary Results of the Longitudinal Study Component in Malawi and Cambodia.* Rome: Food and Agriculture Organization (FAO).

Kaufmann, A. and V. Scherbaum. 2003. "Geeigneter Zeitpunkt für die Gabe von Beikost [Appropriate Time for the Delivery of Complementary Foods]." In *Stillen [Breastfeeding],* edited by V. Scherbaum, F. M. Perl and U. Kretschmer, 348–53. Cologne: Deutscher Ärzte-Verlag.

Kent, G. 2002. "WABA Global Forum II." Arusha, Tanzania, September 23–27, 2002.

———. 2005. *Freedom from Want: The Human Right to Adequate Food.* Advancing Human Rights. Washington, D.C.: Georgetown University Press.

———. 2014. "Rights and Obligations in International Humanitarian Assistance." *Disaster Prevention and Management* 23 (3): 214–21.

Khan, M. U. and M. H. Munshi. 1983. "Clinical Illnesses and Causes of Death in a Burmese Refugee Camp in Bangladesh." *International Journal of Epidemiology* 12 (4): 460–64.

Kramer, M. S. and R. Kakuma. 2012. "Optimal Duration of Exclusive Breastfeeding." *Cochrane Database of Systematic Reviews* 8 (CD003517).

Koletzko, B. 2006. "Long-Term Consequences of Early Feeding on Later Obesity Risk." *Nestlé Nutrition Workshop Series. Paediatric Programme* (58): 1–18.

Kolinsky, H. M. 2010. "Respecting Working Mothers with Infant Children: The Need for Increased Federal Intervention to Develop, Protect, and Support a Breastfeeding Culture in the United States." *Duke Journal of Gender Law and Policy* Spring: 17.

Krawinkel, M. B. 2011a. "Benefits from Longer Breastfeeding: Do We Need to Revise the Recommendations?" *Current Problems in Pediatric and Adolescent Health Care* 41 (9): 240–43.

———. 2011b. "Vom Nutzen des Stillens: Konsensus und weitergehende Überlegungen." *Kinder- und Jugendmedizin* 11 (2): 88–91.

———. 2012. "Overcoming Undernutrition with Local Resources in Africa, Asia and Latin America." *Journal of the Science of Food and Agriculture* 92 (14): 2757–59.

Labbok, M. H., P. H. Smith, and E. C. Taylor. 2008. "Breastfeeding and Feminism: A Focus on Reproductive Health, Rights and Justice." *International Breastfeeding Journal* (3): 8.

Lagrone, L., S. Cole, A. Schondelmeyer, K. Maleta, and M. J. Manary. 2010. "Locally Produced Ready-to-use Supplementary Food Is an Effective Treatment of Moderate Acute Malnutrition in an Operational Setting." *Annals of Tropical Paediatrics* 30 (2): 103–108.

Lamberti, L. M., C. L. Fischer Walker, A. Noiman, C. Victora, and R. E. Black. 2011. "Breastfeeding and the Risk for Diarrhea Morbidity and Mortality." *BioMed Central Public Health* 11 (Suppl. 3): S15.

Lhotska, L. 2008. *Whatever Happened to Health for All? Ups and Downs of Protection of Breastfeeding. Regulation of Transnational Corporations and Health for*

All. Geneva: International Baby Food Action Network (IBFAN); Geneva Infant Feeding Association (GIFA).

Lhotska, L., A. C. Bellows, and V. Scherbaum. 2012. "Conflicts of Interest and Human Rights-based Policy-Making: The Case of Maternal, Infant, and Young Children's Health and Malnutrition." *Right to Food and Nutrition WATCH* 2012: 31–36.

LINKAGES: Breastfeeding, LAM, Related Complementary Feeding, and Maternal Nutrition Program. 2001. *Lactation Amenorrhea Method (LAM): Frequently Asked Questions (FAQ).* Washington, D.C.: LINKAGES: Breastfeeding, LAM, Complementary Feeding, and Maternal Nutrition Program.

———. 2009. *Maternal Nutrition during Pregnancy and Lactation.* Washington, D.C.: LINKAGES: Breastfeeding, LAM, Related Complementary Feeding, and Maternal Nutrition Program.

Lo, B. and M. J. Field, eds. 2009. *Conflict of Interest in Medical Research, Education and Practice.* Washington, D.C.: National Academics Press.

Loewenberg, S. 2011. "Fighting Child Malnutrition in Africa Through the Use of Micronutrient Supplements." *Health Affairs* 30 (6): 1160–64.

Lozano, R., M. Naghavi, K. Foreman, S. Lim, K. Shibuya, V. Aboyans, J. Abraham, . . . C. J. L. Murray. 2012. "Global and Regional Mortality from 235 Causes of Death for 20 Age Groups in 1990 and 2010: A Systematic Analysis for the Global Burden of Disease Study 2010." *The Lancet* 380 (9859): 2095–128.

Lozoff, B., M. Castillo, K. M. Clark, and J. B. Smith. 2011. "Iron-fortified vs. Low-Iron Infant Formula: Developmental Outcome at 10 Years." *Archives of Pediatrics and Adolescent Medicine* 166 (3): 208–15.

Ludwig, D. S. and J. Currie. 2010. "The Association Between Pregnancy Weight Gain and Birthweight: A Within-Family Comparison." *The Lancet* 376 (9745): 984–90.

Maastricht University and International Commission of Jurists (ICJ). 2011. *Maastricht Principles on Extraterritorial Obligations of States in the Area of Economic, Social and Cultural Rights.* Maastricht; Geneva: Maastricht University; International Commission of Jurists (ICJ).

MacLaine, A. and M. Corbett. 2006. "Infant Feeding in Emergencies: Experiences from Indonesia and Lebanon." *Field Exchange* (29): 3.

Manary, M. J. 2006. "Local Production and Provision of Ready-to-use Therapeutic Food (RUTF) Spread for the Treatment of Severe Childhood Malnutrition." *Food and Nutrition Bulletin* 27 (Suppl. 3): S83–89.

Manary, M. J., M. J. Ndekha, P. Ashorn, K. Maleta, and A. Briend. 2004. "Home Based Therapy for Severe Malnutrition with Ready-to-use Food." *Archives of Disease in Childhood* 89 (6): 557–61.

Maren, M. 1997. *The Road to Hell: The Ravaging Effects of Foreign Aid and International Charity.* New York: Free Press.

Marriott, B. P., A. White, L. Hadden, J. C. Davies, and J. C. Wallingford. 2012. "World Health Organization (WHO) Infant and Young Child Feeding Indicators: Associations with Growth Measures in 14 Low-Income Countries." *Maternal and Child Nutrition* 8 (3): 354–70.

Mason, K. 2012. "The Unequal Weight of Discrimination: Gender, Body Size, and Income Inequality." *Social Problems* 59 (3): 411–35.

Maternal and Child Nutrition Study Group. 2008. *Maternal and Child Nutrition. Executive Summary of* The Lancet *Maternal and Child Nutrition Series.* Lancet.

Matilsky, D. K., K. Maleta, T. Castleman, and M. J. Manary. 2009. "Supplementary Feeding with Fortified Spreads Results in Higher Recovery Rates Than with a Corn/Soy Blend in Moderately Wasted Children." *Journal of Nutrition* 139 (4): 773–78.

Monteiro, C. 2010. "The Big Issue Is Ultra Processing: There Is No Such Thing as a Healthy Ultra-Processed Product." *World Nutrition* 2 (7): 333–49.

Moodie, R., D. Stuckler, C. Monteiro, N. Sheron, B. Neal, T. Thamarangsi, P. Lincoln, and S. Casswell. 2013. "Profits and Pandemics: Prevention of Harmful Effects of Tobacco, Alcohol, and Ultra-Processed Food and Drink Industries." *The Lancet* 381 (9867): 670–79.

Moyo, D. and N. Ferguson. 2009. *Dead Aid: Why Aid Is Not Working and How There Is a Better Way for Africa.* New York: Farrar, Straus and Giroux.

Mulford, C. 2008. "Is Breastfeeding Really Invisible, or Did the Health Care System just Choose Not to Notice It?" *International Breastfeeding Journal* 3 (13): August 4, 2008. doi: 10.1186/1746-4358-3-13.

Muytjens, H. L., H. Roelofs-Willemse, and G. H. Jaspar. 1988. "Quality of Powdered Substitutes for Breast Milk with Regard to Members of the Family Enterobacteriaceae." *Journal of Clinical Microbiology* 26 (4): 743–46.

Nestlé Union Network. 2006. *Nestlé Sells Off Two Thai Factories as Part of Regional Restructuring.* Nestlé Union Network.

Olbricht, I. 1985. *Verborgene Quellen der Weiblichkeit: Die Brust, das enteignete Organ [Hidden Sources of Femininity: the Breast, the Expropriated Organ].* Freiburg: Kreuz Verlag.

Ollila, E. 2003. "Health-related Public-Private Partnerships and the United Nations." In *Global Social Governance: Themes and Prospects*, edited by B. Deacon, E. Ollila, M. Koivusalo and P. Stubbs, 36–76. Helsinki: Hakapaino Oy.

Owino, V. O., A. H. Irena, F. Dibari, and S. Collins. 2012. "Development and Acceptability of a Novel Milk-free Soybean-Maize-Sorghum Ready-to-use Therapeutic Food (SMS-RUTF) Based on Industrial Extrusion Cooking Process." *Maternal and Child Nutrition* 10 (1): 126–34.

Palmer, G. 2009. *What Is Complementary Feeding? A Philosophical Reflection to Help a Policy Process. A Discussion Paper Developed for the International Baby Food Action Network (IBFAN).* Geneva: International Baby Food Action Network (IBFAN); Geneva Infant Feeding Association (GIFA).

———. 2011. *Complementary Feeding: Nutrition, Culture and Politics.* London: Pinter & Martin.

Papart, J. P. 2010. "Le Marché Mondial Des Enfants Affamés (The Global Market of Starving Children)." *Le Temps. L'Avis des Experts.* 24 September 2010.

Paruzzolo, S., R. Mehra, A. Kes, and C. Ashbaugh. 2010. *Targeting Poverty and Gender Inequality to Improve Maternal Health.* Washington, D.C.: International Center for Research on Women (ICRW).

Patel, M. P., H. L. Sandige, M. J. Ndekha, A. Briend, P. Ashorn, and M. J. Manary. 2005. "Supplemental Feeding with Ready-to-use Therapeutic Food in Malawian Children at Risk of Malnutrition." *Journal of Health Population and Nutrition* 23: 351–57.

Paul, K. H., M. Muti, B. Chasekwa, M. N. Mbuya, R. C. Madzima, J. H. Humphrey, and R. J. Stoltzfus. 2012. "Complementary Feeding Messages that Target Cultural Barriers Enhance Both the Use of Lipid-Based Nutrient Supplements and Underlying Feeding Practices to Improve Infant Diets in Rural Zimbabwe." *Maternal and Child Nutrition* 8 (2): 225–238.

Phelan, S. 2010. "Pregnancy: A 'Teachable Moment' for Weight Control and Obesity Prevention." *American Journal of Obstetrics and Gynecology* 202 (2): 135. e1–8.

Phuka, J. C., M. Gladstone, K. Maleta, C. Thakwalakwa, Y. B. Cheung, A. Briend, and P. Ashorn. 2012. "Developmental Outcomes Among 18-Month-Old Malawians after a Year of Complementary Feeding with Lipid-based Nutrient Supplements or Corn-Soy Flour." *Maternal and Child Nutrition* 8 (2): 239–48.

Poppendieck, J. 1999. *Sweet Charity? Emergency Food and the End of Entitlement.* New York: Penguin Books.

Poston, L. 2012. "Maternal Obesity, Gestational Weight Gain and Diet as Determinants of Offspring Long Term Health." *Best Practice & Research Clinical Endocrinology and Metabolism* 26 (5): 627–39.

Purwestri, R. C., V. Scherbaum, D. A. Inayati, N. N. Wirawan, J. Suryantan, M. A. Bloem, R. V. Pangaribuan, W. Stuetz, V. Hoffmann,, M. Qaim,, H. K. Biesalski, and A. C. Bellows. 2012. "Supplementary Feeding with Locally Produced Ready-to-use Food (RUF) for Mildly Wasted Children on Nias Island, Indonesia: Comparison of Daily and Weekly Program Outcomes." *Asia Pacific Journal of Clinical Nutrition* 21 (3): 374–79.

Purwestri, R. C., V. Scherbaum, D. A. Inayati, N. N. Wirawan, J. Suryantan, M. A. Bloem, R.V. Pangaribuan, M. Koeniger, V. Hoffmann, H. K. Biesalski, M. Qaim, and A. C. Bellows. 2012. "Cost Analysis of Community-based Daily and Weekly Programs for Treatment of Moderate and Mild Wasting among Children on Nias Island, Indonesia." *Food and Nutrition Bulletin* 33 (3): 207–16.

Purwestri, R. C., V. Scherbaum, D. A. Inayati, N. N. Wirawan, J. Suryantan, M. A. Bloem, R. V. Pangaribuan, V. Hoffman, M. Qaim, and H. K. Biesalski. 2013. "Impact of Daily versus Weekly Supply of Locally Produced Ready-to-use Food on Growth of Moderately Wasted Children on Nias Island, Indonesia." *International Scholarly Research Notices Nutrition.* doi:10.5402/2013/412145.

Rapley, G. 2006. "Baby-led Weaning: A Developmental Approach to Introduction of Complementary Foods." In *Maternal and Infant Nutrition and Nurture Controversies and Challenges*, edited by V. Hall Moran and F. Dykes, 275–98. London: Quay Books.

Rawas, S. 2008. "Challenges of Dealing with Unsolicited Donations during Emergencies." *Field Exchange* (34): 42.

Rice, A. 2010. "The Peanut Solution." *The New York Times*, September 2, 2010.

Richter, J. 1996. " 'Vaccination' against Pregnancy: The Politics of Contraceptive Research." *The Ecologist* 26 (2): 53–60.

———. 2001. *Holding Corporations Accountable: Corporate Conduct, International Codes, and Citizen Action.* London: Zed Books.

———. 2003. *Building on Quicksand: The Global Compact, Democratic Governance and Nestlé.* Geneva and Zürich: Centre Europe-Tiers Monde (CETIM), International Baby Food Action Network/Geneva Infant Feeding Association (IBFAN/GIFA) and Berne Declaration.

———. 2004. *Public-Private Partnerships and International Health Policy Making: How Can Public Interest Be Safeguarded?* Helsinki: Development Policy Information Unit of the Ministry for Foreign Affairs of Finland.

Right to Food and Nutrition WATCH Consortium. 2011. *Right to Food and Nutrition WATCH 2011. Claiming Human Rights: The Accountability Challenge.* Berlin; Heidelberg; Utrecht: Brot für die Welt; FIAN International; Interchurch Organisation for Development Cooperation (ICCO).

Roberts, L., C. Hale, F. Belyakdoumi, L. Cobey, R. Ondeko, M. Despines, and J. Keys. 2001. *Mortality in Eastern Democratic Republic of Congo.* New York: International Rescue Committee.

Rohrer, S. and J. W. Dietrich. 2014. "Das Refeeding-Syndrom—Eine Literaturübersicht [Refeeding Syndrome: A Review of the Literature]." *Zeitschrift für Gastroenterologie* 52 (6): 593–600.

Rosenberg, K. D., C. A. Eastham, L. J. Kasehagen, and A. P. Sandoval. 2008. "Marketing Infant Formula through Hospitals: The Impact of Commercial Hospital Discharge Packs on Breastfeeding." *American Journal of Public Health* 98 (2): 290–95.

Rothman, B. K. 2008. "New Breast Milk in Old Bottles." *International Breastfeeding Journal* 3 (9). doi:10.1186/1746-4358-3-9.

Rouw, E., E. Hormann, and V. Scherbaum. 2015. "The High Cost of Half-Hearted Breastfeeding Promotion in Germany." *International Breastfeeding Journal* 9 (22). doi:10.1186/s13006-014-0022-5.

Ruchat, S. M. and M. F. Mottola. 2012. "Preventing Long-Term Risk of Obesity for Two Generations: Prenatal Physical Activity Is Part of the Puzzle." *Journal of Pregnancy* 2012. doi:10.1155/2012/470247.

Sachs, J., J. Fanzo, and S. Sachs. 2010. "Saying 'Nuts' to Hunger." *The Huffington Post*, September 6, 2010.

Sagoe-Moses, C., K. Mwinga, P. Habimana, I. D. Toure, and T. Ketsela. 2012. "Implementation of the New WHO Recommendations on HIV and Infant Feeding: Challenges and the Way Forward." *African Journal of Food, Agriculture, Nutrition and Development* 12 (4): June 2012.

Save the Children. 2006. *State of the World's Mothers 2006: Saving the Lives of Mothers and Newborns.* London: Save the Children.

Scaling Up Nutrition (SUN) Movement Secretariat. 2012a. *SUN Movement Progress Report: 2011–2012.* Scaling Up Nutrition (SUN) Movement Secretariat.

———. 2012b. *SUN Movement: Revised Road Map.* Scaling Up Nutrition (SUN) Movement Secretariat.

Scaling Up Nutrition (SUN) Road Map Task Team. 2010. *A Road Map for Scaling-Up Nutrition (SUN). September 2010. First Edition.* Scaling Up Nutrition (SUN) Road Map Task Team.

Schellenberg, J. A., C. G. Victora, A. Mushi, D. De Savigny, D. Schellenberg, H. Mshinda, and J. Bryce. 2003. "Inequities Among the Very Poor: Health Care for Children in Rural Southern Tanzania." *The Lancet* 361 (9357): 561–66.

Scherbaum, V. 1996. "Wen Gott wachsen läßt, der wächst. Lebensweisen von Müttern und Kleinkindern in West-Wollega, Äthiopien, unter besonderer Berücksichtigung der Ernährungssituation." [*"Whom God Allows to Grow, Grows. Lifestyles of Mothers and Infants in West-Wollega, Ethiopia, with special focus of the food situation."*] *Curare* 9: 49–66.

———. 1997. "The Interrelationship Between Health- and Nutritional Status for Girls, Mothers and Grandmothers." In *Women and Health, Ethnomedical Perspectives*, edited by C. E. Gottschalk-Batschkus, J. Schuler, and D. Iding. Berlin: VWB–Verlag für Wissenschaft und Bildung.

———. 2003. "Infant Formula Distribution in Northern Iraq." *Field Exchange* (20): 6.

Scherbaum, V. and A. C. Bellows. 2009. "Förderung des Stillens—Ein Beitrag zur Prävention von Übergewicht. [*Promotion of Breastfeeding—A Contribution to the Prevention of Overweight*] *Ernährungs Umschau* 7: 388–394.

Scherbaum, V., E. Rouw, and E. Hormann. 2011. "Förderung des Stillens. Mütter frühzeitig und kompetent beraten." [*Promotion of Breastfeeding—Advising Mothers at an Early Stage and Competently*] *Pädiatrie Kinder und Jugendmedizin Hautnah. Sonderheft Ernährung* 23 (S1): 6–8.

Scherbaum, V., O. Shapiro, R. C. Purwestri, D. A. Inayati, D. Novianty, W. Stütz, Y. Yusran, T. Müller, N. N. Wirawan, and J. Suryantan. 2009. "Locally Produced Ready-to-use Food (RUF): Piloting in Mild and Moderately Wasted Children, Nias Island, Indonesia." *Sight and Life Magazine* (1): 29–37.

Scherbaum, V., R. C. Purwestri, W. Stuetz, D. A. Inayati, J. Suryantan, M. A. Bloem, and H. K. Biesalski. 2015. "Locally Produced Cereal/Nut/Legume-based Biscuits versus Peanut/Milk-based Spread for Treatment of Moderately to Mildly Wasted Children in Daily Programs on Nias Island, Indonesia: an Issue of Acceptance and Compliance?" *Asia Pacific Journal of Clinical Nutrition* 24 (1): 152–61.

Schuftan C. 2011. "The Millennium Development Goals, and the Scaling Up Nutrition Initiative [Column]." Website of the World Public Health Nutrition Association, July 2011, (http://www.wphna.org/htdocs/2011_july_col_claudio.htm; accessed June 3, 2014).

Schuftan, C. and T. Greiner. 2013. "The Scaling Up Nutrition (SUN) Initiative." *Right to Food and Nutrition WATCH* 2013: 22–23.

Schuftan, C. and R. Holla. 2012. "Two Contemporary Challenges: Corporate Control over Food and Nutrition and the Absence of a Focus on the Social Determinants of Nutrition." *Right to Food and Nutrition WATCH* 2012: 24–30.

Sedgh, G., S. Singh, I. H. Shah, E. Hman, S. K. Henshaw, and A. Bankole. 2012. "Induced Abortion: Incidence and Trends Worldwide from 1995 to 2008." *The Lancet* 379 (9816): 625–32.

Sen, S., A. H. Carpenter, J. Hochstadt, J. Y. Huddleston, V. Kustanovich, A. A. Reynolds, and S. Roberts. 2012. "Nutrition, Weight Gain and Eating Behavior in Pregnancy: A Review of Experimental Evidence for Long-Term Effects on the Risk of Obesity in Offspring." *Physiology and Behavior* 107 (1): 138–45.

Sherriff, N. and V. Hall. 2011. "Engaging and Supporting Fathers to Promote Breastfeeding: A New Role for Health Visitors?" *Scandinavian Journal of Caring Sciences* 25 (3): 467–75.

Singh, S., G. Sedgh, and R. Hussain. 2010. "Unintended Pregnancy: Worldwide Levels, Trends, and Outcomes." *Studies in Family Planning* 41 (4): 241–50.

Slesak, G., P. Douangdala, S. Inthalad, B. Onekeo, S. Somsavad, B. Sisouphanh, L. Srour, and H. Barennes. 2009. "Misuse of Coffee Creamer as a Breast Milk Substitute: A Lethal Case Revealing High Use in an Ethnic Minority Village in Northern Laos." Rapid response of 16 January 2009 to Barennes, H., T. Andriatahina, V. Latthaphasavang, M. Anderson, and L. M. Srour. 2008. "Misperceptions and Misuse of Bear Brand Coffee Creamer as Infant Food: National Cross Sectional Survey of Consumers and Paediatricians in Laos." *British Medical Journal* 337: a1379. Website of the *British Medical Journal* (http://www.bmj.com/rapid-response/2011/11/02/misuse-coffee-creamer-breast-milk-substitute-lethal-case-revealing-high-us; accessed June 3, 2014).

Sobel, H. L., A. Iellamo, R. R. Raya, A. A. Padilla, J.-M Olivé, and S. Nyunt-U. 2011. "Is Unimpeded Marketing for Breast Milk Substitutes Responsible for the Decline in Breastfeeding in the Philippines? An Exploratory Survey and Focus Group Analysis." *Social Science and Medicine* 73 (10): 1445–48.

Sowden, M., M. Nutrition, D. Marais, B. Nutrition, M. Nutrition, R. Beukes, and M. Nutrition. 2009. "Factors Influencing High Socio-Economic Class Mothers' Decision regarding Formula-Feeding Practices in the Cape Metropole." *South African Journal of Clinical Nutrition* 22 (1): 37–44.

Sphere Project [The]. 2011. *The Sphere Project: Humanitarian Charter and Minimum Standards in Humanitarian Response*. Rugby, England: Practical Action.

Stieger, R. 2009. "Nestlé's Works to Ensure Appropriate Use of Milk Products." *British Medical Journal* 338 (7688): 189.

Stuebe, A. 2009. "The Risks of Not Breastfeeding for Mothers and Infants." *Reviews in Obstetrics and Gynecology* 2 (4): 222–31.

Suchdev, P. S., L. J. Ruth, B. A. Woodruff, C. Mbakaya, U. Mandava, R. Flores-Ayala, M. E. D. Jefferds, and R. Quick. 2012. "Selling Sprinkles Micronutrient Powder Reduces Anemia, Iron Deficiency, and Vitamin A Deficiency in Young Children in Western Kenya: A Cluster-Randomized Controlled Trial." *American Journal of Clinical Nutrition* 95 (5): 1223–30.

Swinburn, B. A., G. Sacks, K. D. Hall, K. McPherson, D. T. Finegood, M. L. Moodie, and S. L. Gortmaker. 2011. "The Global Obesity Pandemic: Shaped by Global Drivers and Local Environments." *The Lancet* 378 (9793): 804–14.

Thompson, D. F. 2005. *Restoring Responsibility: Ethics in Government, Business and Health Care*. Cambridge: Cambridge University Press.

Thurnham, D. I. 2012. "Adequate Nutrient Intakes for Infancy—Part I: From 0 to 6 Months." *Sight and Life Magazine* 26 (3): 28–39.

Tolhurst, R., J. Raven, and S. Theobald. 2009. "Gender Equity: Perspectives on Maternal and Child Health." In *Maternal and Child Health*, edited by J. E. Ehiri, 151–66. New York: Springer.

Toole, M. J. and R. J. Waldman. 1988. "An Analysis of Mortality Trends Among Refugee Populations in Somalia, Sudan, and Thailand." *Bulletin of the World Health Organization* 66 (2): 237–47.

———. 1997. "The Public Health Aspects of Complex Emergencies and Refugee Situations." *Annual Review of Public Health* 18: 283–312.

Trickey, H. and M. Newburn. 2012. "Goals, Dilemmas and Assumptions in Infant Feeding Education and Support. Applying Theory of Constraints Thinking Tools to Develop New Priorities for Action." *Maternal and Child Nutrition* 10 (1): 72–91.

Uauy, R., M. L. Garmendia, and C. Corvalán. 2014. "Addressing the Double Burden of Malnutrition with a Common Agenda." *Nestlé Nutrition Workshop Series* 78: 39–52.

United Nations (UN). 1945. *Charter of the United Nations, 26 June 1945, 1 UNTS XVI*. San Francisco: United Nations (UN).

———. 2000. *Guidelines on Cooperation Between the United Nations and the Business Community, 17 July 2000*. New York: United Nations (UN).

———. 2003. *Draft Norms on the Responsibilities of Transnational Corporations and Other Business Enterprises with Regard to Human Rights. E/CN.4/Sub.2/2003/12/Rev.2, 26 August 2003*. New York: United Nations (UN).

———. 2009. *Guidelines on Cooperation Between the United Nations and the Business Community, 20 November 2009*. New York: United Nations (UN).

United Nations Administrative Committee on Coordination/Subcommittee on Nutrition (ACC/SCN) and International Food Policy Research Institute (IFPRI). 2000. *Fourth Report on the World Nutrition Situation: Nutrition throughout the Life Cycle*. Geneva: United Nations Administrative Committee on Coordination Subcommittee on Nutrition (ACC/SCN).

United Nations Children's Fund (UNICEF). 2005. *The Innocenti Declaration 2005 on Infant and Young Child Feeding*. Florence, Italy.

———. 2010. *Progress for Children: Achieving the MDGs with Equity (Number 9)*. New York: United Nations Children's Fund (UNICEF).

———. 2011. *Boys and Girls in the Life Cycle: Sex-Disaggregated Data on a Selection of Well-being Indicators, from Early Childhood to Young Adulthood*. New York: United Nations Children's Fund (UNICEF).

———. 2012a. "Country Implementation of the 2010 HIV and Infant Feeding Guidelines: Report on Baseline Information." Unpublished report, last modified September 2012. Text file.

———. 2012b. *The State of the World's Children 2012: Children in an Urban World*. New York: United Nations Children's Fund (UNICEF).

United Nations Children's Fund (UNICEF) and World Health Organization (WHO). 1991. *Baby-Friendly Hospital Initiative*. Geneva: World Health Organization (WHO).

———. 2009. *Baby-Friendly Hospital Initiative: Revised, Updated and Expanded for Integrated Care*. New York and Geneva: United Nations Children's Fund (UNICEF); World Health Organization (WHO).

United Nations Children's Fund (UNICEF), United Nations Global Compact, and Save the Children. 2012. *Children's Rights and Business Principles*. New York and Fairfield: United Nations Children's Fund (UNICEF); United Nations Global Compact; Save the Children.

United Nations Committee on Economic, Social and Cultural Rights (CESCR). 1999. *General Comment No. 12: The Right to Adequate Food (Art. 11 of the Covenant). E/C.12/1999/5, 12 May 1999.* New York: United Nations Economic and Social Council (ECOSOC).

——. 2000. *General Comment No. 14: The Right to the Highest Attainable Standard of Health (Art. 12 of the Covenant). E/C.12/2000/4, 11 August 2000.* New York: United Nations Economic and Social Council (ECOSOC).

——. 2005. *General Comment No. 16: The Equal Right of Men and Women to the Enjoyment of all Economic, Social and Cultural Rights (Art. 3 of the Covenant). E/C.12/2005/4, 11 August 2005.* New York: United Nations Economic and Social Council (ECOSOC).

——. 2009. *General Comment No. 20: Non-Discrimination in Economic, Social and Cultural Rights (Art. 2, Para. 2, of the International Covenant on Economic, Social and Cultural Rights). E/C.12/GC/20, 2 July 2009.* New York: United Nations Economic and Social Council (ECOSOC).

——. 2011. *Statement on the Obligations of States Parties regarding the Corporate Sector and Economic, Social and Cultural Rights. E/C.12/2011/1,2–20 May 2011.* New York: United Nations Economic and Social Council (ECOSOC).

United Nations Committee on the Rights of the Child (CRC Committee). 2013a. *General Comment No. 15 (2013) on the Right of the Child to the Enjoyment of the Highest Attainable Standard of Health (Art. 24). CRC/C/GC/15, 17 April 2013.* Geneva: United Nations Committee on the Rights of the Child (CRC Committee).

——. 2013b. *General Comment No. 16. (2013) State Obligations regarding the Impact of the Business Sector on Children's Rights. CRC/C/GC/16), 17 April 2013.* Geneva: United Nations Committee on the Rights of the Child (CRC Committee).

United Nations Department of Economic and Social Affairs (UN DESA). 2010. *The World's Women 2010: Trends and Statistics.* New York: United Nations (UN).

United Nations General Assembly. 1959. *Declaration of the Rights of the Child. A/RES/1386(XIV), 20 November 1959.* New York: United Nations (UN) General Assembly.

——. 1966. *International Covenant on Economic, Social and Cultural Rights. 16 December 1966, United Nations, Treaty Series, Vol. 993, p. 3.* New York: United Nations (UN) General Assembly.

——. 1979. *Convention on the Elimination of all Forms of Discrimination against Women. 18 December 1979.* Geneva: United Nations (UN) General Assembly.

——. 1989. *Convention on the Rights of the Child, 20 November 1989, United Nations, Treaty Series, Vol. 1577, p. 3.* New York: United Nations (UN) General Assembly.

——. 2006. *Resolution Adopted by the General Assembly on 16 December 2005 [on the Report of the Third Committee (A/60/509/Add.2 (Part II))]: The Right to Food. A/RES/60/165, 2 March 2006.* New York: United Nations (UN) General Assembly.

——. 2007. *Resolution Adopted by the General Assembly [on the Report of the Third Committee (A/61/443/Add.2 and Corr.1)]: The Right to Food. A/RES/61/163, 21 February 2007.* Geneva: United Nations (UN) General Assembly.

United Nations Human Rights Council (HRC). 2008. *Resolution 7/14. The Right to Food.* Geneva: United Nations Human Rights Council (HRC).

——. 2009. *Resolution 10/12. The Right to Food.* Geneva: United Nations Human Rights Council (HRC).

——. 2010. *Human Rights and Access to Safe Drinking Water and Sanitation. A/HRC/15/L.14, 24 September 2010.* Geneva: United Nations Human Rights Council (HRC).

———. 2011a. *Report Submitted by the Special Rapporteur on the Right to Food, Olivier De Schutter, at the Nineteenth Session of the United Nations Human Rights Council. A/HRC/19/59, 26 December 2011.* New York: United Nations (UN) General Assembly.

———. 2011b. *Thematic Study on the Realization of the Right to Health of Older Persons by the Special Rapporteur on the Right of Everyone to the Enjoyment of the Highest Attainable Standard of Physical and Mental Health, Anand Grover. A/HRC/18/37, 4 July 2011.* New York: United Nations (UN) General Assembly.

United Nations Office of the High Commissioner for Human Rights (OHCHR). 2008. *Working with the United Nations Human Rights Programme: A Handbook for Civil Society.* New York and Geneva: United Nations Office of the High Commissioner for Human Rights (OHCHR).

———. 2010. *Fact Sheet No. 34, the Right to Adequate Food.* Geneva: United Nations Office of the High Commissioner for Human Rights (OHCHR).

United Nations Population Fund (UNFPA). 2012. *State of the World Population 2012: Executive Summary.* New York: United Nations Population Fund (UNFPA).

United Nations Standing Committee on Nutrition (SCN). 2010. *Sixth Report on the World Nutrition Situation: Progress in Nutrition.* Geneva: United Nations Standing Committee on Nutrition (SCN).

United Nations Standing Committee on Nutrition (SCN) NGO/CSO. 2010. *Draft Guidelines for the Marketing of Ready to Use Supplemental Foods for Children.* Geneva: United Nations Standing Committee on Nutrition (SCN).

Utting, P. 2002. "The Global Compact and Civil Society: Averting a Collision Course." *Development in Practice* 12 (5): 644–47.

Van Esterik, P. 1999. "Right to Food; Right to Feed; Right to Be Fed. The Intersection of Women's Rights and the Right to Food." *Agriculture and Human Values* 16 (2): 225–32.

Varela-Silva, M. I., F. Dickinson, H. Wilson, H. Azcorra, P. L. Griffiths, and B. Bogin. 2012. "The Nutritional Dual-Burden in Developing Countries—How Is It Assessed and What Are the Health Implications?" *Collegium Antropologicum* 36 (1): 39–45.

Victora, C. G., A. Wagstaff, J. A. Schellenberg, D. Gwatkin, M. Claeson, and J. P. Habicht. 2003. "Applying an Equity Lens to Child Health and Mortality: More of the Same Is Not Enough." *The Lancet* 362 (9379): 233–41.

Votaw, D. 1973. "Genius Becomes Rare." In *The Corporate Dilemma*, edited by D. Votaw and S. P. Sethi. Upper Saddle River, New Jersey: Prentice Hall, quoted in Carroll, A. B. 1999. "Corporate Social Responsibility: Evolution of a Definitional Construct." *Business Society* 38 (3): 268–95.

Weaver, L. T. 2006. "Rapid Growth in Infancy: Balancing the Interests of the Child." *Journal of Pediatric Gastroenterology and Nutrition* 43 (4): 428–32.

Williams, A. F. 2009. "Lifecycle Influences and Opportunities for Change." In *Infant and Young Child Feeding*, edited by F. Dykes and V. Hall Moran, 163–80. Chichester: Wiley Blackwell.

Wolf, J. H. 2008. "Got Milk? Not in Public!" *International Breastfeeding Journal* 3: 11.

"Women's Choice Is Key to Reduce Maternal Deaths." 2012. *The Lancet* 380 (9856): 1791.

World Alliance for Breastfeeding Action (WABA). 1995. *Declaration for Women's Reproductive and Sexual Rights and Health. Issued by the Reproductive Rights Caucus at the NGO Forum and the 39th Session of the Commission on the Status of Women, New York, USA, March-April 1995.* Malaysia: World Alliance for Breastfeeding Action (WABA).

World Breastfeeding Trend Initiatives (WBTi). 2010. *Botswana Assessment Report 2010.* Botswana: Nutrition and Food Control Division.

World Health Assembly (WHA). 1982. *WHA Resolution 35.26. Thirty-fifth World Health Assembly.* Geneva: World Health Assembly (WHA).

———. 1984. *WHA Resolution 37.30. Thirty-seventh World Health Assembly.* Geneva: World Health Assembly (WHA).

———. 1986. *WHA Resolution 39.28. Thirty-ninth World Health Assembly.* Geneva: World Health Assembly (WHA).

———. 1988. *WHA Resolution 41.11. Forty-first World Health Assembly.* Geneva: World Health Assembly (WHA).

———. 1990. *WHA Resolution 43.3. Forty-third World Health Assembly.* Geneva: World Health Assembly (WHA).

———. 1994. *WHA Resolution 47.5. Forty-seventh World Health Assembly. Infant and Young Child Nutrition.* Geneva: World Health Assembly (WHA).

———. 1996. *WHA Resolution 49.15. Forty-ninth World Health Assembly.* Geneva: World Health Assembly (WHA).

———. 2001. *WHA Resolution 54.2. Fifty-fourth World Health Assembly. Infant and Young Child Nutrition.* Geneva: World Health Assembly (WHA).

———. 2002. *WHA Resolution 55.25. Fifty-fifth World Health Assembly. Infant and Young Child Nutrition.* Geneva: World Health Assembly (WHA).

———. 2005. *WHA Resolution 58.32. Fifty-eighth World Health Assembly. Infant and Young Child Nutrition.* Geneva: World Health Assembly (WHA).

———. 2006a. *WHA Resolution 59.11 Fifty-ninth World Health Assembly. Nutrition and HIV/AIDS.* Geneva: World Health Assembly (WHA).

———. 2006b. *WHA Resolution 59.21. Fifty-ninth World Health Assembly. Infant and Young Child Nutrition.* Geneva: World Health Assembly (WHA).

———. 2008. *WHA Resolution 61.20. Sixty-first World Health Assembly.* Geneva: World Health Assembly (WHA).

———. 2010. *WHA Resolution 63.23. Sixty-third World Health Assembly. Infant and Young Child Nutrition.* Geneva: World Health Assembly (WHA).

———. 2011. *WHA Resolution 64.6. Sixty-fourth World Health Assembly. Health Workforce Strengthening.* Geneva: World Health Assembly (WHA).

———. 2012a. *WHA Resolution 65.3. Sixty-fifth World Health Assembly. Strengthening Noncommunicable Disease Policies to Promote Active Ageing.* Geneva: World Health Assembly (WHA).

———. 2012b. *WHA Resolution 65.6. Sixty-fifth World Health Assembly. Comprehensive Implementation Plan on Maternal, Infant and Young Child Nutrition.* Geneva: World Health Assembly (WHA).

———. 2013. *WHA Resolution 66.10. Sixty-sixth World Health Assembly. Follow-Up to the Political Declaration of the High-Level Meeting of the General Assembly on the Prevention and Control of Non-Communicable Diseases.* Geneva: World Health Assembly (WHA).

World Health Organization (WHO). 1981. *International Code of Marketing of Breast-milk Substitutes.* Geneva: World Health Organization (WHO).

———. 1999. *Management of Severe Malnutrition: A Manual for Physicians and Other Senior Health Workers.* Geneva: World Health Organization (WHO).

———. 2000. *Guidelines on Working with the Private Sector to Achieve Health Outcomes. EB107/20, 30 November 2000.* Geneva: World Health Organization (WHO).

———. 2003. *Guiding Principles for Complementary Feeding of the Breastfed Child.* Geneva:: World Health Organization (WHO).

———. 2005. *The World Health Report 2005: Make Every Mother and Child Count.* Geneva: World Health Organization (WHO).

———. 2007. *Evidence on the Long-Term Effects of Breastfeeding: Systematic Reviews and Meta-Analyses.* Geneva: World Health Organization (WHO).

———. 2008. *Integrated Health Services—What and Why?* Geneva: World Health Organization (WHO).

———. 2009. *Infant and Young Child Feeding: Model Chapter for Textbooks for Medical Students and Allied Health Professionals.* Geneva: World Health Organization (WHO).

———. 2010a. *Annex 1: Policy on WHO Engagement with Global Health Partnerships and Hosting Arrangements. A63/44, Annex, 22 April 2010 and A63/44 Corr.1, 13 May 2010.* Geneva: World Health Organization (WHO).

———. 2010b. *Guidelines on HIV and Infant Feeding 2010: Principles and Recommendations for Infant Feeding in the Context of HIV and a Summary of Evidence.* Geneva: World Health Organization (WHO).

———. 2012a. *Executive Board 130th Session. Resolutions and Decisions Annexes. EB130/2012/REC/1, 16–23 January 2012.* Geneva: World Health Organization (WHO).

———. 2012b. *WHO Guidelines on HIV and Infant Feeding 2010: An Updated Framework for Priority Action.* Geneva: World Health Organization (WHO).

———. 2013a. *Consolidated Guidelines on the use of Antiretroviral Drugs for Treating and Preventing HIV Infection: Recommendations for a Public Health Approach. June 2013.* Geneva: World Health Organization (WHO).

———. 2013b. *Draft Terms of Reference for a Global Coordination Mechanism for the Prevention and Control of Noncommunicable Diseases. Second WHO Discussion Paper (Version Dated 1 November 2013).* Geneva: World Health Organization (WHO).

———. 2013c. *Information Concerning the Use and Marketing of Follow-Up Formula.* Geneva: World Health Organization (WHO).

World Health Organization (WHO) and Food and Agriculture Organization of the United Nations (FAO). 2007. *Safe Preparation, Storage and Handling of Powdered Infant Formula: Guidelines.* Geneva:: World Health Organization (WHO).

World Health Organization (WHO) and United Nations Children's Fund (UNICEF). 1979. *Joint WHO/UNICEF Meeting on Infant and Young Child Feeding. Geneva, 9–12 October 1979. Statement, Recommendations, List of Participants.* Geneva: World Health Organization (WHO); United Nations Children's Fund (UNICEF).

———. 1990. *The Innocenti Declaration on the Protection, Promotion and Support of Breastfeeding.* Florence: World Health Organization (WHO); United Nations Children's Fund (UNICEF).

———. 2003. *Global Strategy for Infant and Young Child Feeding.* Geneva: World Health Organization (WHO).

———. 2005. *The Declaration on Infant and Young Child Feeding.* Florence: World Health Organization (WHO); United Nations Children's Fund (UNICEF).

World Public Health Nutrition Association (WPHNA). 2011. *Who Protects Public Health? Governments, or Transnationals?* Rio de Janeiro: World Public Health Nutrition Association (WPHNA).

Ziaei, S., R. T. Naved, and E. C. Ekström. 2012. "Women's Exposure to Intimate Partner Violence and Child Malnutrition: Findings from Demographic and Health Surveys in Bangladesh." *Maternal and Child Nutrition.* doi:10.1111/j.1740-8709.2012.00432.x.

5 Sustainable Food Systems, Gender, and Participation

Foregrounding Women in the Context of the Right to Adequate Food and Nutrition

Stefanie Lemke and Anne C. Bellows

INTRODUCTION

This chapter is guided by the argument that there is a need to integrate gender, nutrition, and the human right to food as well as to promote interscalar governance strategies in support of sustainable livelihoods with enhanced food and nutrition security. This integration can be achieved by promoting local agriculture and food systems, in line with a food sovereignty approach. As outlined in chapters 2 and 4 of this volume, this chapter addresses our concerns with the dominant view that the state and international market systems provide the best or only reasonable support for food security and nutritional well-being and, further, that international distribution and trade of highly technical food production and medicalized food assistance provide the most appropriate response to food insecurity and malnutrition. We claim that these positions foster economic dependency and overlook the capacity for self-determination and for establishing sustainable local and regional food systems that promote nutrition and health.

As was illustrated in detail in chapter 4 of this volume, nutrition security is most often associated with women and children, typically collapsed into the nexus of the maternal-infant life phase. The patronizing impetus to deliver external charitable nutrition "cures," especially in non-emergency situations as a "malnutrition prevention strategy," reifies discrimination against women and communities. It presumes that they are incapable of meeting these challenges themselves, and it impedes their active participation in food and nutrition security. We follow these arguments in this chapter with alternative theoretical and practical frames that integrate food and nutrition security in a food systems approach, among them food sovereignty, sustainable diets, and agroecology. Central to our discussion is a gender perspective that takes into consideration discrimination and violence which women face, posing barriers to their participation in providing food and nutritional security for themselves, their families, and their communities (see chapter 3 of this volume). This chapter presents strategies that have yielded positive results for women in overcoming certain barriers, participating in governance, and gaining a voice. We support the inclusion of social movements and grassroots-based approaches in public policy that can enable the possibility of addressing structural problems, including gender discrimination and power imbalances that perpetuate food insecurity and hunger. We argue that these approaches will ultimately be more cost-effective and sustainable, building capacity and self-determination in local food systems through local governance that foregrounds inclusive participation of all members of society.

Chapter 5 is organized into the following sections:

- Section one, "The need for a systems approach and gender perspective for addressing the right to adequate food and nutrition," discusses the constructed and artificial separation in policy, program, trade, and ideology of "food" as something to produce and "nutrition" as a construction of micro- and macro-nutrient sufficiency. We review the shortcomings of current measures to address malnutrition and hunger that favor paternalistic approaches and perpetuate aid, neediness, and dependency. The separation of food and nutrition security approaches needs to be overcome and replaced by more holistic approaches in support of local and sustainable agriculture and food systems, integrating a gender perspective. Specific emphasis is being laid at the household level, as individual household members—especially women and children, who are often primarily targeted by nutrition programs—cannot be viewed in isolation from other household members. Intra-household dynamics, decision-making, and resource allocation, as well as inter-household relations and their related social networks, are decisive factors for food and nutrition security of household members, often even more important than income, as will be illustrated by case studies.
- Section two, "Food and nutrition governance: interscalar local to global strategies to address the gender gap and enhance rural livelihoods," introduces democratic processes and holistic approaches to integrated local and regional food production and nutritionally sound consumption systems. The paternalism of policy that promotes food and nutrition aid dependencies instead of autonomy reifies structures of uneven economic power that are reflected in uneven social relations, including but not limited to gender discrimination. The decisive questions are: what are appropriate strategies in achieving sustainable, equitable, and participatory local food systems that can enhance food and nutrition security, livelihoods, and local economies, and how are women included in this debate? This section introduces some of the recent concepts that aim to address these questions by promoting alternative approaches, among them local food systems, food sovereignty, community food security, food policy councils, food justice, agroecology and organic agriculture, and sustainable diets. We employ

these concepts to discuss women's *and* men's needs to gain capabilities necessary to protect their and their communities' well-being.

- Section three, "Democratic participation, governance, and mobilization from civil society toward more equitable food systems," discusses challenges at the local and global levels for developing rural agriculture-based livelihoods, and emphasizes the role civil society plays for achieving more equitable food systems. In this context, the ultimate goal is to achieve increased autonomy, strengthen self-reliance, and improve access to resources for the poor. At the same time, we acknowledge that people who have limited self-help capacity might not be reached and, therefore, social protection programs remain necessary. Within the framework of progressively realizing the right to adequate food and nutrition, this refers to the obligation of states to *fulfill* this right, on the one hand by proactively *facilitating* access to productive resources that result in improved livelihoods and food security, and on the other hand by *providing* the necessary resources and social protection directly to those individuals or groups who are unable, due to reasons beyond their control, to enjoy the right to adequate food and nutrition. This does not, however, conflict with the application of a human rights framework that strives for local solutions and local governance, as long as local agriculture and local economies are integrated as far as possible into social security systems.[1] Ironically, and tragically, those who work on large-scale commercial farms and in the food industry worldwide are often among the most food insecure, with women being even more insecure than men. Therefore, in the right to adequate food and nutrition discourse, emphasis needs to be placed on unjust structural conditions in industrial agriculture and food production. This section closes by stressing that the poor, and especially the women among them, must not be patronized as victims of their circumstances. Further, their labors and capacities through social networks and assets must be recognized as valuable experience and knowledge for food governance systems wherein their contribution is paramount. Following this argument, we provide examples of how women can overcome barriers to participation, and argue that women should be regarded as actors, not as vulnerable beneficiaries, acknowledging their capacities to find local solutions. We further argue that men have to be more actively integrated, and provide case studies and initiatives from various regions that aim to address specifically men.
- Section four, "Initiatives for mainstreaming gender in right to adequate food and nutrition work," introduces some of the many recent texts and initiatives that call for mainstreaming gender in right to adequate food and nutrition work.
- In the last section of this chapter we lay out "Conclusions and recommendations for moving forward." We propose that development

needs to engage alternative approaches of building local self-reliance, community food security, and local governance that foreground inclusive participation, with a focus on the household, community, and national levels.

THE NEED FOR A SYSTEMS APPROACH AND GENDER PERSPECTIVE FOR ADDRESSING THE RIGHT TO ADEQUATE FOOD AND NUTRITION

Food and Nutrition Security: Divide of Disciplines and Policy Orientations

The concept of food security has been defined in numerous ways (cf. Maxwell and Frankenberger 1992). At the international level, it was propelled forward in the 1948 *Universal Declaration of Human Rights* (UDHR). However, a shift toward a human rights framework to address issues concerning food security did not really begin to develop until the 1990s.[2] Beginning in the 1960s, food security evolved in largely economic delivery terms, referring to food supply relative to production, trade, marketing, stocks, and reserves at global, regional, and national levels. The macrolevel approach gradually transformed and decentralized in the 1970s and 1980s toward the concept of individual entitlements based on Sen (1981). As described by Maxwell (1996, 155), three main shifts could be observed since the first World Food Conference in 1974: from the global and national levels to the household and individual, from a food first perspective to a livelihood perspective, and from objective indicators to subjective perceptions.[3] According to Bellows and Hamm (2003), the decentralizing focus on food security corresponds with a compounding and globalizing dynamic through grassroots networking within civil society organizations (CSOs). This has asserted the democratic imperative of participation in food governance as well as a sovereign authority to define and protect food and nutrition security at the scale of diverse social collectives.

Today, food security is defined as "a situation that exists when all people, at all times, have physical, social and economic access to adequate, safe and nutritious food that meets their dietary needs and food preferences for an active and healthy life" (FAO 2001). Whereas food insecurity is often but not always characterized by hunger, its principal meaning refers to the *risk* of people being hungry (Kracht 1999, 55). Food security is, therefore, not just about the absence of hunger but also about the absence of risk relating to adequate food consumption as has been highlighted by Webb and von Braun (1993). This also entails the ways in which food or the resources to access food are obtained, referring to "social access" as has been integrated at the World Food Summit 2001 (FAO 2001), an aspect that had not been recognized in the earlier definition of food security (FAO 1996). It further depends on how available resources are used and distributed in the house-hold, as will be outlined later.

Food security has developed in a different direction than has nutritional well-being. The definition of "food security" has been criticized for its narrow focus on "food" and disregard of "nutrition" and health-related aspects. Decisive factors for nutritional status, such as health services and a healthy environment and care for women and children, are illustrated in the widely used malnutrition framework developed by Urban Jonsson (1981) and adopted by the United Nations Children's Fund (UNICEF; UNI-CEF 1990; see also the discussion in chapter 6 of this volume). Gross et al. (2000), in their overview of definitions and concepts of food and nutrition security, highlight that the two most commonly used concepts, namely food security and the malnutrition framework, are significantly different in their approach. While the first emphasizes economic issues with a central focus on food as a commodity, the latter emphasizes a biological approach, with human beings as the starting point. The terms "nutrition security" or "food and nutrition security" have been recommended as they better reflect the complexity of nutrition problems, including utilization of food, care, and health-related and environmental aspects (Klennert 2009, 25; Kracht 1999, 55–56). The concept "food and nutrition security" has only recently been adopted by the Committee on World Food Security (CFS) with the definition as follows: "Food and nutrition security exists when all people at all times have physical, social and economic access to food, which is safe and consumed in sufficient quantity and quality to meet their dietary needs and food preferences, and is supported by an environment of adequate sanitation, health services and care, allowing for a healthy and active life" (CFS 2012, 10).

The separation between nutrition and agriculture in policy and programming to solve hunger and food insecurity is also reflected in academic disciplinary divides. On the one hand, there are agronomy, agricultural economics, food production, and food sciences; on the other hand, nutrition, health, physiology, and medicine. The separation of academic disciplines is duplicated in political frameworks, policy agendas, and practical social discourse. For example, we observe that national nutrition institutions are generally housed *under* either "Departments of Agriculture" or "Departments of Health." The political work of nutrition does not tend to be free-standing, autonomous, and holistic but rather structured and, one could say, patronized or colonized either by agriculture or health interests. We note that recent literature from medicine, health, and law concur that in addressing the rapid growth of largely nutrition-based malnutrition and noncommunicable diseases (NCDs) throughout the world, there must be an end to narrowly constructed medicalized nutrition and a change toward policy and academic approaches that respect and welcome social movement contributions and that integrate analysis of the political economy of nutrition and food systems (Moodie et al. 2013; Thomas and Gostin 2013; see also the discussion in chapter 2 of this volume). Several publications confirm our observation that national nutrition programs are typically located inside national ministries of agriculture or health, limiting the capacity of nutrition to take a program development holistic approach but rather to be geared either toward food production and trade, or toward health care and medicine (Benson 2006, 2012; SCN 2014, esp. chap. 5; World Bank 2007, esp. chap. 6).

Linked to the above discussion on the divide between nutrition and agriculture is the detailed analysis of von Braun, Ruel, and Gillespie (2010), who investigate origins and causes of the sectoral divide and lack of coordination between the agriculture and health sectors. In their recommendations on how to overcome this gap and achieve intersectoral collaboration, the authors state that this requires, among other factors, an enabling policy environment that provides incentives for collaboration, as well as effective institutional arrangements. Further, and maybe most importantly, capacity has to be strengthened, especially among researchers and professionals, who should be encouraged to collaborate across disciplines and to embrace different perspectives. As is concluded by the authors, these relationships between individuals are often the key to successful intersectoral collaboration (von Braun, Ruel, and Gillespie 2010, 300), and, as we emphasize, this refers to relationships both at the professional and personal levels.

At the global level, the field of nutrition sciences has only recently started to adopt a more holistic approach. Two previous congresses of the International Union of Nutritional Sciences (IUNS) shall be highlighted here that illustrate this shift. The 18th IUNS International Congress of Nutrition 2005 in Durban, South Africa was the first to take place on the African continent. Whereas the main focus was on physiological and health-related aspects of nutrition, selected symposia focused on food and nutrition security, HIV/AIDS and nutrition, the right to adequate food and nutrition, and one plenary was on poverty and food and nutrition security (Möser et al. 2005). At this congress, the New Nutrition Science project was introduced, defining nutrition as principally a biological science, now also including nutritional aspects of genomics and adding social and environmental dimensions (Cannon and Leitzmann 2005, 673). This integration had so far been missing in "classic" nutritional sciences. The initiators of this New Nutrition Science project acknowledged "the work already done by institutions, organisations and individuals in Africa, Asia, Europe and the Americas that are already addressing the issues, challenges and resolutions set out here" ("The Giessen Declaration" 2005, 783). The project received, however, criticism from experts in international research on development and nutrition security, where social sciences methodologies and holistic approaches had long been integrated and where nutrition security was already regarded as a core element of development.[4]

The 19th IUNS International Congress of Nutrition 2009 in Bangkok, Thailand, for the first time specifically integrated agriculture into the agenda, with one of the four main conference themes being entitled "Integrating agriculture, food systems, indigenous cuisines and diet quality."[5]

Another important milestone that contributed to linking agriculture and nutrition was the *Sixth Report on the World Food Situation* published in 2010 by the United Nations (UN) Standing Committee on Nutrition (SCN; SCN 2010). The report highlighted the crucial role of the agricultural sector to address food and nutrition problems, emphasizing that nutrition friendly, sustainable agricultural development is key to improving food and nutrition security. These developments led to an attempt of integrating nutrition and agriculture to achieve better health and nutrition outcomes. The concept "nutrition sensitive" or "nutrition responsive" agriculture evolved, linking food, health, and continuous care.[6] Nutrition sensitive agriculture focuses on food-based systems that advocate diets which are rich in nutrients and diversity, thereby enhancing dietary quality and curbing malnutrition; it supports rural livelihoods by emphasizing the social standing of agriculture and food and encourages people to regard their diet in terms of their whole lifestyle and wellbeing (Gerster-Bentaya 2013, 724–25). The ideas underlying this concept are of course not new, but old knowledge and wisdom are being reinvented as will be illustrated in the section of this chapter entitled "Food and nutrition governance: interscalar local to global democratic strategies to address the gender gap and enhance rural livelihoods." Yet, despite this knowledge, whether old or new, and a generally favorable environment for modifying food systems to be nutrition sensitive, why do we not move "from rhetoric to action," as Pinstrup-Andersen (2013a, 375) asks in his comment in *The Lancet*? He provides two main reasons. Firstly, the economic and political agendas in the agricultural and postharvest sector favor dominant stakeholder group interests as opposed to those of the malnourished population, and policy interventions that could link nutrition and economic aims are not pursued. On the contrary, health and nutrition interventions are mostly geared toward treating chronic diseases and nutrition deficiencies when the damage has already been done, instead of creating incentives for farmers, consumers, food processors, and other actors in the food and agricultural system that would promote behavioral change—something that might take time but is ultimately more cost effective and sustainable. Secondly, randomized controlled trials (RCTs), applicable only to smaller projects like home gardens, are considered by the health and nutrition community as the only way to glean evidence. Two main reasons are provided as to why such trials are used only for small-scale schemes: (*a*) the pathways are extensive and numerous variables, for example, the uncontrollable actions of system agents, cause an impact, and (*b*) policy interventions of a larger scale within food systems are not considered suitable for randomization and control groups (Pinstrup-Andersen 2013b, 4). We agree with Pinstrup-Andersen (2013a) in his call for shifting the current focus, as food system policies and programs are impossible to appraise using RCTs, yet it is through these policies that the most auspicious improvement opportunities within health and nutrition can be achieved.

In light of ongoing rapid urbanization, there is a further need to specifically focus on nutrition sensitive urban agriculture. While it is clear that the latter cannot fully accommodate for rising food needs in urban areas (Los Angeles Food Policy Task Force 2010, 26), the various forms of urban agriculture can nevertheless make an important contribution to enhancing food and nutrition security. Urban agriculture further provides an excellent example of the multi-functionality of agriculture, with the latter having been emphasized by the *International Assessment of Agricultural Knowledge, Science and Technology for Development* (IAASTD; IAASTD 2009). Urban agriculture, beyond agricultural production purposes, serves other multiple functions, among them strengthening social interaction and networks by integrating various actors from civil society, providing education, promoting a healthy and active lifestyle, enhancing economic development, and providing leisure activities for urban people (Duchemin, Wegmuller, and Legault 2008, 44).

As this review of the development of the concepts "food security" and "nutrition security" highlights, it is long overdue that the artificial separation between nutrition and agriculture is being replaced by interdisciplinary and intersectoral approaches in order to adequately address current and future challenges of food and nutrition insecurity and hunger. The 20th IUNS International Congress of Nutrition hosted in September 2013 in Granada, Spain, continued the trend of the previous two IUNS congresses toward an integration of nutrition and agriculture (IUNS 2013).[7] These recent developments are going in the right direction and are encouraging.

In his paper "Paradigms in Applied Nutrition" presented at the 19th IUNS International Congress of Nutrition 2009, Urban Jonsson (2009) analyzes the paradigm shifts in applied nutrition over the past sixty years, arguing that we have been in a period of paradigm crisis since 2005 and presenting the current two competing paradigms. Whereas the "investment in nutrition paradigm," according to Jonsson (2009, 19), supports top-down approaches, including aspects such as delivery to beneficiaries, planning for people instead of planning with them, charitable approaches, and privatization of health and education services, the "human rights approach to nutrition paradigm" favors a combination of both bottom-up and top-down approaches, building capacity for empowerment, planning with people instead of planning for them, moving away from charitable approaches, and promoting health and education services as a public good (Jonsson 2009, 21).[8] Jonsson (2009, 26) concludes that the next mainstream paradigm will not be based on new scientific discoveries but rather on power politics and ideology. Arguments in favor of the investment in nutrition paradigm that reflects an individualistic approach in line with a free market ideology include, among others, its sound conceptual basis, support of the World Bank and likelihood of significant funding, and the avoidance of sensitive political causes and consequences of malnutrition. Arguments in favor of the human rights approach to nutrition paradigm that reflects a collective, public health, and democratic ideology are, among others, the increased recognition of economic and social rights, addressing impunity, corruption and social access to justice, and the implication of clear accountability (see also HRC 2011).

We support grassroots approaches that are based inside social movements and favor the human rights approach to nutrition paradigm as this perspective enables the possibility of addressing the structural problems that perpetuate food insecurity and hunger, including, most specifically, gender and power imbalances.[9] We find particular hopefulness in a people's and food sovereignty approach as presented in detail in chapter 6 of this volume that centers problem analysis and attention at the local level by local actors, and in dialogue with human rights-focused constitutional structures. However, gender is not yet adequately addressed and integrated into the discussions, neither in the mentioned IUNS congresses, nor in Jonsson's analysis. The focus on women and children needs to move beyond their portrayal as disempowered victims in a maternal-child and housebound state, and begin to include local populations of women, men, and children with food and nutrition rights and capabilities regardless of their stage in the reproductive cycle and inclusive of their locations in both public and private spaces, as is elaborated in more detail in chapters 2, 3, and 4 of this volume (see also ARROW 2014). Additionally, we argue that a call for a human rights approach to nutrition paradigm should be housed within the right to adequate food and nutrition and possibly other established human rights instruments (e.g., the right to the highest attainable standard of health). We would discourage a move to champion a separate human right to nutrition that might lead to program planning which isolates instead of integrates the diverse aspects of the human right to adequate food and nutrition. The call of the 19th IUNS congress for a closer alliance of nutrition and agricultural systems also needs to be refined to focus on small and regional scale, agroecological farming and farmers, with the objective of promoting greater self-determination, economic autonomy, and the right to adequate food and nutrition at the local and regional scales.

The Shortcomings of Agricultural Production Models for Food and Nutrition Security

The evaluation of the Food and Agriculture Organization of the United Nations (FAO) estimates on how to feed the world population (FAO 2009) observes that the narrow focus on increased production and supply coexists with persisting poverty and ongoing lack of access to food (Grethe, Dembélé, and Duman 2011). As was concluded by the aforementioned IAASTD, in spite of all of the investment and claimed advancement of agricultural technology and production, food insecurity and hunger have increased (IAASTD

2009). The IAASTD report was the work of over four hundred international nutrition and agriculture experts working for approximately five years on a study funded by FAO, Global Environment Facility (GEF), United Nations Development Programme (UNDP), United Nations Environment Programme (UNEP), United Nations Educational, Scientific and Cultural Organization (UNESCO), the World Bank, and the World Health Organization (WHO).[10] The executive summary of the synthesis report was approved by fifty-eight countries, while three countries—Australia, Canada, and the United States of America—held reservations against certain aspects of the executive summary. The IAASTD calls for a need to reexamine the purpose of agricultural knowledge and production in a more democratic and participatory way. Among the main challenges stated are to increase the productivity of agriculture in a sustainable manner and to address the needs of small-scale farms in diverse ecosystems. The IAASTD further calls for attention to women in agriculture, local knowledge and democratic participation in food policy broadly construed, human health, natural resource management, and greater farmer independence vis-à-vis international industrial concerns.

Scoones (2009) gives credit to the IAASTD report for placing complex livelihood concerns at the center, with principles of equity, access, and sustainability guiding the normative frame. He further notes that the report stands in stark contrast to previous reports by the World Bank, wherein the ideal to strive for was agriculture as a business, driven by entrepreneurship and vibrant markets, and linked to a burgeoning urban economy. According to *The Cordoba Declaration on the Right to Food and the Governance of the Global Food and Agricultural Systems*, the IAASTD should form the basis for ongoing discussions on the potential role of agricultural technologies, as it recognizes "the need for complementary and diversified approaches to sustainable agriculture, pointing out that agricultural models based on smallholder farming can present alternatives appropriate for a human rights-based food security" (CEHAP 2008, 3).

Several experts had argued before that agricultural and rural policies need to be reevaluated in order to reverse the negative trends that promote more economic growth while resulting in no substantial benefits for the poor (Cousins 2007; Windfuhr and Jonsén 2005). Adding to this is the fact that 30 to 40 percent of food in both the developed and developing world is lost to waste, although the causes are very different (Godfray et al. 2010). As Godfray et al. (2010) conclude in their review "Food Security: The Challenge of Feeding 9 Billion People," the challenge is to make food production sustainable and to meet the Millennium Development Goal (MDG) 1 of eradicating extreme poverty and hunger while at the same time controlling greenhouse gas emissions and conserving water supplies. They emphasize that this cannot be achieved by maximizing productivity but only by overcoming barriers between different fields and disciplines and by optimizing processes of production as well as environmental and social justice outcomes.

The following case study is one example of how the agroindustrial model can negatively impact food and nutrition security of mothers, infants, and young children, as well as the environment and health of the entire community.

Case study 5.1 Brazil: toxic contamination of agricultural products compromises food and nutrition security of mothers and infants[11]

A master thesis undertaken at the Federal University of Mato Grosso, Brazil, published in 2011,[12] revealed that in Lucas do Rio Verde (Mato Grosso) the breastmilk of sixty-two mothers was directly or indirectly contaminated by agrochemicals. The author attributes this high level of contamination to intense production of grains (soybeans and corn) with abusive utilization of pesticides and herbicides.[13] According to the study, the inhabitants in this municipality are exposed to pesticide levels forty-five times higher than the average resident of Brazil.[14] At least two substances of high toxicity, dichlorodiphenyldichloroethylene (DDE, one of the components of dichlorodiphenyltrichloroethane (DDT)) and beta-endosulfan, among others, were identified in the blood of the affected mothers. The use of DDT, for instance, was forbidden in Brazil in 1998. This means that the contamination of breastmilk with DDE is a direct violation of the right to adequate food and nutrition of mothers, their infants, and young children, and the community as a whole. It is also worrisome that beta-endosulfan was excreted in the breastmilk of 44 percent of the mothers. DDE, beta-endosulfan, and other pesticides identified in the mothers' bodies are dangerous as they can cause cancer, fetal malformation, induce abortion, and deregulate the endocrine system (Colles et al. 2008; Eskenazi et al. 2009; Sanghi et al. 2003).

This is a clear demonstration of how the agroindustrial production model has led to violations of the right to adequate food and nutrition, not only by evicting traditional populations and peasants from their land and reducing biodiversity, but also by compromising the food available to local communities, which notably includes women's breastmilk for their children.

The Gender Gap in Agriculture

Although women have been called the key to household food security (FAO 2011; IFPRI 2005; Kent 2002; Quisumbing et al. 1995; Quisumbing and Smith 2007), gender is not yet adequately addressed and integrated into discussions on how to achieve adequate food supplies. While both men and women smallholder farmers do not have access to adequate resources, it is generally accepted that, due to social norms, female farmers in all regions have less ownership of land and livestock and less access to agricultural inputs, credit, education, extension, and other services than do men (FAO 2011; see also FAO 1997). Further, farm labor for women is often limited to part-time and seasonal work, restraining their income opportunities to certain periods, and their wages are characteristically lower than those of men (FAO 2011; World Bank, FAO, and IFAD 2009). Women's labor is thus absorbed and their ability to profit from it, stymied. The *Gender in Agriculture Sourcebook* (World Bank, FAO, and IFAD 2009) provides numerous references on gender-based inequalities and women's unacknowledged role in agriculture.[15] Women, and often girls, undertake a significant, and sometimes the major, part in food production. They also undertake a significant part in the labors of shopping, the household-based labors of storage, processing, cooking, and caring for the nutritional well-being and dietary-related health status of families, as well as essential reproductive health issues during the pregnancy and the lactation period. Women are engaged and typically overrepresented in the lowest paying jobs related to harvest and postharvest processing of foods destined for domestic and global open markets. Women are further often regarded as family members who "help with farming," while, in fact, they are mainly responsible for food production both for the market and for household consumption needs, especially in many African countries (Schäfer 2012).

There are varying figures on how many women are involved in the agricultural sector worldwide. Whereas previous reports claimed that women perform 60 to 80 percent of agricultural labor in developing countries, according to the FAO report *The State of Food and Agriculture 2010–11—Women in Agriculture: Closing the Gender Gap for Development* (FAO 2011), women comprise on average 43 percent of the agricultural labor force in developing countries, with numbers ranging from 20 percent in Latin America to 50 percent in Eastern Asia and sub-Saharan Africa. Women in sub-Saharan Africa have the highest average agricultural labor force participation rates in the world, comprising over 60 percent in some countries (e.g., Lesotho, Mozambique, and Sierra Leone).[16] In South Africa, as a case in point, according to Altman, Hart, and Jacobs (2009, 357), women represent 61 percent of people involved in farming, and they produce more food for household consumption than men. Further, in a number of countries, the female share of the agricultural labor force has increased in recent decades due to, among others, conflict, HIV/AIDS, and migration (FAO 2011). Women in particular face multiple threats and challenges, as outlined by Schäfer (2012). Civil wars and violent conflicts often prevent female smallholders from engaging in agriculture due to the real danger of being abducted or raped, or because they have been displaced. The HIV/AIDS epidemic results in loss of access to income of male breadwinners and higher costs for medication and funerals. At the same time, in the case of the death of a male household member, women often do not inherit their male partner's rights to the land, and these women might even lose the right to live on that land. Women also commonly care for sick household members, for their own grandchildren, and for children of relatives who have lost one or both parents because of AIDS. If women themselves get infected with HIV, it compromises their ability to engage in agricultural production and to take care of their household's nutritional needs. As Schäfer (2012) emphasizes, these social forces, together with the increasing trend of male migration, lead to changing and more flexible household structures and to growing numbers of women-led households. However, female migration has also drastically increased, impacting network-based (kin and friendship) social sustainability strategies. Despite these challenges and because of them, women develop alternative and resilient resources that enable them to engage actively in processes of demographic and socioeconomic transitions, as will be elaborated further in the section of this chapter entitled "Food and nutrition governance: interscalar local to global democratic strategies to address the gender gap and enhance rural livelihoods."

Political structures, to a large extent, determine women's unequal access to resources and their lack of rights. Gender rights typically conflict with traditional authority and customary laws that treat women as minors, resulting in gender-based disparities in property rights (IFPRI 2005; Quisumbing 2010; Rangan and Gilmartin 2002; UNDESA 2010). However, even where laws addressing gender inequality are in place, traditions and customs play a strong role in determining whether women, for example, actually have rights to land and whether those rights are meaningful.[17]

The following case studies not only highlight discrimination against women due to social norms in Uganda and South Africa, but also provide a positive example of how women's property rights have been strengthened in Kenya.[18]

Case study 5.2 Uganda: women cannot access markets due to social norms

According to case study research carried out by the International Fund for Agricultural Development (IFAD) in Zambia, Mozambique, and Uganda, in female-headed households it is mostly women who market the agricultural produce and control income from the sale. However, some female-headed households in Uganda experience constraints in taking produce to markets because they cannot use bicycles due to strict taboos within some ethnic groups in Central and Western Uganda. As women do not have access to other means of transport, they are forced to sell their produce at low prices at the farm gate and depend upon buyers passing through the village (IFAD 2002, 34).[19]

Case study 5.3 South Africa: insecurity of tenure of female farmworkers

In the agricultural sector in South Africa, wages of female farmworkers are lower than those of men and generally employment and housing contracts are linked to men (Shabodien 2006). As was illustrated in research on gender and livelihoods among South African farmworker households (Lemke, Bellows, and Heumann 2009), this results in several negative consequences for women, including the facts that they depend on their male partner for accommodation and that women's limited decision-making power impacts on resource allocation within the household. The resulting dependency on male partners threatens livelihood security of female farmworkers should the men leave the farm or stop working.[20]

Case study 5.4 Kenya: enforcing women's rights with regard to land ownership

In Kenya, the government adopted a new constitution on August 27, 2010 after it was approved by an overwhelming majority in a national referendum.[21] This achievement was the result of decades of tireless engagement by national women's rights organizations (Wölte 2008). The new constitution enforces women's right to land ownership, land inheritance, and the protection of matrimonial property during and after the termination of marriage. The new constitution further demands that discrimination in laws, customs, and practices related to land and property is eliminated (AWC 2010). It remains to be seen how this will translate into practice, but the fact that the new constitution specifically addresses traditional laws indicates that these structural problems are being acknowledged.

Based on studies carried out by the International Food Policy Research Institute (IFPRI), empowering women and reducing gender disparities promotes better food security and nutrition security for all (IFPRI 2005). Among the main findings were (*a*) targeting women in agricultural technology dissemination can have a greater impact on poverty than targeting men, (*b*) equalizing agricultural inputs between men and women results in significant gains in agricultural productivity, and (*c*) gender disparities in property rights threaten natural resource management. Key recommendations are to target resources to women and to increase women's participation in agricultural education, legal rights, and household decision-making (IFPRI 2005, 2–4). This is supported by Meinzen-Dick et al. (2012) in their investigation of different agricultural development strategies, namely smallholders and markets, large-scale agriculture, and homestead food production. There is evidence that increasing women's access to resources and control over household income and in production and employment scenarios has important implications for the health and nutrition of the family, particularly for the health and nutrition of women and children. For example, Meinzen-Dick et al. (2012, 143) emphasize that the practice and potential of homestead food production is still under-researched, under-promoted, and under-realized; production for domestic consumption can lead to substantial improvements in health and nutrition, especially if combined with educational and related initiatives. The authors conclude that whereas substantial evidence exists on positive health and nutritional outcomes if women's position is strengthened, further research is needed to fully understand the linkages between and impact of alternative agricultural development strategies on health and nutrition (Meinzen-Dick et al. 2012, 142). The women's empowerment in agriculture index (WEAI; IFPRI 2012) could provide a useful tool to measure the empowerment, agency, and inclusion of women in the agricultural sector. The WEAI is based on individual level data collected by interviewing men and women within the same household. It investigates decisions about agricultural production, access to and decision-making power concerning productive resources, control over use of income, leadership in the community, and time allocation. The WEAI further aims to measure gender parity by reflecting the percentage of women who are empowered or whose achievements are at least as high as those of the men in their households.

The FAO report *The State of Food and Agriculture 2010–11* (FAO 2011, 5–6) provides the following key messages for closing the gender gap for development. If women had the same access to productive resources as men, they could increase yields on their farms by 20 to 30 percent. Expressed in terms of production gains, this could reduce the number of hungry people in the world by 12 to 17 percent, varying of course by region and specific conditions. The report further reiterates that benefits go beyond the agricultural sector and relate to human capital and economic growth, as women are known to spend more of their income on food, health, and education for their children. The report then repeats the call for policy interventions that close the gender gap in agriculture and rural labor markets by (*a*) eliminating women's discrimination regarding access to resources, (*b*) creating enabling infrastructure and technologies to provide women with more time for productive activities, and, last but not least, (*c*) by facilitating women's participation in flexible, efficient, and fair rural labor markets. As Jacques Diouf, the former FAO director general, frames it in the foreword to the report: "We must eliminate all forms of discrimination against women under the law, ensure that access to resources is more equal and that agricultural policies and programmes are gender-aware. . . . Achieving gender equality and empowering women is not only the right thing to do; it is also crucial for agricultural development and food security" (FAO 2011, vii). Godfray et al. (2010) argue in the same vein, highlighting that in smallholder agriculture women often take a dominant role in the workforce and that investment in social and economic mechanisms to improve yields can be an important means of increasing both farm and rural non-farm households, especially if targeted at women.

However, despite the reiteration of women's important role for social and economic development and the frequent call to empower women, there is too much emphasis on economic aspects, bearing negative consequences. As the director general of FAO, José Graziano Da Silva, critically remarks, new responsibilities add to the workload of women, with the double and sometimes triple burden of their work in the field, at home, and in the community neither being recognized nor shared by men or other household members.[22] The section "Women, development, gender, empowerment: an evolving debate" will provide a more detailed reflection on these aspects.

The Shortcomings of Medicalized Nutrition Intervention Models for Food and Nutrition Security

Ongoing debates around support for medicalized nutrition intervention models in the case of food aid have evolved to favor the investment in nutrition paradigm. Case in point is the 2008 *The Lancet* series "Maternal and Child Undernutrition" which has provoked civil society criticism and scientific debates.[23] The series rightly identified the outrage of nutrition-related maternal and child mortality rates, but without acknowledging the associated denial of basic human rights over the life span to, among others, basic dignity and self-determination. The series emphasized a need for short-term, private sector-led nutrition strategies with a focus on micronutrient supplementation and the modeling, reconstruction, and medicalization of food delivery instead of the delivery of food-based systems and local, sustainable strategies involving the public and civil sectors. Accordingly, the Scaling Up Nutrition (SUN) initiative (Bezanson and Isenman 2010; Horton et al. 2010) that was developed as a result of *The Lancet* series favors a stronger influence of the private sector (Latham et al. 2011) to the detriment of more holistic and locally based approaches. Food is not, however, just about nutrients but about livelihoods, value, culture, and many other aspects. As has been pointed out at a post-19th IUNS International Congress of Nutrition 2009 symposium hosted by SCN, the cost-effectiveness of supplementation (e.g., with vitamin A or imported, preprocessed complementary foods) requires investigation.[24] Supplementation is designed to achieve a single effect on health versus food-based strategies that seek more diversified nutritional and other livelihood outcomes (e.g., of supporting local food systems and economies). Additionally, the ethics of public-private partnerships (PPPs) associated with supplementation and linked to the undermining of local agriculture and diets as well as to economic dependencies must be questioned.

Case study 5.5 Ready-to-use supplementary food (RUSF)

We return to the example of the large-scale distribution of ready-to-use supplementary food (RUSF) as promoted by the SUN initiative.[25] RUSF is a high energy nutritional food supplement, based on cereals, legumes, or seeds fortified with vitamins and minerals, used to treat or prevent moderate to mild forms of malnutrition. We argue that global circulation of RUSF, as an example of a non-local food and nutrition "cure" and increasingly even as a form of malnutrition prevention, is overemphasized to the advantage of trade interests but to the detriment of developing capacity and autonomy in community and nation-based food and nutrition systems. Opening RUSF markets further introduces highly processed and packaged foods into traditional eating cultures, thereby normalizing the brand names and consumption habits that also support the transglobal trade in snack and "junk" foods (e.g., candy, breakfast cereals, and chips) which tend to be calorie dense and nutrition poor. The question becomes: whose interests are served by SUN and whose livelihoods enhanced? Public and business policy to adopt or promote industrially produced, internationally traded, and non-locally sourced or created RUSF can inhibit local sustainable solutions for food and nutrition security. These "measures" represent a paternalistic approach, indicating a presumption of local incompetence and with an emphasis on aid, neediness, and dependency, instead of being in line with a human rights framework. In contrast, approaches are needed that promote ownership, capacity, autonomy, and self-determination of local food systems as well as tangible outcomes such as improved food and nutrition security, job creation, enhanced livelihoods, and broad social networks.

The Shortcomings of Household Surveys on Food and Nutrition Security in Addressing Gender and Intra-household Dynamics

The concepts of the household and intra-household dynamics have to be investigated closely as it is crucial for the understanding of household's food and nutrition security situation. Further, it needs to be taken into account that individual household members experience different food security risks and often follow different food security strategies. As social scientists such as Netting, Wilk, and Arnould (1984) had already argued in the 1980s with regard to the history of the household concept, there is a need to move away from the concept of the nuclear family and from the search for simplicity. The assumption, however, still often persists that households consist of members with a single economic aim, complementary objectives, and tied to the same social networks within a shared social environment (Mazonde 2000; Prabhu 2010). As several authors have argued, analyzing social processes and transformation using the household as a homogeneous unit where resources are equally distributed derives from and creates oversimplification (Mazonde 2000; Pasteur 2002; Rogers and Schlossman 1990). This assumption is especially misleading in low income households. Changing and often fluid household structures as well as women's position within households are still not adequately reflected in surveys and statistics, and the household as an analytical unit has increasingly been challenged (Gillespie and Kadiyala 2005; Hosegood and Timaeus 2005; Murphy, Harvey, and Silvestre 2005). According to Messer (1990), who argues from an anthropological household perspective, the outsider's perspective of economic models conflicts with the insider's perspective of social conceptualizations. It is this subjective perception that influences behavior and affects the ways in which people respond to a changed environment. Further, the perception of the household as a co-residential unit, as it is still often defined, is an inadequate unit of analysis for exploring social and economic processes. The validity of household surveys that are based on the outlined assumptions, therefore, is questionable. We argue that an anthropological or sociological perspective of the concept of household is needed in the context of food and nutrition security in order to trace the causal relationships between the dynamics within households and the well-being of households and their members.

Access to and utilization of food at the household level and the related impact on nutritional status for household members requires, therefore, much improved data collection. As has been emphasized by Hosegood and Timaeus (2005), the complexities of households, such as fluid household composition, high levels of individual and household mobility, non-resident household members, and multiple household memberships, have to be captured. They used the concepts "multiple household membership," "full members," and "affiliated members" in longitudinal data collection surveys that were developed for the Africa Centre Demographic Information System (ACDIS). In Southern Africa and elsewhere, due to migration and other factors, households often cannot be defined as co-residential but are highly complex with regard to extended networks of kin and relatives (Spiegel, Watson, and Wilkinson 1996). Spiegel, Watson, and Wilkinson (1996) replaced the conventional term "household" with the term "stretched domestic units" which refers to the fact that members of a so-called household are often not co-residential or commensal for most of their lives. Individuals, therefore, may belong to several households that are connected through kinship, social relations, and various other arrangements, creating "multiple household memberships." In research on food and nutrition security among rural populations in South Africa, based on earlier definitions by Murray (1976) and Spiegel, Watson, and Wilkinson (1996), the household was defined as "all people who share income and other resources, possibly also certain obligations and interests, whether they belong to the same or different residential units. In most cases, members of these households are related along kinship links" (Lemke 2001, 109). This definition reflects and takes into account fluid or stretched household boundaries. Among the key findings of previous research were that the stretching of households over several domestic units and the search for migrant labor were among the most important strategies people use for improved food security and survival (Lemke 2001, ix).

How to adequately capture intra-household dynamics and decision-making remains, however, a challenge. According to *The World's Women 2010* report (UNDESA 2010), whereas there has been an increase over the past decade of available gender statistics, data are often not comparable, as concepts, definitions, methods, and also quality of data vary between countries. The report further confirms that statistics are sometimes too broad or are not further disaggregated by relevant characteristics. Shortcomings are especially experienced with data related to international migration, maternal mortality, causes of death, vocational education, access to and use of information and communication technologies, the informal sector, and informal employment, as well as with data on occupations, wages, unemployment and underemployment, decision-makers in government and the private sector, and household poverty. As was stated in the aforementioned FAO report *The State of Food and Agriculture 2010–11*, there are further limitations in data collection of different types of female-headed households, including "de facto female headed households" characterized as women having an adult male partner who is a migrant worker but who remains involved through remittances and other economic and social ties, and "de jure female headed households" defined as having no male partner member and headed instead by women who are widowed, divorced, or never married (FAO 2011). However, this categorization remains limited as it is necessary to determine the actual decision-making power within households in order to provide more accurate data on intra-household resource allocation. Besides intra-household gender dynamics that can lead to conflict, various other power relations exist among different categories of household members, for example, among women and men based on age, marital status, sexual orientation, ethnicity, and religion; among older and younger household members; or between income earners and unemployed household members.

Whereas men are generally still regarded as the household head, in reality many households are led de facto by women. As was confirmed by research in South Africa (Lemke 2001; Lemke et al. 2003), half of households were led by women, with men either being absent because of migrant work, because they were not able to marry due to being unemployed and their resulting low socioeconomic status, or because women had decided to stay single for greater economic and social security. The strive for greater independence of women is largely due to ongoing patriarchal structures and the high incidence of domestic violence against women (van der Vliet 1991; Jones 1999), as is illustrated in the following case study.

Case study 5.6 South Africa: violence against women and women-led households for greater security

In South Africa, violence against women did not gain serious political attention until the 1990s. During apartheid, the struggle against the oppressive regime was at the forefront and the issue of gender did not constitute an obvious element in the political discourse. Women's human rights in South Africa in general, whether among the black, white, colored, or other population groups, were not being recognized or championed (Ramphele and Boonzaier 1988; Schäfer 2005).[26] In other words, oppression against women by men both within and outside of the antiapartheid movement was not addressed, accounting in part for the impunity of violence against women existing today. Only with the political change in the 1990s was the significance of gender issues fully recognized for the first time. The new South African Constitution, passed into law in 1996 (Republic of South Africa 1996), explicitly guarantees freedom from discrimination on the basis of, among other things, race, gender, and disability. Whereas South Africa is committed today to gender rights (Office on the Status of Women [South Africa] 2000), this paper proclamation has not resulted in improvements in the daily life of women, and gender-based discrimination remains widespread. Furthermore, previous social structures, such as paternalism, are still prevalent, reinforcing women's inferior position within the household and community (Reddy and Moletsane 2009).

Due to ongoing patriarchal structures, inequality, poverty, social destitution, and the high incidence of violence against women, including sexual and domestic violence, women may leave their male partner and choose to stay single, adding to the growing number of female-headed households, as has been documented in a number of studies among rural and urban black women (Jones 1999; Lemke et al. 2003; van der Vliet 1991). Singlehood can be seen as a coping strategy of women but also as a strategy for empowerment by resisting male domination, which has been framed by Jones (1999) as the concept "singlehood for security." Another reason why black South African women in particular increasingly prefer to stay single is that they are afraid of contracting HIV from their male partners who, due to migrant work and patriarchal ideals, often pursue multiple relationships (Schäfer 2002). Gender-based violence (GBV), power relationships within households, and greater autonomy of women are therefore directly linked to changes in household composition.

In an example of micro-level in-depth research among South African farmworkers with a focus on gender and sustainable livelihoods, Lemke, Bellows, and Heumann (2009) revealed that female-headed households, although having less access to earned income compared to male-headed households, are able to take better care of the well-being of household members and achieve greater food and nutrition security than comparable households with male headship. Whereas men remain the dominant earners, women have better access to social grants, remittances from relatives, and income obtained through informal employment. This study highlights the crucial role of women's access to resources and power relations within households for greater food and nutrition security and sustainable livelihoods. The findings further reaffirm the need to include household and gender variables in demographic and health surveys to more accurately determine the socioeconomic and food security status of households.

As this section highlights, clearly an anthropological or sociological perspective of the concept of household is needed in order to trace the causal relationships between the dynamics within households and the well-being of households and its members. This underscores the need for a comprehensive gendered perspective and for detailed micro-social research, in order to reveal underlying social factors and how these influence decision-making and resource allocation; factors that largely determine household food and nutrition security (Doss 2013; Leonhäuser et al. 2005; Prabhu 2010; Quisumbing and Smith 2007).

Women, Development, Gender, Empowerment: an Evolving Debate

In current debates, "gender" is often still misunderstood as "being about women." This is more than forty years after the gender debate evolved in the 1970s and more than twenty years after the 1992 UN Conference on Environment and Development in Rio de Janeiro with the Agenda 21 final report that recognized women as key actors in the fight against poverty and in the preservation of the environment (UN General Assembly 1992 a, b).

According to Wichterich (2012), the "green economy," which served as a model for the Rio+20 UN Conference on Sustainable Development, fell sadly behind the achievements of the Agenda 21 as it failed to integrate gender mainstreaming and a feminist perspective into a plan moving forward. Wichterich (2012, 11) attributes this partly to a certain "gender fatigue" that pervaded the early 2000s. For women who worked toward gender mainstreaming this might have been based on their frustrations with the slow progress of institutions that claimed concern about the need for and their ostensible success with mainstreaming women in their organizations but that, nevertheless, made little or no difference to women's progressive access to equality and human rights. As Harcourt (2012) states, the official declaration of the Rio+20 UN Conference on Sustainable Development, *The Future We Want* (UN General Assembly 2012), repressed any reference to support sexuality, reproductive rights, or health, taking women's rights two decades backwards.

In order to understand the current gender debate and its interpretations, it is important to examine how the concepts "gender," "development," and "empowerment" evolved, how they are used, and what they mean today.

The gender debate in the international context was initiated in the 1970s by the women in development (WID) agenda that aimed to increase women's involvement in the market economy and project activities. The WID movement was informed by Ester Boserup's overview in 1970, *Women's Role in Economic Development*.[27] Boserup challenged the assumptions of the previous "welfare approach" that regarded women mainly as wives and mothers and being in need and shifted the perspective to women's importance to the agricultural economy (Razavi and Miller 1995). One of the main shortcomings of the WID approach, however, was that it focused on women in isolation from their social relationships and did little to address the power imbalances rooted in these social relations that lead to women's greater vulnerability to poverty. The WID agenda was followed by the gender and development (GAD) and later the gender mainstreaming (GM) approach. Although the intention of the two latter concepts was to recognize gender differences and to focus on social relationships and interactions between women and men, they partly continued the distorted focus of WID (Benad 2002; Townsend et al. 1999).

The concept "empowerment" that is currently largely being used in policies concerning gender is controversial and has to be regarded with caution. One of our reservations with this concept is that "empowering someone" can entail a passivity that is contradictory and that diverts us from the initial intention of changing social power dynamics. The process of "empowerment" can reinforce inequality by suggesting that the person "to be empowered" lacks certain capacities and capabilities relative to those who promote empowerment and who are "empowered."[28] A second broad concern is that the meaning and use of empowerment has narrowed to an individualized focus on market-oriented productivity (Kabeer 2001; Lutrell et al. 2009).

Examples for this observation are the concepts of empowerment and gender equality as being applied by the World Bank within their MDG strategies, where it is argued that the integration of women into markets will lead to more economic growth and efficiency, with the measure of equality being economic benefits and losses (World Bank 2011). This interpretation of empowerment, however, perpetuates the above-mentioned distorted focus of empowerment being mainly about increasing market-oriented productivity and instrumentalizes women in a neoliberal economic model, instead of recognizing local knowledge and contributions of women *and men* to existing local food systems and their functions as social security measures.[29] This leads to a rather limited focus on women's individual productivity and efficiency, an approach that tends to ignore the impact of a broad range of social divisions and social relations that constrain women's economic choices and opportunities, as had been stated already in 1995 by Razavi and Miller. According to Cornwall and Brock (2005, 1046), the original emphasis of empowerment to build "personal and collective power in the struggle for a more just and equitable world" is being changed by agencies that apply empowerment in the context of gender. As they critically remark in their reflection of the buzzwords "empowerment," "participation," and "poverty reduction," "[w]ords that once spoke of politics and power have come to be reconfigured in the service of today's one-size-fits-all development recipes, spun into an apoliticised form that everyone can agree with" (Cornwall and Brock 2005, 1043), and conclude that an approach "stripped of any engagement with context or culture, politics, power or difference, does violence to the very hope of a world without poverty" (Cornwall and Brock 2005, 1058).

We support Alston's (2009) argument that the key challenge of empowerment and gender mainstreaming is to address structural causes of inequality and discrimination. But, like Moghadam and Senftova (2005), we contextualize "empowerment" within a multidimensional process of civil, political, social, economic, cultural participation and rights, and a human rights framework (see chapters 1 and 6 of this volume), wherein addressing structural causes must begin with empowered dialogue and direction from those marginalized from social power. The radical difference of regarding the concepts of empowerment and gender mainstreaming within a human rights framework lies in the need to change a system to incorporate women rather than attempting to change women to fit the system, as is often promoted by current approaches (Alston 2009, 141; see also chapter 3 of this volume).

We further and strongly suggest that the empowerment of women must be linked to the empowerment of men, who must be enabled and encouraged to break free from the "traditional male roles" ascribed to them. In the context of food and nutrition security, it is therefore critical not to focus on women as a "vulnerable" group in isolation from decisive structural issues at the household and community levels (see chapter 2 of this volume). Men should be integrated into related research and programming, recognizing that not doing so both perpetuates women's "burden" of food-related labors, remains blind to the potential, real, and desperate need for men's changing identities and masculinities, and ultimately results in the limited success of food and nutrition programs. Schäfer (2012) stresses an urgent need to place a stronger focus on socially marginalized men as well as on existing non-gender-based hierarchies, exploitation, and violence among and between men and women. Among men, it is often younger ones who have no access to land, no decision-making power, and no options of establishing a family. This can lead to violence in certain geographic regions and under certain circumstances.[30] The opportunity to address gender power imbalances fully has so far largely been missed, perhaps particularly when considering the lack of inclusion of men in gender mainstreaming practice. Whereas this subsection has focused on the evolving debate around women and gender in the context of development, it is clear that attention should be paid equally to other social categories beyond gender, as has been pointed out earlier, and that acknowledgement should be given to intersectoral analysis that investigates the link between gender, class, age, race, ethnicity, and religion, taking into account the various and complex power dynamics, as is also elaborated by Schäfer (2012, xi).

Sustainable Livelihoods Approaches for Integrated Analysis of Complex Location Specific Processes and Individuals' and Groups' Capacities

Diverse forms of the sustainable livelihoods approach (SLA) enable the investigation of underlying structural conditions of livelihoods at the household and community levels, focusing on individuals' and groups' capacities and access to various livelihood assets. We recommend SLA as an analytical tool as it can serve not only to (re)identify known aspects of discrimination but also to uncover peoples' livelihood assets that policy efforts might augment to leverage transformation of individuals and groups through and beyond the context of their vulnerabilities. The SLA, as developed by the Department for International Development (DFID; DFID 1999) and as adapted to the context of agriculture by Adato and Meinzen-Dick (2002), can serve as a theoretical framework to explore rural livelihoods and the closely connected issues of poverty, hunger, and food insecurity. The initial SLA became increasingly central to the international debate about development, poverty reduction, and environmental management in the 1990s, with a rapid proliferation of livelihood research in the development literature (Scoones 2009). Drawing on the earlier definition of sustainable livelihoods by Chambers and Conway (1992) and as developed further by Scoones (1998), quoted below:

> A livelihood comprises the capabilities, assets (including both material and social resources) and activities required for a means of living.

A livelihood is sustainable when it can cope with and recover from stresses and shocks, maintains or enhances its capabilities and assets, while not undermining the natural resource base. (Scoones 1998, 5)

At the micro- and meso-level, livelihood assets (physical, natural, financial, social, and human capital) play an essential role for households to pursue their livelihood strategies and strive for desired livelihood outcomes, largely influenced by institutional and policy structures at the national and provincial levels, with these structures to a great extent determining the vulnerability context of people. Thus, a SLA must address a full range of access to resources for insecure populations. These comprise, in particular, rural food producers, the rural and urban poor, and, among them, women as a group further discriminated against (Scherr 2003; Windfuhr and Jonsen 2005). The range of often compromised resource access includes not only access to land but also access to social and political assets, all of which are critical to reduce vulnerability.

The SLA has been criticized for not adequately reflecting and addressing social power relations (Scoones 2009). The initial SLA, however, stresses attention to an understanding of social relationships through the institutions, organizations, and embedded power dynamics that maintain them, this focus being crucial to designing interventions that can improve sustainable livelihood outcomes (Scoones 1998). Scoones (2009), in his historical review of livelihoods and rural development, provides an overview of how different approaches and ideas around livelihoods have emerged and how these were influenced by dominant economic paradigms and policy debates. He further critiques simplistic applications of the SLA that have prevailed in development applications, especially over the past decade. He finds that research and policy has generally shifted away from the contextual, transdisciplinary, and cross-sectoral SLA influenced perspective, and back toward a predictable default to macroeconomic analysis. Scoones (2009) points out four main failures of SLA, relating to a lack of engagement with (a) processes of economic globalization, (b) debates about politics and governance, (c) challenges of environmental sustainability, and (d) fundamental transformatory shifts in rural economies. Instead of scrapping SLA, however, he calls for reenergizing more complex livelihoods perspectives. He notes that if SLA is to have continued relevance and application it must both integrate the global policy context to achieve local dynamic change and democratize policy-making by providing a more central and accessible place for considerations of knowledge, power, values, politics, and policy change.

We argue that SLA research continues to offer a valuable and holistic approach for an integrated analysis of complex and highly dynamic contexts. As SLA draws upon diverse disciplinary perspectives and cuts across sectoral boundaries, it is further able to bridge divides, particularly between the natural and social sciences, and to challenge single sector approaches. The importance of local knowledge and the inclusion of participatory research methods both help to understand complex local realities and to facilitate engagement and learning between local people and outsiders. The advantages of SLA research also mirror its challenges. Additional tools and frameworks might have to be integrated and every exploration must be adapted to the respective research context and specific priorities, creating high time and resource demands. Yet, if we seriously aim to address structural and underlying causes of food and nutrition security, this detailed exploration of location specific contexts is absolutely necessary, providing a uniquely viable and sustainable approach.

Especially for poor households, multiple livelihood strategies are often more a response than a coping mechanism. That is to say, these households are often merely able to respond to crises when they happen; the household actors are not "coping" with strategies and flexibility mechanisms prepared in advance for the possibility of crisis (Loevinsohn and Gillespie 2003). In Southern Africa, for example, most households draw upon a diverse portfolio of activities and income sources that not only enhance household income but also food security, health, social networks, and savings and that furthermore bridge the rural-urban divide (Mazonde 2000; Shackleton, Shackleton, and Cousins 2000). While smallholder farming remains an important strategy to contribute to food supplies, these households also depend upon formal and informal employment, remittances from migrant household members, welfare transfers, and microenterprises. The construction of the potential for multiple livelihood strategies depends upon flexibility, access to information, and the negotiation of social relationships, typically both inside and outside the local community. An SLA analysis reflects upon and addresses these complex interactions and processes.

Case study 5.7 **Application of SLA in studies of agricultural programs and women's livelihoods in South Africa**

Research on food security and the right to adequate food and nutrition in the context of land and agrarian reform in South Africa has been carried out since 2010 with several South African based CSOs, exploring the prospects of smallholder agricultural programs for establishing sustainable livelihoods, with a specific focus on the participation of women in such programs (Lemke 2010). Drawing on the sustainable livelihoods framework and employing a mixed methods approach, a research project carried out in the Western Cape, South Africa, explored through participant observation and interviews the prospects of two smallholder agricultural programs for establishing sustainable livelihoods (Lemke et al. 2012). These programs were facilitated by CSOs and focused upon rural black and colored women.[31] One project evolved from a foundation established from a successful ecotourism venture; the other from a grassroots women's NGO with political action roots. Participation in these programs enabled women access to various livelihoods assets: education and capacity building (human assets), land (natural assets), tools and infrastructure (physical assets), stipends and income from selling their produce (financial assets), and networking (social assets). Improvements in livelihood assets further increased women's level of self-confidence and empowerment. This could be shown especially in the case study carried out in cooperation with the grassroots women NGO in their cooperatives program. In this specific research context the integration of the sustainable livelihoods framework with the women empowerment framework by Kabeer (1999) proved especially useful. Operational challenges apparent in both case studies included (a) divergent expectations on the side of project facilitators and participants and inadequate communication between them, (b) participants' financial dependency on the organizations meaning that women's participation time had to translate into income because they did not have the luxury to be unpaid students, interns, or volunteers, (c) historical race dynamics that complicated development objectives through black women's relationship with white male foundation managers in one case and their relationship to white and mostly male farm ownership in the other, (d) programs concentrated on developing agricultural skills without corresponding attention to adequate market access for food produced, and (e) the program's lack of financial sustainability.

The findings suggest that, while these programs are not yet sustainable, they stimulate an awareness of possibilities, visions, ownership, and rights that can have a long-term effect on the livelihoods of these rural women. Further, in evaluating program success, especially in the initiation phases, it must be remembered that structural barriers to the improvement of rural women's livelihoods are formidable and few South African models or alternatives are presently available to help CSOs formulate new opportunities (Lemke et al. 2012).

Among the main challenges described in the above case study is the struggle for autonomy, especially among those women who live on rural white-owned farms where their male partners work, and where they, as women, occasionally receive part-time or seasonal employment as well. This struggle for autonomy and independence partly stems from the previous system of gendered and racial paternalism (Du Toit 1993; van Onselen 1996) that continues to determine relationships on many farms, often leading to ambivalent and unstable situations. Obviously, large-scale farm owners rely on farm laborers to work their land. Farmworkers, on the other hand, become dependent on farm owners for employment and some social benefits, such as education and health services which, however marginal, have otherwise not been publically available in remote areas through the state. Yet in this arrangement, farmworkers still strive for fair and dignified labor practices and, additionally as illustrated in the case above, alternative livelihood strategies that enable them to become more independent.[32]

The findings from the previously illustrated case are in line with Schäfer (2012), who argues that socioeconomic and societal changes take time and often cannot be measured with so-called hard facts, even though institutions of development cooperation require this type of data. In this regard, social anthropological and ethnographic research and participatory and qualitative methods provide alternative approaches to broaden the understanding of success and sustainability of programs as illustrated above. The contributions of ethnographic research in revealing benefits of land reform programs are illustrated in the following case study by Hart (2012) who emphasizes that success or failure is not necessarily determined by the good or bad conception of programs and that an understanding of the actions and experiences of actors involved at different levels is of utmost importance.

Case study 5.8 South Africa: land reform policies
lead to benefits

Land reform in South Africa, through various programs, aims to rectify previously outlined historical injustices.[33] Land reform policy has been strongly criticized as it fails to address broader rural development objectives (e.g., health and education) and to provide the support necessary for emerging farmers to engage in agriculture.[34] Documenting a case study of land redistribution in the southern Cape of South Africa, Hart (2012) argues that, instead of focusing on institutional and organizational aspects of land reform and on the implementation of related policies and intervention programs, an ethnographic lens should be applied that allows insights into the complexities and social processes of land reform and that reveals how policy programs are understood and interpreted differently by different actors. In his analysis, Hart starts by asking the question *how* land reform works instead of asking *whether* it works, thus providing a deeper understanding of complex social relationships between policy and practice. Through ethnographic research, Hart explores how rural residents interpreted land reform policy and used the resources given to them by the state. This revealed that local actors' decisions and actions were based largely on their livelihood requirements and were, further, often determined by their historical experiences and social relationships. Although these beneficiaries acted differently than had been anticipated by officials, a number of them have gained tangible benefits, for example, by pursuing business activities other than agriculture after they had acquired land. This has given credence to the land reform policy and, in this specific case, resulted in state officials continuing to provide support to these beneficiaries (Hart 2012).

Case study 5.9 Sustainable livelihoods, nutrition security, HIV/AIDS, and gender

Especially in sub-Saharan Africa, people are affected by the devastating confluence of AIDS and food scarcity.[35] AIDS attacks exactly those capacities that enable people to resist famine, killing the most productive and reproductively active members of society (Piot and Pinstrup-Andersen 2002; Jackson and Landis 2002) and leading to a vicious circle that links poverty, food insecurity, and HIV/AIDS (UNAIDS 2002). HIV infection increases the risk of malnutrition in the individual; malnutrition exacerbates the effects of AIDS, further deteriorating nutritional status. Good nutrition is therefore regarded as one of the few bulwarks against AIDS-related illnesses and early death.[36] This is particularly the case in regions where access to HIV medicines is rare and, if available, out of economic reach of most poor people for whom AIDS is one additional burden on top of many others (Piot 2001; Fourie 2006). HIV/AIDS is not skewed to those households infected and affected but is systemic and thus affects the social and economic ties upon which communities are built (Budlender 2000). As predominantly the working generation is infected, this negatively impacts livelihoods,[37] resulting in (a) reduced income and divisions of labor in households, (b) families, workplaces, and communities being disrupted, (c) decreased agricultural production, and (e) weakening economies and, thus, undermining the social fabric (Fourie 2006). Social networks that are crucial for the survival of the poor are breaking down, with women bearing the brunt of this destabilization. Women are disproportionately more affected by HIV/AIDS than men because of gender inequality and women's biological, social, cultural, and economic vulnerability. Sexual violence, including selling sex for food, money, and other necessities, contributes to the higher incidence of HIV/AIDS among women. As is stated in article 14 of the *Declaration of Commitment on HIV/AIDS* of the UN (UN General Assembly 2001) that has been transformed into action by the formation of the Global Coalition on Women and AIDS on February 2, 2004 (UNAIDS 2004), gender equality and the empowerment of women are fundamental elements in the reduction of the vulnerability of women and girls to HIV/AIDS (see also HRC 2012).

The former UN secretary general, Kofi Annan, stated that AIDS in Africa has a woman's face (Annan 2002). Data from *The World's Women 2010* report (UNDESA 2010) indicate that in sub-Saharan Africa, North Africa, and the Middle East, women account for more than half of people living with HIV/AIDS. In South Africa, which has the highest incidence of rape worldwide in a country not at war, HIV transmission following rape is of particular concern (Women's Health Project 2000; Smith 2000).[38] South Africa is among the countries hit hardest by HIV, with an estimated prevalence rate of 17.9 percent among adults aged fifteen to forty-nine (UNAIDS 2013)—only Swaziland, Lesotho, and Botswana have a higher prevalence rate.

In this section we reviewed the shortcomings of current measures to address malnutrition and hunger that favor paternalistic approaches and perpetuate aid, neediness, and dependency. We further illustrated the crucial role that intra-household dynamics, decision-making, and resource allocation as well as inter-household relations and their social networks play for food and nutrition security of household members. Progressive realization of the human right to adequate food and nutrition requires the participation of civil society to overcome the limitations of industrial agriculture and medicalized nutrition models. Those most disenfranchised from basic human rights, often but not always nor exclusively women, need to participate in problem analysis and prescriptions for social change. In the following section we lay out democratic processes and holistic approaches to integrated local and regional food production and nutritionally sound consumption systems.

FOOD AND NUTRITION GOVERNANCE: INTERSCALAR LOCAL TO GLOBAL DEMOCRATIC STRATEGIES TO ADDRESS THE GENDER GAP AND ENHANCE RURAL LIVELIHOODS

In the first section of this chapter, we articulated the need to include gender and a systems approach into efforts to address the human right to adequate food and nutrition. Here, we expand this discussion and emphasize the importance of integrating principles of sustainability, social justice, and participatory sovereignty over food systems that nourish communities. Social justice and stability are associated with sustainable and equitable access to human necessities. Food insecurity, malnutrition, and poverty as well as the violation of related human rights correlate with significant polarization in well-being, for example, the size of the gap between rich and poor, between women and men, and also hierarchies within different groups of men and women, respectively, based on ethnicity, social status, age, and other factors. Vulnerability to social conflict is similarly correlated with uneven and unequal distribution of basic tenets of human security: protection, equal standing in the law, sustainable labor, and basic needs such as clean water, adequate food and nutrition, housing, basic and free education, and medical care.

International and local food aid models are similarly designed to provide short-term emergency care. They nevertheless characteristically entrench themselves and can contribute to chronic local dependency on charity and non-locally produced food items. Such dependency can lead to the destruction of originally autonomous economic and food systems where they existed or to an obstruction of new or improved local food and nutrition system planning. Distribution to the "poor" engenders service and food production economies that arguably enrich the well-being of food providers as much or more than the "short-term" food insecure. Resistance to food aid models is famously witnessed in the civil society criticism and scientific debates over the 2008 *The Lancet* series "Maternal and Child Undernutrition" that led to the SUN initiative, as was illustrated in case study 5.5. In emergencies, we need food provision services to deliver short-term relief or ongoing support in particularly difficult conditions. But what we additionally and desperately also need is the concurrent promotion of locally controlled, non-emergency oriented, long-term strategies that respect and integrate gender and social diversity to (*a*) build secure and sustainable local food economies and (*b*) weave nutritional well-being into agriculture, public health, and education programming.[39] This leads to the questions: what are appropriate strategies in achieving sustainable, equitable, and participatory local food systems that can enhance food and nutrition security, livelihoods, and local economies? And how are women included in the debate? This section introduces some of the recent and prominent concepts that aim to address this question: local food systems, food sovereignty and food governance, community food security, food policy councils, food justice, agroecology and organic agriculture, and sustainable diets. We employ these concepts to discuss women's *and* men's needs to gain capabilities necessary to protect their and their communities' well-being.

Local Food Systems and Food Sovereignty

The concept of local or alternative food systems has been framed by various terms and in diverse geographic contexts. Among the terms frequently employed are "local food systems" (Bellows and Hamm 2001; Feagan 2007; Hinrichs 2003; Martinez et al. 2010), "alternative or local food initiatives" (Allen et al. 2003; Connelly, Markey, and Roseland 2011), "alternative agro-food networks" (Brunori 2007; Ortmann and King 2010), or "local food economies" (Kelly and Schulschenk 2011). Kelly and Schulschenk (2011, 463) define a local food economy as "[t]he flow of resources (financial, human, social, environmental and others) within a network of community based enterprises that produce and distribute food at the local scale for local consumption." The challenge remains to define what we understand by "local," with many authors agreeing on the common idea of confining a food system to a particular region or location. Beyond a geographic context, civil society plays a crucial role in the contemporary discourse on local food systems. Localized food systems as we understand them are, therefore, characterized by smaller scale, ecologically oriented, and regionally based farmers and food system actors, with participation of civil society forming an important element of such alternative food systems. Localized food systems erase the divide between food security and nutrition security through an integrated public-private-civil society approach that strives for healthy, just, and sustainable local food economies. To create the space for the development of such participatory local food systems there is a need for the regulation within a human rights framework of public and private sector activities that limit or reduce access to natural resources (see chapter 6 of this volume), often framed within the scope of development and referred to as "large-scale land acquisitions," "landgrabbing," or "earthgrabbing." Although landgrabbing is not a new phenomenon, over the past few years a new type of landgrabbing is taking place where foreign public and private investors create agreements with domestic states involving possession and/or controlling of large surfaces of land relevant for current and/or future food security of the host country (FIAN International 2010, 8).[40] In countries where hunger, vulnerability to climate change, and poverty are prevalent, this practice may result in reduced land availability, besides possible violations of human rights, such as loss of access to adequate food and nutrition, housing, and water. According to FIAN International (2010, 11), "[l]and grabbing, even where there are no related forced evictions, drastically reduces land availability for land scarce groups, reduces the political space for peasant-oriented agricultural policies and gears national markets toward agribusiness interests and global markets, rather than sustainable peasant agriculture for local and national markets and for future generations."[41] In addition, the perception frequently reflected by conventional production models that current land use in marginalized areas is inefficient and underutilized has to be challenged, especially as this might open the door even more to investors to pursue large-scale land acquisitions. This would further contradict international recommendations, as outlined, for example, in the IAASTD (2009), by the former UN special rapporteur on the right to food, Olivier De Schutter (HRC 2011), and in more recent research (e.g., Lambek et al. 2014) emphasizing peasant agriculture as fundamental in the struggle against hunger.[42]

Agricultural policies often do not take into account the concerns, needs, and rights of marginalized groups and, therefore, fail to reduce hunger and malnutrition (Windfuhr 2007). These groups, which have been deprived of their rights, also often feel disempowered to take action about their circumstances. The concept "food sovereignty" that was introduced in 1996 at the World Food Summit,[43] based on the initiative of civil society groups, offered a new and innovative approach as it shifted the emphasis to the rights and specific needs of smallholders and other marginalized groups, addressing core problems of hunger and poverty (Windfuhr and Jonsén 2005). The following excerpt from the definition of food sovereignty highlights some of the key principles:

> Food sovereignty is the right of peoples to healthy and culturally appropriate food produced through ecologically sound and sustainable methods, and their right to define their own food and agriculture systems. . . . Food sovereignty prioritizes local and national economies and markets and empowers peasant and family farmer-driven agriculture, artisanal fishing, pastoralist-led grazing, and food production, distribution and consumption based on environmental, social and economic sustainability. . . . Food sovereignty implies new social relations free of oppression and inequality between men and women, peoples, racial groups, social and economic classes and generations. (Forum for Food Sovereignty 2007, para. 3)

The concept of food sovereignty that promotes local food governance and challenges current food systems has received increasing attention, as is reflected, among others, by the recent international conference Food Sovereignty: A Critical Dialogue at Yale University.[44] As Monsalve Suárez (2012) and also Patel (2012) emphasize, the concept of food sovereignty should not be misunderstood as stopping global trade or for countries to be self-sufficient with regard to food supplies within their own borders. However, the broad scope of food sovereignty lends itself to various interpretations. As Burnett and Murphy (2013, 22) state at the above conference, the food sovereignty movement has so far failed to provide a clear position on trade, which might close political doors, especially with regard to current and future negotiations at the level of the World Trade Organization (WTO). Bernstein (2013) provides a critical review of the food sovereignty movement, where he states that food sovereignty and small-scale farming will not be able to transform the world's food systems. He acknowledges, however, the movement's potential to challenge the materialist (agrarian) political economy and to take environmental change seriously. He further notes that the movement points to important struggles, such as (*a*) opposition to the inequalities of international trade in food and other agricultural commodities and international agribusiness, (*b*) resistance to so-called land-grabbing for producing food, agrofuels, and mining, and (*c*) support for redistributive land reform in certain areas and for rural populations whose farming, although marginal, is crucial for their livelihoods (Bernstein 2013, 30). Further research and a continued discourse at the levels of academia, civil society, and policy makers is needed to identify more clearly to what extent and at which levels food sovereignty can contribute to promoting more sustainable and equitable agriculture and food systems that could enhance food and nutrition security. As Burnett and Murphy (2013) state, the conditions of trade should be negotiated and more democratic structures need to be put in place. Clearly and despite controversially discussed topics (e.g., the role of trade and smallholder farming), food sovereignty has succeeded in stirring a debate concerning various structural problems of existing food systems, especially the power of private corporations and the negative impact of current food systems of industrialized nations on both under- and overnutrition.

Both food sovereignty and the human right to adequate food and nutrition concentrate on access to productive resources to be able to feed oneself and one's family, representing a much more active approach than the most widely used concept of food security that has been criticized for its rather passive approach and its focus on individual access to food (Windfuhr and Jonsén 2005).[45] As Windfuhr and Jonsén (2005) state, food sovereignty can be seen as a condition for genuine food security and the right to adequate food and nutrition as a tool to achieve it. Further, and importantly, both approaches foreground women and gender equality for achieving improved access to productive resources. As Kent (2002) has argued, because women play such an important role in shaping the social conditions of food and nutrition systems, they have to be empowered through achieving their full human rights, which would be the key to realizing the right to adequate food and nutrition for all.[46]

Community Food Security

We reintroduce a community food security approach that prioritizes social justice, including gender equity, and that promotes practical programming, such as nutrition education and local food business development. The concept of community food security evolved during the 1990s (Gottlieb and Fisher 1996), emphasizing long-term, systemic, and broad-based approaches to address food insecurity (McCullum et al. 2005). Community food security has been defined by Hamm and Bellows (2003, 37) as "a condition in which all community residents obtain a safe, culturally acceptable, nutritionally adequate diet through a sustainable food system that maximizes community self-reliance and social justice." Community food security developed in part from theories of food and economic democracy (Koc et al. 1999; Lang 1999) and the concept of civic agriculture (Lyson 2004), as well as the international human right to food (Bellows and Hamm 2003). As with food sovereignty, community food security is rooted in civil society and cross-sectoral partnerships (public, private, and private non-profit) that leverage a "community voice" into traditional power structures to redefine food and nutrition needs, security, and local-based strategies. Similarly, Anderson (2008) introduced the concept of rights-based food systems and their connection with more localized and sustainable agroecological systems that contribute to awareness of the environmental and social costs of current food systems practices.

Block et al. (2008) advanced the concept of so-called value webs as integral to the development of local food systems. The term "value web" indicates that relationships between actors in the food system are multidirectional. The term and related perspective are the antithesis of "value chains" that provide a more unidirectional description of an operating food system. By illustrating case work in various areas of the United States, the authors highlight the following key characteristics: locally based, action-oriented, equity and social values, partnerships and trust relations between partners, engagement, and mutual cooperation. The authors further make a case for higher education-community partnerships where intended beneficiaries at the community level take on active roles instead of being mere recipients of knowledge that is passed on by an actor at a higher education level. This multisided approach to knowledge development in the food system and on behalf of community food and nutrition security can be seen in the recommendations of the IAASTD (2009) and other recent reports that promote the integration of local knowledge and more democratic participation in food policy, especially but not only at the community level.

Food Policy Councils

Food policy councils (FPCs) are a North American phenomenon of the last twenty years wherein neighborhood food initiatives cooperate with diverse civic actors to develop policies for just, healthy food systems that serve local communities through a synergy of social and economic development. FPCs convene citizens, CSOs, government officials, farmers, and other local private sector entrepreneurs for the purpose of providing a comprehensive examination of a state or local food system. This unique, non-partisan form of civic engagement brings together a diverse array of food system actors to develop food and agriculture policy recommendations (Clancy, Hammer, and Lippoldt 2007; Roberts 2010; Winne 2008).[47]

The first FPC started in 1982 in Knoxville, Tennessee, in the United States. The best known, however, might be the Toronto Food Policy Council (TFPC), Canada. The TFPC provided extensive documentation on its developmental experience that helped to replicate the model elsewhere.[48] The NGO Food First writes:

> [Food policy councils] often include anti-hunger and food justice advocates, educators, non-profit organizations, concerned citizens,

government officials, farmers, grocers, chefs, workers, food processors and food distributors. Food Policy Councils create an opportunity for discussion and strategy development among these various interests, and create an arena for studying the food system as a whole. Because they are often initiated by government actors, through executive orders, public acts or joint resolutions, Food Policy Councils tend to enjoy a formal relationship with local, city or state officials. (Harper et al. 2009, 2)

Members of FPCs review local and regional food issues, foster coordination between sectors in the food system, evaluate and influence policy, and launch or support programs and services that address local needs. Rural and urban communities alike build cohesive public policy through inclusive dialogue on food and nutrition issues (Thomson, Maretzki, and Harmon 2007).[49] The emphasis on inclusive and balanced participation of actors in local, regional, and community food systems suggests that FPCs may serve as a model for women's participation in food and nutrition security approaches generally, and also as a model of relevance for other world regions.

Food Justice

Food justice is an emerging new field that addresses inequalities embedded in food systems, considering the "production, distribution and consumption of food, and the ways that communities and social movements shape and are shaped by these inequalities" (Alkon 2012, 295). The food justice movement aims to create local food systems and green jobs in, for, and with marginalized communities, "exercising their right to grow, sell and eat food that is fresh, nutritious, affordable, culturally-appropriate and grown locally with care for the well-being of the land, workers and animals."[50] According to Alkon (2012, 295), food justice research could contribute to social change by responding to, building upon, and helping to inspire grassroots movements. In her overview, Alkon (2012) provides insights into the origins and contributions of this field that emerged out of environmental justice, critical race theory, sustainable agriculture, and food studies. Among the main contributions of food justice, as seen by Alkon (2012), is the fact that food justice research uncovers the unexamined race and class privileges within the sustainable agricultural movement—with mostly white and middle class people being able to build alternative and self-sufficient food systems—thus perpetuating institutionalized racism within the agricultural sector (Alkon 2012, 298). Amid the gaps and limitations are that within the food justice movement family farms and unprocessed food are idealized, neglecting a focus on those who work on farms and in the food industry and not addressing the exploitative power of industrial agriculture (Alkon 2012, 300–301). Further, there is a huge rift with regard to addressing gender inequalities within food systems that needs urgent attention in future research (Alkon 2012, 300).

An initiative originating in the United Kingdom is the Food and Fairness Inquiry resulting in the report entitled *Food Justice: The Report of the Food and Fairness Inquiry* (Food Ethics Council 2010). Apart from revealing the extent of social injustice in the food system within the United Kingdom and at the global level, the report seeks to make recommendations how this can be addressed by pointing to the responsibilities at the levels of government, business, and civil society. According to this report, the food system in the United Kingdom faces three major challenges: (*a*) to ensure food security, domestically and globally, (*b*) to make production and consumption of food environmentally sustainable, and (*c*) to promote public health through food policy. The authors of the report argue that the food policy debate focuses on economic and environmental issues, whereas considerations of fairness and social justice are peripheral, impeding progress toward sustainable food and farming. The ethical framework suggested by the report considers three perspectives on social justice for each of the challenges mentioned above: "fair shares" or equality of outcome, "fair play" or equality of opportunity, and "fair say" or autonomy and voice (Food Ethics Council 2010, 11). The following key messages are outlined by this report to guide the future debate about food policy in order to move toward a more socially just food system (Food Ethics Council 2010, 18):

- Food policy is central to meeting recognized ecological sustainability challenges.
- Social justice issues around food are at the heart of recognized environmental and health challenges.
- Addressing food-related social injustice mainly requires wider social and economic policy solutions.
- Social justice does not mean treating everyone the same.
- We need to find ways to engage people and society as a whole with food policy.
- To enable people to change their behavior, we need to address the inequalities that underpin their behavior.
- "Cheap food" is no longer a legitimate social policy objective.
- The market, including the financial market, has to work differently.
- There are limits to what can be achieved through market mechanisms, so we need government leadership.
- The current international trade regime presents significant obstacles to addressing social injustice in food and farming.
- All actors face limits to what they can achieve themselves but, for their commitment to social justice to be credible, they must openly support whatever measures are necessary, even if they are beyond their own capacity.

These key messages are in line with a human rights framework, emphasizing respect for the right to produce, obtain, and consume food in ways that uphold human dignity. Further, this initiative calls for socially and environmentally sustainable ways of obtaining healthy food through purchase, production, and earning, and for sustainable ways and means of researching, producing, and distributing food, grounded in just, equitable, moral, and ethical social values.

Agroecology and Organic Agriculture

In most developing countries, smallholders perform "de facto organic farming" or "organic farming by default," meaning that they do not use synthetic agriculture inputs or soil building practices because of reliance on traditional ways of farming (Scialabba 2000). This preserves the soil, water reserves, and biodiversity and thus provides sustainable and environmentally sound strategies for farming (Gliessman 2007; Vandemeer 2011). Women smallholders often apply traditional farming methods and agroecological principles that are largely neglected in so-called modern commercial farming (Schäfer 2012). In developing countries, agroecology can provide a strategy for resource poor farmers, especially for the women among them, for enhancing food security and livelihoods in a sustainable way (Hine, Pretty, and Twarog 2008). As the former UN special rapporteur on the right to food, Olivier De Schutter, highlights, "agro-ecology can benefit women most, because it is they who encounter most difficulties in accessing external inputs or subsidies" (HRC 2010, 19). The definition of organic agriculture according to the International Federation of Organic Agriculture Movement (IFOAM) in principle could apply also to agroecology.[51] However, organic agriculture is closely connected with certification and increasingly relates to large-scale conventional and export-oriented farming, while agroecology has been closely related to local agricultural systems. According to Scialabba (2000, 13), "[t]he focus on certified organic products (and attendant costs and risks) has distracted attention on this system's potential to contribute to local food security, especially in low-potential areas in developing countries. Market driven organic agricultural policies need to be complemented with organic agriculture policies that target local food security." The potential of organic or agroecological farming methods for improved food security has also been highlighted by the IAASTD report (IAASTD 2009). As recent findings show, based on empirical evidence, agroecology in the medium or longer term can provide even larger agricultural outputs than conventional agriculture (Pretty et al. 2006; Pretty, Toulmin, and Williams 2011). Through support of smallholder agriculture, previous knowledge systems of agroecological production and traditional means of sustainable livelihoods could be revived.

However, in a recent article by Levidow, Pimbert, and Vanloqueren (2014), it was acknowledged that although agroecology does provide an alternative to the dominant food system, it has lately been embraced by those who advocate the conventional agricultural system. Therefore, agroecology can be seen to either "conform to" or "transform" mainstream methods. As the authors argue, to avoid conformity, it is important that scientists collaborate with farmers and that there is an exchange of knowledge between the two as opposed to a linear transfer from former to latter.

Sustainable Diets

The concept "sustainable diets" had first been introduced in the 1980s, based on the realization that the health of humans and the health of ecosystems are inextricably linked (Gussow and Clancy 1986). Unfortunately, this approach was neglected in the decades to come due to the primary focus on increased food production in order to address world hunger (Burlingame 2012, 7). Only recently has there been a shift in the scientific and political debate on food security, as was outlined in earlier sections of this chapter. The former focus on production and availability of food was extended to issues such as more equitable access to food and adequacy of diets and linked to other societal challenges like health, gender equality, access to productive resources, and environmental protection (Wilkins 2007). According to the former UN special rapporteur on the right to food, Olivier De Schutter (HRC 2011), existing food systems have not only failed to address hunger but at the same time encouraged diets that are a source of overweight and obesity, leading to even more deaths worldwide than does underweight. De Schutter calls for a transition toward sustainable diets that will succeed only "by supporting diverse farming systems that ensure that adequate diets are accessible to all, that simultaneously support the livelihoods of poor farmers and that are ecologically sustainable" (HRC 2011, 1).

The term "diet," which stems from the Greek word *diaita* and goes back to Hippocrates (400 BC), means "order" or "way of living" (Jouanna 2012). The concept was initially understood as a model for a healthy way of life, with nutrition being one of several key elements (Jouanna 2012, 139). The term "diet," therefore, represented a holistic concept different from how it is being used nowadays, that is, limited to specific nutritional requirements or weight reduction. The concept "sustainable diets" was only revived on a larger scale at the International Scientific Symposium Biodiversity and Sustainable Diets: United against Hunger held in Rome in November 2010 and organized by FAO and Bioversity International. Findings of this conference were published two years later (Burlingame and Dernini 2012). Sustainable diets are defined as follows: "diets with low environmental impacts which contribute to food and nutrition security and to healthy life for present and future generations. Sustainable diets are protective and respectful of biodiversity and ecosystems, culturally acceptable, accessible, economically fair and affordable; nutritionally adequate, safe and healthy; while optimizing natural and human resources" (Burlingame 2012, 7). This extended definition implies a strong participation of different actors within the agrofood system in the preservation of existing sustainable diets and in the transformation of unsustainable, insufficient, or even harmful diets to sustainable ones. A mere increase of food production by increasing, for example, smallholder farmers' inputs is not an option in this context.

As Tim Lang stated in his keynote speech at the above FAO/Bioversity International scientific symposium, it is critical to clearly define sustainable diets through scientific and public discourse. Lang emphasizes that, besides the core elements of the concept "sustainability," entailing environmental, economic, and social aspects,[52] policy attention needs to be placed on quality of food, health, and governance, resulting in a six-headed approach (Lang 2012, 22).

In his report on the current agrofood system and sustainable diets, De Schutter (HRC 2011, 1) further makes specific reference to women as the principal caregivers of young children, emphasizing that women must be able to make informed and autonomous decisions about food and feeding, to ensure adequate growth, health, and development of their children.

DEMOCRATIC PARTICIPATION, GOVERNANCE, AND MOBILIZATION FROM CIVIL SOCIETY TOWARD MORE EQUITABLE FOOD SYSTEMS

The growing attention to a human right to adequate food and nutrition approach has moved the discussion about food and nutrition security to individuals' and groups' capacity to engage in a public dialogue around the definition of what constitutes "security" and how states can meet their obligations to realize that security progressively. The former UN special rapporteur on the right to food, Olivier De Schutter, has pressed for attention both to the rights and voices of small farmers, highlighting that the women among them deserve specific attention due to their contributions to the food and agricultural sector, and to agroecological approaches employed particularly by women to achieve food and nutrition security (HRC 2010). De Schutter's focus links production and food security locally and centers women as well as men in the governance of local food and nutrition systems.

Challenges for Developing Local Food Systems and Rural Agriculture-Based Livelihoods

Developing local food systems faces multiple challenges. Rural people and food producers across the urban-rural expanse, and women as a particularly marginalized and violated against population among them, are often disconnected and alienated from the tools and traditions that might develop prosperous local food systems. For example, in South Africa the capacity of rural households to contribute to local economic development has been questioned, especially as some of that population has moved away from agricultural production and embraced various other livelihood strategies (Bank 2005). Insecure land tenure and land rights, rising land costs, and the displacement of rural persons and groups by powerful interest groups through the recent phenomenon known as landgrabbing contribute to a rejection of rural agricultural livelihoods. Concentrated land ownership and control, and with it the means to produce and employ as collateral, is held not only by the rich in general but by men in general. Girls' more limited access to education results in knowledge and traditions of training being more available to men than women. As was outlined in chapter 4 of this volume, crude or uneven access to health care and choices in the reproductive cycle—from autonomy in marriage decisions to control over fertility—impair girls' and women's health and productivity, impacting also on agricultural production.

Not all rural people are able to or want to engage in agricultural production, whether to produce food for their own consumption, to gain an extra income, or as their main source of livelihood. Sometimes people have a desire and a need to gain access to land not with the purpose of agricultural production but to use it for multiple other purposes, as the following case study illustrates.

Case study 5.10 South Africa: the historical legacy and negative perceptions regarding land and farming

Smallholder agriculture in South Africa faces multiple challenges due to historical injustices regarding access to land and resources and to post-apartheid policies that failed to promote rural development. Beginning over one hundred years ago, discriminatory policies uprooted black South Africans from the natural resource base forming their livelihoods. Public policy forced former sharecroppers into rural farm wage labor, preventing the farmworkers from migrating to urban areas or seeking non-rural, off farm employment.[53] These policies largely destroyed the tradition of subsistence farming and resulted in farmworkers and their families being trapped on commercial farms without possibilities for advancement or skills to be involved in the wider economy. Further, the race-based system of paternalism continues today to perpetuate the hierarchical structure that separates commercial farm owners and farmworkers in isolated rural territories. Despite of, or because of the distorted power dynamics, farm owners often constitute the backbone of farm labor's social security mechanisms, from the availability of rudimentary schools to transportation and basic off farm communications. Laws implemented by the South African government that were aimed at protecting and strengthening farmworkers' rights often left farmworkers with even less security than before the formal end of apartheid. As documented by Atkinson (2007), Wegerif, Russel, and Grundling (2005), and Lemke and Jansen van Rensburg (2014), the 1997 implementation of minimum wages in the farming sector had detrimental effects on farmworkers' available benefits and resources as a number of farm owners reacted by diminishing what assistance had been provided and leading to farmworkers evictions. Today, farmworkers belong to the most marginalized social groups and continue to face poverty as well as income and residential insecurity.[54]

Enduring forced agricultural labor with limited alternatives to farm work for basic survival has led, not surprisingly, to some degree of alienation from rural land-based livelihoods. This phenomenon might be even greater among women than among men, with women facing particular discrimination as seasonal or temporary workers, often without a formal contract, receiving lower salaries and being more vulnerable to exploitation because they have even fewer employment alternatives.

Building alternative local food systems in the hopes of achieving greater social equity as opposed to the hierarchy and paternalism found in many commercial and industrial farms requires knowledge, resources, and a commitment to rural livelihoods. In the context of race and economic inequality in industrial agriculture, the challenges have not been thoroughly examined by local food system proponents (Alkon 2012, 300–301). Case study research on black South African smallholders in the Limpopo region north of Johannesburg revealed difficulties in accessing markets due to lack of financial and technical support, lack of consistent production, lack of quality standards, and lack of knowledge on how to approach and access new markets. Significantly, land use was also not restricted to agricultural purposes. More often than a desire to develop autonomous farming ventures, researchers found a demand for rural land to serve residential objectives, to regain access to ancestral land and graves, and to restore land justice.[55] These observations are also confirmed by Ntsebeza and Hall (2007).

Global Challenges and the Need for Mobilization from Civil Society toward More Equitable Food Systems

Community and local food and nutrition systems are not independent from food trade, policy, and traditions at the national, regional, and global scales. Understanding any part of the larger and integrated system requires analysis of how the different scales fit together and affect each other. The recent and still ongoing food crisis highlights yet again how intertwined the respective levels are and how severely an international crisis can exacerbate existing hunger and poverty of marginalized populations at the local level. Schuftan (2010) points to root causes of the global food crisis, including (*a*) food price inflation (not food shortages) caused, among other factors, by the protectionist strategy imposed in Europe and the United States and related subsidy payments to agribusiness corporations, (*b*) the emergence of a middle class in India and China that resulted in changing diets, especially increased meat consumption, (*c*) the increase of oil prices, (*d*) the growing demand for agrofuel, (*e*) water scarcity, (*f*) loss of arable land, and (*g*) speculation in food markets (Schuftan 2010, 18). Godfray et al. (2010) highlight similar causes for rising food prices and call for multifaceted and linked global strategies to ensure sustainable and equitable food security. As Lahiff (2008a) states, the recent dramatic rise in food prices serves as a rude reminder of local dependency on dominant global agribusinesses for staple food needs, demonstrating that an alternative vision of diverse agricultural production and more resilient, less costly, and more environmentally sustainable options urgently needs to be developed.

Today, calls for good governance and accountability of both recipients of aid as well as donors are common. Terms like "development industry" and "job creation for the North" have been introduced, questioning the approach of development aid and highlighting the often concurrent loss of local and national self-determination.[56] Several authors call for alternatives to previous development approaches, all of them highlighting the crucial and still neglected role of women for the reduction of poverty and sustainable livelihoods (Calderisi 2007; Mills 2010; Seitz 2010). It has to be recognized, however, that a change of previous development approaches will also entail a shift in power dynamics and a possible economic loss of certain industries that have so far benefited from paternalistic and charity approaches. As Schuftan (2010, 21) frames it: "Only strong popular pressure will enable the changes needed to eradicate hunger, malnutrition and poverty. Growing mobilization efforts and strong pressure from civil society, including labour unions, farmer and fisherfolk organizations, indigenous people, and women, as well as other broad-based social movements, are indispensable for changing the prevailing power structures and policies that dominate today's decision-making." While civil society engagement is crucial in order to tackle prevailing structures, it has to be acknowledged that civil society does not have one uniform view on how to respond to current development approaches and, therefore, efforts to jointly discuss and identify the issues and common struggles and to bridge the various perspectives and groups will be necessary. Prime examples of such engagement and discourse include the food sovereignty movement and related conferences,[57] and current activities concerned with the worldwide peasant movements like the seminar Human Rights Compliant and Sustainable Food Systems organized by FIAN International in June 2014 in Geneva.[58]

The CFS lays out such processes and provides room for global governance structures that include the participation of civil society and social movements as well as the private sector. In the thirty-fifth session held in October 2009, the members of the CFS agreed to a wide-ranging reform that aimed to make the CFS the foremost inclusive international and intergovernmental platform dealing with food security and nutrition and to be a central component in the evolving Global Partnership for Agriculture, Food Security and Nutrition (FAO 2009).[59]

Case study 5.11 **Application of the human rights framework by grassroots and social movements in the agrarian sector**

Several examples of how grassroots and social movements implement the human rights approach in agrarian struggles are documented by Monsalve Suárez (2012). Her reporting features representatives of grassroots and social movements working in diverse countries (e.g., Uganda, Honduras, Ghana, and Italy) at multiple local, national, and international levels. Monsalve Suárez (2012) provides in-depth analysis into how these groups apply the human rights framework, with all contributions critically reflecting upon the impact and limitations that the application of a human rights framework has had for the advancement of rural peoples. In the case of Uganda, an indigenous community had been violently evicted from their land without receiving compensation. As an alternative strategy of resistance, the community chose to employ a human rights framework to advocate for redress and restitution of the right of tenure on their land rather than to engage in violent protest or armed struggle. This included an advocacy campaign that has moved from the local to the international level and that has helped to make their case heard. Further, a civil suit against the government and a foreign investor has been filed. According to the leader of this grassroots movement, Peter Baleke Kayiira (quoted in Monsalve Suárez 2012), applying a human rights framework has been a peaceful, democratic, and people-centered process that has helped to build confidence among the community, to find allies, and to spread the campaign, making the community stronger. On the other hand, Kayiira states that among the biggest limitations of the human rights framework is the fact that the local constituent rights holders are not aware of their rights due to illiteracy, lack of information, and poverty, resulting in apathy and dependency on the powerful. Also, this approach is largely dependent on the political situation of a country and might not be successful in dictatorial or pseudodemocratic regimes. Resisting oppression and injustice often leads to detention and other conse-quences that can severely impact the socioeconomic situation of the rights claimants and the community. Slow government response to the redress and restitution demands is another limitation, requiring perseverance (Monsalve Suárez 2012, 15–20). As is concluded by the leader of this movement, despite all of these limitations, "the rights-based approach is an option to influence change in a peaceful and civilized manner. Furthermore the success of an oppressed group in one corner of the world can be shared to command the success of another oppressed group in another corner of the world" (Peter Baleke Kayiira, quoted in Monsalve Suárez 2012, 20).

In another account from Monsalve Suárez' (2012) collection from grassroots movements, the Honduran journalist Sandra Maribel Sán-chez documents how poor landless women who are single mothers have applied a human rights framework to reclaim a piece of state land through claims of violations of their right to adequate food and nutri-tion. This case illustrates how the human rights framework served to support marginalized rural women in their struggle for emancipation, both with regard to the state and also vis-à-vis male-dominated peas-ant organizations.[60]

Case study 5.12 FAO *Right to Food Guidelines* and application by civil society

The FAO *Voluntary Guidelines to Support the Progressive Realiza-tion of the Right to Adequate Food in the Context of National Food Security* (2005; hereinafter known as *Right to Food Guidelines*) was designed to support the national implementation of the right to ade-quate food and nutrition through the development of methods and instruments to assist states parties and other actors in establishing food security baselines and measuring progress (or lack thereof) by the state in meeting its treaty obligations for the right to adequate food and nutrition (see also chapter 1 of this volume). By referring to "stakeholders" (plural), the *Right to Food Guidelines* addresses and invites civil society and, for that matter, the private sector to par-ticipate democratically in the governance processes of assessing state progress and making recommendations for change. The 2005 FAO text includes nineteen elaborated guidelines for evaluating national state progress on the right to adequate food and nutrition. Several of these guidelines make specific references to gender, women, and promoting participation in the context of self-determination, human dignity, and freedom, for example:

- Women's involvement and participation in programs for poverty reduction and nutrition (guideline 7.4)
- Highlighting the benefits of local food production on women's incomes (guideline 8.4)
- Promoting women's full and equal participation in the economy and promoting gender sensitive legislation with regard to access to land, property, and other productive resources (credit, land, water, technology, etc.) (guideline 8.6)
- In case food assistance is needed, highlighting women's access to it as a way to enhance their decision-making power and to ensure that food is used to meet food requirements of all household members (guideline 13.4).

With support from and in collaboration with the German development organization Welthungerhilfe, the NGO FIAN International published the workbook *Screen State Action Against Hunger! How to Use the Voluntary Guidelines on the Right to Food to Monitor Public Policy* (Suárez Franco and Ratjen 2007). As stated in the title, FIAN International's publication encourages CSOs to frame their specific issues in human rights terms (i.e., as human rights violations wherein the national state has not respected, protected, or fulfilled people's rights as iterated among the nineteen guidelines in the *Right to Food Guidelines*; Suárez Franco and Ratjen 2007, 16–18). Under guideline number 10, "Nutrition," for example, a question to test is: "Do State policies include programmes or projects aimed at confronting the different nutritional problems of the various social groups?" (Suárez Franco and Ratjen 2007, 39). FIAN International then proposes the following approaches that a CSO might find relevant to its own situation:

- Are there special programs to detect the nutritional problems of the most vulnerable groups and the causes of these problems?
- Are there information systems that register disaggregated data, thus providing the responsible authorities with an overview of the nutritional problems of the different population groups and regions?
- Are programs being carried out to solve the causes of inadequate nutrition among the most vulnerable groups?

Democratizing food and nutrition systems requires participation by all, most especially those traditionally and particularly marginalized, such as women, in food and nutrition governance systems with the objective of building empowered self-determination.

Social Protection: State's Obligations to Fulfill the Right to Adequate Food and Nutrition

Throughout this chapter we emphasize that the ultimate goal of food and nutrition security policies and programs is to achieve increased autonomy, strengthen self-reliance, and improve access to resources for the poor. It must be recognized, however, that people who have limited self-help capacity might not be reached. As was illustrated in previous sections of this chapter on food justice research and challenges for developing local food systems and rural agriculture-based livelihoods, we cannot limit the discussion to building local and sustainable food systems. Large sections of the society have either no or limited access to such initiatives, due to various reasons. Social protection for those who are marginalized, therefore, remains necessary. This does not, however, conflict with the application of a human rights framework that strives for local solutions and local governance, as long as social security programs are integrated into and aimed at strengthening local economies. This would have the added benefit of achieving more sustainable impacts instead of short term solutions.

According to De Schutter (2009) writing in the context of the 2008 global food crisis when food prices were increasing and people were not able to afford food, social protection programs, for example in the form of food vouchers, cash transfers, or employment guarantees, could have eased the situation. As De Schutter elaborates in his 2012 report to the UN Human Rights Council (HRC) *Women's Right and the Right to Food*, "[t]he right to social security as guaranteed under the International Covenant on Economic, Social and Cultural Rights, includes access to health care; benefits and services to persons without work-related income due to sickness, disability, maternity, employment injury, unemployment, old age or death of a family member, including contributory or non-contributory pensions for all older persons; family and child support sufficient to cover food, clothing, housing, water and sanitation; survivor and orphan benefits" (HRC 2012, 10).

De Schutter (HRC 2012) further highlights the specific situation of women, noting that they are often not considered in the design and implementation of social protection programs. Such programs may also reinforce gender stereotyped roles if women's identity in need is limited to "mothers" and "caregivers."[61]

Further, currently not enough importance is given to the recognition, reduction, and redistribution of women's unpaid care work. Unpaid care, which is for the most part invisible within development policy, refers to "meeting the material and/or developmental and emotional needs of one or more other people through a direct relationship" (IDS 2013, 1). The former UN special rapporteur on extreme poverty and human rights, Magdalena Sepúlveda Carmona, states that unequal care obligations are a considerable hindrance to gender inequality and, consequentially, often subject women to a life of poverty (UN General Assembly, 2013). Sepúlveda Carmona concludes that state policies should be introduced that classify care as a responsibility of the collective, not the individual.

Another barrier to women's participation in some social protection programs are the cultural norms that limit their mobility, for example, making it impossible for them to leave the house (for meetings, trainings, etc.), as is often part of compliance with the conditionalities of these programs.

Social protection programs, as necessary for situations wherein not everyone can afford adequate food for a healthy life, can also help stimulate local food and nutrition economies if properly designed (Godfray et al. 2010). The following case study illustrates the example of how the Programa Nacional de Alimentação Escolar (National School Feeding Program) in Brazil is linked to food purchasing from smallholder and traditionally marginalized farmers (e.g., indigenous and *Quilombola*), thereby increasing demand for their products and reducing normal farmer risks.[62]

Case study 5.13 Brazil: the National School Feeding Program

The case of the National School Feeding Program in Brazil provides an example of how social protection programs can be translated into practice through participation of civil society in the monitoring of the program implementation and linking access to food with the promotion of local food production networks. According to the 2009 legal framework of this program, 30 percent of the food products used for school feeding should be supplied either by local farmers, indigenous and/or *Quilombola* organizations, or agrarian reform settlements; all entities that had historically been economically marginalized and specifically excluded from public procurement for school feeding.[63] The program seeks further to include small-scale farmers in local school feeding councils, magnifying the program benefits to democratizing the development of local food and nutrition policy, promoting local production and consumption, respecting regional eating habits, and generating jobs and income. The program also prioritizes organic and agroecological models of food production, which is in line with the right to adequate food and nutrition and a sustainable global food system as recommended by De Schutter (HRC 2009).

There is one particular drawback: namely, that female farmers and their participation in local food production are not specifically mentioned in the National School Feeding Program. In fact Brazil has a separate non-school feeding-related program that promotes women farmers. Unfortunately, as of this writing, they are not linked. A gender differentiated analysis of progress on the existing National School Feeding Program could provide insights into whether female farmers are reached and, if not, what the barriers are that prevent their inclusion in the National School Feeding Program.[64]

A PhD thesis investigated the realization and perception of the human right to adequate food and nutrition within the school feeding program in *Quilombola* communities. Findings reveal both that a violation of the right to adequate food and nutrition was made by the regional judiciary branch which led to a lack of food in the school and that duty bearers and operators of recourse mechanisms dealt with the violation inadequately in part because they did not understand their roles and obligations under national and international laws pertaining to the right to adequate food and nutrition. Dissemination of information on rights, available recourse mechanisms, and duty bearers' related obligations are critical for the enforceability of the right to adequate food and nutrition. Addressing dissemination of same was a primary recommendation of this part of the study (Viana and Bellows 2014). This study provides further insights into whether and how the National School Feeding Program can be implemented into practice to realize progressively the right to adequate food and nutrition and what are its achievements, challenges, and limitations.

Case study 5.14 South Africa: social protection gaps in the agricultural sector?

Another example where social protection is urgently required is the previously mentioned case of South African farmworkers. Despite recently implemented laws that were aimed at protecting and strengthening their rights, the outcome was often unintended detrimental effects and farmworkers left with even less security. Farmworkers are, in most cases, not in a position to claim their rights due to weak organization and a lack of unions, their remote and isolated setting, and a lack of education and access to information (Lemke and Jansen van Rensburg 2014; see also Devereux and Solomon 2011; Human Rights Watch 2011). Here, the state is called upon to provide protective social measures, the focus of which cannot be limited to working conditions and labor issues. Social protection for rural farmworkers must be expanded to include adequate housing, health care, transportation, and communication, as well as other services that are usually inadequate on commercial farms.[65]

Strengthening Women as Actors

To mobilize women as actors in the governance of food systems, a transformation is urgently needed in research and programming that will strengthen resources and coping strategies available to women. As Schäfer (2012) argues, such an effort requires micro-level, in-depth research at community and household levels to provide insight into the conditions necessary for stability and success in women's livelihoods. As has been highlighted in the section of this chapter entitled "The need for a systems approach and gender perspective for addressing the right to adequate food and nutrition," methodologies as they are still often used to date do not capture and analyze the challenges faced and the strategies and capabilities employed by women—especially poor women—and, therefore, provide no reporting that might leverage policy and programs to improve women's and their families' food and nutrition security status. The fact that women are able to mobilize various economic and social resources and actively participate in processes of social transformation needs to be better recognized, as has, for example, been shown by Guyer (1991). Schäfer (2012) further points to the great value of interdisciplinary networks, especially among female researchers in Southern Africa. These networks, which are characterized by strong practical application and policy orientation, could provide important starting points for a reorientation of research programs. In this regard, as we argue throughout this volume, research approaches that recognize marginalized people as actors and rights holders instead of passive beneficiaries, in line with a human rights framework, can contribute considerably to this pressing need for change in research methods. Such a shift will take time and must engage inclusive approaches that involve local institutions, the community, and importantly, male community members instead of focusing on women alone to overcome the multiple barriers that especially women experience when attempting to claim and achieve their rights.

The following set of case studies, supported through the Dutch Government's MDG3 Fund: Investing in Equality (hereinafter, MDG3 Fund), illustrates initiatives that work toward ending social discrimination and rights injustices toward women and demonstrate how they can induce changes in women's lives and their communities.[66]

Case study 5.15 Using law for rural women's empowerment in West Africa: Women in Law and Development in Africa (WiLDAF)[67]

Rural women in West Africa, especially those with limited formal educational experience, are often not well-informed about their legal rights and about how to purchase or lease land in an economic and social environment that is often dominated by men. Studies revealed that women mostly enter into oral land transactions and fail to register their land. Most women do not inherit land but gain access via marriage. Additionally, violence against women by in-laws is a barrier for women to take up their rights. In West Africa, the organization Women in Law and Development in Africa (WiLDAF) is reaching out to women farmers to educate them about their rights. Rural women are assisted in cases of violence and family disputes that research shows are often related to inheritance issues. WiLDAF also works with local authorities toward allocating land to rural women so that they can gain full ownership. To ensure that there is a working legal framework to promote gender equal access to land, WiLDAF undertakes legal education to support the ratification and implementation of the *Protocol to the African Charter on Human and Peoples' Rights on the Rights of Women in Africa* (ACHPR 2003). Through support of the MDG3 Fund, WiLDAF is training 250 women in farmers' organizations in five West African countries (i.e., Benin, Burkina Faso, Côte d'Ivoire, Ghana, and Togo) on how to change gender inequalities, particularly on issues of land inheritance and access to resources and economic opportunities. This includes training of paralegals to work with women farmers to understand the law. WiLDAF aims to involve communities and to include men in the fight to end violence.

Case study 5.16 Mobilizing poor working women for economic equality: Women in Informal Employment Globalization and Organizing (WIEGO)[68]

Women in Informal Employment Globalization and Organizing (WIEGO) does not see women as an investment, as is being promoted by the World Bank, but regards women as the backbone of the so-called informal work force that sustains the livelihoods of millions of poor families and communities. WIEGO aims to support poor women by ensuring that they are informed and can thus mobilize around their human rights to security, safety, and fair incomes. Through the MDG3 Fund, WIEGO was able to assist women informal workers in Asia, Africa, Latin America and the Caribbean, and Central and Eastern Europe, applying a human rights framework and holistic approach to economic equality projects that involve domestic workers, street vendors, waste pickers, construction workers, garment workers, smallholder farmers, and transport workers. Women working in these sectors often receive little social or legal recognition and are among those hit hardest by economic crises. The long-term vision of WIEGO is to achieve democratic organizations in all sectors of the informal economy and, through these organizations, to ensure women acquire visibility, voice, and power. According to WIEGO, policy and donors need to listen and learn from women's informal organizations if appropriate policy agendas are to be set. One example of success in 2010 and 2011 was that domestic workers were supported to form their own network and social mobilizations by providing technical support, strategic advice, research, capacity building, and fundraising assistance. This enabled domestic workers to represent themselves in policy fora and to fight for their rights toward decent working conditions.

Case study 5.17 Building feminist democracy in Mesoamerica: Just Associates (JASS)[69]

Just Associates (JASS) works globally to strengthen women's voice, visibility, and collective organizing power. They do so by supporting women to take leadership roles to fight for their rights, whether working toward economic democracy or fighting gender-based violence (GBV) or political repression. It is crucial for this work to build cross-national alliances and to make known GBV. The MDG3 Fund supports the work of JASS to strengthen the participation of marginalized women in three regions and twenty-four countries. In Mesoamerica (i.e., Costa Rica, El Salvador, Guatemala, Honduras, Mexico, Nicaragua, and Panama), for example, JASS has worked with the support of the MDG3 Fund and other strategic alliances to offer capacity-building programs and networking, solidarity outreach through immediate responses to emergency situations and longer term support, and consciousness raising through radio and online social media. For instance, the feminist political program, Observatorio/Women Crossing the Line, is working with Feminist

International Radio Endeavor (FIRE) to reinforce women's transformative roles and local actions in struggles across Mesoamerica. This is supported through the newsletter and radio program "La Petatera" to ensure that, through radio and social networks, women's voices are heard across countries. A key objective of these activities is to identify, bear witness to, and stop diverse kinds of violence against women from domestic, to workplace, to the multiple threats faced by women human rights defenders. JASS promotes connections among grassroots and local-to-global organizations, among these the Nobel Women's Initiative, that respond to women's demands for the immediate cessation of violence against them.

The Masculinity Crisis and the Need to Integrate Men

If women's social and economic positions change, the consequence is that this will also affect men's position and their self-image. On the one hand, if women take on a more prominent position within the household as a result of pursuing an education, earning an income, or gaining access to resources, this can lead to increased decision-making power and to a reduction of domestic violence (Kabeer 2001, 2005a). On the other hand, increased economic independence of women may have the unintended effect that their male partners or other male household members perceive this as a threat to their masculinity with the consequence that women's greater economic independence has sometimes led to GBV.[70] This has, for example, been documented by the NGO Brot für die Welt (Bread for the World) in their case studies of good practices in gender mainstreaming (Brot für die Welt 2009), and also by a recent report on analyzing gender roles in forest management (Colfer 2013).

In South Africa, the alarmingly high incidence of violence against women, both outside and inside their homes, is seen as a result of a patriarchal society and was explained by Bank (1994) as indicative of a crisis of African masculinity. As was pointed out earlier in this chapter, socially marginalized men, especially younger men, may resort to violence due to their experience of male hierarchies, exploitation, and violence. Schäfer (2012) argues that men have to be integrated much more strongly into transformative economic and social processes. The reason that this is often not pursued is that many traditional societies do not recognize shifts in male self-image or traditional roles. In academic circles, masculinity research has been largely neglected and is only slowly being accepted. This reinforces the status quo of many (male) development and agricultural experts focusing primarily on feasibility and technical solutions and having no training in assessing the role of men (including themselves) in perpetuating male control over social, political, and economic resources (Schäfer 2012, xi).

Case study 5.18 Men speak out against violence against women

A national initiative that aims specifically to address men is the South African NGO Sonke Gender Justice Network.[71] Founded in 2006 by two men who had been activists in the antiapartheid struggle, the Sonke Gender Justice Network speaks out against all forms of violence against women. The goal of this initiative is to reinstate healthy social structures by promoting the need for positive male role models and establishing partnerships between men and women that are based on mutual respect and equality. The Sonke Gender Justice Network works across Africa and has linked up with the international movement MenEngage.

MenEngage was founded in 2004 and is a global alliance of more than four hundred NGOs from sub-Saharan Africa, Latin America and the Caribbean, North America, Asia, and Europe, as well as UN agencies that seek to engage boys and men to achieve gender equality. MenEngage promotes public health and strategies to reduce violence at the global level and addresses the structural barriers to achieving gender equality.[72] MenEngage set out to work toward the fulfilment of the MDGs, with a particular focus on achieving gender equality (MDG 3). Among their activities are information sharing, joint training activities, and national, regional, and international advocacy campaigns. It is encouraging to see the rise of such men-initiated movements as this compounds the message of existing women-led movements and increases the likelihood that the movements' antiviolence message will be heard.

More such initiatives are urgently needed to address underlying causes of GBV and to change perceptions in society at large. Nevertheless, this will require time (Ichaporia and Lawes 2013). Traumatized women still have minimal and yet slowly increasing infrastructure to protect them when reporting attacks. The media are increasingly willing to report such cases, although they too often sensationalize rape instead of imbuing an abomination of the crime. One horrific rape case that had led to the death of a young Indian woman mobilized grassroots support and ignited the global campaign One Billion Rising (OBR; Smallhorne 2013, 37). As several activists and academics express in Smallhorne's *Mail & Guardian* article, campaigns such as OBR can raise awareness and mobilize broader participation of citizens who are already committed to ending GBV, but these campaigns need to be supported by local and national government initiatives and flanked by measures that are embedded in long-term educational strategies, starting from an early age and teaching children about gender equality. Smallhorne

(2013, 37) suggests that acceptance of GBV is learned and compares it to the acceptance of slavery as a normal and, indeed, crucial pillar of many European economies until the nineteenth century: "Violence against women is another ancient, entrenched practice . . . ardent, consistent, stubborn and organized campaigning pushed society to a cusp. Suddenly it was acceptable, even fashionable, for people to support abolition [of slavery]." Similarly, sanctioned and ignored violence against women is a learned social construction that can and must be unlearned.

Another recent global campaign that publicly raised awareness of gender-based discrimination was the social movement Kurdish Men for Gender Equality.[73] An Iranian court punished a man by making him wear traditional Kurdish women's clothes in public, perceiving it as a degradation to a man to be displayed as a woman. To protest against this form of discrimination, Kurdish men dressed in women's clothes and posted their photos on Facebook, making strong statements against patriarchy. This movement received solidarity from women and men in other parts of Kurdistan, Europe, and the United States.[74] What was especially inspiring about this movement was that men started it. As a Kurdish woman, quoted in an article by Dilar Dirik published online in 2013 on the website of *The Kurdistan Tribune*, puts it: "This action is very meaningful and powerful, because it was started by men who stand up for women's rights. This illustrates that women's rights is a societal phenomenon that involves all of society, not just women. These men . . . don't just mentally stand up for women's rights, but do so literally in a physical sense . . . different population groups are active in demanding women's liberation; it is not just an issue that concerns intellectual elitist circles. Feminism can very well root in the broader community."[75]

Examples of Good Practice Integrating Both Men and Women into Rural Development Programs

Some development programs might reconsider focusing on women in isolation from men. Brot für die Welt (Bread for the World) provides cases of good practice in gender mainstreaming from four continents (Brot für die Welt 2009). These case studies especially highlight the inclusion of both women *and* men into such programs to be successful and sustainable. The following two case studies illustrate how gender sensitive development projects can work to the benefit of both men and women.

Case study 5.19 PROMESA: a promise for poor farmers and indigenous communities in Panama

PROMESA stands for Programa de Ministerio y Educación Social and means, literally translated, "promise." PROMESA sees gender equality as a condition for social justice and environmental sustainability. The organization, established in 1989 by the Episcopal Church of Panama, promotes sustainable farming, food security, and gender equality among Panama's peasant and indigenous communities. According to PROMESA, the fact that sustainable farming courses went beyond practical training was crucial to the success of the gender strategy. Training courses applied a "farmer-to-farmer" methodology that provides a space where social, economic, and environmental issues can be considered. A significant step was that masculinity workshops were held at PROMESA, carried out by the Costa Rican organization Instituto WEM—Instituto Costarricense para la Acción, Educación e Investigación de la Masculinidad, Pareja y Sexualidad (Costa Rican Institute for Action, Education and Research on Masculinity, Partnership and Sexuality) that offers these workshops throughout Central America. The workshops contributed to the examination and discussion of established male stereotypes in different areas of work and life and demonstrated to men that, by changing stereotypical roles, they could expect an easing of their own responsibilities and an improved quality of life. Despite challenges, many advances have been made. The report by Brot für die Welt (2009) describes, for example, how among farming groups the division of labor between women and men and the decision-making power within families have shifted, with women working in the fields and men also taking care of cooking and looking after children. Women further have gained self-confidence, whereas men have relinquished some of the burden of responsibility. Decision-making, both within the family and at the producer organization level, is based on more equal participation of men and women, thereby strengthening the community's social cohesion. Whereas both male and female farmers confirm that domestic and other violence against women remain a major problem at the local and national levels, there are no known cases of violence within the producer groups which could be due to their in-depth examination of gender roles and processes of social change.

Case study 5.20 Equipo Mujeres en Acción (EMAS):
a Mexican women's organization integrating men

The Equipo Mujeres en Acción Solidaria (EMAS; Team Women in Solidarity Action) is a women's organization in the state of Michoacán,

Mexico, that works on health, farming, and human rights. EMAS has developed two programs: "Sustainable Local Development with a Gender Perspective" and "Influencing Local Politics and Furthering the Exercise of Women's Political and Civil Rights." For EMAS, gender justice is a prerequisite for a functioning democracy. In order to facilitate gender equality, EMAS began its work in the area of sustainable farming and food sovereignty with a consistent focus on gender and by involving men as a target group in projects. In this case study, men and women discuss the existing balance and dynamic of power and speak out on topics such as domestic violence, the right of women to be masters of their own bodies, and fairer distribution of household tasks. Among the positive changes noted are that women have more self-confidence and are able to work as promoters within their communities and families, whereas men are more aware of the significant contribution made by women in the home and on the land through their increasing involvement in project work. There is an increasing involvement and interest among women and men in the development of and the decisions being made in their communities and towns. EMAS acknowledges, however, that a variety of factors have a negative effect on the implementation of the gender approach, among them machismo, social conservatism, poverty, and people's lack of trust in their own experience and local knowledge. In addition to these barriers, public politics show little concern either for the rural areas or for the implementation of a gender approach. Further, team members are influenced by traditional gender stereotypes and breaking away from these stereotypes, they report, poses the same challenges for them as for any other women and men (Brot für die Welt 2009).

INITIATIVES FOR MAINSTREAMING GENDER IN RIGHT TO ADEQUATE FOOD AND NUTRITION WORK

This section presents some recent initiatives and reports related to the concepts previously outlined in this chapter. The list is not meant to be inclusive but rather introductory.[76]

Center for Women's Global Leadership (CWGL)

Founded in 1989 and located in the School of Arts and Sciences at Rutgers University, the Center for Women's Global Leadership (CWGL) consists primarily of an academic center, but also functions as an NGO in consultative status with ECOSOC.[77] The center works globally to enhance and support women's leadership in regards to social justice and human rights by improving women's economic and social rights within a feminist context, advocating the eradication of GBV and ensuring policy reformation, both nationally and internationally, in regards to the global women's movement through coalition formation and capacity expansion. Its vision is of "a world in which all people are equal and gender equality is systemically realized by the achievement of human rights for all."[78]

In 2011, CWGL organized a two-day consultation on gender and the right to food, the main premise being to contribute to the work being conducted on gender equality by the former UN special rapporteur on the right to food, Olivier De Schutter (CWGL 2011). The central foci of this meeting were (*a*) economic policy conformity with right to food obligations through a feminist lens and (*b*) the relationship between regulatory objectives and human rights realization (CWGL 2011). The main topics discussed included the gendered dimensions of international trade and the right to food and gender equality in regards to fiscal policy, food prices, and financialization. In their recommendations to states, participants of this consultation highlighted (*a*) the need for trade policy to recognize the right to food and the rights of women, (*b*) the need for gender equality within fiscal policy design, subsidies and taxation, and entitlement programs, and (*c*) the importance of identifying gendered dimensions in terms of price volatility and food reserves (CWGL 2011).

Association for Women's Rights in Development (AWID)

The Association for Women's Rights in Development (AWID) began in 1982 as an international, feminist organization working to strengthen the influence of women's rights through capacity building, advocacy, knowledge creation, information sharing, and strategic alliances and meetings.[79] Via dynamic networks of women and men around the world, AWID seeks to achieve gender equality and sustainable development as well as effectively advance the rights of women. AWID consists of various members, among them researchers, academics, students, educators, activists, business people, policy makers, development practitioners, and funders. The mission of AWID is: "strengthening our collective voice, impact and influence to transform structures of power and decision-making and advance human rights, gender justice and environmental sustainability."[80]

Gender in Agriculture Sourcebook

The *Gender in Agriculture Sourcebook* (World Bank, FAO, and IFAD 2009) is a joint project of the World Bank, FAO, and IFAD. It is compiled by over one hundred experts from these organizations as well as external advisers and reviewers. The sourcebook provides a comprehensive overview of the crucial role gender equality plays for agricultural development, sustainable livelihoods, and the attainment of the MDGs. A holistic approach is applied, which is (*a*) attempting to bridge the gap between macro- and micro-level analysis, (*b*) placing emphasis on strengths and opportunities rather than on needs and weaknesses, and (*c*) paying attention to context specific circumstances and heterogeneity among the poor. The *Gender in Agriculture Sourcebook* adopts the SLA to explore sustainable livelihoods through a gender lens. Specific emphasis is placed on selected elements of the SLA, capturing gender inequalities within these areas and conceptualizing sustainable livelihoods as influenced by: (*a*) access to and control over assets, (*b*) access to markets, (*c*) access to information and organization, and (*d*) effective management of risk and vulnerability as well as by the interaction of these factors with policies and institutions at the global, national, and local levels (World Bank, FAO, and IFAD 2009, 4–6).

Landesa Center for Women's Land Rights

The organization Landesa Rural Development Institute (Landesa) launched the Center for Women's Land Rights in 2009 to address the challenges of women's unequal access to resources, especially land, and to unite the global community in support of women's land rights.[81] The center provides resources and training with regard to land rights for women. It further aims to (*a*) connect policymakers, researchers, and practitioners from around the world, (*b*) educate development experts about the gap between customary and institutional law to ensure that these issues are addressed in Landesa's projects, and (*c*) pilot innovative solutions to women's lack of secure land rights.

Inter Press Service (IPS) MDG3 Project "Communicating for Change: Voice, Visibility and Impact for Gender Equality"

The Inter Press Service (IPS) News Agency "is an international communication institution with a global news agency at its core, raising the voices of the South and civil society on issues of development, globalization, human rights and the environment."[82] Through its program IPS—Communicating MDG3, funded by the Dutch Government's MDG3 Fund and started in 2009, IPS seeks to promote the visibility and voice of women in the news through the application of a gender and human rights perspective. The publication "Communicating for Change: Voice, Visibility and Impact for Gender Equality—Summary and Highlights" (IPS—Communicating MDG3 2012) documents how IPS uses its media networks to reveal stories of women's struggles and empowerment. Case studies illustrate how the MDG3 Fund has helped women's organizations fight to overcome violence against women, gain political and economic independence, fight for land rights, and become more involved in public decision-making.[83] A core objective of the IPS—Communicating MDG3 project is to produce news contents for distribution through diverse multimedia platforms and to promote the representation of women in the media. Among the outcomes was that coverage by female reporters increased dramatically (IPS—Communicating MDG32012, 6).

Nobel Women's Initiative

The Nobel Women's Initiative was established in 2006 by Nobel Peace Prize laureates Jody Williams (United States), Shirin Ebadi (Iran), the late professor Wangari Maathai (Kenya), Rigoberta Menchú Tum (Guatemala), Betty Williams (Northern Ireland), and Mairead Maguire (Northern Ireland).[84] These six women, who represented North and South America, Europe, the Middle East, and Africa, decided to work together for peace with justice and equality. Nobel Peace Prize laureates Aung San Suu Kyi (Burma) became an honorary member in 2011 following her release from house arrest, and Leymah Gbowee (Liberia) and Tawakkol Karman (Yemen) joined the Nobel Women's Initiative in 2012. In more than 110 years only fifteen women have been awarded the Nobel Peace Prize. The Nobel Women's Initiative is aimed at strengthening women's rights around the world, using the prestige of the Nobel Peace Prize and their laureates to expand the visibility of women working in countries around the world for peace, justice, and equality. There are three programs, namely: "Women Forging Peace," "Women Advancing Equality and Human Rights," and "Women Achieving Justice." According to the Nobel Women's Initiative, peace is not the absence of armed conflict but is "the commitment to equality and justice; a democratic world free of physical, economic, cultural, political, religious, sexual and environmental violence and the constant threat of these forms of violence against women, indeed against all of humanity."[85]

UN Women

In July 2010, the new UN Entity for Gender Equality and the Empowerment of Women, or UN Women for short, was established to advance the rights of women worldwide.[86] This initiative brought together four separate UN organizations under one roof: the Division for the Advancement of Women (DAW), the International Research and Training Institute for the Advancement of Women (INSTRAW), the Office of the Special Adviser on Gender Issues and Advancement of Women (OSAGI), and the UN Development Fund for Women (UNIFEM).

In September 2010, Oxfam and the Voluntary Services Overseas (VSO) UK, with support of the Gender and Development Network (GADN), commissioned a global civil society survey on UN Women among one hundred CSOs, including grassroots and women's rights organizations from seventy-five countries. The aim was to capture the needs, aspirations, and concerns of women's rights advocates and their organizations at country level with regard to the future operations of UN Women. Among the key recommendations of this survey were, first and foremost, to take action against all forms of violence against women (VAW), to focus on the empowerment of rural women who are least aware of their rights and who have the fewest resources and the least access to services, and to collaborate with CSOs as genuine partners by including them in the political processes of their countries, among other measures (Rosche 2011).

UN Women released their first report in 2014 entitled *World Survey on the Role of Women in Development 2014: Gender Equality and Sustainable Development* (UN Women 2014). The report addresses, among other issues, gender equality in regards to sustainable development, the green economy and care, food security, and the population agenda.

The World's Women Reports

The World's Women reports are produced by the UN Statistics Division of the UN Department for Economic and Social Affairs (UNDESA) every five years, starting in 1990.[87] The *World's Women 2010* report (UNDESA 2010) is organized into eight chapters that highlight the current situation of both women and men worldwide. The chapters are: (1) population and families, (2) health, (3) education, (4) work, (5) power and decision-making, (6) violence against women, (7) environment, and (8) poverty. While the *World's Women 2010* report states that an increase in the availability of gender statistics over the previous ten years can be observed, it also highlights that increasing the capacity to produce reliable, accurate, and timely statistics, in particular gender statistics, remains a formidable challenge for many countries. The latest report was released in 2015 (UNDESA 2015).

MenEngage

The global alliance MenEngage, which was founded in 2004, comprises more than four hundred NGOs from sub-Saharan Africa, Latin America and the Caribbean, North America, Asia, and Europe, as well as UN agencies.[88] Mentioned earlier in this chapter but expanded upon here because of its importance as a transformative initiative, MenEngage seeks to involve boys and men in programs to advance gender equality by promoting health and reducing violence at the global level, including questioning the structural barriers to achieving gender equality. Diverse activities, from dissemination of information to offering training and initiating advocacy campaigns, form part of the work of this initiative. MenEngage seeks to act as a collective voice to promote a global movement of men and boys engaged in and working toward gender equality and questioning violence and non-equitable versions of manhood. International Steering Committee members include the Sonke Gender Justice Network (South Africa;

co-chair), Promundo (Brazil; co-chair), the international organization Engender Health, Family Violence Prevention Fund (United States), International Center for Research on Women (ICRW), International Planned Parenthood Federation (IPPF), Men's Resources International (United States), Salud y Género (Health and Gender, Mexico), Save the Children (Sweden), SAHAYOG (India), the global White Ribbon Campaign, and also WHO, UNDP, the United Nations Population Fund (UNFPA), and UNIFEM.[89]

Women and the Right to Livelihoods

The global network Women and the Right to Livelihoods was founded in 2009 at the annual Brazilian meeting Fórum Social Mundial (World Social Forum) in the city of Belém and established with a report by the global network's name (Sydenham 2009).[90] This network regards the fact that the right to livelihoods is not recognized as a human right as a gap in the human rights system that leaves the conditions necessary to support, sustain, and advance the lives of women and their families with dignity unprotected and unsupported. Women and the Right to Livelihoods works with and engages various groups and social movements including indigenous, Dalits, minority groups, land rights, environment, antipoverty, trade, housing, agriculture, worker's rights, and others focused on women's livelihoods. As stated by this network, its aims include (*a*) to foster a collective voice to articulate the severity of the situation faced by women, (*b*) to develop a common understanding of the right to livelihoods, (*c*) to work to have the right recognized in international law, and (*d*) to develop a strategy to advance women's livelihoods in reality around the world.

The Committee on World Food Security (CFS)

The global Committee on World Food Security (CFS) is the UN's forum for reviewing and following up on policies concerning world food security and related issues that affect the world food situation (see also chapters 1 and 6 of this volume). Upon recommendation from the 1974 World Food Conference, the CFS was established in response to the international economic recession and related food crises of the early 1970s.[91] At the thirty-fifth session held in October 2009 in Rome, members of the CFS agreed on wide-ranging reforms to make the CFS the foremost inclusive international and intergovernmental platform dealing with food security and nutrition. At the thirty-sixth session in October 2010 (FAO and CFS 2010), the Civil Society Mechanism (CSM) was established to operationalize CSOs and social movements' participation in the CFS. The inclusion of women and a gender perspective carries paramount importance with guidelines that require gender-balanced representation and an overarching gender approach in the CFS, especially with regard to small-scale food producers.

The State of Food and Agriculture 2010–11—Women in Agriculture: Closing the Gender Gap for Development

The key conclusions and recommendations of the FAO report *The State of Food and Agriculture 2010–11—Women in Agriculture: Closing the Gender Gap for Development* were highlighted earlier in this chapter. The report provides a comprehensive view of the gender gap in agriculture and rural labor markets and its causes, calling for policy interventions that (*a*) eliminate women's discrimination regarding access to resources, (*b*) create enabling infrastructure and technologies to provide women with more time for productive activities, and (*c*) facilitate women's participation in flexible, efficient, and fair rural labor markets. The report highlights that gender equality and women's empowerment are crucial for agricultural development and food security.

International Assessment of Agricultural Knowledge, Science and Technology for Development (IAASTD)

The *International Assessment of Agricultural Knowledge, Science and Technology for Development* (IAASTD) report was also mentioned earlier in this chapter and is reintroduced here because it represents a paradigm shift in agricultural assessments, with important implications both for smallholder farming and for women in agriculture. The core message of the IAASTD was that food insecurity and hunger have increased in spite of major investments in agricultural technology and increased production (IAASTD 2009). This stood in stark contrast to previous reports by the World Bank, with its emphasis on agriculture as a business, driven by entrepreneurship and vibrant markets, and linked to a burgeoning urban economy (Scoones 2009). The IAASTD highlighted the position of smallholder farmers, with particular emphasis on the women among them, through its call to reexamine the purpose of agricultural production, the sources of related knowledge, the democratization of participation in agricultural sciences, and the needs of small-scale farms in diverse ecosystems.

UNiTE to End Violence against Women

The "UNiTE to End Violence against Women" campaign, or UNiTE for short, was launched in 2008 by the UN secretary general with the aim to raise public awareness and increase political will and resources for preventing and ending all forms of violence against women and girls in all parts of the world.[92] According to UNiTE, this vision can only be realized through meaningful actions and ongoing political commitments of national governments, backed by adequate resources. The campaign calls on governments, civil society, women's organizations, men, young people, the private sector, the media, and the entire UN system to join forces in addressing this global pandemic. In line with international human rights standards, the goals of UNiTE are, among others (*a*) the adoption and enforcement of national laws and the adoption and implementation of multisectoral national action plans to address and punish all forms of violence against women and girls, (*b*) data collection and analysis systems concerned with the prevalence of various forms of violence against women and girls, (*c*) national and local campaigns to engage civil society actors in preventing violence and supporting women and girls who have been abused, and (*d*) systematic efforts to address sexual violence in conflict situations. UNiTE has linked up with several UN entities, among others UN Women, the Inter-Agency Network on Women and Gender Equality (IANWGE), the Office of the United Nations High Commissioner for Human Rights (OHCHR), UNICEF, WHO, UNDP, and the United Nations High Commissioner for Refugees (UNHCR).

Women's Initiatives for Gender Justice

From 1997 to 2003, the coalition of NGOs known as the Women's Caucus for Gender Justice involved women's human rights advocates from around the world.[93] They took part in negotiations toward the creation of the *Rome Statute of the International Criminal Court* (hereinafter, *Rome Statute*; UN General Assembly 1998) with the aim of including principles of gender justice and accountability for crimes of sexual and gender violence in the International Criminal Court (ICC). After completion of the negotiations of the *Rome Statute* and its supplemental documents and the first election of judges, the Women's Caucus for Gender Justice concluded its work.[94] Subsequently, the Women's Initiatives for Gender Justice was established as a women's human rights organization in January 2004 in The Hague to monitor the ICC and advocate for gender inclusive justice through the administration of the ICC. Among the objectives of the initiative are (*a*) to ensure that sexualized violence and gender-based crimes are a priority in the investigations and prosecutions of the ICC, (*b*) to enhance capacity among women, particularly women's NGOs, in countries where the ICC is conducting investigations in the use of international law, specifically the *Rome Statute*, and to consult with women, women's groups, and NGOs most affected by conflict to ensure that their concerns and issues are incorporated into the investigations and prosecutions and in the ICC's work with victims and witnesses, and (*c*) to influence and strengthen the gender competence of the ICC through training and the recruitment and appointment of women to the ICC, including experts on gender and sexual violence.

Women in Law and Development in Africa (WiLDAF)

Women in Law and Development in Africa (WiLDAF) is a Pan-African network of women's rights-based and non-governmental, non-profit organizations dedicated to promoting and strengthening strategies that link law and development to increase women's participation and influence at the local, national, and international levels.[95] Mentioned earlier in this chapter in connection with the documentation of specific cases, the WiLDAF network was conceived through a 1990 conference entitled Women, Law and Development: Networking for Empowerment in Africa held in Harare, Zimbabwe. The aim of the conference was to establish an organization that promotes and strengthens a society that strives to empower women and improve their status in Africa. The network encompasses thirty-one countries, over five hundred organizations, and over 1,200 individual members, with several subregional offices operating in Southern, Eastern, and Western Africa. At the national and international levels, the WiLDAF network lobbies for laws that promote women's rights. At the local level, free legal counselling as well as paralegal training is offered.

CONCLUSIONS AND RECOMMENDATIONS FOR MOVING FORWARD

Policy reforms to eradicate gender discrimination are one major condition to improve women's political voice and participation. However, for laws to translate into changes on the ground, women and men need to be aware of their rights in order to claim them. This emphasizes the need for a strong civil society and social movements that can lead this process.

The case studies illustrated in this chapter show how gender sensitive approaches that involve local communities can translate into change over time, even though barriers are being experienced at various levels. The examples of good practice revealed that women are increasingly represented at both political and grassroots levels, have gained confidence, and are able to stand up for their interests. Especially visible in the case studies provided by Brot für die Welt (2009), gendered approaches can be implemented in various cultural contexts. Some organizations increasingly integrate men and encourage reflection on stereotypical male roles.

In this chapter, we further illustrated the shortcomings of agricultural production and nutrition intervention models and proposed that development needs to engage alternative approaches of building local self-reliance, community food security, and local governance that foreground inclusive participation. Such approaches are perhaps slower and might seem more expensive at first, but they are surely more cost-effective in the longer term. Social and economic transformations take time. These shifts often cannot be measured by so-called hard facts or so-called evidence generated through randomized controlled trials, as is increasingly required in the context of development cooperation or nutrition sciences and related disciplines, respectively. Instead, or in addition, what we need are anthropological and other studies that integrate participatory and qualitative methods that can contribute to a much needed improved understanding of the sustainability of programs. In a context of ongoing conditions of rural, racial, gender, and class structural power inequities, the "success" of single programs should rather be viewed in terms of their ability to leverage, as opposed to shoulder, social change and sustainable livelihoods.

Based on the elaborations in this chapter, we propose the following recommendations:

- A systems approach needs to begin from the perspective of local populations of women, men, and children, regardless of a person's life stage and inclusive of their social locations (i.e., race, ethnicity, gender, income, etc.), in both public and private spaces.
- Research should involve local actors at all stages, from the design of research objectives to the sharing of results and formulating recommendations, applying participatory approaches. Qualitative, quantitative, or mixed methods can be applied.
- There is a need for more gender sensitive and gender disaggregated data at the household and community levels, as well as for an intersectoral analysis that investigates the link between gender, class, age, race, ethnicity, and religion, taking into account the various and complex power dynamics. This would allow for a clearer determination of the food and nutrition security status, as well as of the diverse tasks and responsibilities of different groups of women and men. This broadened perspective can further contribute to an improved understanding of the challenges women or men are facing, and can reveal the different coping strategies women and men adopt.
- Sustainable livelihoods approaches that link people, agroecological principles, and viable local economies should be applied to achieve more resilient local food systems and governance, wherein individuals, women in particular, can become involved.
- A human rights framework should be integrated into local food systems and governance founded on the precept that all individuals have the right to participate in and define food and nutrition security strategies.
- Chronic dependency on food aid and charity designed for emergencies must be avoided and overcome with a shifted goal on the development of local food systems that promote self-determination.
- Local food systems and governance should be simultaneously linked to national and global food governance approaches, assuming they foreground grassroots civil society interests.
- The separation of food production and nutrition objectives needs to be overcome. Instead, a systems approach should be adopted and local food governance promoted in the development of community food security and food and nutrition policy. Promising efforts are underway, with several initiatives having being illustrated in this chapter.

- The focus on women and children in the right to adequate food and nutrition needs to move beyond their portrayal as disempowered victims in a maternal-child and housebound state and requires a proactive approach to protecting and centering women's voices. At the same time, there must be an awareness of the possible cost of participation and negative consequences women might face due to social and gender norms. In this regard, the concept of empowerment needs to be carefully reviewed.
- There is a need for a genuine gendered approach that involves women *and* men, instead of continuing to focus on women in isolation. If the challenges that especially young men are facing in societies in transition are not considered, and if men in general are not integrated into efforts to overcome gender inequalities, these efforts will fail.

NOTES

1. Please refer to chapter 6 of this volume for the argument that one of the fragmentations within the current human rights framework is the lack of integrated implementation of the three levels of state's human rights obligations— to respect, protect, and fulfil.
2. The concept of food security is enshrined in article 25 of the UDHR reading: "Everyone has the right to a standard of living adequate for the health and well-being of himself and of his family, including food" (UN General Assembly 1948, art. 25(1)).
3. For a detailed account of the history and evolution of underlying concepts of food security and nutrition security, see the comprehensive report by Maxwell and Frankenberger (1992) and also the recent report by the Committee on World Food Security (CFS; CFS 2012).
4. The need for more integrated research approaches and specifically qualitative research in nutrition sciences was highlighted in a special congress issue of *Public Health Nutrition* (Steyn 2005, 448–50). A review of papers from studies undertaken in Africa and published in the journal since its inception in 1998 revealed that "only a handful made use of qualitative methodology, implying that nutrition scientists are still not making use of important tools to understand the underlying social reasons for many of the nutritional conditions they face" (Steyn 2005, 442). A paper by the first author of this chapter was among these few studies applying qualitative methods (Lemke et al. 2003).
5. For more details on the 19th IUNS International Congress of Nutrition, please refer to *Annals Nutrition & Metabolism* 2009, volume 55, supplement 1, which is available online at http://www.karger.com/Journal/Issue/253614 (accessed on August 7, 2014).
6. Several international conferences focused on this concept "nutrition sensitive agriculture" over the past years, among them the New Delhi conference Leveraging Agriculture for Improving Nutrition and Health, which took place on February 10–12, 2011, New Delhi, India. For further information on this conference and related documents on various initiatives that aim to integrate agriculture and nutrition, please visit http://2020conference.ifpri.info (accessed August 12, 2014).
7. Further information on the 20th International Congress of Nutrition in Granada can be found online at http://icn2013.com (accessed August 12, 2014).

8. For a critical discussion on the concept "empowerment," see the section "Women, development, gender, empowerment: an evolving debate" later in this chapter.

9. Chapter 6 of this volume entails a more detailed discussion of social movements and their role in the reconceptualization of an integrated framework of the right to adequate food and nutrition. Examples of social movements are the food sovereignty movement including peasants and small farmers, but also traditional populations, landless people, and indigenous peoples. Further examples encompass women's rights groups, children's rights groups, fisherfolks, environmentalists, groups engaging in agroecology, urban agriculture and gardening, farmworkers, and community food security groups. The section of this chapter entitled "Democratic participation, governance, and mobilization from civil society toward more equitable food systems" elaborates on various national and international social movements that engage in the context of discrimination and violence against women.

10. A consultative process, involving over eight hundred constituencies, was begun in 2002 to determine if a full-blown assessment was necessary. In 2004 it was decided to conduct an assessment in which over four hundred experts, nominated by the consultation participants, were involved. For more information, please visit http://www.unep.org/dewa/Assessments/Ecosystems/IAASTD/tabid/105853/Default.aspx/ (accessed August 12, 2014).

11. This case study was provided by a coauthor of chapter 1 of this volume, Roseane do Socorro Gonçalves Viana.

12. The interview with Danielly Palma, author of the Master thesis undertaken at the Federal University of Mato Grosso on the contamination of breastmilk with agrochemicals is available online in Portuguese at http://www.viomundo.com.br/denuncias/exclusivo-a-pesquisadora-que-descobriu-veneno-no-leite-materno.html (accessed August 7, 2014).

13. Lucas do Rio Verde is the second largest grain producer in the state of Mato Grosso which, for its part, is the second largest grain producer in Brazil. For more information (in Portuguese) please visit http://www.viomundo.com.br/denuncias/exclusivo-a-pesquisadora-que-descobriu-veneno-no-leite-materno.html (accessed August 7, 2014).

14. According to data from the Brazilian Sindicato Nacional da Indústria de Produtos para Defesa Vegetal (National Union of Pesticide Industries, SINDIVEG), previously named Sindicato Nacional da Indústria de Produtos para Defesa Agrícola (National Union of Agrochemical Industries, SINDAG), 986,500 tons of pesticides were sold in 2008 and more than a million tons in 2009 (equivalent to 5.2 kg of agrochemical products per Brazilian per year). Although SINDIVEG itself and other agribusiness sources issued statements commemorating these figures, exalting the use of agrochemicals as the application of technology, the national press began to publish news stories connecting the abuse of pesticides to food contamination, environmental damage, and health issues. Undoubtedly because of the negative impact of these media reports, this year SINDIVEG published no data on the volume of pesticides sold in 2010 but merely reported that the value of the sales achieved over the period was US\$ 7.2 billion. SINDIVEG did, however, emphasize that this value represented a 9 percent increase from the previous year. For more information, please read the online article published by AS-PTA Agricultura Familiar e Agroecologia at http://boletimtransgenicos.campanhasdemkt.net/ver_mensagem.php?id=H|774|57167|12445682 4284401400 (accessed November 25, 2014).

15. Gender analysis is not limited to revealing patterns of gender differences and inequalities but examines why disparities exist, whether they are a matter of concern, and how they might be addressed. For elaborations and tools on how

to conduct gender analysis see, for example, Pasteur (2002) for gender analysis in the context of sustainable livelihoods, Buscher (2005) for measuring gender equality in the context of refugees and internally displaced populations, and Colfer (2013) for analyzing gender roles in the context of forest management.

Several of the reports mentioned here frequently refer to "women's roles," implying a rather static concept. We should refer instead to the more dynamic concept "gender relations" to be able to address inherent power imbalances and to avoid the danger of distorting the attention only on women. For a more detailed discussion, see the later section in this chapter entitled "Women, development, gender, empowerment: an evolving debate."

16. According to FAO (2011, 7), the agricultural labor force includes people who are working or looking for work in formal or informal jobs and in paid or unpaid employment in agriculture. That includes self-employed women as well as women working on family farms.

17. For more information on women's land rights, please visit http://www.landesa. org/women-and-land/ (accessed August 7, 2014).

18. More examples of good practices and lessons learned in the context of reforming legal and property systems in sub-Saharan Africa are provided by Quisumbing (2010) in her report to the Commission on the Status of Women.

19. The synthesis report *Gender and Poverty Targeting in Market Linkage Operations* by IFAD (2002) aimed at improving the understanding of gender and targeting issues in market linkage operations and developing practical ideas, approaches, and tools that can be used to mainstream gender and promote poverty targeting in current and future market linkage projects and programs. The authors emphasize that gender and poverty dimensions vary in different places and societies and that, therefore, there is no "one size fits all" recipe for gender mainstreaming in market linkage operations. They conclude that good knowledge of the gender dimensions, and especially the difference in the constraints that women and men face in their societies, will make an important difference in how efficiently different actors can address diverse aspects of business, market access, and development (IFAD 2002, 70–71).

20. The inequalities experienced by women in the agricultural sector in general have been highlighted, among others, by De Schutter (HRC 2012).

21. For more information on the ratification of the Kenyan new constitution, please read the article "Kenya President Ratifies New Constitution" published on the web page "NEWS Africa" on the website of the British Broadcasting Company (BBC) at http://www.bbc.co.uk/news/world-africa-11106558 (accessed August 7, 2014).

22. For the full article by Da Silva "Guardians of life and of the earth" published online March 7, 2013 by Inter Press Service (IPS) News Agency, please visit http://www.ipsnews.net/2013/03/guardians-of-life-and-of-the-earth/ (accessed August 12, 2014). For an elaboration on the limitations of women's empowerment, see also Kabeer (2005b).

23. Please refer to *The Lancet* series on "Maternal and Child Undernutrition," launched January 16, 2008 and available online at http://www.thelancet.com/ series/maternal-and-child-undernutrition (accessed August 7, 2014).

24. Personal comment, Stefanie Lemke. For more information about the conference, please refer to the 2009 edition of *Annals of Nutrition and Metabolism*, volume 55, supplement 1, which is available online at http://www.karger.com/ Journal/Issue/253614 (accessed August 12, 2014).

25. The example of RUSF has been elaborated in more detail in chapter 4 of this volume, with a focus on conflicts of interests in multisectoral public policy-making.

26. We are fully aware that these terms "black," "white," and "colored" are controversial. Yet, they are still widely used in South Africa, although there is an

ongoing debate regarding these categories, especially in academic circles. As there is no alternative yet, the terms "black," "colored," "white," and alternatively "black/white/colored" South Africans will be used in this chapter, in order to situate the specific context. For further information regarding the discourse on race in South Africa, see Durrheim, Mtose, and Brown (2011), Erasmus (2008), Posel (2010), and Seekings and Nattrass (2005).

27. For a comprehensive introduction to the women and development agenda and the way women's issues have been conceptualized in the development context from the 1970s to the 1990s, see *From WID to GAD: Conceptual Shifts in the Women and Development Discourse*, a report by Shahrashoub Razavi and Carol Miller that was written in 1995 as a contribution to the Fourth World Conference on Women in Bejing on behalf of the UN Research Institute for Social Development. Although this report dates back almost twenty years, many of the statements made are still highly relevant for the current discourse on gender and development. See also Christa Wichterich's feminist analysis of the topic of the Rio+20 UN Conference 2012, *The Future We Want: A Feminist Perspective* (Wichterich 2012).

28. For a similar discussion on the use of the concept "vulnerability," see chapter 2 of this volume.

29. The approach of the World Bank that regards women's empowerment as a smart economic strategy was also criticized by IPS in their MDG3 Project "Communicating for Change: Voice, Visibility and Impact for Gender Equality." In their report, IPS argues that supporting gender equality and women's empowerment has to go beyond focusing solely on business concerns and calls for gender and development to be based on women's autonomy and freedom from violence, along with fair and equal access to resources and assets, to achieve their human rights (IPS—Communicating MDG3 2012).

30. For a more detailed elaboration on masculinities, the need to integrate men, and positive examples in this regard, please see the section of this chapter entitled "Democratic participation, governance, and mobilization from civil society toward more equitable food systems."

31. Please see endnote 26 for a discussion on the issue of race in South Africa.

32. White's (2010) study of a farmworkers' movement in the Western Cape emphasizes the social challenges of paternalism, patriarchy, and racism and the need to overcome these constructs to achieve participation and democratic structures. Similarly, Schweitzer (2008) describes the struggle for autonomy among farmworkers in the Western Cape who became wine farmers.

33. For an overview of the South African land reform program, see Department of Land Affairs [South Africa] (1997). For a critical reflection on land reform, see Hall and Ntsebeza (2007).

34. For a detailed discussion on the status and challenges of land reform in South Africa, see Lahiff (2008b) and Greenberg (2010).

35. As stated by in the *Declaration of Commitment on HIV/AIDS* (UN General Assembly 2001), AIDS threatens development, social cohesion, political stability, and food and nutrition security and imposes a devastating economic burden.

36. Good nutrition is further especially important with regard to antiretroviral therapy (ART) that is only effective in combination with adequate food.

37. See Gillespie and Kadiyala (2005) on interactions of HIV/AIDS and food and nutrition security, integrating how HIV/AIDS affects and is affected by livelihoods. See also Murphy, Harvey, and Silvestre (2005) on AIDS' impacts on rural livelihoods in sub-Saharan Africa.

38. For the severity of the incidence of rape in South Africa, please visit http://www.mg.co.za/article/2010–11–26-one-in-three-sa-men-admit-to-rape-survey-finds (accessed August 12, 2014).

39. See chapter 6 of this volume for a more elaborated description of the need for the implementation of state obligations (to respect, protect, and fulfil) in an integrated manner.
40. See chapters 2 and 6 of this volume for further discussion on landgrabbing.
41. See also HRC (2009, 11–14), where De Schutter outlines necessary protective measures for the local population regarding employment, incomes, and access to productive resources in the context of large-scale land acquisitions and leases.
42. Also the first UN special rapporteur on the right to food, Jean Ziegler (mandate holder from 2000 to 2008), had contributed to framing agrarian issues in a human rights context, covering, among other issues, access to land, agrarian reform, agroecology, women's role in agriculture, workers in the agricultural sector, and corporate control over food systems. Ziegler continues to publish on the right to food and related issues; see, for example, *The Fight for the Right to Food: Lessons Learned* (Ziegler et al. 2011).
43. This term "food sovereignty" was initiated in the early 1990s by the global farmers' movement La Via Campesina, which aimed at discussing and promoting alternatives to neoliberal policies for achieving food security. See chapter 6 of this volume for more details on this social movement.
44. The international conference Food Sovereignty: A Critical Dialogue, convened at Yale University from September 14–15, 2013, provided a critical and productive debate around this concept. All papers of this conference are available online on the Yale University website at http://www.yale.edu/agrarianstudies/foodsovereignty/ (accessed August 12, 2014). A follow-up conference on food sovereignty took place on January 24, 2014 in The Hague, The Netherlands. The food sovereignty 2013/2014 conference paper series is available online through the International Institute of Social Studies in The Hague at http://www.iss.nl/research/research_programmes/political_economy_of_resources_environment_and_population_per/networks/critical_agrarian_studies_icas/food_sovereignty_a_critical_dialogue/ (accessed August 12, 2014).
45. Chapter 6 of this volume elaborates further on the concept "food sovereignty" as a principle for the progressive realization of the human right to adequate food and nutrition.
46. In this context, empowerment is referred to in line with its initial emphasis on building personal and collective power in the struggle for a more just and equitable world. Please see Cornwall and Brock (2005).
47. Please visit also the State and Local Food Policy Councils' website at http://www.statefoodpolicy.org/ (accessed August 12, 2014).
48. Toronto has long been at the forefront of public health initiatives and food security research, being one of the originators of and among the first world cities to sign onto the WHO Healthy Cities movement. In 1991, in the absence of federal and provincial leadership on food security, the city created the Toronto Food Policy Council (TFPC). As presented on the council's website at http://tfpc.to/about (accessed August 12, 2014), the mission statement of the TFPC is to connect "diverse people from the food, farming and community sector to develop innovative policies and projects that support a health-focused food system, and provides a forum for action across the food system."
49. For more information on rural food policy councils, please visit http://ruralcommunitybuilding.fb.org/2010/07/19/food-policy-councils-support-local-economy/ (accessed August 12, 2014); http://kansasruralcenter.org/kansas-food-policy-council/ (accessed August 12, 2014); and http://www.farmtotablenm.org/policy/ (accessed on August 12, 2014).
50. Please visit the Just Food website at http://www.justfood.org/food-justice (accessed August 12, 2014).

51. For more information about organic agriculture, please visit http://www.ifoam. org/en/news/2013/04/05/latest-facts-and-figures-organic-agriculture   (accessed August 12, 2014).
52. This concept of sustainability was outlined in the so-called *Brundtland Report* (Brundtland 1987), with each of these three elements (environmental, economic, and social) receiving equal weight.
53. The *Natives Land Act* of 1913 restricted the black peasantry's access to land by preventing them from acquiring property outside designated areas (later the so-called "homelands"), which led to the enriching of the white population and the impoverishment of the black population (van Onselen 1996). Further, black South Africans were displaced from white-owned farms and directed to designated areas by the state's massive relocation program. Black South Africans, constituting 80 percent of the population, were limited to 13 percent of the land (Sharp 1994).
54. For a more detailed elaboration on the destitute working and living conditions of farmworkers on commercial farms in South Africa, see, for example, Du Toit (2004), Atkinson (2007), Human Rights Watch (2011), and Devereux and Solomon (2011).
55. This case study was informed by research carried out for a Master thesis by L. Heine (unpublished), within the earlier mentioned larger research project by Lemke (2010).
56. This "job creation for the North" extends also to countries of the South, East, and developing countries in general, with many NGOs relying heavily on donor support and, with it, not only local livelihoods of the poor these development programs aim to serve but also of the people facilitating such programs and being employed at NGOs.
57. The food sovereignty 2013/2014 conference paper series is available through the International Institute of Social Studies in The Hague: http://www.iss.nl/ research/research_programmes/political_economy_of_resources_environ- ment_and_population_per/networks/critical_agrarian_studies_icas/food_ sovereignty_a_critical_dialogue/ (accessed August 12, 2014); please see also endnote 44.
58. For more information on the synergies created at the seminar Human Rights Compliant and Sustainable Food Systems (June 24–26, 2014), please visit FIAN International's website at http://www.fian.org/news/article/detail/synergies_ created_at_food_systems_conference/ (accessed November 20, 2014).
59. For a detailed discussion of the origins and reform of the CFS, please see chapter 1 of this volume.
60. This case is documented in detail by Sandra Maribel Sánchez, quoted in Monsalve Suárez (2012, 20–25).
61. Chapter 3 of this volume provides numerous examples of social protection programs targeted at women, discussing both benefits and unintended effects, and emphasizing how such programs can both increase or decrease vulnerability to domestic violence and can further reinforce gender stereotypes if not well designed. As Quisumbing (2010) points out in the context of antipoverty programs, these should be evaluated to increase effectiveness, paying specific attention to gender-differentiated impacts.
62. *Quilombola* status and identity are based on self-recognition and identification. Calling oneself a *Quilombola* is considered a reaffirmation of Afro-descendant heritage and part of a historic process of resistance and struggle against black slavery and oppression in Brazil that existed from 1500 until 1888, when slavery was abolished (Viana and Bellows 2014).
63. This provision on the percentage of food products used for school feeding that should be supplied by economically marginalized population groups is found

in *Law No. 11.947* establishing the Programa Nacional de Alimentação Escolar (National School Feeding Programme) in primary schools of Brazil as of June 16, 2009.

64. This case study was provided by coauthor of chapter 1 of this volume, Roseane do Socorro Gonçalves Viana, a PhD candidate at the Food Security Center and the Department of Gender and Nutrition, University of Hohenheim.

65. See also Greenberg (2010) for a critical reflection on the prospects and position of farmworkers within current land reform programs in South Africa.

66. The MDG3 Fund supports women's rights organizations, catalyzing progress toward achievement of the 2015 MDG 3 on gender equality and women's empowerment, and partnering with several other organizations, among them the Nobel Women's Initiative.

These case studies were compiled by Wendy Harcourt for a report published by Inter Press Service (IPS; see IPS—Communicating MDG3 2012) and financed through the MDG3 Fund and the United Nations Entity for Gender Equality and the Empowerment of Women (UN Women). In this chapter, three of ten case studies are illustrated. For the complete article "Women Empowering Women," please visit http://www.ips.org/mdg3/Category/women-empowering-women/ (accessed August 12, 2014).

67. For more information about the West African division of Women in Law and Development in Africa (WiLDAF), please visit http://www.wildaf-ao.org/ (accessed August 12, 2014).

68. For more information about Women in Informal Employment: Globalizing and Organizing (WIEGO), please visit http://wiego.org/ (accessed August 12, 2014).

69. For more information about Just Associates (JASS), please visit http://www.justassociates.org/ (accessed August 12, 2014).

70. Chapter 3 of this volume provides detailed information and various case studies on how women's greater economic independence can actually increase GBV.

71. For more information on the Sonke Gender Justice Network, please read the article by Janine Erasmus "NGO Fights for Gender Equalisation in South Africa" of May 26, 2010 at the *Media Club South Africa* website http://www.mediaclubsouthafrica.com/index.php?option=com_content&view=article&id=1752:sonke-260510&catid=44:developmentnews&Itemid=111#ixzz0sFQaBxxF (accessed July 22, 2014). Also, please visit the Sonke Gender Justice Network website at http://www.genderjustice.org.za/ (accessed August 12, 2014).

72. For a more detailed documentation of the initiative MenEngage, please visit http://www.menengage.org/index.php?option=com_content&view=category&layout=blog&id=4&Itemid=2 (accessed August 12, 2014). Please also refer to the section in this chapter entitled "Initiatives for mainstreaming gender in right to adequate food and nutrition work."

73. For more information on the movement Kurdish Men for Gender Equality, read Dilar Dirik's article "Kurdish Men for Gender Equality: 'Being a Woman is Not a Tool to Punish or Humiliate Anyone—No Free Society without Free Women'" (April 25, 2013) on *The Kurdistan Tribune* website at http://kurdistantribune.com/2013/kurdish-men-for-gender-equality/ (accessed November 20, 2014).

74. As is further elaborated in Dilar Dirik's article (see previous note), degrading prisoners by making them wear Kurdish women's clothes was not only an attack on women but also on Kurdish culture. The protest of Kurdish men by dressing in traditional Kurdish women's clothes was, therefore, a protest against both sorts of oppression. Even though this example might not relate directly to the context discussed here, it demonstrates how joint actions by men and women and global campaigns are able to mobilize people and spread across regions.

75. See previous note 73.

76. For further investigation, please consider the following link taken from the IPS-Communicating MDG3 (2012) report that provides an overview of women's networks and NGOs: http://www.ips.org/mdg3/?s=women%27s+networks+and+NGOs (accessed August 12, 2014).

77. For this and more information about the CWGL, please visit the organization's website at http://www.cwgl.rutgers.edu (accessed November 6, 2014).

78. Please visit the web page "Vision and Mission" on the CWGL's website at http://www.cwgl.rutgers.edu/about-110/vission-a-mission (accessed November 6, 2014).

79. For more information on AWID, please visit the organization's website at http://www.awid.org/About-AWID/ (accessed May 29, 2013). See also the web page "Association for Women's Rights in Development (AWID)" on the Sigrid Rausing Trust website at http://www.sigrid-rausing-trust.org/Grantees/Association-for-Womens-Rights-in-Development-AWID (accessed May 29, 2013).

80. This quote was taken from the web page "Who We Are" on AWID's website at http://www.awid.org/About-AWID/Who-We-Are (accessed May 29, 2013).

81. For more information on Landesa's Center for Women's Land Rights, please visit http://www.landesa.org/women-and-land/ (accessed August 12, 2014).

82. For more information on IPS News Agency, please visit http://www.ipsnews.net/ (accessed August 12, 2014). The quote was taken from the bottom of the web page "Home" at the agency's website (accessed August 12, 2014).

83. For an illustration of case studies from the IPS—Communicating MDG3 (2012) report, see the section of this chapter entitled "Strengthening women as actors."

84. For more information on the Nobel Women's Initiative, please visit http://nobelwomensinitiative.org/about-us/ (accessed August 12, 2014).

85. As quoted on the Nobel Women's Initiative website at http://nobelwomensinitiative.org/about-us/ (accessed August 12, 2014).

86. For more information about UN Women, please visit the organization's website at http://www.unwomen.org/ (accessed August 12, 2014).

87. For more information on the World's Women reports, please visit the website of the UN Statistics Division at http://unstats.un.org/unsd/demographic/products/Worldswomen/WWreports.htm (accessed November 25, 2014)

88. For more information on MenEngage, please visit http://menengage.org/ (accessed August 12, 2014).

89. Other organizations that engage men and boys are referred to as the MenEngage Initiative.

90. For more information on women and the right to livelihoods, visit the website of the Programme on Women's Economic, Social and Cultural Rights (PWESCR) at http://www.pwescr.org/ (accessed August 12, 2014) and the web page "The Human Right to Livelihood and Land" on the People's Movement for Human Rights Education website at http://www.pdhre.org/rights/land.html (accessed August 12, 2014).

91. For the history of the CFS, please visit their homepage at http://www.fao.org/cfs/en/ (accessed August 12, 2014).

92. For more information on UNiTE, please visit http://endviolence.un.org/about.shtml (accessed August 12, 2014).

93. Information about the history and mission of the Women's Caucus for Gender Justice and the Women's Initiative for Gender Justice is available online at http://www.iccwomen.org/aboutus/history.php (accessed August 12, 2014).

94. The *Rome Statue* dates from July 17, 1998. It entered into force on July 1, 2002. For more information, please visit http://www.un.org/law/icc/ (accessed August 12, 2014).

95. For more information on Women in Law and Development in Africa, please visit: http://www.wildaf.org/ (accessed November 5, 2014).

REFERENCES

Adato, M. and R.S. Meinzen-Dick. 2002. *Assessing the Impact of Agricultural Research on Poverty using the Sustainable Livelihoods Framework: Concepts and Methods.* EPTD Discussion Paper 89. Washington, D.C.: International Food Policy Research Institute (IFPRI).

African Commission on Human and People's Rights (ACHPR). 2003. *Protocol to the African Charter on Human and Peoples' Rights on the Rights of Women in Africa. Adopted by the Second Ordinary Session of the Assembly of the Union, Maputo, July 11, 2003.* Maputo: African Commission on Human and People's Rights (ACHPR).

African Woman and Child Feature Service (AWC). 2010. *Women Gains in the Proposed Constitution of Kenya.* Nairobi: African Woman and Child Feature Service (AWC).

Alkon, A.H. 2012. "Food Justice: An Overview." In *Routledge International Handbook of Food Studies*, edited by K. Albala, 295–305. New York: Routledge, Taylor and Francis Group.

Allen, P., M. FitzSimmons, M. Goodman, and K. Warner. 2003. "Shifting Plates in the Agrifood Landscape: The Tectonics of Alternative Agrifood Initiatives in California." *Journal of Rural Studies* 19 (1): 61–75.

Alston, M. 2009. "Drought Policy in Australia: Gender Mainstreaming or Gender Blindness?" *Gender, Place and Culture—A Journal of Feminist Geography* 16 (2): 139–54.

Altman, M., T.G.B. Hart, and P.T. Jacobs. 2009. "Household Food Security Status in South Africa." *Agrekon* 48 (4): 345–61.

Anderson, M.D. 2008. "Rights-Based Food Systems and the Goals of Food Systems Reform." *Agriculture and Human Values* 25 (4): 593–608.

Annan, K.A. 2002. "In Africa, AIDS Has a Woman's Face." *The New York Times*, December 29, 2002.

Asian-Pacific Resource and Research Centre for Women (ARROW). 2014. "Linking Poverty, Food Sovereignty and Security, and Sexual and Reproductive Health and Rights." *Arrow for Change* 29 (1).

Atkinson, D. 2007. *Going for Broke: The Fate of Farmworkers in Arid South Africa.* Cape Town: Human Sciences Research Council.

Bank, L. 1994. "Angry Men and Working Women. Gender, Violence and Economic Change in Qwaqwa in the 1980s." *African Studies* 53 (1): 89–114.

———. 2005. "On Family Farms and Commodity Groups: Rural Livelihoods, Households and Development Policy in the Eastern Cape." *Social Dynamics* 31 (1): 157–81.

Bellows, A.C. and M.W. Hamm. 2001. "Local Autonomy and Sustainable Development: Testing Import Substitution in Localizing Food Systems." *Agriculture and Human Values* 18 (3): 271–84.

———. 2003. "International Origins of Community Food Security Policies and Practices in the U.S." *Critical Public Health, Special Issue: Food Policy* 13 (2): 107–23.

Benad, A. 2002. "Women and Gender in Development Projects: Experiences of Deutsche Welthungerhilfe. Schriften zur Internationalen Entwicklungs- und Umweltforschung." In *Women in the Context of International Development and Co-Operation: Review and Perspectives*, edited by I.-U. Leonhäuser. Vol. 3, 117–24. Frankfurt am Main: Lang.

Benson, T. 2006. "Agriculture and Health in the Policymaking Process. Brief 15 of 16." In *Understanding the Links between Agriculture and Health*, edited by C. Hawkes and M.T. Ruel, 31–32. Washington, D.C.: International Food Policy Research Institute (IFPRI).

————. 2012. "Cross-Sectoral Coordination in the Public Sector: A Challenge to Leveraging Agriculture for Improving Nutrition and Health." In *Reshaping Agriculture for Nutrition and Health*, edited by S. Fan and R. Pandya-Lorch, 145–62. Washington, D.C.: International Food Policy Research Institute (IFPRI).

Bernstein, H. 2013. "Food Sovereignty: A Sceptical Review" (paper presented at the international conference Food Sovereignty: A Critical Dialogue, Yale University, September 14–15, 2013).

Bezanson, K. and P. Isenman. 2010. "Scaling Up Nutrition: A Framework for Action." *Food and Nutrition Bulletin* 31 (1): 178–86.

Block, D.R., M. Thompson, J. Euken, T. Liquori, F. Fear, and S. Baldwin. 2008. "Engagement for Transformation: Value Webs for Local Food System Development." *Agriculture and Human Values* 25 (3): 379–88.

Boserup, E. 1970. *Woman's Role in Economic Development*. London: Earthscan.

Brot für die Welt. 2009. *Gender Mainstreaming in Practice: Nine Examples of Good Practice from Four Continents*. Stuttgart: Diakonisches Werk der EKD e.V..

Brundtland, G.H. 1987. *Our Common Future: Report of the World Commission on Environment and Development (WCED)*. Oxford: Oxford University Press.

Brunori, G. 2007. "Local Food and Alternative Food Networks: A Communication Perspective." *Anthropology of Food [Online]*, S2.

Budlender, D. 2000. "Human Development." In *Poverty and Inequality in South Africa: Meeting the Challenge*, edited by J. May, 98–139. Cape Town: David Philip.

Burlingame, B. 2012. "Preface." In *Sustainable Diets and Biodiversity: Direction and Solutions for Policy, Research and Action*, edited by B. Burlingame and S. Dernini, 6–8. Rome: Food and Agriculture Organization of the United Nations (FAO).

Burlingame, B. and S. Dernini, eds. 2012. *Sustainable Diets and Biodiversity: Direction and Solutions for Policy, Research and Action*. Rome: Food and Agriculture Organization of the United Nations (FAO).

Burnett, K. and S. Murphy. 2013. "What Place for International Trade in Food Sovereignty?" (paper presented at the international conference Food Sovereignty: A Critical Dialogue, Yale University, September 14–15, 2013).

Buscher, D. 2005. *Masculinities: Male Roles and Male Involvement in the Promotion of Gender Equality—A Resource Packet*. New York: Women's Commission for Refugee Women and Children.

Calderisi, R., ed. 2007. *The Trouble with Africa: Why Foreign Aid Isn't Working*. New Haven: Yale University Press.

Cannon, G. and C. Leitzmann. 2005. "The New Nutrition Science Project." *Public Health Nutrition* 8 (6A): 673–94.

Cátedra de Estudios sobre Hambre y Pobreza (Chair of Hunger and Poverty Studies, CEHAP). 2008. *The Cordoba Declaration on the Right to Food and the Governance of the Global Food and Agricultural System: Launched on the Occasion of the Sixtieth Anniversary of the Universal Declaration of Human Rights*. Cordoba: Cátedra de Estudios sobre Hambre y Pobreza (Chair of Hunger and Poverty Studies, CEHAP).

Center for Women's Global Leadership (CWGL). 2011. *The Right to Food, Gender Equality and Economic Policy. Meeting Report. September 16–17, 2011*. New Brunswick: Center for Women's Global Leadership (CWGL).

Chambers, R. and G. Conway. 1992. *Sustainable Rural Livelihoods: Practical Concepts for the 21st Century*. Brighton: Institute of Development Studies (IDS).

Clancy, K., J. Hammer, and D. Lippoldt. 2007. "Food Policy Councils: Past, Present, and Future." In *Remaking the North American Food System: Redefining Foodways in a Changing World*, edited by C.C. Hinrichs and T.A. Lyson, 121–43. Lincoln: University of Nebraska Press.

Colfer, C.J.P. 2013. *The Gender Box: A Framework for Analysing Gender Roles in Forest Management—Occasional Paper 82*. Indonesia: Center for International Forestry Research (CIFOR).

Colles, A., G. Koppen, V. Hanot, V. Nelen, M.C. Dewolf, E. Noël, R. Malisch, A. Kotz, K. Kypke, P. Biot, C. Vinkx, and G. Schoeters. 2008. "Fourth WHO-Coordinated Survey of Human Milk for Persistent Organic Pollutants (POPs): Belgian Results." *Chemosphere* 73 (6): 907–14.

Committee on World Food Security (CFS). 2012. *Coming to Terms with Terminology: Food Security, Nutrition Security, Food Security and Nutrition, Food and Nutrition Security (Revised Draft July 25, 2012)*. Rome: Committee on World Food Security (CFS).

Connelly, S., S. Markey, and M. Roseland. 2011. "Bridging Sustainability and the Social Economy: Achieving Community Transformation through Local Food Initiatives." *Critical Social Policy* 31 (2): 308–24.

Cornwall, A. and K. Brock. 2005. "What Do Buzzwords Do for Development Policy? A Critical Look at 'Participation', 'Empowerment' and 'Poverty Reduction'." *Third World Quarterly* 26 (7): 1043–60.

Cousins, B. 2007. "Agrarian Reform and the 'Two Economies': Transforming South Africa's Countryside." In *The Land Question in South Africa: The Challenge of Transformation and Redistribution*, edited by L. Ntsebeza and R. Hall, 220–45. Cape Town: Human Sciences Research Council.

De Schutter, O. 2009. *Contribution by the Special Rapporteur on the Right to Food at the Seventeenth Session of the UN Commission on Sustainable Development (CSD-17)*, May 4–15, 2009, New York.

Department for International Development [United Kingdom] (DFID). 1999. *Sustainable Livelihoods Guidance Sheets*. London: Department for International Development [United Kingdom] (DFID).

Department of Land Affairs [South Africa] (DLA). 1997. *White Paper on South African Land Policy. Chapter Four: Land Reform Programmes*. Pretoria: Department of Land Affairs [South Africa] (DLA).

Devereux, S. and C. Solomon. 2011. *Shooting the Messenger: Controversy over Farmworker Conditions in South Africa*. Brighton: Institute of Development Studies (IDS).

Doss, C. 2013. "Intrahousehold Bargaining and Resource Allocation in Developing Countries." *The World Bank Research Observer* 28 (1): 52–78.

Du Toit, A. 1993. "The Micro-Politics of Paternalism: The Discourses of Management and Resistance on South African Fruit and Wine Farms." *Journal of Southern African Studies* 19 (2): 314–36.

———. 2004. *Forgotten by the Highway: Globalisation, Adverse Incorporation and Chronic Poverty in a Commercial Farming District*. Working Paper No. 4. Cape Town: Programme for Land and Agrarian Studies.

Duchemin, E., F. Wegmuller, and A.-M. Legault. 2008. "Urban Agriculture: Multi-Dimensional Tools for Social Development in Poor Neighbourhoods." *Field Actions Science Reports* 1 (1), 43–52.

Durrheim, K., X. Mtose, and L. Brown. 2011. *Race Trouble: Race, Identity and Inequality in Post-Apartheid South Africa*. Plymouth: Lexington Books.

Erasmus, Z. 2008. "Race." In *New South African Keywords*, edited by N. Shepherd and S. Robins, 169–81. Ohio: Ohio University Press.

Eskenazi, B., J. Chevrier, L.G. Rosas, H.A. Anderson, M.S. Bornman, H. Bouwman, A. Chen, B.A. Cohn, C. De Jager, D.S. Henshel, F. Leipzig, J.S. Leipzig, E.C. Lorenz, S.M. Snedeker, and D. Stapleton. 2009. "The Pine River Statement: Human Health Consequences of DDT Use." *Environmental Health Perspectives* 117 (9): 1359–67.

Feagan, R. 2007. "The Place of Food: Mapping Out the 'Local' in Local Food Systems." *Progress in Human Geography* 31 (1): 23–42.

FIAN International. 2010. *Land Grabbing in Kenya and Mozambique: A Report on Two Research Missions and a Human Rights Analysis of Land Grabbing.* Heidelberg: FIAN International.

Food and Agriculture Organization of the United Nations (FAO). 1996. *Rome Declaration on World Food Security and World Food Summit Plan of Action.* Rome: Food and Agriculture Organization of the United Nations (FAO).

———. 1997. "Women and Sustainable Food Security." In *Women: The Key to Food Security*, edited by Women and Population Division, Sustainable Development Department, Food and Agriculture Organization of the United Nations (FAO). Rome: Food and Agriculture Organization of the United Nations (FAO). http://www.fao.org/docrep/x0171e/x0171e02.htm#P83_10385

———. 2001. *The State of Food Insecurity in the World 2001.* Rome: Food and Agriculture Organization of the United Nations (FAO).

———. 2005. *Voluntary Guidelines to Support the Progressive Realization of the Right to Adequate Food in the Context of National Food Security.* Rome: Food and Agriculture Organization of the United Nations (FAO).

———. 2009. *Thirty-Sixth Session: Report of the Thirty-Fifth Session of the Committee on World Food Security (CFS) Rome, 14, 15 and 17 October 2009 (C 2009/21-Rev.1).* Rome: Food and Agriculture Organization of the United Nations (FAO).

———. 2011. *The State of Food and Agriculture 2010–11. Women in Agriculture: Closing the Gender Gap for Development.* Rome: Food and Agriculture Organization of the United Nations (FAO).

Food and Agriculture Organization of the United Nations (FAO) and Committee on World Food Security (CFS). 2010. *Final Report of the Thirty-Sixth Session of the Committee on World Food Security (CFS). Rome, 11–14 and 16 October 2010.* Rome: Food and Agriculture Organization of the United Nations (FAO); Committee on World Food Security (CFS).

Food Ethics Council. 2010. *Food Justice: The Report of the Food and Fairness Inquiry.* Brighton: Food Ethics Council.

Forum for Food Sovereignty. 2007. *Declaration of Nyéléni.* Sélingué, Mali.

Fourie, P., ed. 2006. *The Political Management of HIV and AIDS in South Africa: One Burden Too Many?* Hampshire: Palgrave MacMillan.

Gerster-Bentaya, M. 2013. "Nutrition-Sensitive Urban Agriculture." *Food Security* 5: 723–37.

"The Giessen Declaration." 2005. *Public Health Nutrition* 8 (6A): 783–86.

Gillespie, S. and S. Kadiyala. 2005. *HIV/AIDS and Food and Nutrition Security: From Evidence to Action.* Washington, D.C.: International Food Policy Research Institute (IFPRI).

Gliessman, S. 2007. *Agroecology: The Ecology of Sustainable Food Systems.* 2nd ed. Boca Raton, FL: Taylor and Francis Group.

Godfray, H. C. J., J. R. Beddington, I. R. Crute, L. Haddad, D. Lawrence, J. F. Muir, J. Pretty, S. Robinson, S. M. Thomas, and C. Toulmin. 2010. "Food Security: The Challenge of Feeding 9 Billion People." *Science* 327 (5967): 812–18.

Gottlieb, R. and A. Fisher. 1996. "Community Food Security and Environmental Justice: Searching for a Common Discourse." *Agriculture and Human Values* 3 (3): 23–32.

Greenberg, S. 2010. *Status Report on Land and Agricultural Policy in South Africa.* University of the Western Cape: Institute for Poverty, Land and Agrarian Studies (PLAAS).

Grethe, H., A. Dembélé, and N. Duman. 2011. *How to Feed the World's Growing Billions. Understanding FAO World Food Projections and their Implications.* Berlin: Heinrich Böll Foundation (HBF); World Wildlife Fund Germany (WWF).

Gross, R., H. Schoeneberger, H. Pfeifer, and H.-J. A. Preuss. 2000. *The Four Dimensions of Food and Nutrition Security: Definition and Concepts.* European Union;

Internationale Weiterbildung und Entwicklung gGmbH (InWent); Food and Agriculture Organization of the United Nations (FAO).

Gussow, J.D. and K. Clancy. 1986. "Dietary Guidelines for Sustainability." *Journal of Nutrition Education* 18: 1–5.

Guyer, J. 1991. "Female Farming in Anthropology and African History." In *Gender at the Crossroads of Knowledge: Feminist Anthropology in the Post Modern Era*, edited by M. Di Leonardo, 257–77. Berkeley: California University Press.

Hall, R. and L. Ntsebeza. 2007. "Introduction." In *The Land Question in South Africa: The Challenge of Transformation and Redistribution*, edited by L. Ntsebeza and R. Hall, 1–24. Cape Town: Human Sciences Research Council.

Hamm, M.W. and A.C. Bellows. 2003. "Community Food Security and Nutrition Educators." *Journal of Nutrition Education and Behavior* 35 (1): 37–43.

Harcourt, W. 2012. "No Economic Justice without Gender Justice [Editorial]." *Development* 55 (3): 257–59.

Harper, A., A. Shattuck, E. Holt-Giménez, A. Alkon, and F. Lambrick. 2009. *Food Policy Councils: Lessons Learned*. Oakland, California: Institute for Food and Development Policy.

Hart, T.G.B. 2012. "How Rural Land Reform Policy Translates into Benefits." *Development Southern Africa* 29 (4): 563–73.

Hine, R., J. Pretty, and S. Twarog. 2008. *Organic Agriculture and Food Security in Africa*, edited by United Nations Environment Programme—United Nations Conference on Trade and Development (UNCTAD-UNEP) Capacity-Building Task Force on Trade, Environment and Development. New York: United Nations.

Hinrichs, C.C. 2003. "The Practice and Politics of Food System Localization." *Journal of Rural Studies* 19 (1): 33–46.

Horton, S., M. Shekar, C. McDonald, A. Mahal, and J.K. Brooks. 2010. *Scaling Up Nutrition: What Will it Cost?* Washington, D.C.: World Bank.

Hosegood, V. and I.M. Timaeus. 2005. "Household Composition and Dynamics in KwaZulu Natal, South Africa: Mirroring Social Reality in Longitudinal Data Collection." In *African Households: Censuses and Surveys*, edited by E. Van der Walle, 58–77. New York: M.E. Sharpe.

Human Rights Watch. 2011. *Ripe with Abuse: Human Rights Conditions in South Africa's Fruit and Wine Industries*. New York: Human Rights Watch.

Ichaporia, A. and C. Lawes. 2013. *What about the Boys? Raising Men to End Violence Against Women*. Pune: Equal Community Foundation.

Institute of Development Studies (IDS). 2013. *IDS Policy Briefing: Getting Unpaid Care onto Development Agendas*. Issue 31. Brighton: Institute of Development Studies (IDS).

Inter Press Service (IPS)—Communicating MDG3. 2012. *Communicating for Change: Voice, Visibility and Impact for Gender Equality—Summary and Highlights*. Rome: Inter Press Service (IPS).

International Assessment of Agricultural Knowledge, Science and Technology for Development (IAASTD). 2009. *Agriculture at a Crossroads: International Assessment of Agricultural Knowledge, Science and Technology for Development: Synthesis Report*, edited by B.D. McIntyre, H.R. Herren, J. Wakhungu and R.T. Watson. Washington, D.C.: Island Press.

International Food Policy Research Institute (IFPRI). 2005. *Women: Still the Key to Food and Nutrition Security*. Washington, D.C.: International Food Policy Research Institute (IFPRI).

———. 2012. *Women's Empowerment in Agriculture Index*. Washington, D.C.: International Food Policy Research Institute (IFPRI).

International Fund for Agricultural Development (IFAD). 2002. *Synthesis Report: Gender and Poverty Targeting in Market Linkage Operations*. Rome: International Fund for Agricultural Development (IFAD): Gender Strengthening Programme for Eastern and Southern Africa Division.

International Union of Nutritional Science (IUNS). 2013. *IUNS 20th International Congress of Nutrition. Granada (Spain) September 15–20, 2013. "Joining Cultures through Nutrition."* Vienna: International Union of Nutritional Science (IUNS).

Jackson, R. and R. Landis. 2002. "The Impact of HIV/AIDS on Food and Nutrition Security." *Entwicklung und Ländlicher Raum* 36 (1): 9–12.

Joint United Nations Programme on HIV/AIDS (UNAIDS). 2002. *AIDS Epidemic Update.* Geneva: Joint United Nations Programme on HIV/AIDS (UNAIDS); World Health Organisation (WHO).

———. 2004. *A UNAIDS Initiative: The Global Coalition on Women and AIDS.* New York: United Nations (UN) General Assembly.

———. 2013. *Global Report. UNAIDS Report on the AIDS Epidemic 2013.* Geneva: Joint United Nations Programme on HIV/AIDS (UNAIDS).

Jones, S. 1999. "Singlehood for Security: Towards a Review of the Relative Economic Status of Women and Children in Woman-Led Households." *Society in Transition* 30 (1): 13–27.

Jonsson, U. 1981. "The Causes of Hunger." *Food and Nutrition Bulletin* 3 (2): 1–9.

———. 2009. "Paradigms in Applied Nutrition" (paper presented at the International Conference on Nutrition (ICN), Bangkok, Thailand, October 5–9, 2009).

Jouanna, J. 2012. *Greek Medicine from Hippocrates to Galen: Selected Papers.* The Netherlands: Koninklijke Brill NV.

Kabeer, N. 1999. "Resources, Agency, Achievements: Reflections on the Measurement of Women's Empowerment." *Development and Change* 30 (3): 435–64.

———. 2001. *Reflections on the Measurement of Women's Empowerment. Discussing Women's Empowerment—Theory and Practice. SidaStudies No. 3.* Stockholm: Novum Grafiska AB.

———. 2005a. "Gender Equality and Women's Empowerment: A Critical Analysis of the Third Millennium Development Goal." *Gender and Development* 13 (1): 13–24.

———. 2005b. "Is Microfinance a 'Magic Bullet' for Women's Empowerment? Analysis of Findings from South Asia." *Economic and Political Weekly* XL (44–45): 4709–18.

Kelly, C. and J. Schulschenk. 2011. "Assessing the Vulnerability of Stellenbosch's Foodsystem and Possibilities for a Local Food Economy." *Development Southern Africa* 28 (4): 563–78.

Kent, G. 2002. "A Gendered Perspective on Nutrition Rights." *Agenda* 17 (51): 43–50.

Klennert, K., ed. 2009. *Achieving Food and Nutrition Security: Actions to Meet the Global Challenge. A Training Course.* Environment, Natural Resources and Food. Feldafing: Internationale Weiterbildung und Entwicklung gGmbH (InWEnt).

Koc, M., R. MacRae, L. J. A. Mougeot, and J. Welsh, eds. 1999. *For Hunger-Proof Cities: Sustainable Urban Food Systems.* Toronto: International Development Research Centre (IDRC); The Centre for Studies in Food Security, Ryerson Polytechnic University.

Kracht, U. 1999. "Hunger, Malnutrition and Poverty: Trends and Prospects towards the 21st Century." In *Food Security and Nutrition: The Global Challenge*, edited by U. Kracht and M. Schulz, 55–74. New York: St. Martin's.

Lahiff, E. 2008a. "Food Crisis Makes Effective Land Reform an Urgent Priority." *Mail & Guardian*, August 29, 2008.

———. 2008b. *Land Reform in South Africa: A Status Report 2008.* Cape Town: Programme for Land and Agrarian Studies.

Lambek, N. C. S., P. Claeys, A. Wong, and L. Brilmayer, eds. 2014. *Rethinking Food Systems: Structural Challenges, New Strategies and the Law.* Dordrecht: Springer.

Lang, T. 1999. "Food Policy for the 21st Century: Can It Be Both Radical and Reasonable?" In *For Hunger-Proof Cities: Sustainable Urban Food Systems*, edited by M. Koc, R. MacRae, L.J.A. Mougeot and J. Welsh, 216–14. Toronto: International Development Research Centre (IDRC); The Centre for Studies in Food Security, Ryerson Polytechnic University.

———. 2012. "Sustainable Diets and Biodiversity: The Challenge for Policy, Evidence and Behaviour Change." In *Sustainable Diets and Biodiversity: Direction and Solutions for Policy, Research and Action*, edited by B. Burlingame and S. Dernini, 20–26. Rome: Food and Agriculture Organization of the United Nations (FAO).

Latham, M.C., U. Jonsson, E. Sterken, and G. Kent. 2011. "Commentary: RUTF Stuff. Can the Children Be Saved with Fortified Peanut Paste?" *World Nutrition* 2 (3): 62–85.

Lemke, S. 2001. "Food and Nutrition Security in Black South African Households: Creative Ways of Coping and Survival." PhD, Centre of Life Sciences, Technical University Munich-Weihenstephan.

———. 2010. "Food Security and Right to Adequate Food in the Context of Land and Agrarian Reform in South Africa." In *Centre for Agriculture in the Tropics and Subtropics Tropenzentrum. Report 2008/2009*, 39–40. Stuttgart: Centre for Agriculture in the Tropics and Subtropics, University of Hohenheim.

Lemke, S., A.C. Bellows, and N. Heumann. 2009. "Gender and Sustainable Livelihoods: Case Study of South African Farm Workers." *International Journal of Innovation and Sustainable Development* 4 (2–3): 195–205.

Lemke, S. and N.S. Jansen van Rensburg. 2014. "Remaining at the Margins: Case Study of Farm Workers in the North West Province, South Africa." *Development Southern Africa* 31 (6): 843–58.

Lemke, S., H.H. Vorster, N.S. Jansen van Rensburg, and J. Ziche. 2003. "Empowered Women, Social Networks and the Contribution of Qualitative Research: Broadening our Understanding of Underlying Causes for Food and Nutrition Insecurity." *Public Health Nutrition* 6 (8): 759–64.

Lemke, S., F. Yousefi, A.C. Eisermann, and A.C. Bellows. 2012. "Sustainable Livelihood Approaches for Exploring Smallholder Agricultural Programmes Targeted at Women—Examples from South Africa." *Journal of Agriculture, Food Systems, and Community Development* 3 (1): 25–41.

Leonhäuser, I.-U., S. Dreschl-Bogale, S. Lemke, E. Yéo, and S. Petermann. 2005. "Afrika im Blick der Ernährungsforschung. Ernährungssicherung in der internationalen Entwicklungszusammenarbeit—eine Haushalts- und Genderperspektive." ["Africa in the Focus of Nutrition Research. Food Security in International Development Cooperation—A Household and Gender Perspective"] *Spiegel der Forschung* 22 (1/2): 44–52.

Levidow, L., M. Pimbert, and G. Vanloqueren. 2014. "Agroecological Research: Conforming—or Transforming the Dominant Agro-Food Regime?" *Agroecology and Sustainable Food Systems* 38: 1–29.

Loevinsohn, M. and S. Gillespie. 2003. *HIV/AIDS, Food Security and Rural Livelihoods: Understanding and Responding*. Washington, D.C.: International Food Policy Research Institute (IFPRI).

Los Angeles Food Policy Task Force. 2010. *The Good Food for all Agenda: Creating a New Regional Food System for Los Angeles*. Los Angeles: Los Angeles Food Policy Task Force.

Luttrell, C., S. Quiroz, C. Scrutton, and K. Bird. 2009. *Understanding and Operationalising Empowerment*. Working Paper No. 308. London: Overseas Development Institute.

Lyson, T.A. 2004. *Civic Agriculture: Reconnecting Farm, Food, and Community*. Massachusetts: Tufts University Press.

Martinez, S., M. Hand, M. Da Pra, S. Pollack, K. Ralston, T. Smith, S. Vogel, S. Clark, L. Tauer, S.A. Low, and C. Newman. 2010. *Local Food Systems: Concepts,*

Impacts, and Issues, ERR 97. Washington, D.C.: U.S. Department of Agriculture, Economic Research Service.

Maxwell, S. 1996. "Food Security: A Post-Modern Perspective." *Food Policy* 21 (2): 155–70.

Maxwell, S. and T. R. Frankenberger. 1992. *Household Food Security: Concepts, Indicators, Measurements—A Technical Review.* New York: United Nations Children's Fund (UNICEF); International Fund for Agricultural Development (IFAD).

Mazonde, I. N. 2000. "Social Transformation and Food Security in the Household: The Experience of Rural Botswana." In *Botswana—Alltagswelten im Umbruch: Facets of a Changing Society,* edited by F. Krueger, G. Rakelmann and P. Schierholz, 53–73. Hamburg: Lit Verlag.

McCullum, C., E. Desjardins, V. I. Kraak, P. Lapido, and H. Costello. 2005. "Evidence-Based Strategies to Build Community Food Security." *Journal of the American Dietetic Association* 105 (2): 278–83.

Meinzen-Dick, R., J. Behrman, P. Menon, and A. R. Quisumbing. 2012. "Gender: A Key Dimension Linking Agricultural Programs to Improved Nutrition and Health." In *Reshaping Agriculture for Nutrition and Health,* edited by S. Fan and R. Pandya-Lorch, 135–44. Washington, D.C.: International Food Policy Research Institute (IFPRI).

Messer, E. 1990. "Intra-Household Allocation of Resources: Perspectives from Anthropology." In *Intra-Household Resource Allocation: Issues and Methods for Development Policy and Planning,* edited by B. L. Rogers and N. P. Schlossmann, 51–62. Tokyo: United Nations University Press.

Mills, G. 2010. *Why Africa Is Poor and What Africans Can Do about It.* Johannesburg: Penguin.

Moghadam, V. M. and L. Senftova. 2005. "Measuring Women's Empowerment: Participation and Rights in Civil, Political, Social, Economic, and Cultural Domains." *International Social Science Journal* 57 (184): 389–412.

Monsalve Suárez, S. 2012. "The Human Rights Framework in Contemporary Agrarian Struggles." *The Journal of Peasant Studies* 40 (1): 1–52.

Moodie, R., D. Stuckler, C. Monteiro, N. Sheron, B. Neal, T. Thamarangsi, P. Lincoln, and S. Casswell. 2013. "Profits and Pandemics: Prevention of Harmful Effects of Tobacco, Alcohol, and Ultra-Processed Food and Drink Industries." *The Lancet* 381 (9867): 670–79.

Möser, A., I.-U. Leonhäuser, U. Zander, and U. Meier-Gräwe. 2005. "Employment Rate of Women and Everyday Life Food Routines—An International Comparison. Abstracts—18th International Congress of Nutrition, Durban, South Africa, September 19–23, 2005." *Annals of Nutrition & Metabolism* 49 (Suppl. 1): 1–440.

Murphy, L. L., P. Harvey, and E. Silvestre. 2005. "How Do We Know What We Know about the Impact of AIDS on Food and Livelihood Insecurity? A Review of Empirical Research from Rural Sub Saharan Africa." *Human Organization* 64 (3): 265–75.

Murray, C. 1976. Keeping House in Lesotho. Unpublished Ph.D. thesis, Cambridge: University of Cambridge.

Netting, McC. R., R. R. Wilk, and E. J. Arnould, eds. 1984. *Households: Comparative and Historical Studies of the Domestic Group.* Berkeley, Los Angeles: University of California Press.

Ntsebeza, L. and R. Hall, eds. 2007. *The Land Question in South Africa: The Challenge of Transformation and Redistribution.* Cape Town: Human Sciences Research Council.

Office on the Status of Women [South Africa]. 2000. *South Africa's National Policy Framework for Women's Empowerment and Gender Equality.* Johannesburg: Office on the Status of Women [South Africa].

Ortmann, G. F. and R. P. King. 2010. "Research on Agri-Food Supply Chains in Southern Africa Involving Small-Scale Farmers: Current Status and Future Possibilities." *Agrekon* 49 (4): 397–417.

Pasteur, K. 2002. *Gender Analysis for Sustainable Livelihoods—Frameworks, Tools and Links to Other Sources.* Eldis.

Patel, R. C. 2012. "Food Sovereignty: Power, Gender and the Right to Food." *PLoS Medicine* 9 (6): 1–4.

Pinstrup-Andersen, P. 2013a. "Nutrition-Sensitive Food Systems: From Rhetoric to Action." *The Lancet* 382 (9890): 375–76.

Pinstrup-Andersen, P. 2013b. *Preparatory Technical Meeting for the International Conference on Nutrition (ICN2). Nutrition-Enhancing Food and Agricultural Systems.* PTM-ICN2 2013/05, 13–15 November, 2013. Rome: Food and Agriculture Organization of the United Nations (FAO); World Health Organization (WHO).

Piot, P. 2001. *Keynote Address: Nutrition and HIV/AIDS.* Geneva: United Nations Administrative Committee on Co-ordination/ Sub-Committee on Nutrition (ACC/SCN).

Piot, P. and P. Pinstrup-Andersen. 2002. *IFPRI Annual Report Essay 2001–2002.* Washington, D.C.: International Food Policy Research Institute (IFPRI).

Posel, D. 2010. "Races to Consume: Revisiting South Africa's History of Race, Consumption and the Struggle for Freedom." *Ethnic and Racial Studies* 33 (2): 157–75.

Prabhu, V. S. 2010. "Tests of Intrahousehold Resource Allocation using a CV Framework: A Comparison of Husbands' and Wives' Separate and Joint WTP in the Slums of Navi-Mumbai, India." *World Development* 38 (4): 606–19.

Pretty, J. N., A. D. Noble, D. Bossio, J. Dixon, R. E. Hine, F. W. Penning De Vries, and J. I. Morison. 2006. "Resource-Conserving Agriculture Increases Yields in Developing Countries." *Environmental Science and Technology* 40 (4): 1114–19.

Pretty, J., C. Toulmin, and S. Williams. 2011. "Sustainable Intensification in African Agriculture." *International Journal of Agricultural Sustainability* 9 (1): 5–24.

Quisumbing, A. R. 2010. *Implementing the Internationally Agreed Goals and Commitments in Regard to Gender Equality and Empowerment of Women. Gender Equality and Poverty Eradication: Good Practices and Lessons Learned. Commission on the Status of Women, Fifty-Fourth Session.* New York: United Nations (UN).

Quisumbing, A. R., Lynn R. Brown, H. S. Feldstein, L. Haddad, and C. Peña. 1995. *Women: The Key to Food Security.* Washington, D.C.: International Food Policy Research Institute (IFPRI).

Quisumbing, A. R. and L. C. Smith. 2007. "Case Study No. 4–5. Intrahousehold Allocation, Gender Relations, and Food Security in Developing Countries." In *Food Policy for Developing Countries: Case Studies*, edited by P. Pinstrup-Andersen and F. Cheng, 13 pp. Ithaca, New York: Cornell University.

Ramphele, M. and E. Boonzaier. 1988. "The Position of African Women: Race and Gender in South Africa." In *The Uses and Abuses of Political Concepts*, edited by E. Boonzaier and J. Sharp, 153–66. Cape Town: David Philip.

Rangan, H. and M. Gilmartin. 2002. "Gender, Traditional Authority, and the Politics of Rural Reform in South Africa." *Development and Change* 33 (4): 633–58.

Razavi, S. and C. Miller. 1995. *From WID to GAD: Conceptual Shifts in the Women and Development Discourse.* Occasional Paper No. 1. Geneva: United Nations Research Institute for Social Development (UNRISD); United Nations Development Programme (UNDP).

Reddy, V. and R. Moletsane. 2009. *The Gendered Dimensions of Food Security in South Africa: A Review of the Literature.* Pretoria: Human Sciences Research Council (HSRC).

Republic of South Africa. 1996. *The Constitution of the Republic of South Africa. No. 108 of 1996.*

Roberts, W. 2010. "Food Policy Encounters of a Third Kind: How the Toronto Food Policy Council Socializes for Sustain-Ability." In *Imagining Sustainable Food Systems: Theory and Practice*, edited by A. Blay-Plamer, 173–200. Farnham and Burlington: Ashgate.

Rogers, B. L. and N. P. Schlossmann, eds. 1990. *Intra-Household Resource Allocation: Issues and Methods for Development Policy and Planning.* Tokyo: United Nations University Press.

Rosche, D. 2011. *A Blueprint for UN Women.* Oxford; London: Oxfam; Voluntary Service Overseas (VSO).

Sanghi, R., M. K. K. Pillai, T. R. Jayalekshmi, and A. Nair. 2003. "Organochlorine and Organophosphorus Pesticide Residues in Breast Milk from Bhopal, Madhya Pradesh, India." *Human and Experimental Toxicology* 22 (2): 73–76.

Schäfer, R. 2002. "Gender und ländliche Entwicklung in Afrika." *Politik und Zeitgeschichte* B13–14: 31–38.

———. 2005. *Im Schatten der Apartheid. Frauen-Rechtsorganisationen und geschlechtsspezifische Gewalt in Südafrika.* Münster: Lit Verlag.

———. 2012. *Gender und ländliche Entwicklung in Afrika. Eine Kommentierte Bibliographie. [Gender and Rural Development in Africa. An Annotated Bibliography]* 3. aktualisierte und erweiterte Auflage. Münster: Lit Verlag.

Scherr, S. 2003. *Halving Global Hunger. Background Paper of the Millennium Project Task Force on Hunger.* New York: United Nations Development Programme (UNDP).

Schuftan, C. 2010. "Governments in Times of Crisis: Seeking an Excuse to Brush-Off Their Responsibility in Upholding the Human Right to Nutrition?" In *Right to Food and Nutrition WATCH 2010*: 18–21.

Schweitzer, E. 2008. "How Black Farm Workers Become Land and Business Owners: Actors, Resources, Contexts and Outcomes of Black Empowerment Projects in the South African Wine Industry." *Stichproben. Wiener Zeitschrift für kritische Afrikastudien* 8 (15): 31–53.

Scialabba, N. 2000. "Factors Influencing Organic Agriculture Policies with a Focus on Developing Countries" (paper presented at the IFOAM 2000 Scientific Conference, Basel, Switzerland, August 28–31, 2000).

Scoones, I. 1998. *Sustainable Rural Livelihoods: A Framework for Analysis.* Sussex: Institute for Development Studies (IDS).

———. 2009. "Livelihoods Perspectives and Rural Development." *Journal of Peasant Studies* 36 (1): 171–96.

Seekings, J. and N. Nattrass. 2005. *Class, Race, and Inequality in South Africa.* London: Yale University Press.

Seitz, V. 2010. *Afrika wird armregiert oder wie man Afrika wirklich helfen kann.* München: Deutscher Taschenbuch Verlag.

Sen, A. 1981. *Poverty and Famines: An Essay on Entitlements and Deprivation.* Oxford: Clarendon Press.

Shabodien, F. 2006. *Livelihoods Struggles of Women Farm Workers in South Africa.* Stellenbosch, South Africa: Women on Farms Project (WFP).

Shackleton, S., C. Shackleton, and B. Cousins. 2000. *Re-Valuing the Communal Lands of Southern Africa: New Understandings of Rural Livelihoods.* London: Overseas Development Institute.

Sharp, J. 1994. "A World Turned Upside Down: Households and Differentiation in a South African Bantustan in the 1980s." *African Studies* 53 (1): 71–88.

Smallhorne, M. 2013. "The Tide Is High—Is This a Historic Moment in the Fight Against Gender-Based Violence?" *Mail & Guardian*, 37.

Smith, C. 2000. "A Society of Rapists." *Weekly Mail & Guardian*, April 7, 2000.

Spiegel, A. D., V. Watson, and P. Wilkinson. 1996. "Domestic Diversity and Fluidity among Some African Households in Greater Cape Town." *Social Dynamics* 22 (1): 1–30.

Steyn, N.P. 2005. "The 18th International Congress of Nutrition Takes Place on African Soil." *Public Health Nutrition* 8 (5): 441–43.

Suárez Franco, A. M. and S. Ratjen. 2007. *Screen State Action against Hunger! How to Use the Voluntary Guidelines on the Right to Food to Monitor Public Policy.* Bonn and Heidelberg: Welthungerhilfe; FIAN International.

Sydenham, E. 2009. *Women and the Right to Livelihoods: World Social Forum 2009. Testimonies and Discussions.* New Delhi: Programme on Women's Economic, Social and Cultural Rights (PWESCR).

Thomas, B. and L.O. Gostin. 2013. "Tackling the Global NCD Crisis: Innovations in Law and Governance." *Journal of Law, Medicine and Ethics* Spring: 16–27.

Thomson, J.S., A.N. Maretzki, and A.H. Harmon. 2007. "Community-Initiated Dialogue: Strengthening the Community through the Local Food System." In *Remaking the North American Food System: Redefining Foodways in a Changing World*, edited by C.C. Hinrichs and T.A. Lyson, 183–98. University of Nebraska Press.

Townsend, J., E. Zapata, J. Rowlands, P. Alberti, and M. Mercado. 1999. *Women and Power: Fighting Patriarchy and Poverty.* London: Zed Books.

United Nations Children's Fund (UNICEF). 1990. *A UNICEF Policy Review: Strategy for Improved Nutrition of Children and Women in Developing Countries.* New York: United Nations Children's Fund (UNICEF).

United Nations Department of Economic and Social Affairs (UNDESA). 2010. *The World's Women 2010: Trends and Statistics.* New York: United Nations (UN).

———. 2015. *Progress of the World's Women 2015–2016: Transforming Economies, Realizing Rights.* New York: United Nations (UN).

United Nations Entity for Gender Equality and the Empowerment of Women (UN Women). 2014. *World Survey on the Role of Women in Development 2014: Gender Equality and Sustainable Development.* New York: United Nations (UN).

United Nations General Assembly. 1948. *Universal Declaration of Human Rights, Adopted by General Assembly Resolution 217 A(III) of 10 December 1948.* Geneva: United Nations Office of the High Commissioner for Human Rights (OHCHR).

———. 1992a. *Report of the United Nations Conference on Environment and Development, Rio de Janeiro, 3–14 June 1992, A/Conf.151/26 (Vol. 1).* New York: United Nations (UN) General Assembly.

———. 1992b. *Report of the United Nations Conference on Environment and Development, Rio de Janeiro, 3–14 June 1992, A/Conf.151/26 (Vol. 2).* New York: United Nations (UN) General Assembly.

———. 1998. *Rome Statute of the International Criminal Court. Text of the Rome Statute Circulated as Document A/CONF.183/9 of 17 July 1998 and Corrected by Process-Verbaux of 10 November 1998, 12 July 1999, 30 November 1999, 8 May 2000, 17 January 2001 and 16 January 2002. The Statute Entered into Force on 1 July 2002.* New York: United Nations (UN) General Assembly.

———. 2001. *Declaration of Commitment on HIV/AIDS. 2 August 2001, A/RES/S-26/2.* New York: United Nations (UN) General Assembly.

———. 2012. *Resolution Adopted by the General Assembly on 27 July 2012 [Without Reference to a Main Committee (A/66/L.56)]. 66/288. The Future We Want. A/RES/66/288, 11 September 2012.* New York: United Nations (UN) General Assembly.

———. 2013. *Extreme Poverty and Human Rights. Note by the Secretary-General. Report of the Special Rapporteur on Extreme Poverty and Human Rights, Magdalena Sepúlveda Carmona. A/68/293, 9 August 2013.* New York: United Nations (UN) General Assembly.

United Nations Human Rights Council (HRC). 2009. *Report Presented by the Special Rapporteur on the Right to Food [Olivier De Schutter] at the 12th Session of the United Nations Human Rights Council. A/HRC/12/31, 21 July 2009.* New York: United Nations (UN) General Assembly.

———. 2010. *Agroecology and the Right to Food. Report Presented [by the Special Rapporteur on the Right to Food, Olivier De Schutter,] at the 16th Session of the United Nations Human Rights Council. A/HRC/16/49, 20 December 2010*. New York: United Nations (UN) General Assembly.

———. 2011. *Report Submitted by the Special Rapporteur on the Right to Food, Olivier De Schutter, at the Nineteenth Session of the United Nations Human Rights Council. A/HRC/19/59, 26 December 2011*. New York: United Nations (UN) General Assembly.

———. 2012. *Report Submitted by the Special Rapporteur on the Right to Food, Olivier De Schutter: Women's Rights and the Right to Food. A/HRC/22/50, 24 December 2012*. New York: United Nations (UN) General Assembly.

United Nations Standing Committee on Nutrition (SCN). 2010. *Sixth Report on the World Nutrition Situation: Progress in Nutrition*. Geneva: United Nations Standing Committee on Nutrition (SCN).

———. 2014. *Findings from a Review of Country Level Programming in Nutrition-Sensitive Agriculture*. Geneva: United Nations Standing Committee on Nutrition (SCN).

van Der Vliet, V. 1991. "Traditional Husbands, Modern Wives? Constructing Marriages in a South African Township." In *Tradition and Transition in Southern Africa*, edited by A.D. Spiegel and P.A. McAllister, 219–41. Johannesburg: Witwatersrand University Press.

van Onselen, C. 1996. *The Seed Is Mine: The Life of Kas Maine, A South African Sharecropper 1894–1985*. New York: Hill and Wang.

Vandemeer, J.H. 2011. *The Ecology of Agroecosystems*. Sudbury, MA: Jones and Bartlett.

Viana, R.S.G. and A.C. Bellows. 2014. " 'Teacher, We Are Hungry.' The Violation of *Quilombola* Students' Right to Adequate Food: A Case Study." *International Journal of Human Rights*. DOI: 10.1080/13642987.2014.932773.

von Braun, J., M.T. Ruel, and S. Gillespie. 2010. "Bridging the Gap: Linking Agriculture and Health to Achieve the Millennium Development Goals." In *The African Food System and its Interaction with Human Health and Nutrition*, edited by P. Pinstrup-Andersen, 279–303. London: Cornell University Press; United Nations University.

Webb, P. and J. von Braun. 1993. *Ending Hunger Soon: Concepts and Priorities. Background Paper Prepared for the Conference on Overcoming Global Hunger, November 29-December 1*. Washington, D.C.: World Bank.

Wegerif, M., B. Russel, and I. Grundling. 2005. *Still Searching for Security: The Reality of Farm Dweller Evictions in South Africa*. Johannesburg: Nkuzi Development Association and Social Surveys.

White, F. 2010. "Deepening Democracy: A Farm Workers' Movement in the Western Cape." *Journal of Southern African Studies* 36 (3): 673–91.

Wichterich, C. 2012. *The Future We Want: A Feminist Perspective*. Publication Series on Ecology. Volume 21. Berlin: Heinrich Böll Stiftung.

Wilkins, J. 2007. "Eating Right Here: The Role of Dietary Guidance in Remaking Community-Based Food Systems." In *Remaking the North American Food System: Redefining Foodways in a Changing World*, edited by C.C. Hinrichs and T.A. Lyson, 163–82. University of Nebraska Press.

Windfuhr, M. 2007. "Experiences from Case Related Right to Food Work: Lessons Learned for Implementation." In *Food and Human Rights in Development, Volume II: Evolving Issues and Emerging Applications*, edited by W.B. Eide and U. Kracht, 331–58. Antwerpen: Intersentia.

Windfuhr, M. and J. Jonsén. 2005. *Food Sovereignty: Towards Democracy in Localized Food Systems*. Warwickshire: ITDG.

Winne, M. 2008. *Closing the Food Gap: Resetting the Table in the Land of Plenty.* Boston: Beacon Press.

Wölte, S. 2008. *International—National—Lokal, FrauenMenschenrechte und Frauenbewegung in Kenia.* Königstein: Ulrike Helmer Verlag.

Women's Health Project. 2000. *Violence Against Women: It's Importance for HIV/ AIDS Prevention and Care. News and Views.* Johannesburg: Women's Health Research Centre, University of the Witwatersrand.

World Bank. 2007. *From Agriculture to Nutrition: Pathways, Synergies and Outcomes.* Washington, D.C.: The International Bank for Reconstruction and Development; World Bank.

———. 2011. *World Development Report 2012: Gender Equality and Development.* Washington, D.C.: The International Bank for Reconstruction and Development; World Bank.

World Bank, Food and Agriculture Organization of the United Nations (FAO), and International Fund for Agricultural Development (IFAD). 2009. *Gender in Agriculture Sourcebook.* Washington, D.C.: World Bank Publications.

Ziegler, J., C. Golay, C. Mahon, and S.A. Way. 2011. *The Fight for the Right to Food: Lessons Learned.* International Relations and Developments. Hampshire and New York: Palgrave Macmillan.

6 Closing Protection Gaps through a More Comprehensive Conceptual Framework for the Human Right to Adequate Food and Nutrition

Flavio L. S. Valente, Ana María Suárez Franco, and R. Denisse Córdova Montes

INTRODUCTION

In this chapter, we concentrate on the role of human rights in improving women's food and nutrition security and in reducing overall hunger and malnutrition. In an effort to do this, we delve into the existing disconnects and fragmentations present in the current human right to adequate food and nutrition concept and why the manner in which human rights are defined and applied by some sectors might have contributed to a failure in protection due to conceptual limitations induced by social and political pressures. Nonetheless, we are guided by the argument that human rights promote a more precise diagnosis of, and help overcome, the root causes of inequities observed in society, which are linked to abuses of power. In this context, we put forward some constructive ways to surmount the limitations in the existing conceptual framework of the right to adequate food and nutrition through the proposal of a more holistic concept for this human right. In relation to political processes regarding the redefinition and implementation of this human rights framework, we call for increasing coordination with and among social movements and make recommendations for the use of this new framework through the creation of precedent through casework at the national and international levels.

Building upon material discussed in earlier chapters of this volume, we propose the food sovereignty framework, which calls for a more explicit integration of self-determination, women's rights and a gender perspective, and nutrition, as the framework for the right to adequate food concept. Based on this, we argue that the right to adequate food should be renamed the human right to adequate food *and nutrition*. At the same time, we seek to demonstrate that working within the core principles of indivisibility and interrelatedness of human rights is fundamental to support policy coherence that maintains people at its center in global, national, regional, and local food and nutritional security governance. This effort, applied in a participative manner, is intended to sharpen our human rights tools, adjusting them to the current challenges in order to provide adequate mechanisms for ensuring a life of dignity for each and every human being and especially for the most disadvantaged and marginalized ones in our societies.

In our analysis and proposals we are guided by the understanding that the human rights approach is not immune to social and political interests—especially of the powerful elites—present in our societies, and must, therefore, be constantly updated in order to continue serving its purpose of providing universal protection. The principle of evolutive interpretation and the effectiveness principle call for existing human rights treaty clauses to be interpreted in light of contemporary conditions when monitoring bodies and other legal operators apply human rights treaties in order to tackle upcoming promotion and protection challenges.[1] As such, these principles of interpretation are significant throughout our chapter because they call for the human rights framework to incorporate new dimensions that are made visible by the continued struggles of different social groups and movements against oppression and discrimination in order to remain effective.[2]

This chapter is organized into five main parts. The first part, "Historical overview of conceptual limitations in the human rights framework as a reflection of the use and abuse of power," discusses the limitations in the current conceptual framework of the right to adequate food and nutrition. This first section links these limitations to the abuse of power and emphasizes the importance of adjusting the framework to the new dimensions made visible by social struggles in order to overcome the structural causes of hunger and malnutrition. The second part, "Advances and missed opportunities in the development of the legal concept of the human right to adequate food and nutrition," describes conceptual advances made over the years that should have pointed to the need for a shift in the understanding of the human right to adequate food and nutrition. It also describes missed opportunities to incorporate these advances into a more inclusive right to adequate food and nutrition and the resulting conceptual foundations that contributed to the authors' new proposed framework. The third part, "The food sovereignty framework for the human right to adequate food and nutrition: a proposal for a more advanced and integral framework incorporating women's rights and nutrition," introduces the authors' new proposed framework for the human right to adequate food and nutrition and presents the People's and Food Sovereignty Matrix, which visually captures the new proposed conceptual framework. The fourth part, "Collaborating with social movements in the reconceptualization of a unifying framework," emphasizes the importance of fostering coordination with and among social movements in order to develop a unifying conceptual framework for the human right to adequate food and nutrition. Finally, "Moving from theory to practice: recommendations," offers specific recommendations at the national and international levels on how to practically move the proposed conceptual framework from mere theory to reality.

HISTORICAL OVERVIEW OF CONCEPTUAL LIMITATIONS IN THE HUMAN RIGHTS FRAMEWORK AS A REFLECTION OF THE USE AND ABUSE OF POWER

Despite the great potential of the human rights system, human rights instruments—especially those adopted through political negotiations between states—often reflect the conflicts of interests permeating national and international communities. The human rights system must, therefore, be constantly updated in order to incorporate the advances achieved in different fronts of the struggle by different social groups against oppression and discrimination, covering old and emerging promotion and protection gaps.

In this section, we present a brief historical overview of the concept of the human right to adequate food and nutrition as a social construct (for a more comprehensive review, please see chapter 1 of this volume), discuss the limitations that arise from social influences defining the framework, and analyze the role of the principle of evolutive interpretation in overcoming these fragmentations. Furthermore, we analyze the structural causes of hunger and malnutrition that are kept invisible by these processes.

The Human Right to Adequate Food and Nutrition: A Social Construct

Beyond the historically—and socially—constructed ideological divides between economic, social, and cultural rights and civil and political rights resulting in the creation of two separate international human rights covenants during the twentieth century, the concept of the human right to adequate food and nutrition has suffered from further rifts (see Gross et al. 2000; Maxwell 1996; Maxwell and Frankenberger 1992; Maxwell and Smith 1992; see also chapter 5 of this volume). One trend has mainly identified the right to adequate food and nutrition as the right to be free from hunger and associated it with food aid or assistance. From another set of perspectives, the human right to adequate food and nutrition has been historically associated with the right to have access to productive resources to produce food, or to have resources to buy food (see W. B. Eide and Kracht 2005, 2007). However, the nutritional dimension has not been effectively or clearly incorporated into either one of these two main trends. Similarly, the special situation and role of women in relation to the human right to adequate food and nutrition is not fully taken into account in *General Comment 12 on the Right to Adequate Food* (hereinafter, *General Comment 12*) issued by the United Nations Committee on Economic, Social and Cultural Rights (CESCR; see CESCR 1999b).[3] Ideological disconnects related to the human right to adequate food, its nutritional dimension, and women's rights are also evident in the *Convention on the Elimination of All Forms of Discrimination against Women* (CEDAW; see UN General Assembly 1979) and the *Convention on the Rights of the Child* (CRC; see UN General Assembly 1989; and see also chapter 2 of this volume).

Social Determinants of the Conceptual Limitations in the Human Rights Framework

As previously illustrated, human rights instruments are social constructs and reflect social conflicts which are then mirrored in conceptual limitations in the human right to adequate food and nutrition. In chapter 2 of this volume, two main structural disconnects in the human rights system were identified and discussed. The authors identified the structural isolation of women's rights from the right to adequate food and nutrition through the very reduced reference to women in the language of the *International Covenant on Economic, Social and Cultural Rights* (ICESCR; see UN General Assembly 1966), which leads to the invisibility of women in this document, as well as the reduction of women to motherhood in relation to food and nutrition security under CEDAW and the CRC as a structural disconnect in the current human rights framework to the right to adequate food and nutrition. As part of this first structural disconnect, the authors also identified the resulting disempowerment of women that is in turn reflected in the human rights system's lack of acknowledgment of the power and capacity of women throughout their life spans and across their diverse life roles. A second disconnect was the isolation of the right to adequate food from its nutritional component through the inconsistent role nutrition plays in the right to adequate food under the ICESCR, CEDAW, and the CRC.

In addition to these two structural disconnects, the following fragmentations have been identified—in the previous chapters of this volume as well as in this chapter—in the human rights approach to public policies, in implementation practices, and in the legal and conceptual frameworks related to the right to adequate food and nutrition:

- *The present analysis of hunger and malnutrition does not fully address structural root causes.*[4] This results in proposed policy solutions that, in a reductionist and simplified manner, mainly deal with the symptoms through the use of the "business as usual" isolated tools.[5] These inadequate solutions to hunger and malnutrition include calls to increase food production,[6] nutritional education initiatives that do not engage local knowledge and participatory pedagogy,[7] micronutrient supplementation,[8] and more political will,[9] among others.
- *Different sets of rights are addressed separately.*[10] The lack of recognition in the current practical application of the legal framework of the right to adequate food and nutrition of the interdependence of civil and political rights, economic, social, and cultural rights, women's rights, children's rights, maternal rights, the right to adequate food, and the right to nutrition, among others, overlooks the complexity of the links

existing among them in reality. The root causes of social exclusion and deprivation, associated with political and economic oppression, can be missed if these links are not adequately analyzed. Only by taking these into account will we be able to identify more holistic solutions for overcoming hunger and malnutrition.

- *Compliance with the three levels of human rights: state obligations are addressed in a disconnected or unbalanced manner.* Measures adopted to comply with the obligations to respect, protect, and fulfill (facilitate, promote, and provide) must be implemented in an integrated manner. For example, the provision of food by governments, in situations in which people cannot feed themselves for reasons beyond their control, should be *implemented* while also ensuring that the food is safe and adequate. Furthermore, these efforts should also be accompanied by measures that promote the recovery of the capacity to feed oneself, such as the promotion of access to productive resources (land, seeds, technical assistance, etc.), of job opportunities and income generation, as well as of unemployment insurance and social security programs. At the same time, while states should take into account the fact that there are people who will require social protection throughout their whole lives, social protection programs should not replace the obligations to respect, protect, and promote the access of all to natural resources and/or the necessary income to feed themselves.
- *Human beings are separated from nature through public policies, state conducts, and current legal frameworks.*[11] This fragmentation is expressed in human beings' lack of control and sovereignty over access and use of natural resources for the production of food. It is further connected to the lack of social control over the manner in which these resources are put to use, and for what, and to the limited physical and economic access people have over their products, including their lack of choice and of freedom to choose.
- *Human beings, in particular women, are separated from their own human nature through public policies, state conducts, current legal frameworks, and social and cultural practices.*[12] This fragmentation is depicted through women's restricted access to food to guarantee their adequate growth and development, as well as their limited freedom of choice and self-determination over what to do with their own lives and bodies, such as restrictions of their reproductive rights and eating practices, and their restricted capabilities to enjoy nutritional and health well-being and human dignity.
- *The collective and independent subjectivities of women and children are reflected in an inadequate and often imbalanced way in human rights instruments.*[13] This fragmentation in public policies and legal frameworks does not adequately embrace the intertwined collective and independent subjectivities of mother and child during pregnancy and breastfeeding. In order to address this, there is the need for legal

and programmatic attention that expressly articulates the interconnectedness and concurrent independence of mother and child, as well as the time dependent and specific food and nutrition rights and needs of women in pregnancy and children up to the age of two. However, it is also crucial that these efforts do not result in the neglect of women's, men's, and children's individual food and nutrition rights and specific needs over their life spans nor, more generally, of their human rights over their life spans (i.e., reproductive rights, the right to self-determination, and the right to participation).

- *Food sovereignty is not taken into account by the decision-making power mostly at the service of the interests of transnational corporations (TNCs) and national and international elites.* This is reflected in the lack of effective and coordinated participation of relevant female, as well as male social actors, in the elaboration and implementation of policies and regulations in the fields of trade, finance, job generation, agriculture, social security, environment, health, food security, and nutrition policies.[14]

  - *Unbalanced emphasis is placed on rural—over urban—women's right to adequate food and nutrition issues.* This is reflected in the various human rights standards, where the focus is on rural women's right to adequate food and nutrition, while ignoring the unique situations that lead urban women to be food insecure.[15] Furthermore, the relationship between threats and violations of the right to adequate food and nutrition of rural women and the migration of these women to urban environments, where they continue to be food insecure, is often overlooked in the analysis of women's right to adequate food and nutrition.

The Invisibility of Violence as a Central Component of the Structural Causes of Hunger and Malnutrition

As exemplified above, the fragmentations present in the current human rights framework result in the invisibility of a number of structural causes of hunger and malnutrition, and the related invisibility and silencing of those affected by these processes. These fragmentations have as one of their central components the invisibility of violence as a common thread that unites these structural causes of hunger and malnutrition.[16]

The ongoing grab of land and natural resources, or "earthgrab"—which is a consequence of the current production model and investment policies, among other things—results in peoples' violent separation from their individual and collective natural resources, such as land, water, forests, and minerals. The violent eviction of "invisible" social groups, as well as the exclusion of affected parties from decision-making processes, is a structural component of the hegemonic international model of development not compliant with the primacy of human rights. Powerful elites, often making use of armed forces, forcefully evict the traditional populations that have occupied the territories for generations, or close their eyes to forceful evictions carried out by private militias. These events are seen as part of the natural course of "development," which is supported by the present international governance structure to guarantee cheaper access to raw materials to maintain rates of profit. This violence is usually justified by property and use laws, historically established by the national and international powerful elites, and by their alleged use for the benefit of the public good, such as mega development projects (e.g., dams, special economic zones, tourist resorts, mining sites, etc.). What happens in reality is that national elites make use of concessions to private corporate interests and to foreign governments for their own benefit and continued enrichment, which results in overall inequalities among rich and poor countries, as well as within developing and developed countries. Furthermore, social groups and peoples who resist and defend their territories and cultures are stigmatized as "backward," an impediment to progress and development, and even criminalized.[17]

Additionally, powerful interests, through economic policies and practices, have also caused many states' violent separation from their own capacity and authority to employ social protection programs to fulfill the capabilities and rights of their populace to achieve food security and nutrition (see A. Eide 2005, 12–17). Behind this, one can find structural adjustment policies implemented since the 1970s by the International Monetary Fund (IMF) and the World Bank as a condition for international financial loans. Since 1994 and the finalization of the Uruguay Round of the General Agreement on Tariffs and Trade (GATT), states' tools to protect the rights of those in their territory, including through the use of subsidies, tariffs, and regulation, have been further compromised. States ability to meet their *protect* obligations in the trade context was stifled at the very same time as the right to adequate food and nutrition system started to develop. The 1994 GATT reduced the ability of states to protect their own food systems and economies, promising that international trade and a free market optimize food supply. The Uruguay Round facilitated industrial monopolies to expand delivery of commercialized forms of medical cures for malnutrition, be it folic acid for pregnant women or ready to use foods (RUFs) for young children, without addressing the structural conditions of rights violations that instigate malnutrition and hunger and without consideration of the role of nutrition in local food systems and economies (see Madeley 2000).

The present agroindustrial, capital, and chemical input intensive agricultural model of production results in the violent separation of peoples from their culturally traditional eating patterns. This model of food production, which is based on extensive production, monocultures, genetically modified organisms (GMOs), reduced biodiversity, monopolization, and verticalization of production, has a direct effect on water and soil contamination, rural exodus, climate change, and the reduction of diet diversity, safety, and nutritional quality. This violent destruction of the manner in which individuals and peoples have traditionally fed themselves is a structural cause of hunger and malnutrition for current and future generations. Hunger results from the eviction, landgrab, and low wages, among other grievances, that are caused by such violence, while malnutrition results from the lower quality of food, reduction of food diversity, and food contamination prevalent in the current model of food production. The present model does not take into account the real social, cultural, environmental, health, climate change, and other human costs that heavily subsidize the profits of the food and agricultural corporate sector, and, instead, transfers these human costs to the directly affected populations (i.e., agricultural workers, consumers, evicted populations, etc.) and to society as a whole. Furthermore, this model has also subsidized the industrial and services sectors by increasing their profits through the maintaining of food costs artificially low and excluding small-scale producers from the markets through dumping practices (see also chapter 5 of this volume).[18]

In a similar manner, the marketing and advertising practices of the corporate food sector also result in the violent separation of peoples from their traditional eating and nutrition patterns, which is a structural cause of hunger and malnutrition. Through the inappropriate advertising practices directed at parents of infants, children, and adolescents, which combine the closely linked interests of the agribusiness and food industry, an increase in malnutrition has resulted in both developing and developed countries (see also chapter 4 of this volume).[19]

Another structural cause of hunger and malnutrition is the blatant structural violence against women and girls. This violence is sometimes enshrined in the law and/or policies; however, it remains especially present in the cultural practices of diverse societies. Cultural violence is invisible due to the patriarchal lens that is still very much hegemonic in present-day global society, with variations among countries and cultures, but still pervasive overall. Structural violence against girls and women takes place at the community and household levels in the form of child marriage, genital mutilation, and domestic violence, among others. These forms of structural violence are often hidden under the justification of cultural practices. This violence is further expressed through gender discrimination, limits on women's rights to participation, self-determination, control over their lives and bodies, food, equal remuneration, education, and lack of equitable access to natural and productive resources, policies, and social services, with severe consequences on women's nutritional status. Moreover, this violence is also a structural cause of the intergenerational reproduction of poverty and malnutrition, resulting in children's poor nutritional status at birth and throughout their lives, even affecting their chances for survival (see also chapter 3 of this volume).

The structural violence against women and girls is also reflected in the attempts to collapse diverse aspects of women's lives into their biological capacity, cultural roles, and emotional connection to motherhood. These violences place on them the brunt of responsibility for ensuring the food and nutritional security of their family, in particular of their children, without effectively guaranteeing any of the needed prerequisites to fulfill this task or acknowledging the inequality of carrying the multiple roles assigned to them by society. For example, instead of ensuring that nutritionally depleted pregnant women and breastfeeding mothers have access to enough food to meet their nutritional requirements as part of the fulfillment of the rights of every woman, women's human rights to adequate food and nutrition and to self-determination are subjected to the fluctuating whims and demands of public policy and the medical field, which make women responsible for their children's health even to the detriment of their own health. The extreme expression of this violence is reflected in a phrase once heard by one coauthor of this chapter from a medical doctor in the field, certainly imbued with good intentions: "Even the most malnourished mother can still adequately breastfeed her baby, and she should." Women are furthermore targeted by unethical marketing from breastmilk substitute industries that profit from poor women's crises in spite of women's right to have the best possible information about their and their children's rights, health, and optimal nutritional practices, especially in emergency situations, as well as women's right to protection from commercial pressures. Respecting, promoting, and fulfilling women's rights, including their right to self-determination, will have repercussions beyond their own persons and will allow them to exercise the powers they already have, which include the power to care for and feed their children and households (see Van Esterik 1999, 229; please see also chapters 3 and 4 of this volume).

Similarly, de jure or de facto discrimination—which is a form of structural violence—of different groups in regards to access to productive resources, to markets, to jobs, to wages, to public services, and to justice is a structural cause of the cycle of hunger and malnutrition around the world. Discrimination of certain groups, based on gender, socioeconomic status, race, ethnicity, geography, religion, sexual orientation, age, sickness, and other forms of discrimination have an enormous impact on the perpetuation of hunger and malnutrition throughout a person's life span.

Finally, the medicalization of nutrition, leading to assumptions that the health sector must intervene mainly with technical support, results in the violent separation of peoples from their local knowledge and governance capacity (see also chapters 2 and 5 of this volume). This form of violence depreciates the link to local food production as the best strategy to enhanced nutrition, and neglects preventive health strategies, including breastfeeding which we characterize as the most local of food systems (see also chapter 4 of this volume). This vision overwhelms people's self-determination and excludes nutrition education as a key tool to improve nutritional status, especially when enhanced nutritional knowledge can promote autonomy. The medicalization of nutrition also tends to deal exclusively with pregnant and breastfeeding women and children, in particular by targeting these groups and ignoring the nutritional status of all women, men, and the elderly throughout their respective life spans as an important determinant of malnutrition for all.

ADVANCES AND MISSED OPPORTUNITIES IN THE DEVELOPMENT OF THE LEGAL CONCEPT OF THE HUMAN RIGHT TO ADEQUATE FOOD AND NUTRITION

The violences exemplified in the previous section end up being ignored by the human rights instruments and system, including the field of the right to adequate food and nutrition. The invisibility of violences allows for huge cracks through which violations of human rights continue to be perpetrated without being identified as such, especially when policy implementers and human rights defenders lose sight of, or neglect the relevance of the indivisibility principle.[20]

Over the last decades, different academics and practitioners have pointed to the need for a shift in the conceptual framework of the human right to adequate food and nutrition in order to adequately address the structural causes of hunger and malnutrition.[21] In spite of the limitations of the human rights system, we argue that human rights continue to be the best tool to address hunger and malnutrition. Human rights are the most powerful tool developed by humankind as a result of millennia of struggles against oppression and discrimination, against abuses of power, and for the promotion of human dignity for all. Sometimes we tend to forget that the human rights system is very young, and is and will always be in a process of development (see also chapter 1 of this volume). Even with its limitations, it has already demonstrated its capacity to limit the worst forms of abuse, and to keep a close monitoring eye on potential new forms of abuse, guaranteeing prevention of violations, sanctions for responsible authorities and other perpetrators, and remedies for victims. Through its identification of rights holders and duty bearers, the human rights approach provides a tool for those most affected to fight for justice, and it can be put to use for promoting a more just and equitable society. Nevertheless, this potential relies on the capacity of individuals and peoples to become aware of their nature as rights holders and to transform themselves into claim holders and thus denounce violations, and for governments, as duty bearers, to fulfill their obligation to provide effective and accessible recourse and accountability mechanisms for rights holders to make their rights enforceable.

Call to Revise the Conceptual Framework of the Right to Adequate Food and Nutrition

Aware of the failures in the fragmented conceptual framework of the right to adequate food and nutrition and of the need to make it more coherent with human rights principles, Asbjørn Eide, during his tenure as a member of the United Nations (UN) Sub-commission on Prevention of Discrimination and Protection of Minorities, proposed changes in the 1980s. These proposed changes reflect the ideas that a collective of practitioners and academics working on the right to adequate food and nutrition had been theorizing.[22] A. Eide's first public attempt at incorporating the nutrition and women's rights dimensions into the conceptual framework of the human right to adequate food and nutrition appears in a report commissioned by the UN Sub-commission on the Promotion and Protection of Human Rights and published in 1989 (see A. Eide 1984a, b, c, 1989). In 1999, A. Eide updated his 1989 report upon request by the sub-commission (see A. Eide 1999).

In his 1999 updated report, A. Eide affirms that:

> [T]he ultimate purpose of promoting the right to adequate food is to achieve nutritional well-being for the individual child, woman and man. (A. Eide 1999, para. 44)

In the same report, he goes on to say that:

> [H]uman nutritional status is determined by at least three major clusters of conditions which interact in a dynamic fashion, relating to food, health and care, and with education as a *cross-cutting* dimension. Food alone is not sufficient to ensure good nutrition for the individual. (A. Eide 1999, para. 44; emphasis added)

A. Eide's 1999 report to the sub-commission points to the need to shift the framework on the human right to adequate food to the human right to adequate food *and nutrition*, and to take into consideration the data related to child and adult malnutrition, as well as the impact of hunger and malnutrition on morbidity and mortality rates. At the same time, A. Eide emphasizes the importance of incorporating the results of several related UN global conferences, such as the International Conference on Nutrition (Rome 1992), the World Conference on Human Rights (Vienna 1993), the Copenhagen Summit on Social Development (1995), and the Fourth World Conference on Women (Beijing 1995), among others, into the comprehensive understanding of the human right to adequate food and nutrition. He also based most of his arguments on the literature documenting the intergenerational reproduction of poverty and malnutrition and the life cycle approach, revised by the UN Standing Committee on Nutrition (SCN; see Commission on the Nutrition Challenges of the 21st Century 2000).

The central thesis of A. Eide's reports, that the realization of the right to adequate food and nutrition is intrinsically linked to nutritional outcomes and requires the full realization of women's rights, exhibits the complex structural conditions necessary to achieve the human right to adequate food and nutrition. The structural causes of hunger are relevant all along the food chain, from access to land, seeds, and water, to food processing, marketing and publicity, and to income and consumption patterns, up until the very moment in which food is effectively consumed, individually or in community with others by dignified and healthy human beings across their life spans. Moreover, this whole process is mediated by gender- and power-biased social structures. Ignoring this holistic reality of the human right to adequate food and nutrition, as part and as result of social processes, leads to the fragmented understanding of food that was already identified in the earlier chapters of this volume.

A. Eide's reports also reaffirms the understanding that the human rights approach to food and nutrition establishes rights for individuals, groups, and peoples, as well as obligations for states, and that these obligations must be seen in a holistic context. A. Eide's view, which reflects the contributions of various members of the SCN working on the right to adequate food and nutrition, was depicted in the Food Security Matrix (see figure 6.1). The matrix, conceived by Asbjørn Eide jointly with Arne Oshaug and Wenche Barth Eide in 1987 (see W. B. Eide 2005, 77), captures the different levels of state obligations to guarantee the human right to adequate food and nutrition. Looking at this simplified matrix, we can appreciate the complexity of the process of the realization of this right, and how that realization cannot depend on the fulfillment of one obligation alone, or on the fulfillment of an isolated dimension of the right.

Missed Opportunities Posed by *General Comment 12 on the Right to Adequate Food* and the *Voluntary Guidelines to Support the Progressive Realization of the Right to Adequate Food in the Context of National Food Security*

Unfortunately, an opportunity was missed when members of the CESCR did not listen to the alert reaffirmed in A. Eide's 1999 report, in which he calls for the need to promote the human right to adequate food and nutrition, within a much broader spectrum of understanding:

> The lesson to be drawn, however, in assessing the nutritional status of populations is that the underlying causality is often much more complex than a single-factor explanation such as overall lack of food. And yet, adverse nutritional trends are all too often used to "demonstrate" the need for increased food production as the remedy. The "right to adequate food" may be as much a question of the full realization of the rights of women as of ensuring a bundle of nutrients handed over through food supplementation schemes. (A. Eide 1999, para. 28)

The decision—made by states parties at the World Food Summit (Rome 1996) and stated in their Plan of Action—to request from the UN Office of the High Commissioner for Human Rights (OHCHR) and related treaty bodies

guiding principles / level of national obligations	FOOD ADEQUACY			VIABILITY IN PROCUREMENT (consistent (not conflicting) with the realization of other Basic Human Needs)	SUSTAINABILITY OF ACCESS
	Nutritional Adequacy	Safety	Cultural Acceptability		
RESPECT	recognize the positive nutritional aspect of existing food patterns	n.a.	recognize the significance of food culture as part of a wider cultural identity	recognize customary rights to means of food procurement, consistent with Basic Human Needs; recognize the significance of informal and non-governmental institutions in facilitating food procurement	recognize the positive ecological significance of existing food production systems; recognize the significance of informal and NGO institutions in crisis management ("buffer systems")
PROTECT	prevent distortion of positive nutritional aspects of existing food patterns	develop national legislation on food safety; participate in developing international legislation on food safety ("Codex Alimentarius")	counteract when necessary influences which may negatively erode positive aspects of existing food culture	develop national legislation and administrative mechanisms and procedures to protect and facilitate a viable food procurement for all	develop national legislation to: counteract activities that may erode ecological balance; protect ecologically sound buffer systems in crisis management
FULFILL	correct negative aspects of existing food patterns; guide dietary change when necessary, consistent with the above; incorporate nutritional considerations in relevant development activities	establish a nationwide system of food control and inspection	incorporate positive aspects of food culture into relevant development activities (IRD, agricultural, health, educational, industrial, etc.)	formulate and execute policies, plans and programs to facilitate and assist all groups in society (with emphasis on the socio-economically most vulnerable) in obtaining viable procurement of food, consistent with Basic Human Needs	formulate and execute policies, plans and programs to facilitate the restoration of ecological balance; support and strengthen effective existing institutions and as necessary develop new ones for crisis management

Figure 6.1 The Food Security Matrix. (Source: A. Eide 1989, 29)

a clarification of the content of the human right to adequate food and nutrition (see FAO 1996, objective 7.4(e)),[23] opened up the possibility of a broad revision of the conceptual framework of this right. CESCR *General Comment 12* and the UN Food and Agriculture Organization (FAO) *Voluntary Guidelines to Support the Progressive Realization of the Right to Adequate Food in the Context of National Food Security* (hereinafter, *Right to Food Guidelines*), approved by the FAO Council in 2004 and published in 2005 (see FAO 2005), were responses to the 1996 states parties' request. These two new human rights documents nevertheless failed to effectively incorporate, in a comprehensive manner, women's rights, gender, and nutrition into the revised framework.[24] Despite the fact that paragraphs 7–11 of *General Comment 12* address adequacy and sustainability (with special emphasis on dietary needs, adverse substances, and cultural and consumer acceptability, respectively), they do not tackle women's rights, gender, or the relevant links between food and how, by whom, and for what food is socially produced, and their nutritional implications (see also chapters 1 and 2 of this volume).

The opportunity posed by *General Comment 12* and the *Right to Food Guidelines* to understand the adequacy dimension of the human right to adequate food and nutrition in a comprehensive manner, as proposed by A. Eide and colleagues, was missed. These two documents failed to define the human right to adequate food and nutrition as more than just the right to adequate *food stuffs*, which might compose a safe, culturally, and nutritionally adequate diet. In fact, a comprehensive understanding of the human right to adequate food and nutrition requires understanding it also as a *social process* of producing food, of preparing food for oneself and others, and of eating and promoting nutritional well-being, as a capability required for the full achievement of the human development potential, and for an active and healthy social life, with self-determination and autonomy.[25] The full realization of the human right to adequate food and nutrition must be regarded as a social process of how people, women and men, decide in sovereignty how to transform natural resources—that is, nature—into food that is adequate to produce and reproduce their human nature and cultural identity, how to care for each other, in particular for those with special needs, both as an individual responsibility and a collective obligation, how to achieve human growth and development, as well as nutritional well-being, and an active and healthy social life. This holistic approach must devote special attention to women and children with respect to their equal, interconnected, yet independent rights in the context of their specific nutritional needs (see also chapter 4 of this volume).

Fundamentals for a New Conceptual Framework for the Human Right to Adequate Food and Nutrition

In formulating a new conceptual framework for the human right to adequate food and nutrition, we also utilize aspects of the capability approach, which was pioneered by Amartya Sen and further developed by a growing number of scholars, such as Martha Nussbaum (see Nussbaum 1988;

Nussbaum and Sen 1993) and Bina Agarwal (see Agarwal, Humphries, and Robeyns 2006). Based on the capability approach, we depart from the understanding that the realization of the human right to adequate food and nutrition requires the fulfillment of entitlements, freedoms, and capabilities.[26] Entitlements include access to natural resources, access to traditional land and territories, and to the set of foods that compose an adequate diet for the specific person. Freedoms include freedom of choice, freedom from violence, deprivation, and fear, as well as freedom to use natural resources to guarantee a sustainable livelihood and development that is in line with the rights to self-determination, to freely dispose of natural wealth and resources (see UN General Assembly 1966, art. 1, paras. 1, 2), and to exert food sovereignty. Finally, we consider nutritional well-being as a capability that enables growth and an active life, fulfills the development potential by allowing people to take advantage of educational, cultural, and other opportunities, and fosters sustainable livelihoods and agroecologically sustainable food systems, which, in turn, confer people the ability to choose adequate and safe food stuffs, reinforcing again local communities' capabilities.

Based on this, we argue that the human right to adequate food and nutrition includes both the entitlement to access adequate food *and* the capability of being well nourished, which implies the ability to work, be healthy, grow and develop to the individual's full potential, and lead a healthy and active social life. As such, the human right to adequate food should be renamed the human right to adequate food *and nutrition*. The core element of the right must lie in the social, collective, and participatory processes of identifying and defining what adequate food means for specific social groups, communities, or peoples. In defining what adequate food means, culturally, nutritionally, safety-wise, environmentally, and socially, peoples will need to determine (*a*) the adequate way of producing it in order to guarantee social, environmental, and economic sustainability, (*b*) who should produce it, (*c*) how it should be distributed, and (*d*) how people could have adequate options to satisfy their culturally defined personal food habits, nutritional, and other needs, in an informed way and protected from abusive and false propaganda.

Therefore, the understanding of the human right to adequate food and nutrition should never be limited to the mere access to food stuffs, to a nutritionally balanced diet, or to relevant public services such as nutrition education or health care. The human right to adequate food and nutrition must extend beyond guaranteeing freedom from hunger to encompass how societies organize to feed themselves adequately and sustainably, in a participatory way. It must guarantee the right of all—women and men, young and old—to have the access to and the choice of adequate food, and to enjoy a healthy and active life according to their potentials. It should incorporate the concept of adequacy that relates to all social, cultural, climatic, and nutritional dimensions of the available foods to compose an adequate diet. The human right to adequate food and nutrition should further relate to the sustainability of human livelihoods, of food production, and of economic systems, thinking about present and future generations. Thus, nutritional quality and safety of the food produced should also be adequately incorporated in local, regional, and national agricultural planning. Furthermore, this right must include those who cannot feed themselves for reasons beyond their control.

This means that the core elements of the human right to adequate food and nutrition would be the exercise of the freedom to:

- Collectively and sovereignly, with the equitable participation of all, define the ways, policies, and programs through which a society wishes to use its natural resources to produce, organize, and guarantee the sustainable access to adequate, safe, and nutritious food for all. This must be in line with cultural and religious practices, taking into account the social, economic, political, and environmental sustainability of the system, and exercising people's food sovereignty.
- Individually—women and men—exert the self-determination to choose, and the entitlement to have access to nutritious and safe food that is adequate to meet individual specific needs, to achieve nutritional well-being and capabilities, to reaffirm cultural identity, and to lead an active and healthy life. Female and male children need to learn these rights and freedoms, and have them fulfilled and protected, to carry forward the concept and implementation of self-determination.

The expanded concept of the human right to adequate food and nutrition cannot be seen in isolation, if it is to be fully understood and effectively put to use. Rather, it must be seen in connection with the promotion of the realization of related rights, such as the right to health, the right to use natural resources, the right to work, the right to education, and the right to social security, as well as other civil and political rights. We further need to pay special attention to groups identified as discriminated against in, or excluded from, the enjoyment of universal human rights as a whole, including women (CEDAW; see UN General Assembly 1979), children (CRC; see UN General Assembly 1989), indigenous peoples (*Declaration of Rights of Indigenous Peoples*; see UN General Assembly 2007b), displaced populations (*Convention Relating to the Status of Refugees*; see UN General Assembly 1951), people with special needs and disabilities (*Convention on the Rights of Persons with Disabilities*; see UN General Assembly 2007a), as well as food producers and providers, including peasants.[27]

THE FOOD SOVEREIGNTY FRAMEWORK FOR THE HUMAN RIGHT TO ADEQUATE FOOD AND NUTRITION: A PROPOSAL FOR A MORE ADVANCED AND INTEGRAL FRAMEWORK INCORPORATING WOMEN'S RIGHTS AND NUTRITION

This section continues to build upon the idea that the human rights system in general and the right to adequate food and nutrition in particular are not immune to social, political, and cultural pressures. As this volume has tried to demonstrate, hunger and malnutrition are not natural; they are mostly the result of social processes. We could even say, provocatively, hunger and malnutrition are socially produced or "man-made."[28] The only way to confront hunger and malnutrition, therefore, is through social processes, such as international and national governance, democratic participation of all, legislation, public policies and regulations, and accountability. However, the current proposed policies to combat food insecurity and malnutrition, in particular of girls and women, are to a large extent ineffective and lead, at best, to partial solutions for social injustice. These proposed solutions are fragmented and based on conceptual frameworks that present several limitations, which do not allow for a comprehensive and holistic analysis of the causes of the problems. The fragmentations are the result of powerful interventions by political, social, cultural, ideological, and scientific hegemonic forces that naturalize violence, disqualify opposing views, and make structural violence invisible.

The failure of the international community, national governments, and societies to overcome hunger and malnutrition, and, in particular, to promote and protect the food and nutritional security of women and children, is not accidental. It is not caused by a lack of political will or lack of policy coherence. In fact, there is a high level of political will to promote coherence among the international financial, trade, investment, and development cooperation, among agricultural, industrial, employment, energy, and climate change mitigation policies, and even among compensatory social policies, such as safety nets, cash transfer, and food assistance policies, and to avoid coherence with human rights (see A. Eide 2005). This coherence, in turn, is closely linked with the interests of the small international financial, industrial, and agroindustrial elite, associated with national elites, and is facilitated and monitored not by the UN as a whole with all the states parties, but by the Group of Eight (G8), and legitimized by the Group of Twenty Finance Ministers and Central Bank Governors (G20), in close cooperation with the Bretton Woods Institutions and the World Trade Organization (WTO).[29] In reality, these policies are the main cause for continued hunger and malnutrition and represent violations of the human right to adequate food and nutrition and related rights.

By proposing the food sovereignty conceptual framework to be used for the human right to adequate food and nutrition, which incorporates the nutritional and women's rights dimensions, we seek to overcome the reductionism in which the human rights framework is being applied to public food and nutrition policies influenced by the above-mentioned groups of power. Furthermore, the new framework must resist the pressure to fragment itself, if it is to become a conceptual framework capable of confronting the structural pattern of violations of the human right to adequate food and nutrition linked to the present hegemonic model. We elucidate how human rights covenants and treaties, if adequately interpreted and implemented under the good faith principle,[30] can remain the guiding framework toward a society based on the promotion and protection of human dignity for all, in which governance and policies are coherent with the interests of the majority, while also seeking to eliminate all forms of discrimination and respecting the rights of discriminated against, marginalized, and disadvantaged groups.

Incorporating the Nutritional Dimension into the Human Right to Adequate Food and Nutrition

The human right to adequate food and nutrition is realized when individuals and communities have a healthy, productive, and active life, made possible, among other things, by their nutritional well-being.[31] Thus, a more prominent inclusion of the nutritional dimension in the conceptual framework of the human right to adequate food and nutrition is central for the proper understanding and realization of this right.

The human right to adequate food and nutrition entails the full process from increasing the yield in the field, to guaranteeing access to adequate food, and the promotion of nutritional well-being for all. The nutritional dimension must be taken into account at all phases of the food system, from the production of seeds, cultivation, harvesting, transformation, marketing, and purchase, all the way to consumption and biological and cultural utilization at the individual level, if nutritional well-being and human dignity are to be achieved. Nutrition, which is established at the interface between the food consumed and its utilization by the human body, guarantees the right to nutritional well-being. If we focus separately either on the harvesting fields that feed us or on the human bodies that consume the food, we may witness the reduction of the fulfillment of the human right to adequate food and nutrition either to the sole increment of food production or to the development of institutions operating compensatory food assistance programs or cash transfers alone. Furthermore, if instead of a holistic approach, we opt to delink the human right to adequate food and nutrition from its nutritional dimension, we run the risk of taking a medicalized and reductionist approach to nutrition and malnutrition.

This inadequate, medicalized, and fragmented approach, which thinks more in terms of quantifiable micro- and macro-nutrients, runs counter to a food sovereignty approach that focuses on sustainable food systems that support sustainable communities (see also chapters 2, 4, and 5 of this volume). It leverages the expansion of the global nutrition industry through short-term nutrition fixes, as is the case with the range of largely under-supervised RUFs distribution that can have negative impacts on local agriculture, breastfeeding, and food practices, and lead to global dependency instead of local autonomy. In this context, civil society movements have voiced concerns in relation to international programs, such as the Scaling Up Nutrition (SUN) program proposed by the World Bank with the support of the Bill Gates Foundation and the United States and Irish governments, among others.[32]

From our analysis, such fragmented approaches also neglect the social and cultural dimensions of the human right to adequate food and nutrition, which are essential to guarantee social cohesion and peace in our societies.[33]

Building upon A. Eide's remarks, we would like to add another dimension and remind the reader that not all types of food are able to lead to nutritional well-being.[34] In reality, the food produced and circulated in the global food economy by the industrial agriculture and food processing can be highly monotonous and of limited nutritional diversity and value. Just as food alone is not enough to promote nutritional well-being and human dignity, neither are health and care alone, especially without access to food produced within a sustainable, healthy, and agroecological process that allows for nutritionally rich, culturally sensitive, and diversified diets.

The nutritional dimension of the right to adequate food and nutrition represents the interface between food, social conditions, and human health. The act of feeding oneself, one's own family, and others, when analyzed in depth, is one of the human activities that best reflects the wealth and complexity of human life in society (see Valente 2002a). The eating practices and habits of an individual and family, the way food is produced, which food is produced, how food is commercialized, and which food is consumed and how, are the result of the history and the lives of ancestors. These practices are a reflection of complex relations between climate, environment, and decisions on what food is best for the health of the family and community, agricultural practices, how each society organizes the access to productive resources, both agricultural and otherwise, and how human beings produce and reproduce themselves as healthy and productive individuals and communities. Eating also involves a strong sense of socialization, creativity, caring, religiousness, and spirituality. Food is marked by a strong symbolic link of humanity to nature. It is no accident that several religions involve food in their rituals, and that many national celebrations are linked with special food preparations that reaffirm cultural identity (see Valente 2002b). All these aspects constitute the social and cultural dimensions of the human right to adequate food and nutrition. How food is produced and how human beings eat in different societies and cultures is, therefore, a central component of their human, economic, and social development, as well as a key component of their cultural identity. These cultural and social patterns concurrently include gender roles and duties that are often heavily biased against women, producing stereotypes which reproduce inequalities in social life.

Having economic and physical access to adequate and safe food and water, having access to healthy eating and life practices, and having guaranteed the enabling conditions to exert the appropriate choices in life are key elements of generating the adequate conditions for health and nutritional well-being for all members of a society. Directly producing food for consumption, working to have income to purchase adequate food, the act of feeding oneself, one's own family, and others, guaranteeing that those who cannot feed themselves are fed, and how this is organized at the community and societal level directly influence the capacity of these communities and societies to support the growth and development of their populations. These rights guarantees enable populations to lead healthy lives, work, actively participate in social life, and have adequate conditions to conceive and raise healthy children capable of taking advantage of educational possibilities to fully develop their potentials. In turn, these serve to further develop the well-being of these communities and societies. The nutritional dimension is intrinsic to this process. As our societies become more complex, the nature of food production, the social determination of eating practices, and their consequences in nutritional well-being become more intricate. At the same time, more and more individuals and families must rely on societal mechanisms to promote and protect their capacity to maintain adequate eating practices and nutritional well-being. This is the central role that must be played by public institutions—collectively instituted and managed—at the local, national, and international levels.

A revised conceptual framework of the human right to adequate food and nutrition could also provide an excellent analytical tool to approach the different new forms of malnutrition, which affect millions of people in the world, including the growing epidemics of overweight and obesity, as well as eating disorders. These epidemics and their impact on life quality, morbidity, and mortality must be analyzed from a human right to adequate food and nutrition perspective and the patterns of violations of the right identified. There is enough evidence in the literature of the links of obesity with the increased production, availability, and consumption of energy rich, nutrient poor, and ultra-processed foods, associated with inappropriate marketing and advertising practices, particularly with those directed at children, adolescents, and pregnant and lactating women (see Commission on the Nutrition Challenges for the 21st Century 2000; HRC 2011b; see also chapters 4 and 5 of this volume). The present practices of the agroindustrial and corporate food systems are essentially geared to profit-making based on overconsumption of highly processed, energy dense foods and lead to an increase in morbidity and a reduction in life expectancy, especially for the poorer segments of the population in both developing and developed countries (see Hesse-Biber et al. 2006). The double burden of malnutrition, as well as the links between malnutrition *intra uterus* and in early childhood with the increased risk of later development of overweight, obesity, and chronic degenerative diseases have been broadly documented and discussed in the literature (see Doak et al. 2005; FAO 2006; SCN 2006). There is a strong need for the discussion of possible human rights-based regulatory frameworks for consumer protection in this area, covering all phases of food production, processing, marketing, and consumption (see HRC 2011b). The responsibility for regulating and monitoring the system and for sanctioning in case of abuses is a public one, and it falls within the obligations of the state to protect and fulfill the human right to adequate food and nutrition.

Incorporating the Women's Rights Dimension into the Human Right to Adequate Food and Nutrition

One structural bottleneck toward the eradication of hunger and malnutrition that has been systematically overlooked, if not very frequently forgotten, is the inclusion of women's rights into the human right to adequate food and nutrition (see chapter 2 of this volume). Central to the inclusion of women's rights is the understanding of the role of structural violence committed against women and girls when they are deprived of the totality of their rights and their freedom to choose how to live their lives, as a barrier to the realization of women's human right to adequate food and nutrition (see chapter 3 of this volume). As a result of the invisibility of structural violence, many girls and women fall victims to child marriage, bonded labor, and adolescent pregnancy.[35] These girls and young women suffer the consequences of the double or triple burden of work from a very early age. They are deprived of their rights (e.g., their right to education, reproductive rights, etc.) and loaded with household chores and with the nutritional demands of bearing a child, while being themselves still in the growing period. These young women are also prone to having successive pregnancies, increasing the risk of maternal and infant malnutrition and mortality. The infant mortality and malnutrition rates associated with adolescent pregnancies are higher than those of adult pregnancies and the risk of maternal death is three to four times higher (see UNICEF 2011). Adolescent pregnancies are among the most important causes of death for women in this age group. Similar consequences can be observed for adult women, when their right to self-determination, including their reproductive rights, are not adequately respected, protected, and promoted, even if to a lesser extent.

Case study 6.1 Women's human right to adequate food and nutrition in India

According to official India government data, cited in the website of the United Nations Children's Fund (UNICEF) India (2010), 36 percent of Indian women were chronically undernourished and 70 percent were anemic in 2005–2006.

India is an example that illustrates how serious the impact of the socially attributed low status of women and of violations of their human right to adequate food and nutrition can be, leading to hunger, malnutrition, and infant and maternal mortality. Recent UNICEF data show that 68 percent of the children admitted to programs for the severely malnourished ones were girls (UNICEF India 2010). Also according to the "Statistics" webpage at the UNICEF website, 47 percent of the marriages in India were child marriages in the period between 2002 and 2011, reaching 57 percent in rural areas

(UNICEF 2013). Medical literature indicates that adolescent mothers have a higher risk of having low birthweight babies. India has one of the highest rates of low birthweight in the world, reaching 28 per 1000 live births between 2007 and 2011 (UNICEF 2013). Low birthweight babies have a much higher risk of dying before reaching age five, of developing more severe malnutrition, specially stunting,[36] and of developing chronic degenerative diseases in adult age (see UNICEF 2006, 9). Close to 50 percent of the malnourished children in the world live in India (approximately seventy million), the prevalence of malnutrition among children under five years of age in India is among the highest in the world (43 percent for moderate and severe underweight and 48 percent for moderate and severe stunting between 2007–2011; see UNICEF 2013).

Identifying the neglected women's rights and gender equity dimensions in the human right to adequate food and nutrition conceptual framework and making them more visible and detailed in the legal framework would make the links between violations of the rights of women and children and hunger and malnutrition more visible. The acknowledgement of these links could make it easier to confront violations of the human right to adequate food and nutrition. By protecting and promoting women's autonomy and self-determination, the human right to adequate food and nutrition will be better able to be used as a tool to overcome the structural violence and discrimination that prevent women and their families from realizing their human rights. The result of the lack of inclusion of the women's rights dimension into the human right to adequate food and nutrition can have drastically negative consequences, not only for women's food and nutrition security, but also for that of their children and their entire families. Whereas interventions aimed at supporting women's nutrition must be continued, their impact will remain limited if not associated with more structural policy and legal measures that protect women's rights and are based on women's human dignity.

An example of the negative consequences of the exclusion of the women's rights dimension into the human right to adequate food and nutrition can be seen through the limitations of the interventions carried out by UNICEF. Despite all of the evidence linking malnutrition to a low socioeconomic status of women, UNICEF continues to prioritize limited interventions that neglect structural causes. For example, UNICEF interventions attempt—in a reductionist way—to improve adolescent girls' nutrition, maternal nutrition during pregnancy and lactation, breastfeeding, and children's nutrition during the first two years of life, without due attention to the extreme structural violence and exclusion to which these girls and women are submitted throughout their lives. Under UNICEF, emphasis is also placed on the empowerment of women, but again not enough attention is given to guaranteeing the needed social and legal protection against discrimination of women and girls, against femicide, against child marriage, nor to promoting gender equity in access to food, land, work, remuneration, education, inheritance, and other related rights.

The *Sixth Report on the World Nutrition Situation* of the SCN (2010) revisits the issue of the relationships among women's nutrition and the intergenerational cycle of growth failure (see Shrimpton 2010). Adding a human rights lens to the points raised by the report allows us to state that the main causes of the failure of public policies and programs to reduce child malnutrition, including low birthweight, wasting, and stunting, with the consequences of impaired cognitive development and obesity in adulthood primarily revolve around the lack of attention to the women's rights dimension in the human right to adequate food and nutrition. First, the concentration of public programs on "after the fact" interventions such as rehabilitation, exclusive breastfeeding, and supplementary feeding places the center of the responsibility for this on the household and on the mothers and ignores the role of governments as duty bearers with the obligation to respect, protect, promote, facilitate, and provide the right to adequate food and nutrition. Similarly, the SCN report exemplifies the fact that insufficient attention is given to women's nutritional status prior to conception and to the social conditions and role of adolescent pregnancy, which results in violations of women's human rights. Adolescent pregnancy places a severe burden on the nutritional well-being, growth, and development of the still growing girl, even if provided with an adequate diet. This lack of public policy attention to the nutritional well-being of women and adolescent girls throughout their life spans results in the violation of their human rights, including the human right to adequate food and nutrition.

If we go deeper into reading the SCN report, the data go even further, pointing to the fact that public policies do not take into account violations of other dimensions of women's rights. The report points to the negative health and nutritional impacts of adolescent pregnancy for the woman, which includes lower stature and malnutrition. It also points to the fact that such an early pregnancy represents a risk for her life, which is four times as high as for an adult pregnancy. Finally, the report highlights the magnitude of child marriage in the developing world and the role it plays in leading to adolescent pregnancy by reporting that 33 percent of weddings overall, and in some countries more than 50 percent, are child marriages, involving children below the age of eighteen. The report discusses the case study of India, where child marriage represents almost 50 percent of all marriages, despite its illegal status according to Indian National Law and the fact that involuntary child marriage is a violation of CRC and CEDAW, in clear violation of women's and children's rights (see de Silva-de-Alwis 2008).

This SCN report, therefore, gives clear leads as to the links among the different types of violence against women. It links child marriage to early and adolescent pregnancy, associated nutritional deprivation and stunting, risk of death, distancing from family, workload, and imposed obligations of child care and breastfeeding.

Taking into account that a significant percentage of low birthweight infant mortality and stunting is associated with adolescent pregnancies, and that this malnutrition in early childhood will have clear consequences in terms of reduced cognitive and working capacities, a significant part of child malnutrition and hunger in the world, at least that of women and children, is directly linked to women's rights violations. These structural causes of hunger and malnutrition include non-compliance with obligations related to women's rights in the form of inadequate protection against violence and discrimination, violations of partnership and reproductive rights, violations of the freedom of choice, as well as violations of the human right to adequate food and nutrition.

To aggravate the situation, policies tend to make women invisible, in particular when they ignore the diversity of women's roles throughout their life spans and instead reduce them to that of motherhood. Women are, in many official documents, viewed as "future mothers" from conception or birth onwards, and are often not taken into account in policies and programs in other phases of life or if they decide not to become mothers (see also chapter 2 of this volume).

The SCN report also identifies the UNICEF conceptual framework on the causes of child malnutrition as partly responsible for the invisibility of women's rights.[37] The UNICEF framework, as utilized today, does not capture the significant role that women's good nutritional status prior to, and independently of, becoming a mother has for the offspring. The UNICEF report takes on a particularly strong medical sector approach and, within that, a clear prioritization for the curative approach that emphasizes disease, death, and provision of health services, instead of one more conducive to the promotion of health and prevention of malnutrition. It further concentrates the focus of the underlying causes at the household level and, within that, on the role of the woman, here seen in her role as the mother. The possible causes for inequalities among the households are mentioned, but the focus is on the isolated household.[38] The framework also tends to hide, or make invisible, the relationship of the household situation with the distribution of land, power, and income in the local society, and neglects the role of power and social relations that lead the woman to be in that household, to become a mother, and to stay there under particular conditions. This narrow and inadequate approach therefore "imprisons" or "captures" the woman in her role as a mother, and stresses her role as a provider of breastfeeding, child care, and food security. As a result, this framework neglects to recognize that she, as a woman, has rights and should have the freedom to decide whether she wants to get married and to have a child and when.

We recognize that the UNICEF framework, if well used, represents a potent tool to support a more in-depth analysis of the social determinants of child and maternal malnutrition, especially if it fully takes into account the applicable underlying and basic causes to the case under study. Unfortunately, its present use seems to be very limited to a preconceived set of causes. We, therefore, strongly recommend that researchers and others interested in the framework use it in conjunction with the original framework proposed by Urban Jonsson (1981). Jonsson's framework provides good guidance on how to identify the relevant causes at all levels—underlying, basic, and immediate—and thus provides a more holistic review of the structural causes of malnutrition.

The promotion of girls' and women's overall rights across their life spans, which, among others, include access to self-determination and autonomy, education, productive resources, jobs, income, sexual and reproductive rights, reproductive-related information and services, adequate preventive and curative health care, and fair and unbiased partnerships, not only enables women and girls to freely decide whether and when to become mothers, but it also has a positive impact on their overall nutritional status, on their pregnancy outcomes, and on their babies' survival and health. For example, the above-mentioned SCN *Sixth Report on the World Nutrition Situation* provides case studies of how universal programs that benefit women with cash transfers, independently of whether they are pregnant or not, have a very positive effect in terms of increased overall birthweight, when the women decide to have babies (SCN 2010). Furthermore, this improved pregnancy outcome should be accompanied by information and support to the mothers and their families on best possible infant, baby, and young child feeding practices.

The People's and Food Sovereignty Framework for the Human Right to Adequate Food and Nutrition

The people's and food sovereignty framework for the right to adequate food and nutrition emerges from the right of people and peoples to self-determination and the control over their essential resources and relates to decisions to overall food and nutrition (see *Declaration of Nyéléni*; Forum for Food Sovereignty 2007a). The inclusion of this concept into the legal framework of the human right to adequate food and nutrition could represent an additional tool to foster conditions for the local populations to participate in political discussions related to overall food, nutrition, economic, financial, labor, health, and agricultural policies. These discussions could revolve around land utilization and tenure, social, economic, and environmental sustainability, access to local and regional markets, access to jobs and adequate remuneration, and adoption of agricultural production models that result in adequate, nutritious, and safe food, less contamination of soil and water, and the increased protection of the health of producers and surrounding communities.

The inclusion of this concept is also associated with the perspective of the right to sustainable livelihoods, food and nutrition systems, and economies, based on agroecological principles. These principles guarantee the reduction of agricultural workers and surrounding communities' exposure to toxic substances and the reduction of soil and water contamination and support the production of safe and nutritious foods and the protection and promotion of the human right to adequate food and nutrition of present and future generations.[39] It is not enough to talk about nutrition and sustainable livelihoods separately, we must work with them in an integrated manner (see also chapter 5 of this volume). Nutritional and health concerns of producers and consumers must be reflected in the decision of what foods to produce and how, guaranteeing at the same time in each region or territory the maximum possible food quality and diversity for local trade, local consumption, and the nutritional health and well-being of local and regional populations. This would also reduce dependence on imports and vulnerability to food price fluctuations (see HRC 2010).

Concrete Proposal for the Redefinition of the Conceptual Framework of the Human Right to Adequate Food and Nutrition

Our proposal entails a three-pronged approach based on a holistic concept of the human right to adequate food and nutrition that uses the food sovereignty framework and includes nutrition and women's rights while promoting more internal coherence and inclusiveness within the conceptual framework, as well as external coherence with other related human rights:

- *People's and food sovereignty.*[40] First, we propose moving from a food security framework to a food sovereignty framework by:

    i. *Placing peoples' and communities' right to self-determination at the center.* Peoples and communities should have the capability to use their natural resources to guarantee their development and to freely dispose of and utilize their natural wealth and resources in order to realize their human right to adequate food and nutrition (see UN General Assembly 1966, art. 1, paras. 1 and 2). This capability should be recognized in the legal framework. Furthermore, the practical implementation of food sovereignty as the right's framework should include the establishment of a set of practices and policies that guarantee peoples' and communities' ability to establish sustainable local, regional, and national food systems and the capability to feed themselves, their families, and their communities with healthy and safe foods that guarantee their nutritional well-being, in accordance with what they jointly decide. Peoples and communities should also have the right to directly participate in the elaboration, budgeting, decision-making, implementation, and monitoring of related public policies and programs, at all levels.

    ii. *Incorporating the dimension of environmentally sustainable food systems.* Incorporating the dimension of sustainable livelihoods and agroecological principles to food systems, with reduced climate change impact, will guarantee the human right to adequate food and nutrition for the present and next generations.

- *Internal coherence.* Second, we call for the strengthening of the internal coherence of the conceptual framework defined by CESCR *General Comment 12* (CESCR 1999b), and for making it more comprehensive by:

    i. *Fully incorporating the nutritional dimension.* Inseparably linking the nutritional dimension, including its dietary adequacy component, into the human right to adequate food, understood as a capability and thus, renaming the right to adequate food "the right to adequate food *and nutrition*," is a necessary step for properly developing its normative content and for its full realization. The incorporation of the nutrition dimension would also include the recognition of the close linkage and indivisibility between food, nutrition, and health. In line with this, and departing from a holistic approach, the reframing of the conceptual framework should also take into consideration the content of CESCR *General Comment 14 on The Right to the Highest Attainable Standard of Health* (CESCR 2000), *General Recommendation 24 on Women and Health* issued by the United Nations Committee on the Elimination of Discrimination against Women (CEDAW Committee; see CEDAW Committee 1999), as well as *General Comment 15 on The Right of the Child to the Enjoyment of the Highest Attainable Standard of Health* issued by the United Nations Committee on the Rights of the Child (CRC Committee; see CRC Committee 2013, as well as chapter 2 of this volume).

    ii. *Reaffirming the interconnection among specific state obligations and general obligations.*[41] At the analytical and implementation levels, it is important to recognize the interconnection between the specific state obligations to (*a*) respect, (*b*) protect, and (*c*) fulfill, including their extraterritorial dimension,[42] and the general obligations to (*a*) not discriminate, (*b*) progressive realization, including the prohibition of retrogression and the existence of minimum core obligations,[43] which should be implemented immediately, and (*c*) international cooperation.

    iii. *Incorporating women's rights and promoting gender equity dimensions.* The right should effectively recognize the need to promote and protect the self-determination and autonomous development of girls and women. Promoting women's human and reproductive rights and choices, including their protection against structural violence and discrimination, is a prerequisite to reduce violations of the human right to adequate food and nutrition (see also chapters 3 and 4 of this volume). Ensuring recognition of this dimension within the right would protect women's human right to adequate food and nutrition, whether or not they are mothers, as well as reduce infant, child, and maternal malnutrition.

iv. *Incorporating the dimensions that enable individuals and peoples to have stable access to adequate food.* The right should reaffirm the dimensions of access to natural resources, jobs, and adequate, fair, and equal pay, adequate working conditions, social security and emergency assistance, as well as the dimension of sustainable livelihoods and agroecological principles to food systems.

v. *Affirming people's and food sovereignty.* Affirming this within the right will serve as an enabling condition for, and integral part of, the promotion and protection of the human right to adequate food and nutrition at local, national, and international levels, within the framework of self-determination to empower sustainable food systems.

- *External coherence.* Third, we call for the strengthening of the external coherence of the right with the human rights approach, within the indivisibility of rights by:

  i. *Demonstrating links between documented cases of violations of the human right to adequate food and nutrition with violations of other economic, social, and cultural rights.* Explicitly linking violations of the right to adequate food and nutrition with other economic, social, and cultural rights violations, such as violations of the right to water and sanitation, health, work, adequate, fair and equal pay, access to resources, education, and social security—all taking into account the gender perspective—in case documentation and civil society national reports will promote the development of new standards by the CESCR and other UN human rights and technical organizations. Within this, establishing the links between violations of the right to adequate food and nutrition and other economic, social, and cultural rights will also enable the development of bridges between the conceptual frameworks of the various rights and serve to unify the struggles of affected populations.

  ii. *Demonstrating links between violations of the human right to adequate food and nutrition and of civil and political rights.* Making explicit the links between violations of the right to adequate food and nutrition and violations of rights related to the protection of human rights defenders, extralegal executions and other forms of criminalization, democratic participation, and personal integrity, among others, in case documentation and national reports will enable the development of bridges between the conceptual frameworks of these rights. Within this, special attention should be paid to the links between violations of the human right to adequate food and nutrition and those of women's and children's rights, among other discriminated against, marginalized, and disadvantaged populations.

The People's and Food Sovereignty Matrix: Capturing the New Proposed Conceptual Framework for the Human Right to Adequate Food and Nutrition

In a previous section of this chapter, we introduced the Food Security Matrix proposed by A. Eide in his 1989 report. With this matrix, A. Eide attempted to demonstrate how the obligations of the states must be looked at from a holistic point of view, based on the pillars of food security. In the revised matrix presented in this section—the People's and Food Sovereignty Matrix—we try to depict state obligations within the people's and food sovereignty framework, as proposed in our broadened understanding of the human right to adequate food and nutrition.

A. Eide's Food Security Matrix concentrates on state obligations related to guaranteeing food adequacy (nutritional, safety, and cultural), viability in procurement (access and availability), and sustainability of access, all of which are directly related to intrinsic characteristics of the food stuffs and how to access them. However, the new proposed matrix broadens the obligations from a food sovereignty perspective (see table 6.1).[44] These expanded obligations include four dimensions. The first column, "Sustainable supply of adequate food," depicts the social and political processes toward a sustainable supply of adequate food, which include participatory policy elaboration, decision-making, implementation, and monitoring (see table 6.2). Secondly, with its second column entitled "Stable access to adequate food," the matrix focuses on how to guarantee stable access to adequate food, which encompasses access to resources, income and livelihoods, food supply public policies, and social security (see table 6.3). The third column, "Adequate food," details how to guarantee food adequacy through an adequate quantity and nutritional quality of food that is safe and culturally acceptable (see table 6.4). Finally, the fourth and last column, "Eating, self-determination, and well-being," illustrates how to guarantee that individuals realize their human right to adequate food and nutrition in line with self-determination, freedom of choice, and human dignity, from the moment in which the food is produced to the moment it is eaten and digested, and transformed into nutritional well-being (see table 6.5).

Table 6.1 People's and food sovereignty conceptual framework of the human right to

Normative principles (people's and food sovereignty attributes)	Sustainable supply of adequate food	Stable access to adequate food			
Categories of state obligations	Collectively managed, participatory, social, economic, political, environmentally sustainable food systems	Natural and productive resources	Work, livelihoods, and income	Food supply management public policies	Social security
Respect	See table 6.2		See table 6.3		
Protect					
Fulfill[i]					
Facilitate					
Provide					
Non-retrogression, non-discrimination, and use of maximum funds available	These core obligations apply for all levels of specific state obligations				

[i] Although under *General Comment 12* "the right to adequate food . . . imposes three types of level of obligations on States parties: the obligation to *respect*, to *protect* and to *fulfil*" and, "[i]n turn, th obligation to *fulfil* incorporates both an obligation to *facilitate* and an obligation to *provide*" (CESC 1999b, para. 15), *General Comment 12* should be interpreted using an evolutive perspective and w should infer that it should have also evolved to entail all three levels of the obligation to fulfill (facilitat provide, and promote) incorporated into later CESCR general comments. Nonetheless, whereas w believe that we should move in that direction, this matrix only focuses on the two levels of fulfill (facil tate and provide) listed in *General Comment 12* and the missing level (promote) is subsumed under th obligation to fulfill/facilitate.

[ii] See A. Eide and Rosas (2001, 22, 26, 65–67, 154–5, 176, 185, 282, 367, 542, 547), Klee (2000, 104 Rossi (2006, 83), Sepúlveda Carmona (2003, 117), and Suárez Franco (2010, 60, 268). See also CESC *General Comment 3 on the Nature of States Parties' Obligations* (CESCR 1990, paras. 2, 9), *Ge eral Comment 5 on Persons with Disabilities* (CESCR 1994, para. 9), *General Comment 11 on Plar of Action for Primary Education* (CESCR 1999a, para. 10), *General Comment 12 on the Right t Adequate Food* (CESCR 1999b, para. 14), *General Comment 13 on the Right to Education* (CESC 1999c, para. 43), *General Comment 14 on the Highest Attainable Standard of Health* (CESCR 200(para. 30), *General Comment 15 on the Right to Water* (CESCR 2003, para. 18), *General Comment 1 on the Equal Right of Men and Women to the Enjoyment of All Economic, Social and Cultural Righ* (CESCR 2006a, para. 39), *General Comment 17 on the Right of Everyone to Benefit from the Prote tion of the Moral and Material Interests Resulting from Any Scientific, Literary or Artistic Production (which He or She is the Author* (CESCR 2006b, paras. 25, 26), and *General Comment 18 on the Righ to Work* (CESCR 2006c, para. 19).

adequate food and nutrition: the People's and Food Sovereignty Matrix

Adequate food			Eating, self-determination, and well-being			
Dietary adequacy (quantity and nutritional quality)	Food safety	Cultural acceptability	Autonomy and self-determination	Freedom to choose food to consume and feed	Nutritional well-being	Human dignity
See table 6.4			See table 6.5			

nd for all dimensions of the human right to adequate food and nutrition included in this matrix[ii]

Table 6.2 The People's and Food Sovereignty Matrix: sustainable supply of adequate food

Normative principles (people's and food sovereignty attributes)	Sustainable supply of adequate food
Categories of state obligations	Collectively managed, participatory, social, economic, political, environmentally sustainable food systems
Respect	No interference with the positive social, political, economic, and ecological significance of diversified small-scale production systems and breastfeeding, in the state's own country, as well as in other countries
Protect	Development of national and international regulation to counteract activities that may erode social, economic, political, and environmental sustainability of food systems (including breastfeeding)
	Protection of diversified sustainable small-scale food production systems in the state's own country as well as in third countries, against third-party initiatives
Fulfill	
Facilitate	Participatory formulation and execution of a national and an international food sovereignty strategy toward the consolidation of collectively managed, nutrition sensitive, participatory, social, economic, political, and environmentally sustainable food systems
	Support breastfeeding education
Provide	

The People's and Food Sovereignty Matrix can serve to guide efforts to analyze and/or elaborate public policies and programs within the new broadened framework of the human right to adequate food and nutrition, fully integrating gender, women's rights, and nutrition, as well as the food sovereignty principles.

Under the proposed people's and food sovereignty framework, in order for states to respect, protect, and fulfill the human right to adequate food and nutrition in an integrated manner, they must ensure that all under their jurisdiction—individually or in community with others—have continued and stable physical and economic access to a sustainable supply of adequate food and that all enjoy the right to self-determination and well-being. Below, we detail the three levels of state obligations for meeting the human right to adequate food and nutrition in an integrated manner, specifically taking into account the different dimensions of the people's and food sovereignty framework depicted in the proposed People's and Food Sovereignty Matrix.[45]

Table 6.3 The People's and Food Sovereignty Matrix: stable access to adequate food

Normative principles (people's and food sovereignty attributes) Categories of state obligations	Stable access to adequate food			
	Natural and productive resources	Work, livelihoods, and income	Food supply management public policies	Social security
Respect	No interference with or destruction of customary rights to means of food production No undermining of breastfeeding	No interference with the realization of the right to equal work, livelihood, and income of women and men	No interference with the exercise of the right of all to an adequate, safe, and affordable diet, throughout the lifecycle	No interference with the exercise of the right of all to social security No reduction of funds allocated to social security in periods of budget cuts without the adequate rationality and proportionality tests
Protect	Development of national legislation and administrative mechanisms to protect access to productive resources by all Regulation of negative and potentially negative third-party initiatives Regulation of marketing of breastmilk substitutes	Development of national legislation and administrative mechanisms to protect against inadequate and unequal pay Regulation of negative and potentially negative third-party initiatives	Development of national legislation and administrative mechanisms to protect producers and consumers against abusive prices Regulation of negative and potentially negative third-party initiatives	Regulation to ensure the adequate compliance of employers and non-state actors with their contributions

(Continued)

Table 6.3 (Continued)

Normative principles (people's and food sovereignty attributes) Categories of state obligations	Stable access to adequate food			
	Natural and productive resources	Work, livelihoods, and income	Food supply management public policies	Social security
Fulfill				
Facilitate	Participatory formulation and execution of a national and an international food sovereignty strategy toward the consolidation of collectively managed, nutrition sensitive, and participatory social, economic, political, and environmentally sustainable food systems Support breastfeeding education	Formulation and execution of policies, plans, and programs to facilitate and assist all social groups to have access to work, livelihoods and income, giving priority to women and marginalized and disadvantaged groups Promotion of labor laws to protect the right of women to breastfeed	Formulation and execution of policies, plans, and programs to facilitate an adequately priced food supply	Formulation and execution of social security policies, plans, and programs to allow all people to realize their right to adequate food and nutrition
Provide				

Table 6.4 The People's and Food Sovereignty Matrix: adequate food

Normative principles (people's and food sovereignty attributes) Categories of state obligations	Adequate food		
	Dietary adequacy (quantity and nutritional quality)	Food safety	Cultural acceptability
Respect	No interference with the recognition of the positive nutritional aspects of existing food patterns, intrinsic to diversified food systems, with breastfeeding as superior food for infants and young children	No interference with the recognition of positive safety aspects of agroecological production systems	No interference with the recognition of the significance of food culture as part of a wider cultural identity
Protect	Prevention of distortion of the perception of positive nutritional aspects of existing food patterns (e.g., protection of breastfeeding) Regulation of negative and potentially negative third-party initiatives (e.g., marketing practices, publicity, etc.)	Development of national and international regulation on food safety Regulation of negative and potentially negative third-party initiatives (e.g., agro-chemicals, junk food, etc.)	Counteraction of non-state actors' influences which may erode positive aspects of food culture Regulation of negative and potentially negative third-party initiatives (e.g., introduction of GMOs against the precautionary principle or without the needed public information)

(*Continued*)

Table 6.4 (Continued)

Normative principles (people's and food sovereignty attributes) Categories of state obligations	Adequate food		
	Dietary adequacy (quantity and nutritional quality)	Food safety	Cultural acceptability
Fulfill			
Facilitate	Correction of negative aspects of existing food patterns Incorporation of nutritional considerations in all relevant policies and programs Promotion of positive food practices, including breastfeeding	Establishment of a national and international system of food control and inspection	Promotion and support of positive food culture aspects (e.g., seed banks) in all relevant policies and programs
Provide	Formulation and execution of policies and programs aimed at guaranteeing the right to adequate food and nutrition of individuals, groups, and communities which, for reasons beyond their control, are found in conditions of food insecurity, hunger, and malnutrition. These programs should respect all other dimensions of the right to adequate food and nutrition, avoid interfering with the right to adequate food and nutrition of other communities, incorporate a strong component toward promoting the capacity of the affected communities to feed themselves in dignity, and protect them against abuses from non-state parties		

Specific obligations: the obligation to respect. At the first level, the obligation to respect requires states, as representatives of the public interest and managers of public resources, to abstain from negatively impacting the realization of individuals' and peoples' right to adequate food and nutrition, both in their own territories and in other territories, in recognition of their extraterritorial state obligations. Under the new proposed matrix, in order to ensure a sustainable supply of adequate food and nutrition, states should respect the positive social, political, economic, and ecological significance of diversified small-scale production systems (see table 6.2).

Normative principles (people's and food sovereignty attributes)	Eating, self-determination, and well-being			
Categories of state obligations	Autonomy and self-determination	Freedom to choose food and to consume and feed	Nutritional well-being	Human dignity
Respect	No interference with the realization of all women and men of all ages of autonomy and self-determination in relation to their lives and bodies, noting also responsibility for the absolute autonomy of women breastfeeding their children	No interference with the exercise of the right of all women and men of all ages to choose their eating patterns and to feed their children in the best way possible	No interference with the exercise of the right of all women and men to nutritional well-being throughout the lifecycle as a prerequisite to their right to fully develop their human potential	No interference with the right of all women and men to human dignity
Protect	Development of national and international legislation and administrative mechanisms to counteract third-party initiatives that erode and abuse autonomy and self-determination of all, with special attention to girls and women	Prevention of distortion of positive nutritional aspects of existing food patterns (e.g., protection of breastfeeding) Regulation of negative and potentially negative non-state actors' initiatives (e.g., marketing practices)	Development of national programs and administrative mechanisms to assess the food and nutritional status of the population, especially those with special nutritional needs	Development of national and international legislation and administrative mechanisms to monitor, investigate, sanction, and redress eventual violations of the right to adequate food and nutrition and human dignity, while holding involved third-parties accountable for their abuses of human rights

(Continued)

Table 6.5 (Continued)

Normative principles (people's and food sovereignty attributes)	Eating, self-determination, and well-being		
Categories of state obligations	Autonomy and self-determination	Freedom to choose food and to consume and feed	Nutritional well-being	Human dignity
	Regulation of negative and potentially negative non-state actors' conducts affecting self-determination (e.g., structural and domestic violence, patriarchal and cultural patterns affecting autonomy, arresting women's and communities' autonomy in superior child nutrition through the introduction of artificial feeding)		Elaboration and execution of a set of policies and programs to prevent nutritional disorders (e.g., water and sanitation, health, care support, etc.) derived from non-state actors' conducts	

Fulfill

Facilitate	Revision and reformulation of existing policies and programs to reduce structural violence and discrimination against women and other affected social groups, which engender violations of women's rights and have a negative impact on the right to adequate food and nutrition of women and children Adaptation of the *International Code of Marketing of Breast-milk Substitutes* into national legislation	Formulation and execution of policies, plans, and programs to inform and stimulate healthy adequate food choices, while at the same time respecting cultural values	Participatory formulation and execution of a national and international food and nutrition sovereignty strategy toward the consolidation of a collectively managed, integrated food and nutrition sovereignty system	Formulation and execution of a human rights education and empowerment program that specifically refers to the principle of human dignity Mainstreaming of human rights principles in all food and nutrition security and sovereignty related policies
Provide	Formulation and execution of policies and programs aimed at guaranteeing the right to adequate food and nutrition of individuals, groups, and communities which, for reasons beyond their control, find themselves suffering from food insecurity, hunger, and malnutrition. These programs should respect all other dimensions of the right to adequate food and nutrition, avoid interfering with the right to adequate food and nutrition of other communities, incorporate a strong component for promoting the capacity of affected communities to feed themselves in dignity, and protect them against abuses by non-state parties			

In addition, states should respect customary rights to means of production, such as customary land, fishing, and hunting rights of indigenous peoples and rural communities in order to make it possible for these peoples to satisfy their right to a stable access to adequate food (see table 6.3). States' obligation to respect the right to adequate food and nutrition further implies respecting the right to breastfeed as a natural resource that ensures children's access to adequate and nutritious food. At the same time, states should ensure recognition of the right of individuals and communities to seek an income, which includes the right to equal income for equal work by both men and women, in order to enable them to feed themselves and secure their basic needs. States' food supply public policies should ensure the recognition of the right to an adequate, safe, and affordable diet, throughout individuals' life cycles. States' recognition of the right of all to social security, including ensuring that the budget allocation to social security is not reduced irrationally, disproportionally, or against the law during budget cuts is also necessary for a stable access to adequate food.

Simultaneously, individuals and peoples need to have access to adequate food that is nutritious, safe, and culturally acceptable (see table 6.4). Under this dimension, states' obligation to respect should ensure the recognition of the positive nutritional aspect of existing food patterns, intrinsic to diversified food systems. At the same time, states should ensure that the food is safe for human beings to consume by recognizing the positive safety aspects of agroecological production systems. States also have the responsibility to ensure that the food is culturally acceptable by recognizing the significance of food culture as part of a wider cultural identity.

Under the eating, self-determination, and well-being dimension of the framework (see table 6.5), states should respect the right of all, women and men of all ages, to autonomy and self-determination in relation to their lives and bodies. Furthermore, states should respect the right of all to choose their eating patterns and to feed their children and their families in the best way possible,[46] to human dignity, and to nutritional well-being throughout their life cycles as a prerequisite to their right to fully develop their human potential.

The obligation to protect. Under the obligation to protect, states shall adopt regulations, implement monitoring mechanisms, establish investigation procedures, make available accessible remedy mechanisms, put in place sanction mechanisms in order to avoid abuses by non-state actors of the right to adequate food and nutrition, and enable rights holders—especially but not only women and children and those from disadvantaged and low income groups—to hold their authorities accountable and to end impunity of state and non-state perpetrators. To ensure a sustainable supply of adequate food (see table 6.2), states ought to develop national and international legislation to counteract activities by third parties that may erode the social, economic, political, and environmental sustainability of food systems. Similarly, states should protect diversified sustainable small-scale food production systems in their own country as well as in third countries against third-party initiatives by regulating the expansion of the industrial agricultural model and by forbidding landgrab.

In order to ensure a stable access to adequate food (see table 6.3), states are called to develop national legislation and administrative mechanisms to protect access to productive resources by all, to protect against inadequate and unequal pay, and to protect producers and consumers against abusive prices. Within this framework, states should also regulate negative and potentially negative third-party initiatives, including labor violations by private employers and the marketing of breastmilk substitutes, among others.

To ensure access to adequate food for all (see table 6.4), states are called to prevent a distortion of the perception of positive nutritional aspects of existing food patterns, with special attention to protecting breastfeeding practice and culture, which are in line with human dignity. Similarly, states ought to develop national and international legislation on food safety and counteract influences which may negatively erode positive aspects of food culture. In addition, states should regulate negative and potentially negative third-party initiatives, such as harmful marketing practices, the replacement of traditional seeds,[47] and the introduction of agrochemicals, "junk food,"[48] or GMOs.

The obligation to protect the right to self-determination and well-being of all (see table 6.5) implies that states should develop national and international legislation and administrative mechanisms to counteract third-party initiatives that erode and abuse autonomy and self-determination or instrumentalize people for their own aims. Mechanisms should also be created to assess the food and nutritional status of the population and to monitor, investigate, and redress potential violations of the right to adequate food and nutrition in line with the principle of human dignity. All of these legislations and mechanisms should pay special attention to girls and women, those with special nutritional needs, and those subject to other existing forms of discrimination and violence, which hinder the enjoyment of their human rights and in turn engender further violations of the right to adequate food and nutrition, not only of women, but also of infants and children. Furthermore, states should also regulate negative and potentially negative non-state actor initiatives and hold these non-state actors accountable for their human rights abuses, which include structural and domestic violence. States also have the obligation to prevent distortion of positive nutritional aspects of existing food patterns, such as breastfeeding, and to elaborate and execute policies and programs to prevent nutritional disorders, such as those related to water, sanitation, health, and care support, among others.

The obligation to fulfill. At the third level, we present two dimensions of the obligation to fulfill: the obligation to facilitate and the obligation to provide.[49] Under the obligation to facilitate, states shall adopt as soon as possible all necessary measures in order to allow people to feed themselves in an adequate manner. Under the obligation to provide, states should guarantee the access to food for people who are, for reasons beyond their control, not able to feed themselves. Such provision of food should be coherent with the nutritional needs and culture of the targeted population and accompanied by specific middle- and long-term strategies and measures that allow those who are capable to do so to recover their food autonomy.

Facilitate. In order for states to facilitate a sustainable supply of adequate food (see table 6.2), states will have to formulate and execute, in a participatory manner, a national and international food and nutrition sovereignty strategy toward the consolidation of collectively managed and nutrition sensitive social, economic, political, and environmentally sustainable food systems.

With the aim of fulfilling (facilitate and promote) their obligation to ensure a stable access to adequate food (see table 6.3), states ought to formulate and execute plans, programs, and policies, including social security policies, that facilitate and assist all social groups to have access to production resources, to work and seek an income, to an adequately priced food supply, and to adequate food and nutrition. In addition, states ought to elaborate legislation to promote breastfeeding, including labor laws to protect the right of women to breastfeed.

States' obligation to facilitate the access to adequate food for all (see table 6.4) consists of correcting negative aspects of existing food patterns, incorporating nutritional considerations in all relevant policies and programs, and promoting positive practices, which would include breastfeeding, with the aim of ensuring that everyone has access to a diet that is adequate in terms of quantity and nutritional quality. In addition, states should establish national and international systems of food control and inspection in order to ensure the safety of its food supply. Finally, to ensure that food is culturally acceptable, states should recognize, promote, and protect positive food culture aspects in all relevant policies and programs.

This obligation would also entail states' revision and reformulation of existing policies and programs to reduce violence and discrimination against women and other social groups affecting their right to adequate food and nutrition. In addition, states should formulate and execute policies, plans, and programs to inform and stimulate healthy adequate food choices that respect cultural values, a national and international food and nutrition sovereignty strategy toward the consolidation of collectively managed and integrated food and nutrition sovereignty systems that include breastfeeding promotion and the adoption of appropriate complementary foods that introduce children to their cultures (see Palmer 2011), and a human rights education and empowerment program. To facilitate human dignity, states should also mainstream human rights principles into all food and nutrition-related policies, avoiding the instrumentalization of rights holders and placing special emphasis on the most disadvantaged and marginalized groups (see table 6.5).

Provide. In order for states to provide adequate food and the rights to self-determination and well-being (see tables 6.4 and 6.5), they should formulate and execute policies and programs aimed at guaranteeing the right to adequate food and nutrition of individuals, groups, and communities which, for reasons beyond their control, are found in conditions of food insecurity, hunger, and malnutrition. These programs should respect all other dimensions of the right to adequate food and nutrition, avoid interfering with the right to adequate food and nutrition of other communities, incorporate a strong component toward promoting the capacity of the affected communities to feed themselves in dignity, and protect them against abuses from the part of non-state actors (see also HRC 2012).

General obligations. Moreover, the general obligations of using the maximum available resources for the progressive implementation of the right to adequate food and nutrition,[50] non-retrogression,[51] and non-discrimination,[52] are crosscutting at all levels of the specific state obligations and all dimensions of the human right to adequate food and nutrition included in the proposed matrix (see table 6.1). These obligations call for states to implement strategies that allow them to progressively realize the rights of an ever larger and wider range of people, to refrain from deliberately taking steps backwards in the realization of these rights, to ensure that rights are being realized in a non-discriminatory manner, and to allocate the resources necessary to realize these rights and implement these strategies.[53]

COLLABORATING WITH SOCIAL MOVEMENTS IN THE RECONCEPTUALIZATION OF A UNIFYING FRAMEWORK

The revised and strengthened human right to adequate food and nutrition can become a powerful unifying tool for orienting the new holistic approach to global governance for food and nutrition security, including policies against hunger and malnutrition, all within a gender perspective. In our opinion, the success of our proposal will ultimately depend on the capacity of the new suggested framework to attract the support of social movements to work together toward a unified conceptual framework of the human right to adequate food and nutrition. These social movements should include those engaged in the struggle against the different violations of rights, directly or indirectly linked to the food and nutritional issues discussed in this volume. Examples of these include movements involving food sovereignty, peasants, small-scale farmers, traditional populations, landless, indigenous peoples, women's rights, children's rights, fisherfolks, environmentalists, agroecology, urban agriculture and gardening, farm workers, and community food security, among others. Furthermore, an alliance among these different movements would help build further cohesion and cooperation across north-south civil society groups and across urban-rural divides.

The starting point for an increased coordination among social movements could be an effort to jointly discuss and develop, in an inclusive manner, a new, clear diagnosis of where previous policy approaches have failed.[54]

These discussions could center on where policy approaches, including the conceptual framework of the human right to adequate food and nutrition, have been unable to capture the full complexity of the issue, have led us to fall into different sectorial traps in our artificially divided struggles, and have made it difficult to achieve increased unity. Furthermore, this reconceptualization effort by social movements should have two priorities: to overcome the fragmentations in the conceptual understanding of the causality of hunger and malnutrition and to overcome the social invisibility of root causes of hunger and malnutrition. As previously discussed, fragmentations in the conceptual understanding of the causes of hunger have several coexisting presentations, which include undernutrition, micronutrient malnutrition, overnutrition and obesity, and eating disorders. Within this frame, it is especially important to tackle the phenomena of nutrition transition, present in both industrialized and poorer countries.[55] The second priority, overcoming the social invisibility of the root causes of hunger and malnutrition, requires particular attention to the invisibility of the situation lived by the most affected groups.

Our belief is that the new proposed framework will be effective only if it is able to successfully respond to the specific needs of the different sectors of the social movements and overcome violations and growing challenges of protection against new forms of violations faced by members of these movements. By addressing the specific concerns of social movements, this new proposal will be effectively perceived by the affected populations as a tool to guarantee the realization of their human rights and achieve their goals. Simultaneously, through the identification of links among the various struggles, new strategic alliances among the social movements will be forged and the collective capacity to increase pressure on governments, multilateral fora, and international institutions toward increased human rights-based accountability, including extraterritorial obligations and the regulation of the private for-profit sector, will be strengthened.[56] A social movement-led reconceptualization of the human right to adequate food and nutrition framework will enable the push for a unified conceptual framework and place pressure on the national and UN human rights systems to adopt the new proposed concept in their new legal standards, such as in the form of resolutions, recommendations, and general comments. Furthermore, the understanding that any shift in power could result in a backlash by powerful corporate interests against social movements involved and their supporting actors requires any human rights framework to also ensure that human rights defenders are provided with the appropriate protection.

MOVING FROM THEORY TO PRACTICE: RECOMMENDATIONS

While cooperating with social movements in the reconceptualization of a holistic framework is an essential component of ensuring the success of our proposed framework for the human right to adequate food and nutrition, there are additional recommendations that we would like to make in order to advance our new comprehensive framework from mere theory to practice.

Closing the Gaps in the Human Rights System

An analysis of existing hard and soft law and international human rights standards allows us to affirm that most of the current challenges and gaps identified in this volume are still not adequately handled in a comprehensive and coordinated manner. An updated conceptualization of the human right to adequate food and nutrition is needed to close protection gaps that have been overlooked for a long time and have weakened the effectiveness of strategies and policies to combat hunger and malnutrition. It is known that the change of main binding instruments—such as the human rights covenants ICESCR, CEDAW, and CRC—is, politically, very difficult.[57] This change would require a huge investment of energy and would not necessarily guarantee effective protection. Nevertheless, this should not be seen as an insurmountable obstacle to further advance and update legal protection and to further a reconceptualization of the human right to adequate food and nutrition. We consider that the treaty bodies, which are in charge of the clarification of the content of human rights enshrined in the treaties through their general comments and recommendations, are competent authorities to take steps forward in the task of evolutive interpretation, advancing toward a more comprehensive conceptual framework of the human right to adequate food and nutrition.

Recommendations for the United Nations Committee on Economic, Social and Cultural Rights (CESCR)

First, we recommend that the CESCR come up with a new *General Comment on the Right to Adequate Food and Nutrition*. This would entail an update of the conceptual framework based on the holistic concept of the human right to adequate food and nutrition, which uses the peoples' and food sovereignty framework and incorporates nutrition, women's rights, and gender.

- *Incorporating peoples' and food sovereignty into a new general comment.*

    i. This principle should be included in the new general comment as a condition of people to be able to feed themselves in an adequate manner. This reference should be linked to the existing recognition of non-discriminatory access to productive resources and income for all persons and peoples, and should include the obligation of states to adopt affirmative measures to guarantee this access for the most marginalized and disadvantaged rural and urban individuals and communities.

ii. Moreover, a mention should be included that refers to the obligations of states to respect, protect, and fulfill the access of traditional communities and peasants to their territories, taking into account the definition of territories that social movements have developed.[58] In this sense, states' obligation to respect these territories as a condition for these communities to be able to maintain their livelihoods and to feed themselves in a sustainable manner should be mentioned in an explicit manner in the revised general comment.

iii. Under the obligation to protect, the proposed general comment would recognize that states should adopt regulations, monitoring, sanction, and remedy mechanisms to avoid threats and damages caused to individuals' and communities' livelihoods by the current agribusiness centered production model, including the practice of resource- or land-grab, which affects the human dignity of peoples and deprives them of their access to adequate food and nutrition.

iv. Also, under the obligations to protect and fulfill/facilitate, the new general comment would recognize that states should adopt measures regarding agroecological production models developed by peoples, thereby allowing them to maintain their traditional seeds, production, marketing, and consumption practices and traditions in order to guarantee food sustainability and a better use of natural resources.

v. Furthermore, states' obligation to adopt adequate measures and coping mechanisms to avoid further climate change-related negative consequences on food and nutrition security should be included under the obligation to fulfill the right to adequate food and nutrition.

- *Incorporating nutrition into the new general comment.* Under the legal attribute of food adequacy, the nutritional dimension (nutritional well-being) should be fully included as a needed capability for people to realize their right to an adequate standard of life in dignity, for which nutritional well-being is a prerequisite.

  i. Due to the linkage between food, nutrition, and health, the new general comment should be drafted in line with the content of CESCR *General Comment 14 on the Right to the Highest Attainable Standard of Health* (CESCR 2000), CEDAW Committee *General Recommendation 24 on Women and Health* (CEDAW Committee 1999), as well as in line with the content of CRC Committee *General Comment 15 on the Right of the Child to the Enjoyment of the Highest Attainable Standard of Health* (CRC

Committee 2013), so as to ensure that the strong linkage between food, nutrition, and health is highlighted.

ii. When dealing with state obligations, the new general comment should include the state obligation to adopt measures to combat the structural causes of hunger and malnutrition under the obligation to fulfill, both territorially and extraterritorially.

iii. Under the obligation to protect, states should adopt measures (regulations, monitoring, sanction, and remedy mechanisms) to protect people from negative consequences that marketing and advertising practices of the food corporate sector have on nutrition, including the development of dependencies on globalized, commercialized, and medicalized production that replaces local capacities to achieve food and nutrition self-reliance.

iv. Nutrition must be linked to local, regional, and national food systems and economies, promoting autonomy, health, and sovereignty with particular attention to the participatory rights and needs of women, infants, and small children in the development of sustainable livelihoods and food/production systems based on agroecological principles that respect and improve dietary traditions.

v. Non-pregnant and non-breastfeeding women and adult men should be included and particular attention should be given to the nutritional needs of children below two years of age, as well as of children after age two.

vi. Culturally adapted, regionally appropriate nutritional education to all human beings, independent of gender and age should be promoted.

- *Incorporating gender into the new general comment.* The strong gender dimension of the violations of the right to adequate food and nutrition leading to infant, child, and women malnutrition should be well-developed in the proposed general comment, especially in relation to:

  i. Gender discrimination in access to productive resources, inheritance, jobs, salaries, education, and public services in general

  ii. Structural and open violence against girls and women, which includes the institution of child marriage, household-bonded labor, sexual abuse, adolescent pregnancies, limited physical and social mobility, etc., which have negative consequences on the realization of the right to adequate food and nutrition

  iii. Strong gender-biased imposition of responsibilities on women within food and nutrition security policies, without due recognition and promotion of overall women's rights to self-determination, autonomy, freedom of choice, and equality, and without protection against structural/cultural and overt societal and household violence

iv. Women's equal right to participate in the design, adoption, implementation, and monitoring of food and nutrition policies at local, regional, national, and international levels

v. The concurrently independent and intertwined legal, biological, and cultural subjectivities of women and children during pregnancy/fetal development and lactation/infancy, particularly as they concern rights to self-determination, dignity, and well-being.

Secondly, the CESCR should take into consideration the approaches developed by the UN special rapporteur on the right to food and by other rapporteurs working with related issues.[59] The committee could highlight the efforts that states should put in place in order to take into account general and national recommendations produced by such special procedures with regard to the human right to adequate food and nutrition and related rights. During the analysis of national reports to the committee, the way in which states are complying with such recommendations could be revised, especially those derived from official visits and subsequent reports of the UN special rapporteur on the right to food or on related rights.

Recommendations for the United Nations Committee on the Elimination of Discrimination against Women (CEDAW Committee)

Similarly, we recommend that the CEDAW Committee issue a *General Recommendation on the Human Right to Adequate Food and Nutrition and Women*—with a similar approach to the one proposed to the CESCR and departing from the perspective of the rights of women—and take into account the proposed conceptual framework in its *General Recommendation on Rural Women*, which is being prepared by the Committee at the time of this writing.[60] Especially relevant would be to address more fully the consequences of violence and discrimination on the rights to adequate food and nutrition of women and the need for policies to tackle these issues in all phases of women's lives. Policies should take into account the specific nutritional and food needs of all children, women, and men of all ages, as well as women's special needs during pregnancy and breastfeeding, and for infants and young children through age two.

Recommendations for the United Nations Committee on the Rights of the Child (CRC Committee)

We recommend the evaluation of the adoption of a general comment developing the topic of children's human right to adequate food and nutrition, with a similar approach to the proposal to the CESCR and CEDAW Committee, especially recognizing the interdependency among mother and child and the need to protect mothers' human dignity, even when policies to overcome child malnutrition and hunger are addressed.

Recommendations for the United Nations Office of the High Commissioner for Human Rights (OHCHR)

We recommend that the OHCHR support the review of *General Comment 12* by the CESCR, promote the adoption of a *General Recommendation on the Right to Adequate Food and Nutrition and Women* by the CEDAW Committee, and promote the adoption of a general comment on the issue by the CRC Committee. We consider that the OHCHR could play an important coordinating role during the process of adoption of such treaty body standards in order to guarantee adequate institutional coordination and coherence and to facilitate adequate consultations with civil society.

Fostering Institutional Coordination

A new conceptual rights-based framework for food and nutrition security must be elaborated, departing from the conceptual clarification presented in this chapter, in order to overcome the limitations of previous fragmented frameworks. Institutional coordination to carry out a diagnosis of bottlenecks on the basis of the revised conceptual framework is necessary in order to better identify specific conceptual and political challenges to be tackled, and to have an adequate basis for the definition of pragmatic strategies and guidelines to overcome them, including the identification of risks, which could negatively affect the process and the way to avoid or minimize them. A condition sine qua non for the effective achievement of this aim is the inter-institutional coordination between the diverse bodies working on economic, social, and cultural rights, gender and women, including mainly but not exclusively the competent treaty bodies. These could include the Working Group on the Issue of Discrimination against Women in Law and in Practice (WG DAW), the UN Entity for Gender Equality and the Empowerment of Women (UN Women), the Commission on the Status of Women (CSW), and the OHCHR. Once the specific objectives of elaboration and implementation of such framework are defined, local, regional, national, and international strategies—in line with the process of elaboration of the Committee on World Food Security (CFS) Global Strategic Framework for Food Security and Nutrition (GSF; see chapter 1 of this volume)—should be adopted.[61]

Fostering Full and Democratic Participation of all Constituencies

The strategies developed with the full participation of all relevant social groups and constituencies, in particular those most affected, will serve to guide the needed public and private activities to reach democratically established goals related to overcoming the identified bottlenecks, at all levels. To this end, these strategies should ensure that the competent institutions, at all levels, establish mechanisms to guarantee permanent and autonomous participation of all relevant social groups,[62] with special attention to those historically excluded and socially "invisible." Moreover, the reorientation and coordination of public policies and programs toward the defined goals should be done in accordance with the principles of participation, accountability, transparency, empowerment, non-discrimination, and the rule of law, with the understanding of the priority of human rights and human dignity. Strategies developed should recommend the revision or establishment of new institutional and governance mechanisms, as well as new legislations and regulatory instruments as needed. Similarly, these should call for democratic and transparent public budget elaboration, public funds allocation, execution, and monitoring in line with public goals, which allow social control. Finally, there should be a reorientation of UN activities related to the theme, on the basis of the revised conceptual framework, based on adequate consultation with civil society, and with adequate representation of small-scale food producers, providers, and those most affected by food and nutrition insecurity, as guaranteed in the reform document of the CFS (see chapter 1 of this volume).

Strengthening Accountability Systems

Increasing accountability, from the local to the global level, is one of the best ways to ensure that public policies do not result in the preferential treatment of the already privileged sectors of society. In order to ensure that everyone, and in particular the most affected by food and nutrition insecurity, benefits from public food and nutrition policies, it is necessary for governments to establish, and inform its inhabitants of the creation of, national and international mechanisms of accountability that are accessible to all groups, that allow for the right to adequate food and nutrition to be a truly claimable right, and that provide effective protection for all those who speak against human rights violations.

Fostering Accessible and Non-Discriminatory Accountability Systems

In order to ensure effectiveness, institutions must guarantee that accountability mechanisms are accessible, non-discriminatory, and consider the specific conditions needed to allow real influence of diverse constituencies. In establishing these mechanisms, it is important to take into account that, at least in the so called "not well ordered societies" (Rawls 1993, 15) and in the international food security governance structures, traditional representative democracy has failed to answer to the interests of the most affected communities. In order to guarantee the exercise of communities' food sovereignty, as well as the realization of their human rights, it is necessary to establish participatory mechanisms that allow the direct participation of different social groups and peoples in the design, adoption, implementation, and monitoring of food and nutrition-related public policies. These mechanisms are essential to avoid abuse of power at all levels. Similarly, in order to ensure inclusion, cultural and context specificities have to be taken into account. Context specific factors to consider during the establishment of these mechanisms could include communicational culture, self-organization mechanisms, languages, infrastructure, communication possibilities, levels of knowledge, economical constraints, distances between communities, and administrative or political centers, among others.

Fostering Access to Recourse Mechanisms

Strengthening human rights accountability at the local, regional, national, and international levels will guarantee that the human right to adequate food and nutrition, within a gender equity perspective, does not remain as mere written clause, but is a truly claimable right. For that, people should have adequate rights, based on political, administrative, and quasi-judicial and judicial tools, at all levels, to make their authorities responsible for failures in the design, adoption, and/or implementation of food and nutrition-related public policies, strategies, and programs. These mechanisms should allow for social control of national and local management of public recourses to regulate authorities' negligence, inefficiency, ineffectiveness, and corruption practices. Furthermore, to allow for effective participation, adequate information tools and the primacy of material rights over procedural hurdles should be guaranteed. Therefore, several existing procedures should be revised and adapted to make them accessible to the most disadvantaged sectors of society.[63]

Strengthening National Human Rights Systems

Moving toward the establishment of human rights national institutions based on the Paris Principles should be a priority.[64] Institutions, such as national human rights commissions and ombudsman systems, should not just concentrate on civil and political rights, but better focus their work also on economic, social, and cultural rights, including the human right to adequate food and nutrition. These institutions should have the competencies and autonomy needed to ensure the better promotion and protection of the human right to adequate food and nutrition, including its gender dimension, and should count with adequate budgetary resources to exercise such competencies. Moreover they should be engaged in the presentation of independent national reports on the realization of the human right to adequate food and nutrition and its gender dimension to the UN treaty bodies, independently from other state authorities.

Strengthening Protection of Human Rights Defenders

All states have the obligation to inform all inhabitants of their territory about their rights, as well as about the existing available recourse mechanisms. States must also train their public officers at national, regional, and local levels, on how to fulfill their obligations under national law and international human rights law. At the same time, strong attention must be given by states to the protection of human rights defenders, particularly women and other strongly discriminated and excluded social groups, against public and private violence linked to their mobilization for their rights. Open violence and criminalization of social movements, human rights defenders and organizations, many times linked to private corporate interests, is dangerously on the rise in the world. The reformed CFS could be seen as a space that allows for the accountability process to take place. This process could occur in close cooperation with the UN human rights system and with similar mechanisms at regional and national levels.

Encouraging the Ratification of the *Optional Protocol to the International Covenant on Economic, Social and Cultural Rights*

All states parties to the ICESCR should be called on to sign and ratify the *Optional Protocol to the International Covenant on Economic, Social and Cultural Rights* (see UN General Assembly 2009), which includes three new mechanisms adequate to make accountable the human right to adequate food and nutrition at the international level: (*a*) the communications procedure, (*b*) the inquiry procedure, and (*c*) the interstate procedure. Moreover, the CESCR should ensure that the rules of procedure for the optional protocol (see CESCR 2013) truly allow the effective access of people and non-governmental organizations (NGOs) advocating for their rights to this international justice, that is, allowing the participation of NGOs, strategic litigating lawyers to the claims, and amicus curiae advocating for the human right to adequate food and nutrition.[65]

Promoting the Creation of a Universal Human Rights Court

The proposal to create a universal human rights court, which would constitute a binding justiciability mechanism for violations of the human right to adequate food and nutrition and other rights, should be further discussed and adopted at the international level. States should make possible this level of justiciability, which has a huge potential of protection for those most affected by violations of their human right to adequate food and nutrition, especially against causes of violations and abusing power structures that go beyond the competence of a single state or a regional group of states (see Kozma, Nowak, and Scheinin 2010).

Fostering Better Regulations and Accountability Mechanisms Regarding Extraterritorial Human Rights Obligations (ETOs)

Better regulations and accountability mechanisms should be foreseen toward the compliance of ETOs of states in coherence with the *Maastricht Principles on Extraterritorial Obligations of States in the Area of Economic, Social and Cultural Rights* (Maastricht University and ICJ 2011). These should cover diverse policy fields, mainly: (*a*) investment, trade, and development cooperation, (*b*) activities of intergovernmental organizations (IMF, World Bank, and WTO, among others), (*c*) state responsibility for violations caused by corporate private sector activities, with special attention to the food and agriculture international system, nutrition, health, and access to natural resources (among others, land, seeds, water, and raw materials), (*d*) border conflicts, and (*e*) climate change and environment with the objective, inter alia, of:

- Stopping all plundering activities of land, water, forests, and other natural resources by foreign and private corporate initiatives, and regulating the role of International Finance Institutions (IFIs) and other governmental and intergovernmental bodies involved in its promotion (e.g., European Commission, G8, WTO, etc.)
- Promoting peoples' sovereignty over their natural resources above described and their right to decide how to use them for their own equitable human development
- Regulating and curbing the abuses of the chemical intensive industrial agricultural model of production, including its impact on soil degradation, soil and water contamination, labor abuses, agricultural workers' and human health in general, and monopoly practices in seed and retail control
- Regulating marketing and advertising practices of food corporations, with special attention to those involved in the production of "junk food,"[66] and prohibiting any food publicity directly or indirectly aimed at children in all means of communication[67]
- Further strengthening regulation of marketing and advertising of breastmilk substitutes[68]
- Create an international enabling environment for agroecology and food sovereignty. This is to be achieved through measures including the review of multilateral and bilateral agreements in the area of trade investment
- In order to comply with their ETOs related to the right to adequate food and nutrition, states have to prioritize the nutritional needs of the disadvantaged and marginalized groups, with special attention to women in those groups.

CONCLUSION

We have attempted to demonstrate that hunger and malnutrition are prima facie a consequence of the lack of fulfillment of states' human rights obligations under the right to adequate food and nutrition and are reflections of the inequalities in our societies. While many work toward ensuring that all human beings have their human right to adequate food and nutrition guaranteed, so that they are capable of leading a socially productive, healthy, active, and dignified life, independently of their social status, ethnicity, religion, gender, etc., unfortunately, this is not yet the case for a significant proportion of people. Women, men, and children have been and continue to be excluded from the benefits of economic and social development. The results of this exclusion are especially visible in food-related areas and disproportionately affect more women and children.

As discussed above, the failure to elaborate effective strategies to overcome hunger and malnutrition originates from a set of complex issues. These issues, which are the fragmentation of the conceptual, legal, and institutional frameworks, the associated reductionism of solutions, and the invisibility and underestimation of structural processes, have led to ineffective policies against hunger and malnutrition. To a certain extent, all these factors are related to the fact that it is not in the interest of the hegemonic elites to question and really change these structural processes, inherent to a global model that clearly works in their favor. The present strategies and policies against hunger and malnutrition are, in essence, coherent with the strengthening of the global model that promotes more inequities. The great challenge we have tried to address is how to make these strategies and policies coherent with human rights principles and objectives to which states are obliged.

We have argued that the human rights system, while imperfect and subject to social and political influences, continues to be the best tool for addressing hunger and malnutrition. This tool faces the challenge of needed continuous evolution, which will allow it to close existing and emerging gaps in protection. In this context, our proposed conceptual framework for the human right to adequate food and nutrition would enable the human rights system to become a more effective tool to support human rights governance and coherent, people-centered, and gender sensitive policies to reduce hunger and malnutrition, while promoting healthy and dignified lives. This framework has the potential to more effectively address the structural causes of hunger and malnutrition that are strongly linked to poverty, reduced capabilities and associated deprivations, power relations, and violations of women's rights, causes which cannot be overcome with merely compensatory measures. These causes must be tackled through holistic and integrated human rights-based policies aimed at redistributive measures and reduction of inequities in access to productive resources, public services, and social security, and by applying the principle of peoples' and food sovereignty.

We also recognize that an essential component of the success of the new proposed conceptual framework is its ability to allow social movements to bring their experiences and knowledge to decision-making and implementation processes. Through institutional coordination and democratic participation of the various constituencies, strengthening of accountability systems, and better regulation of ETOs, our framework can be further advanced from theory to practice.

NOTES

1. The principle of evolutive interpretation assumes that human rights are not static and, therefore, effective protection of these rights involves taking into account developments in law and society. For a deeper analysis of the evolutive interpretation of human rights treaties see, inter alia, Sepúlveda Carmona (2003, 81). The effectiveness principle is a legal principle of interpretation that states that law should be effective, as to its operation. Since the overriding function of human rights treaties is the protection of individuals' rights, their interpretation should make that protection effective (see, inter alia, Sepúlveda Carmona 2003, 79). As to the effectiveness principle as a rule of treaty interpretation, see the International Court of Justice (1950, 229). As to legal interpretation according to the development of international public law, see European Court of Human Rights (ECHR 2011), the website of the Icelandic Human Rights Centre (2012), as well as Sepúlveda Carmona (2003, 73–112).
2. It is important to mention that there are other principles of interpretation that could be considered; however, because other principles do not directly result from the special object and purpose of human rights treaties, their analysis is beyond the scope of this chapter.
3. See paragraph 26 of *General Comment 12* (CESCR 1999b), which introduces an explanation mainly dealing with non-discrimination "particularly for women" in access to resources; however, this paragraph does not refer to the nutritional dimension of the right to adequate food of women.
4. For concrete examples of structural root causes of hunger and malnutrition, please see previous chapters of this volume. For example, see chapter 3 for an in-depth discussion of violence against women and girls (such as lack of protection at the workplace, child marriage, and early pregnancy, among others) as a structural root cause of hunger and malnutrition.
5. For an example of "business as usual" reductionist approaches and how to overcome them, see the *International Assessment of Agricultural Knowledge, Science and Technology for Development* (IAASTD 2009).
6. See chapter 5 of this volume for a discussion of paternalistic policies calling for global food production, which result in the promotion of food and nutrition aid dependencies instead of autonomy, in contrast to approaches to integrated local and regional food production and nutritionally sound consumption systems, which have as their ultimate goal to achieve increased autonomy, strengthen self-reliance, and improve access to resources for the poor.
7. For a discussion about the introduction of RUFs into communities without adequate local knowledge and participation, in particular without the mention of the best practice of continued breastfeeding and a gradual introduction of semi-solid and solid foods from the traditional food the family eats, please see chapter 4 of this volume.

8. For an in-depth discussion about emergency interventions aiming at micronutrient supplementation through the provision of micronutrient fortified foods, please see chapter 4 of this volume.

9. Political will is not the decisive action that needs to be taken; policy coherence with people at its center instead of being linked with the interests of the small international financial, industrial, and agroindustrial elite is crucial in order to adequately address hunger and malnutrition. For examples of how erroneous policy presumptions can further contribute to hunger and malnutrition, please see chapter 5 of this volume.

10. For a discussion about the disconnect between the right to adequate food and nutrition and women's and children's rights, please see chapters 2 and 4 of this volume.

11. For the public policy presumption that the state and international market systems provide better support for food security and nutritional well-being than do local and regional systems and the impact of this presumption on women's food security, please see chapter 5 of this volume.

12. For a discussion about the structural isolation of women's rights from the human right to adequate food and nutrition within the legally binding language of key international human rights treaties, please see chapter 2 of this volume. For violence against women and girls as an under-examined barrier to women's right to adequate food and nutrition and their participation as autonomous and participatory members of efforts to address hunger and malnutrition, please see chapter 3. For a discussion on the current focus on malnutrition during pregnancy and infancy and the accompanying neglect of women's overall nutritional needs throughout their life spans, see chapter 4.

13. For the exploration of the problems associated with the structural and legal separation of the rights of (*a*) women and their control over reproductive choice and nutritional needs before, during, and after pregnancy; and (*b*) foeti, infants, and young children during the most crucial time of human nutrition and health, a period generating short and long term developmental consequences, please chapter 4 of this volume.

14. For how violence against women and girls impedes their participation in food and nutrition policies, see chapter 3 of this volume. For a discussion on how global market systems prevent women's food security by focusing away from gender, nutrition, and inter-scalar governance approaches that promote and integrate small farmers and agroecology in food systems, see chapter 5.

15. Whereas all contributors to this volume recognize the need to emphasize the situation of rural women (cf. e.g., chapter 5), the specific situation of urban women also suffering from violations of the right to adequate food and nutrition has been mostly neglected. For examples of this unbalanced emphasis, please refer to article 14 of CEDAW, where only the right of rural women to land is expressed as the only indirect mention to the right to adequate food and nutrition (see UN General Assembly 1979). Also see guidelines 2.5, 8.4, 8.6, and 8.10 of the *Voluntary Guidelines to Support the Progressive Realization of the Right to Adequate Food in the Context of National Food Security* (FAO 2005), where there is an emphasis on the right to adequate food and nutrition of women primarily as rural food producers.

16. Violence here is understood as encompassing more than overt directed and aggressive forms of violence. It includes the broader concepts of structural violence (such as gender discrimination) and cultural violence (such as those aspects of structural or direct violence that are legitimized by culture and tradition). Please see chapter 3 of this volume for a more in-depth description of our understanding of violence.

17. According to the former UN special representative of the secretary general on human rights defenders, Ms. Hina Jilani, and the former special rapporteur on

the situation of human rights defenders (2008–2014), Ms. Margaret Sekaggya, the second most vulnerable group of human rights defenders are those working on land, natural resources, and environmental issues (see HRC 2007, 2011a; see also APRODEV et al. 2012; Global Witness Limited 2012).

18. For an in-depth discussion of why agriculture should be fundamentally redirected toward modes of production that are more environmentally sustainable and socially just, and how this can be achieved, see HRC (2010).

19. For a framework on how to achieve protection for children against the commercial promotion of foods and beverages, please see the webpage "The Sydney Principles" at the International Obesity Taskforce website (IOTF 2013).

20. The indivisibility principle refers to the notion that human rights, whether they are civil, political, economic, social, or cultural rights, cannot be separated from one another. The fulfillment of one right depends on the fulfillment of others. The holistic approach of the human rights system, which recognizes the indivisibility and interdependence of all human rights, allows for the issuance of comprehensive guidelines for public action toward the promotion of people centered, equitable, and sustainable human development. For further discussion on the indivisibility principle, see A. Eide and Rosas (2001, 3) and UN General Assembly (1993b, part I, para. 5).

21. Practitioners and academics that have pointed to the need for a shift in the conceptual framework of the right to adequate food and nutrition include Asbjørn Eide, Urban Jonsson, Arne Oshaug, Penny Van Esterick, Wenche Barth Eide, Uwe Kracht, and Flavio Valente, among others. For a sample of articles written by these individuals, please see W. B. Eide and Kracht (2005, 2007).

22. See previous note 21.

23. Objective 7.4(e) of the *World Food Summit Declaration and Plan of Action* "[i]nvite[s] the UN High Commissioner for Human Rights, in consultation with relevant treaty bodies, and in collaboration with relevant specialized agencies and programmes of the UN system and appropriate intergovernmental mechanisms, to better define the rights related to food in Article 11 of the Covenant and to propose ways to implement and realize these rights as a means of achieving the commitments and objectives of the World Food Summit, taking into account the possibility of formulating voluntary guidelines for food security for all" (FAO 1996).

24. Only paragraph 26 of *General Comment 12* establishes that: "The strategy should give particular attention to the need to prevent discrimination in access to food or resources for food. This should include: guarantees of full and equal access to economic resources, *particularly for women*, including the right to inheritance and the ownership of land and other property, credit, natural resources and appropriate technology; measures to respect and protect self-employment and work which provides a remuneration ensuring a decent living for wage earners and their families (as stipulated in article 7(a)(ii) of the Covenant); maintaining registries on rights in land (including forests)" (CESCR 1999b, para. 26; emphasis added).

25. Capability here is used as defined by Drèze and Sen (1999, vii): "Expansions of basic human capabilities, including such freedoms as the ability to live long, to read and write, to escape preventable illnesses, to work outside the family irrespective of gender, . . ., not only influence the quality of life that the Indian people can enjoy, but also affect the real opportunities they have to participate in economic expansion."

26. Please see previous note 25 for our understanding of the concept of capabilities. Entitlements, according to Amartya Sen (1983, 2–3), include all ownership relations that are legitimized in a specific society, over specific commodities and/or services. They can be inheritance-related, production-based, own labor-based, trade-based, social security-based, etc. Human rights can also be a source of

entitlements, for instance, the right to the promotion or protection of cultural or religious identity through the ingestion of culturally adequate food.

27. According to article 1 of the *Declaration on the Rights of Peasants and Other People Working on Rural Areas* (UN General Assembly 2013), "[a] peasant is a man or woman of the land, who has a direct and special relationship with the land and nature through the production of food or other agricultural products. Peasants work the land themselves and rely above all on family labour and other small-scale forms of organizing labour. Peasants are traditionally embedded in their local communities and they take care of local landscapes and of agro-ecological systems."

28. Other academics who have argued that hunger and malnutrition are "man-made" include Amartya Sen, Olivier De Schutter, and Jean Ziegler, among others.

29. For an example of such coherence, see the G8's New Alliance for Food Security and Nutrition. For more information about this alliance, see the webpage "Advancing the New Alliance for Food Security and Nutrition" at the United States Agency for International Development (USAID) website (USAID Press Office 2012).

30. The *Vienna Convention on the Law of Treaties* establishes that a general rule of interpretation calls for "[every] treaty [to] be interpreted in good faith in accordance with the ordinary meaning to be given to the terms in their context and in the light of its object and purpose" (UN 1969, art. 31, para. 1).

31. The core elements of the human right to adequate food and nutrition entail the collective and individual exercise of rights and freedoms. Please see the section of this chapter "Fundamentals for a new conceptual framework for the human right to adequate food and nutrition" for a further discussion.

32. For a criticism of the current policies around maternal, infant, and young children's nutrition, see Lhotska, Bellows, and Scherbaum (2012, 31).

33. For an example of anthropological studies of the social and cultural dimensions of food, please see Camacho (2006).

34. Please see the previous section of this chapter "Advances and missed opportunities in the development of the legal concept of the human right to adequate food and nutrition" for a review of Asbjørn Eide's proposals.

35. For a concrete example of the links between violations of the right to adequate food and nutrition and structural violence against women and girls, see FLORAISON et al. (2012).

36. Stunting, or low height for age, is usually caused by continued insufficient nutrient intake and frequent infections, with higher prevalence below age two. Wasting, or low weight for height, is a strong predictor of infant or child mortality and is usually associated with acute lack of adequate nutrient intake and disease. For more information, see UNICEF (2007).

37. In 1990, UNICEF adapted Urban Jonsson's conceptual framework on the causes of malnutrition, developed in the 1970s, into the Conceptual Framework for Malnutrition and Death for UNICEF's *Strategy for Improved Nutrition of Children and Women in Developing Countries* (see UNICEF 1990).

38. This situation can be linked to an observation collected by FIAN Mexico (2007–2009) during the development of a project with women in the Mexican states of Guerrero and Morelos. Women participating in a diagnosis exercise to determine their perception of violence and discrimination against women highlighted the fact that public programs, which supposedly are in place to support women, instead of alleviating the heavy workload of women in the household, burden the female beneficiaries of state programs even more. Thus, these public programs place additional responsibilities on these women; among these, the responsibility to serve their communities as a condition of receiving the proposed benefits. For more information, see FIAN International et al. (2012).

39. Food sovereignty is based on six principles: (*a*) focus on food for people, (*b*) valuing food producers and providers, (*c*) localization of food systems, having providers and consumers at the center of decision-making, (*e*) recognition of producers' right to control over local territory, (*f*) building on traditional and local knowledge, and (*g*) working in harmony with nature (see Forum for Food Sovereignty 2007b).

40. Priscilla Claeys (2012, 849) states that food sovereignty should be considered a right evolving, inter alia, from the principles of self-determination and access to resources. The authors of this chapter are of the opinion that, since currently food sovereignty has not been recognized as a human right in any international law source, this concept should be understood as a set of principles that can be used to form the framework for the right to adequate food and nutrition highlighting self-determination as a crosscutting principle of human rights.

41. We reaffirm the interconnection among specific state obligations and general obligations according to the categorization used by the CESCR from its *General Comment 14 on The Right to the Highest Attainable Standard of Health* onwards. This classification was still not adopted when *General Comment 12* was drafted. For more information, see Suárez Franco (2010, 250).

42. See the *Maastricht Principles on Extraterritorial Obligations of States in the Area of Economic, Social and Cultural Rights* (Maastricht University and ICJ 2011). For further information on this extraterritorial dimension, please see Coomans and Künnemann (2012) as well as the website of the ETO Consortium (2013).

43. On the prohibition of retrogression, please see CESCR *General Comment 4 on the Right to Adequate Housing* (CESCR 1991, para. 11), *General Comment 12 on the Right to Adequate Food* (CESCR 1999b, para. 19), *General Comment 13 on the Right to Education* (CESCR 1999c, paras. 45, 59), *General Comment 14 on the Right to the Highest Attainable Standard of Health* (CESCR 2000, paras. 32, 48), *General Comment 15 on the Right to Water* (CESCR 2003, paras. 19, 42), *General Comment 16 on the Equal Right of Men and Women to the Enjoyment of All Economic, Social and Cultural Rights* (CESCR 2006a, para. 42), *General Comment 17 on the Right of Everyone to Benefit from the Protection of the Moral and Material Interests Resulting from Any Scientific, Literary or Artistic Production of which He or She is the Author* (CESCR 2006b, para. 44), *General Comment 18 on the Right to Work* (CESCR 2006c, paras. 21, 34), and *General Comment 19 on the Right to Social Security* (CESCR 2008, para. 42). See also, van Boven, Flinterman, and Westendorp (1998, para. 14). On the existence of minimum core obligations, see CESCR *General Comment 3 on the Nature of States Parties' Obligations* (CESCR 1990, paras. 2, 9), *General Comment 5 on Persons with Disabilities* (CESCR 1994, para. 9), *General Comment 11 on Plans of Action for Primary Education* (CESCR 1999a, para. 10), *General Comment 12 on the Right to Adequate Food* (CESCR 1999b, para. 14), *General Comment 13 on the Right to Education* (CESCR 1999c, para. 43), *General Comment 14 on the Right to the Highest Attainable Standard of Health* (CESCR 2000, para. 30), *General Comment 15 on the Right to Water* (CESCR 2003, para. 18), *General Comment 16 on the Equal Right of Men and Women to the Enjoyment of All Economic, Social and Cultural Rights* (CESCR 2006a, para. 39), *General Comment 17 on the Right of Everyone to Benefit from the Protection of the Moral and Material Interests Resulting from Any Scientific, Literary or Artistic Production of which He or She is the Author* (CESCR 2006b, paras. 25, 26), and *General Comment 18 on the Right to Work* (CESCR 2006c, para. 19).

44. We should note that this new matrix does not seek to eliminate the existing human rights standards related to the right to adequate food and nutrition

concept which include access, availability, adequacy, and sustainability, but rather complement and broaden it from a food sovereignty perspective.

45. The explanation of these three levels of state obligations is in reference to the Peoples' and Food Sovereignty Matrix presented in this chapter. For more general information on the specific state obligations, please refer to chapter 1 of this volume.

46. Nonetheless, the obligation of states to respect individuals' right to choose their eating patterns is limited by their obligation to also protect the human rights of children and other family members who might be discriminated against because of traditional and culturally acceptable intra-household eating patterns. For an in-depth discussion of discrimination—in special against women and girls—in intra-household feeding patterns as structural violence and as human rights violation, see chapter 3 of this volume.

47. In this chapter, we use the term "traditional seeds" to refer to seeds that have adapted to local realities through local knowledge over generations.

48. The term "junk food" throughout this chapter refers to foods of poor nutritional value that are high in salt, fat, and simple sugar. For a more in-depth description of "junk food" and its effects on health, see Bayol, Farrington, and Stickland (2007).

49. Although under CESCR *General Comment 12* "the right to adequate food . . . imposes three types of levels of obligations on States parties: the obligation to respect, to protect and to fulfill" and, "[i]n turn, the obligation to fulfill incorporates both an obligation to facilitate and an obligation to provide" (CESCR 1999b, para. 15), *General Comment 12* should be interpreted using an evolutive perspective and we should infer that it should have also evolved to entail all three levels of the obligation to fulfill (facilitate, provide, and promote) incorporated into later CESCR general comments. Nonetheless, whereas we believe that we should move in that direction, this matrix only focuses on the two levels of fulfill (facilitate and provide) listed in *General Comment 12* and the missing level (promote) is subsumed under the obligation to fulfill/facilitate.

50. See CESCR *General Comment 12* establishing the obligation of a state party "to take the necessary steps to the maximum of its available resources" (CESCR 1999b, para. 17). For more information on the general obligation to take appropriate measures toward the full realization of economic, social, and cultural rights to the maximum of states' available resources, see Sepúlveda Carmona (2003, 313–19).

51. See CESCR *General Comment 12* establishing that "[v]iolations of the right to food can occur through the direct action of States or other entities insufficiently regulated by States" (CESCR 1999b, para. 19). For more information on the general obligation of non-retrogression toward the full realization of economic, social, and cultural rights, see Sepúlveda Carmona (2003, 319–32).

52. See CESCR *General Comment 12* establishing that "any discrimination in access to food, as well as to means and entitlements for its procurement, on the grounds of race, colour, sex, language, age, religion, political or other opinion, national or social origin, property, birth or other status . . . constitutes a violation of the Covenant" (CESCR 1999b, para. 18). For more information on the general obligation of non-discrimination in regards to the realization of economic, social, and cultural rights, see Sepúlveda Carmona (2003, 379–419).

53. Please note that in spite of the principle of progressive realization of economic, social, and cultural rights, governments, no matter what level of resources are at their disposal, are obligated to ensure that people living under their jurisdiction enjoy at least an essential level of protection of these rights. For more information on minimum core obligations, see Klee (2000, 104), Sepúlveda Carmona (2003, 313–19), and Suárez Franco (2010, 60).

54. Such a process of increased coordination has already been started by the Global Right to Food and Nutrition Network of civil society organizations (see The Right to Food website of the FAO; FAO 2013).
55. Nutrition transition is a product of dietary intake that even in the context of adequate food availability is nevertheless deficient in high quality vitamins, minerals, and nutrients. Whole grains, fresh fruits, and vegetables relinquish the center of intake to foods high in fats, sugars, and salt. The outcome is an increase in chronic diseases, especially obesity, high blood pressure, heart disease, and diabetes, among others. Whereas originally associated with northern and richer countries, the globalized food economy has spread poor food culture and habits to middle and lower income countries which increasingly experience high rates of both under- and overnutrition, even at the household level.
56. A first step toward the identification of links among the various struggles has already been accomplished by the establishment of the Global Right to Food and Nutrition Network. See previous note 54.
57. For general rules regarding the modification of treaties, see the *Vienna Convention on the Law of Treaties* (UN 1969, part IV).
58. For examples of social movements' definitions of territories, see guidelines 1.1 and 1.2 of the *Civil Society Organizations' Proposal for the FAO Guidelines on Responsible Governance of Land and Natural Resources Tenure* (FIAN International 2011, 17); see also the *Synthesis Report [of the Nyéléni Forum for Food Sovereignty, (23–27 February 2007)]* (Forum for Food Sovereignty 2007b) and the final declaration of the "Land, Territory and Dignity" Forum (IPC 2006).
59. For Olivier De Schutter's reports as UN special rapporteur on the right to food during the years 2008–2014, please visit his website (De Schutter 2014).
60. For more information on the process of the drafting of the *General Recommendation on Rural Women* by the CEDAW Committee, visit the webpage of the CEDAW Committee at the OHCHR website (OHCHR 2014).
61. For more information on the civil society assessment of the Global Strategic Framework for Food Security (GSF), visit the website of the International Food Security & Nutrition Civil Society Mechanism (CSM; CSM 2012).
62. For more information about the CSM to the Committee on World Food Security (CFS) as an example of mechanisms to ensure the permanent and autonomous participation of all relevant social groups in food and nutrition strategies, please see chapter 1 of this volume.
63. As a practical example of how to implement the right to adequate food and nutrition at the country level, see Burity, Cruz, and Franceschini (2011).
64. The Paris Principles set out the minimum standards required for national institutions seeking to protect and promote human rights (see UN General Assembly 1993a).
65. Amicus curiae, or literally "friend of the court," refers to specialized opinions, often in the form of letters, that inform the judge about the possibly broad legal effects of the decision. These letters often contain international legal standards applicable to the case at hand, sources proceeding from comparative law, and the manner in which these could be applied to the specific case. See also Abregú and Courtis (1997, 387).
66. For a definition of "junk food," see note 48 above.
67. See note 19.
68. For more information on the recommendation to further strengthen the regulation of marketing and advertising of breastmilk substitutes, please visit the website of the International Baby Food Action Network (IBFAN; see IBFAN 2013).

REFERENCES

Abregú, M. and C. Courtis. 1997. "Perspectivas y Posibilidades del Amicus Cur-iae en el Derecho Argentino." *["Amicus Curiae Perspectives and Possibilities in Argentinian Law"]* In *La Aplicación de los Tratados sobre Derechos Humanos por los Tribunales Locales [The Implementation of Human Rights Treaties by Local Courts]*, edited by M. Abregú and C. Courtis, 387–404. Buenos Aires: Centro de Estudios Legales y Sociales (CELS).

Agarwal, B., J. Humphries, and I. Robeyns. 2006. *Capabilities, Freedom and Equality: Amartya Sen's Work from a Gender Perspective*. India: Oxford University Press.

Association of World Council of Churches related Development Organisations in Europe (APRODEV), Coopération Internationale pour le Développement et la Solidarité (CIDSE), Copenhagen Initiative For Central America and Mexico (CIFCA), FIAN International, Observatory for the Protection of Human Rights Defenders (OBS), Oficina Internacional de Derechos Humanos Acción Colombia (OIDHAC), Peace Brigades International (PBI) Guatemala & Colombia Projects, and Plataforma Holandesa contra la Impunidad. 2012. *The Criminalization of Human Rights Defenders in Latin America: An Assessment from International Organisations and European Networks*.

Bayol S.A., S.J. Farrington, and N.C. Stickland. 2007. "A Maternal 'Junk Food' Diet in Pregnancy and Lactation Promotes an Exacerbated Taste for 'Junk Food' and a Greater Propensity for Obesity in Rat Offspring." *British Journal of Nutrition* 98: 843–51.

Burity, V., L. Cruz, and T. Franceschini. 2011. *Exigibilidade: Mechanisms to Claim the Human Right to Adequate Food in Brazil*. Rome: Food and Agriculture Organization of the United Nations (FAO).

Camacho, J. 2006. "Bueno para Comer, Bueno para Pensar." *["Good for Eating, Good for Thinking."]* In *Desarrollo con Identidad: Comunidad, Cultura y Sustentabilidad en los Andes [Development with Identity: Community, Culture and Sustainability in the Andes]*, edited by R. Rhoades, 237–62. Quito: Abya Yala.

Claeys, P. 2012. "The Creation of New Rights by the Food Sovereignty Movement: The Challenge of Institutionalizing Subversion." *Sociology* 46 (5): 844–60.

Commission on the Nutrition Challenges for the 21st Century. 2000. *Ending Malnutrition by 2020: An Agenda for Change in the Millennium. Final Report to the ACC/SCN by the Commission on the Nutrition Challenges of the 21st Century*. Geneva: United Nations Administrative Committee on Coordination/Sub-Committee on Nutrition (ACC/SCN).

Coomans, F. and R. Künnemann. 2012. *Cases and Concepts on Extraterritorial Obligations in the Area of Economic, Social and Cultural Rights*. Cambridge: Intersentia.

De Schutter, O. 2010. *Addressing Concentration in Food Supply Chains: The Role of Competition Law in Tackling the Abuse of Buyer Power*. Briefing Note 3.

———. 2014. "Documents." Olivier De Schutter: UN Special Rapporteur on the Right to Food, accessed January 21, 2014, http://www.srfood.org/en/documents.

de Silva-de-Alwis, R. 2008. *Child Marriage and the Law: Legislative Reform Initiative Paper Series*. New York: United Nations Children's Fund (UNICEF).

Doak, C.M., L.S. Adair, M. Bentley, C. Monteiro, and B.M. Popkin. 2005. "The Dual Burden Household and the Nutrition Transition Paradox." *International Journal of Obesity* 29: 129–36.

Drèze, J and A. Sen. 1999. *India: Economic Development and Social Opportunity*. Oxford: Clarendon Press.

Eide, A. 1984a. *The New International Economic Order and the Promotion of Human Rights (Study on the Right to Adequate Food as a Human Right)*, E/CN.4/Sub.2/1984/22, 29 June 1984.

————. 1984b. *The New International Economic Order and the Promotion of Human Rights (Study on the Right to Adequate Food as a Human Right)*, E/CN.4/Sub.2/1984/22/Add.1, 29 June 1984.

————. 1984c. *The New International Economic Order and the Promotion of Human Rights (Study on the Right to Adequate Food as a Human Right)*, E/CN.4/Sub.2/1984/22/Add.2, 3 July 1984.

————. 1989. *Right to Adequate Food as a Human Right*. Human Rights Study Series 1. New York: United Nations/Center for Human Rights.

————. 1999. *The Right to Adequate Food and to be Free from Hunger: Updated Study on the Right to Food, Submitted by Mr. Asbjørn Eide in Accordance with Sub-Commission Decision 1997/108*, E/CN.4/Sub.2/1999/12, 28 June 1999.

————. 2005. "The Importance of Economic and Social Rights in the Age of Economic Globalisation." In *Food and Human Rights in Development, Volume I: Legal and Institutional Dimensions and Selected Topics*, edited by W. B. Eide and U. Kracht, 3–40. Antwerpen, Oxford: Intersentia.

Eide, A. and A. Rosas. 2001. "Economic, Social and Cultural Rights: A Universal Challenge." In *Economic, Social and Cultural Rights: A Textbook*, edited by A. Eide, C. Krause and A. Rosas. 2nd ed., 3–7. The Hague: Kluwer Law International.

Eide, W. B. 2005. "From Food Security to the Right to Food." In *Food and Human Rights in Development, Volume I: Legal and Institutional Dimensions and Selected Topics*, edited by W. B. Eide and U. Kracht, 67–97. Antwerpen, Oxford: Intersentia.

Eide, W. B. and U. Kracht, eds. 2005. *Food and Human Rights in Development, Volume I: Legal and Institutional Dimensions and Selected Topics*. Antwerpen, Oxford: Intersentia.

————. 2007. *Food and Human Rights in Development, Volume II: Evolving Issues and Emerging Applications*. Antwerpen, Oxford: Intersentia.

ETO Consortium. 2013. "ETOs for Human Rights Beyond Borders." ETO Consortium, accessed February 5, 2013, http://www.etoconsortium.org.

European Court of Human Rights (ECHR). 2011. *Dialogue Between Judges 2011: "What Are the Limits to the Evolutive Interpretation of the Convention?"* Strasbourg : European Court of Human Rights (ECHR).

FIAN International. 2011. *Civil Society Organizations' Proposals for the FAO Guidelines on Responsible Governance of Land and Natural Resources Tenure*. Heidelberg: FIAN International.

FIAN International, FIAN Mexico, Colectivo de Mujeres Campesinas, and Unión de Pueblos de Morelos. 2012. *Construyendo la Política Alimentaria Comunitaria desde una Perspectiva de Género y Derechos Humanos [Framing Community Food Policy from a Gender and Human Rights Perspective]*. Mexico City: FIAN Mexico.

FLORAISON, Groupe de Recherche-Action pour le Développement Socio-Economique (GRADSE), Réseau Africain Pour le Droit à l'Alimentation (RAPDA) Togo, and FIAN International. 2012. *Alternative Written Report Submitted on Behalf of Rural Women in Gnita, Togo and Togo-Based NGOs, FLORAISON, GRADSE and RAPDA-Togo, with the Support of FIAN International, to the Committee on the Elimination of Discrimination against Women during its Fifty-Third Session (October 2012)*.

Food and Agriculture Organization of the United Nations (FAO). 1996. *Rome Declaration on World Food Security and World Food Summit Plan of Action*. Rome: Food and Agriculture Organization of the United Nations (FAO).

————. 2005. *Voluntary Guidelines to Support the Progressive Realization of the Right to Adequate Food in the Context of National Food Security*. Rome: Food and Agriculture Organization of the United Nations (FAO).

————. 2006. *The Double Burden of Malnutrition: Case Studies from Six Developing Countries*. Food and Nutrition Paper. Vol. 84. Rome: Food and Agriculture Organization of the United Nations (FAO).

————. 2013. "Coherent Food Security Responses: Incorporating Right to Food into Global and Regional Food Security Initiatives—Global Right to Food and Nutrition Network of Civil Society Organizations." The Right to Food, accessed January 27, 2013, http://www.fao.org/righttofood/our-work/current-projects/rtf-global-regional-level/grtfn/en/.

Forum for Food Sovereignty. 2007a. *Declaration of Nyéléni (27 February 2007)*. Sélingué, Mali.

————. 2007b. *Synthesis Report [of the Nyéléni Forum for Food Sovereignty, (23–27 February 2007)]*. Sélingué, Mali.

Global Witness Limited. 2012. *A Hidden Crisis? Increase in Killings as Tensions Rise Over Land and Forests*. Global Witness Briefing, 19 June 2012. London: Global Witness.

Gross, R., H. Schoeneberger, H. Pfeifer, and H.-J. A. Preuss. 2000. "Four Dimensions of Food and Nutrition Security: Definition and Concepts." *SCN News* 20: 20–25.

Hesse-Biber, S., P. Leavy, C. E. Quinn, and J. Zoino. 2006. "The Mass Marketing of Disordered Eating and Eating Disorders: The Social Psychology of Women, Thinness and Culture." *Women's Studies International Forum* 29 (2): 208–24.

Icelandic Human Rights Centre (IHRC). "Interpretation of Human Rights Treaties." The Concepts of Human Rights: An Introduction, accessed October 31, 2012, http://www.humanrights.is/the-human-rights-project/humanrightscasesandmaterials/humanrightsconceptsideasandfora/theconceptsofhumanrightsanintroduction/interpretationofhumanrightstreaties/.

International Assessment of Agricultural Knowledge, Science and Technology for Development (IAASTD). 2009. *Agriculture at a Crossroads: International Assessment of Agricultural Knowledge, Science and Technology for Development: Executive Summary of the Synthesis Report*. Washington, D.C.: Island Press.

International Baby Food Action Network (IBFAN). "IBFAN." International Baby Food Action Network (IBFAN), accessed February 05, 2013, http://ibfan.org/.

International Court of Justice (ICJ). 1950. *Advisory Opinion Concerning the Interpretation of Peace Treaties with Bulgaria, Hungary, and Romania; Second Phase (18 July 1950)*.

International Food Security & Nutrition Civil Society Mechanism (CSM). 2012. "Final Assessment of the GSF from a Civil Society Perspective." International Food Security & Nutrition Civil Society Mechanism (CSM), last modified October 31, 2012, accessed February 23, 2013, http://www.csm4cfs.org/news/final_assessment_of_the_gsf_from_a_civil_society_perspective-91/.

International NGO/CSO Planning Committee for Food Sovereignty (IPC). 2006. *"Land, Territory and Dignity" Forum, Porto Alegre, March 6–9, 2006. For a New Agrarian Reform Based on Food Sovereignty!* Porto Alegre: International NGO/CSO Planning Committee for Food Sovereignty (IPC).

International Obesity Taskforce (IOTF). 2013. "The Sydney Principles," accessed January 25, 2013, http://www.iaso.org/iotf/obesity/childhoodobesity/sydneyprinciples/.

Jonsson, U. 1981. "The Causes of Hunger." *Food and Nutrition Bulletin* 3 (2): 1–9.

Klee, K. 2000. *Die progressive Verwirklichung wirtschaftlicher, sozialer und kultureller Menschenrechte [The Progressive Realization of Economic, Social and Cultural Rights.]*. Ulm: R. Boorberg.

Kozma, J., M. Nowak, and M. Scheinin. 2010. *A World Court of Human Rights: Consolidated Statute and Commentary*. Vienna: Neuer Wissenschaftlicher Verlag.

Lhotska, L., A.C. Bellows, and V. Scherbaum. 2012. "Conflicts of Interest and Human Rights-Based Policy-Making: The Case of Maternal, Infant, and Young Children's Health and Malnutrition." *Right to Food and Nutrition WATCH* 2012: 31–36.

Maastricht University and International Commission of Jurists (ICJ). 2011. *Maastricht Principles on Extraterritorial Obligations of States in the Area of Economic, Social and Cultural Rights.* Maastricht; Geneva: Maastricht University; International Commission of Jurists (ICJ).

Madeley, J. 2000. *Hungry for Trade: How the Poor Pay for Free Trade.* London: Zed Books.

Maxwell, S. 1996. "Food Security: A Post-Modern Perspective." *Food Policy* 21 (2): 155–70.

Maxwell, S. and T.R. Frankenberger. 1992. *Household Food Security: Concepts, Indicators, Measurements. A Technical Review.* New York: United Nations Children's Fund (UNICEF); International Fund for Agricultural Development (IFAD).

Maxwell, S. and M. Smith. 1992. "Household Food Security: A Conceptual Review." In *Household Food Security: Concepts, Indicators, Measurements, A Technical Review*, edited by S. Maxwell and T.R. Frankenberger, 1–72. New York: United Nations Children's Fund (UNICEF); International Fund for Agricultural Development (IFAD).

Nussbaum, M. 1988. "Nature, Functioning and Capability: Aristotle on Political Distribution." *Oxford Studies in Ancient Philosophy* Supplement: 145–84.

Nussbaum, M. and A. Sen, eds. 1993. *The Quality of Life.* New York: Oxford Clarendon Press.

Palmer, G. 2011. *Complementary Feeding: Nutrition, Culture and Politics.* London: Pinter & Martin.

Rawls, J. 1993. *Political Liberalism.* New York: Columbia University Press.

Rossi, J. 2006. "La Obligación de No Regresividad en la Jurisprudencia del Comité de Derechos Económicos, Sociales y Culturales de la ONU." ["The Obligation of Non-Retrogression within the Jurisprudence of the United Nations Committee on Economic, Social and Cultural Rights."] In *Ni Un Paso Atrás: La Prohibición de Regresividad en Materia de Derechos Sociales [Not a Single Step Backward: The Prohibition of Retrogression in the Context of Human Rights]*, edited by C. Courtis. Buenos Aires: Centro de Asesoría Laboral (CEDAL), Centro de Estudios Legales y Sociales (CELS).

Sen, A. 1983. *Poverty and Famines: An Essay on Entitlement and Deprivation.* Oxford: Oxford University Press.

Sepúlveda Carmona, M. 2003. *The Nature of the Obligations under the International Covenant on Economic, Social and Cultural Rights.* Antwerpen, Oxford: Intersentia.

Shrimpton, R. 2010. "Maternal Nutrition and the Intergeneration Cycle of Growth Failure." In *Sixth Report on the World Nutrition Situation: Progress in Nutrition*, edited by United Nations Standing Committee on Nutrition (SCN), 62–75. Geneva.

Suárez Franco, A. M. 2010. *Die Justiziabilität wirtschaftlicher, sozialer und kultureller Menschenrechte: Eine Untersuchung über den aktuellen Zustand in Lateinamerika unter Beachtung der völkerrechtlichen Menschenrechtsstandards: Kolumbien als Beispiel [The Justiciability of Economic, Social and Cultural Rights: An Analysis of the Current State in Latin America under Consideration of International Human Rights Law: The Case of Colombia].* Berlin: P. Lang.

United Nations (UN). 1969. *Vienna Convention on the Law of Treaties (23 May 1969) Treaty Series, Vol. 1155, p. 331.* United Nations Treaty Series. New York: United Nations (UN).

United Nations Children's Fund (UNICEF). 1990. *Strategy for Improved Nutrition of Children and Women in Developing Countries. A UNICEF Policiy Review.* New York: United Nations Children's Fund (UNICEF).

———. 2006. *Progress for Children: A Report Card on Nutrition. Number 4, May 2006.* New York: United Nations Children's Fund (UNICEF).

———. 2007. *Progress for Children: A World Fit for Children Statistical Review. Number 6, December 2007.* New York: United Nations Children's Fund (UNICEF).

———. 2011. *The State of the World Children—2011. Adolescence: an Age of Opportunity.* New York: United Nations Children's Fund (UNICEF).

———. 2013. "India, Statistics," accessed February 3, 2013, http://www.unicef.org/ infobycountry/india_statistics.html#73.

United Nations Children's Fund (UNICEF) India. 2010. "Child Undernutrition in India: A Gender Issue," last modified August 18, 2010, accessed February 3, 2013, http://www.unicef.org/india/nutrition_5901.htm.

United Nations Committee on Economic, Social and Cultural Rights (CESCR). 1990. *General Comment No. 3: The Nature of States Parties' Obligations (Art. 2, Para. 1, of the Covenant).* E/1991/23, 14 December 1990. New York: United Nations Economic and Social Council (ECOSOC).

———. 1991. *General Comment No. 4: The Right to Adequate Housing (Art. 11 (1) of the Covenant).* E/1992/23, 13 December 1991. New York: United Nations Economic and Social Council (ECOSOC).

———. 1994. *General Comment No. 5: Persons with Disabilities.* E/1995/22, 9 December 1994. New York: United Nations Economic and Social Council (ECOSOC).

———. 1999a. *General Comment No. 11: Plans of Action for Primary Education (Art. 14 of the Covenant).* E/1992/23, 10 May 1999. New York: United Nations Economic and Social Council (ECOSOC).

———. 1999b. *General Comment No. 12: The Right to Adequate Food (Art. 11 of the Covenant).* E/C.12/1999/5, 12 May 1999. New York: United Nations Economic and Social Council (ECOSOC).

———. 1999c. *General Comments No. 13: The Right to Education (Art. 13 of the Covenant).* E/C.12/1999/10, 8 December 1999. New York: United Nations Economic and Social Council (ECOSOC).

———. 2000. *General Comment No. 14: The Right to the Highest Attainable Standard of Health (Art. 12 of the Covenant).* E/C.12/2000/4, 11 August 2000. New York: United Nations Economic and Social Council (ECOSOC).

———. 2003. *General Comment No. 15: The Right to Water (Arts. 11 and 12 of the Covenant).* E/C.12/2002/11, 20 January 2003. New York: United Nations Economic and Social Council (ECOSOC).

———. 2006a. *General Comment No. 16: The Equal Right of Men and Women to the Enjoyment of all Economic, Social and Cultural Rights (Art. 3 of the Covenant).* E/C.12/2005/4, 11 August 2005. New York: United Nations Economic and Social Council (ECOSOC).

———. 2006b. *General Comment No. 17: The Right of Everyone to Benefit from the Protection of the Moral and Material Interests Resulting from any Scientific, Literary Or Artistic Production of which He Or She is the Author (Art. 15, Para. 1 (c) of the Covenant).* E/C.12/GC/17, 12 January 2006. New York: United Nations Economic and Social Council (ECOSOC).

———. 2006c. *General Comment No. 18: The Right to Work (Art. 6 of the Covenant).* E/C.12/GC/18, 6 February 2006. New York: United Nations Economic and Social Council (ECOSOC).

———. 2008. *General Comment No. 19: The Right to Social Security (Art. 9 of the Covenant).* E/C.12/GC/19, 4 February 2008. New York: United Nations Economic and Social Council (ECOSOC).

————. 2013. *Provisional Rules of Procedure under the Optional Protocol to the International Covenant on Economic, Social and Cultural Rights, Adopted by the Committee at Its Forty-Ninth Session (12–30 November 2012).* E/C.12/49/3, 15 January 2013. New York: United Nations Economic and Social Council (ECOSOC).

United Nations Committee on the Elimination of Discrimination against Women (CEDAW Committee). 1999. *CEDAW General Recommendation No. 24: Article 12 of the Convention (Women and Health) (A/54/38/Rev.1, Chapter 1).* Geneva: United Nations Office of the High Commissioner for Human Rights (OHCHR).

United Nations Committee on the Rights of the Child (CRC Committee). 2013. *General Comment No. 15 (2013) on the Right of the Child to the Enjoyment of the Highest Attainable Standard of Health (Art. 24).* CRC/C/GC/15, 17 April 2013. New York: United Nations (UN).

United Nations General Assembly. 1951. *Convention Relating to the Status of Refugees (28 July 1951).* United Nations Treaty Series. Vol. 189. New York: United Nations (UN) General Assembly.

————. 1966. *International Covenant on Economic, Social and Cultural Rights (16 December 1966).* United Nations Treaty Series. Vol. 993. New York: United Nations (UN) General Assembly.

————. 1979. *Convention on the Elimination of all Forms of Discrimination against Women (CEDAW), 34/180, Adopted in the General Assembly,* 18 December 1979. New York: United Nations (UN) General Assembly.

————. 1989. *Convention on the Rights of the Child.* A/RES/44/25, 20 November 1989. New York: United Nations (UN) General Assembly.

————. 1993a. *National Institutions for the Promotion and Protection of Human Rights,* A/RES/48/134, 20 December 1993. New York: United Nations (UN) General Assembly.

————. 1993b. *Vienna Declaration and Programme of Action,* A/CONF.157/23, 12 July 1993. Vienna: United Nations (UN) General Assembly.

————. 2007a. *Convention on the Rights of Persons with Disabilities: Resolution / Adopted by the General Assembly.* A/RES/61/106, 24 January 2007. New York: United Nations (UN) General Assembly.

————. 2007b. *Declaration on the Rights of Indigenous Peoples: Resolution / Adopted by the General Assembly [without Reference to a Main Committee (A/61/L.67 and Add.1)].* A/RES/61/295, 2 October 2007. New York: United Nations (UN) General Assembly.

————. 2009. *Optional Protocol to the International Covenant on Economic, Social and Cultural Rights: Resolution / Adopted by the General Assembly [on the Report of the Third Committee (A/63/435)],* A/RES/63/117, 5 March 2009. New York: United Nations (UN) General Assembly.

————. 2013. *Declaration on the Rights of Peasants and Other People Working on Rural Areas.* A/HRC/WG.15/1/2, 20 June 2013. New York: United Nations (UN) General Assembly.

United Nations Human Rights Council (HRC). 2007. *Report Submitted by the Special Representative of the Secretary-General on Human Rights Defenders, Hina Jilani, at the Fourth Session of the Human Rights Council.* A/HRC/4/37, 24 January 2007. Geneva: United Nations Human Rights Council (HRC).

————. 2010. *Report Submitted by the Special Rapporteur on the Right to Food, Olivier De Schutter, at the Sixteenth Session of the United Nations Human Rights Council.* A/HCR/16/49, 20 December 2010. New York: United Nations (UN) General Assembly.

————. 2011a. *Report of the Special Rapporteur on the Situation of Human Rights Defenders, Margaret Sekaggya, at the Nineteenth Session of the United Nations Human Rights Council.* A/HRC/19/55, 21 December 2011. New York: United Nations (UN) General Assembly.

————. 2011b. *Report Submitted by the Special Rapporteur on the Right to Food, Olivier De Schutter, at the Nineteenth Session of the United Nations Human Rights Council*. A/HRC/19/59, 26 December 2011. New York: United Nations (UN) General Assembly.

————. 2012. *Final Draft of the Guiding Principles on Extreme Poverty and Human Rights, Submitted by the Special Rapporteur on Extreme Poverty and Human Rights, María Magdalena Sepúlveda Carmona*. A/HRC/21/39, 18 July 2012. New York: United Nations (UN) General Assembly.

United Nations Office of the High Commissioner for Human Rights (OHCHR). 2013. "Committee on the Elimination of all Forms of Discrimination against Women: General Discussion on Rural Women, 7 October 2013." United Nations Human Rights: Office of the High Commissioner for Human Rights, accessed January 21, 2014, http://www.ohchr.org/EN/HRBodies/CEDAW/Pages/Rural-Women.aspx.

United Nations Standing Committee on Nutrition (SCN). 2006. *Double Burden of Malnutrition—A Common Agenda*. Thirty-third Annual Session. Geneva: United Nations Standing Committee on Nutrition (SCN).

————. 2010. *Sixth Report on the World Nutrition Situation: Progress in Nutrition*. Geneva: United Nations Standing Committee on Nutrition (SCN).

United States Agency for International Development (USAID) Press Office. 2012. "Advancing the New Alliance for Food Security and Nutrition." United States Agency for International Development (USAID), last modified August 20, 2012, accessed February 6, 2013, http://www.usaid.gov/news-information/press-releases/advancing-new-alliance-food-security-and-nutrition.

Valente, F. L. S. 2002a. "Do Combate à Fome à Segurança Alimentar e Nutricional: O Direito à Alimentação Adequada." ["The Struggle against Hunger and for Food and Nutrition Security: The Right to Adequate Food"] In *Direito Humano à Alimentação: Desafíos e Conquistas [The Human Right to Food: Challenges and Achievements]*, 37–70. São Paulo: Cortez.

————. 2002b. "Segurança Alimentar e Nutricional: Transformando Natureza em Gente." ["Food and Nutrition Security: Transforming Nature into People"] In *Direito Humano à Alimentação: Desafíos e Conquistas [The Human Right to Food: Challenges and Achievements]*, 103–36. São Paulo: Cortez.

van Boven, T. C., C. Flinterman, and I. Westendorp. 1998. *The Maastricht Guidelines on Violations of Economic, Social and Cultural Rights*. SIM Special No. 20. Utrecht.

Van Esterik, P. 1999. "Right to Food; Right to Feed; Right to be Fed. The Intersection of Women's Rights and the Right to Food." *Agriculture and Human Values* 16 (2): 225–32.

Glossary of Abbreviations and Acronyms

ACC/SCN	Administrative Committee on Coordination / Subcommittee on Nutrition
ACDIS	Africa Centre Demographic Information System
AFASS	affordable, feasible, acceptable, sustainable, and safe
ART	antiretroviral therapy
ARV	antiretroviral
AWC	African Woman and Child Feature Service
AWID	Association for Women's Rights in Development
BAPEN	British Association for Parenteral and Enteral Nutrition
BFHI	Baby-Friendly Hospital Initiative
BINGO	Business Interest Non-Governmental Organization
CARE	Cooperative Assistance and Relief Everywhere
CAT	*Convention against Torture and Other Cruel, Inhuman or Degrading Treatment or Punishment*
CDC	Center for Disease Control, United States
CEDAW	*Convention on the Elimination of All Forms of Discrimination against Women*
CEDAW Committee	United Nations Committee on the Elimination of Discrimination against Women
CESCR	United Nations Committee on Economic, Social and Cultural Rights
CFS	Committee on World Food Security
CGIAR	Consultative Group on International Agricultural Research
CHR	United Nations Commission on Human Rights
CIDSE	International Cooperation for Development and Solidarity
CIM	Inter-American Commission of Women (Comisión Interamericana de Mujeres)
CIMMYT	International Maize and Wheat Improvement Center (Centro Internacional de Mejoramiento de Maiz y Trigo)

CIRAD	Agricultural Research Centre for International Development (Centre de Coopération en Recherche Agronomique pour le Développement), France
CLEP	United Nations Commission on Legal Empowerment of the Poor
CLOC	Latin-American Coordination of Farm Organizations (Coordinadora Latinoamericana de Organizaciones del Campo)
CPED	*International Convention for the Protection of All Persons from Enforced Disappearance*
CPG	consumer packaged goods
CRBP	*Children's Rights and Business Principles*
CRBPI	Children's Rights and Business Principles Initiative
CRC	*Convention on the Rights of the Child*
CRC Committee	United Nations Committee on the Rights of the Child
CRPD	*Convention on the Rights of Persons with Disabilities*
CSM	International Food Security & Nutrition Civil Society Mechanism
CSO	civil society organization
CSR	corporate social responsibility
CSW	(United Nations) Commission on the Status of Women
CWGL	Center for Women's Global Leadership, Rutgers University
DAPEN	Danish Association of Parenteral and Enteral Nutrition
DAW	(United Nations) Division for the Advancement of Women
DDE	dichlorodiphenyldichloroethylene
DDT	dichlorodiphenyltrichloroethane
DEVAW	*Declaration on the Elimination of Violence against Women*
DFID	Department for International Development, United Kingdom
DH	Department of Health, United Kingdom
ECOSOC	United Nations Economic and Social Council
EMAS	Women in Joint Action Team (Equipo Mujeres en Acción Solidaria)
ENN	Emergency Nutrition Network
EPA	Economic Partnership Agreement
ERA	*Equal Rights Amendment*
ECHR	European Court of Human Rights
ESPEN	European Society for Clinical Nutrition and Metabolism
ESPGHAN	European Society for Paediatric Gastroenterology, Hepatology and Nutrition
ETO	extraterritorial (human rights) obligations of states

F&N	Fraser and Neave
FAO	Food and Agriculture Organization of the United Nations
FDI	foreign direct investment
FGM	female genital mutilation
FIRE	Feminist International Radio Endeavor
FPC	food policy council
FSA	Food Standards Agency, United Kingdom
G8	Group of Eight (the governments of eight of the world's wealthiest countries)
G20	Group of Twenty Finance Ministers and Central Bank Governors
G77	Group of Seventy-Seven
GAD	gender and development
GADN	Gender and Development Network
GAIN	Global Alliance for Improved Nutrition
GATT	General Agreement on Tariffs and Trade
GBV	gender-based violence
GCCRB	*General Comment on Children's Rights and Business* (CRC Committee)
GCAR	Global Campaign for Agrarian Reform
GEF	Global Environment Facility
GIZ	German Society for International Cooperation (Deutsche Gesellschaft für Internationale Zusammenarbeit)
GM	gender mainstreaming
GMO	genetically modified organism
GPAFS	Global Partnership on Agriculture, Food Security and Nutrition
GRESPEN	Greek Society for Clinical Nutrition and Metabolism
GRtFN	Global Right to Food and Nutrition Network
GSF	*Global Strategic Framework for Food Security and Nutrition*
GSO	Global Social Observatory
HFSS	high in fats, sugar, and salt
HKP	Nestlé's Healthy Kids Programme
HLTF	High Level Task Force on the Global Food Crisis
HRC	United Nations Human Rights Council
HRI	Hagen Resources International
IAASTD	*International Assessment of Agricultural Knowledge, Science and Technology for Development*
IAFN	International Agri-Food Network
IANWGE	Inter-Agency Network on Women and Gender Equality
Ibase	Brazilian Institute of Social and Economic Analyses (Instituto Brasileiro de Análises Sociais e Econômicas)

IBFAN	International Baby Food Action Network
ICC	International Criminal Court
ICCPR	*International Covenant on Civil and Political Rights*
ICERD	*International Covenant on the Elimination of All Forms of Racial Discrimination*
ICESCR	*International Covenant on Economic, Social and Cultural Rights*
ICJ	International Commission of Jurists
ICMW	*International Convention on the Protection of the Rights of All Migrant Workers and Members of Their Families*
ICN	(First) International Conference on Nutrition
ICN2	Second International Conference on Nutrition
ICRW	International Center for Research on Women
IFAD	International Fund for Agricultural Development
IFI	international finance institution
IFOAM	International Federation of Organic Agriculture Movements
IFPRI	International Food Policy Research Institute
IGWG	intergovernmental working group
ILO	International Labour Organization
IMCI	integrated management of childhood illness
IMF	International Monetary Fund
INE	intensive nutrition education
INRA	National Institute for Agricultural Research (Institut National de Recherche Agronomique), France
INSTRAW	International Research and Training Institute for the Advancement of Women
IPC	International Planning Committee on Food Sovereignty
IPPF	International Planned Parenthood Federation
IPS	Inter Press Service
IPV	intimate partner violence
IrSPEN	Irish Society for Clinical Nutrition and Metabolism
IUNS	International Union of Nutritional Sciences
IYCF	infant and young child feeding
JASS	Just Associates
JIU	United Nations Joint Inspection Unit
LAM	lactational amenorrhea method
LBW	low birth weight
MAM	moderate acute malnutrition
MDG	Millennium Development Goal
MIJARC	International Movement of Catholic Agricultural and Rural Youth (Mouvement International de la Jeunesse Agricole et Rurale Catholique)

MNI	Medical Nutrition International Industry
MNP	micronutrient powder
MNT	medical nutrition therapy
MSI	multistakeholder initiative
MVVFS	Mango Valley Visionaries Friendly Society
NAP	national action plan
NCD	noncommunicable disease
NE	(non-intensive) nutrition education
NESPEN	Netherlands Society for Parenteral and Enteral Nutrition
NFHS-3	Third National Family Health Survey, India
NGO	non-governmental organization
OAS	Organization of American States
OBR	One Billion Rising
OECD	Organisation for Economic Co-operation and Development
OHCHR	United Nations Office of the High Commissioner for Human Rights
OSAGI	(United Nations) Office of the Special Adviser to the Secretary-General on Gender Issues and Advancement of Women
PIF	powdered infant formula
PINGO	public interest non-governmental organization
PPP	public-private partnerships
PROGRESA	Program for Education, Health and Food (Programa de Educación, Salud, y Alimentación), Mexico
PROMESA	Program for Ministry and Social Education (Programa de Ministerio y Educación Social), Episcopal Church of Panama
QPM	quality protein maize
RBFS	rights-based food systems
RCT	randomized controlled trial
RDA	recommended daily allowance
ROPPA	Network of Farmers' and Agricultural Producers' Organisations of West Africa (Réseau des Organizations Paysannes et de Producteurs de l'Afrique de l'Ouest)
RUF	ready-to-use complementary food
RUSF	ready-to-use supplementary food
RUTF	ready-to-use therapeutic food
SAM	severe acute malnutrition
SCN	United Nations Standing Committee on Nutrition
SENPE	Spanish Society for Parenteral and Enteral Nutrition (Sociedad Española de Nutrición Enteral y Parenteral)

Sida	Sweden's International Development Cooperation Agency
SLA	sustainable livelihoods approach
SUN	Scaling Up Nutrition
TFPC	Toronto Food Policy Council
TNC	transnational corporation
UDHR	*Universal Declaration of Human Rights*
UN	United Nations
UN DESA	United Nations Department of Economic and Social Affairs
UNDG	United Nations Development Group
UNDP	United Nations Development Programme
UNEP	United Nations Environment Programme
UNESCO	United Nations Educational, Scientific and Cultural Organization
UNFPA	United Nations Population Fund
UNHCR	United Nations High Commissioner for Refugees
UNICEF	United Nations Children's Fund
UNIFEM	United Nations Development Fund for Women (Fonds de Développement des Nations Unies pour la Femme)
UN Women	United Nations Entity for Gender Equality and the Empowerment of Women
US	United States
USAID	United States Agency for International Development
VAW	violence against women
VSO	Voluntary Services Overseas
WANAHR	World Alliance for Nutrition and Human Rights
WBTi	World Breastfeeding Trends Initiative
WEAI	women's empowerment in agriculture index
WFP	United Nations World Food Programme
WG DAW	Working Group on the Issue of Discrimination against Women in Law and in Practice
WHA	World Health Assembly
WHO	World Health Organization
WIC	Special Supplemental Nutrition Program for Women, Infants and Children, United States
WID	women in development
WIEGO	Women in Informal Employment: Globalizing and Organizing
WiLDAF	Women in Development and Law and Development in Africa
WTO	World Trade Organization

Chronological Glossary of Human Rights Instruments and Other International Frameworks and Documents Mentioned in This Volume

1923 *Equal Rights Amendment* (ERA) introduced to United States Congress
1928 ERA adopted as regional platform for national action by the Inter-American Commission of Women—the first intergovernmental agency dealing with women's rights in the world
1945 *United Nations Charter* signed in San Francisco, United States
1948 *Universal Declaration of Human Rights* (UDHR) adopted by the United Nations (UN) General Assembly
1959 *Declaration of the Rights of the Child* adopted by the UN General Assembly
1966 *International Covenant on Economic, Social and Cultural Rights* (ICESCR) adopted by the UN General Assembly
       International Covenant on Civil and Political Rights (ICCPR) adopted by the UN General Assembly
1969 *Vienna Convention on the Law of Treaties* adopted by the United Nations Conference on the Law of Treaties
1974 World Food Conference held in Rome under the auspices of the Food and Agriculture Organization of the United Nations (FAO) held in Rome, Italy
1976 ICESCR and ICCPR enter into force
1979 *Convention on the Elimination of All Forms of Discrimination against Women* (CEDAW) adopted by the UN General Assembly
1981 *International Code of Marketing Breast-milk Substitutes* (*Code*) adopted by the World Health Organization (WHO)
       CEDAW enters into force
1985 Third World Conference on Women by the UN to review the achievements of the United Nations Decade for Women, held in Nairobi, Kenya
1986 World Health Assembly (WHA) *Resolution 39.28* to endorse use of the *Code* adopted at the 39th WHA
1987 Committee on Economic, Social and Cultural Rights (CESCR) established under *Resolution 1985/17* of the United Nations Economic and Social Council (ECOSOC)

1988   *Additional Protocol to the [1969] American Convention on Human Rights in the Area of Economic, Social and Cultural Rights* adopted in San Salvador, El Salvador, by the General Assembly of the Organization of American States (OAS)

1989   Asbjørn Eide authors report *Right to Adequate Food as a Human Right* commissioned by the UN Sub-Commission on the Promotion and Protection of Human Rights

Convention on the Rights of the Child (CRC) adopted by the UN General Assembly

General Comment 1 on Reporting by States Parties issued by the CESCR

1990   *Convention on the Rights of All Migrant Workers and Members of Their Families* (ICMW) adopted by the UN General Assembly

CRC enters into force

World Summit for Children, endorsed by WHA, United Nations Educational, Scientific and Cultural Organization (UNESCO), and United Nations Children's Fund (UNICEF), held in New York, United States

Innocenti Declaration on the Protection, Promotion, and Support of Breastfeeding adopted by WHO and UNICEF

General Recommendation 15 on Women and AIDS issued by the Committee on the Elimination of Discrimination against Women (CEDAW Committee)

1991   Baby-Friendly Hospital Initiative (BFHI) launched by WHO and UNICEF

General Recommendation 18 on Disabled Women issued by the CEDAW Committee

1992   First International Conference on Nutrition (ICN) by FAO and WHO, held in Rome, Italy

United Nations Conference on Environment and Development, held in Rio de Janeiro, Brazil

Integrated Management of Childhood Illness (IMCI) strategy established by WHO and UNICEF

General Recommendation 19 on Violence against Women issued by the CEDAW Committee

1993   CESCR *Rules of Procedure* revised

La Via Campesina (The Peasants' Way) established by farmers' organizations from Latin America, Asia, Africa, Europe, and North America, with the headquarters located in Belgium (now Jakarta, Indonesia)

1994   International Conference on Population and Development by the United Nations Population Fund (UNFPA), held in Cairo, Egypt

WHA *Resolution 47.5* on infant and young child nutrition adopted at the 41st WHA

General Comment 5 on Persons with Disabilities issued by the CESCR

1995   Fourth World Conference on Women: Action for Equality, Development and Peace by the UN, which resulted in the adoption of the *Beijing Declaration and Platform for Action*, held in Beijing, China

World Summit for Social Development, organized principally by the United Nations Department for Policy Coordination and Sustainable Development, which saw the adoption of the *Copenhagen Declaration*, the *Ten Commitments*, and the *Programme of Action* of the World social Summit, held in Copenhagen, Denmark

Declaration for Women's Reproductive and Sexual Rights and Health issued by the Reproductive Rights caucus at the NGO Forum at the 39th session of the Commission on the Status of Women held in New York, United States

General Comment 6 on The Economic, Social and Cultural Rights of Older Persons issued by the CESCR

1996   World Food Summit by FAO, which resulted in the adoption of the *Rome Declaration on World Food Security*, held in Rome, Italy

Civil Society Forum on Food Security runs parallel with the World Food Summit, organized by the ad hoc International Planning Committee for Food Sovereignty (IPC), in Rome, Italy

Second United Nations Conference on Human Settlements, which saw to the adoption of the *Habitat Agenda* and the *Istanbul Declaration*, held in Istanbul, Turkey

Constitution of the Republic of South Africa adopted, including explicit recognition of the right to food

1997   *International Code of Conduct on the Right to Adequate Food (Code of Conduct)* drafted and endorsed by FIAN International, the World Alliance for Nutrition and Human Rights (WANAHR), and the International Jacques Maritain Institute

Human rights-based approach introduced by UN secretary general's 1997 report, *Renewing the United Nations: A Programme for Reform*

General Comment 7 on the Right to Adequate Housing: Forced Evictions issued by the CESCR

1998   *Humanitarian Charter and Minimum Standards in Humanitarian Response* issued by the Sphere Project based in Geneva, Switzerland

General Comment 10 on the Role of National Human Rights Institutions in the Protection of Economic, Social and Cultural Rights issued by the CESCR

1999   *General Comment 12 on the Right to Adequate Food (Article 11 of the Covenant)* issued by the CESCR

The Right to Adequate Food and to Be Free from Hunger: Updated Study on the Right to Food submitted by Asbjørn Eide to ECOSOC

General Recommendation 24 on Women and Health issued by the CEDAW Committee

General Comment 13 on the Right to Education issued by the CESCR

2000 *General Comment 14 on the Right to the Highest Attainable Standard of Health* issued by the CESCR

Resolution 2000/10 to appoint a special rapporteur on the right to food adopted by the United Nations Commission on Human Rights (CHR) at its 56th session

UN Global Compact officially launched at the UN headquarters in New York, United States

Guidelines on Cooperation between the United Nations and the Business Community issued by the UN secretary general

Guidelines on Working with the Private Sector to Achieve Health Outcomes issued by WHO at its 107th session

Maternity Protection Convention, 2000 (No. 183) and its accompanying *Maternity Protection Recommendation, 2000 (No. 191)* adopted by the International Labour Organization (ILO) in Geneva, Switzerland

UN Millennium Declaration adopted by the UN General Assembly at the Millennium Summit at the UN headquarters in New York, United States

2001 *Declaration of Commitment on HIV/AIDS* adopted by the UN General Assembly at its 26th special session

2002 World Food Summit: five years later by FAO, at which the *Declaration of the World Food Summit: five years later* was adopted by member states, held in Rome, Italy

2002 Forum for Food Sovereignty organized by the ad hoc IPC in Rome, Italy

ILO *Maternity Protection Convention, 2000 (No. 183)* enters into force

2003 UN *Statement of Common Understanding on Human Rights-Based Approaches to Development Cooperation and Programming* adopted by the United Nations Development Group (UNDG)

Draft Norms on Responsibilities of Transnational Corporations and Other Business Enterprises with Regard to Human Rights submitted by the Working Group on the Working Methods and Activities of Transnational Corporations and approved by the UN Sub-Commission for the Promotion and Protection of Human Rights

Global Strategy for Infant and Young Child Feeding (IYCF) published by WHO and UNICEF

General Comment 15 on The Right to Water issued by the CESCR

IPC officially established

ICMW enters into force

2004 *Voluntary Guidelines to Support the Progressive Realization of the Right to Adequate Food in the Context of National Security* adopted at the 127th session of the FAO Council

Protocol to the African Charter on Human and Peoples' Rights enters into force
General Recommendation 25 on Temporary Special Measures issued by the CEDAW Committee

2005   *General Comment 16 on the Equal Right of Men and Women to the Enjoyment of All Economic, Social and Cultural Rights* issued by the CESCR
Innocenti Declaration on Infant and Young Child Feeding updated and endorsed by the UN Standing Committee on Nutrition (SCN) after the 15th anniversary of the first *Innocenti Declaration.*
18th International Congress on Nutrition by the International Union of Nutrition Sciences (IUNS), held in Durban, South Africa

2006   *Convention on the Rights of Persons with Disabilities* (CRPD) adopted by the UN General Assembly
Maria da Penha Law (Federal Law 11340), sanctioned in Brazil by President Luiz Inácio Lula da Silva, defines domestic violence, including inadequate food, as a human rights violation
Resolution 60/165 on the right to food adopted by the UN General Assembly at its 60th session
General Comment 17 on the Right of Everyone to Benefit from the Protection of the Moral and Material Interests Resulting from any Scientific, Literary or Artistic Production of Which He or She Is the Author issued by the CESCR

2007   *United Nations Declaration on the Rights of Indigenous Peoples* adopted by the UN General Assembly at its 61st session
Screen State Action against Hunger! How to Use the Voluntary Guidelines on the Right to Food to Monitor Public Policies published by FIAN International and Welthungerhilfe (Aid for World Hunger)
Safe Preparation, Storage and Handling of Powdered Infant Formula Guidelines (PIF Guidelines) adopted by WHO and FAO
Resolution 61/163 on the right to food adopted by the UN General Assembly at its 61st session

2008   *Resolution 7/14* on the right to food adopted by the United Nations Human Rights Council (HRC) at its 40th meeting
WHA Resolution 61.20 on infant and young child nutrition adopted at the 61st WHA
The Cordoba Declaration on the Right to Food and the Governance of the Global Food and Agricultural Systems launched on the occasion of the 60th anniversary of the UDHR
General Recommendation 26 on Women Migrant Workers issued by the CEDAW Committee
CRPD enters into force

2009   *General Comment 20 on Non-Discrimination in Economic, Social and Cultural Rights* issued by the CESCR
Guidelines on Cooperation between the United Nations and the Business Community issued by the UN secretary general

Resolution 10/12 on the right to food adopted by the HRC at the 10th session of its 42nd meeting

International Assessment of Agricultural Knowledge, Science and Technology for Development (IAASTD), initiated by the World Bank and co-sponsored by FAO, Global Environment Facility (GEF), United Nations Development Programme (UNDP), United Nations Environment Programme (UNEP), UNESCO, the World Bank, and WHO, is published

Gender in Agriculture Sourcebook published by the World Bank, FAO, and the International Fund for Agricultural Development (IFAD)

Reform of the Committee on World Food Security adopted at the 35th session of the Committee on World Food Security (CFS), held in Rome, Italy

Women and the Right to Livelihoods published by the Programme on Women's Economic, Social and Cultural Rights (PWESCR)

General Comment 21 on The Right of Everyone to Take Part in Cultural Life issued by the CESCR

2010   *Sixth Report on the World Nutrition Situation: Progress in Nutrition* published by the SCN

Policy on WHO Engagement with Global Health Partnerships and Hosting Arrangements issued by WHO

Every Woman Every Child initiative launched by the UN secretary general

Healthy Kids Program launched by Nestlé

WHA *Resolution 63.23* adopted at the 63rd WHA

Operational Guidance on Infant and Young Child Feeding in Emergencies endorsed by WHA *Resolution 63.23*

Guidelines on HIV and Infant Feeding 2010 published by WHO

World Breastfeeding Trends Initiative (WBTi): Botswana Assessment Report published by Botswana's Nutrition and Food Control Division, Ministry of Health

Draft Guidelines for the Marketing of Ready to Use Supplemental Foods for Children developed by the SCN NGO/CSO constituency

WHO publishes online "Continuum of Care Fact Sheet: Reproductive, Maternal, Newborn and Child Health"

WHA Resolution 63.14 to reduce food marketing exposure to children adopted by the WHA at its 63rd session

19th International Congress on Nutrition by the IUNS on Nutrition Security for All, held in Bangkok, Thailand

The World's Women 2010: Trends and Statistics published by the United Nations Department of Economic and Social Affairs (UNDESA)

Food Justice: The Report of the Food and Fairness Inquiry published by the Food Ethics Council based in the United Kingdom

General Recommendation 27 on Older Women and Protection of their Human Rights issued by the CEDAW Committee

General Recommendation 28 on the Core Obligations of States Parties under Article 2 of the Convention on the Elimination of All Forms of Discrimination against Women issued by the CEDAW Committee

2011 CRC Committee launches process to develop a *General Comment on Children's Rights and Business* (GCCRB)

Baby Milk Action Statement of Concern developed by the Conflicts of Interest Coalition

The State of Food and Agriculture 2010–11: Women in Agriculture: Closing the Gender Gap for Development published by FAO

Maastricht Principles on Extraterritorial Obligations of States in the Area of Economic, Social and Cultural Rights published by Maastricht University and the International Commission of Jurists (ICJ)

WHO updates its online "Continuum of Care Fact Sheet: Reproductive, Maternal, Newborn and Child Health"

2012 First version of the *Global Strategic Framework for Food Security and Nutrition* (GSF) adopted by the CFS at its 39th session

Children's Rights and Business Principles Initiative (CRBPI) launched by UNICEF

Resolution EB130.R7, "Prevention and Control of Noncommunicable diseases: Follow-up to the High-level Meeting of the United Nations General Assembly on the Prevention and Control of Non-communicable Diseases," adopted by WHO at its 130th session

Revised consumer recommendations endorsing breastfeeding issued by the Centers for Disease Control and Prevention (CDC), United States

Maternity Protection Resource Package: From Aspiration to Reality published by ILO

WHO Guidelines on HIV and Infant Feeding 2010: An Updated Framework for Priority Action published by WHO

SUN Movement: Revised Road Map released by the secretariat of the Scaling Up Nutrition (SUN) Movement

Rio+20, United Nations Conference on Sustainable Development held in Rio de Janeiro, Brazil

Report *Women's Right and the Right to Food* submitted by the special rapporteur on the right to food, Olivier De Schutter, to the HRC

Voluntary Guidelines on the Responsible Governance of Tenure of Land, Fisheries and Forests in the Context of National Food Security published by FAO

2013   *ICESR Optional Protocol* enters into force after Uruguay provides the tenth ratification
CESCR *Rules of Procedure* revised
General Comment 15 on the Right of the Child to the Enjoyment of the Highest Attainable Standard of Health issued by the CRC Committee
General Comment 16 on State Obligations regarding the Impact of the Business Sector on Children's Rights issued by the CRC Committee
Information Concerning the Use and Marketing of Follow-up Formula published by WHO
20th International Congress on Nutrition, Joining Cultures through Nutrition, by the IUNS, held in Granada, Spain
Conference Food Sovereignty: A Critical Dialogue, sponsored by the Program in Agrarian Studies at Yale University and the Journal of Peasant Studies, held at the Macmillan Center at Yale University in Connecticut, United States
General Recommendation on Article 16 of the Convention on the Elimination of All Forms of Discrimination against Women (Economic Consequences of Marriage, Family Relations and Their Dissolution) issued by the CEDAW Committee

2014   Second International Conference on Nutrition (ICN2) held in Rome, Italy, by FAO and WHO

Contributors

Anne C. Bellows is professor and graduate program director of the Food Studies Program in the Department of Public Health, Food Studies and Nutrition at Syracuse University, where she began in 2013 after having chaired the Department of Gender and Nutrition, Faculty of Agriculture, at the University of Hohenheim since 2007. A geographer and planner by training, Bellows focuses on food and nutrition systems and economies, and, more specifically, on curricular development, research, and collaborative advocacy to support the growing field of human rights and the right to adequate food and nutrition.

R. Denisse Córdova Montes coordinates FIAN International's work on gender and women's rights as well as its program on income, nutrition, and related policies. She holds a juris doctor (JD) degree from the University of Pennsylvania Law School, a master of public health (MPH) degree from Boston University, and a bachelor of arts (BA) in international studies from the University of Miami. She has previously worked on issues related to access to reproductive health, immigrant rights, gender-based violence, and HIV/AIDS and human rights.

Anna Jenderedjian is a doctoral candidate at the University of Hohenheim's Institute of Social Sciences in Agriculture, where she conducts research on food security and civil society organizations (CSOs) in Armenia and Georgia, with a special focus on women. She has an MSc in environmental sciences and policy from the Central European University in Budapest, and an MA in psychology from Yerevan State University. Her research builds upon five years of work experience with CSOs in South Caucasus. She is also involved in consulting work on social impact assessments for private and public companies in Armenia.

Stefanie Lemke holds an MSc in nutrition sciences and home economics and a PhD in rural sociology (University of Munich-Weihenstephan) and obtained her habilitation and venia legendi in "Gender and Nutrition" from the University of Hohenheim. In 2015, she joined the Centre for

Agroecology, Water and Resilience at Coventry University. From 2013 to 2015, she was acting chair in the Department of Gender and Nutrition, Faculty of Agriculture, at the University of Hohenheim. She was a senior research fellow at the same department from 2008 to 2012, and from 2003 to 2007 at the Center for International Development and Environmental Research at the Justus Liebig University of Giessen. Her work focuses on food and nutrition security, gender, sustainable livelihoods, right to adequate food and nutrition, sustainable agriculture, and food systems. She applies qualitative, participatory, mixed method, and rights-based approaches in inter- and transdisciplinary research. Besides academia, she has worked as a nutrition and consumer consultant for various German civil service organizations.

Lida Lhotska, who holds a BSc in biology and a PhD in physical anthropology, started her working career at the National Institute of Public Health in Prague. In 1994, she took a position as infant feeding advisor in the UNICEF Headquarters in New York. In 2001, she joined the Geneva Infant Feeding Association (GIFA), the liaison office of the International Baby Food Action Network (IBFAN) in Geneva. She has followed with concern the increase of conflicts of interest in the global health and nutrition arena and has been trying to raise awareness of their problematic impacts, such as decreasing spaces for holding corporations accountable for their harmful marketing practices and human rights violations.

María Daniela Núñez Burbano de Lara holds a graduate engineer degree in food technology from the University of Bonn and an MSc in environmental protection and agricultural food production from the University of Hohenheim. She is a research and teaching associate at the Institute of Social Sciences in Agriculture at the University of Hohenheim, where she also pursues a doctoral degree focusing on the incorporation of human rights education into higher education curricula as an advocacy strategy for non-governmental and civil society organizations engaged in the advancement of the human right to adequate food and nutrition and food sovereignty.

Veronika Scherbaum is a senior researcher at the Institute of Social Sciences in Agriculture, Department of Gender and Nutrition, at the University of Hohenheim. As a diploma graduate in nutrition science, she earned her MSc in mother and child health at the University of London, and her PhD at the Institute of Biological Chemistry and Nutrition, University of Hohenheim. In December 2014 she was granted a German habilitation degree in nutrition science, specifically in international child nutrition, from the Faculty of Natural Sciences of the same university. She is the editor and co-author of a book on breastfeeding and nutrition in early childhood and reproductive health (original German title:

Stillen—frühkindliche Ernährung und reproduktive Gesundheit). Her research focuses on treatment and preventive strategies regarding child malnutrition, as well as nutrition during pregnancy, lactation, and the complementary feeding period, under special consideration of locally grown foods rich in micronutrients.

Ana María Suárez Franco holds degrees in law from the Universidad Javeriana (Bogotá) and in public policies from the Universidad de los Andes (Bogotá). She further received the titles master of laws (LLM) from the University of Heidelberg and juris doctor (JD) from the University of Mannheim. As a human rights practitioner, she has worked on the justiciability of the human right to adequate food and nutrition and related country casework at FIAN International. Currently, she is the permanent representative of this organization in Geneva. In this position, she has participated in the processes toward the adoption of, among others, the *Maastricht Principles on Extraterritorial Obligations of States in the Area of Economic, Social and Cultural Rights*, of an international declaration of peasants rights, and of a legally binding human rights instrument on transnational corporations and other business enterprises, and has supported the preparation of parallel reports to the CESCR and CEDAW Committee.

Flavio Luiz Schieck Valente has, since February 2007, been the secretary general of FIAN International which is based in Heidelberg. He is a medical doctor with an MPH from Harvard School of Public Health. From 2002 to 2007, he acted as the national rapporteur on the human rights to adequate food, water, and rural land in Brazil. Over the last decade his work has concentrated on the development and implementation of administrative, quasi-judicial, and judicial recourse mechanisms toward the realization of the human right to adequate food. For many years he was the technical coordinator of ABRANDH (Brazilian Action for Nutrition and Human Rights) and, from 1998 until 2006, a member of the coordination team for the Brazilian Forum for Food and Nutritional Security (FBSAN). He was the civil society representative in the steering committee of the United Nations Standing Committee on Nutrition from 2001 to 2006 and, before this, nutrition and public health professor at the Federal University of Bahia (master's program on community health from 1979 until 1982) and at the Federal University of Santa Catarina (1983 to 1995). He was also the advisor to the president of the Brazilian National Food Security Council (CONSEA) from 1992 to 1994.

(†2015) Roseane do Socorro Gonçalves Viana held a degree from the University of Pará in nutrition sciences. From 2005 to 2006, she served as rapporteur for the Black Population Committee at the Brazilian National Food and Nutritional Security Council. She also worked at the Ministry of Health and the Ministry of Social Development and Fight against Hunger of Brazil. She was a Global Food Security Program PhD student at the Department of Gender and Nutrition and a German Academic Program (DAAD) scholar (2010–2015), focusing her research on the application of the human rights framework on the National School Feeding Program of Brazil.

Index

1000 days *see* window of opportunity

accountability: within *CFS Private Sector Modalities* 36, 38; within the Committee on World Food Security (CFS) 35, 392; within the *Declaration on the Elimination of Violence against Women* (DEVAW) 146; as a duty bearer obligation 36; regarding food aid 296; and gender mainstreaming 139; in human rights research 113; within the *International Covenant on Economic, Social and Cultural Rights* (ICESCR) 60; within the International Criminal Court (ICC) 317; mechanisms 28, 115, 167, 350, 390–1, 393, 395; within the nutrition paradigm 262; within the *Optional Protocol to the Convention on the Elimination of All Forms of Discrimination against Women* 126; within the *Optional Protocol to the International Covenant on Economic, Social and Cultural Rights* 392; within public policy 390; as a strategy to confront hunger and malnutrition 357; within United Nation (UN) instruments 6; within the *Voluntary Guidelines to Support the Progressive Realization of the Right to Adequate Food in the Context of National Food Security* 31, 32; *see also* corporate private sector accountability, state

extraterritorial human rights obligations, *Global Strategic Framework for Food and Nutrition Security* (GSF), human rights-based framework, human rights principles, recourse mechanisms, state accountability, state human rights obligations

Additional Protocol to the [1969] American Convention on Human Rights in the Area of Economic, Social and Cultural Rights (Protocol of San Salvador) 91; article 12 77; *see also* democracy, food production, nutrition

Africa 142, 205, 259, 265, 305, 313: Algeria 132, 133; Botswana 206–7; Ethiopia 117, 124, 197; Ghana 124; Jordan 117; Kenya 216, 267; Lesotho 265; Liberia 132; Mauritania 119; Mozambique 265; North Africa 283; Sierra Leone 265; Southern 271, 279, 303; Sub-Saharan 165, 265, 282–3, 307, 314; Sudan 140; Tanzania 132, 140; Uganda 216, 266, 297; West 304; West Sahara 196; Zambia, 216, 133; *see also* HIV/AIDS, South Africa, United Nations Children's Fund (UNICEF), Women in Law and Development in Africa (WiLDAF)

Agenda 21 274, 275

agrarian reform: under the *Convention on the Elimination of All Forms of Discrimination against Women* (CEDAW) 62; regarding discrimination against women

120; under Brazil's National
School Feeding Program 301;
within South Africa 121, 279;
see also human rights-based
framework, Global Campaign
for Agrarian Reform (GCAR),
International Seminar Agrarian
Reform and Gender, rural
women, women in agriculture
Agreement on Agriculture (AoA) 81
agribiotechnology 86; genetic
engineering 85, 90, 221,
347; marketing of 89; and
pharmaceuticals 85–6; state
human rights obligation to
protect against 381; *see also*
biofortification
agribusiness: civil society and 18–19;
and the contamination of
breastmilk 264; and its effect
on the environment 264, 347;
and its effect on food and
nutrition security 264; and
the food production model
72, 386; and food sovereignty
286; and the global food crisis
296; the global power of 18,
34; marketing *see* corporate
private sector marketing; as
a market-led system 72, 285;
and micronutrient deficiency
85; and its structural link to
overweight 196; use of pesticides
and chemicals by 264, 347;
regulation of 167; *see also*
local food systems, traditional
practices
agriculture *see* agriculture and
nutrition, agroecology, food
production, organic agriculture,
urban agriculture
agriculture and nutrition: 81–2, 90;
under the Committee on World
Food Security (CFS) 33; under
a food systems approach 81;
nutrition sensitive (responsive)
agriculture 260–1; sectoral
divide of 258–9, 261; *see also*
agroecology, International Union
of Nutritional Sciences (IUNS),
*Sixth Report on the World
Nutrition Situation*, Global
Partnership on Agriculture, Food
Security and Nutrition (GPAFS)

agroecology: under Brazil's National
School Feeding Program 301;
within a food sovereignty
framework 367; in a food
systems approach 254,
387; compared to industrial
agriculture 291–2; and nutrition
262, 355, 359; production
models 386, 387; as a rights-
based food system 288;
safety aspects of 380; state
extraterritorial human rights
obligations to ensure an enabling
environment for 393; under the
state human rights obligation to
fulfill 386; under the state human
rights obligation to protect 386;
under the state human rights
obligation to respect 380; and
sustainable livelihoods 319,
365–6, 367, 368, 387; and trade
investment 393; and women 291,
293; *see also* De Schutter, O.,
food (in)security, *International
Assessment of Agricultural
Knowledge, Science and
Technology for Development*
(IAASTD), local food systems,
people's and food sovereignty,
women's food and nutrition
security
Americas 9, 11, 259; Argentina 140;
Belize 133; Caribbean 305, 307,
314; Chile 132; Haiti 10, 133;
Honduras 298; Latin America
142, 265, 305, 307, 314;
Mesoamerica 305–6; Mexico
121–2, 123–4; North America
213, 288, 307, 313, 314;
Panama 308–9; Peru 124; South
America 313; *see also* Brazil,
Canada, United States
Annan, K. 172, 283
Asia 110, 142, 259, 305, 307, 314;
China 202, 296; Democratic
People's Republic of Korea 202;
Eastern 265; Indonesia 202,
215–16, 218–19; Iran 308; Iraq
202; Israel 119; Lao People's
Democratic Republic 194–5;
Lebanon 202; Middle East 283,
313; Mongolia 134; Myanmar
216; Nepal 119; South 141;
Thailand 195, 259; Vietnam 125;

see also Baby-Friendly Hospital
Initiative (BFHI), Bangladesh
Association for Women's Rights in
Development (AWID) 311
Australia 131–2, 139, 263

Baby-Friendly Hospital Initiative
(BFHI) 193; training package
217; in China 203; *see
also* breastmilk substitutes,
breastfeeding
Bangladesh: and cash transfer programs
125; and microfinance programs
141; violence against women
112, 119, 124–5; *see also* rural
women
*Beijing Declaration and Platform for
Action* 127, 128, 130, 144
biofortification 89; *see also*
agribiotechnology, medicalized
nutrition
Bolsa Família 124, 125
Boserup, E. 275
Brazil: agroindustrial model in 264;
National School Feeding
Program 301–2; *Quilombola*
301, 302; social protection
policies in 124; in an *Updated
Study on the Right to Food*
15; violence against women in
11; *see also* agrarian reform,
agroecology, Bolsa Família,
Freire, P., *Inter-American
Convention on the Prevention,
Punishment, and Eradication
of Violence against Women*,
recourse mechanisms, Women
and the Right to Livelihoods
Bread for the World *see* Brot für die
Welt
breastfeeding: under the Baby-Friendly
Hospital Initiative (BFHI) 217;
as part of the best nutrition
practices 129, 181, 183, 214,
218, 223, 228; as a biological
norm 163, 183; compared to
animal milk 188; under the
*Convention on the Elimination
of All Discrimination against
Women* (CEDAW) 62, 74–5;
under the *Convention on the
Rights of the Child* (CRC)
74, 76, 191, 199; corporate
challenges to 21, 85, 171–9,
180, 181–2, 188–96, 223;
in emergencies 201–3; under
the *Declaration of the Rights
of the Child* 165; feeders 59,
111, 112; under the *Fourth
Report on the World Nutrition
Situation: Nutrition throughout
the Life Cycle* 183; and
gender discrimination 166;
under *General Comment 15
on the Right of the Child to
the Enjoyment of the Highest
Attainable Standard of Health*
192; impacts of 184–5; in
regard to infant and young child
feeding 162, 164, 198; under
the *Innocenti Declaration on
the Protection, Promotion and
Support of Breastfeeding* (2005)
163; and the International
Conference on Population and
Development 165; as an isolated
period of the life span 164, 166;
and medical nutrition 72, 349;
and nutrition interventions 225;
and nutritional status 66, 71,
226, 349; within the People's
and Food Sovereignty Matrix
372–7; and ready-to-use foods
(RUFs) 210, 214, 215, 358; the
right to 181, 182, 199, 228,
380; under Scaling Up Nutrition
(SUN) 222, 224; social and
cultural challenges to 196–200;
as social wealth equity 202;
under the state human rights
obligation to fulfill (facilitate)
382; under the state human
rights obligation to protect
381; under the state human
rights obligation to respect
380; and the United Nations
Children's Fund (UNICEF) 362,
364; and the United Nations
Committee on the Elimination of
Discrimination against Women
(CEDAW Committee) 388; and
the United Nations Committee
on the Rights of the Child (CRC
Committee) 191; under the
*Voluntary Guidelines to Support
the Progressive Realization of
the Right to Adequate Food in
the Context of National Food*

Security 79; and the *Sixth Report on the World Nutrition Situation* 183, 363; and World Alliance for Breastfeeding Action (WABA) 181; a women's decision to 163, 164, 181; *see also* breastmilk substitutes, complementary foods, HIV/AIDS, *International Code of Marketing of Breast-milk Substitutes*, intertwined subjectivities, local food systems, Nestlé, nutrition, overnutrition, noncommunicable diseases, rural women, state human rights obligations, traditional practices, United States, vulnerability, window of opportunity, women's autonomy, women's reproductive rights, women's human right to adequate food and nutrition

breastmilk substitutes 163; Baby-Friendly Hospital Initiative (BFHI) on 193; and commerciogenic malnutrition 188, 224; corporate private sector marketing of 21, 112, 188–91, 196–8, 215, 224–5, 349; under the *Draft Guidelines for the Marketing of Ready to Use Supplemental Foods for Children* 215; economic impact of 185; use during emergency situations 202–3, 206–7; health risks of 163, 188; under the *International Code of Marketing of Breast-milk Substitutes* 172, 181, 189; and powdered infant formula (PIF) 189–91; public health approach to 206; regulations on the marketing of 129, 229, 381; under the state extraterritorial human rights obligation to regulate 393; World Health Association (WHA) Resolution 47.5 193; *see also* De Schutter, O., *Convention on the Rights of the Child (CRC)*, *HIV and Infant Feeding 2010: An Updated Framework for Priority Action*, *Innocenti Declaration on the Protection, Promotion and Support of Breastfeeding*, *Safe Preparation, Storage and Handling of Powdered Infant Formula Guidelines*, Nestlé

Brot für die Welt 142, 306, 308, 309, 318; *see also* democracy, food (in)security, gender equality, gender mainstreaming

Canada 10, 132, 198–9, 263; Toronto Food Policy Council (TFPC) 288
CARE International 139, 195
Center for Women's Global Leadership (CWGL) 310–11
Charter of the United Nations (UN) 2, 22, 164
child malnutrition: failure of policies and programs to reduce 363; low birth weight (LBW) 182, 362, 363, 364; moderate acute malnutrition (MAM) 209, 211, 212, 213; under Scaling Up Nutrition (SUN) 219, 225; severe acute malnutrition (SAM) 210, 211, 213; social determinants of 71; stunting 182, 186, 194, 362, 363, 364; therapeutic care for acute malnutrition 210, 213; prevention of undernutrition 213–14; wasting 194, 210, 363, 364; and its link to women's human rights within the human right to adequate food and nutrition 363–4; *see also* complementary foods, United Nations Children's Fund (UNICEF)
child marriage 134, 166; and child mortality 361; as a violation of the *Convention on the Rights of the Child* (CRC) 363, as a violation of the *Convention on the Elimination of All Forms of Discrimination against Women* (CEDAW) 363; under *General Comment on the Right to Adequate Food and Nutrition* 387; in India 134–6, 361–2; and maternal mortality 180, 361; under the *Sixth Report on the World Nutrition Situation* 363–4; as structural violence 348, 361, 387; and the United Nations Children's Fund (UNICEF) 363; *see also*

pregnancy, *The Prohibition of Child Marriage Act*, rural women, women's human right to adequate food and nutrition

child mortality: 165, 179, 184; and adolescent pregnancy 361; due to Bear Brand coffee creamer misleading marketing 194, 195; due to breastmilk substitutes in emergencies 202, 206–7; and *Children's Rights and Business Principles* (CRBP) 172–3; in emergency and chronic health crises 202, 206; under India's *National Plan of Action for Children 2005* 134; due to intimate partner violence (IPV) 135;neonatal 184; linked to powdered infant formula (PIF) 190; and the right to dignity 136, 269; *see also* child marriage

children's human rights: under the *Convention on the Rights of the Child* (CRC) 76; and *General Comment 16 on the Equal Right of Men and Women to the Enjoyment of All Economic, Social and Cultural Rights* 166, 173; and human rights indivisibility 25; adoption of a new general comment on the right to adequate food and nutrition 388; to nutrition 75, 76, 81; see also United Nations Committee on the Rights of the Child (CRC Committee)

chronic health crises 200; and dependency 200–1; infant and young child feeding in 202, 208–9; local knowledge for dealing with 201, 202; and local self-determination 201, 214; and processed nutrition 201; and women's participation 201; *see also* emergencies

chronic malnutrition: as human rights violation 88; and local food systems 216; and the micronutrient deficiency paradigm 81; use of ready-to-use supplementary foods (RUSFs) for 213; *see also* hunger and malnutrition, India, malnutrition

civic agriculture 287; *see also* community food security

civil and political rights 4; under the *Convention on the Elimination of All Forms of Discrimination against Women* (CEDAW) 62; and the human right to adequate food and nutrition 227, 356, 368–9; within the national human rights systems 391; *see also* economic, social, and cultural rights, *International Covenant on Civil and Political Rights* (ICCPR)

civil society: alternative national reports by 145, 168–9, 368; empowerment of 27, 32; within gender mainstreaming 146–7; concern over the global nutrition industry 358; criticism of *The Lancet* "Maternal and Child (Under)Nutrition" series 269, 284; within national action plans (NAPs) 146–7; participation *see* civil society participation; as rights (claim) holders 23, 25–7, 350; separation from nature 345; *see also* agribusiness, conflicts of interest, corporate private sector, evolution of the human right to food and nutrition concept, *General Comment 12 on the Right to Adequate Food*, *Handbook for Legislation on Violence against Women*, rights holders, state human rights obligations

Civil Society Forum on Food Security 19

Civil Society Forum on Food Sovereignty 31

civil society participation 2; impact of charitable nutrition on 254; within the International Food Security & Nutrition Civil Society Mechanism (CSM) 35, 39; within the Committee on World Food Security (CFS) 33, 34, 35, 38, 39, 297; and community food security 287; and implementation of the conceptual framework of the human right to adequate food and nutrition 395; under the *Convention on the Elimination of All Forms of Discrimination against Women* (CEDAW) 62; and corporate social responsibility (CSR) 171; under the *Declaration on the Elimination of Violence against Women* (DEVAW) 146; and empowerment 276; and equitable food systems 295–300; within food policy councils (FPCs) 288; and food security 257; and food sovereignty 286, 287; within a food sovereignty framework 365, 366; and gender discrimination 318; and gender mainstreaming 144, 145, 146; under the Committee on Economic, Social and Cultural Rights (CESCR) general comments 23; under the governance paradigm 81; as a core element of the human right to adequate food and nutrition 355–6; and human rights defenders *see* human rights; and the human rights-based framework (approach) 26, 27, 138, 262; to confront hunger and malnutrition 357; under the *International Assessment of Agricultural Knowledge, Science and Technology for Development* (IAASTD) 263; and the creation of the *International Code of Conduct on the Right to Adequate Food* 30; and local food systems 76, 255, 285, 288, 319; and multistakeholder initiatives (MSIs) 168; through national action plans (NAPs) 146; in Brazil's National School Feeding Program 301; and participatory and action-based research methods 147, 278–9, 281, 318, 319; and participatory mechanisms 391; promotion and strengthening of 26; in public policy 255, 258, 389–90; and public-private partnerships (PPPs) 168; public-private-civil society approach 285, 288; within recourse mechanisms 391; within Scaling Up Nutrition (SUN) 219; under *Screen State Action against Hunger! How to Use the Voluntary Guidelines on the Right to Food to Monitor Public Policies?* 32, 299; in social protection programs 301; and structural violence 146; and the United Nations (UN) 390; and the United Nations Committee on Economic, Social and Cultural Rights (CESCR) 17; and the United Nations Office of the High Commissioner for Human Rights (OHCHR) 389; and urban agriculture 261; under the *Voluntary Guidelines to Support the Progressive Realization of the Right to Adequate Food in the Context of National Food Security* 32, 79, 145, 298–9; *see also* Association for Women's Rights in Development (AWID), Civil Society Forum on Food Security, Civil Society Forum on Food Sovereignty, Equipo Mujeres en Acción Solidaria (EMAS), evolution of the human right to food and nutrition concept, *Global Strategic Framework for Food Security and Nutrition* (GSF), human rights principles, *Optional Protocol to the International Covenant on Economic, Social and Cultural Rights*, people's and food sovereignty, "UNiTE to End Violence against Women," United Nations Entity for Gender Equality and the Empowerment of Women (UN Women), Women and the Right to Livelihoods

climate change 83, 285, 347–8, 357, 367, 386, 393

Codex Alimentarius 173, 353

commercialized nutrition *see* medicalized nutrition

Committee on World Food Security (CFS) 90, 92; *CFS Private Sector Modalities* 36, 38; on food and nutrition security 33–6, 258, 315; and human rights defenders

392; Intergovernmental Working Group 19, 31; the private sector within 36–9; reform of 33–6, 79, 297, 315, 390; *see also* accountability, agriculture and nutrition, civil society participation, corporate private sector, democracy, food (in)security, food production, gender equality, *Global Strategic Framework for Food Security and Nutrition (GSF)*, human rights violations, local food systems, *Proposal for an International Food Security and Nutrition Civil Society Mechanism for Relations with CFS*, women's human rights, World Bank

community food security 257, 284, 287–8, 318, 319, 383

complementary foods: in combination with breastfeeding 163, 185–7, 197, 205, 225; under the *Consolidated Guidelines on the Use of Antiretroviral Drugs for Treating and Preventing HIV Infection* 205; under the *Convention on the Rights of the Child* (CRC) 186; corporate marketing of 186; in emergency situations 208–16; as industry-based food violence 112; under the *Maternity Protection Convention* (No. 183) 192; and the pharmaceutical-based approach to micronutrient supplementation 72; safety and adequacy of 162, 186–7; and severe acute malnutrition (SAM) 211; *see also Global Strategy for Infant and Young Child Feeding* (IYCF), infant and young child feeding, local food systems, malnutrition

conflicts of interest: civil society on 175–6; and the Conflicts of Interest Coalition 176–7; definitions 175; within the Global Social Observatory (GSO) 223; under *HIV and Infant Feeding 2010: An Updated Framework for Priority Action* 207–8; and human rights instruments 343; within multistakeholder initiatives (MSIs) 175; in *The Lancet* "Maternal and Child (Under) Nutrition" series 176; between public policy and corporate sector 173–9, 225; within public-private partnerships (PPPs) 175, 220; within Scaling Up Nutrition (SUN) 220, 221, 222; within the United Nations (UN) 228; and the World Health Organization (WHO) 176–7, 222

Consensus of Washington 18

Consolidated Guidelines on the Use of Antiretroviral Drugs for Treating and Preventing HIV Infection 204–5

Consultative Group on International Agricultural Research (CGIAR) Consortium 34, 81

consumer packaged goods (CPG) companies 86; *see also* Nestlé

"Continuum of Care Fact Sheet: Reproductive, Maternal, Newborn and Child Health" 217

Convention on the Elimination of All Forms of Discrimination against Women (CEDAW) 165, 356; article 5 199; article 11 199; article 12 62, 63, 75–6; article 14 62–4; on childbearing 179; conceptual limitations of 344; entry into force 9; evolution 6–8, 164; regarding the fulfillment of women's and girls' right to dignity 145; regarding the highest attainable standard of health 75; on maternity 199; and nutrition *see* nutrition; omission of women's human right to adequate food and nutrition *see* structural isolation of women's human rights from the human right to adequate food and nutrition; protection gaps 385; on the role of women in relation to the human right to adequate food and nutrition 343; on state party periodic reports 92, 146; and the United Nations Children's Fund (UNICEF)

25; *see also* agrarian reform, breastfeeding, child marriage, civil and political rights, civil society participation, economic, social, and cultural rights, gender equality, gender mainstreaming, *General Recommendation on Rural Women, General Recommendation 24 on Women and Health, General Recommendation 25 on Temporary Special Measures,* highest attainable standard of health, human rights instruments, local food systems, optional protocols, pregnancy, rural women, state human rights obligations, United Nations Committee on the Elimination of Discrimination against Women (CEDAW Committee), violence against women, vulnerability, women's human right to adequate food and nutrition
Convention on the Nationality of Married Women 7, 10; *see also* human rights instruments
Convention Relating to the Status of Refugees 356; *see also* human rights instruments
Convention on the Rights of the Child (CRC) 356; adoption 6, 16; article 18 199; article 24, 74, 75, 76, 186, 188; article 27 75, 76; on breastmilk substitutes in emergencies 202; development 75; on human right to full and accurate information about best nutrition and feeding practices for infants and young children 188, 349; and nutrition *see* nutrition; nutritional dimension 344, 345; protection of children 165; relationship to the *International Code of Marketing of Breast-milk Substitutes* 189; and the United Nations Children's Fund (UNICEF) 25; on women as passive feeders of infants 59, 344; *see also* breastfeeding, child marriage, children's human rights, evolution of the human right to

food and nutrition concept, food production, highest attainable standard of health, human rights instruments, optional protocols, pregnancy, state human rights obligations, United Nations Committee on the Rights of the Child (CRC Committee), vulnerability
Convention on the Rights of Persons with Disabilities 6, 356; *see also* human rights instruments
Convention against Torture and Other Cruel, Inhumane or Degrading Treatment or Punishment 6; *see also* human rights instruments
Copenhagen Summit on Social Development 351
The Cordoba Declaration on the Right to Food and the Governance of the Global Food and Agricultural Systems 263
corporate private sector 30, 39; accountability *see* corporate private sector accountability; civil society struggle against 18–19, 27, 39; within the Committee on World Food Security (CFS) 34, 36, 39; under *General Comment 12 on the Right to Adequate Food* 23; growth of 5, 83–85; interests versus civil society 85, 92, 168, 346, 347, 384, 392; and landgrabbing 129, 347; and malnutrition 166, 360; power of 26, 33, 84, 91, 168, 287, 384; marketing *see* corporate private sector marketing; power relationship with rights holders 23, 26, 33, 38; resistance to the human right to adequate food 27; and cooperation with the United Nations (UN) 177; *see also CFS Private Sector Modalities,* Eide, A., food and nutrition security, food sovereignty, *General Comment 12 on the Right to Adequate Food, General Comment 16 on State Obligations Regarding the Impact of the Business Sector on Children's Rights, Global*

Strategic Framework for Food Security and Nutrition (GSF), human rights-based framework, intertwined subjectivities, medical nutrition, open-ended intergovernmental working groups

corporate private sector accountability 27, 171–9; and corporate social responsibility (CSR) 171–2, 222; legal 21; mandatory regulatory guidelines on 171; under the *SUN Movement: Revised Road Map* 224; within the United Nations Global Compact 172–3; and voluntary initiatives 167, 170, 172; *see also Children's Rights and Business Principles* (CRBP), *Draft Norms on Responsibilities of Transnational Corporations and Other Business Enterprises with Regard to Human Rights*, *Global Strategy for Infant and Young Child Feeding*, infant and young child feeding, state human rights obligations

corporate private sector marketing: of the Bear Brand *see* Nestlé; of food (and nutrition) substitutes 40, 112; of foods high in saturated fats, trans-fatty acids, sodium and sugar (HFSS foods) 196; regulation regarding foods of poor nutritional value 192–3; regulation under *General Comment 15 on the Right of the Child to the Enjoyment of the Highest Attainable Standard of Health* 192; regulation under *General Comment 16 on State Obligations Regarding the Impact of the Business Sector on Children's Rights* 192–3; regulation under *Innocenti Declaration on Infant Young Child Feeding* (2005) 193; state extraterritorial human rights obligation to regulate 393; state human rights obligation to protect against 381, 387; and traditional feeding practices 348; regulation under World Health

Association (WHA) resolutions 193, 229; *see also* breastmilk substitutes, De Schutter, O., medical nutrition, ready-to-use foods (RUFs), structural causes of hunger and malnutrition

corporate private sector obligations: and corporate social responsibility (CSR) 171, 179; under the *International Code on Marketing of Breast-milk Substitutes* 192, 229; under the *International Covenant on Economic, Social and Cultural Rights* (ICESCR) 166–7; regarding nutrition-based interventions 229; regarding the progressive realization of the human right to adequate food and nutrition 167; under World Health Association (WHA) resolutions 229; under World Health Organization (WHO) recommendations on the marketing of foods and non-alcoholic beverages to children 229; *see also Draft Norms on Responsibilities of Transnational Corporations and Other Business Enterprises with Regard to Human Rights*, state human rights obligations

corporate social responsibility (CSR) *see* corporate private sector accountability, corporate private sector obligations

crises *see* chronic health crises, emergencies

cultural practices *see* traditional practices

cultural violence *see* violence against women

De Schutter, O.: on agroecology 291, 293; on breastmilk substitutes 225–6; on food production and marketing 83, 196; on the global food crisis 24, 33; on the *Global Strategic Framework for Food and Nutrition Security* (GSF) 37; on the *International Code of Marketing of Breast-milk Substitutes* 225, 226; on local food security 293; on nutrition initiatives 224, 226; on peasant agriculture 285; on regulating corporate private sector marketing practices 226; on social protection 300; on the structural causes of hunger 33; on sustainable diets 292, 293; on a sustainable global food system 301; on women and gender 63, 109, 293, 311; on World Health Assembly (WHA) resolutions 225, 226; on World Health Organization (WHO) recommendations on the marketing of breastmilk substitutes and of foods and non-alcoholic beverages to children 226

Declaration of Commitment on HIV/ AIDS 283

Declaration on the Elimination of Violence against Women (DEVAW): introduction 11; article 1 127, 146; article 2 127, 146; article 3 127, 146; article 4 127, 146; *see also* accountability, civil society participation, gender mainstreaming, human rights instruments, *International Covenant on Economic, Social and Cultural Rights* (ICESCR), local food systems, violence against women

Declaration of the Rights of the Child 165; *see also* human rights instruments

Declaration on the Rights of Indigenous Peoples 6, 356; *see also* human rights instruments

Declaration for Women's Reproductive and Sexual Rights and Health 179

Declaration of the World Summit on Food Security 37

democracy: under the *Additional Protocol to the [1969] American Convention on Human Rights in the Area of Economic, Social and Cultural Rights (Protocol of San Salvador)* 77; and Brot für die Welt 142; and the Committee on World Food Security (CFS) 34, 92; and corporate social responsibility (CSR) 171; democratic participation 2, 17, 23, 357, 368, 389–90; and food and nutrition systems 300; and food governance 257; in food policy 288; and human rights 18; and the human rights-based framework 262, 297; under the *International Assessment of Agricultural Knowledge, Science and Technology for Development* (IAASTD) 263, 316; democratic governance 26, 39, 84, 257; and multistakeholder initiatives (MSIs) 168; and public-private partnerships (PPPs) 168; and state human rights obligations 267; and the sustainable livelihoods approach (SLA) 278; under the *Voluntary Guidelines to Support the Progressive Realization of the Right to Adequate Food in the Context of National Food Security* 145; *see also* agroecology, civil society participation, community food security, Equipo Mujeres en Acción Solidaria (EMAS), food justice, food policy councils, food sovereignty, local food systems, organic agriculture, Nobel Women's Initiative, sustainable diets, state obligations, Women in Informal Employment Globalization and Organizing (WIEGO)

Department for International Development (DFID) 277

domestic violence: under the *Beijing Declaration and Platform for Action* 127; and Equipo Mujeres en Acción (EMAS) 310; need for law on 118; and microcredit interventions 141; in national action plans (NAPs) 131–2; within the People's and Food Sovereignty Matrix 378; as a risk to women's health 128; and social protection 125; state human rights obligation to protect 381; as structural violence 116–17, 348; and women's independence 273; and women's position in the household 273, 306; evaluation by the World Health Organization (WHO) on 127; *see also* structural violence, violence against women

Draft Guidelines for the Marketing of Ready to Use Supplemental Foods for Children 215, 227; *see also* breastmilk substitutes, corporate private sector marketing

Draft Norms on Responsibilities of Transnational Corporations and Other Business Enterprises with Regard to Human Rights 171–2; *see also* human rights instruments

duty bearers: and accountability 36; and Brazil's National School Feeding Program 302; within food and nutrition policies 90; under *The Future We Want* 224; and gender mainstreaming 146; under *General Comment 12 on the Right to Adequate Food*; 23; within the human rights framework 26–7; within the human rights-based approach 25, 116, 162, 350; under international law 168–9; under Scaling Up Nutrition (SUN) "Principles of Engagement" 224; within the *Sixth Report on the World Nutrition Situation* 363; *see also* corporate private sector obligations, state human rights obligations

economic, social, and cultural rights 4, 145; relationship to civil and political rights 5, 17, 19, 74, 343, 344, 391; under the *Convention on the Elimination of All Forms of Discrimination against Women* (CEDAW) 62; within national human rights systems 391;indivisibility with human right to adequate food and nutrition 368; state obligations under 21–2; under the *Universal Declaration of*

Human Rights (UDHR) 16; and structural violence 144; *see also International Covenant on Economic, Social and Cultural Rights* (ICESCR), human rights instruments

Eide, A. 16, 359; on corporate power 18; on the human right to adequate food and nutrition conceptual framework 350–2; on the human rights-based approach to food 25, 352; on human rights principles 350; *The Right to Adequate Food and to Be Free From Hunger: Updated Study on the Right to Food* 16, 20, 22, 23, 25, 351–2; and the United Nations Children's Fund (UNICEF) 25; on women's human rights 351, 352; *see also* Food Security Matrix

emergencies: acute 200; chronic 200; coexistence of overweight and underweight in protracted 196; and household power relations 118; use of the infant and young child feeding (IYCF) approach 217; use of ready-to-use foods (RUFs) in 87, 213, 214, 216; response programs to 143, 209–10; sudden 200; urgent 200; *see also* breastfeeding, breastmilk substitutes, child mortality, complementary foods, food aid, HIV/AIDS, human right to adequate food and nutrition, human rights-based framework, infant and young child feeding, *Infant and Young Child Feeding in Emergencies: Operational Guidance for Emergency Relief Staff and Programme Managers, International Code of Marketing of Breast-milk Substitutes*, Just Associates (JASS), local food systems, state human rights obligations

empowerment: concept 138, 275, 320; key challenge to 276; of women *see* women's empowerment; *see also* civil society, civil society participation, gender, gender equality, gender mainstreaming,

HIV/AIDS, human rights-based approach, human rights principles, human rights-based framework, local food systems, United Nations Entity for Gender Equality and the Empowerment of Women (UN Women), women in agriculture, World Bank

Equal Rights Amendment 9

Equipo Mujeres en Acción Solidaria (EMAS) 309–10

Europe 213, 259, 296, 307, 308, 313, 314; Albania 134; Armenia 117–18; Central 305; Denmark 119; Eastern 142, 305; Ireland 132, 358; Moldova 132; Northern Ireland 139–40; Spain 261; Sweden 133; Ukraine 132; United Kingdom 86, 119, 190, 290

Every Woman Every Child 177–8

evolution of the human right to adequate food and nutrition concept: role of civil society 2, 12, 16–20, 40; through treaty bodies 385; *see also General Comment 12 on the Right to Adequate Food, Global Strategic Framework for Food and Nutrition Security* (GSF), human right to adequate food and nutrition, human right to adequate food and nutrition conceptual framework, human rights-based framework, *Voluntary Guidelines to Support the Progressive Realization of the Right to Adequate Food in the Context of National Food Security*

extraterritorial human rights obligations *see* state extraterritorial human rights obligations

FIAN International 19, 32, 63, 285, 296, 299

Fiji 119

food aid: as charitable nutrition 254; dependency on 84, 200, 214–15, 229, 284, 296, 319; as malnutrition prevention strategy 254; under the *Voluntary*

Guidelines to Support the Progressive Realization of the Right to Adequate Food in the Context of National Food Security 214; *see also* accountability, gender equality, human rights violations, local food systems, violence against women

Food and Fairness Inquiry 290; *Food Justice: The Report of the Food and Fairness Inquiry* 290–1

food and nutrition (in)security: and agroecology 291; and Brot für die Welt 142; community food security 287–8; concept of 19, 79, 257–8, 287; and the conceptual human rights-based framework 383, 389; under the *Convention on the Rights of the Child* (CRC) 76; and corporate involvement 21, 33; current state of 1; dimensions (pillars) of 20, 22–3, 76, 79, 369; and equality 72, 296; and the global food crisis 32; and food sovereignty 18, 73, 287; and the free market 18; human rights perspective of 35; and gender mainstreaming 139, 143, 145; gender perspective in 2, 58, 72, 108, 113, 143, 145; under *General Comment 12 on the Right to Adequate Food* 63, 77; under *General Comment 14 on the Right to the Highest Attainable Standard of Health* 91, 129; under *General Recommendation 24 on Women and Health* 64; household surveys on *see* household; and human rights principles 38; and individual entitlements 257; and international governance structure 390; at the 18th International Union of Nutritional Sciences (IUNS) 259; and landgrabbing 285; in local food systems 85, 92, 285; and medical nutrition 89; and nutrition sensitive urban agriculture 261; production oriented 19, 72, 80, 257, 262; and ready-to-use supplementary foods (RUSFs) 214; shortcomings of agricultural models for 262–4; shortcomings of medicalized nutrition intervention models for 269–70; meaning of "security" 293; within the *Sixth Report on the World Food Situation* 260; and sustainable diets 292; and the *Universal Declaration of Human Rights* (UDHR) 257; and the *Voluntary Guidelines to Support the Progressive Realization of the Right to Adequate Food in the Context of National Food Security* 30–1, 298; of women *see* women's food and nutrition security; women's (key) contribution to 1, 72, 111, 117, 256, 264, 276, 293, 310; *see also* agribusiness, De Schutter, O., Committee on World Food Security (CFS), Civil Society Forum on Food Security, civil society participation, *Declaration of the World Summit on Food Security*, food policy councils (FPCs), food production, Food Security Matrix, food sovereignty, food systems approach, gender equality, gender perspective, *Global Strategic Framework for Food Security and Nutrition* (GSF), household, human right to adequate food and nutrition, human rights-based approach, human rights-based framework, indigenous peoples, *International Assessment of Agricultural Knowledge, Science and Technology for Development* (IAASTD), local food systems, PROMESA, state human rights obligations, *The State of Food and Agriculture 2010–11—Women in Agriculture: Closing the Gender Gap for Development*, sustainable livelihoods, traditional practices, United Nations High-Level Task Force (HLTF) on the Global Food Security Crisis, violence against women, vulnerability, women's empowerment,

women's food and nutrition security, women
food policy councils (FPCs)) 255, 284, 288–9
food production: under the *Additional Protocol to the [1969] American Convention on Human Rights in the Area of Economic, Social and Cultural Rights (Protocol of San Salvador)* 78; and the child's right to adequate food 76; under the Committee on World Food Security (CFS) 33, 81; under the *Convention on the Rights of the Child* (CRC) 77; under *General Comment 12 on the Right to Adequate Food* 63; under *General Comment 16 on State Obligations Regarding the Impact of the Business Sector on Children's Rights* 61; under *General Recommendation 24 on Women and Health* 64; industrial scale 32–3, 58, 73, 74, 85, 254, 347–8; under the *International Covenant on Economic, Social and Cultural Rights* (ICESCR) 13, 74; market-based approaches of 81; as separate from nutrition 73–85, 258–9, 319, 358, 360; overproduction 85; rural agriculture-based livelihoods 293–4; sustainable 163, 214, 263, 355, 380–1, 387; and sustainable diets 292–3; under the *Universal Declaration on the Eradication of Hunger and Malnutrition* 14; under the *Voluntary Guidelines to Support the Progressive Realization of the Right to Adequate Food in the Context of National Food Security* 80; and women and the household 65; and women's role 265, 268; *see also* agribusiness, De Schutter, O., food sovereignty, *International Assessment of Agricultural Knowledge, Science and Technology for Development* (IAASTD), local food systems, traditional practices
Food Security Matrix 22–3, 352, 353, 369; *see also* Eide, A.

food sovereignty: concept 286; and control over means of production 80, 85, 91, 113, 355, 356, 366; and the core elements of the human right to adequate food and nutrition 355–6, 366–9; and corporate interests 346; Equipo Mujeres en Acción Solidaria (EMAS) 310; in food and nutrition practices 89, 90; Food Sovereignty: A Critical Dialogue at Yale University 286; and gender equality 287; and the human rights-based approach 26, 31, 72, 80; integration of gender, nutrition, and the human right to adequate food within 254, 287; and medical nutrition 358; movement 286, 296; state extraterritorial obligation to ensure an enabling environment for 393; *see also* agribusiness, civil society participation, democracy, food and nutrition (in)security, food production, food sovereignty framework, food systems approach, gender perspective, *International Assessment of Agricultural Knowledge, Science and Technology for Development* (IAASTD), International Planning Committee on Food Sovereignty (IPC), La Via Campesina, local food systems, people's and food sovereignty, People's Food Sovereignty Forum, People's and Food Sovereignty Matrix, traditional practices, United Nations Entity for Gender Equality and the Empowerment of Women (UN Women), women's human rights, World Food Summit
food sovereignty framework 39, 91, 341, 356–8, 365–6, 394; *see also* food sovereignty, Peoples' and Food Sovereignty Matrix
food systems approach 129; and food sovereignty 254; integrating food and nutrition security 254, 319; local governance 76,

77, 319; and nutrition 75, 85; and sustainable diets 254; *see also* agriculture and nutrition, agroecology, traditional practices
formula feeding *see* breastmilk substitutes
Fourth Report on the World Nutrition Situation: Nutrition throughout the Life Cycle 183
Fourth World Conference on Women 16, 126, 127, 138, 351; *see also Beijing Declaration and Platform for Action*, gender mainstreaming
fulfill (facilitate) *see* state human rights obligations
fulfill (provide) *see* state human rights obligations
functional foods 87, 88, 89, 90; *see also* nutraceuticals, medicalized nutrition

gender: and (mal)nutrition 2, 91, 182; under the International Food Security & Nutrition Civil Society Mechanism (CSM) 38, 39; debate on 274; and development (GAD) 275; dimension within human rights national institutions 391; and empowerment 276; fatigue 275; gender disaggregated data *see* household; under *General Comment 12 on the Right to Adequate Food* 61, 354; International Union of Nutritional Sciences (IUNS) on 262; 19th International Union of Nutritional Sciences (IUNS) on 262; within a new general comment on the right to adequate food and nutrition 387–8; within the People's and Food Sovereignty Matrix 372; research 113; sensitive approaches 299, 318, 319, 394; stereotypes 65, 74, 300, 310, 359; under the *Voluntary Guidelines to Support the Progressive Realization of the Right to Adequate Food in the Context of National Food Security* 354; *see also* De

Schutter, O., gender equality, gender mainstreaming, gender perspective, gender-based discrimination, violence against women, women in agriculture, women's empowerment, women's human rights

Gender in Agriculture Sourcebook 139, 265, 311–12; *see also* women in agriculture

gender-based discrimination 1, 2, 59, 74, 109–10; in childhood 165, 166; under *General Comment 16 on The Equal Right of Men and Women to the Enjoyment of All Economic, Social and Cultural* 61; in household and community oriented nutrition work 80; and hunger and malnutrition 349; andKurdish Men for Gender Equality 308; and maternal mortality 179–80; and medical nutrition 89; and the nutrition paradigm 262; and human rights principles 28; policy reforms on 318–20; systematic 116; as a form of violence *see* violence against women; *see also* breastfeeding, child marriage, civil society participation, De Schutter, O., *The Lancet* "Maternal and Child (Under) Nutrition" series, patriarchal structure, pregnancy, rural women, structural isolation of women's human rights from the human right to adequate food and nutrition, vulnerability

gender-based violence *see* violence against women

gender discrimination *see* gender-based discrimination

gender equality: in agriculture 264–9; and Brot für die Welt 142; under the Committee on World Food Security (CFS) 92; under the *Convention on the Elimination of All Forms of Discrimination against Women* (CEDAW) 63; and community food security 287; and empowerment 276; and food aid 201; and food and nutrition security 267, 269; and food justice 289; under gender mainstreaming 138, 142; as part of the human rights system 2; within the human right to adequate food framework conceptual framework 362, 367–8; and microfinance 140; under national action plans (NAPs) 134; and natural resource management 267; within recourse mechanisms 391; and structural violence 124; and sustainable diets 292; within trade and policy 311; under the United Nations Children's Fund (UNICEF) 363; and unpaid care 301; *see also* Association for Women's Rights in Development (AWID), Center for Women's Global Leadership (CWGL), De Schutter, O., *Declaration of Commitment on HIV/AIDS*, food sovereignty, *Gender in Agriculture Sourcebook*, *Global Strategic Framework for Food and Nutrition Security* (GSF), MenEngage, Nobel Women's Initiative, PROMESA, *The State of Food and Agriculture 2010–11—Women in Agriculture: Closing the Gender Gap for Development*, United Nations Entity for Gender Equality and the Empowerment of Women (UN Women), World Bank

gender mainstreaming 120; and Brot für die Welt 142; concept 138–40; under the *Convention on the Elimination of All Forms of Discrimination against Women* (CEDAW) 145–6; under the *Declaration on the Elimination of Violence against Women* (DEVAW) 146; education 144; and empowerment 276–7; evolution 275; and the Fourth World Conference on Women in Beijing 126; inclusion of men in 277, 308–10, 320; in legal systems 144; in human right to adequate food and nutrition work 310–18; and MenEngage 307, 314; and microfinance programs 140–1; operational implementation level of 139–40; at the Rio+20 United Nations Conference on Sustainable Development 275; and structural violence 147; and the United Nations Committee on Economic, Social and Cultural Rights (CESCR) 145; United Nations (UN) definition of 137–8; and women's human right to adequate food and nutrition 146, 147; *see also* Association for Women's Rights in Development (AWID), Center for Women's Global Leadership (CWGL), civil society, civil society participation, Committee on World Food Security (CFS), Equipo Mujeres en Acción Solidaria (EMAS), gender equality, *Gender in Agriculture Sourcebook*, Inter Press Service (IPS) MDG3 Project, *International Assessment of Agricultural Knowledge, Science and Technology for Development* (IAASTD), Landesa Center for Women's Land Rights, Nobel Women's Initiative, PROMESA, *The State of Food and Agriculture 2010–11—Women in Agriculture: Closing the Gender Gap for Development*, "UNiTE to End Violence against Women," United Nations Entity for Gender Equality and the Empowermentof Women (UN Women), violence against women, Women and the Right to Livelihoods, Women in Law and Development in Africa (WiLDAF), Women's Caucus for Gender Justice, World's Women reports

gender perspective: within the International Food Security & Nutrition Civil Society Mechanism (CSM) 315; within the conceptual human right to adequate food framework 368, 383; in food and nutrition security 58, 108, 254; and food sovereignty 39, 341; mainstreaming of 2, 110, 137; and public policy 255; *see also* Equipo Mujeres en Acción Solidaria (EMAS), gender mainstreaming, food and nutrition (in)security, food sovereignty, People's and Food Sovereignty Matrix, women's food and nutrition security

General Agreement on Tariffs and Trade (GATT) *see* Uruguay Round of the General Agreement on Tariffs and Trade (GATT)

General Comment 12 on the Right to Adequate Food: on the adequacy dimension of the human right to food and nutrition 354; adoption and development of 19, 2; civil society responsibilities 23; and the human right to adequate food and nutrition conceptual framework 354, 367–8, 389; definition of the right to adequate food and nutrition 20–1; and gender discrimination *see* structural isolation of women's human rights from the human right to adequate food and nutrition; and the role of women in relation to the human right to adequate food and nutrition 343; state human rights obligations 21–2, 23; on the regulation of corporate activity 23; women's human right to adequate food 145; *see also* corporate private sector, food and nutrition (in)security, food production, gender, *General Comment on the Right to Adequate Food and Nutrition*, *Global Strategic Framework for Food Security and Nutrition* (GSF), human rights instruments, *International Covenant on Economic, Social and Cultural Rights* (ICESCR), nutrition, patriarchal structure, PROMESA, state human rights obligations, United Nations

Committee on Economic, Social
and Cultural Rights (CESCR),
World Food Summit
*General Comment 14 on the Right to
the Highest Attainable Standard
of Health*: adoption of 169;
article 10 128; and the human
right to adequate food and
nutrition 91, 367; on indigenous
peoples 78–9, 91, 128; and the
nutritional dimension 367; state
human rights obligations 22;
see also food and nutrition (in)
security, *General Comment on
the Right to Adequate Food
and Nutrition*, human rights
instruments, *International
Covenant on Economic, Social
and Cultural Rights* (ICESCR),
nutrition, state human rights
obligations, traditional practices,
United Nations Committee on
Economic, Social and Cultural
Rights (CESCR), violence against
women
*General Comment 15 on the Right of
the Child to the Enjoyment of
the Highest Attainable Standard
of Health* 191–2, 226, 367; *see
also* breastfeeding, *Convention
on the Rights of the Child*
(CRC), corporate private sector
marketing, *General Comment
on the Right to Adequate Food
and Nutrition*, *Global Strategy
for Infant and Young Child
Feeding* (IYCF), human rights
instruments, *International Code
of Marketing of Breast-milk
Substitutes*, state human rights
obligations, United Nations
Committee on the Rights of the
Child (CRC Committee)
*General Comment 16 on The Equal
Right of Men and Women to
the Enjoyment of All Economic,
Social and Cultural* 61, 67–9,
169; *see also* gender-based
discrimination, human rights
instruments, *International
Covenant on Economic,
Social and Cultural Rights*
(ICESCR), local food systems,

United Nations Committee on
Economic, Social and Cultural
Rights (CESCR)
*General Comment 16 on State
Obligations Regarding the
Impact of the Business Sector
on Children's Rights* 169–70,
173, 192–3; *see also Convention
on the Rights of the Child*
(CRC), corporate private
sector, corporate private sector
marketing, food production,
*International Code of Marketing
of Breast-milk Substitutes*, local
food systems, non-governmental
organizations (NGOs), state
human rights obligations,
traditional practices, United
Nations Committee on the
Rights of the Child (CRC
Committee), World Health
Assembly (WHA) resolutions
*General Comment 20 on Non-
Discrimination in Economic,
Social and Cultural Rights*
169; *see also* gender-based
discrimination, human rights
instruments, *International
Covenant on Economic, Social
and Cultural Rights* (ICESCR),
United Nations Committee on
Economic, Social and Cultural
Rights (CESCR)
*General Comment on the Right
to Adequate Food and
Nutrition*(new) 385–9;
incorporation of gender 387–8;
in line with *General Comment
14 on the Right to the Highest
Attainable Standard of Health*
386; in line with *General
Comment 15 on the Right of
the Child to the Enjoyment of
the Highest Attainable Standard
of Health* 386; in line with
*General Recommendation 24
on Women and Health* 386;
and the nutritional dimension
386–7; and people's and
food sovereignty 385; *see
also* human right to adequate
food and nutrition conceptual
framework, human rights

instruments, *International Covenant on Economic, Social and Cultural Rights* (ICESCR), United Nations Committee on Economic, Social and Cultural Rights (CESCR), United Nations Committee on the Rights of the Child (CRC Committee)
general comments 17, 23, 66–70, 169, 384, 385; *see also* civil society participation, *General Comment 12 on the Right to Adequate Food, General Comment 14 on the Right to the Highest Attainable Standard of Health, General Comment 15 on the Right of the Child to the Enjoyment of the Highest Attainable Standard of Health, General Comment 16 on The Equal Right of Men and Women to the Enjoyment of All Economic, Social and Cultural, General Comment 16 on State Obligations Regarding the Impact of the Business Sector on Children's Rights, General Comment 20 on Non-Discrimination in Economic, Social and Cultural Rights, General Comment on the Right to Adequate Food and Nutrition*, United Nations Committee on Economic, Social and Cultural Rights (CESCR), United Nations Committee on the Rights of the Child (CRC Committee), vulnerability
General Recommendation on the Human Right to Adequate Food and Nutrition and Women 92, 146, 169, 388, 389; *see also Convention on the Elimination of All Forms of Discrimination against Women* (CEDAW), human rights instruments, structural isolation of women's human rights from the human right to adequate food and nutrition, United Nations Committee on the Elimination of Discrimination against Women (CEDAW Committee)

Rural Women 91, 388; *see also Convention on the Elimination of All Forms of Discrimination against Women* (CEDAW), human rights instruments, United Nations Committee on the Elimination of Discrimination against Women (CEDAW Committee)
General Recommendation 24 on Women and Health 63–4, 126; and a new *General Comment on the Right to Adequate Food and Nutrition* 386; and the nutritional dimension 367; *see also Convention on the Elimination of All Forms of Discrimination against Women* (CEDAW), food and nutrition (in)security, *General Comment on the Right to Adequate Food and Nutrition*, human rights instruments, local food systems, United Nations Committee on the Elimination of Discrimination against Women (CEDAW Committee)
General Recommendation 25 on Temporary Special Measures 71–2; *see also Convention on the Elimination of All Forms of Discrimination against Women* (CEDAW), human rights instruments, United Nations Committee on the Elimination of Discrimination against Women (CEDAW Committee), vulnerability
general recommendations 66, 145, 169, 385; *see also Convention on the Elimination of All Forms of Discrimination against Women* (CEDAW), *General Recommendation on Rural Women, General Recommendation on the Human Right to Adequate Food and Nutrition and Women, General Recommendation 24 on Women and Health, General Recommendation 25 on Temporary Special Measures*, human rights instruments, United

Nations Committee on the Elimination of Discrimination against Women (CEDAW Committee), vulnerability
Geneva Conventions 16; Additional Protocols 16
Global Partnership on Agriculture, Food Security and Nutrition (GPFAS) 33, 34, 35
Global Social Observatory (GSO) 223; Announcement for a Consultation Process on Conflict of Interest in the Scaling Up Nutrition Movement 223; *see also* conflicts of interest
green economy 275, 314
Group of Eight (G8) 33, 357
Group of Seventy-Seven (G77) 33
Group of Twenty Finance Ministers and Central Bank Governors (G20) 33, 357
Global Alliance for Improved Nutrition (GAIN) 174, 221, 224
global food crisis 1, 24, 32–3, 296; *see also* agribusiness, De Schutter, O., food and nutrition (in) security, India, United States
global food governance 26, 36, 80, 319
Global Partnership for Agriculture, Food Security and Nutrition 297
Global Strategic Framework for Food Security and Nutrition (GSF) 389; and accountability 38; and civil society participation 37, 38, 79; and the corporate private sector 38, 79; and the evolution of the human right to food and nutrition concept 8; on food (in)security 36–7, 79; on gender equality 92; and *General Comment 12 on the Right to Adequate Food* 37; and the human rights-based approach to adequate food 37–8; on indigenous peoples 38; on nutrition 79–80; on structural causes of hunger and malnutrition 38; and the *Voluntary Guidelines to Support the Progressive Realization of the Right to Adequate Food in the Context of National Food Security* 37; and women's human

rights 92; *see also* Committee on World Food Security (CFS), De Schutter, O.
Global Strategy for Infant and Young Child Feeding 173, 174, 178, 217; on complementary foods 186–7; under *General Comment 15 on the Right of the Child to the Enjoyment of the Highest Attainable Standard of Health* 192
green revolution 81, 83
Guidelines on Cooperation between the United Nations and the Business Community 174–5
Guidelines on HIV and Infant Feeding: 2010 edition 205–6; 2013 edition 205–6
Guidelines on Working with the Private Sector to Achieve Health Outcomes 174

Handbook for Legislation on Violence against Women 130
HIV/AIDS: situation in Africa 274, 282, 283; antiretroviral (ARV) interventions 204–5; under the Baby-Friendly Hospital Initiative (BFHI) 217; and breastfeeding by infected mothers 165, 203–8; in crises 200, 206–7; and empowerment 125; in girls and women 165, 282–3; and food and nutrition insecurity 165, 282; and infant feeding *see* infant and young child feeding; and the 18th International Union of Nutritional Sciences (IUNS) 259; public health approach 204, 206; and maternal nutritional health status 165; human right to adequate food and nutrition for affected infants and young children 207; and sexual violence 282–3; and women in agriculture 265–6; and women's right to make an informed decision on infant feeding 203, 204, 206; *see also* breastmilk substitutes, *Consolidated Guidelines on the Use of Antiretroviral Drugs for Treating and Preventing HIV Infection, Declaration of*

*Commitment on HIV/AIDS,
Guidelines on HIV and Infant
Feeding, HIV and Infant Feeding
2010: An Updated Framework
for Priority Action*, human
rights-based framework, national
action plans (NAPs), World's
Women reports
*HIV and Infant Feeding 2010: An
Updated Framework for
Priority Action* 207–8; *see
also* breastmilk substitutes,
conflicts of interest, HIV/AIDS,
*International Code of Marketing
of Breast-milk Substitutes*
household: food and nutrition security
269–70, 274; concept 271, 272;
female-headed 272–3, 274;
gender disaggregated data on
270–4, 319; intra-household
dynamics of 270, 272, 274;
see also food and nutrition
(in)security, food production,
gender-based discrimination,
South Africa, *The State of Food
and Agriculture 2010–11—
Women in Agriculture:
Closing the Gender Gap for
Development*, women in
agriculture, women's autonomy,
women's empowerment, World's
Women reports
human dignity: within *Food Justice:
The Report of the Food and
Fairness Inquiry* 291; under
*General Recommendation 24
on Women and Health* 64; and
human rights covenants and
treaties 357; within the human
rights-based framework 3;
human rights promotion of 350;
under the *International Code
of Marketing of Breast-milk
Substitutes* 192; and medicalized
nutrition 82; mother's 388;
under a new general comment
on the right to adequate food
and nutrition 386; and the
nutritional dimension 358, 359;
as a PANTHER principle 27,
29; within the People's and Food
Sovereignty Matrix 369, 377–9,
380, 381, 382; within public

policies and programs 390;
under the *Universal Declaration
of Human Rights* (UDHR) 4;
under the *Voluntary Guidelines
to Support the Progressive
Realization of the Right to
Adequate Food in the Context
of National Food Security* 299;
women's 362; *see also* human
rights principles
human right to adequate food and
nutrition: under the capability
approach 354–5; and the Center
for Women's Global Leadership
(CWGL) 311; and civil society
participation 23, 283; and
community food security
287; conceptual framework
see human right to adequate
food and nutrition conceptual
framework; cultural dimension
of 359; definition 355–6; as an
economic, social, and cultural
right 4, 21; in emergencies
143; evolutive nature 2–5, 40,
59, 72; need for "food *and*
nutrition" 3, 262, 341, 355,
367; and gender mainstreaming
138; under the *Global Strategic
Framework for Food Security
and Nutrition* (GSF) 37, 38; of
infants 182; as international law
12; at the 18th International
Union of Nutritional Sciences
(IUNS) 259; interrelatedness
with other human rights 25, 33,
59, 137, 145, 344–5, 356; legal
foundation 12–16; nutritional
dimension of 2, 39, 58, 72–4,
91, 343–4, 355, 358–60, 367,
386; and the need to identify
discriminated against groups
356; and public policy 27, 58,
72, 91, 110, 129, 131; as a social
construct (process) 343–4, 354;
in social protection programs
125, 143; role of women in
2, 64, 91, 145, 343; and the
Uruguay Round on General
Agreement on Tariffs and Trade
(GATT) 18; women's human
rights dimension 361–5; women
and progressive realization of

1, 2, 137, 287; *see also* civil and political rights, Eide, A., evolution of the human right to food and nutrition concept, food sovereignty, food sovereignty framework, Food Security Matrix, food and nutrition (in) security, *General Comment 12 on the Right to Adequate Food*, national action plans (NAPs), People's and Food Sovereignty Matrix, state human rights obligations, *Voluntary Guidelines to Support the Progressive Realization of the Right to Adequate Food in the Context of National Food Security*, *Updated Study on the Right to Food*

human right to adequate food and nutrition conceptual framework 12, 14, 77, 344–6; development of 354–6; and the human rights system 394; and justiciability 12, 17, 392; redefinition of 341, 350–2, 366–9; *see also* civil society participation, Eide, A., evolution of the human right to adequate food and nutrition concept, food sovereignty framework, gender equality, gender perspective, *General Comment 12 on the Right to Adequate Food*, *General Comment 14 on the Right to the Highest Attainable Standard of Health*, *General Comment on the Human Right to Adequate Food and Nutrition*, human right to adequate food and nutrition, nutrition, overnutrition, People's and Food Sovereignty Matrix, state human rights obligations, structural causes of hunger and malnutrition, *Voluntary Guidelines to Support the Progressive Realization of the Right to Adequate Food in the Context of National Food Security*

human rights: approach *see* human rights-based approach; characteristics *see* human rights characteristics; of children *see* children's human rights; claiming 4, 12, 29; conceptual limitations of 341; defenders 24, 30, 224, 350, 368, 384, 392; instruments *see* human rights instruments; legal framework 2, 15, 59, 72, 92, 116, 224; national systems 391; principles *see* human rights principles; as best tool to address hunger and malnutrition 341, 350, 394; as best tool to address inequality 341, 350; universal court 392; of women *see* women's human rights; *see also* human right to adequate food and nutrition, human right to adequate food and nutrition conceptual framework, women's human right to adequate food and nutrition

human rights-based approach 2, 14, 20, 24, 27; within the Committee on World Food Security (CFS) 36; compared to the human rights-based framework 26; discourse on 26; and empowerment 138; and food and nutrition security 26, 27; and the Global Alliance for Improved Nutrition (GAIN) 224; within legal and conceptual frameworks 344–6; mainstreaming of 25; to nutrition paradigm 261–2; within public policy 344–6; and Scaling Up Nutrition (SUN) 224–5; to addressing structural violence 116; and social and political interests 342; within the *Voluntary Guidelines to Support the Progressive Realization of the Right to Adequate Food in the Context of National Food Security* 32; *see also* accountability, civil society participation, duty bearers, Eide, A., food sovereignty, *Global Strategic Framework for Food and Nutrition Security* (GSF), human rights, human rights principles, human rights-based framework, rights holders, state human rights obligations, *United*

Nations Statement of Common
Understanding on Human
Rights-Based Approaches to
Development Cooperation and
Programming
human rights-based framework: and
accountability 26, 262; and
agrarian struggles 297–8;
and breastfeeding and HIV/
AIDS 204, 206; conceptual
framework *see* human right to
adequate food and nutrition
conceptual framework; and
the corporate private sector
34; in emergency situations
209; and empowerment 276;
evolution 19, 72, 342; for food
and nutrition security 25–30,
72, 257; and the *Food Justice:
The Report of the Food and
Fairness Inquiry* 290–1; and
gender mainstreaming 146, 276;
and global food governance
80; and the invisibility of
structural causes of hunger
and malnutrition 346–50; and
multistakeholder initiatives
(MSIs) 171; and local food
systems 285, 300, 319; and
the inclusion of marginalized
groups 303; and public-private
partnerships (PPPs) 171; social
determinants of the conceptual
limitations in 344–6; and trade
policy 40; in the *Voluntary
Guidelines to Support the
Progressive Realization of the
Right to Adequate Food in
the Context of National Food
Security* 31, 32; and Women
in Informal Employment
Globalization and Organizing
(WIEGO) 305; *see also* civil
society participation, democracy,
duty bearers, human rights,
human rights principles, human
rights-based approach, rights
holders, state human rights
obligations
human rights characteristics 3, 4, 5, 25,
61; of inalienability 4, 5, 14, 59,
163, 165; of indivisibility 4, 5,
25, 80, 137, 341, 350, 368; of

interdependence 4, 5, 59, 137,
344; of interrelatedness 4, 341;
of universality *see* universality
Human Rights Compliant and
Sustainable Food Systems 296
human rights instruments 1, 6, 72, 72;
and intertwined subjectivities
of mother and child 164; and
invisibility of violences 350; as
social constructs 343–4; *see also*
conflicts of interest
human rights principles: of
accountability *see* accountability;
of empowerment *see*
empowerment; as foundation
for the progressive realization
of human rights 3, 5; of human
dignity *see* human dignity;
mainstreaming of 379, 382; of
non-discrimination *see* non-
discrimination; PANTHER
27–30, 38; of participation 23,
27, 28, 78, 276, 348, 390; and
policies against hunger and
malnutrition 394; of rule of law
27, 29–30, 31, 390; and social
movements 12; of transparency
23, 27, 28–9, 390; and the
*Voluntary Guidelines to Support
the Progressive Realization of
the Right to Adequate Food in
the Context of National Food
Security* 32; see also Eide, A.
human rights treaty bodies *see*
United Nations Committee on
Economic, Social and Cultural
Rights (CESCR), United Nations
Committee on the Elimination
of Discrimination against
Women (CEDAW Committee),
United Nations Committee on
the Rights of the Child (CRC
Committee)
human rights violations: and the
Committee on World Food
Security (CFS) 39; domestic
violence as 11, 273; and food
aid 64; under the human
rights-based framework 27;
and the Second International
Conference on Nutrition (ICN2)
82; and the indivisibility of
human rights 368–9; and the

need for a legal mechanism 6; and landgrabbing 285; and medicalized nutrition 88, 89; and the *Optional Protocol to the International Covenant on Economic, Social and Cultural Rights* 17, 40; social support against 114; within state parties' and civil society reports 145, 146; state human rights obligation to protect against 21; systematic 114–115; and the *Voluntary Guidelines to Support the Progressive Realization of the Right to Adequate Food in the Context of National Food Security* 32; *see also* micronutrient supplementation, recourse mechanisms, structural violence, violence against women, vulnerability

hunger and malnutrition: freedom from 25, 74, 77, 355; global problem of 1, 16, 34, 83; and international financial, trade and investment 357; invisibility of violence and 346–50; and medicalized nutrition 80; policy strategies to overcome 286, 344, 357–8, 363, 383, 385, 394; and Scaling Up Nutrition (SUN) 220; social movement involvement in 384; as a result of social processes 357; and state human rights obligations 394; status of women 165; as systematic human rights violations 115; and traditional feeding practices 348; as a form of violence 108; and women's public participation 138; inclusion of women's human rights into the human right to adequate food and nutrition conceptual framework 361–2, 364; *see also* accountability, child malnutrition, food and nutrition (in)security, gender-based discrimination, human rights, human rights-based framework, structural causes of hunger and malnutrition, *Universal Declaration on the Eradication of Hunger and Malnutrition*, violence against women

inalienability *see* human rights principles

India: global food crisis 296; solutions to moderate and mild chronic malnutrition in 216; social protection in 124–5; Third National Family Health Survey (NFHS-3) 135; violence against women in 119, 307; women's human right to adequate food and nutrition in 361–2; women's milk production in 185; *see also* child marriage, One Billion Rising

indigenous peoples: in the Civil Society Forum for Food Sovereignty 30; in the International Food Security & Nutrition Civil Society Mechanism (CSM) 35; cooperative 121–2; equality 164–5; food and nutrition security 129; lands 129; in Mexico 121–2; in Panama 308–9; state human rights obligations to respect customary rights to means of production 380; in Uganda 279–8; *see also Declaration on the Rights of Indigenous Peoples, General Comment 14 on the Right to the Highest Attainable Standard of Health, Global Strategic Framework for Food and Nutrition Security* (GSF), traditional practices, Women and the Right to Livelihoods

indivisibility *see* human rights principles

infant and young child feeding: in emergencies 201–3, 208–16; best practices of 163, 197, 217–19; commercial and social challenges to 188–96, 196–200; in regard to HIV/AIDS 162, 203–8; infant and young child feeding (IYCF) approach 217; and marketing 170, 196; right to full and complete information about best practices for 163, 188, 197;in *see also* chronic health crises, emergencies,

Global Strategy for Infant and Young Child Feeding (IYCF), *Infant and Young Child Feeding in Emergencies: Operational Guidance for Emergency Relief Staff and Programme Managers, International Code of Marketing of Breast-milk Substitutes,* Scaling Up Nutrition (SUN), United Nations Children's Fund (UNICEF)

Infant and Young Child Feeding in Emergencies: Operational Guidance for Emergency Relief Staff and Programme Managers 202, 203; *see also* chronic health crises, emergencies, infant and young child feeding

infant malnutrition *see* child malnutrition

infant mortality *see* child mortality

inheritance: and gender discrimination 387; of land 129, 267, 304; right to 61, 363; and women 111, 129, 133, 267, 304, 363

Innocenti Declaration on the Protection, Promotion and Support of Breastfeeding: 1990 edition 193, 199, 202; 2005 edition 163, 193, 199, 202; *see also* breastfeeding, breastmilk substitutes

Integrated Management of Childhood Illness (IMCI) strategy 217

Integrating the Rights of Women into the Human Rights Mechanisms of the United Nations 126

Inter-American Commission of Women (CIM) 10, 11

Inter-American Convention on the Nationality of Women 10; *see also* human rights instruments, Organization of American States (OAS)

Inter-American Convention on the Prevention, Punishment, and Eradication of Violence against Women (Convention of Belém do Pará) 11; *see also* human rights instruments, Organization of American States (OAS)

Inter Press Service (IPS) MDG3 Project 312–13; "Communicating for Change: Voice, Visibility and Impact for Gender Equality— Summary and Highlights" 312–13

interdependence *see* human rights principles

International Assessment of Agricultural Knowledge, Science and Technology for Development (IAASTD) 163, 261, 262–3, 285, 288, 291, 316; *see also* agroecology, civil society participation, democracy, food and nutrition (in)security, food production, food sovereignty, local food systems, sustainable livelihoods, urban agriculture, women in agriculture, World Bank

International Baby Food Action Network (IBFAN): 173; *see also* breastfeeding, breastmilk substitutes, children's human rights, complementary foods, corporate private sector accountability, corporate private sector marketing, conflicts of interest, infant and young child feeding, *International Code of Marketing of Breast-milk Substitutes*

International Code of Conduct on the Right to Adequate Food 19, 30, 31; *see also* civil society participation

International Code of Marketing of Breast-milk Substitutes: adoption 188–9; article 1 188–9; article 4 188; on breastfeeding 189; on breastfeeding in emergencies 202; in *General Comment 15 on the Right of the Child to the Enjoyment of the Highest Attainable Standard of Health* 192, 226; in *General Comment 16 on State Obligations Regarding the Impact of the Business Sector on Children's Rights* 170, 193, 226; under the *Global Strategy for Infant and Young Child Feeding* 173–4; in

HIV and Infant Feeding 2010: An Updated Framework for Priority Action 207–8; in the *Innocenti Declaration on Infant Young Child Feeding* (2005) 193; and Scaling Up Nutrition (SUN) 220, 221, 222; state implementation of 193, 225; and the World Health Assembly (WHA) resolutions 189; *see also* breastmilk substitutes, corporate private sector marketing, *Convention on the Rights of the Child* (CRC), De Schutter, O., Nestlé, non-governmental organizations (NGOs), state human rights obligations

International Conference on Nutrition (ICN): first conference (ICN) 82, 351; second conference (ICN2) 82, 88, 92

International Conference on Population and Development 16, 165

International Covenant on Civil and Political Rights (ICCPR) 4; article 1 16; article 6 16; *see also* human rights instruments

International Covenant on Economic, Social and Cultural Rights (ICESCR) 4, 19, 23, 30, 37; article 1 16; article 2 14–15, 22, 60; article 10 199; article 11 13, 60, 73, 145, 188, 200; articles 16–22 15; and the *Declaration on the Elimination of all Forms of Violence against Women* (DEVAW) 127; and *General Comment 14 on the Right to the Highest Attainable Standard of Health* 128; invisibility of women's right to adequate food and nutrition *see* structural isolation of women's human rights from the human right to adequate food and nutrition; as legally binding instrument 21, 59, 385; and national legislation 167; on maternity leave 199; on the mother-infant/young child dyad 181; and nutrition 73–5, 344; patronizing language 60; ratification 392; *see also* accountability, corporate private

sector obligations, economic, social, and cultural rights, *General Comment 12 on the Right to Adequate Food*, human rights instruments, nutrition, optional protocols, state human rights obligations, state extraterritorial human rights obligations, United Nations Committee on Economic, Social and Cultural Rights (CESCR)

International Covenant on the Elimination of All Forms of Racial Discrimination 5; *see also* human rights instruments

International Federation of Organic Agriculture Movement (IFOAM) 291, *see also* organic agriculture

International Food Policy Research Institute (IFPRI) 183, 267

International Food Security & Nutrition Civil Society Mechanism (CSM) 35, 39, 315; Coordination Committee 35; *see also* civil society participation, gender, gender perspective

International Fund for Agricultural Development (IFAD) 139, 266; *see also Gender in Agriculture Sourcebook*

International Monetary Fund (IMF) 18, 347, 393

International Planning Committee on Food Sovereignty (IPC) 30, 31; *see also* Civil Society Forum for Food Security, Civil Society Forum for Food Sovereignty, civil society participation, evolution of the human right to food and nutrition concept, food sovereignty

International Scientific Symposium Biodiversity and Sustainable Diets: United against Hunger 292

International Seminar Agrarian Reform and Gender 120

International Union of Nutritional Sciences (IUNS): 18th IUNS International Congress of Nutrition 259, 262; 19th IUNS International Congress of Nutrition 259–62; 20th

IUNS International Congress of
Nutrition 261–2; New Nutrition
Science project 259;"Paradigms
in Applied Nutrition" 261;
see also gender, HIV/AIDS,
human right to adequate food
and nutrition, Jonsson, U.,
medicalized nutrition
intertwined subjectivities (of women
and children) 71–2, 112,
165–6, 179–87; and best
feeding practices217–19; and
breastfeeding 164–6, 179–87;
concept 164, 180; under the
"Continuum of Care Fact
Sheet: Reproductive, Maternal,
Newborn and Child Health"
217; and corporate abuse 166;
framework for 179, 227–8;
under *General Comment on
the Right to Adequate Food
and Nutrition* 388;*ex utero*
183–7; *in utero* 182–3; policies
and programs for 227, 228;
see also breastfeeding, Baby-
Friendly Hospital Initiative
(BFHI), children's human
rights, corporate private sector
marketing, *Global Strategy for
Infant and Young Child Feeding*,
human rights instruments,
Integrated Management of
Childhood Illness (IMCI)
strategy, pregnancy, state human
rights obligations, structural
isolation of women's human
rights from the human right to
adequate food and nutrition,
women's human rights, women's
right to adequate food and
nutrition, women's reproductive
rights

Jonsson, U. 258, 261, 262, 365
Just Associates (JASS) 305; *see also*
MDG3 Fund: Investing in
Equality

Kurdish Men for Social Violence 308

La Via Campesina: on food sovereignty
18; Global Campaign for
Agrarian Reform (GCAR) 120
lactation *see* breastfeeding

The Lancet "Maternal and Child
(Under)Nutrition" series:
criticism of 269; focus on the
window of opportunity 219,
284; *see also* civil society, Scaling
Up Nutrition (SUN)
land: evictions 21, 83, 264, 297;
ownership 61, 265, 267, 294,
304; rights *see* land rights; use
295, 365
land rights: under *General Comment
12 on the Right to Adequate
Food* 61; and Landesa Center
for Women's Land Rights
312; in national action plans
(NAPs) 133; and the progressive
realization of the right to
adequate food and nutrition 79;
and rural agricultural livelihoods
294; and state human rights
obligation to respect 380;
and women 129, 265–6, 267;
and Women and the Right to
Livelihoods 315
Landesa Center for Women's Land
Rights 312
landgrabbing 285, 286, 294, 346–7,
348, 381, 386; *see also* corporate
private sector, food and nutrition
(in)security, human rights
violations, land, land rights
local food economies 187, 284, 285; *see
also* local food systems
local food systems: and agribusiness
296; and agroecology 262,
355; breastfeeding as 113, 185,
197, 349; under the Committee
on World Food Security (CFS)
80; and complementary foods
187;under the *Declaration on
the Elimination of All Forms of
Discrimination against Women*
(DEVAW) 64; definition 285;
challenges for development of
293–4; in emergency situations
208; and empowerment 276;
and food aid 214, 215, 284,
296, 319; and food justice
289–91;and food sovereignty
18, 78, 91, 113, 262, 284–8;
under *General Comment 16 on
State Obligations Regarding the
Impact of the Business Sector on
Children's Rights* 170; under the

Global Alliance for Improved Nutrition (GAIN) 174; under *General Recommendation 24 on Women and Health* 64; under the *Global Strategy for Infant and Young Child Feeding* 217; and global market approaches 33, 72, 73, 84, 112, 223, 229; and medicalized nutrition 269–70, 349, 387; and nutrition 72, 73, 75, 214–15, 359–60, 387; and organic agriculture 291; and power imbalances 82, 84; and public-private partnerships (PPPs) 270; and ready-to-use foods (RUFs) 210, 213–15, 229, 270, 347, 349, 358; rights-based food systems 288; and Scaling Up Nutrition (SUN) 220, 223, 224, 269; and the need for social protection programs 300–2; and state human rights obligations; and ultra-processed food 112; United Nations Children's Fund's (UNICEF) framework 364; under the Uruguay Round of the General Agreement on Tariffs and Trade (GATT) 347; and values webs 288; *see also* chronic crises, chronic malnutrition, civic agriculture, community food security, civil society participation, De Schutter, O., Equipo Mujeres en Acción (EMAS), food and nutrition (in)security, food policy councils (FPCs), human rights-based framework, *International Assessment of Agricultural Knowledge, Science and Technology for Development* (IAASTD), local food economies, local knowledge, nutraceuticals, nutrition education, people's and food sovereignty, People's and Food Sovereignty Matrix, rural livelihoods, sustainable livelihoods approach (SLA), "UNiTE to End Violence against Women", women, women in agriculture, women's empowerment
local knowledge: in emergencies 201–2; and the concept of

empowerment 276; and Equipo Mujeres en Acción Solidaria (EMAS) 310; under the *International Assessment of Agricultural Knowledge, Science and Technology for Development* (IAASTD) 263, 288; and medicalized nutrition 74, 213, 349; and participatory research methods 278; and inadequate solutions to hunger and malnutrition 344

Maastricht Guidelines on Violations of Economic, Social and Cultural Rights 22
Maastricht Principles on Extraterritorial Obligations of States in the Area of Economic, Social and Cultural Rights 167, 393; *see also* state extraterritorial human rights obligations
malnutrition: and biofortification 90; child *see* child malnutrition; chronic *see* chronic malnutrition; cyclical 136; double burden of 196, 360; fetal programming theory of 183; in industrialized states 287; infant *see* child malnutrition; intergenerational cycle 182, 196, 348, 351, 363; maternal 183, 365, 368; and maternal mortality 180; physical causes of 348; undereating 119; United Nations Children Fund's (UNICEF) framework of 258, 362, 364, 365; *see also* complementary foods, corporate private sector, Jonsson, U., medicalized nutrition, noncommunicable diseases (NCDs), overnutrition, ready-to-use foods (RUFs), undernutrition
Maria da Penha Law (law 11.340/2006) 11; *see also* domestic violence, *Inter-American Convention on the Prevention, Punishment, and Eradication of Violence against Women*
masculinity crisis 306; *see also* gender mainstreaming, Sonke Gender Justice Network

maternal mortality 179–80, 184; and adolescent pregnancy 361–2, 364; due to childbirth 165; *see also* child marriage, gender-based discrimination

maternity protection 199–200; *Maternity Protection Convention* (No. 183): 192, 200; *Maternity Protection Recommendation* (No. 191) 200; *Maternity Protection Resource Package— From Aspiration to Reality* 199–200

MDG3 Fund: Investing in Equality 303–5

medical nutrition 58, 86; and the corporate sector 72, 80, 85, 89–90; as inappropriate approach to combat malnutrition 88–9; Medical Nutrition International Industry (MNI) 87; research 82, 85, 86–7; therapy (MNT) 86–7; *see also* functional foods, medicalized nutrition, micronutrient supplementation, nutraceuticals, ready-to-use foods (RUFs)

medicalized nutrition 85–90, 254, 269, 349–50; marketing 65; as medicalized health interventions 58, 213, 347, 364; and research 258; and Scaling Up Nutrition (SUN) 220; as separate from food production 72, 81–3; shortcomings of 269–70, 283, 349–50, 358–9; and state human rights obligation to protect 387; *see also* breastfeeding, biofortification, food and nutrition (in)security, food production, functional foods, gender-based discrimination, local food systems, medical nutrition, micronutrient supplementation, nutraceuticals, nutrition, nutritionism, ready-to-use foods (RUFs), structural disconnects, structural isolation of women's human rights from the human right to adequate food and nutrition

Méndez, J. E. 108

MenEngage 307, 314–15; *see also* gender mainstreaming

Mercy Corps 139

micronutrient supplementation 72, 86, 88, 352; as short-term relief 136, 269–70; *see also* functional foods, medical nutrition, medicalized nutrition, nutraceuticals, nutrition, nutritionism, ready-to-use foods (RUFs)

Millennium Development Goals (MDGs) 219, 276, 307, 312; goal 1 (MDG1) 34, 263; *see also Gender in Agriculture Sourcebook*, Inter Press Service (IPS) MDG3 Project, MDG3 Fund: Investing in Equality, MenEngage

multistakeholder initiatives (MSIs) 168, 171

national action plans (NAPs) 130, 131, 146; on the correlation of abuse and malnutrition 132, 146; extra-national development policy 133; on food deprivation 131, 146; on forced sex for food and punishment related to food work expectations 132, 146; on gender violence and economic insecurity 132–3, 146; on HIV/ AIDS, gender-based violence, and food insecurity 133, 146; on isolated rural livelihoods 133; on the right to adequate food and nutrition 133; on women in prisons 133; *see also* civil society participation, civil society, gender-based discrimination, gender equality, nutrition education, rural women, violence against women

Nestlé: Bear Brand marketing 194–5; on Every Woman Every Child 177–8; food safety problems in baby foods 191; Healthy Kids Global Programme (HKP) 178, 179; Scaling Up Nutrition (SUN) member 221; and the United Nations (UN) 178, 179; and violation of the *International Code of Marketing of Breast-milk Substitutes* 177–9, 194–5; *see also* breastmilk substitutes, child mortality, corporate private sector accountability, corporate private sector marketing, *International Code of Marketing of Breast-milk Substitutes*, nutrition education

Nobel Women's Initiative 306, 313; *see also*

noncommunicable diseases (NCDs) 82, 89, 112, 174, 196, 258; and breastfeeding 225; and Global Alliance for Improved Nutrition (GAIN) 174; World Health Organization (WHO) *Resolution EB130.R7* 176–7; *see also* conflicts of interest, malnutrition, overnutrition, United Nations High-Level Meeting on Prevention and Control of Non-Communicable Diseases by the Conflicts of Interest Coalition, WHO Global NCD Action Plan 2013–2020

non-discrimination: and accountability mechanisms 390; within the *International Covenant on Economic, Social and Cultural Rights* (ICESCR); regarding women 137, 144; as a PANTHER principle 27, 28; within the People's and Food Sovereignty Matrix 383, 385; within public policies and programs 390; under the *Universal Declaration of Human Rights* (UDHR) 60; under the *Voluntary Guidelines to Support the Progressive Realization of the Right to Adequate Food in the Context of National Food Security* 79; *see also General Comment 20 on the Non-Discrimination in Economic, Social and Cultural Rights*; *see also* human rights principles

non-governmental organizations (NGOs): alternative reports by 168–9; on breastmilk substitutes 202; business interest non-governmental organizations (BINGOs) 176; on *Children's Rights and Business Principles* (CRBP) 173; and *International Code of Conduct on the Right to Adequate Food* 19, 31; and the Committee on World Food Security (CFS) 35; and gender mainstreaming 144; and *General Comment 16 on State Obligations Regarding the Impact of the Business Sector on Children's Rights* 170; on the Global Alliance for Improved Nutrition (GAIN) 174; and the human rights framework 26; and the International Food Security & Nutrition Civil Society Mechanism (CSM) 39; and the *Optional Protocol to the International Covenant on Economic, Social and Cultural Rights* 392; public interest non-governmental organizations (PINGOs) 176; within the public sector 168; under *Rules of Procedure of the Committee* 17; on Scaling Up Nutrition (SUN) 221; *see also* civil society, evolution of the human right to food and nutrition concept

Nussbaum, M. 66, 354

nutraceuticals 86–89; *see also* functional foods, medical nutrition, medicalized nutrition

nutrition: under the *Additional Protocol to the [1969] American Convention on Human Rights in the Area of Economic, Social and Cultural Rights* (*Protocol of San Salvador*) 77; and breastfeeding 65, 78, 81, 163, 184; of the child 75–6; and the Committee on World Food Security (CFS) 79, 80; under the *Convention on the Elimination of All Forms of Discrimination against Women* (CEDAW) 74–5, 343–4; under the *Convention on the Rights of the Child* (CRC) 74–6, 344; under *General Comment 12 on the Right to Adequate Food* 77; under *General Comment 14 on the Right to the Highest Attainable Standard of Health* 77; under the *Global Strategic Framework for Food Security and Nutrition* (GSF) 79–80; as a human right 74–7; within

the human right to food and
nutrition conceptual framework
358–60; under the *International
Covenant on Economic, Social
and Cultural Rights* (ICESCR)
73, 77, 344; knowledge 73,
187, 213, 218, 226; life cycle
approach to 183; medicalization
see medicalized nutrition;
New Nutrition Science project
259; paradigm 261–2; during
pregnancy 66, 71, 164, 182–3,
227–8, 346, 362–5; under the
*Voluntary Guidelines to Support
the Progressive Realization of
the Right to Adequate Food in
the Context of National Food
Security* 79; science 74, 259,
318; security *see* food and
nutrition (in)security; under the
*Universal Declaration of Human
Rights* (UDHR) 73; *see also*
agriculture, child malnutrition,
*Fourth Report on the World
Nutrition Situation: Nutrition
throughout the Life Cycle*,
human right to adequate food
and nutrition, malnutrition,
medical nutrition, medicalized
nutrition, nutrition education,
nutrition interventions,
overnutrition, *Sixth Report on
the World Nutrition Situation*,
undernutrition, window of
opportunity
nutrition education 75, 136, 202,
287, 349; intensive nutrition
education (INE) 218–19; and
local food systems 208, 217–18,
344, 349; as a tool for the
progressive realization of the
human right to adequate food
and nutrition 73; and traditional
practices 217–19, 228, 387;
within national action plans
(NAPs) 134; and Nestlé 178–9;
see also women's reproductive
rights
nutrition interventions 134, 136, 217,
225, 260;*see also* biofortification,
micronutrient supplementation,
medical nutrition, medicalized
nutrition, nutrition education

nutrition medicalization *see* medicalized
nutrition
nutrition transition 82, 384
nutritionism 89;*see also* medicalized
nutrition

obesity *see* overnutrition
One Billion Rising 307
open-ended intergovernmental working
groups: on a Legally Binding
Instrument on Transnational
Corporations and Other Business
Enterprises with Respect to
Human Rights 6; on a United
Nations Declaration on the
Rights of Peasants and Other
People Working in Rural Areas 6
optional protocols 17; to the
*Convention on the Elimination
of All Forms of Discrimination
against Women* (CEDAW) 8,
17, 126; to the *International
Covenant on Civil and Political
Rights* (ICCPR) 17; to the
*International Covenant on
Economic, Social and Cultural
Rights* (ICESCR) 17, 18, 40, 392
organic agriculture 255, 284, 291,
301, *see also* agroecology,
International Federation of
Organic Agriculture Movement
(IFOAM), local food systems
Organization of American States (OAS)
10, 91
overnutrition 81, 89, 196, 287, 360,
363, 384: and breastfeeding
184, 185, 225; as consequence
of food-related cultural violence
119–20; *leblouh* 119–20;
coexistence with undernutrition
81–2, 196; and functional foods
89; under Nestlé Healthy Kids
Global Programme (HKP) 178;
within the nutritional dimension
of the human right to food
and nutrition 360; *see also*
agribusiness, malnutrition
overweight *see* overnutrition
Oxfam 139, 195, 313

Papua New Guinea 125
paradigm: food systems 81; governance
81; micronutrient deficiency

81, 85; investment in nutrition 261–2, 269; production 81; sustainability 81

Paris Principles 391

participation *see* human rights principles; *see also* civil society participation

patriarchal structure 60, 61, 273, 348; under *General Comment 12 on the Right to Adequate Food* 61; under the *International Covenant on Economic, Social and Cultural Rights* (ICESCR) 60; within non-governmental organizations (NGOs) 142; in South Africa 273–4, 306; under the *Universal Declaration of Human Rights* (UDHR) 60; *see also* structural isolation of women's human rights from the human right to adequate food and nutrition, violence against women, vulnerability

peasants: agriculture 285; as a discriminated against group 356; as a food and nutrition insecure group 1; and food sovereignty 286; and land 264, 285; movements 296, 383; Open-ended Intergovernmental Working Group on a United Nations Declaration on the Rights of Peasants and Other People Working in Rural Areas 6; state human right obligations under a new general comment on the right to adequate food and nutrition regarding 386; women 120; see also PROMESA

People's Food Sovereignty Forum 35

People's and Food Sovereignty Matrix 365–6, 369, 372; adequate food 375–6; eating, self-determination, and well-being 377–9; incorporation of the nutritional dimension 358–60, 367; incorporation of women's human rights 361–5; layout 370–9; use within public policy 372, 384; importance of social movements 383–5; stable access to adequate food 373–4; specific state human rights

obligations *see* state human rights obligations; sustainable supply of adequate food 372; *see also* Food Security Matrix, food sovereignty framework, gender, human right to adequate food and nutrition conceptual framework

Policy on WHO Engagement with Global Health Partnerships and Hosting Arrangements 174

pregnancy: adolescent 361, 363–4; and a child's health and nutrition 164; and child marriage 135; death due to 165; in the *Convention on the Elimination of All Forms of Discrimination against Women* (CEDAW) 62, 74–5; under the *Convention on the Rights of the Child* (CRC) 74, 75, 76; under the *Declaration of the Rights of the Child* 165; of female prisoners 133; and gender discrimination 166; at the International Conference on Population and Development 165; as an isolated period of life span 164, 166, 227; and public participation 122; and the United Nations Children's Fund (UNICEF) 362; United Nations Committee on the Elimination of Discrimination against Women (CEDAW Committee) policy recommendations on 388; *see also* breastfeeding, child marriage, intertwined subjectivities, nutrition, structural isolation of women's human rights from the human right to adequate food and nutrition, vulnerability, women's reproductive rights

(obligation of) progressive realization 5, 64, 167, 169, 293, 367, 383; under the *International Covenant on Economic, Social and Cultural Rights* (ICESCR) 14–15, 21; and non-state actors 167; monitoring by United Nations treaty bodies 168; and the World Food Summit 19; *see also* human right to adequate food and nutrition

The Prohibition of Child Marriage Act 136

PROMESA (Programa de Ministerio y Educación Social) 308–9

Promoting Pro-Poor Growth: Social Protection 125

Proposal for an International Food Security and Nutrition Civil Society Mechanism for Relations with CFS 35, 36; *see also* Committee on World Food Security (CSM), International Food Security & Nutrition Civil Society Mechanism (CSM)

protect *see* state human rights obligations

Protocol of San Salvador see Additional Protocol to the [1969] American Convention on Human Rights in the Area of Economic, Social and Cultural Rights (Protocol of San Salvador)

public participation *see* civil society participation, women's public participation

public-private partnerships (PPPs) 2, 40, 168, 171, 219–21, 270; *see also* conflicts of interest, Global Alliance for Improved Nutrition (GAIN), Scaling Up Nutrition (SUN)

ready-to-use foods (RUFs) 86, 87, 210, 211, 212, 213, 215; ready-to-use-therapeutic foods 88, 210, 211, 212, 213 (RUTFs); ready-to-use supplementary foods (RUSFs) 88, 211, 213, 214, 270; Plumpy'nut 213; marketing of 214, 216, 220, 223; RUF-Nias 215–16; under the Uruguay Round of the General Agreement on Tariffs and Trade (GATT) 347; *see also Draft Guidelines for the Marketing of Ready to Use Supplemental Foods for Children*, chronic malnutrition, food and nutrition (in)security, local food systems, medicalized nutrition, micronutrient supplementation

recourse mechanisms 29, 31, 115–6, 146–7, 167, 350, 391–2; under the *International Covenant on Economic, Social and Cultural Rights* (ICESCR) 15; within Brazil's National School Feeding Program 302; under the state human rights obligation to protect 381; *see also* accountability, human rights, gender equality, optional protocols

Renewing the United Nations: A Programme for Reform 25

Resolution 7/14 on the Right to Food 165

respect (obligation) *see* state human rights obligations

rights holders: and accountability mechanisms 115, 380; within the *CFS Private Sector Modalities* 36; within the Civil Society Mechanism (CSM) 39; within the Committee on World Food Security (CFS) advisory group 34; under the *UN Statement of Common Understanding on Human Rights-Based Approaches to Development Cooperation and Programming* 27; and the corporate private sector 23; within food and nutrition policies 382; under *The Future We Want* 224; and gender mainstreaming 138, 146–7; under *General Comment 12 on the Right to Adequate Food* 22; within the *Global Strategic Framework for Food Security an Nutrition* (GSF) 38; within the human rights framework 3, 27, 40, 297; within the human rights principles 28–9; in regard to human rights universality 163; within the human rights-based approach 25–6, 116, 138, 350; and HIV/AIDS and emergency situations 162; under the *International Covenant on Economic, Social and Cultural Rights* (ICESCR) 60; and local governance 226; marginalized people as 303; and medicalized nutrition 85; and nutrition policy 65; within research 303; and the Food Security Matrix 23; under Scaling Up Nutrition (SUN) 223; under Scaling Up Nutrition (SUN) "Principles of Engagement" 224; under the *Universal Declaration of Human Rights* (UDHR) 60; under the *Voluntary Guidelines to Support the Progressive Realization of the Right to Adequate Food in the Context of National Food Security* 79; women as 59, 60, 166; *see also* civil society, civil society participation

Rio+20 United Nations Conference on Sustainable Development 275; *The Future We Want* 275; *see also* gender mainstreaming

Rome Declaration on World Food Security and World Food Summit Plan of Action 30, 37, 352; *see also* World Food Summit

Rome Statute of the International Criminal Court 317

rule of law *see* human rights principles

rural livelihoods: and alternative local food systems 294–5; and food and nutrition governance 283–4; and nutrition sensitive agriculture 260; and the sustainable livelihoods approach (SLA) 277; *see also* food and nutrition (in)security, food sovereignty, local food systems, national action plans (NAPs), peasants, rural women

rural women: in the agrarian sector 278, 298; in Bangladesh 141; and breastfeeding 197; and child marriage 361; under the *Convention on the Elimination of All Forms of Discrimination against Women* (CEDAW) 62–3; female-headed households 273; and gender discrimination 129; under national action plans (NAPs) 133; in South Africa 121, 279–80; and the United Nations Entity for Gender Equality and the Empowerment of Women (UN Women) 314; versus urban women's food insecurity 346; and Women in Law and Development in Africa (WiLDAF) 304; *see also General Recommendation on Rural Women*, Landesa Center for Women's Land Rights

Safe Preparation, Storage and Handling of Powdered Infant Formula Guidelines 190

Save the Children 166, 195, 315; *see also Children's Rights and Business Principles* (CRBP)

Scaling Up Nutrition (SUN) 219–27, 358; and breastfeeding 222, 224; on genetic modification 221; Principles of Engagement 224; "Private Sector Engagement Tool Kit" 220; and public health policy 174; as public-private-partnership (PPP) 219–220, 221; and ready-to-use supplementary foods (RUSFs) 270; *SUN Movement Progress Report: 2011–2012* 221; *SUN Movement: Revised Road Map* 222; *see also* "Announcement for a Consultation Process on Conflict of Interest in the Scaling Up Nutrition Movement," child malnutrition, civil society participation, conflicts of interest, *The Lancet* "Maternal and Child (Under)Nutrition" series, local food systems, window of opportunity

Screen State Action against Hunger! How to Use the Voluntary Guidelines on the Right to Food to Monitor Public Policies 32, 299; *see also* civil society participation

Second United Nations Conference on Human Settlements 16

Security Council Resolution 2106 (2013) [on Sexual Violence in Armed Conflict] 131

Sen, A. 74, 82, 83, 84, 257

Sixth Report on the World Nutrition Situation 183, 363–4, 365; agriculture and nutrition 260;

see also child marriage, food and nutrition (in)security

smallholder farmers: and access to resources 264; and agroecology 291; and the Civil Society Mechanism (CSM) 35; under *The Cordoba Declaration on the Right to Food and the Governance of the Global Food and Agricultural Systems* 263; as entrepreneurs 39; and food sovereignty 286; and the *Global Strategic Framework for Food Security and Nutrition* 38, 80; within the *International Assessment of Agricultural Knowledge, Science and Technology for Development* (IAASTD) 316; as livelihood strategy 279; and Brazil's National School Feeding Program 301; and organic farming 291; in South Africa 294, 295; and sustainable livelihoods 279, 291; women 265, 269, 291; and Women in Informal Employment Globalization and Organizing (WIEGO) 305

small-scale farmers 83, 301; *see also* smallholder farmers, peasants

Sonke Gender Justice Network 307, 314

South Africa: female-headed households 272–4; 18th IUNS International Congress of Nutrition 259; land reform policies 281–2; livelihoods 279–80, 293–5; national action plans (NAPs) 133; smallholder farming 294–5, 302–3; social protection 302–3; in *Updated Study on the Right to Food* 25; women and public participation 121; microfinance 141; violence against women 273–4, 306; women in agriculture 265, 267; *see also* agrarian reform, rural women, Sonke Gender Justice Network

special rapporteur on the right to food 24; Office of the High Commission for Human Rights (OHCHR) resolution 2000/10

24; *see also* De Schutter, O., Ziegler, J.

state: accountability *see* state accountability; power 26, 33, 38; as duty-bearer 350, 363; and the corporate private sector 347, 357; obligations *see* state human rights obligations; *see also* duty bearers

state accountability: and civil society reports 168–9; in the human rights-based framework 26, 27; under the *International Covenant on Economic, Social and Cultural Rights* (ICESCR) 60; through international treaties 169; monitoring by the United Nations (UN) treaty bodies 168; for progressive realization of the human right to adequate food and nutrition 167; as state human rights obligation 89, 115; through state reports 168; United Nations Committee on Economic, Social and Cultural Rights (CESCR) on 168; United Nations Committee on the Elimination of Discrimination against Women (CEDAW Committee) on 168; United Nations Committee on the Rights of the Child (CRC Committee) on 168; under the *Voluntary Guidelines to Support the Progressive Realization of the Right to Adequate Food in the Context of National Food Security* 31; *see also* accountability, *General Comment 12 on the Right to Adequate Food*

state extraterritorial human rights obligations (ETOs) 167, 367, 376, 384, 387, 393; within the evolution of human rights 40; under *General Comment 12 on the Right to Adequate Food* 22; and the implementation of the human right to adequate food and nutrition conceptual framework 395; under the *International Covenant on Economic, Social and Cultural*

Rights (ICESCR) 14, 22; under the *Maastricht Principles on Extraterritorial Obligations of States in the Area of Economic, Social and Cultural Rights* 167, 393; and non-state actors 167, 382, 393; regulations and accountability mechanisms of 393; *see also* agroecology, breastmilk substitutes, corporate private sector marketing, food sovereignty

The State of Food and Agriculture 2010–11—Women in Agriculture: Closing the Gender Gap for Development 316: on access to resources 268, 269; on female-headed households 272; on gender equality 269, 316; on market access 268; on technology dissemination 268; on women's empowerment 269; on women and food security 269, 316; on women's participation in agriculture 265

state human rights obligations 3, 20–3, 25, 31–2, 64–5; as opposed to charity 3, 4, 26, 73, 80; to empower civil society 89, 115, 226; under Committee on World Food Security (CFS) 92; regarding community and peasant territories 386; under the *Convention on the Elimination of All Forms of Discrimination against Women* (CEDAW) 62, 71, 126; under the *Convention on the Rights of the Child* (CRC) 63, 75, 76, 181; and democratic dialogue 167; in emergencies 202; extraterritorial *see* state extraterritorial human rights obligations; regarding freedom from hunger 74, 200; to fulfill (facilitate) 22, 65, 381–2; to fulfill (provide) 22, 65, 381–3; and gender mainstreaming 146; general obligations 383; under *General Recommendation 24 on Women and Health*, 63; indivisibility of 345, 367, 369; under *Innocenti Declaration on Infant Young Child*

Feeding (2005) 193; under the *International Code of Marketing of Breast-milk Substitutes* 202, 229; under the *International Covenant on Economic, Social and Cultural Rights* (ICESCR) 63, 77, 166, 200; under *General Comment 12 on the Right to Adequate Food* 77; under *General Comment 14 on the Right to the Highest Attainable Standard of Health* 78, 129; under *General Comment 15 on the Right of the Child to the Enjoyment of the Highest Attainable Standard of Health* 191–2; under *General Comment 16 on State Obligations Regarding the Impact of the Business Sector on Children's Rights* 193; under *Global Strategic Framework for Food Security and Nutrition* (GFS) 80–79–80; and national action plans (NAPs) 146; and non-state actor influence 168, 347; to regulate non-state actors 181, 191, 228–9, 360, 380–1, 386, regarding pregnancy and breastfeeding 63, 228; of progressive realization of the human right to adequate food and nutrition 167; to protect 21, 65, 380–1, 386; to protect human rights defenders 24, 392; to regulate ready-to-use foods (RUFs) use226, 228–9; to provide recourse and accountability mechanisms 350, 380, 386; to respect 21, 64, 376–7; and social protection programs 143, 346; and structural violence 115–16; and trade 347; of transparency 167; and women's human rights 137; *see also* breastmilk substitutes, civil and political rights, democracy, Food Security Matrix, human right to adequate food and nutrition conceptual framework, human rights-based framework, People's and Food Sovereignty Matrix

structural adjustment policies 347; *see also* International Monetary Fund (IMF), World Bank
structural causes of hunger and malnutrition 344, 394: corporate private sector marketing 348; de jure/facto discrimination 349; dealing with 91; along the food chain 351–2; inequality 394; invisibility of violence 346–50, 357, 384; structural violence against women and girls 348–9, 361; and medicalized nutrition 88, 89, 349–50; overcoming 384; state obligation to combat 387, 394; *see also* De Schutter, O., *Global Strategic Framework for Food Security and Nutrition* (GSF), human right to adequate food and nutrition conceptual framework, landgrabbing
structural disconnects *see* food production, medicalized nutrition, structural isolation of women's human rights from the human right to adequate food and nutrition
structural isolation of women's human rights from the human right to adequate food and nutrition 58–61; under the *Convention on the Elimination of All Forms of Discrimination against Women* (CEDAW) 62–3, 343–44; under *General Comment 12 on the Right to Adequate Food* 61, 63, 354; under the *International Covenant on Economic, Social and Cultural Rights* (ICESCR) 59–61, 63, 344; and state accountability 59, 60; under the *Universal Declaration of Human Rights* UDHR 59–61; *see also* intertwined subjectivities, women's human rights, women's right to adequate food and nutrition
structural violence 113–15; adolescent pregnancy as 387; de jure/facto discrimination as 349; domestic violence as 116–17, 118, 140, 348, 381; withholding food as 119, 131–2; in food

and nutrition policy 91, 143, 144; under *General Comment on the Right to Adequate Food and Nutrition* 387; using the human right to adequate food and nutrition to prevent 362, 367; as a human rights violation 114–19, 128, 129; and maternal mortality 180; measuring of 130; and the role of motherhood 348–9, 364; and paradigm shift 144; roots of 143–4; and the United Nations Children's Fund (UNICEF) 362; *see also* child marriage; domestic violence, economic, social, and cultural rights, gender-based discrimination, gender mainstreaming, violence against women
Supplement to the Handbook for Legislation on Violence against Women: Harmful Practices against Women 130
supplementary food *see* micronutrient supplementation
sustainable agriculture 263, 289; *see also International Assessment of Agricultural Knowledge, Science and Technology for Development* (IAASTD)
sustainable diets 292–3; *see also* De Schutter, O., food and nutrition (in)security, gender equality
sustainable livelihoods 254, 355–6, 387: approach *see* sustainable livelihoods approach (SLA); within a food sovereignty framework 365–6, 367; *see also* agroecology, democracy, food sovereignty, *International Assessment of Agricultural Knowledge, Science and Technology for Development* (IAASTD)
sustainable livelihoods approach (SLA): criticisms of 278; development 277–9; within the *Gender in Agriculture Sourcebook* 312; and local food systems 319, 355; and multiple livelihood strategies 279; *see also* rural livelihoods, sustainable livelihoods

Third World Conference on Women 138

traditional practices: and agribusiness 85; breastfeeding as 72, 113, 188, 197–8, 215, 224, 381; and community food security 287; of discrimination 72, 144; food as 269, 354, 359; current food production model versus 347–8; in food security policy 80; and food sovereignty 90, 91; within a food systems approach 129; and food taboos 146, 180; in *General Comment 14 on the Right to the Highest Attainable Standard of Health* 77–78; in *General Comment 16 on State Obligations Regarding the Impact of the Business Sector on Children's Rights* 61; and human rights 136–7; and the human right to adequate food and nutrition 162–3, 355–6; of indigenous peoples 78–9, 91, 129; and medicalized nutrition 90, 359; and microfinance 141; and pregnancy and breastfeeding 164, 180, 183, 187, 188, 196–200, 226; and ready-to-use foods (RUFs) 214, 216, 270, 358; under state human rights obligation to respect 380; under state human rights obligation to fulfill (facilitate) 382; in the *Voluntary Guidelines to Support the Progressive Realization of the Right to Adequate Food in the Context of National Food Security* 79; and ultra-processed food 112; and violence against women 61, 114, 116, 142, 144, 348; and women's reproductive rights 136; *see also* infant and young child feeding, child marriage, chronic health crises, *leblouh*, nutrition education, patriarchal structure, women's participation

transnational corporations (TNCs) *see* corporate private sector

transparency *see* human rights principles undernutrition: and food and nutrition crises 209;

due to food-related cultural violence 119–20; and the green revolution 83; in infants 194, 202; intergenerational cycle of 196; and policy 82; as a presentation of hunger 384; prevention of 213; and ready-to-use foods (RUFs) 223; and Scaling Up Nutrition (SUN) 219; and the World Food Conference 81; *see also The Lancet*" Maternal and Child (Under) Nutrition" series, malnutrition

"UNiTE to End Violence against Women" 130, 316–17

United Nations Administrative Committee on Co-ordination/ Sub-Committee on Nutrition (ACC/SCN) 81, 183

United Nations Children's Fund (UNICEF): on the right to nutrition 75; [India's] Third National Family Health Survey (NFHS-3) 135; Meeting on Infant and Young Child Feeding 188; on the adoption and implementation of the 2010 WHO *Guidelines on HIV and Infant Feeding* in the African setting 205; integrated infant and young child feeding (IYCF) approach 217; malnutrition framework 258, 364–5; exclusion of women's human rights dimension from the human right to adequate food and nutrition 362–3, 354; *see also* child marriage, *Children's Rights and Business Principles* (CRBP), Baby-Friendly Hospital Initiative (BFHI), Eide, A., gender equality, *Global Strategy for Infant and Young Child Feeding, Innocenti Declaration on the Protection, Promotion and Support of Breastfeeding,* Integrated Management of Childhood Illness (IMCI) strategy, Jonsson, U., local food systems, Scaling Up Nutrition (SUN)

United Nations Commission on Human Rights (CHR) 18, 19, 126, 172

United Nations Commission on the
Status of Women (CSW) 7, 9,
126, 389
United Nations Committee on
Economic, Social and Cultural
Rights (CESCR): establishment
of 17; regarding a *General
Comment on the Right to
Adequate Food and Nutrition*
385–8; on state party periodic
reports 17, 92, 145, 168, 388;
Rules of Procedure 17; *see
also* civil society participation,
gender mainstreaming, general
comments, *International
Covenant on Economic, Social
and Cultural Rights* (ICESCR),
women's human right to
adequate food and nutrition
United Nations Committee on the
Elimination of Discrimination
against Women (CEDAW
Committee): development of
*General Recommendation 24
on Women and Health* 63,
126; development of *General
Recommendation 25 on
Temporary Special Measures*
71; regarding a *General
Recommendation on the Human
Right to Adequate Food and
Nutrition and Women* 91; on
state party periodic reports
168; need to address violence
against women 388; *see also
Convention on the Elimination
of All Forms of Discrimination
against Women* (CEDAW),
*General Recommendation
on Rural Women*, general
recommendations, women's
human rights
United Nations Committee on the
Rights of the Child (CRC
Committee): on *General
Comment 16 on State
Obligations Regarding the
Impact of the Business Sector
on Children's Rights* 169–70,
192; recommendation for a new
general comment 388; on state
party periodic reports 92, 168;
see also breastfeeding, children's

human rights, *Convention on the
Rights of the Child* (CRC), state
accountability
United Nations Conference on
Environment and Development
16, 274–7
United Nations Department of
Economic and Social Affairs (UN
DESA) 116; *see also* World's
Women reports
United Nations Development Fund for
Women (UNIFEM) 313, 315
United Nations Development Group 25
United Nations Development
Programme (UNDP) 25, 263,
315, 317
United Nations Economic and Social
Council (ECOSOC) 311
United Nations Educational, Scientific
and Cultural Organization
(UNESCO) 263
United Nations Entity for Gender
Equality and the Empowerment
of Women (UN Women) 109,
131, 313–14, 317, 389; *World
Survey on the Role of Women
in Development 2014: Gender
Equality and Sustainable
Development* 314
United Nations Environment
Programme (UNEP) 263
United Nations Food and Agriculture
Organization (FAO) 33, 139,
292; on feeding the world
population 82–3, 262; on
powdered infant formula (PIF)
190; publications of 31, 37,
59, 79, 82–3, 263, 311; *see
also* Committee on World
Food Security (CFS), *Gender
in Agriculture Sourcebook*,
International Conference
on Nutrition (ICN), *Safe
Preparation, Storage and
Handling of Powdered Infant
Formula Guidelines, The
State of Food and Agriculture
2010–11: Women in Agriculture:
Closing the Gender Gap for
Development, Voluntary
Guidelines on the Responsible
Governance of Tenure of
Land, Fisheries and Forests in*

the Context of National Food
Security, Voluntary Guidelines
to Support the Progressive
Realization of the Right to
Adequate Food in the Context of
National Food Security, World
Food Conference, World Food
Summit, World Food Summit:
five years later
United Nations Fourth World Conference
for Women in Beijing 2
United Nations General Assembly 25,
130, 131, 169
United Nations General Assembly
Special Session on Children 174
United Nations Global Compact
172–3, 174; see also Children's
Rights and Business Principles
(CRBP), corporate private sector
accountability
United Nations High-Level Meeting
on Prevention and Control of
Non-Communicable Diseases see
Conflicts of Interest Coalition
United Nations High-Level Task Force
(HLTF) on the Global Food
Security Crisis 33, 34
United Nations Human Rights Council
(HRC) 6, 17, 24, 165, 169, 172,
187
United Nations Joint Inspection Unit
(JIU) 172–3
United Nations Millennium Declaration
25; see also vulnerability
United Nations Office of the High
Commissioner for Human Rights
(OHCHR) 317, 352, 389
United Nations Security Council 131
United Nations Standing Committee on
Nutrition (SCN) 215, 260, 351,
352; see also Draft Guidelines
for the Marketing of Ready to
Use Supplemental Foods for
Children, Sixth Report on the
World Nutrition Situation
United Nations Statement of Common
Understanding on Human
Rights-Based Approaches to
Development Cooperation and
Programming 25
United Nations Sub-Commission on
the Promotion and Protection of
Human Rights 16, 171, 351

United States: on breastfeeding 197–8;
and the global food crisis
296; and the invisibility of
marginalized women 123–4; and
Kurdish Men for Social Violence
308; market driven ideology of
74; and undereating 119; and
national action plans (NAPs)
132, 133; on powdered infant
formula (PIF) 190–1; and Scaling
Up Nutrition (SUN) 358; and
value webs 288; see also Equal
Rights Amendment (ERA)
Universal Declaration on the
Eradication of Hunger and
Malnutrition 13–14; see also
food production
Universal Declaration of Human
Rights (UDHR) 4, 16, 27, 59;
article 25 13, 60; invisibility of
women see structural isolation
of women's human rights from
the human right to adequate
food and nutrition; and nutrition
see nutrition; see also civil and
political rights, economic, social,
and cultural rights, evolution
of the human right to adequate
food and nutrition concept, food
and nutrition (in)security, human
rights principles
universality: under the *Additional*
Protocol to the [1969] American
Convention on Human Rights
in the Area of Economic, Social
and Cultural Rights (Protocol
of San Salvador) 77; under the
Convention on the Elimination
of All Forms of Discrimination
against Women (CEDAW) 62,
74; under the *Convention on the*
Rights of the Child (CRC) 74;
and enjoyment by discriminated
against groups 356; under
General Comment 12 on the
Right to Adequate Food 61; as
a human rights characteristic
5; and the human rights-based
framework 26; and the human
rights-based approach 25;
evolution of 5, 9, 59; as part
of international law 3; and the
progressive realization of the

human right to adequate food 40; and the identification as all rights holders as equal 163; under the *Universal Declaration of Human Rights* (UDHR) 4; *see also* human rights characteristics
urban agriculture 261, 383
Uruguay Round of the General Agreement on Tariffs and Trade (GATT) 18, 81, 347

Vienna Convention on the Law of Treaties 3
violence against women 11; and access to human rights 111; and child care 165; under the *Convention on the Elimination of All Forms of Discrimination against Women* (CEDAW) 126, 145–6; cultural violence 113, 348; under the *Declaration on the Elimination of Violence against Women* (DEVAW) 127, 128, 146; development organizations and violence against women initiatives 142–3; direct violence 113; and economic insecurity 132–3; female genital mutilation (FGM) 180, 348; and food aid 64, 133, 140, 143, 201, 229; food violences 111; and food and nutrition (in)security 72, 124, 131, 134, 139, 142–3, 145; and food-based work 111–2, 117, 132; food-related 109, 111–13, 130, 133, 119–20; forced sex for food 132; as part of gender discrimination 109–13; and gender mainstreaming 131, 137, 138–44, 146–7; under *General Comment 12 on the Right to Adequate Food* 126; under *General Comment 14 on the Right to the Highest Attainable Standard of Health* 128–9; under *General Recommendation 24 on Women and Health* 126, 127–8; and the human right to adequate food and nutrition 108, 109, 111, 113–20, 129, 131; as human rights violation 125–30, 134, 146; as industry-based food violence 112; within the International Criminal Court (ICC) 317; international institutional recognition of 125–30; intersectionality 111; intimate partner violence (IPV) 112, 135; invisibility 122–4; law enforcement against 130; male initiatives against 307–8; and maternal mortality 180; national institutional recognition of 130–7; in public policy 127, 131, 144; recommendations against 145–7; in research and policy 122–4, 145; within the *Sixth Report on the World Nutrition Situation* 363–4; as social construct 308; in social protection programs 124–5; under the state human rights obligation to fulfill (facilitate) 382; under the state human rights obligation to protect 381; as structural cause of hunger and malnutrition 348, 364; symbolic violence 115, 117–18; rape 131, 307; unrecognized 140; *see also* Bangladesh, *Beijing Declaration and Platform for Action*, Brazil, Center for Women's Global Leadership (CWGL), child marriage, *Convention on the Elimination of All Forms of Discrimination against Women* (CEDAW), *Declaration on the Elimination of All Forms of Violence against Women* (DEVAW), domestic violence, Equipo Mujeres en Acción Solidaria (EMAS), *Handbook for Legislation on Violence against Women*, *Promoting Pro-Poor Growth: Social Protection*, India, *Inter-American Convention on the Prevention, Punishment, and Eradication of Violence against Women (Convention of Belém do Pará)*, Inter Press Service (IPS) MDG3 Project, Just Associates (JASS), Kurdish Men for Social Violence, masculinity crisis, MenEngage, national action plans (NAPs), Nobel Women's Initiative, One Billion

Rising, PROMESA, *Security Council Resolution 2106 (2013) [on Sexual Violence in Armed Conflict]*, Sonke Gender Justice Network, South Africa, structural causes of hunger and malnutrition, *Supplement to the Handbook for Legislation on Violence against Women: Harmful Practices against Women*, structural violence, traditional practices, "UNiTE to End Violence against Women," United Nations Committee on the Elimination of All Forms of Discrimination against Women (CEDAW Committee), women's public participation, Women's Caucus for Gender Justice, World Health Organization (WHO)

Voluntary Guidelines on the Responsible Governance of Tenure of Land, Fisheries and Forests in the Context of National Food Security 37; *see also* land, land rights, vulnerability

Voluntary Guidelines to Support the Progressive Realization of the Right to Adequate Food in the Context of National Food Security: on food adequacy 354; and the Committee on World Food Security (CFS) 35; development of 30–2; state party periodic reporting 145; voluntary nature 31; *see also* accountability, civil society, civil society participation, democracy, evolution of the human right to adequate food and nutrition concept, food aid, food and nutrition (in)security, gender, *Global Strategic Framework for Food Security and Nutrition Security* (GSF), human right to adequate food and nutrition, human right to adequate food and nutrition conceptual framework, human rights-based framework, nutrition, vulnerability, Ziegler, J.

vulnerability: under the *Convention on the Elimination of All Forms of Discrimination against Women* (CEDAW) 66, 71; under the *Convention on the Rights of the Child* (CRC) 66; and food and nutrition (in)security 65, 91, 276; under *General Comment 12 on the Right to Adequate Food* 67–9; under *General Comment 14 on the Right to the Highest Attainable Standard of Health* 67–9; and the human rights-based framework 65; and human rights violations 65, 66, 68–72, 115; under the *International Covenant on Economic, Social and Cultural Rights* (ICESCR) 66; language 65–6, 72; regarding pregnancy, breastfeeding and reproduction 66, 71–2; and structural violence 115–16; under the *United Nations Millennium Declaration* 66; under the *Voluntary Guidelines to Support the Progressive Realization of the Right to Adequate Food in the Context of National Food Security* 66; and women's autonomy 64, 65, 66, 72; see also gender-based discrimination, patriarchal structure, violence against women

window of opportunity 219, 225
women: in agriculture *see* women in agriculture; autonomy *see* women's autonomy; as caregivers 164; and food and nutrition (in)security *see* women's food and nutrition (in)security; discrimination *see* gender-based discrimination; empowerment *see* women's empowerment; human rights *see* women's human rights; informal employment 304–5; key to food security 1, 111, 117, 264; and local food systems 66, 76, 113; participation *see* women's participation; in prisons 133; reproductive rights *see* women's reproductive rights;

right to adequate food and nutrition *see* women's human right to adequate food and nutrition; rural *see* rural women; unpaid care 300–1; urban 11, 63, 64, 114, 141, 196, 273; *see also* violence against women

women in agriculture: and access to resources 265, 266, 267, 268, 304; additional responsibilities of 265, 269; as farm labor 265, 280–1; gender gap in 264–9; and head of the household 266; importance of 269, 275; market access 266; and the effect of migration 265, 166; and agricultural education 167–8; and technology dissemination 267; women's empowerment in agriculture index (WEAI) 268; *see also* food production, *Gender in Agriculture Sourcebook*, HIV/AIDS, Inter Press Service (IPS) MDG3 Project, *International Assessment of Agricultural Knowledge, Science and Technology for Development* (IAASTD), Landesa Center for Women's Land Rights, rural women, South Africa, *The State of Food and Agriculture 2010–11—Women in Agriculture: Closing the Gender Gap for Development*, Women in Law and Development in Africa (WiLDAF)

women in development (WID) 275

Women in Informal Employment Globalization and Organizing (WIEGO) 304–5; *see also* MDG3 Fund: Investing in Equality

Women in Law and Development in Africa (WiLDAF) 304, 317–18; *see also* MDG3 Fund: Investing in Equality

Women and the Right to Livelihoods 315

women's autonomy: and cash transfer programs 125; and connection to society 59; and decisions about food 293; and food and nutrition security policies 387;

under *General Recommendation 24 on Women and Health* 64; in the household 74, 274; and the human right to adequate food and nutrition 136, 355, 367; in marriage decisions 294; and medicalized nutrition 58; and microfinance programs 140–1; in the People's and Food Sovereignty Matrix 377; regarding pregnancy and breastfeeding 71; and separation from own human nature 345; under the state human rights obligation to protect 381; under the state human rights obligation to respect 380; struggle for 280–1; *see also* breastfeeding, child marriage, Food and Fairness Inquiry, infant and child nutrition, intertwined subjectivities, women's empowerment, women's human rights, women's reproductive rights

Women's Caucus for Gender Justice 317

women's empowerment 304–5: concept 138; under the *Declaration of Commitment on HIV/AIDS* 283; economic 141, 268; and food and nutrition (in)security 139, 267, 268, 274; and gender mainstreaming 138–9; within the governance of food systems 303; through human rights 287, 344; and men's empowerment 276–7; as opposed to market-based approaches 223; and singlehood 273; social protection 124–5; and structural violence 137; sustainable livelihoods 280; integration with the framework 280; under United Nations Children's Fund (UNICEF) 363; *see also* Center for Women's Global Leadership (CWGL), empowerment, gender mainstreaming, human rights-based approach, HIV/AIDS, Inter Press Service (IPS) MDG3 Project, Just Associates (JASS), Kurdish Men for Social Violence,

PROMESA, United Nations Entity for Gender Equality and the Empowerment of Women (UN Women), women in agriculture, Women in Informal Employment: Globalizing and Organizing (WIEGO), Women in Law and Development in Africa (WiLDAF), World Bank

women's food and nutrition security: through agroecology 293; challenges to 61, 201, 303; within food policy councils (FPCs) 289; and gender mainstreaming 134, 137, 139, 145; and gender-biased policies 387; and *General Recommendation 24 on Women and Health* 64; reduced to motherhood 344, 348–9; and human rights 341, 362; status 2, 58, 108, 143, 303, 319; and structural violence 124, 131, 144; *see also Convention on the Elimination of All Forms of Violence against Women* (CEDAW), *Declaration on the Elimination of Violence against Women* (DEVAW), *Global Strategic Framework for Food Security and Nutrition* (GSF)

women's human rights 2, 39, 62; within the Committee on World Food Security (CFS) 92; within the human right to adequate food and nutrition conceptual framework 366, 167–8; to dignity 136, 144; access to 164–5; under *The Future We Want* 275; to health 63, 128, 179; institutional framework for realizing 6–12; throughout the life span 72, 90, 134, 162, 225, 365; lobbying for 9–10; within public policy 362, 363, 364; under Scaling Up Nutrition (SUN) 223; to self-determination 90, 91, 92, 144, 227; sexual 179, 181; *see also* Association for Women's Rights in Development (AWID), *Convention on the Elimination of All Forms of Violence against*

Women (CEDAW), *Convention on the Rights of the Child* (CRC), *Declaration on the Elimination of Violence against Women* (DEVAW), Eide, A., *Global Strategic Framework for Food Security and Nutrition* (GSF), human right to adequate food and nutrition conceptual framework, *Inter-American Convention on the Prevention, Punishment, and Eradication of Violence against Women*, Nobel Women's Initiative, state human right obligations, structural isolation of women's human rights from the human right to adequate food and nutrition United Nations Entity for Gender Equality and the Empowerment of Women (UN Women), women in agriculture, Women in Law and Development in Africa (WiLDAF), women's human right to adequate food and nutrition

women's human right to adequate food and nutrition: and best feeding practices 90; and child marriage 166; of child-age mothers 137; under the *Convention on the Elimination of All Forms of Discrimination against Women* (CEDAW) 59, 91; holistic approach to 80, 91, 129, 354, 366; in the context of reproduction 71–2; inalienable from other human rights 163; interrelatedness to other human rights 134, 137, 145, 227; instrumentalization and patronization of 64–72; throughout the life span 64, 65, 72, 164, 227, 346, 363; and motherhood 164, 179, 227; obstacles to 129, 361; realization of 2, 109; and the right to (breast)feed 162–3, 164, 228; rural versus urban 346; 59–60; United Nations Committee on Economic, Social and Cultural Rights (CESCR) on 90, 91, 145; United Nations Committee on the Rights of the Child (CRC Committee) on 90; *see also* food sovereignty framework, gender mainstreaming, human right to adequate food and nutrition, intertwined subjectivities, People's and Food Sovereignty Matrix, structural isolation of women's human rights from the human right to adequate food and nutrition, women's autonomy, women's empowerment, women's public participation

women's public participation: cultural and social barriers 120, 122, 123–4, 139, 147, 320; within food and nutrition security strategies 108, 113, 142, 144, 254–5; under *General Comment on the Right to Adequate Food and Nutrition* 388; under *General Comment 14 on the Right to the Highest Attainable Standard of Health* 128–9;and gender mainstreaming 138; and the *Handbook for Legislation on Violence against Women* 130; through microfinance programs 140–1; in nutrition and food systems 387; in public policy 111, 126, 129, 138, 318, 388; in social protection programs 300–2; strengthening women as actors 303–6; and the *Supplement to the Handbook for Legislation on Violence against Women: Harmful Practices against Women* 130; within sustainable livelihoods approaches (SLA) 279–80; and violence against women 66, 120–5, 108–9, 117–18, 129, 138–40, 348; within the *Voluntary Guidelines to Support the Progressive Realization of the Right to Adequate Food in the Context of National Food Security* 299; regarding women's human right to adequate food and nutrition 120, 128; *see also* chronic crises, Fourth World Conference on Women, Inter Press Service (IPS) MDG3

Project, *The State of Food and Agriculture 2010-11—Women in Agriculture: Closing the Gender Gap for Development*, structural isolation of women's human rights from the human right to adequate food and nutrition, violence against women and public participation, Women in Law and Development in Africa (WiLDAF)

women's reproductive rights: breastfeeding best framed as 181; in *The Future We Want* 275; at the International Conference on Population and Development 165; over the life span 225, 346, 365; in regard to Nestlé's nutrition education 178; promotion of 367; restriction of 346; state human rights obligation to protect 137; and structural violence 361; violation as structural cause of hunger and malnutrition 364; *see also* traditional practices

Working Group on the Issue of Discrimination against Women in Law and in Practice (WG DAW) 389

World Alliance for Breastfeeding Action (WABA) 181

World Bank: agriculture as a business 316, 393; within the Committee on World Food Security (CFS) 34; on empowerment and gender equality 276; and the *International Assessment of Agricultural Knowledge, Science and Technology for Development* (IAASTD) 263; on noncommunicable diseases (NCD) 176; on the nutrition paradigm 261; on Scaling Up Nutrition (SUN) 219; on structural adjustment 18, 347; *see also Gender in Agriculture Sourcebook*

World Conference on Human Rights 5, 11, 16, 126, 130, 351; Preparatory Committee 17

World Food Conference (13–14, 81, 257, 315

World Food Program (WFP) 201, 219

World Food Summit 16; and the *International Code of Conduct on the Right to Adequate Food* 31; on food sovereignty 286; on *General Comment 12 on the Right to Adequate Food* 169; on the human right to adequate food concept 19, 20, 352–3; Plan of Action *see Rome Declaration on World Food Security and World Food Summit Plan of Action*; on a set of voluntary guidelines for right to adequate food realization 30; *see also* evolution of the human right to adequate food and nutrition concept

World Food Summit: five years later 19, 31, 257

World Health Assembly (WHA) resolutions 112, 170, 173–4, 181, 189; European Union on 193; in *General Comment 16 on State Obligations Regarding the Impact of the Business Sector on Children's Rights* 193; in the *Innocenti Declaration on Infant Young Child Feeding* (2005) 193; *Resolution 61.20* 190; *Resolution63.14* 226; *Resolution 63.23 on Infant and Young Child Nutrition* 189, 202, 215, 226; *Resolution 64.6* 222; and Scaling Up Nutrition (SUN) 220, 222; state implementation of 193; under-enforcement of 225; *see also* breastmilk substitutes, corporate private sector marketing, corporate private sector obligations, De Schutter, O., *International Code of Marketing of Breast-milk Substitutes*, state human rights obligations

World Health Organization (WHO): on continuum of care 180–1; on infant food manufacturers 178; on follow-up formulas 194; on food marketing 196; *Guidelines on Working with the Private Sector to Achieve Health Outcomes* 174; *Policy on WHO Engagement with Global Health Partnerships and Hosting Arrangements* 174; on powdered infant formula (PIF) 190; and Scaling Up Nutrition (SUN) 219; and violence against women 127, 131, 146; World Health Organization (WHO) Global NCD Action Plan 2013–2020 177; *see also* Baby-Friendly Hospital Initiative (BFHI), conflicts of interest, *Global Strategy for Infant and Young Child Feeding, Innocenti Declaration on the Protection, Promotion and Support of Breastfeeding*, Integrated Management of Childhood Illness (IMCI) strategy, *International Code of Marketing of Breast-milk Substitutes*, International Conference on Nutrition (ICN)

World Summit for Children 16

World Summit for Social Development 16

World Trade Organization (WTO) 18, 286, 357, 393; *see also* Agreement on Agriculture (AoA)

World's Women reports 314: on HIV/AIDS 283; on household surveys 272; *The World's Women 2010: Trends and Statistics* 116–17, 314

Ziegler, J. 24